BROADCASTING AND THE BBC IN WALES

BROADCASTING AND THE BBC IN WALES

John Davies

UNIVERSITY OF WALES PRESS
CARDIFF
1994

British Library Cataloguing-in-Publication Data.
A catalogue record for this book is available from the British Library.

ISBN 0-7083-1273-X

Published with the financial support of the Arts Council of Wales.

Cover design by Design Principle, Cardiff
Printed in Great Britain by the Cromwell Press, Melksham, Wiltshire

For
Janet

Contents

Illustrations

Preface

'To try to write the history of broadcasting', wrote Asa Briggs, '. . . is . . . to try to write the history of everything else.' This is particularly true of Wales, where, to a greater extent than perhaps in any other country in Europe, broadcasting has played a central role, both positive and negative, in the development of the concept of a national community. This study focuses on BBC broadcasting in Wales. Yet, as the greater part of the Welsh people's experience of radio and television has consisted of BBC broadcasting to Wales, the activities of the Corporation as a whole and the central role of London must necessarily loom large. Since the 1950s, that experience has also included the output of the commercial sector; this study, however, is concerned with independent commercial companies only in so far as their development impinged upon the history of the BBC.

While the book was in the press, the White Paper, *The Future of the BBC*, was published. It expresses the government's belief that 'the BBC should be able to evolve into an international multi-media enterprise . . . separate from its public services'. It recommends that the Charter should be renewed and should run until 31 December 2006 – a ten-year term compared with the fifteen-year term granted in 1981. 'Of all the possible ways of financing the BBC at present,' notes the White Paper, 'the licence fee has the fewest drawbacks, [but] in the longer term, it might be possible to transfer all or some of the BBC's services to a subscription system.' Thus, funding from the licence fee 'should be reviewed before the end of 2001'. *The Future of the BBC* also argues that 'there should be a new definition of the role of the National Councils' and recommends that they should have responsibilities similar to those of the Board of Governors 'for audiences in their country and the public services provided for them'.

Preface

In preparing this book, I have gathered a large number of obligations. My first is to Geraint Talfan Davies, controller Wales, who asked me to undertake the work and who arranged for the BBC to provide me with a degree of sustenance while I was writing it. My second is to the University of Wales Press, particularly to Ned Thomas, the director, and to Ceinwen Jones, who was impressively thorough in dealing with my typescript. I received a warm welcome at the BBC's Written Archives Centre at Caversham and recall with especial gratitude the assistance of Jacqueline Kavanagh, Guinevere Jones and Joanne Cayford. Members of the staff at Llandaf were equally welcoming, and I am much indebted to Gareth Morris, the BBC's librarian, to Ann Goddard, to Meinir Rees and her colleagues at the Wales Record Centre and to Sue Gress and Margaret Lock at the BBC Library. In addition, I received many kindnesses from the staff of the National Library of Wales, Aberystwyth. The book was written in Iberia and its islands and a list of the bars, restaurants and hotels in which my scribbling was genially regarded would be long indeed.

As always, my chief obligation is to my wife, Janet Mackenzie Davies, with whom I discussed virtually every sentence. She typed the whole work, prepared the index and saved me from the solecisms which can be committed when writing in a language one rarely speaks. To dedicate the book to her is not only a pleasure; it is a recognition of a debt – of many debts.

John Davies
Cardiff
October 1994

A Note on Sources

The two main collections of unpublished material relating to the history of the BBC in Wales are those at the Wales Record Centre at Tŷ Oldfield, Broadcasting House, Llandaf, and at the BBC's Written Archives Centre at Caversham near Reading.

The archive at Llandaf contains little on the 1920s and early and mid 1930s apart from a useful collection of press cuttings and the volume 'Programmes as Broadcast'. Its holdings increase rapidly following the full establishment of the Welsh Region in 1937; indeed, from 1937 onwards it seems that virtually every memorandum produced at Cardiff has been preserved. There were many thousands of large boxes of records at Tŷ Oldfield containing tens of thousands of files and hundreds of thousands of pieces of paper. To make any sense of them would have been impossible but for the succinct lists compiled by Ann Goddard. The files contain minutes of meetings such as those of the regional controllers, material which is also available at Caversham. The minutes of the Broadcasting Council for Wales (1953 onwards) are particularly informative, especially after 1974 when comments cease to be anonymous; they are at their fullest and most interesting in the late 1970s and 1980s when they were compiled by Michael Brooke. Copies of the scripts broadcast in Wales have been deposited at the National Library at Aberystwyth where they have been admirably catalogued. There are still, however, large quantities of scripts at Tŷ Oldfield, those of the wartime Welsh-language news bulletins among them.

The Caversham material is invaluable, particularly where the early history of the BBC in Wales is concerned. The diary of John Reith, the papers relating to the University of Wales Committee and the memoranda on the splitting of the West Region are, for a Welsh historian, the highlights of the archive. Caversham also has a collection of press cuttings on the 'Welsh Controversy'. Memoranda concerning broadcasting in Wales during the Second World War are of outstanding interest, as are the audience research reports of the immediate post-war period. Central to the Caversham collections are the minutes of the BBC Board of Governors. On those occasions when other sources indicate that the governors were discussing Welsh issues, I have examined the Board minutes, but, as I have not worked through them systematically, there may well be further rich lodes to mine.

Among publications, the basic source is the *Radio Times*, a complete run of which is available at the BBC Library at Llandaf. The books and articles I have consulted are listed in the notes. Pre-eminent are Asa Briggs's four volumes which bring the story up to the mid 1950s. A further volume is soon to be published and, when the series is complete, the history of the BBC will have been chronicled in a manner unequalled by any other institution. Having been on the fringes of broadcasting in Wales for almost three decades, I have heard the reminiscences of countless broadcasters, not all of whom would be happy to see their words in print. I had hoped to conduct a series of more formal interviews but, with deadlines approaching and being passed, that proved impossible. I wish, however, to express particular gratitude to Elwyn Evans for his engrossing memories of the BBC in Wales in the 1930s.

1

The Beginnings:
Broadcasting in Wales, 1923–1927

Public broadcasting began in Wales on Tuesday, 13 February 1923, when an evening of programmes was transmitted from an aerial at Eldon Street in Cardiff. Transmission started at 5 p.m. with an hour of children's stories. There was then an interval of half an hour which was followed by the Wireless Orchestra's rendition of Fucik's *Entry of the Gladiators*. At 6.50 John Reith, the manager of the British Broadcasting Company, introduced Lord Gainford, the chairman of the Company's board of directors, who read a message from Lloyd George and expressed the hope that the transmissions of the new station 'would be enjoyed throughout the Principality'. At 7.00 p.m., Gainford's fellow director, Sir William Noble, introduced the lord mayor of Cardiff, Dr J. J. E. Biggs. The lord mayor declared the station open, foresaw the invention of television and delighted in the prospect that 'the highest form of culture will be taken into the homes of the poorest in the land'.[1]

At 7.15, the ceremonies over, a sequence of music, punctuated by a quarter of an hour of news and weather reports, continued until 9.00 p.m. At 9.30, broadcasting recommenced with Mostyn Lewis singing 'Dafydd y Garreg Wen', the first Welsh words to be broadcast publicly. After more music and a second news bulletin, the station closed down at 10.30. The inauguration of broadcasting at Cardiff was extensively reported in the press, the *Western Mail* seeing the event as ushering in a 'Ministry of Happiness'.[2]

Although the Cardiff station was the first to be sited on Welsh soil, some of the inhabitants of Wales had had the opportunity to hear public broadcasting before 13 February 1923. Broadcasting from Manchester, with the call sign 2ZY, had begun on a regular basis on 16 May 1922, and when conditions were favourable Manchester's transmission could be heard in the eastern parts of the counties of Flint and Denbigh. The Birmingham station, 5IT, began regular daily broadcasts on 15 November 1922, and they were audible on occasion in the easternmost districts of the mid Wales border counties. Thus, even before the opening of the Cardiff station, one of the difficulties of broadcasting to Wales as a whole was already apparent: that some Welsh communities could be more easily reached by radio from conurbations in England than from the chief urban centre of Wales.

The stations at Manchester and Birmingham predated the creation of the British Broadcasting Company, as did 2LO, the London station. The London station had been built by Marconi, that at Manchester by Metropolitan Vickers, and that at Birmingham by the Western Electric Company, three of the six major firms that came together, along with a myriad of minor ones, to establish the British Broadcasting Company on 18 October 1922. Of the six companies, Marconi was by far the most important. Employees of Marconi – the Honourable R. T. B. Wynn, the brother of the sixth Baron Newborough and a native of Rhug near Corwen, among them – had begun regular nightly broadcasting from Writtle near Chelmsford on 14 February 1922. The Writtle experiment was a hugely enjoyable and informal venture in which the programmes were put together in the bar of the Cock and Bull Inn minutes before they were broadcast. Transmissions from Writtle continued until 17 January 1923, but by then most of the pioneers had left for London where they launched 2LO at Marconi House in the Strand on 11 May 1922.[3]

The involvement of companies such as Marconi underlines the fact that public broadcasting came into being in Britain, not because of a desire to enlighten, educate and entertain the citizenry, but because manufacturers of wireless receivers were concerned to sell their products. They were only likely to do so on a large scale if the receivers received something, and the public could not be offered anything without the sanction of the Post Office. The telegraph wire service, which was seen as an extension of the letter, had been under the control of the Post Office since 1869. Wireless telegraphy was considered to be a development of line telegraphy, and wireless telephony yet a further advance. They were all therefore deemed to be within the province of the Post Office. Thus, public broadcasting in Britain was the responsiblity of the postmaster-general, a minister who 'was unlikely by appointment and temperament to welcome any great originality'.[4] The Post Office was the government's largest money-earner, and for successive postmasters-general the main purpose of broadcasting was to enhance the Post Office's profitability.[5] The Wireless Telegraphy Act of 1904 had authorized the postmaster-general to grant licences to wireless enthusiasts; thus the principle of the licence – as a payment to the government for the right to receive (and to transmit) broadcast material – was established long before public broadcasting was born.

With the advent of wireless telephony, it was within the power of the postmaster-general to issue licences to a multitude of organizations capable of broadcasting programmes. That is what happened in the United States where over a thousand stations had been licensed by 1924. Yet, as public broadcasting was a late entry in the wireless field, most wavelengths had already been allotted to other interests such as the armed forces, shipping, aviation, the fire service and the police. Initially, the government was only prepared to allocate the wavelengths between 350 and 400 metres to public broadcasting; as each band used for broadcasting was six metres wide, the allocation allowed for no more than eight stations in Britain, assuming that each had its own exclusive wavelength. In the United States in the immediate post-war years the authorities were more indiscriminate; in many parts of that country it was possible to pick up at least three hundred stations, the reception of none of which was wholly satisfactory.

Fear of 'chaos on the ether' – chaos which had much impressed itself on F. J. Brown, the assistant secretary of the Post Office, during a visit to the United States in the winter of 1921–2 – was a central factor in determining the attitude of the Post Office to public broadcasting. Indeed, British broadcasting took the shape it did, not for ideological reasons, but because of one technological fact: that wavelengths (before the coming of VHF) were a very limited commodity. Scarcity of wavelengths did not preclude the establishment of several broadcasting companies. That option, however, was ruled out by the reluctance of the Post Office to choose between companies. Even more important was the power enjoyed by the Marconi Company, which owned most of the relevant patents. To hand over monopoly control of a national resource to Marconi was unacceptable; to grant some stations to other companies would be difficult because the Marconi Company could deny them the use of its patents. The government therefore felt that the only option open to it was to persuade the wireless receiver manufacturers to create a cartel, and this was achieved in a series of meetings between April and October 1922. The creation of a single service was thus fortuitous and the result of much confused thinking.[6]

Equally fortuitous was the creation of a service free from advertising – a factor which came to be considered the hallmark of British broadcasting. Advertising was rejected, not because of basic principles, but because of the likely resistance of the newspapers, which in the 1920s were at the height of their power. As the government did not intend to provide the new service with any money from general taxation, it was to be financed by part of the licence money paid to the Post Office, together with a levy of 10 per cent on the sale of wireless receivers. In addition, an outside body could pay for a programme and use the fact of its sponsorship for publicity purposes. This provision had lapsed by 1926, but not before the *Western Mail* had sponsored two concerts and five recitals during its Wireless Exhibition at Cardiff's Drill-hall in October 1925.[7]

In the discussions between the manufacturers in the early part of 1922, the allocation of the responsibility for building the transmission stations loomed large. Marconi agreed to waive its patents for two of the stations if it were permitted to build the rest. The number and location of the stations was laid down by F. G. Kellaway, the postmaster-general, in a statement to the House of Commons on 4 May 1922. There were to be eight – a figure dictated by the grant of fifty metres of wavelength – and they were to be located in London, Birmingham, Manchester, Cardiff, Newcastle, Plymouth, Aberdeen and Glasgow or Edinburgh. (Glasgow, which had 1,050,000 inhabitants compared with 420,000 in Edinburgh, was eventually chosen.) As Manchester was built by Metropolitan Vickers and Birmingham by the Western Electrical Company, all the other stations were built by Marconi. On 4 January 1923, the General Report of the British Broadcasting Company noted: 'Regarding Cardiff, the Marconi Company have selected a site and construction has started.' Even after the completion of the transmission facilities and the opening of the station, the engineers at Cardiff continued to be employed by Marconi; they did not join the staff of the British Broadcasting Company until June 1923.[8]

The choice of Cardiff as one of the eight centres of British broadcasting does not seem to have aroused any controversy at the time. Nevertheless, it was in some ways unexpected. In 1922, the city, with a population of 220,000, was twenty-first in size among the urban centres of Britain. A hundred years earlier it had had only 3,000 inhabitants, and because of the rapidity of its growth it lacked many of the civic amenities possessed by more venerable centres of population. Although its prosperity as a coal-exporting port was at its height in the immediate post-war years, the nature of its chief economic activity caused it to have a far smaller urban patrician class than had cities with a more varied economic base.[9] It was a larger city than Aberdeen, but that city had no rival in north-east Scotland. This was not the case with Cardiff which was intended to serve both sides of the Severn Estuary. A rival was readily available in Bristol, a city of 377,000 people with a civic tradition far older than that of Cardiff.

No evidence survives relating to the choice of Cardiff, although it was stated in 1936 that Bristol had spurned the opportunity of having a wireless station.[10] The most probable explanation for the choice was the feeling that, as Scotland was to have two stations, Wales should at least have one. The Cardiff station was given the call sign 5WA, implying that (on the analogy of 2LO for London) it had been conceived of as some kind of gesture to Wales. It should be remembered that the decision concerning the location of the stations was made by a government headed by Lloyd George. Although Lloyd George's interest in broadcasting was fitful at best, and although he had fallen from power by the time the Cardiff station was opened, he sent warm greetings on that occasion, and in subsequent years his interventions in Welsh broadcasting matters were to be of crucial importance.[11]

But, if there were to be a station in Wales, was Cardiff necessarily the obvious choice? The city was not to be recognized as the capital of Wales until 1955. Its emergence as the largest urban centre in Wales was very recent; in 1861, there were 49,794 people living in Merthyr Tydfil and 40,862 in Swansea, compared with 32,954 in Cardiff. Civic leaders in Swansea, aware of the town's richer cultural history, its more extensive economic base and its role as the centre of communities imbued with a greater sense of Welsh awareness, were particularly resentful of the new role granted to the parvenu city of Cardiff, an issue discussed *ad nauseam* in the newspapers of Swansea in the 1920s and 1930s. But whatever the considerations which led to the choice of Cardiff, the decision was redolent with consequences. The fact that Cardiff was the headquarters of broadcasting activities in Wales greatly assisted its ambition to be recognized as the capital of Wales and led, in more recent times, to the development of the city as a media centre of international importance. The fact that one of the main stations of British broadcasting was located in Wales dictated the course of the debate over the nature of the broadcasting services which should be provided for the Welsh people.

The choice of Cardiff was made by the government for, when the decision was announced, the British Broadcasting Company had not yet come into existence. The first task of the Company, following its inauguration on 18 October 1922, was to choose the officials who would run it. It began its operations on 14 November 1922 in Magnet House, the offices of the General Electric Company in Kingsway, London. It had two employees, A. R. Burrows, one of the Writtle pioneers, who was head of programmes, and his deputy, Cecil Lewis, later a well-known dramatist. In October 1922 the Company advertised for a manager and on 14 December 1922 the post was offered to John Reith, a 34-year-old Scottish engineer.

The appointment was fateful. John Reith was successively manager, general manager and managing director of the British Broadcasting Company, and from 1927 to 1938 director-general of the British Broadcasting Corporation. Reith, a towering man of six foot four in height, is one of the most remarkable figures in twentieth-century British history; indeed, of the public figures of the century, probably only Lloyd George and Churchill have attracted more published studies. He was a mass of contradictions. The son of a moderator of the United Free Church of Scotland, he was imbued with the moral seriousness of the Kirk.[12] He declared that the broadcasting of religion was the most important task of the new medium, yet there is little evidence that he was an orthodox Christian believer. Despite his Scottish patriotism, his great ambition was to be accepted by the English upper class, and he retired to a grace-and-favour tower in the grounds of Lambeth Palace. Although he presided over the establishment of sound broadcasting and the inauguration of television, his diary suggests that he neither listened to the one nor viewed the other. A stern critic of the sexual transgressions of others, he himself had affairs with lovers of both sexes.[13] Although he was the founding father of Britain's greatest source of intellectual – and less intellectual – pleasure, the concept of pleasure was alien to him, eaten up as he was by a self-absorbing accidie. He despised the rewards of this world, yet the vituperative remarks he wrote in his diary when the honours lists were published make remarkable reading.[14] The medium with which he dealt could be considered to be inherently democratic, but his cast of mind was distinctly authoritarian. 'He believes in irresponsible power,' wrote the distinguished Welsh educationalist, Ben Bowen Thomas; 'his temper is Fascist.'[15] These contradictions are particularly evident in his dealings with Wales. He was impressed on discovering that a shared knowledge of the Welsh language allowed people 'of the farmer type' to converse naturally with Lloyd George, yet that comment is embedded in writings which pulsate with a deep dislike of Wales and the Welsh.[16] Nevertheless, despite (or perhaps aided by) his failings, Reith was the creator of the British system of public broadcasting, and he is thus one of the twentieth century's greatest benefactors.

In the early days, Reith at his office – first at Magnet House and then at the Institute of Electrical Engineers in Savoy Hill – impinged little upon the day-to-day running of the Cardiff station. He chose the employees and allocated the funds, but the programmes broadcast were entirely the responsibility of the station director and his staff. In the first months of its existence, everything transmitted by the Cardiff station was unique to Cardiff. The work of the early stations was local radio in its fullest sense, a form of broadcasting which was dispensed with following the creation of a more

centralized system in the late 1920s. It did not re-emerge until the
1960s; even then, the British Broadcasting Corporation's local radio
was by no means as fundamentally local as was that of the British
Broadcasting Company in the early 1920s.

During the Cardiff station's first week – 13 to 19 February 1923 –
programme transmissions amounted to 21 hours 15 minutes. Apart
from Sunday, the usual pattern was for the station to be on the air for
three hours each evening: 5.00 to 5.30, 7.30 to 9.00 and 9.30 to 10.30.
Sunday programmes were transmitted from 8.30 p.m. to 10.05 p.m. Of
the first week's output, 4 per cent consisted of talks, 13 per cent of
news and 17 per cent of children's programmes. The rest, 66 per cent
of the total material broadcast – fourteen hours in all – was music. In
the early days, this was the pattern in all the stations, giving rise to the
belief that the transmission of music was virtually the sole function of
the new medium. The station orchestra – five instrumentalists drawn
from among Cardiff musicians – was responsible for over half the
station's musical output. The rest was provided by soloists and by
local groups such as the Cymric Octette. The music consisted largely
of light airs, folk songs and arias from popular operas, causing early
broadcast music to be described as a 'potted palm court' affair.[17] Such
music took up most of the evening, but on every night except Sunday
it was usual for all stations to broadcast dance music between the
second news bulletin and close-down, a vital contribution to the dance
craze which was such a feature of the 1920s.

The setting up of the Cardiff station was undertaken by Rex
Palmer, the first director of 2LO, who had been sent to Cardiff soon
after the establishment of the Company to search for studio
accommodation and to liaise with the Marconi engineers who were
already at work in the city. The premises he leased were situated in
19 Castle Street above Mr Kinshot's music shop.[18] They consisted of
two rooms, one eighteen foot square and the other considerably
smaller. The larger room was the station director's office during the
day, and the production studio while transmission was in progress;
the smaller was used by the engineers and by visitors. The studio
was draped with blankets to muffle the sound of the traffic of Castle
Street, and therefore had no ventilation. On occasions when it was
crammed with an orchestra and a male-voice choir – thirty
performers in all – it became unbearably hot and smelly. Percy Pitt,
the Company's head of music, nearly collapsed when conducting in
Castle Street; a fan was then installed, but that also had to be
blanketed to stop the hum.[19] The station remained at Castle Street
until May 1924 when more commodious offices at 39 Park Place
were leased from the University College of Cardiff.

Rex Palmer appears to have left Cardiff immediately after the opening of the station. The volume 'Programmes as Broadcast' notes on 14 and 15 February 1923 that the station director was Frederick Roberts, who also conducted the orchestra. He was dismissed after forty-eight hours, apparently because he had been found drunk in his office.[20] Rex Palmer returned to Cardiff and managed the station for a few weeks until he was succeeded by Cecil Lewis, also an emissary from Head Office. Then, on 26 March 1923, six weeks after it was opened, the station came under the management of Major Arthur Corbett-Smith. The new director was to be paid an annual salary of £500 and his working hours were to be 8.45 a.m. to 10.30 p.m., Saturdays and Sundays included. The other staff at the time were a deputy at £260, a secretary at £130, a clerical assistant at £104, an evening typist at £100 and a filing clerk at £39.[21]

Of all the station directors of the British Broadcasting Company, Corbett-Smith must surely have been the most original. Born in 1880, he was the son of Sir William Corbett-Smith, a leading public health reformer. After education at Winchester and Oxford, he turned his hand to a variety of occupations; he had been the deputy secretary of the Shanghai Municipal Council, the producer of *Mr Wu* at the Strand Theatre in London, the founder of an educational movement concerned with sexual diseases and the director of publicity for the British National Opera. His experience as an artillery officer in the First World War provided the basis of his book, *The Retreat from Mons*, a highly regarded military study. Among his friends were General Smuts, Lord Jellicoe and Lord Leverhulme, all of whom testified to his ability. In 1921, he married Tessie Thomas of Neath, a skilled violinist, whose father, Oscar Thomas (Oliver Raymond), was responsible for the musical output of the Cardiff station. Corbett-Smith, a man of huge exuberance, had a marked manic streak; one of his habits was to make periodic announcements in the press concerning his imminent suicide, a threat he ultimately carried out on the promenade at Margate in 1945.[22]

As station director at Cardiff, Corbett-Smith considered that his role was to energize and innovate. The composer Grace Williams described him as 'short and dapper, agile as an acrobat, darting over and under and in and out'.[23] He was assisted by his deputy, Norman Settle, the executive officer and programme announcer, about whom opinions differ. Grace Williams remembered Settle as 'very tall, very courteous and very English', but in 1927 he was described as having 'a generally overbearing nature, frequent tempers and an unpleasantly officious manner', the consequence, it was suggested, of the fact that he 'was one of the early employees [and thus] has not the social or the educational advantages that more recent people in similar positions have'.[24]

Whatever the defects of Corbett-Smith and Settle, they had, by the end of 1923, succeeded in making the Cardiff station one of the most interesting centres of British broadcasting. Corbett-Smith disliked formality; talks became chats; the station greeting was changed from 'Hullo Everybody' to 'Hullo Comradios' (or sometimes 'Cymradios'.) *Children's Hour* became the *Hour of the Kiddiewinks*. Several times a week, the station director took to the microphone to air his views as Mr Everyman. Whole evenings were devoted to a single theme, rather on the lines of the early programming of BBC2: Irish nights with Synge's plays, Yeats's poems and traditional music; army nights (helped no doubt by Corbett-Smith's fame as a military historian) with concerts by the bands of well-known regiments; sports nights, including 'chats' by boxing promoters; countryside nights, when people with rustic accents were permitted to broadcast; popular nights, offering what a Wykehamist believed the people really wanted. He also established *Women's Hour* (half an hour every night) and gave considerable prominence to children's programmes. The Scouts, the Guides and the Boys' Brigade – which had its origins in the church of which Reith's father had been minister – were given extensive publicity, but Urdd Gobaith Cymru (the Welsh League of Youth) was totally ignored.[25] Emphasis upon programmes for children was a marked feature of early broadcasting generally and virtually all the senior employees of the British Broadcasting Company were pressed into service as uncles and aunts.

Music at Cardiff became more ambitious, with greater attention to Mozart, Dvořák and Sibelius and fewer renditions of 'In a Monastery Garden'. The resources of the city itself were exploited: Syd Lewis's Syncopated Dance Orchestra was regularly featured, at a time when London viewed syncopated music as barbaric; Richard Treseder, the Cardiff horticulturist, gave gardening talks, and social workers were invited to broadcast on themes such as 'The colliery boy and his hours of leisure'. On St David's Day 1923 – before the arrival of Corbett-Smith – Huw J. Huws, a Cardiff inspector of schools, gave a ten-minute talk in Welsh, and earlier in the same day Gwilym Davies quoted two lines of Welsh verse in a talk on the League of Nations – the first spoken Welsh to be broadcast from Cardiff.[26] During Corbett-Smith's directorship, however, spoken Welsh never emanated from the Cardiff transmitter. In other spheres, Corbett-Smith was highly innovative. His *Magic Carpet* series was a mixture of speech, song and music arranged around a central theme; it marked the invention of the feature programme and was rapidly copied by other stations. In addition to giving his Everyman talks, acting in plays, doing much of the announcing, conducting the orchestra and being avuncular to the 'kiddiewinks', Corbett-Smith put on one-man shows, written, produced and performed by himself; on 6 October 1923, for example, he broadcast his recital on the first Battle of Ypres.[27]

Peter Eckersley, the company's chief engineer and the one true genius involved in the early history of British broadcasting, was delighted with Corbett-Smith's activities. Reith, however, was less appreciative. In his *Broadcast over Britain* (1924), Reith noted that the appointment of station directors was 'a matter of trial and error, and initially many mistakes were made' – and he almost certainly had the Cardiff director in mind.[28] On 27 March 1924, Corbett-Smith was replaced by E. R. Appleton, of whom more – much more – later. An account of the development of broadcasting at Cardiff, compiled in the mid 1930s, noted that Corbett-Smith's 'exuberant personality was found to be a little overwhelming for a Station Director's post, and he was transferred to Head Office as Programme Adviser or Artistic Director'.[29] Eckersley put the matter differently: '[Corbett-Smith] was asked to come to Head Office to be given more scope; he was given less and so he left.'[30] He ceased being artistic director in December 1924, when he was attached to Intelligence, a section of the Company concerned with the criticism of programmes. In that capacity, he seems to have continued on his wayward path. The Company's Control Board noted on 18 May 1926 that 'in view of Major Corbett-Smith's general attitude, brought to a head during the recent emergency [the General Strike], it was decided to dispense with his services as critic at the earliest possible moment'.[31] He ceased to have any connection with the Company on 30 September 1926.

The volume 'Programmes as Broadcast' in the Wales Record Centre lists the Cardiff Station's transmissions from the beginning. With the launching of the *Radio Times* on 28 September 1923, a more accessible but less reliable source became available. In the early months the totality of what was transmitted was produced in Castle Street. There was no outside broadcast until 25 June 1923 when Cardiff broadcast a thirty-minute performance from the Capitol Cinema by Lionel Falkman and his orchestra.[32] In the early days of the Company, the use of gramophone records was eschewed, partly because the practice was considered an objectionable characteristic of American radio and partly because of the poor quality of the records produced in the immediate post-war years. Quality improved rapidly in the mid 1920s. Cardiff first broadcast a gramophone record on 12 March 1925; by the summer of that year, records constituted about five hours a month of the station's transmissions.

As the entire early output was live, everything was destroyed at the moment of transmission. Nothing was recorded, for the day of cheap recording tape had not yet dawned; wax records could be made, but the process was so expensive that it was only used under very exceptional circumstances. The earliest extant BBC recording is that of a speech made by the prince of Wales in May 1931; the earliest relating to Wales is Lloyd George's speech at the proclamation of the Caernarfon National Eisteddfod in July 1934. Some of Corbett-Smith's nightly fifteen-minute talks may have been unscripted, but the Company soon adopted the rule that all words transmitted should be read from a script, even those which purported to be the broadcast of a spontaneous discussion. There are no surviving scripts of the output of the Cardiff station of the 1920s; the earliest script in the collection of BBC scripts at the National Library of Wales is dated 2 January 1937.

With little information available apart from the listings provided by the *Radio Times* and by the volume 'Programmes as Broadcast', the early programmes can seem to be beyond recovery. Yet it is possible to have some idea of their nature. There was a contraction in the proportion of the transmission time devoted to music with the 66 per cent of the early days declining to 55 per cent in the last weeks of Corbett-Smith's regime. The scores, librettos and song sheets of the music that was played and sung are generally available, and thus the content of the greater part of what was broadcast is known, although its quality is not. What was said in the talks is surmisable; furthermore, some of them were commented upon in the press although the publication of Cardiff talks in newspapers did not occur on any scale until the 1930s. Cardiff began to broadcast plays on 10 April 1923 when an extract from *King John* was performed; as most of them were classic works, their content is known. Some plays, however, were the work of the station staff and they, like the feature programmes and the items for children, have disappeared beyond recall.

Equally irrecoverable are the early news programmes, although it is unlikely that they contained anything surprising. Opposition from newspapers had ensured that the Company was not allowed to have its own news-gathering staff or to broadcast news until seven o'clock in the evening, after the appearance of evening newspapers. News programmes consisted of statements prepared by news agencies, Reuters in particular. Corbett-Smith introduced a nightly five-minute bulletin of south Wales news, but as Reuters' news-gathering activity in Wales was slight, its content must have been thin.

If knowledge of the content of the early broadcasts is scanty, knowledge of their audience is even more sparse. Unlike broadcasting companies in the United States, where the number and the nature of those listening were of vital interest to advertisers, the British broadcasting authorities felt no urgent need systematically to study their audience. Indeed, Reith long resisted any suggestion of audience research, for he feared that the evidence collected would be used to press for more popular programmes. Regular surveys of the pattern of listening were not undertaken until the late 1930s, and even then little material specifically relevant to Wales was collected.[33] Sales of licences and of the *Radio Times* are important indicators, but the figures are not always available for Wales. Thus, much of the evidence concerning the welcome the Welsh people gave to broadcasting tends to be anecdotal.

In February 1923, wireless telephony was not a total novelty to the Welsh. Shakespeare suggests that Owain Glyndŵr had foreseen the invention.[34] In 1868, Moses Griffiths, a Holyhead electrician, published an essay in which he discussed the possibility of broadcasting. David Hughes, whose family hailed from Bala, patented a microphone in 1878. There was much local interest in Marconi's successful attempt in 1897 to transmit words without wires from Lavernock to Flatholm, an experiment prompted by Sir William Preece, the Post Office's chief engineer and a native of Y Bontnewydd near Caernarfon. Marconi successfully contacted Australia from Waunfawr in Caernarfonshire in August 1918. The *Western Mail* was strongly wireless-minded. It had conducted its own experiments in wireless telephony in 1911 and in the early days of the Cardiff station it co-operated closely with the British Broadcasting Company, unlike the newspapers of cities such as Birmingham and much of the London popular press.[35] In 1922, crowds gathered at the Park Hall Cinema to hear a broadcast from a studio in St Mary's Street, and in the same year the Writtle experimenters were invited to give a demonstration at the Cardiff YMCA.[36] Merthyr's Radio and Scientific Society attracted large numbers to its weekly meetings at Cyfarthfa Castle and Swansea's Radio Society received the active support of many of the town's leading inhabitants.[37]

Early broadcasts could be received in four ways: by group listening inside and outside the shops of wireless receiver retailers or in halls and vestries at occasions organized by societies or retailers; by purchasing a valve set; by purchasing a crystal set; by buying the components and constructing a crystal set. In 1923, mass listening in the streets was a common phenomenon, the *Western Mail* noting the crowds standing around the shop of Cross Brothers in St Mary's Street. Wireless evenings were frequently organized; the *Merthyr Express*, for example, reported 'listening-ins' at Calfaria Chapel, Abercynon, on 19 February and at the Ystrad Mynach Workmen's Hall on 13 March. Indeed, as late as 1927, a report to the Board of

Education assumed that group listening was the most usual way of receiving broadcasts.[38]

A valve set in the home – the almost universal form of listening by the mid 1930s – was rare in 1923. In that year, the cheapest two-valve set cost £13.10s. (£13.50), the equivalent of at least £700 by 1994 prices. Furthermore, valve sets needed power. Few houses were wired for electricity in 1923; even in Cardiff, a pioneer in the field, less than half the city's private houses had electricity and most of those were only wired for light. With the establishment of the National Grid in 1926, the number of urban dwellings with electricity increased rapidly. By 1935, the great majority of the houses of urban Wales had the facility; some rural communities had a locally produced supply – often dependent upon weird and wonderful contraptions – but the majority of the houses of the Welsh countryside were not connected to the grid until the second half of the twentieth century. Most of the early valve sets were therefore battery-driven. Each set needed a dry battery of almost a foot wide and also a wet battery, about the size of a large jam-jar, which had to be recharged every ten days or so. If power to recharge the battery were not conveniently available, the set could be out of commission for lengthy periods. A survey of the ownership of sets in rural Denbighshire in 1937 noted that in many villages up to half the sets were not in use.[39]

The year 1923 was fairly prosperous in industrial Wales. Unemployment was lower in Wales than in any other part of Britain; coal exports from Cardiff, at 30 million tons, were the highest ever recorded, and the level of wages in the south Wales coalfield caused its 213,000 miners to be among the best paid of the members of the British working class. Nevertheless, as a valve set in 1923 cost the equivalent of several weeks' wages, very few were bought by working-class families. The price of the cheapest valve set fell to about £6 in 1925 and to about £4 by 1930, but the severe depression which began in the south Wales coalfield in 1925 and the distress attendant upon the conflicts of 1926 meant that increasing penury prevented most Welsh families from taking advantage of the declining prices. The majority of the households of Wales able to receive radio programmes did not have a valve set until the 1930s.

Thus, in the early years of broadcasting, possession of a valve set was very much a middle-class phenomenon. Indeed, some of the British Broadcasting Company's employees – in London more than elsewhere – assumed that their audience was exclusively middle-class, or rather, upper middle-class. There was no point, believed Roger Eckersley, the Company's organizer of programmes and the brother of Peter Eckersley, in broadcasting between 7 and 8 p.m.

because everyone would be dressing for dinner. In 1925, the London *Women's Hour* broadcast a lengthy series of talks on 'Manners at Bridge', and, on *Children's Hour*, listeners intending to go on a picnic were advised to ask Cook to prepare their sandwiches.

The fragile evidence available suggests that it was the less articulate members of the middle class who bought valve sets. Intellectuals did not hasten to buy them for, as in the early days of television, video recorders and satellite dishes, the educated class did not warm to the new invention. John Davies, the secretary of the Workers' Educational Association in south Wales, was still radio-less in 1930 although he had long been in regular contact with the BBC's education officers. W. J. Gruffydd, the professor of Welsh at Cardiff and the leading advocate of an improved radio service for Wales, did not acquire a set until 1934 when he informed the readers of his journal *Y Llenor* that he had bought a *teleffon diwifr*. Thus those most prone to record their opinions were the least likely to have daily experience of broadcasting, although that did not prevent them from making their opinions known.[40]

As valve sets were expensive, reception of broadcasts at home generally meant listening to a crystal set. Depending as it did upon the power of the transmitting signal, the crystal set needed neither mains electricity nor batteries. The cheapest already-assembled crystal set cost about £3.15s. (£3.75), but the components could be bought for 7s.6d. (37.5p), with the headphones costing a further 2s. (10p) and the hundred-foot aerial 1s.8d. (8.3p). Assembling a crystal set and inducing it to pick up broadcasts by warming its 'whiskers' with a lighted match was not difficult, but it required patience and dexterity. In 1923, it was estimated that three-quarters of those listening to broadcasts were receiving them on crystal sets they had made themselves. The vast majority of the listeners were young hobbyists – almost exclusively male – with mechanical tastes. They were not, perhaps, the most obvious audience for the 'potted palm court' music provided for them, but for the crystal-set user the appeal was not in the content of the programmes but in the excitement of tracking them down.[41]

The 5WA station was initially powered by 1.5 kilowatts and broadcast on 353 metres.[42] In daylight, reception on a valve set was about forty miles, but during the hours of darkness, Cardiff, under favourable conditions, could have an outreach of hundreds of miles. Seventeen days after the station opened, the *Western Mail* reported that it had been heard in Paris.[43] Throughout the 1920s, reception of most stations was rarely wholly satisfactory. Oscillation – a humming noise which affected all the sets in a neighbourhood if one of them was incorrectly tuned – was a constant problem. There was much concern over heterodyne; the operation of trams could cause serious interference and there were many complaints about the elaborate aerials which festooned the houses and gardens of the more dedicated enthusiasts.

Reception of the Cardiff station was particularly problematic, partly because of the unusual shape of its aerial; it extended for 200 feet from a 70-foot cooling tower to a 120-foot chimney, from which it descended to the ground by a series of right-angle turns.[44] But if the reception of programmes was frequently unsatisfactory, the success in transmitting them was remarkable. In the first six months of the Cardiff station, transmission time lost because of breakdown amounted to 3 hours 50 minutes, less than 0.5 per cent of its output of over 800 hours. The engineers were the true, if unsung, heroes of the early days of broadcasting. 'We were', as Peter Eckersley put it, 'on trial against the measure of our ambitions.'[45]

By 17 October 1923, when Bournemouth (which had been substituted for Plymouth) was opened, all the eight stations announced by Kellaway in May 1922 were in operation; a ninth, Belfast, was opened on 24 October 1924. In many parts of Britain, a good valve set could pick up all of them, although with varying degrees of audibility. Changing atmospheric conditions could produce unexpected results, with distant stations sometimes offering clearer listening than those closer to hand. There were occasions when there was good reception of Aberdeen in Glamorgan, of Bournemouth in Lothian and of Newcastle in Devon. London, which operated on a higher power of 10 kilowatts, compared with the 1.5 kilowatts of the other stations, was widely heard, the *Western Mail* noting that, at Abergavenny, it was easier to listen to London than to Cardiff. In addition, a number of the stations of mainland Europe could be clearly heard, and in October 1923 the *Radio Times* began listing the programmes of one Dutch and three French stations; by October 1924, it was listing forty stations broadcasting from nine states. On occasion, even American stations could be picked up, but Cardiff's attempt in March 1925 to have an exchange session with Illinois proved unsuccessful.[46]

Owners of crystal sets were much more circumscribed in their listening. For them, the range of the British Broadcasting Company's stations was generally about twenty miles; it could be more for transmissions crossing the sea, but it was considerably less where there were hills in the way. Thus the Cardiff station could be heard on crystal sets on the coast of Somerset; in the south Wales coalfield, however, it was difficult to pick up north of Pontypridd, although the Cardiff aerial had been specifically designed to reach the industrial valleys. Reith was particularly anxious that broadcasts should be available in the coalfield, for they could, he believed, 'do much to combat the doctrines of Communism and Bolshevism so sedulously preached there'. For this reason, Cardiff was among the first of the provincial stations to operate on the higher power of ten kilowatts. This virtual sevenfold increase in power did not mean a sevenfold increase in the outreach of the station for, as Reith explained, 'power output is only proportionate to the square root of the obtainable range, [and thus] to double the range we must quadruple the power'.[47]

With higher power, crystal-set users up to forty miles away could hear Cardiff. Its output could be picked up on crystal sets in most of the industrial areas of Monmouthshire and east Glamorgan, except in those districts – much of the Rhondda among them – where transmission was blocked by the lie of the land.[48] Higher power also meant better reception in south-western England where valve-set users, in Bristol in particular, were already getting a satisfactory service from Cardiff. Although Bristol was by 1925 demanding its own station, Cardiff was increasingly seen as the station serving both sides of the Severn Estuary, although it was not formally recognized as the 'West' station until 9 June 1927. The first major programme from Cardiff featuring performers from the south-west of England was *The Bristol Pageant*, broadcast on 20 May 1924, and thereafter such programmes multiplied rapidly despite complaints about the cost and inconvenience of the 86-mile return train journey from Bristol, or the 172-mile journey from and to Taunton.

Even with higher power, reception by crystal-set users remained very limited. Large towns such as Swansea offered them no service, and at Swansea and other major urban centres the service for valve-set users was frequently unsatisfactory. The answer seemed to be the establishment of a number of low-power town stations, a development strongly advocated by Peter Eckersley, who wanted broadcasting to provide 'poorer people with entertainment rather than to pander to the better off'.[49] He was equally concerned to find a way of serving those areas where there were no towns large enough to enable them to claim a low-power station – rural Wales being perhaps the most obvious example outside the Highlands and Islands of Scotland. Along with his plans for town stations, Eckersley developed the notion of establishing a high-power station on long wave which could reach virtually every corner of the kingdom. Broadcasting in the United States – the pioneer of radio telephony – was restricted to short and medium waves and there were doubts whether long-wave transmission was practicable. Furthermore, the establishment of low-power stations and of a long-wave service was not possible as long as the Post Office restricted public broadcasting to the 350- to 400-metre waveband.[50]

Frustration over that restriction fed the antagonism between the British Broadcasting Company and the postmaster-general which became evident in the early months of 1923, antagonism which was intensified by Reith's annoyance at having to deal with so lowly a government minister. A more important ingredient in that antagonism was the growing realization that the system for financing the new service was seriously flawed. The levy on sets applied only to those of British manufacture and was not paid by those who assembled their crystal sets, generally using cheap imported components. They could be considered experimenters rather than 'listeners-in' and as such were subject to a different kind of licence. In fact, few of them paid any kind of licence; by 1 March 1923, only 80,000 licences had been bought in Britain, representing less than a quarter of those availing themselves of the service. The postmaster-general, Joynson-Hicks, later to win fame as a pleasure-hating home secretary, doubted whether he had the authority to punish those who did not pay. There were only two prosecutions for non-payment between March 1923 and March 1925. Reith was seriously displeased. 'Every condition and regulation', he wrote, 'is being infringed and evaded.'[51]

The issues were put before a committee chaired by Major-General Sir Frederick Sykes; it was appointed on 24 April 1923 and was charged with the duty to 'consider the whole question of broadcasting, not merely the question of licences, but [also] the desirability of existing contracts'. Its report was submitted in August 1923, but was not published until October. The report recommended that the levy should be abandoned and that every household receiving programmes should pay a uniform licence fee of 10s. (50p – the equivalent of £25 by 1994 prices), of which 75 per cent (not 50 per cent, as hitherto) should be handed over to the British Broadcasting Company. It urged that the Company's licence, which was originally to last for two years, should be extended for a further two years, and that public broadcasting should be permitted on most of the bands between 300 and 500 metres. The government accepted its recommendations. With the matter of the licence fee clarified and with the Post Office showing some willingness to prosecute non-payers, licence-paying boomed; 595,000 had been bought by the end of 1923, and 1,129,000 by the end of 1924.[52]

While the Sykes Committee was sitting, the officials of the Company were considering the implications of running a service with nine main stations and possibly a further dozen smaller stations. If all the twenty or more stations were to have their own exclusive programmes, the Company, it was believed, would be subject to intolerable demands, particularly where money was

17

concerned. There was thus an urgent need to link all the stations together through the Post Office's land lines; it would then be possible for any station to broadcast simultaneously programmes produced by other stations. Although the land links were not fully completed until early in 1924, simultaneous broadcasting began on 29 August 1923, when all stations transmitted the London news. Over the next few months, SBs, as the *Radio Times* called them, were virtually restricted to the two, nightly, ten-minute news bulletins from London, but by November 1923 talks from London were becoming increasingly numerous. On 5 November, all stations carried a Mozart concert produced at Newcastle. The first Cardiff production to be carried by all British stations was *Children's Corner*, broadcast on 20 January 1924.[53] In 1924, with land lines much improved, SBs multiplied. Of the 34 hours 30 minutes transmitted from Cardiff in the first week of February, 22 hours 50 minutes was locally produced; of the 11 hours 40 minutes of SBs, 78 per cent came from London and 22 per cent from other provincial stations.

The concept of a provincial station was the direct result of simultaneous broadcasting, and it was one which was to transform the nature of broadcasting in Britain. Initially, the nine original stations were seen as more or less equal, each with its own exclusive pattern of programmes. With simultaneous broadcasts, the concept of London as the main provider emerged. It did not happen immediately. Even after simultaneous broadcasting had begun, Reith was still thinking in terms of the nine stations being dominant, with London offering metropolitan material on 'Special Nights'. In December 1923, he suggested that London should be taken by all stations on Mondays, and that each station should in turn prepare a programme for simultaneous broadcasting on Fridays; during the rest of the week, the stations would produce their own material, with the exception of the main news bulletin. To finance the output, each station was to receive a programme allowance of £140 a week, plus a special grant of £40 for the extra programme every seven weeks.[54]

Reith's plan of December 1923 was not implemented. On 14 January 1924, less than a month after it had been formulated, the five-man Control Board was established. Among its members was A. R. Burrows, the 2LO head of programmes – the beginning of the subsumation of the London station staff into Head Office staff.[55] A more centralist attitude rapidly gained ground, at the urging, in particular, of Charles Carpendale, Reith's deputy, and of Roger Eckersley. Reith became increasingly enamoured of the concept of a uniform service, imprinted with the stamp of authority. The Programme Board was set up in May 1924 to monitor the activities of the provincial stations, and J. C. Stobart, the Company's director of education, was authorized to inspect them without advance notice.[56] Announcers were to be anonymous, and in March 1924 Reith decreed that the style of announcing was to be the same in all stations in order to assert the collective personality of the service. The announcers' evening dress, of which so much has been made, was primarily a London phenomenon. Elsewhere, it was left to the discretion of the station director; there is no evidence that evening dress was worn by radio announcers at Cardiff.[57]

These developments were accompanied by a determined effort to stamp out the informal jollity of early broadcasting, with its competitions, its prizes, its requests and its marked encouragement of audience participation. Only persons of distinction, insisted Reith, should be allowed to broadcast. It 'harmed the dignity' – dignity, he thought, was the highest virtue – of station directors to be uncles in children's programmes, and the letters written to those programmes were an entire waste of time.[58] In 1923, Cardiff was receiving 2,000 letters a week, but with the greater formality the number declined rapidly. As Scannell and Cardiff put it, 'the attitudes and values . . . [of the early days] were quite deliberately eradicated by the policy of centralization'.[59] Yet London's emergence as the provider of the greater part of the material transmitted by the other stations should not be predated. Of the 65 hours 50 minutes broadcast from Cardiff in the first week of June 1926, 60 per cent was produced there; the rest was SB from London, for the intention that the provincial stations should provide a considerable proportion of the material on what was beginning to be called the network was not fulfilled. Instead, the BBC followed 'all the other mass media of the early twentieth century in bolstering London's supremacy [and further eroding] the proud provincialism of the Victorian age'.[60]

The first phase of the centralization policy coincided with Corbett-Smith's departure from Wales; indeed, it may have been partly inspired by his brief tenure of office at Cardiff. The tenure of his successor, Ernest Robert Appleton, was to be rather more lengthy; he took up his post on 27 March 1924 and did not sever his connection with Cardiff until 19 October 1936. Appleton was a native of Malvern and had graduated in natural sciences at Oxford. Before coming to Cardiff he had been an instructor at the Royal Naval College at Dartmouth. A man of wide culture, he had been involved with the Shakespeare Head Press at Stratford-upon-Avon, and had founded *The Beacon*, a magazine devoted to the arts. Primarily, however, he saw himself as a guide on spiritual matters, a fact which caused him, initially at least, to enjoy Reith's approbation.[61] He claimed that he had been anointed by the bishop of Oxford, and in the mid thirties his attempt to use broadcasting as a means of advertising his own spiritual movement was among the factors which led Reith to insist upon his resignation.[62] His best-known contributions at Cardiff were Bible stories which he read to his daughters, Joan and Betty, and his *Silent Fellowship* programme – fifteen minutes of comforting words and music directed particularly at the sick and lonely. Alun Llywelyn-Williams, who joined the Cardiff staff in 1935, considered Appleton to be a superlative broadcaster; yet 'yn ei ymwneud â phobl eraill . . . ef oedd un o'r bobl fwyaf digrefydd, a diegwyddor a adnabûm i erioed'*.[63]

Appleton did not think highly of Cardiff. With the exception of the civic centre, he considered it to be an ugly city, and the only way 'it could be made beautiful is to destroy it and build again'. He informed J. C. Stobart that 'the branch of the University of Wales situated at Cardiff happens to be the weakest of the colleges', and that the bishop of Llandaf was 'not a very powerful personality'.[64] He knew nothing about the communities of the coalfield. Such ignorance was not unusual among early broadcasters; indeed, lack of contact with the working class seems to have been a prime qualification for employment at the higher levels of the British Broadcasting Company.

As Cardiff station director, Appleton's primary duty was to provide programmes for east Glamorgan, Monmouthshire, Gloucestershire and Somerset. He was impressed by the need to conciliate opinion in Bristol where there was a strong feeling that the British Broadcasting Company had treated the city in a cavalier manner. The 5WA staff organized a summer carnival in Weston-super-Mare in August 1925 at which children delighted in the company of Cardiff's uncles and aunts. An advisory committee for Bristol was established in 1925 and Appleton organized an elaborate radio week there in November 1927, the first event of its kind in Britain.[65]

At Cardiff, Appleton's first task was to eliminate Corbett-Smith's more eccentric innovations. Chats became talks again and kiddiewinks and comradios were consigned to oblivion. Some of the innovations were retained, in particular the *Magic Carpet* feature programmes. Appleton extended Corbett-Smith's practice of having 'special nights', in particular by his introduction of 'Women's Nights', when only female voices were broadcast. Cardiff's most urgent need was better accommodation. On 17 March 1924, two months after Appleton's appointment, the station moved from

---

*'In his dealings with other people . . . he was one of the most irreligious and unprincipled people I have ever met.'

Castle Street to Park Place and Reith attended the official opening of the new premises five days later. They consisted of a one-storey building in the garden of 39 Park Place, together with the former kitchen and scullery of the main building. The one-storey building contained a large studio, a control room, an office apiece for the director and his deputy and two rooms for visiting performers. A Head Office report of July 1924 considered the interior of the 5WA studio to be 'perhaps the most impressive of all the provincial studios' and approved of its location in 'a good residential area [where the houses] have been converted into offices . . . for professions of the discreeter sort'.[66]

The acquisition of a more spacious studio – although it was initially affected by the rumblings of the coal wagons on the Taff Vale Railway – offered an opportunity to improve the station's chief function, the broadcasting of music. In May 1924, Warwick Braithwaite, a member of the Head Office staff, was appointed director of music at Cardiff. Braithwaite was not universally popular. 'He has no use for Wales or Welshmen, only as objects to be cursed at', wrote John Davies of the WEA.[67] His musical abilities, however, were not in doubt. By June 1924, he had set up a station orchestra of seventeen players. Braithwaite's tastes were highbrow; in July 1926, he provided Cardiff's listeners with a programme of Hungarian music, much of it by little-known composers. In south-western England, where there was general agreement that Cardiff was the best of all the stations, criticism of his choice of music was frequently expressed. 'Throughout the Cardiff programmes,' wrote the *Bristol Evening Echo* in November 1926, 'there is a bias towards ultra-classical music . . . It is not entertainment.'[68]

Braithwaite's achievement was remarkable, particularly in view of the fact that, of the nine centres granted stations under the original plan, Cardiff, in terms of its music-making potential, ranked near the bottom of the list. It had nothing comparable with the Hallé at Manchester, or even with the municipal orchestra at Bournemouth. There was a vigorous Cardiff Music Society, but its members had ceased to co-operate with the station following tactless treatment by Corbett-Smith. As all halls suitable for performances were fully used during the week, ambitious works could only be performed on Sundays; as woodwind instrumentalists hardly existed in Wales, players of flutes, oboes and clarinets had to be imported from London. They also were only available on Sunday; thus the Sabbath was a day of much activity among Cardiff's broadcasters, a matter of concern in a nation anxious to keep the 'continental Sunday' at bay.[69] Sabbath-breaker and cambrophobe though he may have been, Braithwaite must be considered one of the most remarkable figures in the early history of broadcasting at Cardiff. In the first week of January 1925, for example, he was on the air with his orchestra for a total of 12 hours 15 minutes.

Appleton came to the conclusion that Braithwaite's work could be the basis of more elaborate music-making activities at the Cardiff station. In November 1925, the *Radio Times* listed performances by the Cardiff Symphony Orchestra which consisted of Braithwaite's players, augmented by local instrumentalists. Cardiff's lord mayor organized meetings to discuss the establishment of a permanent civic orchestra for the city financed by a limited liability company, but the scheme had collapsed by the spring of 1926. Walford Davies, who since 1919 had been the University of Wales's director of music, was closely involved in planning the proposed orchestra and was much distressed by its failure. Davies was 'one of the first stars' of broadcasting; his series on musical appreciation, launched in January 1926, brought an enormous response and was proof of the existence of a great desire, in Wales as in the rest of Britain, for a fuller understanding of music. His office at the headquarters of the Welsh National Council of Music was in the Cardiff Law Courts, a brief stroll across Cathays Park from the radio station in Park Place. Early in 1926, Appleton began discussing with Davies the possibility of a national orchestra for Wales, a far more ambitious project than the 1925 plan for a Cardiff civic orchestra.[70]

Cyril Fox, the director of the National Museum, who had a great interest in broadcasting, was also closely involved, and he offered the almost completed main building of the museum, with its excellent acoustics, as a centre for concerts, provided they were free. On 6 December 1926 Walford Davies, who had been authorized by Reith to negotiate on behalf of the Company, met Appleton and the lord mayor of Cardiff to discuss the arrangements. There would be an orchestra with thirty permanent members at a cost of £11,000 a year; it would provide the greater part of the Cardiff station's musical output and would give regular concerts at Cardiff and elsewhere in Wales. The Company would contribute £6,000 a year (£300,000 by 1994 prices) on the undertaking that Cardiff and other Welsh local authorities would find the remaining £5,000. The generosity of the Company should not be exaggerated. It was already paying £6,000 a year for Braithwaite's orchestra; in the event, however, its commitment in December 1926 was to involve it in expenditure on the National Orchestra of Wales considerably in excess of the £6,000 a year which Reith had authorized Walford Davies to promise.[71]

Appleton's early years at Cardiff coincided with a considerable increase in transmission hours. In January 1924, the station broadcast on weekdays from 3.30 to 4.30 and from 5.0 to 10.15 (sometimes to 11.15). By 1926, it was broadcasting from 12.30 to 1.30, 2.30 to 4.30 and 5.0 to 11.0 (sometimes to 12.0). The pattern was different on Sundays, in accordance with Reith's strict Sabbatarianism. Broadcasting began at 3.0 but there was an interval between 5.15 and 8.15, in order that transmission should not clash with the usual time of evening service. Broadcasts from outside the studio became common. Cardiff's Capitol Cinema was wired for broadcasting and its cinema organ regaled listeners for an hour three times a week; the Bute Room in Cox's Café and the Carlton Restaurant were also wired and the Café Trio and the Carlton Orchestra became staple elements in Cardiff's output. Appleton was particularly proud of his station's plays. He gathered a group from among Cardiff's drama enthusiasts, amateur players who were prepared to offer their services without payment. Chief among them was Dr Worsley, the dean of Llandaf, whose son Francis (later the producer of the famous *ITMA*), joined the station staff in June 1928. The Cardiff group provided the basis of the station's repertory company, which is first mentioned in the *Radio Times* on 5 February 1924. Appleton also used the Gwent Players, a drama company based at Newport. He was constantly searching for new plays and noted that 'twenty books of plays are read before two are chosen . . . and there is a minimum of five rehearsals'.[72] He himself acted in most of them; he also wrote plays, including a saga on Owain Glyndŵr broadcast on 18 December 1925.

Much attention continued to be lavished on children's programmes, with Appleton, despite Reith's disapproval, regularly taking part as Uncle Felix. He established the Radio Sunbeams in May 1926, a children's club which sought to inculcate 'a love for the beautiful'; three months later it had 45,000 members, many of whom frolicked at the garden parties organized by 5WA at Sophia Gardens. Broadcasts for schools from Cardiff were launched on 14 October 1924 when Walford Davies gave a talk on 'Rhythm, Melody and Chords'. The Glamorgan County Council proved uncooperative, but by 1925 Appleton was in active correspondence with sixty schools, and Cardiff was considered 'second only to London as a successful school broadcasting station'.[73] Reith was concerned that listening to the wireless should not be a passive activity; he wanted the audience to listen intently and to join groups to discuss the programmes. Cardiff had a Listeners' Society by 1924 – one of the three early stations to have such a society – and in January 1926 Appleton founded a magazine, the *Radio Beacon*, as the organ of the society.[74] Talks multiplied, with considerable use being made of the staff of the National Museum. Those who offered to talk were not paid, but those who had to be persuaded to do so received between one and two guineas for a fifteen-minute discourse, the beginning of a practice which would help to enhance the income of impecunious – and not so impecunious – academics. Cardiff's talks were considered to be excellent value for money. 'Cardiff', noted a memorandum of 30 November 1925, 'has done 54 excellent talks for 58 guineas, whereas Glasgow has spent 100 guineas on 50 talks.'[75]

There was an obvious need to ensure that this increasing variety of broadcasts should be available to crystal-set users living beyond the reach of the original stations. The establishment of additional transmitters working on low power was feasible following the government's acceptance of the Sykes Committee's recommendation that more wavebands should be released for public broadcasting. Furthermore, the development of simultaneous broadcasting meant that the Company would not be burdened with the need to finance a pattern of programming exclusive to each of the additional stations. The new stations would be relay stations, producing very little original material. The relay system was financially very attractive to the Company; a relay station cost £2,000 to build and £1,500 a year to run, but its existence could lead to the purchase of additional licences worth £50,000 a year.[76] The first relay station, that at Sheffield, opened in November 1923; Plymouth followed in March 1924, Edinburgh in May, Liverpool in June, a joint station in Bradford and Leeds in July and Hull in August. The new stations were powered by 100 watts, which for crystal-set users gave them a range of about five miles – essentially the town itself and its suburbs. For valve-set users, the range was greater, and thus the opening of the Liverpool station on 11 June 1924 provided some degree of service to the more prosperous wireless owners along the north Wales coast, an area where, hitherto, the reception had been highly unsatisfactory.

News of the Company's intention to build relay stations brought demands from towns not included on the original list. Swansea was particularly vocal, and in February 1924 the County Borough Council requested the postmaster-general to include the town in its future plans. On 30 April 1924, the Company's Broadcasting Board agreed that it was 'right to proceed on the principle that all towns of considerable population should eventually have facilities which would enable them to receive the broadcast programmes on inexpensive sets'. On 28 May, the Board decided to build further stations at Nottingham, Stoke-on-Trent, Dundee and Swansea and to give consideration to possible stations at Norwich, Bristol, Portsmouth and Brighton. Nottingham was opened in September, Dundee and Stoke in November and Swansea in December.[77]

The opening of the Swansea station on 12 December 1924 was the occasion of much celebration, with the *Cambria Leader*, Swansea's morning paper, waxing lyrical on the delights which awaited its readers. Unlike the opening ceremony at Cardiff, which had occurred before the coming of simultaneous broadcasting, that at Swansea was transmitted by most of the stations of Britain.[78] The mayor, Councillor John Lewis, gave much of his address in Welsh, the first time for the language to be broadcast to the greater part of the United Kingdom. He took the opportunity to urge his listeners to attend the National Eisteddfod at Swansea in 1926 and then went on to wonder how much greater the influence of John Elias and Christmas Evans would have been had they been able to address 'y genedl gyfan mewn un oedfa'*.[79] The premises of the new station were on the corner of Union Street and Oxford Street, on the first floor of the Oxford Buildings, and consisted of a studio, a waiting room and five offices. Its director was C. K. Parsons, who had been employed at Cardiff as an announcer; he remained at Swansea until October 1932, when he became director of the Plymouth station, a post he held until he left broadcasting in 1936. Parsons was not highly regarded. It was believed that he would fall in with any Head Office plan, for he 'is a faithful man, if not a great inspiration'. Reith was characteristically more blunt. He wrote in his diary in December 1930: 'Saw Parsons of Swansea, a relic of the old days and of whom we should be rid.'[80] Swansea soon acquired a deputy director; he was Ernest Jenkins, who had graduated at Aberystwyth, the first native of Wales, apart from domestic and clerical workers, to be employed by the Company. The station was to have a further Welsh employee in June 1926 when Miss F. M. Morgan, a Swansea graduate, became women's assistant, with special responsibility for *Children's Hour*.[81]

The nature of the programmes Swansea would relay was much discussed in the town's newspapers in the months preceding the opening of the station. When the Sheffield relay station opened in November 1923, it was intended that it should relay the programmes transmitted from Manchester, for the shorter the land lines the lower the Post Office fees and the rarer the breakdowns. There was an outcry in Sheffield. London programmes were demanded, for, as Reith put it, 'no city counted sufficiently important to have a relay station could listen to the programmes of any station other than London without loss of dignity'.[82] The issue arose with the subsequent relay stations, particularly with Edinburgh, a city even less willing to knuckle under to Glasgow than was Sheffield to

---

*'The entire nation at one service'.

Manchester. Reith, a Glaswegian, was annoyed, particularly as he intended the four Scottish stations – Glasgow, Aberdeen, Edinburgh and Dundee – to provide a national service for Scotland. In March 1925, he wrote that 'as the Welsh are a nation distinct from the English, our present policy in Scotland might be advantageously applied to Cardiff'.[83] Thus he felt no sympathy for the much reiterated demand that Swansea should relay London rather than Cardiff. That demand arose, not, as one correspondent put it, 'as a slight on the Cardiff station . . . but [because] Swansea people are satisfied with nothing less than the best'.[84]

Reith referred to the Swansea agitation in his *Broadcast over Britain*, the manifesto for British public broadcasting which he wrote in great haste between June and August 1924. 'It seems absurd', he stated, 'that Swansea . . . should relay from London instead of from Cardiff, or Dundee from London instead of from a Scottish main station . . . [for] a much more satisfactory service will be given [if] stations are grouped by areas according to characteristics, national or local.'[85] In the case of Sheffield, the Company yielded to local demand, and the Sheffield precedent was followed at the other relay stations established in England. Different arrangements were made at Swansea: it would broadcast Cardiff on three nights, London on three nights and its own programme once a week.

These arrangements could lead to curious anomalies. There were occasions when London featured a singer with Swansea connections at a time when Swansea was broadcasting Cardiff's programmes; on the other hand, there were occasions when Cardiff was broadcasting material of specific Welsh interest while Swansea was transmitting London's programmes. The Swansea newspapers – the *Cambria Leader* in particular – made much of these absurdities. Their comments reflected Swansea's bitterness that the town had, somehow, been upstaged by Cardiff. They stressed that Swansea was the capital of 'Welsh Wales', and the *Cambria Leader* suggested mischievously that, when the town's mayor had spoken in Welsh at the opening ceremony, listeners at Cardiff must have thought that they had picked up a Spanish station.[86]

Swansea was the last of the relay stations, for the tentative plan to build stations at Bristol and elsewhere was abandoned. Fear that Bristol would be a permanent adjunct of Cardiff led to the launching of a campaign for 'broadcasting justice' for the city. Swansea was delighted by the Bristol agitation. 'Bristol', stated the *Cambria Leader*, 'is probably more badly served in the matter of broadcasting than any centre of great population in the country.' The paper urged that Bristol should become a main station with a relay for the 'English' population of Cardiff. The main station at Cardiff should be transferred to Swansea which was ideally suitable to be the centre of broadcasting for 'Welsh Wales'.[87] Where broadcasting was concerned, the plan involved the absorption of south-east Wales into south-western England. Its proposal by a newspaper which emphasized its commitment to Welsh issues suggests that the territorial integrity of Wales was not a strongly held concept in the 1920s. The Swansea agitation was ignored by the Company. Indeed, as will be seen, Swansea, far from replacing Cardiff, became more firmly subject to Cardiff's tutelage.

With the opening of the Swansea station, about 70 per cent of the inhabitants of Britain could receive programmes on inexpensive valve sets.[88] By the end of 1924, 1,129,578 licences had been sold, representing almost 10 per cent of the households of the United Kingdom; in addition, it was believed that hundreds of thousands of households were receiving programmes on unlicensed sets.[89] Details of licence sales are not available for Wales until 1930, but by the end of 1924 Cardiff offered reception on inexpensive sets to about 500,000 people in mid and east Glamorgan and to some 200,000 of the inhabitants of Monmouthshire; Swansea offered a similar service to the town's 160,000 inhabitants, as did Manchester and Liverpool to some tens of thousands of the inhabitants of Denbighshire, Flintshire and parts of coastal Caernarfonshire. In addition, when conditions were favourable, owners of expensive sets in south-west, north-west and mid Wales could receive some sort of service. Such owners, however, were not numerous, the *South Wales Daily News* claiming in December 1924 that 'for the one family who can buy a valve set . . . there are hundreds who can only run to crystal outfits'.[90]

The eagerness to receive London programmes, evinced by the controversy over the relay stations, could lead to the view that programme production outside London was unnecessary and that provincial transmitters should do nothing but broadcast London's output. There were those at Head Office who put forward that view, but Reith, although his attitudes were becoming more metropolitan, was not prepared to countenance such extreme centralization. Yet the agitation proved that there would be a welcome for an additional service exclusively devoted to the transmission of programmes produced in London. If that service could be made available to the United Kingdom as a whole, it would help to relieve the deprivation felt by the 30 per cent of the population who could not receive the transmissions of the main and relay stations.

Peter Eckersley's belief that a high-power single transmitter on long wave could reach most parts of Britain was vindicated by experiments conducted at Chelmsford in the early months of 1924. From 21 July to 9 August, the London service was broadcast from

Chelmsford on 1600 metres, an experiment which was widely reported in the newspapers of Wales. The Post Office, under pressure from the armed services, was reluctant to release any long wavebands for public broadcasting, but it yielded to the request of the Company in September 1924. The postmaster-general at the time was Vernon Hartshorn, the Welsh miners' leader and MP for Ogmore, who held the office during the first Labour government (January to November 1924). A 500-foot mast was erected at Daventry in Northamptonshire, near the geographical centre of England. The Daventry transmitter was opened by Stanley Baldwin, the prime minister, on 27 July 1925, an occasion marked by a celebratory poem by the Aberystwyth-born poet, Alfred Noyes. Powered by twenty-five kilowatts, its output, under the call sign 5XX, could be received by at least 80 per cent of the population of Britain. It was audible on inexpensive sets over virtually the whole of Wales. Thus, for the inhabitants of the greater part of the surface area of Wales, the first experience of wireless listening came not from the transmissions of Cardiff but from those of Daventry. Daventry's initial transmissions were identical with those of the London station, but by September 1925 it was broadcasting ten hours a week of its own programmes, the beginning of the concept of a national programme distinct from the offerings of the main and relay stations.[91]

By the summer of 1925, the Company had the facilities to offer two separate services to the majority of the inhabitants of the United Kingdom. The time therefore seemed opportune to review the whole pattern of its activities. There were also other factors encouraging the Head Office to undertake such a review. One of them was the demand for London programmes. Although the extreme centralizers were resisted, there was a strong feeling that, as simultaneous broadcasting was proving so effective, to permit the eight main stations outside London to produce the greater part of their output involved wasteful duplication. London, it was believed, could provide the best of everything. In May 1924, the station directors were asked to consider whether it was desirable to have local talks, as 'the most well-known authorities . . . were to be found in London'.[92] In March 1925, Burrows informed the Control Board that 'in the majority of cases, we have reached saturation point in the use of local performers at provincial stations. Any considerable extension of programme allowance . . . for . . . local talent may be regarded as wasted . . . The whole entertainment industry is centred in London and this fact has to be recognized.'[93] Because of what Head Office considered to be the dearth of local talent, the Company began the practice of sending London artists to take part in programmes at provincial stations, but as such artists could perform more conveniently and cheaply in London, this practice came to be deemed particularly wasteful.

With eight main stations (apart from London) and ten relay stations, there were eighteen station directors with access to the Company's managing director. Reith, using the British civil service as his model, was anxious to concentrate authority in as few hands as possible. As he wanted only a very small number of the London staff directly responsible to him, he sought a similar arrangement outside London. From the point of view of the Head Office, the future lay in a considerable increase in the London input into the 'provinces' and a regrouping of the provincial stations so as markedly to reduce the number of station directors with access to the managing director. These factors, taken together, pointed to one conclusion: that broadcasting outside London, which had begun as local broadcasting, should henceforth be regional broadcasting.[94]

Technological factors were even more pressing in emphasizing the need to regroup the provincial stations. By 1925, Britain was using seventeen medium wavelengths and one long wavelength. As a medium-wave station could often be heard hundreds of miles away, it became apparent that every station in Europe would have to have its own separate wavelength. Indeed, to ensure reception free from gross interference, this might prove to be necessary over a zone including not only Europe but also North Africa and the Near East. Even with the greatest ingenuity and the sharing of wavelengths by low-powered stations there were only two hundred channels available for a zone which contained at least forty separate states. If they were all to make use of channels on the British scale (or even on a far lesser scale), without any consideration of the usage of other states, the New World's 'chaos on the ether' would be far surpassed by that of the Old. It was chiefly because of this factor that the building of relay stations came to an end with the opening of Swansea. Concern over competition for wavelengths led to the Geneva Conference of April 1925 when the Union International de Radiophone was founded. The Geneva Plan, adopted by the Union in July 1926, allocated Britain one long wavelength, nine exclusive medium wavelengths and five 'common' wavelengths below 300 metres. Even before the acceptance of the plan, it was obvious that British broadcasting had made use of too many wavelengths. By accepting the plan, the Company was recognizing that it would have to reduce the number of its transmitters and that there could be no possibility of adding to its range of relay stations. Thus, within a few months of the opening of the Swansea relay station, the entire relay system was doomed.[95]

In the summer of 1925, the Company's officials worked on their regional scheme. Foreseeing the outcome of the Geneva discussions, they planned on the assumption that no more than ten exclusive wavelengths would be available. Peter Eckersley devised a scheme which would allow for six regions, each with two wavelengths; one would transmit the regional programme and the other would supplement the service from Daventry. The plan was adopted by the Control Board on 17 November 1926. The regions were to be London, West (based on Cardiff), Midland (based on Birmingham), North (based on Manchester), Scotland (based on Glasgow) and Northern Ireland (based on Belfast). All were to work on sufficient power so as to make relay stations unnecessary.[96]

Apart from Scotland and Northern Ireland, the regions had little coherence for, as Scannell and Cardiff put it: 'The design of the regional scheme and the siting of the transmitters and stations were determined by administrative, technical and economic considerations before any notion of what regionalisation might actually mean in terms of people, places and cultural characteristics.'[97] The oddest was London, which was not a region at all, but an extension of the Head Office. The North was vast, extending from the Cheviot Hills to the Potteries and containing a third of the population of Britain. In describing the resources of his proposed region in September 1927, Edward Livening, the Manchester station director, listed the bishop of St Asaph among its ecclesiastical dignitaries and the performances on Llandudno pier among its entertainment resources, thus implying that much of north Wales was *de facto*, if not *de jure*, part of the proposed North Region.[98] The Midland Region extended from Oswestry to Lowestoft, although East Anglia was something of a no man's land. The West was south Wales and south-western England; mid and north-west Wales do not seem to have belonged to any region at all.

Peter Eckersley revealed the outline of his plan in October 1925, arousing an angry reaction from all the towns with relay stations, Swansea among them. Reith reacted loftily. He informed the station directors on 9 October 1925, 'I shall be disappointed if local Station Directors are unable to handle hostile embryo local agitation. Such a reflection on their ability will, I am sure, not arise . . . I feel sure that your close association with local affairs will not give rise to any mistaken misconceptions in your minds that such an indiscriminating loyalty to them might detract from your loyalty to the Company and to the service generally.'[99] The co-ordination necessary to implement the plan had been completed by June 1927, but its implications were apparent by 1926. They were proof that regional broadcasting is the enemy of local broadcasting. They were also proof that Reith had abandoned the policy that he had advocated in March 1925 of applying the Scottish model to Wales. South Wales was to be yoked with south-western England; the north-east was to receive an overspill from the North Region, and in the rest of Wales, owners of inexpensive sets would only receive the Daventry programmes.

The abandonment of the intention to create a service for Wales as a whole did not mean that the Company was denying that it had an obligation to provide programmes of specific interest to Welsh listeners. Much was made of the Welsh musical tradition and, as has been seen, the Company was actively concerned to ensure that the country had an orchestra. Welsh history, particularly that of the distant past, provided material for a number of feature programmes, and the topography of Wales was extensively explored. The country's social and economic problems received scant attention, but this was also true of all other parts of the United Kingdom. Major Welsh events were punctiliously broadcast. At the Pontypool National Eisteddfod of 1924, the crowning ceremony was broadcast, but the other ceremonies were not. (The crowning was performed by the prince of Wales.) Considerable coverage was given to the proclamation in 1925 of the Swansea National Eisteddfod of 1926. Five of the presidential addresses delivered (in English) at the National Eisteddfod at Pwllheli in 1925 were broadcast, and several programmes of performances by winning choirs and soloists were transmitted. After-dinner speeches, a staple item of early broadcasting, provided the Company with opportunities to transmit much sentimentally patriotic oratory, particularly from the St David's Day dinners of the Cardiff Cymmrodorion.[100]

From the beginning, however, the Company's officials were insistent that such recognition of Wales should be subservient to one of the primary aims of British broadcasting – the projection of the unity of the British nation. Broadcasting, state Scannell and Cardiff, 'allows the nation to become a knowable community'.[101] That the nation which becomes knowable should be the nation of the Welsh was a concept beyond the comprehension of Corbett-Smith and Appleton. Equally incomprehensible to them was any notion that the 922,000 Welsh-speakers of Wales (37.1 per cent of the population enumerated in 1921) should be provided with programmes produced specifically for them in their own language.

The Welsh dimension to broadcasting (or the Welsh Controversy, to quote the name of a file at the Caversham archives) did not loom large in the first few years of the Cardiff station. The need for broadcasts in Welsh was stressed in an article in the *Western Mail* on 8 March 1923, but there were few such demands until the later 1920s. This may be because the new medium was chiefly perceived as a means of broadcasting music, and in the early years Welsh folk songs and pot-pourris of Welsh airs were liberally provided by the Cardiff and Swansea stations. Furthermore, educated opinion-makers were only dimly aware of the existence of the wireless. However, as the speech element increased, and as transmissions became more readily available in the Welsh-speaking parts of Wales, there was growing concern that a service almost totally English in language constituted a dire threat to the survival of Welsh-speaking communities.

Initially at least, Appleton gave the impression that he was sympathetic towards the Welsh language. He took lessons in Welsh, and, although the claim that he spoke it fluently is based on very little evidence, he had a sufficient command of the language to enable him to recite the Lord's Prayer in Welsh in his *Silent Fellowship* programmes. At the National Eisteddfod of 1925, he was received into the Gorsedd of the Bards as 'Goleuni'r Bannau' (the Beacon Light), an honour which gave him much pleasure. 'I am not an honorary bard like the Queen of Roumania', he wrote, 'but a full acting member of the Circle.'[102]

By 1925, however, Appleton was becoming increasingly aware that his conception of the Welsh language as a quaint folkloric survival was being challenged by Welsh-speakers determined to seek a more dynamic role for their language. 'It is unfortunate', he wrote in 1935, 'that the BBC [came] into being at a time of such rapid development in Wales . . . when the leaders of Wales . . . were becoming nationally conscious.'[103] He pointed to the foundation in 1922 of Urdd Gobaith Cymru (the Welsh League of Youth), which rapidly gained over 50,000 members. Plaid Genedlaethol Cymru (the National Party of Wales), founded in 1925, made nothing like such rapid progress, but Appleton was deeply concerned by the way in which the 'extreme' political Nationalists were seizing the initiative from the 'moderate' cultural nationalists.[104] The cultural nationalists were also becoming more assertive as leading university figures such as Ernest Hughes and Henry Lewis of Swansea and W. J. Gruffydd of Cardiff were becoming, as Appleton put it, 'fully alive to the possibilities of broadcasting'.[105]

Early in December 1924, Appleton met the members of Cylch Dewi (the Circle of St David), a group of Cardiff cultural nationalists. He asked them to prepare a series of programmes, the contents of which were to be submitted six weeks beforehand. The programmes were to be an hour long and Cylch Dewi was to be paid twelve guineas (£12.60p) for each offering. The songs they contained could be in Welsh, but as Appleton was reluctant to permit the broadcast of spoken Welsh by the Cardiff station, any talk, poem or drama would have to be in English. Under the title *A Welsh Hour*, the first of the Cylch Dewi programmes was broadcast on 14 January 1925. There were others on 6, 11 and 28 February, 8 April and 6 May 1925. Saunders Lewis, later Appleton's most severe critic, was invited to give a talk on St David in the programme of 28 February. 'Deuaf ar yr amod y caf siarad yn Gymraeg', he informed Mrs Abel Jones, the producer of the programmes. 'Gellwch hefyd roi fy ngair i'r BBC na ddywedaf i ddim o gwbl o natur boliticaidd anheg.'*[106] Appleton acquiesced but retaliated by offering no timings for March. Mrs Abel Jones accused him of 'treating these Welsh Hours very halfheartedly'. 'If we fail to get a certain amount of justice at your hands', she wrote on 1 May 1925, 'we shall have to consider what else we can do to secure our ends.' Appleton described her letter as 'most unkind and unjust'. 'The "Hours" ', he wrote, 'have been considered not quite cheerful enough and . . . our English-speaking audience simply switches off . . . I doubt very much whether the Welsh-speaking portion of our audience switches off for the English part of the programme, and this fact had to be taken into consideration.' His letter of 2 May offered no future dates and co-operation with Cylch Dewi came to an end.[107]

In addition to the venture by Cylch Dewi, the Cardiff station broadcast a few other items in Welsh during the early years of Appleton's directorship. Eighteen Welsh lessons were transmitted between May and October 1924; extracts from D. T. Davies's play, *Y Pwyllgor*, were heard on 31 July 1924; there were readings from the poetry of T. Gwynn Jones and R. Williams Parry on 14 February and 6 March 1925; a service was broadcast from Tabernacl Welsh Baptist Chapel in The Hayes on 31 May 1925 (with Appleton insisting that it should not be wholly in Welsh); Cardiff transmitted one of the Welsh talks produced at Swansea on 2 October 1925.

By the mid 1920s, Appleton became increasingly involved with the broadcasting needs of south-western England where the number of licence-holders was growing more rapidly than in Wales. This factor convinced him that the minor concessions hitherto granted to spoken Welsh should cease. Where Wales was concerned, he came to conceive of himself as something of a colonial governor or an imperial proconsul, viewing his 'subjects' with a mixture of irritation and condescension. In the Corporation's *Handbook* for 1928, the Cardiff report (presumably written by Appleton) notes that 'broadcasting in Wales is an adventure set with pitfalls . . . but there is a spirit in the people that makes it a lovable business'.[108]

*'I shall come on condition that I may speak in Welsh. You can give my word to the BBC that I will say nothing of an unfairly political nature.'

The Swansea station was not obliged to consider the susceptibilities of listeners in England. As a relay station, its output was less than half that of Cardiff. Of the forty-four hours a week broadcast from Cardiff in the first months of 1925, twenty-eight hours were Cardiff's productions; the equivalent figures for Swansea were forty-two and thirteen. Swansea's basic output consisted of daily transmissions lasting about ninety minutes which included children's programmes, schools programmes, local news, sports commentaries and an occasional talk. In addition the station broadcast one full evening of its own productions once a week – usually on a Friday – drawing on resources such as the local Territorial Army Band, the Tawe Glee Singers and Dr Vaughan Thomas's Octet. Some of the station's broadcast music was not highly regarded, a listener remembering 'an evening of certain sounds, supposed to have been produced by an orchestra in the Swansea studio, that still produce shudders in those who unhappily listened'.[109] Swansea offered an occasional *Welsh Night*, a programme in which all the songs were in Welsh and which included a brief talk in Welsh; in 1925, there were half a dozen such talks, including one by Saunders Lewis on *Y Ddrama Gymraeg*. In that year, the station broadcast three Welsh-language plays, together with two perform-ances of Joseph Parry's *Blodwen* and one of his *Ceridwen*. Its programmes for schools and for children included occasional items in Welsh and, in January 1926, it launched a series of lessons in 'Conversational Welsh'. Welsh hymns were sung in its studio services, and on 22 February 1925 Swansea broadcast a complete Welsh-language religious service from Capel Gomer, the Baptist chapel near the town centre.

These developments received the approval of the *Cambria Leader* which continued to insist that 'Welsh needs will never be served from Cardiff'. The newspaper was profoundly disturbed by the implications of the Regional Scheme for 'it means the end of our fond dream of a special broadcasting station paying attention, in moderation, to the special needs of Wales'. 'We shall be left', wrote its editor, 'with a microphone somewhere and a telephone line to Cardiff, just enough of a concession to local feeling to allow the BBC to say that Swansea is not entirely ignored.'[110]

The *Leader*'s forebodings were not fully realized – at least, not in the 1920s. The Regional Scheme involved the ultimate close-down of the Swansea transmitter; in their public statements, Head Office officials denied that the Swansea studio was also faced with closure, but internal memoranda prove that this was the original intention. The closure was not carried out, because 'in view of the difficult Welsh situation, it was decided that Swansea should be allowed to broadcast on special occasions of Welsh interest'.[111] Nevertheless, the demotion of the relay stations implicit in the Regional Scheme led to a severe curtailment of programme production at Swansea. 'From a Welsh point of view', wrote Ernest Hughes in 1930, '[the putting] of Swansea in its "proper" place . . . has been a calamitous loss.'[112]

The Regional Scheme not only involved the demotion of Swansea. As has been seen, it also meant that the Company was reneging on its promise to provide Wales with a service comparable with that planned for Scotland. The transmissions from the Cardiff and Swansea transmitters could not be heard on inexpensive sets in mid and north Wales. In public, Head Office gave the impression that the output of the powerful transmitter which would be built for the West Region would be able to reach most parts of Wales, but in private this was doubted. Furthermore, unless they travelled to Cardiff or Swansea, the inhabitants of mid and north Wales could not contribute to programmes of Welsh interest provided by those stations, a consideration which caused Appleton to appeal to the Control Board in the autumn of 1926 to establish in north Wales an 'open microphone, similar to that in the Oxford studio'.[113]

On 15 November 1926, the issue of a transmitter and a studio for the north was raised in the House of Commons, the first of many parliamentary speeches on broadcasting in Wales. Ellis Davies, the Liberal MP for Denbigh, demanded a relay station at Colwyn Bay to enable 'Welsh addresses, lectures and religious services' to be broadcast. His request for broadcasts in Welsh caused much merriment among MPs and received no answer from the postmaster-general.[114] By the autumn of 1926, Ellis Davies was not alone in his protests. The *Radio Times* published a passionate appeal for Welsh-language broadcasts on 10 October 1926 and similar appeals were made by the Gorsedd of the Bards and the Union of Welsh Societies.[115] Thereafter, such appeals and protests loom so large that there may be a tendency, in discussing the history of broadcasting in Wales, to give them disproportionate attention.

As the Regional Scheme precluded the possibility of providing a service for Wales as a whole, the Company felt obliged to ensure that occasional programmes of Welsh interest should be available outside the reach of the Cardiff and Swansea transmitters. On 5 February 1926, the Company decided that Daventry should broadcast programmes consisting of songs in Welsh and talks of Welsh interest in English.[116] Thus, in order that the programmes should reach the entire population of Wales, they also had to be available to virtually the entire population of Britain. The first of the 45-minute programmes was broadcast on Thursday, 6 April 1926; introduced by Elfed, the archdruid, it consisted of songs by the London Welsh Male

Octet and scenes from J. O. Francis's play *The Poacher*. Further programmes were broadcast at four- or five-week intervals; they contained no Welsh speech and most of them were produced in London or Birmingham. Letters poured into Savoy Hill from appreciative Welsh residents in England, and from many listeners with no Welsh connections at all. Head Office staff, however, viewed the programmes as a nuisance. 'If it were practicable', wrote Noel Ashbridge, the deputy chief engineer, 'I should be delighted to have all Welsh stuff off Daventry, and what fun Appleton would have!'[117]

Much of north Wales was within the reach of the Manchester and Liverpool transmitters, and they also provided an occasional programme of Welsh interest. Manchester broadcast a *Welsh Night* on 8 October 1924 and again on 29 December 1925; Liverpool provided a *Noson Gymreig* on 3 April 1925 with songs by the Liverpool Cymric Vocal Union. The offerings were little enough but broadcasters believed that it was commendable that they were doing anything at all. There were in Wales those who agreed with them. Reviewing the work of the British Broadcasting Company in 1926, the journalist J. C. Griffith Jones noted that 'it had made offerings on the altar of Welsh national ideals and aspirations'. He went on to write: 'Whether they have yet successfully disposed of this very difficult issue is a debatable point' – a breathtakingly optimistic remark in view of what was to come.[118]

The year 1926 was the last year of the Company, for its licence was to expire on 31 December. Reith had provided a blueprint for its replacement in his *Broadcast over Britain*, in which he had argued that British broadcasting should be a monopoly undertaken by an institution under public control. In July 1925, the government appointed a committee, chaired by the twenty-seventh earl of Crawford, to consider the matter. The committee, which reported on 5 March 1926, endorsed virtually the whole of Reith's blueprint.[119] The Company should connive in its own extinction and be replaced by a Corporation answerable to a board of governors and financed by the licence fee. The case against monopoly was not effectively presented, and thus the report was a recommendation to a Conservative government that, to all intents and purposes, it should nationalize broadcasting. The only opposition to the proposal came from doctrinaire Liberals such as Hore-Belisha. By the late 1920s, the Labour Party was increasingly corporatist in its views, and it was generally in favour of the Crawford Report. Of the Conservatives, the more patrician among them disliked the notion of potentially vulgar competing stations; some of them had heard American radio and had been appalled by its vulgarity – or possibly by its innate democracy. Furthermore, the Conservatives saw themselves as the upholders of national institutions; they were, after all, the champions of the Established Church.

On 14 July 1926, the postmaster-general announced that the government broadly accepted the Crawford proposals. As the Corporation was to be created through royal charter, no legislation was necessary. Reith disliked some of the new arrangements, in particular the financial details, the continued role of the postmaster-general, the excessive (as he saw it) salaries of the governors and the lack of any provision allowing the Corporation to raise money through advertising. On the whole, however, he had reason to feel content, although contentment was alien to his character.[120]

Between the publication of the Crawford Report and the statement of the postmaster-general, Britain was convulsed by the General Strike of 1 to 12 May 1926. As the strike was the consequence of a lock-out in the coal industry, it was of greater importance in Wales than in any other part of the kingdom, for in 1926 27 per cent of the Welsh male work-force was employed in coal-mining compared with less than 10 per cent in the United Kingdom as a whole. As the strike was a profoundly controversial issue – although less so in industrial Wales than in the rest of Britain – broadcasters were forbidden to discuss it, for the Company's licence specifically forbade the broadcast of controversy. Admittedly, Vernon Hartshorn had authorized party political broadcasts during the general election campaign of 1924, but that decision served to restrict broadcast debate to those issues on which the three major parties were at variance.[121] The General Strike was a totally different matter. Much has been written about Reith's activities in May 1926, and there is a widespread belief that his firmness and sagacity saved the independence of British broadcasting. The argument should not be pressed too far, for a great deal of the pusillanimity of British broadcasters in subsequent years may be ascribed to their awareness of how fragile their independence had been in 1926. '[After 1926]', wrote Jonathan Dimbleby, 'the tyranny of safety first stifled adventurous talent . . . Reith never recovered from the Strike.' [122]

As most newspapers did not appear during the strike, the Company was allowed to put out five bulletins a day. Their content was supplied by the agencies, although some broadcasters, contrary to the Company's licence, went in search of news. The aim was to provide the unvarnished truth, and during the strike the broadcasts were almost certainly a moderating influence. The organized working class, however, assumed that the Company was ranged against them and the TUC advised its members not to listen to the bulletins. Whatever the news given – and there is no surviving record of it – it can be assumed that it offered no portrait of the impressive unity of the workers nor any insight into the basic issues which had caused the conflict; indeed, such matters would have been wholly outside the experience of almost all the Company's more senior employees.[123]

In Wales, evidence of broadcasting during the strike is available in the volume 'Programmes as Broadcast'. As the pattern of programming was decided upon weeks before transmission, any change in the scheduling resulting from the strike would be apparent by comparing the lists of programmes in the *Radio Times* with those in 'Programmes as Broadcast'. The comparison shows that on 5 and 11 May the Cardiff station broadcast programmes of gramophone records instead of live performances from Cox's Café. On 4 and 6 May, it transmitted additional fifteen-minute news bulletins and on 9 and 10 May it transmitted longer bulletins than had been originally planned. The only other change to the schedule was that on Saturday evening, 6 May, when an address by the prime minister replaced a talk on athletic training. Otherwise, the planned schedule, including a talk on *The Home Life of a Carrion Crow*, was broadcast undisturbed.[124]

The Company's activities during the strike do not seem to have affected the government's readiness to accept the essentials of Reith's view of public broadcasting. Indeed, within eight weeks of the end of the strike, that view was endorsed by the postmaster-general. The events of May 1926 may have encouraged the government to view more sympathetically the demand that broadcasting should have its own news-gathering service. A clause permitting such a service was included in the licence of the new Corporation.

As the four-year existence of the British Broadcasting Company drew to its end, its directors could look back upon a period of astonishing development. This must also be the feeling of the historian of those years, for the cascade of new ventures seems almost too rapid to record. As Reith put it, 'almost weekly new prospects were revealed'.[125] He believed that, during the four years of the Company, the pattern of British broadcasting had been laid down for years to come, and that the output of the new Corporation would be enthusiastically received by a grateful populace. Where Wales was concerned, he was greatly mistaken, for the launching of the Corporation on 1 January 1927 ushered in an era in Wales during which broadcasting would be one of the most contentious of all issues.

2

The Struggle for the Welsh Region: Broadcasting in Wales, 1927–1937

I The Regional Scheme

New Year's Day 1927, the first day of the British Broadcasting Corporation, did not usher in a revolution, for since early 1925 at least Reith had been managing the Company as if it were a public corporation. Crawford's intention that there should be constitutional change with institutional continuity was fulfilled. In the last months of the Company, Reith wrote to the station directors enquiring whether their staff members were worthy to be employees of the Corporation. He also enquired whether their number could be reduced, for, ironically, the Regional Scheme involved an increase in London programmes and a corresponding decrease in the amount of material produced elsewhere.[1]

The full implementation of the scheme was the first task of the new Corporation. Its central feature was the regrouping of the main and relay stations. In the embryo West Region, there were transmitters and studios at Cardiff, Swansea and Plymouth. On 8 June 1927, Appleton and Parsons each received a lengthy memorandum from Head Office informing them that 'Wales and England south and west of a line from Hereford through Worcester to Bournemouth will . . . be served by a station centred on Cardiff'. The Regional Scheme was presented as the answer to complaints that broadcasting had not recognized the legitimate rights of Wales. It involved the merging of the operations of Cardiff and Swansea, because 'it is advisable to consider Wales as a nation and a distinct section of the proposed region'. Wales, it was argued, would be adequately served when a powerful new transmitter had been built for the West region as a whole. As soon as it was operational, the transmitters at Swansea and Cardiff would be closed.[2]

As has been seen, the original intention of closing the Swansea studio, as well as the town's transmitter, was not carried out. The proposed West transmitter did not come into operation until 1933; Swansea therefore continued to be capable of broadcasting its own programmes for six years after the drawing up of the memorandum of June 1927. That memorandum laid down that Swansea productions broadcast exclusively on the town's transmitter should be phased out and operations at Swansea brought under Cardiff's supervision. The Swansea station director – soon to be known as the Swansea representative – was to visit Cardiff once a week and copies of all correspondence between him and Head Office were to be sent to Cardiff. Swansea's programme planning, noted the memorandum, was to be co-ordinated with that of Cardiff, but as such 'activities are already so largely centralized in London, a sub-centralization at Cardiff will not be a radical alteration'.[3]

In June 1927, Swansea was producing 10 hours 20 minutes of programmes a week. The programmes included forty-five minutes of *Children's Hour* six times a week, announcements, local news, sports commentaries, two concerts and a sixty-minute weekly programme which was also carried by Cardiff. The pattern was much the same a year later, but by June 1929, when the Swansea *Children's Hour* had been reduced to fifteen minutes a week, the station's main function was the production of two weekly programmes which were also transmitted by Cardiff. By the early 1930s, when its fifteen-minute *Morning Service* was the sole broadcast exclusive to Swansea, the *Radio Times* was giving the station only an intermittent listing. Its last listing was 25 May 1933. The West's regional transmitter came into operation on 28 May 1933; its broadcasts from Swansea consisted of an occasional talk and a weekly concert. Swansea's newspapers pointed out that by then less than 5 per cent of the transmitter's output originated west of Cardiff. It would be to the BBC's financial advantage, argued the *Herald of Wales*, to produce more programmes in Swansea. 'There is more employment in the west,' noted the paper. 'Therefore there is more money here to spend on sets.'[4]

Despite the protests of the town's newspapers, the internal arrangements for the merging of Swansea's broadcasting operations with those of Cardiff were carried out smoothly and were cited as an example to be followed elsewhere.[5] Appleton frequently reminded Head Office of Swansea's subjection to him, and also of his responsibilities at Bristol. The reminders were part of his campaign to be recognized as West regional director, a grander title than that of Cardiff station director and one which would make him equal to the North and the Scottish regional directors. His ambition was realized on 4 February 1929.[6]

The Regional Scheme not only involved the attenuation – or, in some cases, the extinction – of programme production at the relay stations; it also involved a contraction in the output of centres such as Cardiff. Even before the full implementation of the scheme in 1928, London programmes had come to constitute almost half the offerings of the regional stations. In the first week of May 1927, the fifty-nine hours broadcast from Cardiff consisted of twenty-seven hours of Cardiff productions, twenty-nine hours of London's and three hours from other stations. In May 1929, of the sixty-four hours transmitted weekly by Cardiff, forty-two were produced in London, twenty-one in Cardiff and one elsewhere. The overwhelmingly dominant role of London meant that it was the work-place of the great majority of the Corporation's employees. In 1927, when the Corporation had a total of 989 employees, Cardiff had an administrative and programme staff of six. The London staff were better paid than those in the regions. In 1924, when Appleton's salary was £550 a year, that of Percy Pitt, the Head Office's director of music, was £1,500. It was noted in 1936 that 'all the best staff' gravitated to London; that gravitation was at least partly the result of financial bait.[7]

London's predominance was also reflected in the programme allowances. In 1927, the London service (2LO) and the Daventry service (5XX) jointly received £1,450 a week; at that time the two stations did not have distinct programme schedules, for 80 per cent of Daventry's output was identical with that of London. Cardiff, with a programme allowance of £190, was in the middle range of provincial stations; Glasgow, with £230, was the most generously treated.[8] The programme allowances are the only form of expenditure which is documented as being allocated to the different regions. The salaries and wages of station staffs, transmission and other engineering costs, the maintenance of premises and all capital investment were London matters. Thus it is impossible to establish the precise cost to the Corporation of its activities in Wales, or in any other part of the United Kingdom, an example of the many obfuscations in the financial history of the BBC.

The implementation of the Regional Scheme involved the curtailing of the power of the regional directors. That was not accompanied by any diminution in their self-esteem. Cleghorn Thomson, the Scottish regional director, was much struck by their 'increasing pomp and decreasing influence'.[9] In 1930, when their salaries ranged from £1,150 to £1,350, Appleton organized a petition to Head Office requesting a substantial pay rise. (By the early 1930s, Reith was being paid £7,500 a year.) V. H. Goldsmith, the assistant controller, informed Charles Carpendale, the controller:

[The regional directors] are certain of the need to keep up appearances. They are considered arbiters of taste in their localities and are believed to be 'big people' . . . They say it is impossible for then to live in a fashion which enables them to return invitations to people like Vice Chancellors of Universities and so forth . . . They think that £2,000 a year is the sort of grade in which one can keep a competent cook and maintain the appearances of decency which are requisite. They say that they have no money to educate their children . . . I suppose a Regional Director should be able to afford three children and one, if not more, should be sent to the University.

Reith was unmoved. The regional directors, he wrote, suggest that their 'executive functions have greatly increased. I am surprised to hear this; nothing of the kind was intended.'[10]

Peter Eckersley, who had devised the Regional Scheme, was appalled by the way it was implemented. His intention of having one wavelength offering the National Service from Daventry and another offering a contrasting group of services reflecting the culture of the different regions of the United Kingdom was, he claimed, totally subverted. The National and the Regional Services became a double outlet for the same kind of programme, with the Regional Scheme used as a way of broadcasting 'material which has accumulated, so to speak, in the Head Office's store department'. Reith dismissed Peter Eckersley in 1929 because he had been cited as a co-respondent in a divorce case, but before his dismissal Eckersley 'sneaked the Regional Directors together . . . and tried to make them revolt'.[11] There were protests from the Manchester, Glasgow and Swansea directors, and also from J. C. Stobart who, in addition to his work as the Corporation's director of education, was responsible for the liaison between Head Office and the regional stations. 'I visit the regions', he wrote to Head Office on 21 May 1928, 'and I state that local activity is to be encouraged; [this] new policy is a breach of faith.'[12] The protests were ignored and centralization continued apace under the leadership of Peter's brother, Roger Eckersley. To Cleghorn Thomson, Roger was 'the greatest enemy of regional initiative and independence, and an enthusiast for just that bloated centripetal "mugwumpery" that his brother feared'.[13]

In view of the Corporation's increasing commitment to centralization, it is surprising that Head Office officials allowed Appleton to continue with the plans to create a national orchestra for Wales. Reith, however, looked favourably upon the project and gave Appleton every encouragement. The prince of Wales agreed to become the orchestra's president and Warwick Braithwaite was appointed its conductor. The orchestra was to provide ten broadcast concerts a week, three from the studio, five from the National Museum and two from Cardiff's City Hall.[14]

It soon became apparent that Cardiff and the other Welsh local authorities were unable to raise the £5,000 required of them, and thus the Corporation, for the first year at least, agreed to contribute the entire £11,000. Reith visited Cardiff to finalize the arrangements on 6 July 1927, and he noted in his diary that Appleton and Walford Davies 'thought that my visit today had saved the scheme'.[15] The orchestra gave its first performance on 12 April 1928, when, conducted by Sir Henry Wood, the thirty players (ten of whom had been recruited from the old station orchestra) gave a rapturously received performance at Cardiff's City Hall.

The BBC's commitment to an orchestra for Wales was viewed with suspicion by several powerful figures at Head Office. By the late 1920s, the Corporation was anxious to allocate a considerable amount of its income to enable London to have a symphony orchestra comparable in quality with those of Vienna and Berlin, an ambition achieved by the mid 1930s when the BBC Symphony Orchestra was winning recognition as one of the finest orchestras in the world. To Roger Eckersley, the extra subsidy received by the National Orchestra of Wales in 1928 was money which could be better spent in London. In November 1928 he sought to convince Reith that 'many of the programmes which provincial stations now do, such as symphony concerts . . . should not properly be attempted by them'. He then went on to make a specific attack upon the subsidy to the National Orchestra of Wales.[16] The doubts of the centralizers were intensified in 1929 when the Welsh local authorities again failed to raise the money expected of them, thus obliging the BBC to fund the orchestra's entire costs for a second year. The *Cambria Leader* exulted in the problems of the Cardiff-based orchestra. 'We can just imagine', wrote the editor, 'the fervour that would be shown [were it based] in Swansea.'[17]

By 1930, the orchestra was in crisis. In May, Reith, accompanied by Thomas Jones, the deputy secretary of the Cabinet and the leading figure in a wide array of Welsh social and educational movements, attended a meeting at Cardiff to discuss its problems. Reith promised that the BBC would underwrite most of the orchestra's costs for a third year if the Welsh local authorities raised £2,000. With the depression tightening its grip, the impoverished authorities failed to raise half that sum. By the end of the year, Thomas Jones was seeking subventions from wealthy Welshmen.[18]

In December 1930, a deputation led by Lord Howard de Walden visited Savoy Hill to appeal to the BBC to continue its subsidy. The Corporation offered £6,000, a sum which would decrease by £1,000 a year and urged that an appeal should be launched by the Welsh National Council of Music to raise the rest of the money. Fearing for the future of his orchestra, Warwick Braithwaite launched his own separate appeal. Neither appeal was successful and the orchestra was disbanded in October 1931. It was replaced by a group of nine musicians, eight of whom had been members of the National Orchestra. Braithwaite was dismissed and was succeeded by his deputy, Reginald Redman. Appleton, who believed that the creation of the orchestra had been his greatest achievement, was much depressed by the episode. It caused him to be cynical about claims that Wales as a whole was yearning for its own national broadcasting service; 'Wales', he wrote, 'was given every opportunity [to have a national orchestra] and by default implied that it was not required.'[19]

The reluctance to finance the National Orchestra of Wales was a reflection of the growing centralization implicit in the way the Regional Scheme was implemented. Roger Eckersley's opposition to regional orchestras was part of his general hostility to what he considered to be wasteful diffusion of effort and resources. 'More has been made of civic pride and *amour propre* than has been necessary,' he wrote. 'This is surely evidenced by the comparative lack of protest in the towns where we have recently curbed the activities of relay stations.'[20] He was not alone in his views. Reith in 1926 had expressed doubts whether provincial stations should do any drama beyond plays of specific local interest, and Val Gielgud, who became productions manager in January 1929, was convinced that metropolitan plays were the only ones worth considering.[21] Every one of the five initial governors of the Corporation lived in London or the English 'home counties' and as they hardly ever heard the programmes of the provincial stations, they could not be expected to have any clear views about them.[22] The early years of the Corporation were a period of financial difficulty. In 1928, 2,384,000 licences were bought at a cost of £1,192,000, but the Post Office and the Treasury retained £411,000, and the BBC's extensive capital investment programme precluded it from having much of a reserve fund; indeed, by 1931, the Corporation had a deficit of £250,000, a sum which would have been twice as large but for the profits of the *Radio Times*.[23] Thus, there were financial as well as ideological arguments in favour of limiting expenditure in the regions. It would be cheaper, it was argued, for the regions to concentrate on matters regional; this would release resources to allow London to deal with matters universal.

The clearest statement of the implications of centralization came in a memorandum from Roger Eckersley sent to the station directors on

28 November 1928. It had clearly been endorsed by Reith, for it contained some of the arguments which Eckersley had put before Reith a fortnight earlier. Eckersley concluded with the frequently quoted sentence: 'The moral of this memorandum could be shortly read as saying: Take from London what you cannot do better yourself, and do yourself what London cannot give you.'[24] The policy was put into operation. Although in theory regional directors were free to broadcast whatever they chose, except on those rare occasions when London's output was mandatory, Head Office's rulings on staff and programme allowances left them with little choice but to concur. In 1930, Arthur Blanche, Cardiff's drama producer, was transferred elsewhere and was not replaced.[25] Cardiff's programme allowance, £190 a week in 1927, was only marginally increased over the following six years although the number of listeners licensed to receive Cardiff's broadcasts more than quadrupled between 1927 and 1933. Despite the acquiescence of the regional directors, there was a constant fear in London that the regions would somehow wrest autonomy for themselves. 'The tendency now', wrote Charles Siepmann, the BBC's director of talks, in 1932, 'is for the Regional Directors to pull gradually away towards independence in programme policy, which we shall live to regret unless we scotch it now.'[26]

Centralization did not only occur in programme ouput. By the early 1930s, regional directors had virtually no power to spend money over and above the programme allowance allotted to them, and the situation worsened in 1933 when the Corporation adopted a rigid distinction between the functions of administrators and those of programme creators. The BBC came to be so bureaucratic that broadcasters were referred to as 'creative helots'.[27] The BBC's employees, argued Peter Eckersley, 'have learned how to keep a job by making the job into the kind they can keep'. He wrote sarcastically of the 'wad of papers in London concerning the placing of a tap in Leeds', and the material relating to Wales offers similar examples.[28] A correspondence between Cardiff and Head Office concerning the employment of a part-time tea-maker at 12s. 6d. (52.5p) a week continued for eighteen months. A large file on a cleaner at Cardiff ends with a Head Office note: 'For sheer inconsequence this is hard to beat.' Another file was then opened in which to put letters discussing who was responsible for the inconsequence.[29]

The bewilderment of a present-day researcher into this mass of paper is increased by the BBC's practice in the early 1930s, and for decades to come, of referring to all employees by the initials of the office they held. Thus, the heading of a typical memorandum reads DOA to DPA and PRE with copies to DSA, MRD, NRD, WRD,

WERD, SRD and NIRD. Alongside the typewritten memorandum there is usually a series of handwritten comments, the initials of the titles of their authors being either absent or illegible. Centralization was accompanied by an urge to issue regulations on everything. The archives contain memoranda declaring that 'plus fours should not be worn in the office except on Saturday morning' and that 'while shirt sleeves are undesirable in wearers' own offices, they should on *no* account be worn about the corridors'. Such regulations reached their apogee in a memorandum circulated to the Cardiff staff: 'Please note in future that Red Pencils should not be used in these offices other than by the [regional director].'[30]

II   Demands from Wales

While the activities of the Corporation, in Wales as elsewhere, were coming under centralized control, a demand fundamentally hostile to that centralization was being increasingly heard.[31] Concern about the lack of programmes in the Welsh language, voiced in 1925 and 1926, has already been noted. It swelled into a loud chorus in 1927. Indeed, the creation of the Corporation probably encouraged its expression for, compared with a company, a public corporation may have been perceived as more amenable to pressure. In February 1927, the Court of Governors of University College, Cardiff, agreed virtually unanimously to demand 'a broadcast station wholly for Wales, with a view to preserving the individuality and the culture of the Welsh nation'. The chief speaker in the discussion was Professor W. J. Gruffydd, who assumed that the proposed station would be in addition to the existing provision. The courts of the other University colleges adopted similar motions, as did that of the University of Wales as a whole.[32]

Moves by the University and its colleges were accompanied by similar moves by the local authorities. In March 1927, Councillor A. Gray Jones of Ebbw Vale, who had proposed the motion at the Cardiff Court, persuaded the Ebbw Vale Education Committee to adopt the Cardiff motion and to distribute it for endorsement by the other Welsh local authorities, a tactic that would be much favoured by advocates of an improved broadcasting service for Wales.[33] As Wales had over 150 local authorities, and as their meetings were very fully reported in the inter-war years, the local press in the spring of 1927 contained a vast amount of discussion of the activities of the BBC in Wales.

The agitation became known as the demand for an all-Welsh station, and that was widely interpreted to mean a station broadcasting programmes that were exclusively in the Welsh language. As the motion was originally brought forward by Ebbw Vale and endorsed immediately and unanimously by Abertyleri – areas where less than 10 per cent of the inhabitants had a knowledge of Welsh – this can hardly have been the case. What Gray Jones and his associates were seeking was a BBC service exclusive to Wales and available throughout Wales, on the analogy of the service being planned for Scotland. Yet the semantic confusion over an all-Welsh and an all-Wales station served to divide Welsh opinion, and the imprecision of the aims of the protesters allowed the Corporation to refute or to ridicule many of their arguments. The *Cambria Leader* poured scorn on the idea of an all-Welsh station, largely on the grounds that there was not enough Welsh music to provide a full service.[34] Whereas British music constituted only a small proportion of the music broadcast by Daventry 5XX, the 'all-British' station, there was a curious assumption that an 'all-Welsh' station would have to restrict itself to Welsh music – an indication, perhaps, that the concept that London alone should deal with the universal was widely held.

The lack of a consensus in Wales was seized upon by the BBC. Cardiff's publicity officer, Margaret Mackenzie, a Scotswoman who was highly suspicious of any Welsh demands, issued a press release noting that there was 'not an unanimous demand for an entirely Welsh programme in Wales itself'. The Welsh were not, she tartly reminded them, 'a separate entity giving them the power to install a station of their own'.[35] Demands for Welsh-language programmes aroused some hostility within Wales itself, although, in the 1920s, newspaper correspondence expressing such hostility was slight compared with what it would be in later decades. A letter in the *Western Mail* in February 1927 urged that an aerial for the transmission of Welsh programmes should be built on Cadair Idris. 'It would have the merit of being well over a hundred miles away from Cardiff.'[36] Opposition to broadcasts in English making use of the Welsh accent and Welsh idioms was more vehement than opposition to broadcasts in the Welsh language. Plays have been broadcast from Cardiff, complained a *Western Mail* correspondent, containing 'woefully silly Welsh voices'.[37]

An intriguing attempt to provide programmes of Welsh interest was made in 1927 with broadcasts from the Irish Free State. (Irish radio had begun as a shoestring operation on 1 January 1926. It would become increasingly sophisticated and make programmes of the highest quality, but condescension towards it was, and is, a characteristic of British broadcasters.) The first of the Dublin programmes was transmitted in April 1927 and they continued monthly

47

until March 1928. None of the Welsh offerings of British stations had been broadcast at fixed times, and thus those from Dublin were the first regular programmes of Welsh interest. They consisted largely of songs sung by the Welsh residents of Dublin and by the crews of the Holyhead ferry boats; the speech element was slight and was mainly in English. The programmes were arranged by W. S. Gwynn Williams, the editor of *Y Cerddor Newydd*, who later won fame as the founder of the Llangollen International Eisteddfod.[38] The Dublin broadcasts aroused great interest in Wales. Ernest Hughes considered writing to Dublin to urge the Irish authorities to provide a more extensive service for Wales, but he desisted because, 'as the increased revenues arising from the multiplication of licences . . . would have gone into the coffers of the indifferent BBC, it seemed unfair even to put forward the suggestion'.[39]

The programmes from Ireland were referred to in *Welsh in Education and Life*, a report commissioned by the president of the Board of Education and published in August 1927. 'It is a rather pathetic comment on the position of Welsh in its own country that the only regular Welsh programme is that given once a week from the Dublin Station by the Irish Government.'[40] The comment contained several errors and was bitterly attacked by Appleton.[41] It was part of a sweeping attack upon the BBC, the work, almost certainly, of W. J. Gruffydd. *Welsh in Education and Life* was widely reported, with most of the press comment concentrating upon the one paragraph (out of 399) which discussed broadcasting. The report stated:

> Wireless is achieving the complete anglicisation of the intellectual life of the nation. We regard the present policy of the British Broadcasting Corporation as one of the most serious menaces to the life of the Welsh language . . . The English officials of the [Corporation may] suppose that a ceremoniously punctilious recognition of Wales is all that is required to silence all protest [but] . . . nothing short of the full utilisation of the Welsh language in broadcasting will meet the case.[42]

The BBC, centrally, issued a brief reply to the report. It noted that Cardiff and Swansea had broadcast programmes in Welsh, as had Daventry, Manchester and Liverpool. The Corporation did not envisage the possibility of a station exclusive to Wales, but stated that when the twin-wave station for Wales and south-western England had been built, 'no doubt a somewhat greater proportion of Welsh could be broadcast'. At Cardiff, Appleton issued a more forthright reply:

Wales, of her own choice is part of the commonwealth of nations in which the official language is English. When His Majesty's Government decided to form a corporation for the important function of broadcasting, it was natural that the official language should be used throughout . . . If the extremists who desire to force the language upon listeners in the area . . . were to have their way, the official language would lose its grip.

He saw no reason to provide news or talks in Welsh, but rather 'let us reserve for Welsh broadcast nights gems of poetry and immortal songs . . . Let us have [Wales's] music, which is national but not secret.'[43] W. J. Gruffydd snorted in disgust. 'Daeth Mr Appleton allan i'w amddiffyn ei hun', he wrote in *Y Llenor*, 'ac yn ei amddiffyniad dangosodd fod pethau'n fil gwaith nag yr ofnau'r Pwyllgor.'*[44]

In his statement that it was natural for the Corporation to make exclusive use of the official language, Appleton could have cited examples from elsewhere in Europe. By 1927, a total of twenty-one European states had acquired broadcasting services, and they were all services operating directly (or in the case of the BBC, somewhat less directly) under government control. France made no provision for its Breton,[45] Basque, Flemish, Alsatian and Provençal-speaking inhabitants. Likewise, Spain ignored the claims of the Basques, Catalans and Galicians, and Italy those of its Friulian, Sard, French and German speakers. On the other hand, Switzerland, Czechoslovakia, the Soviet Union and the Irish Free State provided regular programmes in more than one language. Those were countries with constitutions specifically protecting the linguistic rights of inhabitants whose mother tongue was not the major language of the state. The Welsh language enjoyed no such protection; indeed, in the courts of law, it was more disadvantaged in Wales than was any other language.[46] Although Welsh had won some degree of recognition, especially in education, its lack of legal recognition placed it in a very different position from that of Slovak in Czechoslovakia or of French in Switzerland.

Furthermore, the analogy with Scotland, much pressed by advocates of an improved broadcasting system for Wales, was not fully valid. The kingdom of Scotland had its own legal system; it was to a large extent separately administered and its territorial integrity was wholly beyond dispute. The principality of Wales, as a commentator put it in 1925, was an 'extinct palatinate'.'The average Englishman', wrote an emissary from Head Office in 1935, 'who is

---

*'Mr Appleton came out to defend himself and in his defence he showed that matters were a thousand times worse than the Committee had feared.'

perfectly prepared to regard the Scotch and the Irish as being essentially different in outlook and character from the English . . . is seldom prepared to believe that the Welsh are a different nation – in fact, if there is any general attitude towards the Welsh, it is that they are a nuisance.'[47]

Thus the BBC, in its treatment of the Welsh language and of Wales, was merely following the normal practice of the time. If this is borne in mind, it is remarkable that the campaign launched in 1927 had won its objective by 1937. That success would be the springboard for even greater successes in the future. Indeed, it could be argued that the entire national debate in Wales, for fifty years and more after 1927, revolved around broadcasting, and that the other concessions to Welsh nationality won in those years were consequent upon the victories in the field of broadcasting.

When the agitation began, the BBC had no intention of acceding to it. So enamoured was the Corporation of the neatness of its scheme for twin transmitters offering a service to the whole of the United Kingdom that it considered any criticism of the scheme as being the result of wilful ignorance and ungrateful bigotry. As the BBC had decided how it would use all the wavelengths allotted to it by international agreement, the Corporation insisted that it was impossible for Wales to have a service of its own. The linkage of south Wales with south-western England was sacrosanct. In the late 1920s, the Corporation's officials gave the impression that the proposed new transmitter would allow Cardiff's programmes to be heard in every part of Wales. Therefore, all those demanding a more satisfactory Welsh service were told that such a service would be available when the new transmitter was opened.

The proposed transmitter was intended to serve the West Region as a whole. Thus, even if its output was available throughout Wales, the amount of specifically Welsh material it would broadcast would necessarily be small, for licensed listeners in south-western England were considerably more numerous than they were in Wales.[48] This realization caused growing concern. It was voiced by, among others, W. J. Burdon Evans, the 'major-domo' of David Davies of Llandinam, the coal-owner, peace activist and patron of the monthly magazine *The Welsh Outlook*. Burdon Evans sought to engage the interest of Thomas Jones, a close associate of the Davies family.[49] Thomas Jones contacted Reith in January 1928, and thereafter Reith and Appleton viewed Jones, together with Wynn Wheldon, the secretary of the Welsh Board of Education, and Emrys Evans, the principal of University College, Bangor, as the spokesmen of the 'reasonable' Welsh, as opposed to the 'extremists', such as W. J. Gruffydd, Ernest Hughes and William George – Lloyd George's brother and a particularly vehement critic of the Corporation. Jones urged Reith to request Appleton to seek advice from Welsh cultural leaders. Reith apparently did so, despite his strong dislike of advisory bodies.[50] Early in 1928, Appleton invited societies such as the Cymmrodorion to nominate representatives to a committee which he was forming to offer him guidance on Welsh programmes. The 26-member Welsh Advisory Committee persuaded Appleton to relax his ban on spoken, as opposed to sung, Welsh.[51] On 21 March 1928, the first *Welsh Interlude* was broadcast, a fifteen-minute talk given by Ernest Hughes. As the BBC was by then groping towards the concept of a fixed pattern of programming, the *Interlude* became a series, regularly broadcast on Wednesday nights between 6.00 and 6.15 p.m.

In the autumn of 1928, the registrar of the University of Wales requested Reith to receive a deputation to discuss the possibility of providing Wales with its own station. 'I hardly think we could refuse to see them', wrote Reith, 'but we could easily refuse to give them what they ask for.' The meeting was held on 30 November, and the deputation was told of the scarcity of wavelengths and of the better reception which would be available from the proposed new transmitter. In his diary Reith's only comment was 'silly Welsh deputation'.[52]

Criticism of the BBC increased in 1929. The University Council reacted with hostility to the announcement of the Central Council for Schools Broadcasts that schools broadcasts everywhere except in Scotland would henceforth be supplied by London.[53] Concern was also expressed over the BBC's decision not to broadcast the 1929 peace message of the children of Wales, a message transmitted by most of the broadcasting services of Europe. It had been devised in 1922 by Gwilym Davies, a self-publicist in whom even Corbett-Smith would have found a match. The League of Nations Union had many branches in Wales; in 1929, and for several years to come, Gwilym Davies persuaded virtually all of them to bombard the BBC with protests. Many branches in England also protested, and the Corporation received enquiries from leading peace advocates such as Lord Cecil of Chelwood, causing Reith to write: 'I wish we had [broadcast] the miserable thing . . . when it was first suggested. It would certainly have saved us an immense amount of trouble.'[54]

In the late 1920s, Plaid Genedlaethol Cymru became closely involved in broadcasting politics. In 1929, the party's president, Saunders Lewis, declared that it would soon be necessary to arrange 'for thousands of Welshmen to be prosecuted for refusing to pay for English programmes'.[55] His statement was widely reported, the *Western Mail* noting that 'so strong is public opinion on the matter that drastic measures are likely to be taken to overcome official apathy'.[56] Some of the younger party members were advocating measures far more vigorous than the refusal to pay the licence fee and were calling for Nationalists to block transmissions and court prison sentences. One of them, E. G. Bowen, a physics student at University College, Swansea, sought to counter the BBC's statement that no wavelengths were available. In an article in the *Western Mail* in March 1930, he argued that the Corporation's plan for a twin transmitter for the West Region was fundamentally misguided. As the area to be served could receive Daventry without difficulty, it was unnecessary to devote one of the wavelengths to the transmission of the 5XX service. The wavelength thus released could be used to provide separate services for Wales and for south-western England. A transmitter should be built on the Brecon Beacons to serve south Wales and another – using the same wavelength – would reach most of the inhabitants of the north. His plan, claimed Bowen, would enable up to 97 per cent of the population of Wales to receive a service specifically designed for them.[57]

In October 1929, the University registrar requested another meeting. Reith scribbled on the request: 'No point – nothing has changed.' Appleton urged him to reconsider and, as a result, a University delegation visited Savoy Hill on 15 November 1929. The members were provided with a reiteration of the arguments of the previous year, although Reith was more positive than he had been in 1928 concerning the likelihood that the proposed new transmitter would broadcast a significant number of Welsh programmes.[58] A further meeting with Reith was held on 23 May 1930, when the familiar arguments were again repeated. 'I had three hours with some perfervid Welsh at the University,' he wrote in his diary. 'Their criticisms were extraordinarily ignorant, but Jones was very good.'[59] Reith may have found Thomas Jones commendable, but his effectiveness may be doubted. 'Thomas Jones's cautious tactic of reasoned argument behind the scenes', wrote his biographer E. E. Ellis, 'made no serious inroad into the BBC's settled policy of centralization and metropolitan cultural imperialism.'[60]

By the late summer of 1930, the location of the much-promised twin transmitter for the West Region became known. It was to be at Washford on the Somerset coast twelve miles east of Ilfracombe. The choice led to much criticism, for in the early years of broadcasting there was considerable confusion between transmitters and studios, and there were many who believed that the decision meant that the Cardiff station would be closed and that the whole operation would be moved to England.[61] This was not the case, for Cardiff continued to be the production centre for the West Region, although Bristol acquired a talks studio in 1933 and more elaborate premises in September 1934. Nevertheless, the Washford decision served to strengthen the suspicion that the West Region was primarily intended to serve south-western England. The arrangements for Scotland, where a transmitter was opened in 1932 at Falkirk, near the demographic centre of the country, fed the already widely held view that the BBC was more sensitive to the needs of Scotland than to those of Wales.[62] Because of lack of wavelengths and the mountainous nature of the country, argued the Corporation, it was impossible for comparable arrangements to be made in Wales. 'Everybody knows', commented J. E. Jones, the general secretary of Plaid Genedlaethol Cymru, 'that Scotland is flat.'[63]

The BBC's references to mountains had some substance. Scotland's demographic centre is close to its geographic centre; that is not the case in Wales. Washford was chosen as the site of the West's transmitter partly in order to give Wales – or more specifically the more heavily populated parts of the country – a better service. Transmissions from the Somerset coast would fan more effectively into the valleys of Monmouthshire and Glamorgan than would those from an aerial sited in south Wales. Yet, the further south the transmitter, the less likely it was to offer a service on cheaper sets to the inhabitants of mid and north Wales. By 1930, the BBC had tacitly abandoned the argument that the proposed transmitter would serve the whole of Wales; thus the assurances that Reith had given to the University committee in 1928 and 1929 were, to a large extent, invalid. Aware that the Corporation's policy was under attack, Reith commissioned a pamphlet explaining the BBC's activities in Wales. Published in January 1931, it was not well received.[64]

Appleton was particularly annoyed by accusations that the BBC staff included hardly any natives of Wales and that the Corporation employed no one capable of speaking Welsh. He insisted that Ernest Jenkins, Parsons's deputy at Swansea, was a fluent Welsh-speaker, but in 1930 Reith discovered 'that he could not converse in it at all'.[65] In 1927, Jenkins had been given the title of Welsh representative and was instructed to divide his time equally between Swansea and Cardiff. Thomas Jones, concerned that Appleton lacked a staff member who had the confidence of Welsh cultural leaders, urged Reith to appoint a Welsh-speaking consultant at Cardiff. Prompted by John Davies of the WEA, he suggested the name of Major Edgar Jones, a native of Llanrhaeadr-ym-Mochnant in Montgomeryshire, who was shortly to retire from the headship of the Barry Grammar School for Boys, a post in which he had been spectacularly successful. Edgar Jones became Welsh consultant on 1 July 1931; as he had not yet retired, he originally applied himself to the task on one afternoon a week. He was given additional duties in July 1932 when the Central Council for Schools Broadcasting created a Welsh subcommittee charged with the duty of reviving schools broadcasts for Wales. Thereafter, he was employed on a half-time basis.[66]

The day after Edgar Jones's appointment, Reith met a deputation of Welsh MPs at the prompting of Lloyd George. Although Reith recorded that Lloyd George's 'sole interest' seemed to be the broadcasting of religious services in Welsh, his intervention was undoubtedly important in convincing Corporation officials that the agitation in Wales was not merely the fringe activity of 'extremists' like Lloyd George's brother William. Reith was mesmerized by Lloyd George, contemplating with rapture the power that the former prime minister had once enjoyed. At the meeting of 2 July 1931, the Welsh Parliamentary Party established a broadcasting committee consisting of Megan Lloyd George (Liberal, Anglesey), Wil John (Labour, Rhondda West) and Leslie Forrestier-Walker (Conservative, Monmouth – then the only Conservative constituency in Wales).[67]

Some of the committee's recommendations infuriated Reith, in particular its demand that the Board of Governors should include a member specifically representative of Welsh interests, a notion strongly advocated by Megan Lloyd George and supported by many leading Welsh public figures, Thomas Jones among them. The governors, argued Reith, were appointed because of their general, not their specific, interests and, if the claims of Wales were acceded to, similar claims would be forthcoming from Scotland and Northern Ireland.[68] On the matter of programmes, however, the parliamentary committee's discussions with Corporation officials went smoothly. It was agreed that the Daventry transmitter would broadcast a Welsh programme every fortnight, instead of every month as hitherto; it would also broadcast a regular Welsh-language religious service. If other Welsh programmes of sufficient quality were produced, their transmission would be considered.[69]

The appointment of Edgar Jones and the establishment of the parliamentary committee fed rather than abated the agitation. On 22 June 1931, Appleton informed Reith that 'the Welsh situation is getting more acute . . . I understand Welsh nationalists – not political Nationalists – have decided to adopt suffragette tactics with regard to our work.' Margaret Mackenzie was more explicit:

A new and much more aggressive form of Welsh Nationalism is about to appear, possibly under the leadership of Mr Lloyd George and Miss Lloyd George. The focus of this movement is the demand for separate broadcasts for Wales . . . Young fanatics are making plans to become martyrs by taking violent action against the BBC; there are some fairly well substantiated stories of contemplated raids on our transmitters [and plans] for jamming the Cardiff and Swansea transmissions from a ship off the coast.[70]

Reith thought the staff at Cardiff – 'the dreadful Miss Mackenzie' in particular – were over-reacting. 'Sir John', Appleton was informed, 'thinks it should be perfectly easy to deal with the situation in a way that these perpetual requests and demands . . . should cease.' 'I do hope', replied Appleton, 'that you are not expecting me to keep all these small Welsh organisations quiet. If you are expecting this, I would quote the various national meetings say of the TUC, NUT, NUR etc.; always the Welshmen are expected to jump up with troublesome questions.'[71]

By the autumn of 1931, ten of the thirteen county councils of Wales, and a large number of lesser councils, had passed resolutions calling for an improved broadcasting service for Wales. The initiative came from Plaid Genedlaethol Cymru and deputations of party members argued their case before the councils.[72] At its 1931 conference, the party condemned the Corporation's Regional Scheme as a plan to 'tear a part of south Wales from the rest of Wales and . . . join it in a permanent cultural association with the south west of England, leaving the remainder of Wales to be expeditiously anglicised from Daventry'.[73] In August 1932, it gave sympathetic consideration to a campaign to withhold licence fees. It adopted as its broadcasting policy proposals prepared by its Cardiff branch, which drew heavily upon the ideas of E. G. Bowen. The Cardiff proposals owed much to the work of the branch secretary, Mrs Nansi Peate, whose husband, Dr Iorwerth Peate, was involved in a highly acrimonious correspondence with Appleton. Acrimony was expressed in other quarters also, with a leading minister stating that the letters BBC stood for Bradwyr Budr Cymru (the vile traitors of Wales), William George declaring that 'the BBC is the arch-enemy of the Welsh language' and the Union of Welsh Societies calling for an inquiry into broadcasting in Wales. The *News Chronicle* expressed its surprise that 'Wales is so patient . . . An occasional highbrow talk and an occasional song would not be tolerated elsewhere'.[74]

Parliamentary questions were mainly concerned with the lack of an adequate service in north Wales, the issue which Appleton believed to be the main bone of contention. 'We should attempt', he wrote, 'to give [a better service there] before the attack is upon us.' He proposed a small studio in the north, for 'at present a speaker from north Wales has to spend about three days in getting down to Cardiff and back again'. The best place, he suggested, would be Caernarfon, the centre of 'the intellectual reading population of the

. . . quarrying districts [where] they are most intelligent people, accustomed to speak Welsh in all their affairs'.[75] He was told that, as there was no wavelength available for north Wales, a studio there would be pointless, for any programmes it might produce for transmission from Cardiff would not be audible in north Wales. In 1932, a wavelength (214 metres) outside the British allocation was brought into service at Aberdeen; it was borrowed from Poland and was used to enable the Scottish regional programme to be heard in the north of Scotland. Protests from Wales were answered with the argument that the two cases were not analagous. The north of Scotland could not get Daventry; therefore, if special provision were not made for its inhabitants, they would not get any programmes at all. Where Wales was concerned, noted the *BBC Handbook* of 1932, 'the limitation of the available wavelengths makes the granting of minority demands definitely impossible'.[76]

Instead of pressing for a transmitter and a studio in north Wales, Appleton was urged to discuss with Livening, the North Region director, the possibility of regular Welsh broadcasts from Manchester, a development of an idea tentatively tried in the 1920s. Livening joined him in a tour of the north in the spring of 1932, when Appleton was impressed by 'the earnest desire of thoughtful and well-disposed Welshmen for more Welsh programmes'. A few programmes of Welsh interest were broadcast from Manchester in the autumn of 1932, a service which was expanded in September 1933 when Manchester joined Cardiff in broadcasting two Welsh-language schools programmes a week.[77]

The demand for more Welsh programmes created manpower problems, for the Corporation employed no one capable of producing them. In the spring of 1932, an advertisement appeared in the press seeking applications for the post of part-time general Welsh assistant. Thomas Jones was closely associated with the appointment, and sought opinions of the two main contenders: Sam Jones, a reporter on the *Western Mail*, born at Clydach, near Swansea, and Haydn Davies, a teacher and a native of the Rhondda. John Davies of the WEA, a Calvinistic Methodist with Maerdy and Llangeitho connections, was strongly in favour of Haydn Davies, who gave WEA lectures and was a Calvinistic Methodist with Maerdy and Llangeitho connections. Sam Jones, wrote Davies, 'was a "witwat", with a certain cheap facility of speech and writing, but no cultural standards'. Thomas Jones accepted Davies's assessment and told Carpendale on no account to appoint Sam Jones. Haydn Davies, he wrote, 'is of much heavier metal'. Edgar Jones and Appleton, however, had warmed to Sam Jones and insisted upon appointing him, a decision which would be triumphantly vindicated. Jones began on a half-time basis on 1 November 1932, and became a full-time employee of the Corporation on 1 February 1933.[78]

Appleton, who was holding regular meetings with the Broadcasting Committee of the Welsh Parliamentary Party, informed Head Office that it approved of Sam Jones's appointment. Its attitude to the Corporation, however, caused him anxiety. 'The members of the Committee', he wrote, 'definitely stated that they, and the people whom they represent, would continue to struggle desperately until Welsh had the same position in Wales that English has in England.' In November 1932, Appleton asked Reith to meet the Broadcasting Committee to explain 'the wavelength business [as] I myself am a little hazy on the present state of things'.[79]

The meeting took place on 21 December 1932 when the three committee members were joined by David Lloyd George and his secretary, A. J. Sylvester. Lloyd George made a fierce attack upon Appleton and 'was altogether in a most unfriendly mood'. That experience caused Reith to prefer to hold discussions with the members of the University Council rather than with the Welsh MPs. On his own initiative, he met representatives of the University on 19 July 1933, and was pleasantly surprised that their 'attitude was quite different from previously and they had the grace to admit that we had made very considerable improvements'. He was anxious that there should be only one Welsh organization with which he would be involved and, impressed by the moderation of such men as Emrys Evans, the University's vice-chancellor from 1933 to 1935, he urged that it should be a committee of the Council. 'We evolved a system', he wrote in his diary, 'that we might deal with the Council or a committee of them, meeting them twice a year.'[80]

Reith considered that his readiness to meet the University's representatives was a marked concession on his part. 'It is the only Regional Committee that the Head Office does meet,' he noted. The University's insistence on discussions with the director-general, he believed, reflected poorly upon the ability of the West regional director. 'We should have been delighted', he told Appleton, 'if you could have dealt with such troubles, representing as you do in every way the Corporation.' In its meeting in October 1933, the Council appointed a ten-man committee; much to the annoyance of Reith and Appleton, it included David Lloyd George, William George, W. J. Gruffydd and Saunders Lewis.[81]

The establishment of the University Committee coincided with the opening of the Washford twin-wave transmitter. It began broadcasting the West Regional Service on 28 May 1933 and the National Service on 13 August. The latter service was also broadcast on long wave by the 'big national' transmitter at Daventry; regional transmitters broadcasting the National Service on medium wave came to be known as the 'little nationals'. The West Service was transmitted on the 309.9 wavelength previously used by Cardiff but, as the BBC had exhausted the wavelengths granted to it by international agreement, the National Service was broadcast on 261 metres, the same wavelength as was used by the London National transmitter at Brookman's Park. The opening of the West regional transmitter, powered by seventy kilowatts, made the transmitters at Cardiff and Swansea redundant. Appleton was delighted by the improved reception and by the fact that transmissions penetrated further north than the engineers had expected. Nevertheless, it was in no sense a service for Wales as a whole, for it was not available to owners of ordinary sets living beyond Aberystwyth.[82] The *Western Mail* was less enthusiastic. Six months after the opening of Washford, it declared that the new transmitter 'has been a keen disappointment . . . Some of the so-called concessions made by the BBC have not been free from the character of insult. The Welsh Nationalists are not always reasonable in their demands, but no one can question the justice of their complaint in this regard.'[83]

Endowed with a powerful transmitter, the Region was granted additional staff. In October 1933, J. T. Sutthery became the West's first director of programmes. Sutthery was a man of great ability but he rapidly won the enmity of Appleton and in December 1934 he was moved to Belfast to become the Northern Ireland programme director. 'I am at the end of my tether,' he wrote in January 1934. '[I feel] that nobody seemed to care whether the staff here cracked up or not.'[84] As he was incapable of being involved in Welsh-language programmes, his appointment meant that, to all intents and purposes, Sam Jones was the Welsh-language director of programmes. With the West Region an accomplished fact, and no prospect of change on the matter of wavelengths, Appleton felt it was incumbent upon him to present the region as a natural and cohesive unit. He commissioned Redman to arrange a West signature tune which began with 'Ar Hyd y Nos' ('All Through the Night') and ended with 'Admiral Benbow'. In preparing his report for the *BBC Handbook* of 1934, he took the opportunity to argue that Wales and south-western England did not constitute an artificial region. Its unity had deep historical roots; it represented in fact the re-creation of the kingdom of King Arthur. The 1934 *Handbook* also contained an article entitled 'Some Thoughts about Welsh', which included the comment: 'What the world needs today is more dead languages.'[85]

The notion of the kingdom of King Arthur led to much adverse comment in Wales but, although Appleton's appeal to early British history was specious, his argument was not total nonsense. Those among the Welsh whose early experiences included visits to Weston-super-Mare and trips to Bristol Zoo – and they perhaps represented most of the inhabitants of Monmouthshire and east Glamorgan and therefore over half the inhabitants of Wales – did not view south-western England in the same light as it was viewed by W. J. Gruffydd, a native of Caernarfonshire, or by Saunders Lewis, a member of the Welsh diaspora of Merseyside. In the 1930s, there were over sixty thousand people born in south-western England living in Wales and nearly fifty thousand people born in Wales living in south-western England. Yet Appleton's determined attempts to create a West identity were undermined by the fact that the contrasts between the two sides of the Severn Estuary were greater than the similarities. Apart from Bristol and Plymouth, south-western England was a largely agricultural area, still much influenced by the squirearchical class. In Wales, the squires had been defeated and had departed, while in the industrial south iron-making and coal-mining had created communities wholly different from the villages of Somerset and Devon. When the BBC began studying its audience, it discovered that the contrasts in lifestyles were more marked between south-western England and Wales than they were between any other contiguous regions of the United Kingdom. Furthermore, if many of the Welsh of south-east Wales regarded Bristol and Weston with affection, the feeling was not reciprocated. The authors of the fascinating volume *Mental Maps* note that the index of disapproval felt by the inhabitants of south-western England for those of Wales is 'one of the steepest gradients on any mental map we have ever examined'. 'The West Country', wrote R. A. Rendall, Sutthery's successor, 'has a clearly defined character of its own, and that character is entirely antipathetic to the Welsh character, more so probably than any other section of England that might be yoked to Wales.'[86]

Bristol's annoyance at being dependent upon Cardiff for its programmes became characteristic of south-western England as a whole as the number of Welsh-language programmes increased. 'The West is weary of Wales,' the *Evening World* wrote in 1931. 'The West wants wireless home rule.' By 1934, the antagonism had deepened. There was an assumption that Welsh was given a great deal of air time, for some listeners assumed that any broadcast they did not understand was a broadcast in Welsh. A meeting of south-western England mayors at Plymouth in February 1934 demanded a better service and condemned what they considered to be the imposition of Welsh-language programmes. The *Evening World* expressed the hope that 'this Welsh business is just a passing phase' and that the BBC would 'realise that the pistol that the Welsh Nationalists are pointing at its head is loaded with blank cartridges'.[87]

While Appleton was writing his article on the kingdom of King Arthur, the University Committee was preparing its list of demands, in readiness for the meeting with Reith to be held on 9 February 1934. The BBC argued that it already served the bilingual inhabitants of Wales because they could understand programmes in English; the monoglot Welsh population was too small to merit more programmes than were being provided already. The memorandum prepared by the University Committee declared that such an argument was like stating that 'French-speaking Englishmen only need French programmes'. It demanded ten hours a week in Welsh, and urged that particular attention should be paid to programmes for children.[88] Before the meeting, his officials urged Reith to resist such demands, because 'as nothing short of a separate service will allay discontent [in Wales]', protests would continue even if more Welsh programmes were provided. 'The potential increase in licences in Wales', he was told, 'is definitely less than in the West Country . . . Therefore West Regional programme policy should be orientated . . . more definitely than it is to please the West Country as distinct from the Principality.'[89]

When the members of the University Committee met Reith, they were accompanied by E. G. Bowen, who by 1934 was studying for a doctorate at King's College, London. Bowen's ideas, which he spelled out in greater detail in a closely argued but offensively phrased article in the *Welsh Nationalist*, received considerable publicity. The Corporation's practice of broadcasting the National Service from one of the twin regional transmitters represented, he wrote, 'a squandering of wavelengths'. Bowen also argued that if the wavelength of a station in north Wales were synchronized with that of a Welsh service from Washford, both north and south Wales could receive Cardiff's programmes. He contacted the Marconi Company in January 1934, asking its engineers for their comments on his ideas and stating that 'I believe the BBC's excuses are all moonshine'.[90]

The BBC archives has a 'Bowen file' which contains a copy of his article together with comments on his ideas. 'They are misleading, inaccurate and scurrilous', wrote Noel Ashbridge, the Corporation's director of engineering, although he admitted that 'the attack on the Regional Scheme . . . is rather . . . difficult to handle'. Appleton agreed with Ashbridge's criticism. Indeed, he had suggested in 1930 that those attacking the statements of the BBC's engineers should be sued for libel. Reith was somewhat more circumspect, noting that 'the squandering of wavelengths in England needs a careful reply'.

He was particularly incensed by the letter to Marconi. 'A bumptious young man', he wrote in his diary, '. . . sent a letter to the Marconi Company, which fortunately [has] been passed by them to us.'[91]

To Reith's great annoyance, 'the bumptious young man' turned up at the meeting of 9 February 1934 as the University Committee's technical expert. Reith, an engineer himself, was always concerned to defend the dignity of the Corporation's engineers and he was appalled when Bowen sought 'to corner Ashbridge'. He was even more annoyed when Saunders Lewis, who took a leading role in the discussion, accused the BBC of 'assisting the disintegration of civilization in Wales'. (The confrontation must have been remark-able: the 6 ft 4 in Reith giving the case for the British Corporation in his gruff Doric and the 5 ft 1 in Saunders Lewis giving the case for Wales in his over-polished English.) 'Saunders Lewis', wrote the director of programme administration, 'is a very cantankerous man' – a view with which Reith entirely concurred. Lewis was equally critical of Reith. In a letter to David Jones written in 1968, he stated: 'I had quite a bit to do with the then Sir John Reith at the time of the setting up of the Welsh Region and before. I found him utterly devoid of humour, and his self-esteem and conceit as huge as his frame, a sort of incredible Malvolio and as intelligent.'[92]

Although Reith in February 1934 resisted the demand for an increased number of hours to be devoted to Welsh programmes, he did promise that the Corporation would open a studio in the north. Bangor was chosen, a decision which owed much to the fact that Emrys Evans, the principal of University College, Bangor, was the vice-chancellor of the University; a further factor was the city's role as an important centre of the Post Office's activities. As has been seen, Appleton in 1931 had suggested Caernarfon; he had earlier favoured Wrexham as the centre of the BBC's activities in the north, but as the main issue under consideration in 1934 was the provision of Welsh programmes, the case for locating the studio in an area which had a high proportion of Welsh-speakers seemed irrefutable.[93]

Reith considered that providing a studio in Bangor was a somewhat futile gesture, for in February 1934 he was still convinced that no wavelength would be available for north Wales; thus programmes produced at Bangor would not be heard there. On 18 September 1934, however, the Director-General's Meeting, as the Control Board was then called, discussed the possibility of a north Wales transmitter working on the same wavelength as that of the West Region, precisely the scheme suggested by Bowen. If sited at Beaumaris and powered by two kilowatts, it, together with the Washford transmitter, would serve 80 per cent of the inhabitants of Wales.[94] No public mention was made of this discussion. At the second meeting with the University Committee held on 26 October 1934, the Corporation stated that there were in Britain five areas with populations larger than that of north and mid Wales which could not receive a regional service. Lloyd George responded by 'begging the Corporation to give up its habit of measuring the claims of Wales by purely technical and numerical standards'. At the meeting, Saunders Lewis was deliberatively provocative. Lloyd George was much impressed and informed his brother of Lewis's 'cyfraniad arbennig o effeithiol . . . a'i fedr a'i wroldeb wrth . . . drafod ffeithiau'r achos'*.[95]

At the meeting of the University Court held on 13 December 1934, Emrys Evans read out a lengthy statement giving the committee's reactions to the October discussion with the Corporation's officials. 'I cannot pretend', he said, 'that the Committee was satisfied with the results of this second Conference.' The request for ten hours of Welsh-language programmes a week was answered with an offer of six. The basic problem was that 'as Wales is unequally yoked with the West Country . . . [and as] the BBC tries to satisfy both regions by giving them a roughly equal number of hours . . . Welsh programmes are retarded to keep pace with the slower partner.' There would be no studio at Bangor until the end of 1935. 'There is not much value', said Evans, 'in extracting a promise, if its fulfilment was to be delayed over a period of years.' As 'the West Programme Director knows nothing of Wales . . . he leaves the Welsh programmes to the Welsh Assistant who thus has all the responsibility . . . while devoid of the status'. If the Welsh staff at Cardiff were not increased, 'we can only conclude that the retention of a limited and overworked staff seems to the [BBC] to be an effective method of checking the quantity and diluting the quality of the Welsh programmes'.[96] This forthright statement by a man considered to be a moderating influence caused Appleton great concern. Precisely what he had feared had come about; the 'cultural nationalists', as he termed Emrys Evans and his kind, had coalesced with the political nationalists. The BBC had lost the middle ground.

In all these discussions, there was one body of people which was hardly considered at all. They were the monoglot English-speaking inhabitants of Wales, who constituted, according to the Census of 1931, 63.2 per cent of the country's population. Most advocates of Welsh broadcasts argued that their transmission did not lead to deprivation among those who did not understand them. Some of the Welsh programmes, particularly in the early years, were transmitted during otherwise silent hours, and were therefore an additional, not

---

*'[His] particularly effective contribution . . . and his skill and courage in . . . discussing the facts of the case.'

a displacing, service; many of them, again particularly in the early years, consisted chiefly of Welsh songs, and it was argued that if people could listen to Verdi in Italian, they could listen to Joseph Parry in Welsh. By the mid 1930s, the leading argument was the availability of an alternative. Virtually all the households which could receive broadcasts could get the National Service from Daventry. In many parts of north Wales, it was also possible to pick up the North Regional Service or even that of Northern Ireland, while along the border and in northern Monmouthshire the Midland Service could be clearly heard. Most areas of Glamorgan could not receive a regional service other than that from Washford, but if Wales and south-western England were given a wavelength apiece – as advocates of Welsh-language programmes ardently wished – then those areas would be able to get the West of England Regional Service, thus allowing the inhabitants of the most thickly populated districts of Wales to have a choice, when programmes in Welsh were broadcast, of two alternative programmes. Even if the full demand of the University Committee were acceded to, Welsh-speakers would have ten hours a week of broadcasting in their mother tongue compared with up to 164 hours – or, where other regional services could be heard – as much as 250 hours available to English-speakers in their mother tongue. When put in these terms, it could hardly be claimed that Welsh-language broadcasts represented a serious deprivation for those unable to understand them.

What this argument ignored was the possibility that the English-speakers of Wales would want their own service. Was the advantage that broadcasting could make the nation of Wales a 'knowable community' an advantage to be enjoyed by Welsh-speakers but not by English-speakers? Most of the members of the University Committee did not see the issue in these terms. Joseph Jones, a committee member, stated that the English-speaking inhabitants of Wales preferred programmes from England to Welsh programmes in English, a statement supported by most of the letters to the press. In the large collection of press cuttings at Cardiff and Caversham relating to the 'Welsh Controversy' there is hardly a letter concerning the need for a service for the English-speakers of Wales. Almost all the letters fall into one of two categories, either demanding more Welsh-language programmes or doubting the need for them. The advisory committee convened by Appleton in 1928 contained members of what he called 'the new Anglo-Cymric school of writing', but that committee became defunct in 1929 and thereafter there is little evidence that the Anglo-Welsh writers involved themselves in the 'Welsh Controversy'.[97]

It was usual for those whom Appleton termed the 'cultural

nationalists' to refer to the English-speakers of Wales as 'Saeson'. (What they meant was Anglophones, but the word was usually translated as the English people of Wales.) Some of them were indeed English and had only the dimmest awareness that they were not living in England. The great majority, however, were not, deeply rooted as they were in their communities in Wales. Gwyn Jones describes the inter-war years as the first period in the history of Wales when there was a great reservoir of Anglo-Welshness. 'Anglo-Welsh literature', he wrote, '. . . is the rendering articulate of that majority of Welshmen who cannot, do not, and will not make Welsh their first language.'[98] The same argument could be applied to broadcasting.

As the English-speaking Welsh were not part of the agitation for an improved broadcasting service for Wales, the demand for an increase in Welsh staff inevitably meant a demand for more Welsh-speaking staff. This was only the case with production staff. Where Welsh engineers were concerned, there is evidence that the fact that they were Welsh could be a hindrance to their advancement. J. P. K. Williams, appointed assistant maintenance engineer at Cardiff in 1928, was denied promotion because the superintendent engineer 'did not consider that the Welsh temperament [was] as suited to supervisory duties as the English temperament'.[99]

As the production staff expanded, the belief arose that BBC posts in Wales were the exclusive preserve of Welsh-speakers. That was hardly the case. 'There is no rule', it was stated in 1956, 'that an applicant for a post with the BBC in Wales must be bilingual. Our programme producers are bilingual in varying degrees, the variation being in their command of Welsh rather than of English.'[100] Nevertheless, as the BBC in Wales did not have the resources to employ parallel staff for English and Welsh programmes, and as Welsh-speaking staff were also fluent in English, it was more economical if they produced the English-language as well as the Welsh-language broadcasts. The experience of the Welsh-speaking staff could be very different from that of the mass of Wales's English-speakers, although it was probably less different than was that of most London producers from that of the mass of the people of Britain. The almost exclusive recruitment of production staff from among Welsh-speakers, at least until the 1950s, meant that the English-speaking Welsh were not given the opportunity to interpret themselves to themselves through the medium of their own people. It also meant that Welshmen and women with English as their mother tongue (with the exception of those who gained fluency in Welsh in adulthood – and they were rare in the early years), and who wanted a career in broadcasting, were aware that they were unlikely to be able to pursue that career in their own country. On the other hand, had there not been a perceived need for Welsh-speaking staff, it does not follow that the BBC in Wales would have drawn its employees from the country's monoglot English-speakers. With the exception of Scotland, the Corporation's regions were largely staffed by natives of south-eastern England, often people who had proved to be inadequate at Head Office. 'The Regions', noted the deputy director of the regions in 1936, 'suffer from [being treated] as a dumping ground for failures among the London . . . staff.'[101] The bilingual stipulation meant that that was not the fate of Wales. Nevertheless, although those agitating for a distinct Welsh broadcasting service were concerned above all to unite Wales, implicit in their campaign were factors which would tend to divide it. This may have been inevitable, but, to say the least, it was unfortunate.

While most of the men (and they were all men) involved in the discussion between the Corporation and the University Committee were oblivious to the claims of the English-speaking Welsh, this was not true of all of them. Concern was expressed by those representing the 'extreme' wings of the debate – by Appleton, the champion of the concept of the 'West', and by Saunders Lewis, whose ultimate aim was the entire removal of Wales from the embrace of the British Broadcasting Corporation. While the 'cultural nationalists' were solely concerned with the Welsh-speakers, the political nationalists were concerned with Wales as a whole. In the University Committee, Lewis frequently raised the issue of English programmes. 'What we mean by a Welsh national programme', he wrote in 1933, 'is an all-Welsh programme every day for every part of Wales, as well as an English programme based on Welsh national consciousness, in exactly the same way as the present programmes are based on English national consciousness.' 'We do not propose,' he declared in 1935, 'that the people who cannot speak Welsh should be either ostracised or ignored. On the contrary, I say very emphatically that their interests . . . as English-speaking Welsh people [must] be adequately served.' While Appleton's plans for Wales were far less ambitious than those of Lewis, he constantly rebutted the statements of those who claimed that the English-speaking Welsh could be adequately served by broadcasts transmitted from England. 'It is obvious,' he wrote in 1935, 'that [in view of the linguistic statistics, we should] give about 60 per cent of our Welsh programmes in English.'[102]

The implications of the decisions of the meetings of February and October 1934 soon became apparent. The Corporation, which was still in its extreme centralizing phase, had laid down that the West

Region should not initiate more than twenty hours a week of its own material. Appleton considered that this meant ten hours a week apiece to Wales and south-western England; as the University Committee was demanding ten hours a week in Welsh there would be no opportunity at all to broadcast English programmes for Wales. R. A. Rendall, whose father had been one of the Corporation's first governors, replaced Sutthery as West programme director in November 1934. Soon after his appointment Rendall wrote:

> The Welsh staff of the West Region [are] almost entirely . . . concerned with producing the Welsh language material which we promised the Committee to include in the programmes, and the English staff [are] almost entirely concerned with West Country material. The result is that . . . Welsh material [in the English language] has . . . been neglected.[103]

III   The establishment of the Welsh Region

The appointment of Rendall as the West's director of programmes in November 1934 proved to be a crucial factor in the chain of events leading to the establishment of the Welsh Region of the BBC. Partly in order to avoid attacks similar to those which occurred when Sutthery took up his duties at Cardiff, Rendall was appointed to work from Bristol. He rapidly came to the conclusion that for a regional director of programmes to be wholly ignorant of the greater part of the programme material produced at the region's headquarters was a bizarre situation. In February 1935, he prepared a lengthy memorandum for Appleton with the view that the West director should submit it to Head Office.

In the memorandum, Rendall described the 'extremely uncomfortable atmosphere' on both sides of the Severn Estuary:

> Some means [must] be found of producing a separate wavelength for Wales . . . [or] failing this . . . at least Bristol and Cardiff should have entirely separate programme and administrative staffs. We are giving a very indifferent service to two important sections of the listening community . . . The treatment which the Broadcasting Committee of the University has received at the hands of the BBC has been such as to throw the moderate men into an unholy alliance with the extremists . . . The West Country MPs . . . are restive, and might easily join hands with the Welsh to attack the BBC in the House of Commons; such an attack might be highly prejudicial to the Corporation, with the renewal of the Charter in the offing . . . I know

that there are great technical difficulties to contend with, but I cannot bring myself to believe that it would be beyond the wit of man to devise a solution . . . *if* the fitness and expediency of such provision were fully realized.[104]

The final draft of Rendall's memorandum was written at Sam Jones's house at Roath. As it undermined the West director's defence of his region, it undoubtedly represented a revolt against Appleton. Nevertheless, Appleton felt obliged to send it unchanged to Basil Nicolls, Head Office's director of internal affairs, who was already 'convinced that the present association of the West of England with Wales is anomalous and impermanent'. In his covering letter, Appleton stated that 'as I find myself in complete agreement with [the memorandum], I am submitting it to you just as it was written . . . I cannot stress too strongly the necessity for immediate action. Swift and generous action now would do much to change Welsh criticism into friendly appreciation.'[105]

Reith read Rendall's memorandum on 5 March 1935. By then he was already incensed by a letter sent to him on 22 February by Wil John, requesting him to meet the Welsh MPs, because 'we understand that the technical difficulties with respect to a separate broadcasting station to supply the needs of Wales do not now exist' – a reference, no doubt, to the ideas put forward by E. G. Bowen. Reith was further infuriated by a leading article in the *Western Mail* highly critical of the BBC and by Saunders Lewis's claim that the Corporation was 'intent upon killing the Welsh language'. On 28 February he had written an angry letter to Appleton, accusing him of being unable to control the situation. Appleton answered on 2 March stating that the situation in Wales was 'dangerous and unsound'. The agitation, he wrote, was not controllable because 'nearly all the steps that I have recommended in the past we have since conceded under the influence of outside pressure . . . We have therefore given the impression that we do not want to help Wales, but that we concede to force.'[106]

Having read Appleton's letter and Rendall's memorandum, Reith, on 6 March, composed a lengthy diatribe. 'I do not remember', he informed Appleton, 'that you have advocated before that the Welsh and Western sections should be divorced . . . I have neither heard nor read before anything like Rendall's memorandum, particularly with respect to the impossibility of working the two sections.' Reith declared that he would have pursued the matter of a wavelength for Wales 'with much more determination than I have done had I had such a memorandum from you as has come from Rendall . . . Your remarks to me about the [Welsh] . . . were that they were most unreasonable people . . . never content with anything [and that we should] not pay attention to the grumblers.' Appleton retorted with an eleven-page memorandum listing the warnings he had sent to Head Office since 1927; in it he argued that there is 'little point in separating the West Country from Wales until North Wales is served'.[107]

Having become convinced that something needed to be done, Reith moved quickly. He informed Carpendale, the controller (administration), that he was asking the engineers whether they were 'still quite satisfied that our attitude was right'. 'There is no doubt', he wrote, 'that the matter is serious . . . It does not appear to have been realised here that the national entity of Wales . . . ought to have given Wales a considerable start as against population figures.' 'I do not know', he informed Nicolls, 'whether Ashbridge is going to be able to produce a technical separation of the region or not. I have conversations with him about this and he is doing a lot of thinking. This, however, is very private.' The notion discussed in October 1934 that synchronization would enable north Wales to be served was re-examined and the argument that the north should wait until more populous areas had been provided with transmitters was cast aside. There was also a readiness to look again at the use of the 'little nationals', particularly as a reduction in their number had been made more feasible by the replacement in October 1934 of Daventry on 100 kilowatts by Droitwich on 150 kilowatts.[108]

On 2 April 1935, the Director-General's Meeting decided that a transmitter should be provided for north Wales, and that, subject to further tests, a separate wavelength for Wales was a practical pro-position. The BBC was seeking to synchronize the Scottish National transmission, broadcast on 285.7 metres, with the London and West National transmissions, broadcast on 261.1 metres. The experiment, if successful, would release the 285.7 wavelength for the use of a West of England Regional Service; the 373 wavelength on which the West Regional Service was transmitted could then become the wavelength of a Welsh Regional Service.[109] As Washford was not a completely satisfactory centre from which to broadcast to south-western England, a new transmitter – probably sited in south Devon – should be built to serve that region.

There was great anxiety within the Corporation that the public should not believe that the proposed new arrangements had long been possible and that they were only being adopted because of outside pressure. Reith was to address a joint meeting of the Welsh MPs and the University Committee on 11 April 1935, when the de-cision regarding the wavelength would be announced. In the notes briefing him for the meeting he was told to stress that the practic-ability of the arrangements had only become apparent very recently.

In his statement he declared that our 'conclusions had only been arrived at within the last fortnight and could not have been formed earlier'. The separation of the programme and administrative staffs of Wales from those of south-western England, urgently requested by Rendall in February 1935, was decided upon at the Director-General's Meeting of 13 March, and that decision was also to be announced on 11 April.[110]

Reith recorded his impressions of the meeting with the Welsh MPs and the University Committee both in a memorandum and in his diary. 'I think they are', he wrote, 'the most unpleasant and unreliable people with whom it has ever been my misfortune to deal.' He had wanted to fulminate at great length against Saunders Lewis, who had been making speeches accusing the BBC of seeking the destruction of the Welsh language, but he was dissuaded by the chairman, D. R. Grenfell, MP for Gower. The meeting was told that, as a result of the separation, Cardiff would have a full complement of Welsh staff under the leadership of Appleton, who would be the director of both the Wales and the West of England Regions.[111]

The reaction to the announcement of 11 April 1935 was hardly flattering to the BBC. 'The wonder', noted the *Western Mail*, 'is not that this act of common justice has been done, but that the BBC has been such a prodigious time doing it. We must leave it to the experts to explain by what miracle they have overcome the difficulties which hitherto have baffled them.' 'Hitherto', stated the *North Wales Chronicle*, 'the BBC sheltered behind technical difficulties, [but] these are no longer an excuse because the University Committee had taken care to have expert opinion.' Furthermore, it was apparent that the north Wales relay and the separate wavelength would not be immediately available. Extensive work would be needed to connect Bangor to the Corporation's simultaneous broadcasting system. Even if the Scottish tests were successful, south-western England would continue to share the Washford twin transmitter with Wales until a new transmitter had been built near Plymouth; as that would be incapable of serving Bristol, a relay near Clevedon would be necessary. Bristolians, who had satisfactory reception from Washford, were annoyed. 'What is the strange secret influence these Welsh zealots have over the BBC?' asked the *Bristol Evening News*. 'The BBC is running roughshod over the West, intimidated by the howls of fervid Welsh Nationalists.'[112]

While BBC officials accepted the need for the organizational division of Wales and south-western England, many of them continued to oppose the granting of an exclusive wavelength to Wales. Six weeks after the April meeting, a BBC memorandum argued that 'a wavelength can only be provided for Wales at the expense of another region . . . An exclusive wavelength for Wales would mean too generous treatment for a minority.'[113] In Wales, as in south-western England, the April statement was seen as a Welsh Nationalist victory. 'I had always accepted Reith's explanation', wrote R. T. Evans, Liberal MP for Carmarthen, '[but now] Saunders Lewis can claim a triumph.' 'It is far too early to talk of a triumph,' retorted Lewis. 'Our ambitions go much further than anything that has been conceded. There is a grudging tone to the whole statement. It exhibits English officialdom in its typical obdurate arrogance.'[114]

The 'everlasting Welsh trouble', as he put it, was not Reith's only concern in the early months of 1935. The Corporation's Charter, granted for ten years from 1 January 1927, was due to expire on 31 December 1936. In March 1935, the government announced the appointment of a committee under the chairmanship of the 79-year-old Lord Ullswater, speaker of the House of Commons from 1905 to 1921. Reith was incensed to discover that it included 'that villain', Lord Selsdon, who had been postmaster-general in 1925. He was further incensed on 15 April on discovering that the committee was to have two additional members, one of whom was Clement Davies, Liberal MP for Montgomeryshire. To have a Welshman on the committee was, he thought, wholly unnecessary, because 'I settled Wales last Thursday'. The matter still rankled fourteen years later when he wrote his autobiography. 'Why should the Welsh have a member', he wrote in 1949, '. . . when there was no-one specifically for Scotland. The usual political criterion: there had been no parliamentary complaints from Scotland.'[115] The fact that the Ullswater Committee was sitting may have served to modify the BBC's centralist tendencies. The committee showed considerable interest in decentralization. It questioned three of the regional directors and Head Office would have been embarrassed had they been openly critical; in the event, they loyally endorsed Corporation policy.[116]

In May 1935, applications were invited for the new posts which were to be established in Wales as a result of the creation of a separate Welsh Region. There were nine on offer, and the advertisement aroused great interest, for glamorous and relatively well-paid jobs for Welsh-speaking graduates were not plentiful in 1935. There were seven hundred applications, a figure swelled by press speculation to three thousand. Because the Corporation did not feel competent to assess the qualifications of Welsh-speaking applicants, Nicolls established a committee consisting of Emrys Evans, Jenkin James and Wynn Wheldon to advise him. Appleton was unenthusiastic. 'They are primarily educationalists', he wrote, '[and are therefore] somewhat removed from the hurly burly of everyday affairs in Wales.'[117]

The files of the advisory committee, containing as they do pertinent – and sometimes impertinent – comments on virtually everyone who would be prominent in the life of Welsh-speaking Wales over the following half century, make fascinating reading.[118] The successful applicants would join the BBC's existing Welsh staff, consisting of Ernest Jenkins, Edgar Jones and Sam Jones, together with Dafydd Gruffydd and Owen Parry, appointed in 1933, and Elwyn Evans, appointed in 1934. Finding announcers proved particularly difficult. As they would have to announce in English as well as in Welsh, they were expected to pass the stringent tests of the BBC's phonetics adviser, who championed the clipped accent, regionless and (in theory) classless, characteristic of the Corporation's output in the 1930s. (The adviser was Alfred Lloyd James, professor of phonetics at the School of African and Oriental Studies and a native of Penrhiwceibr.) Few Welsh-speakers had such accents, and the applicants tested were considered to speak in a manner that was 'educated but not cultured'. The best applicant was a woman, but she was turned down because she could not 'swear or be sworn at by London when things go wrong'.[119]

Seven appointments were made in the summer of 1935; two more were made at the end of the year, and another in 1937. As the early staff of the Welsh Region included T. Rowland Hughes, Alun Llywelyn-Williams, Geraint Dyfnallt Owen, Arwel Hughes and Mansel Thomas, they represented the cream of the Welsh-speaking intelligentsia of the 1930s. What struck the press, however, was the degree to which the BBC in Wales was being staffed by the progeny of what would later be called the Welsh-speaking Establishment. By 1936, the BBC was employing the son of a professor of Welsh and the offspring of three archdruids. Over half the appointees were the children or grandchildren of Nonconformist ministers. To Reith, this no doubt appeared unexceptionable; in 1964, on reviewing his leadership of the BBC, he noted 'and it all comes from the Manse'.[120] In England, senior posts at the BBC went disproportionately to the sons of clerics (mostly of the Church of England), but the disproportion in Wales, in 1935 and subsequently, was far more marked. In the early twentieth century, Nonconformist ministers were virtually the only professional group whose work was done mainly through the medium of Welsh; children of the manse were expected to perform in public from their earliest days, and as religious belief waned the secular faith of the BBC could seem an adequate substitute for the religious faith of the forefathers of many of its staff.

Appleton objected to only one of those recommended by Emrys Evans's committee. He was Alun Llywelyn-Williams, perhaps the ablest of the suggested appointees. Appleton recognized Llywelyn-Williams's ability but 'I ought to point out', he wrote to Nicolls, 'that he is an ardent young Nationalist, and in view of the extremely unpleasant attacks which the Welsh Nationalist Party continues to make upon us, I do not think it would be advisable to have a member of this party on our staff'. Llywelyn-Williams had discussed his application with his professor, W. J. Gruffydd, who had advised him to find other referees, 'gan fod Appleton yn meddwl mai enw arall ar y diafol oedd W. J. Gruffydd'*.[121] (It should be noted that Appleton had accepted Gruffydd's son, Dafydd, as a member of the Cardiff staff in 1933.) In the event, Llywelyn-Williams was given a temporary post; he became a permanent employee of the Corporation after Appleton had left Cardiff.

As Appleton, for the time being at least, was to be the director of the Welsh Region, the most important post on offer was that of director of programmes. There were many in Wales who assumed it would go to Sam Jones, who had been *de facto* director of Welsh-language programmes since 1932. Even his warmest admirers, however, ackowledged that Jones lacked *savoir-faire*. Nicolls was determined not to appoint him. 'He is deaf,' he informed Reith, 'he cannot write English . . . [and] he is a bit provincial – rather the kind who has never been outside Wales, except for a big Cup Tie.' Rendall demurred. 'While I agree with the disadvantages of Sam Jones,' he wrote, 'I hope it will not be thought that he has not also some excellent qualities and real achievements to his credit as well.' Appleton also felt moved to add a comment. 'Sam Jones is not illiterate in English,' he informed Nicolls. He believed, however, that Jones was unfit for a permanent senior post. 'Appleton', wrote Reith, 'does not consider Sam Jones nearly good enough to be . . . the Welsh Programme Director.' Jones, it was noted, 'suffers from the usual fault of the Welsh character, namely a certain amount of instability'. Appleton was convinced that no one who pursued a career exclusively in Wales could possibly fill a responsible position. He informed Reith:

I have . . . been searching quietly for some really brilliant Welshmen . . . I have kept in mind the need for such men to have artistic standards higher than those usually obtaining in Wales, and therefore . . . they must have had additional training elsewhere . . . I have searched the records of places like Jesus College Oxford . . . Sam Jones does not believe that we shall be able to find a man who is more competent than he is; he states that if we can find a man whom he really respects as

---

*'Since Appleton thinks that W. J. Gruffydd is another name for the devil.'

being better than himself, he will gladly serve him but . . . if the new man [is] inferior he will have to consider resigning his position.[122]

The man appointed was William Hughes Jones, the son of a Flintshire minister, who for ten years and more had been an education officer with the RAF. He was known as 'Elidir Sais' (Elidir the Englishman, or perhaps the Anglophone) because of his insistence upon speaking English to his Welsh-speaking friends. Shortly after his appointment was announced, he addressed the Cymmrodorion at the National Eisteddfod at Caernarfon. He chose to speak in English, devoting his talk to an attack upon the Welsh because they did not, in his opinion, have sufficient regard for the British Empire. There was an outcry. 'We shall now', declared the veteran Nationalist, D. J. Williams, 'be fighting the Philistines within our gates.' Hughes Jones was transferred to the Empire Service in London in February 1936; the archives contain little concerning the decision to transfer him, apart from a note recording that he could not control his staff. His removal was not supported by all prominent Welsh-speakers. Iorwerth Peate, later the curator of the Welsh Folk Museum, whom Appleton had banned from broadcasting, saw virtue in Hughes Jones and condemned the attacks upon him. Hughes Jones was temporarily replaced by Owen Parry, who had been appointed talks and schools assistant in June 1933.[123]

The procedure for appointing the new staff had been announced at the meeting of the Corporation and the University Committee held on 22 May 1935. As Wales was formally constituted a separate region on 4 September 1935, Head Office believed that further meetings with the committee were unnecessary. As the wavelength issue had not been fully resolved, its members pressed for further meetings. Appleton agreed with them, for he felt that others should occasionally share his experience of the 'unreasonableness of the Welsh'. 'I know that the Committee members', he informed Head Office on 26 September, 'do like to get up to town as frequently and for as long as possible. Any excuse for a London meeting is hailed in Wales with much delight.' A further meeting was held on 24 October 1935, when it was announced that the Bangor studio would be open within about a month and that the north Wales relay station would be operational in nine to twelve months.[124]

The Bangor studio was opened on 1 November 1935. Its opening provided an opportunity to remove Sam Jones from Cardiff to become Bangor representative. He acquiesced with reluctance. Appleton thought that Jones would be more suitable as the representative at Swansea in his native west Glamorgan, a post which carried fewer responsibilities, but, as Appleton informed

Nicolls, 'he is so angry about this decision that he is . . . reluctant to make a definite choice'. By the summer of 1935, however, he had opted to become Bangor representative, a title which was changed to north Wales representative on 15 February 1937. The Bangor studio was located at Bryn Meirion, a large house half-way between the city centre and the University College, which the Corporation had bought in March 1935. As the control room was not fully operational until 11 December, Bangor's earliest productions were transmitted to Daventry by outside broadcast equipment. The first of them was a party political broadcast by Lloyd George, given on 8 November and carried on the National Service. That was unusual, for Bangor had been established with the intention that it should be almost exclusively concerned with making programmes for the Welsh Regional Service. Yet, as the north Wales relay station did not become operational until 1 February 1937, the first fifteen months of Bangor's productions for that service could only be heard in the southern half of Wales. The new studio laboured under considerable handicaps. Ordinary telephone contact with Bangor was often difficult. The link with Washford was a vulnerable land line which went via Manchester, Birmingham, Gloucester and Bristol. Bangor was due to make its first contribution to the Welsh Regional Service on 30 November when the agriculturalist Alun R. Roberts was to give a talk. As the land line had been broken by a falling tree at Llanfairfechan, Roberts's script was read by an announcer at Cardiff. In the event, the first Welsh regional broadcast from Bangor was given on 11 December 1935 by Mrs Grace Wynne Griffith. Bangor had no recording equipment; any programme which was intended to be repeated had to be recorded off the air in Cardiff and then the record was sent to Bangor by train. Despite the handicaps, Sam Jones was determined to make Bangor the chief centre of Welsh-language broadcasting. Indeed, so ambitious were his plans that less than two months after his transfer the Control Board was discussing his activities and seeking assurances from Appleton that Jones would not attempt programmes 'for which Bangor was not designed'.[125]

The opening of Bangor coincided with a modification of the ultra-centralist policies of the Corporation. In June 1935, Charles Siepmann, the director of talks, was made director of regional relations, largely because Reith wanted to move him to a post where his left-wing views would be less intrusive. The appointment was widely attacked in Wales, for it was assumed that it meant that the day-to-day activities of all the regions would be centralized under Siepmann in London.[126] Siepmann had been an ardent centralist, but he changed his opinions after a thorough investigation of the BBC's regional activities. In his report on the regions, submitted in January 1936, he declared:

> Among thinking men and women in all parts of the country, I found a common preoccupation with the dangers resulting from the increasing tendency for administrative, cultural and industrial concentration on the London area . . . The strength of this feeling cannot be exaggerated . . . The provinces are the seedground of talent and the ultimate source of our supply for London programmes. There is a need for a Charter of Rights for the Regions . . . [They have] only a bare skeleton of what is necessary.

He drew attention to the 'huge anomaly of our present system of regional broadcasting – the absence of any interpretation of the country – excluding London – which extends from Norfolk to . . . Hampshire'. In Scotland he discovered 'a self consciousness that is best left alone'. The West Region was 'rather dreamy, backward and feudal' and he suggested that it should be abolished. He urged that 'developments in Wales should be gradual' in order to give a 'raw and inexperienced staff time to prove their capacities and to allow the cooling of political and racial passions provoked by past controversies over our Welsh policy'.[127]

The Corporation, helped by the departure in 1935 of the arch-centralizer, Alan Dawnay, the controller (programmes), saw the force of Siepmann's arguments and acted on many of his recommendations. Charles Carpendale, the deputy director-general, began holding monthly meetings with the regional directors, and the most senior of them – Percy Edgar, the Midland director – was invited to join the Control Board when regional issues were discussed.[128] Programme allowances were increased, as were the hours during which the regions were permitted to opt out of London's productions. As Siepmann had described the BBC's premises at Swansea as 'disgraceful', the Corporation began discussing with the County Borough Council the acquisition of more suitable accommodation. Ernest Jenkins, who had divided his time between Swansea and Cardiff, joined the Cardiff staff in 1935. He was replaced at Swansea by the talented tenor, Tom Pickering. Pickering received the title of west Wales representative on 15 February 1937, the day on which Sam Jones became known as the north Wales representative.[129]

While Siepmann was preparing his report, Reith was digesting the conclusions of the Ullswater Committee. The committee had received submissions from several Welsh bodies. The University of Wales had asked it 'to register the Corporation's decision concerning wavebands'; the Welsh MPs had urged that the Board of Governors should include a representative of Wales, and Plaid Genedlaethol Cymru had demanded that Wales should have its own corporation. In its report, published in March 1936, the Ullswater Committee noted with approval that 'the BBC has already recognised in principle [that] Wales (hitherto associated with the West Country) should as soon as possible be constituted a distinct broadcasting region'. The two, thought the committee, had been a 'mutually uncomfortable partnership'. It rejected the request for a Welsh governor because it would be 'inconsistent with our concept of the Board of Governors'; it was even more emphatic in its rejection of a Welsh corporation. The report was discussed by the House of Commons in July 1936, when Megan Lloyd George and Ernest Evans (Liberal MP for the University of Wales) pressed for the appointment of a Welsh governor. The government accepted the committee's recommendation that the BBC's Charter be renewed for another ten years and thus the constitutional position of the Corporation was ensured until 31 December 1946.[130]

Although the Ullswater Report took it for granted that the 'Welsh Controversy' had been settled, the Corporation had still not made any specific decision as to when a separate wavelength was likely to be provided. Wales and the West of England became separately organized regions in September 1935 but they continued to share the Washford regional transmitter. The hours allotted to productions by the two regions and broadcast on their joint transmitter were increased to twenty-five a week and the use made of those hours was decided by correspondence between the programme directors at Bristol and Cardiff. Head Office, aware of the increasing press protests from south-western England, was anxiously monitoring the situation, for its officials feared that pressures from Wales could lead to a serious imbalance between the hours taken by Cardiff and those taken by Bristol. In March 1936, Lindsay Wellington, the regional liaison officer, informed Rendall, who since 1935 had been the programme director of the West of England:

> At a casual glance, it seemed to me that Welsh programmes [are] overwhelmingly preponderant. I am very ready to be told that your programme builders have been adhering faithfully to the mathematical percentage which the Corporation has agreed should be allotted to Welsh programmes, but I think you may consider it worthwhile to have this comment of mine, since I suspect the listeners in the West of England will have a similar reaction to mine.[131]

As director of both the Wales and the West of England Regions, Appleton had the task of ensuring that the two were kept in harmony. The Corporation had originally intended to postpone the appointment of a regional director for Wales until the granting of separate wavelengths to each of the two regions was imminent, for, while they shared the same transmitter, it was sensible for them to share the same director. By 1936, however, Reith was becoming increasingly dissatisfied with Appleton. The precise cause of the dissatisfaction is not clear, but there is some suggestion that Appleton was orchestrating a campaign to ensure that his programme, *Silent Fellowship*, which had ceased to be broadcast on the National Service, should again be carried by the Droitwich transmitter. By the summer of 1936, he was on prolonged leave for health reasons, and on 29 August 1936 Reith noted in his diary that he had written a 'long-hand letter to Appleton giving him notice'. In fact, Appleton did not cease to be a Corporation employee until 30 June 1937, when he demanded, and received, £5,000 'to go quietly'. By then, Reith was enraged by 'that crook Appleton', but was obliged to accept his terms because Sir James Rae of the Treasury advised the Corporation that in confronting Appleton with charges, his case had been unsatisfactorily handled. Appleton, wrote Reith, had sought the support of the other regional directors, but 'Edgar said his surprise was only that we had tolerated him so long'.[132]

His annoyance with Appleton led Reith to bring forward the appointment of a Welsh regional director. In February 1936, seventeen months before Wales had its own wavelength, the post was advertised in the press. The advertisement led to a flurry of speculation. Reith insisted that the appointment was his alone. He interviewed six of the applicants on 1 May but considered none of them satisfactory. On 26 May, he informed the Control Board that he was going to discuss the post with Rhys Hopkin Morris and on 16 June he informed the Board that Hopkin Morris had been appointed regional director for Wales.[133]

It was a strange appointment. Hopkin Morris had no interest in broadcasting as such, and, as a doctrinaire Liberal, his willingness to be the employee of a state monopoly is very odd. He was the son of a Congregational minister from Maesteg, and had studied law at Aberystwyth and London. In 1923, he had been elected MP for Cardiganshire as the representative of the anti-Lloyd George faction of the Liberal Party, and during the campaign he had stated that the imposition of a tariff was, morally, no different from a declaration of war. In 1929, when the fifty-nine members of the Parliamentary Liberal Party met to re-elect Lloyd George as their leader, Hopkin Morris's was the only dissenting vote.[134] As MP for Cardiganshire, he had frequently criticized the BBC. In 1931 he had stated that there was no reason why the postmaster-general should not grant a licence to an exclusively Welsh station, for he argued, correctly, that the charter of 1927 to 1936 did not grant the Corporation a monopoly of public broadcasting. In 1932, he had accused the BBC of being an 'essentially English corporation'.[135] In that year he left Parliament to become a metropolitan magistrate, a well-paid position from which it was thought unlikely that he could be prised.

Attracting Hopkin Morris to the BBC gave Reith much satisfaction. 'A Welshman', he wrote, 'was appointed as regional director for Wales, of a calibre I had long sought . . . He [gave] up a position of responsibility, security and dignity in the judicature at my rather pressing invitation.'[136] Reith's satisfaction was Hopkin Morris's strength. As he had been 'headhunted' by Reith and as his appointment was greeted – in Welsh-speaking Wales at least – with something akin to rapture, his position in relation to the director-general was different from that of other regional directors, all of whom were in constant fear of dismissal.[137] 'Hopkin Morris is a great idea in many ways,' Professor T. H. Parry-Williams wrote to Thomas Jones. 'If Lloyd George failed to tame him, what chance will John Reith have?'[138] Parry-Williams was correct. Hopkin Morris's great virtue, wrote Alun Llywelyn-Williams, '[oedd ei fod yn mynnu] mai iddo ef yr oedd holl aelodau staff y Rhanbarth Cymreig yn gyfrifol . . . Unwaith iddo benderfynu ar yr hyn oedd yn iawn yn ei olwg, ni wnâi dim oll ei syflyd.'*[139]

Hopkin Morris joined the staff of the BBC on 31 August 1936. He was not Cardiff's only new appointee in that month. On 10 August, J. Gwynfryn Roberts became the Welsh regional executive officer, a post held previously by Norman Settle, who was also executive officer for the West of England Region. Following Roberts's appointment, Settle's duties were restricted to the West of England, thus bringing to an end an association with Cardiff which dated back to the beginnings of broadcasting in the city. Hopkin Morris spent September 1936 at Broadcasting House in London, that mixture of a liner and a lunatic asylum, as Cleghorn Thomson put it, into which Head Office had moved in 1932.[140] He then made a tour of the regions and was not formally installed in his office until 19 October 1936. The occasion was marked by a broadcast during which the new director was introduced by Carpendale. Hopkin Morris chose to speak entirely in Welsh, understandably perhaps in view of the nature of the agitation which had led to his appointment, but unwisely in view of the nature of that appointment. The leading newspapers of Wales acclaimed his speech, but the *Cardiff Times* drew

---

*'He insisted that all the staff of the Welsh Region were responsible to him. Once he had decided what was right in his view, nothing at all would move him.'

attention to the fact that 'Rhys Hopkin Morris did not use a word of English. If that is a sign of the times . . . [then for the great majority] the Welsh station will become not a blessing but a nuisance . . . The unfortunate introduction of the new Director . . . cannot possibly go unchallenged for long.' The *Herald of Wales* agreed. 'The future contingency', it wrote, 'is not that distinctively Welsh interests will not receive sufficient attention. It is that they may be overstressed.'[141]

On 1 May 1936, shortly before Reith began discussions with Hopkin Morris, the University Committee held another of its meetings with the Corporation. There was yet another on 27 November 1936, when it was announced that, as Hopkin Morris had been appointed, the BBC, in any future meetings with a Welsh committee, would be represented not by a London official but by the Welsh director. The November meeting was therefore the last occasion when the University Committee met senior Head Office figures. The Ullswater Report had recommended that the regions should have advisory committees, but as the suggestion was not made mandatory, the recommendation, where Wales was concerned, was left to Hopkin Morris. He chose to ignore it. The meetings of May and November were mainly concerned with demands that the separate wavelength should be provided as soon as possible. At the November meeting it was announced that the synchronization in Scotland was proceeding satisfactorily and that the transmitter for south-western England at Start Point in south Devon would be ready by 1938. The meeting was also told that an unmanned studio would shortly be provided at Aberystwyth, a facility which Sir Stuart Jones, the principal of the University College of Wales, had been particularly anxious to secure. The Aberystwyth studio was opened on 28 December 1936; it was located in a small room in the College's music department, and in its three years of existence it was not extensively used.[142]

The members of the University Committee were dismayed to hear that there would be a delay of up to two years before Start Point was completed and before Wales had its own wavelength. They were heartened, however, by one other piece of news given to them at the November meeting: the north Wales relay station would be operational early in 1937. The station, named after the village of Penmon outside Beaumaris, was opened on 1 February 1937 by Lord Davies of Llandinam, whose journal, *The Welsh Outlook* (by then defunct) had played some part in securing it. At last, the north could hear the programmes produced in the north, thus causing Sam Jones to be even more ambitious in his plans.

Sam Jones's early productions at Bangor were a contribution, not only to the regional service of Wales, but also to that transmitted to communities from Cornwall to the borders of Hampshire. Press comment from south-western England protesting against the imposition of programmes in 'a foreign language', and increasingly strongly worded appeals from the Bristol staff, led Head Office to reconsider its wavelength plans.[143] On 8 December 1936, the Control Board decided that because 'feeling at present existing both in Wales and in the West of England demanded early action', the Corporation would not wait until the completion of Start Point before providing Wales with its own wavelength. There were two transmitters at Washford – the 'little national' broadcasting the National Service and the other broadcasting the joint service of the two regions. The Control Board ruled that Washford would cease to broadcast the National Service, obliging listeners in the two regions to rely exclusively on the service from Droitwich. The transmitter broadcasting the joint service would become the transmitter for Wales Regional Service and, until Start Point had been completed, the Washford transmitter previously offering the National Service would broadcast the West of England Regional Service. The decision represented the final vindication of the ideas which E. G. Bowen had been advocating since 1930. The regional service was in fact the London Regional Service with opt-outs by Wales and the West of England. Cardiff and Bristol were ordered not to opt out at the same time, thus enabling the area served by the Washford transmitters to receive the entire London Regional Service. Until the opening of Start Point – which did not occur until 14 June 1939 – Cardiff and Bristol would therefore continue to be obliged to co-operate extensively over programme scheduling.[144]

These plans were put into operation during the first half of 1937. On 3 July, Reith, accompanied by Noel Ashbridge, the controller (engineering), and Cecil Graves, Dawnay's successor as controller (programmes), travelled to Cardiff to attend the inauguration of the exclusive wavelength for Wales. Reith showed no satisfaction at being present at an occasion which represented a solution to a problem which had been plaguing him for a decade. 'An absurd affair,' he wrote in his diary. '[I am] aggrieved that half my weekend should have been filched by the Cardiff visit . . . I spoke . . . Ashbridge said afterwards it was pearls before swine.' In his speech, he denied that the Corporation had been influenced by the protests from Wales:

Unless I have been hearing wrongly . . . Wales appears for a change to be pleased with the BBC. We have been used to so many fulminations, agitations and deputations from Wales in the last fifteen years that it has been a novel and refreshing experience to listen to what the . . . speakers have said. And not one of those fulminations, agitations and deputations has brought this occasion one day earlier.[145]

There were no representatives from the West of England Region at the wavelength ceremony. 'Is it not usual', Hopkin Morris was asked, 'for both parties to be present at divorce proceedings?' 'Not in an undefended suit,' he replied.[146]

The opening ceremony was performed by G. C. Joyce, the bishop of Monmouth, who, as pro-chancellor of the University, had chaired most of the meetings of the University Committee. It was followed by a luncheon provided by the lord mayor of Cardiff. 'Terrible city hall function', wrote Reith. 'How sad it is that Municipal Government is entering into the hands of the common tradespeople type.' He visited Cardiff's Broadcasting House in Park Place and was aggrieved that 'it didn't seem to have occurred to Hopkin Morris that with a visit from the Director-General, let alone with two Controllers, the whole of his staff should have been on parade'.[147] Although the opening ceremony was held on 3 July 1937, separate broadcasting by the two regions did not begin until the following day. Various dates can therefore be offered as denoting the inauguration of the Welsh Region. The title was first used on 4 September 1935; it became more meaningful with the appointment of Rhys Hopkin Morris on 1 September 1936. The term 'Radio Cymru' (Radio Wales) – wholly unauthorized at the time – first appears in the press on 7 December 1936.[148] Nevertheless, it could be argued that the region only truly came into existence on 4 July 1937, a date which marks the end of one chapter in the history of broadcasting in Wales and the beginning of another.

An addendum must be added to the chapter which came to a close on 4 July 1937. In December 1937, Hopkin Morris persuaded Reith to attend a conference on broadcasting held at Gregynog, the home of Margaret and Gwendoline Davies, the sisters of Lord Davies of Llandinam. 'It is all very odd,' he wrote in his diary; 'big house, very valuable pictures, millionaire hostesses, meals plain.' The first lecture was given by Gwilym Davies, who 'raked up past rows . . . a deplorable start to the weekend'. 'I spoke to them for an hour and twenty minutes, without notes and practically without preparation . . . It went down excellently.' Reith summed up his Gregynog experience with the phrase: 'I thoroughly dislike the Welsh.'[149] In December 1937, Reith's reign had only six months to run. Feeling that he was 'understretched' – 'I have', he wrote, 'maybe an hour's effective work daily' – he resigned as director-general on 30 June 1938.[150] He was succeeded by Frederick Ogilvie, who, like Reith, was of Scottish Presbyterian stock. A distinguished academic, Ogilvie had been in turn the professor of political science at Edinburgh and principal of Queen's University, Belfast.

IV   Listeners and programmes, 1927–1937

The sheer bulk of the evidence relating to the efforts to establish a Welsh region with its own wavelength, and the vast body of material concerning the administration of the Corporation can seduce the historian of broadcasting in Wales away from what sound broadcasting is fundamentally about: people listening to programmes. As Maurice Gorham put it: 'The habit of thinking that what is broadcast is the least important thing about broadcasting is one that grows all too easily among officials everywhere.'[151]

The notion that every household had access to broadcasting – an assumption basic to broadcasting policy in the 1990s – was by no means valid in the 1930s. Indeed, as has been seen, the Corporation's assessment of the claims of Wales and the West of England was influenced by a consideration of which of the two regions was likely to produce the greater increase in licence revenue. Details of licence-holders in Wales are not available until 1930. During the 1930s, the number grew rapidly:[152]

1930	136,320	1935	321,956
1931	165,881	1936	347,782
1932	211,915	1937	373,900
1933	240,817	1938	395,500
1934	295,662	1939	405,954

The 136 per cent increase between 1930 and 1935 is especially remarkable in view of the fact that those years were a time of severe depression, with unemployment among the insured male workers of Wales rising to 42 per cent in the summer of 1932. Initially, the Corporation expressed the figures in terms of percentages of licences to the population, a misleading concept, for licences were held by households rather than by individuals. For example, it claimed that on 31 July 1930 only 4 per cent of the Welsh people had licences.[153] According to the Census of 1931, there were 638,000 households in Wales; thus the proportion of households with licences in that year was 26 per cent, a figure which would rise to 59 per cent by 1937. Half the households of Wales had licences by 1935, a proportion which had been reached in the United Kingdom as a whole in 1933. Within Wales, there were curious regional differences; in 1931, 37.6 per cent of the households of Caernarfonshire had licences, compared with 9.2 in Breconshire. Indeed, throughout the 1930s, the percentage of licensed households was lower in Breconshire than in any other British county. There were marked regional differences in England also, the proportion in 1931 varying from 56 per cent in Hertfordshire to 13 in County Durham. English percentages were consistently higher than Welsh, causing the Corporation to argue that as Wales was not supporting the BBC, the BBC was not obliged to support Wales. 'What material concession can be made to the fact of nationality', asked the *BBC Handbook* of 1932, '. . . in the face of the relative lack of support for broadcasting?' 'No man', retorted the University Committee, 'pays for his goods until he gets them.' The committee pointed out that the percentages in Wales were similar to those in Scotland where specific national provision had been made. They were far higher than they were in Northern Ireland, a province which had its own exclusive wavelength.[154]

In addition to the licensed listeners, there were undoubtedly many households in Wales which used unlicensed sets, although it is unlikely that they were as numerous as they were in Northern Ireland where, in the mid 1930s, the circulation of the *Radio Times* exceeded the number of licence-holders.[155] In the United Kingdom as a whole, purchases of licences were about three times greater than the sales of the *Radio Times*, but no figures relating to its circulation in Wales are available until the 1940s. The ten-shilling (50p) licence undoubtedly represented a considerable outlay, particularly to the families of the unemployed; in the early 1930s, an unemployed man with a wife and two children received £1.9s.9d. (£1.48) a week.

The cost of a licence was a minor part of the expense of equipping a household to receive broadcasts. Crystal sets, by far the commonest means of reception in the early days of broadcasting, were being phased out in the early 1930s. The *Radio Times* ceased to advertise them in 1927; they were still in common use in 1930 but had come to be rare by 1935. There were 600 different types of wireless sets on sale by 1937. Families of limited means bought sets like the Philco, which cost between £5.5s. and £6.6s., generally through hire purchase, a method of acquiring goods which became very popular in the 1930s. The cheaper sets did not have the range of the more expensive ones, particularly if their owners lacked the resources to install an elaborate aerial. Thus, less prosperous Welsh families were more dependent upon the service provided by Washford than were those who were able to buy dearer receivers.[156]

In much of industrial south Wales, the lie of the land caused reception, even from Washford, to be unsatisfactory. The deficiency was made good by the relay companies which provided a service by wire to disadvantaged communities at a cost per household of about

1s.6d (7.5p) a week. In 1935, a quarter of a million British households were relay subscribers. They represented 4 per cent of the licence-holders; in much of south-east Wales, however, the proportion was considerably higher. When the relay companies were licensed in 1929, the Corporation had sought to ensure that they would only be allowed to relay the BBC's services, but no such restriction was placed upon them. Radio Normandie, launched in 1931, and Radio Luxembourg, launched in 1933, broadcast English programmes of a more populist character than those of the BBC, and by the mid 1930s Radio Luxembourg had won a large following, particularly in south Wales.

The licence of the relay companies, like that of the Corporation, was due to expire at the end of 1936. The BBC feared that the relay companies' new licence might allow them to concentrate on transmitting the 'pirate' stations at the expense of the BBC. The relay companies were also of concern to the members of the University Committee, for the companies were markedly hostile to any notion of an all-Welsh service – assuming, as many people did, that it meant a service that broadcast exclusively in Welsh. Enquiries by relay companies in east Glamorgan and Monmouthshire led them to the conclusion that only 6 per cent of their customers would want such a service, and at the staff dinner of the Pontypridd, Merthyr, Bargoed and Rhondda Central Exchanges in 1934 the chairman stated that, if an all-Welsh service were provided, his company would refuse to relay it. Both the BBC and the University Committee were relieved that the relay licence of 1936 laid down that, whatever else the relay companies provided, they were obliged to provide the service which would normally be provided by the BBC in their area of operation.[157]

The increase in the number of households owning sets meant that the public transmission of broadcasts – occasions when people gathered in a hall or vestry to listen to an evening of programmes, a widespread phenomenon in the early 1920s – had become rare by the 1930s. It did not disappear, for even in 1935 half the inhabitants of Wales lacked sets, and there were many who gathered in places such as centres for the unemployed to listen to the wireless. Furthermore, the BBC was anxious to encourage more formal group listening, for it believed that among its programmes were those which deserved to be thoughtfully absorbed and discussed rather than considered as a supply 'on tap'. 'Tap listeners', wrote Graves in 1936, 'warrant no further provision in programmes.' The Corporation regularly broadcast programmes specifically for listening groups and J. C. Stobart, the Corporation's head of education, hoped that such programmes could be the basis for a wireless university, a notion which was shelved following his death in 1933. E. H. F. Mills, the West Region's education officer, maintained contact with the groups, a duty which passed to Owen Parry on his appointment as the Welsh Region's education officer in 1935. By 1937, there were 110 such groups in Wales; some were closely associated with the WEA, and the South Wales Council for Social Services helped to pay the expenses of group leaders. In 1937, the BBC broadcast two series aimed at Welsh-medium listening groups, such as that established by the members of Cardiff's Minnie Street Congregational Chapel.[158]

By far the greater part of the BBC's audience, however, listened at home, and Raymond Williams saw the coming of radio as one of the factors which led to 'the privatisation of life' so characteristic of modern society. When the BBC began surveying its audience in 1936, it discovered that the average wireless-owner listened to the radio for four hours a day, although some acknowledged that, when they were at home, they had the wireless on almost all the time. More people were at home. The early years of broadcasting were not only a time of very high unemployment; they were also a period which saw a marked contraction in working hours – from sixty a week in 1922 to forty-five by 1939.[159] In industrial Wales in particular, the number of women who were at home all day was very high; the activity rate among women in Glamorgan in 1939 was 16 per cent, compared with 39 per cent for Britain as a whole. Little consideration was given to their daytime listening; as Rendall put it: 'Having once run a flat on my own for a week, I had no time at all to listen, so housewives can be ignored as daytime listeners.'[160] The most convenient time for listening was the weekend, a fact blithely ignored by the Corporation, at least until the mid 1930s. In the early 1930s, morning broadcasts on Saturdays were restricted to one thirty-minute transmission, and there was no choice of programmes until 6.0 p.m. Sunday broadcasting began at 3.0 p.m. and there was generally an interval between 5.50 and 7.55. The BBC offered nothing light-hearted on Sunday, thus boosting the popularity of Radio Luxembourg; in 1935, 66 per cent of radio listeners stated that they listened to Radio Luxembourg on Sundays, compared with 11 per cent during the rest of the week.[161]

Although a study of the history of broadcasting in Wales must be primarily concerned with the activities of the BBC's centres in Wales, it must be borne in mind that the great majority of the programmes the Corporation made available in Wales were not produced in Wales. Output increased markedly between the early and the mid 1930s. Virtually all the programmes of the National Service were produced in London. By 1935, the service was on the air from 10.15 a.m. to midnight on weekdays; on Sundays it broadcast for two hours in the morning and then continuously from 12.30 p.m. to 11.00 p.m. – a total weekly output of ninety-five hours. The function of the

National Service was to be the vehicle of the 'national' culture, which meant that it was the disseminator of the attitudes and values of the upper middle classes of the English 'home counties'. This was particularly true of the manner of speaking of those who contributed to it, a manner which followed the dictates of the Corporation's Committee on English Pronunciation, a body consisting of an Englishman, an Irishman, an American and three Welshmen.[162]

Until the opening of the Penmon transmitter, the National wavelength broadcast occasional programmes in Welsh. For instance, it broadcast a religious service in Welsh on 13 October, 10 November and 8 December 1935. In addition, as the Corporation considered that there were some happenings in Wales which the inhabitants of the rest of the United Kingdom should know about, it broadcast occasional English-language programmes of Welsh provenance. The National Service paid marked attention to St David's Day. In 1934, its microphones were at the Cardiff Cymmrodorion dinner when Lord Sankey, the lord chancellor, was guest speaker. The occasion was a disaster, for the society's president spent so much time on his opening remarks that only part of Lord Sankey's speech was broadcast. In 1934, as a further St David's Day celebration, Cardiff offered a programme scheme which included weird Welsh kitsch by the former archdruid, Wil Ifan, and an 'awful script' by A. G. Prys-Jones. Sutthery sent the scheme to London and appealed to Lawrence Gillian, later the head of features, 'to do something with it; my heart bleeds for you'. Matters improved in 1935 when Sam Jones and T. Rowland Hughes produced a programme which greatly delighted the *Western Mail*. 'By London standards,' wrote Rendall to Roger Eckersley, 'it was nothing exciting, but I am satisfied it presented a great step forward in Welsh broadcasting which is still some years behind . . . We have neither the staff nor the equipment [here] to attempt a programme of such a sort without grave risk . . . I suggest HQ should write a note to Sam Jones . . . to dispel the idea of Head Office aloofness.'[163]

Such Welsh offerings on the National Service were very rare indeed, for virtually the whole output of the Welsh Region was produced for transmission on the Regional Service. By 1935, that service was on the air for much the same number of hours as the National Service. As has been noted, Peter Eckersley's notion of two services with distinct identities and parity of esteem had been cast aside. To his brother Roger, the Regional Service should only have the resources which were available after the needs of the National Service had been satisfied, and he and his colleagues in London referred to it as a 'supplementary' service. In 1933, when Sutthery wanted the West Regional Service to broadcast a concert given by

Arthur Rubinstein at Dartington Hall, his request was refused because 'it is against BBC policy, from the financial as well as the programme point of view, to broadcast international artists from regional stations'.[164]

Thus, most Regional Service broadcasts were paler versions of those of the National Service. Of the ninety-three hours broadcast by the West Region's transmitter in the first week of October 1935, 58 per cent was contributed by the London Regional Service, 8 per cent by the Midland, North, Scottish and Northern Irish Regions, and 9 per cent consisted of National Service programmes. The remaining 25 per cent were the productions of the Welsh and West of England Regions, with Wales providing rather more than half. In 1924, Cardiff had produced 66 per cent of its transmissions, a figure which decreased to 45 in 1927 and to 33 in 1929. In 1935, Wales was producing about 15 per cent of the broadcasts of the Washford Regional transmitter. As transmission hours had increased, the decrease in production hours was less than the percentage decrease. Although the percentage declined from 66 in 1924 to 15 in 1935, the average weekly hours produced in Wales only declined from 22 to 14.[165]

The decline was not accompanied by a reduction in the weekly programme allowance. Indeed, it increased. The Cardiff station received £190 a week in 1924; Wales and the West of England jointly received £510 in 1935. (The purchasing power of the pound sterling was considerably higher in 1935 than it had been in 1924.) Furthermore, Wales had twelve programme and administrative staff in 1935 compared with six in 1927. The explanation of this apparent paradox lies in the change in the nature of the programmes produced. In 1927, output was only beginning to move beyond the 'potted palm court' tradition, and non-musical items consisted largely of talks by unpaid speakers, plays performed by unpaid amateurs and many contributions by the station's employees for which they did not receive additional remuneration. By 1937, virtually all speakers were paid, plays were performed by professional or quasi-professional actors and Corporation employees such as the regional director, the director of programmes and the executive officer did not broadcast at all. In the increase in costs and the need for a larger staff, a central factor was the expansion of outside broadcasting; that had hardly existed in 1927, but by 1937 programme directors felt it incumbent upon them fully to exploit the resources of their region, even to the extent of sending the outside broadcasts van a hundred miles and more from the home base, accompanied, if areas lacking electricity were to be visited, by another van carrying generators.[166]

By the mid 1930s, arrangements for the programme schedule were working like a well-oiled machine. Eight weeks before transmission,

London sent its plans to the regions, and the programmes which the regions were obliged to transmit were marked with three stars. Seventeen days later, the regions were required to inform London which of its programmes they did not intend taking and to describe in detail the material which would replace the London productions. London could object, and frequently did. When Sutthery was the West's director of programmes, Lindsay Wellington, Head Office's presentation director, raised constant queries, causing Sutthery to answer sullenly: 'I am quite prepared, of course, to take . . . out [whatever you wish.] Please let me know what you want done.'[167]

The main interest centred upon the period 6.30 to 11 p.m. The day-time programmes of the regional services came mainly from London; thus regional material constituted over half the trans-missions at peak listening time, a major factor in the hostility to Welsh-language programmes in south-western England. The West Region (and the subsequent Wales and West of England Regions, which were jointly financed) was considered profligate. 'We have overspent by £220,' wrote Appleton in 1934; 'there is no hope of recouping the money.'[168] W. J. Coatman, who replaced Livening as North of England regional director in 1936, and whose programme allowance was only marginally higher than the joint allowance of Wales and the West of England, was annoyed by what he saw as the Corporation's indulgence towards over-expenditure at Cardiff and Bristol. The North, he pointed out, was almost four times more populous than the two regions put together, and eight times more populous than Wales. 'The North', he wrote, 'is not a Region; it is the other half of England.'[169]

Although the 'potted palm court' tradition was less prominent under the Corporation than it had been in the early days of the Company, music remained by far the most important element in the BBC's output. In 1929, it constituted 64 per cent of the transmissions of the National Service and 76 per cent of those of the basic (London) Regional Service, causing the Northern Ireland programme director to comment that for much of the time the only choice offered by the two services was a choice between two music programmes.[170]

Until its demise in 1931, the National Orchestra of Wales provided up to half the musical output of the Cardiff station. Its repertoire consisted, in the main, of the lighter classics, but, temporarily aug-mented, it did give the second performance in Britain of Mahler's Fourth Symphony. With the extinction of the orchestra and the departure of Braithwaite, Redman, his successor, had to be content with a nine-piece orchestra. London was dismissive of Wales's music-making capacity. 'There is really no first class Welsh music', wrote Sutthery in 1934, 'and not even second class means of expressing it in Wales even though it existed.'[171] Redman, however, was eager to encourage Welsh music and was remembered with gratitude by the distinguished composer, Grace Williams.[172] Following the division of the West Region in 1935, Redman became the West of England Region's head of music. With the formal establishment of the Welsh Region on 4 September 1935, more resources became available for broadcast music in Wales. In February 1936, Idris Lewis, the musical director of British International Films, became the new region's head of music, with Mansel Thomas as his deputy. Lewis considered that his primary duty was to encourage the new school of composers which was arising in Wales. 'Lewis', wrote Roger Eckersley, 'prefers Welsh music, however bad, to music speaking generally.'[173]

As well as heading the Music Department, Lewis also conducted the Welsh Symphony Orchestra which came into existence on 1 December 1935. On that day, Cardiff's nonet was expanded into an orchestra of twenty players; the development was warmly greeted, although Wales's musicians looked with envy at the 35-strong orchestras of the Midland, North and Scottish Regions. By the later months of 1936, the Welsh Symphony Orchestra was broadcasting for up to four hours a week. Many had assumed that when classical music became readily available, it would win universal popularity. 'What indeed will be left for the highbrow to boast of', the *Cambria Leader* had asked in 1926, 'when the labourer and his children will be as familiar with Beethoven as he?' That development did not come about. Cardiff broadcast a symphony concert at peak listening hours once a week, but the listeners to the performances were not numerous. Hopkin Morris, when touring Wales incognito in 1936, was told that there was no enthusiasm for the BBC's 'sympathy' concerts. In 1937, the Welsh Chamber Music Players were established and they offered performances of a form of music that was even less popular.[174]

The expansion of the BBC Welsh Chorus into a choir of thirty-two voices in 1935 was far more enthusiastically greeted, although BBC employees were distressed to find that what the listeners wanted was 'the same old things over and over again'.[175] In 1937, the Corporation divided its music-making activities into three categories: dance, entertainment and connoisseur. The definition of 'entertainment' had its limits: 'crooning' was greatly deprecated; dance music was broadcast frequently, but not as frequently as many listeners would have wished; jazz, but not experimental jazz, was provided, giving rise to hostile and overtly racist comments from Welsh organizations. Connoisseur music could be highly exotic, for as Scannell and Cardiff put it, the BBC provided presentation of 'all forms of music that had any appreciable audience – and of some that had none'. But whatever the criticism of the Corporation's musical output, the importance of the BBC as a provider of music was beyond doubt. By the late 1930s, well over half the revenue received by the Performing Rights Society came from broadcasting. Even in London, the BBC was easily the largest employer of musicians. In Wales it was virtually the only employer.[176]

Next in importance to music were talks. The BBC talk of the 1930s developed into a distinct art form, with drafting and redrafting of the script and elaborate rehearsals. The talk, stated Siepmann, was a double artifice, for what had begun as the natural statement of the speaker had to be made artifical before it became natural again. In organizational terms, talks included discussions, which were also scripted. One of the few surviving scripts of a discussion broadcast in the 1930s is the one prepared for 'college celebrities' at Aberystwyth in January 1937. The programme was *In Quad Tonight* and consisted of hearty banter by the rugger (*sic*) captain at the expense of the captains of other teams.[177] Features came under the same broad umbrella. In view of the dire problems facing Wales in the early years of the Corporation, it could be considered that the talk, the discussion and the feature offered admirable opportunities for airing current concerns and for making the population as a whole aware of the sufferings of the country's depressed communities. It was an opportunity that was not seized. Current issues are invariably controversial. Although the ban on controversy in broadcasting had been lifted in 1928, memories of the General Strike, fear of attacks by the right-wing press and Reith's increasingly establishmentarian attitudes caused the Corporation to interpret the lifting of the ban in a very faint-hearted way.

Fear of controversy was particularly prevalent at Head Office, where the activities of the radicals, Hilda Matheson and Charles Siepmann, caused grave concern. Nevertheless, the National Service did broadcast some programmes dealing with current social problems. In 1933, the reporter, S. P. B. Mais, gave detailed accounts of the conditions in the Rhondda and Bryn-mawr, and in 1934 the series *Time to Spare* considered the prospects of the unemployed. The comments of one contributor, John Evans, a native of the Rhondda resident in Birmingham, led to questions in the House of Commons and the summoning of Reith to Downing Street. Among the Regions, the North was the most enterprising, but in Wales, where most of the advocates of a separate Welsh region considered broadcasting to be a carrier of culture rather than a forum for debate, the issues of the day received scant attention.[178]

They were not entirely ignored, however. In 1934, six talks on the coal industry were broadcast; in accordance with BBC practice in the 1930s, the contributors were anonymous. They were described as the Coalowner, the Miner, the Economist and so on, but the *Daily Herald* discovered the identity of the Miner and was annoyed to find that he was not a member of the South Wales Miners' Federation. In 1935, the chairman of the Merthyr Tydfil Lodge of Unemployed Miners gave a graphic description of conditions in the town in a discussion with Professor Marquand. In 1936, an unscripted debate entitled *Conflict in the Coalfield* included the prominent Welsh Communist, Arthur Horner, at the very time when London was placing a ban on broadcasts by Communists. Such programmes attracted considerable attention in the press, which is indicative of the fact that they were very rare indeed.[179]

The Corporation preferred historical programmes. 'If a programme is to be done on Merthyr', noted a memorandum in 1933, 'it would be better to do it on old Merthyr, because a programme on present-day Merthyr would be difficult to do without referring to its poverty.' Even old Merthyr had its problems. In 1935, a Welsh-language feature programme was prepared on Dic Penderyn, the Merthyr man hanged for treason in 1831. In London, Dawnay noticed it in the list of proposed programmes sent to him by the regions. He demanded a translation and a rough English draft was sent to him. It contained a scene in which a Merthyr worker gave vent to a fine anti-capitalist rant. Dawnay demanded that it should be deleted, for the 'material strikes just that disruptive note that we should seek in our programmes to avoid'. That Cardiff was planning such a programme, he wrote, was proof of the need for London to receive full translations of the contents of all Welsh-language programmes well before it was proposed that they be broadcast. Rendall demurred. 'Latter-day history in South Wales is industrial history,' he informed Dawnay. It would be impossible to provide full translations, stated Appleton, 'for our Welsh staff is already seriously overworked'.[180] In 1935, Dawnay left the BBC to become commanding officer of the Irish Guards and the issue was not pursued.

Resistance to the portrayal of the history of the industrial areas was not unique to the BBC. In 1936, Cardiff proposed a series of three programmes based on Jack Jones's *Black Parade*, a novel which portrays nineteenth-century Merthyr as a somewhat bawdy and intemperate society. Merthyr organizations protested loudly, believing, as the mayor put it, 'that all the work that has been done to improve the image of the town will be wasted if the programmes are broadcast'. The BBC bowed to the pressure; it postponed the broadcasts and won a rebuke from the distinguished Anglo-Welsh writer, Gwyn Jones. 'Immature and ill-informed minds', he wrote, 'think *Black Parade* is an immoral book – and worse, the immorality is Welsh immorality. The BBC is naturally not guilty of this kind of stupidity. It is guilty of the greater stupidity of deferring to those who are.'[181]

There was a belief that pre-industrial Welsh history was a less dangerous subject. In 1934, Sutthery proposed a series of twenty-six programmes portraying the history of Wales 'as a kind of sound pageant'. At the time, W. J. Gruffydd, Iorwerth Peate and others were criticizing the BBC for presenting Welsh history in a ludicrous light, particularly in the notes in the *Radio Times* on the eisteddfod and the Gorsedd. Rendall abandoned the project because 'we want to get right away from Welsh history which has, I understand, provided more than one bone of contention in the past'.[182]

The archives contain many instances of scripts being sent back to their authors for redrafting. In 1937, for example, Caradoc Evans, the *bête noire* of Wales, was asked to recast entirely a talk he had prepared on the influence of Nonconformity on Welsh art. (Probably the least offensive sentence in the talk was: 'A Welsh choir's preliminary coughing is often the most musical part of the performance.')[183] They only contain one clear example of a talk that was banned altogether. In 1930, Appleton invited Saunders Lewis to explain Welsh Nationalism to the listeners of the Cardiff station. Lewis prepared a talk in which he argued that political nationalism was the only nationalism which had any substance; cultural nationalism divorced from any considerations of political power was 'merely glorified provincialism'. Appleton, after consultation with London, refused to broadcast the talk on the grounds that it was too controversial and because it was important not to inflame Welsh national sympathies. The talk was published as a pamphlet, the author stating that 'he fervently hopes that its publication . . . may have that effect'.[184]

With so many taboo subjects, the talks, discussions and features produced in Wales in the early and mid 1930s could be considered to be somewhat anodyne. Yet, the fact that talks were rarely controversial did not mean that they lacked interest. They were frequently highly polished literary pieces and in 1989 Gwyn Erfyl lamented that, by then, the unscripted chat had almost completely ousted the elegance of the more formal productions of an earlier age.[185] There was a widespread desire that at least some of the talks should have a more permanent form, a desire fulfilled by the launching of *The Listener* in 16 January 1929. *The Listener* published some of the talks produced in Wales. At the University Committee's meeting with the Corporation in October 1934, Emrys Evans suggested there should be a Welsh-language *Listener*. Appleton pursued the matter. He recognized that it would not pay its way, but he believed that the project would be feasible if a subsidy were forthcoming from a wealthy Welshman such as Lord Davies of Llandinam. Fearing the hostility of existing Welsh periodicals, Appleton abandoned the idea in 1935. Several volumes of BBC Welsh talks were published in the 1930s and the question of a Welsh-language *Listener* was revived in the 1950s.[186]

The chief reason for the Welsh Region's lack of involvement with current events was the peculiar position of news within the BBC, particularly in the regions. In the first months of the Corporation, an agreement with the press and the news agencies had allowed the BBC to broadcast its first news bulletin at 6.30 instead of 7.00 p.m., and the bulletins were permitted to include some eye-witness descriptions. Most of the contents of the bulletins remained the responsibility of the agencies, which until the early 1930s also edited the greater part of what was broadcast. In 1934, News and Topicality were separated from Talks and became the responsibility of John Coatman, previously a professor at the London School of Economics and later to be North regional director. He instituted independent BBC reporting, although news programmes remained very timid, much to the frustration of young reporters such as Richard Dimbleby.[187]

These arrangements only applied to London. Following the development of simultaneous broadcasting in the mid 1920s, Cardiff carried the London bulletins; in the early years, it also broadcast five minutes of south Wales news twice a night. The enlargement of the area centred upon Cardiff to include both sides of the Severn Estuary raised the question of the validity of regional news. Except perhaps in Scotland, Reith considered regional news to be no more than an amalgam of the happenings in the towns within the region. 'As it is not possible', he stated, 'to satisfy listeners in every particular town, it is therefore better to make no such attempt.' The station directors informed him that the discontinuance of local news would be unpopular. 'Such clamour', he declared, 'is unimportant. It is not our policy to submit to popular clamour, but rather to take up the standpoint which we ourselves felt to be in the interests of the general public.' By 1927, problems had already arisen in the area served by the Cardiff station, where Bristolians were complaining that the station's news, apart from the London bulletins, was of interest only to Cardiffians. 'News', stated Reith, 'should be a dignified announcement of the more important happenings in the world. This cannot be reconciled with the practice of disseminating details of petty local happenings ... A murder, as such, is not an item for dissemination, unless the victim was a person in whom public interest centred to a high degree.' 'What', asked Appleton, 'of the closure of a colliery ... a matter which was obviously not worthy of general broadcast but which could be of great local interest?'[188] He was given no direct reply, but indicative of the attitude of the BBC was the fact that when it began developing its news-gathering service in the early 1930s, it made no provision for regional centres to have their own correspondents. Furthermore, the Welsh appointments of 1935 and 1936 included no one with responsibility for news.

Compared with Scotland, the problem in Wales was particularly acute. Unlike Scotland, where the *Scotsman* newspaper had established a tradition of news-gathering on a national scale, the morning newspapers of Wales were regional south Wales publications; two of them – the *Cambria Leader* and the *South Wales Daily News* – became defunct in the late twenties, leaving the *Western Mail* as the only daily morning newspaper in Wales. The north was covered by the Welsh edition of the *Liverpool Daily Post*, and, in the inter-war years, by the Welsh edition of the *Manchester Guardian*. Other newspapers, the *News Chronicle* and the *Daily Herald* in particular, also had Welsh editions but the specific Welsh material they contained was very small.

In accordance with Reith's instructions, local news was discontinued in 1927 and was replaced by five minutes of local announcements. On 7 April 1929, however, Cardiff began a daily transmission of five minutes of West regional news at 10.15 p.m., and the bulletin was expanded to ten minutes in 1930. The content, which consisted largely of happenings in Bristol, Cardiff and Swansea, was supplied by Reuters via Hills' Press Agency and cost £6.15s. a week. As the *Manchester Guardian* published a Welsh edition, efforts were made to obtain from Manchester occasional items relating to north Wales but the matter was not vigorously pursued. The West Region's news bulletin came to an end in December 1932 and its place was taken by two five-minute programmes of Welsh and West of England announcements broadcast at 6.30 p.m., together with 'periodic reviews of events in the region'.[189]

Five-minute bulletins in English and Welsh were instituted on 1 January 1934. Broadcast at 10.30 p.m., they consisted of items telephoned from London together with material supplied by Hills'. The agency was paid £8.8s. a week for its services and Owen Parry thought that 'for an extra four guineas we could do it ourselves'. The Welsh bulletin was a translation of its English predecessor; no attempt was made to include news of specific interest to Welsh-speakers and the standard of the translation was, according to Alun Llywelyn-Williams, 'yn wallus ac yn ddi-raen'*.[190] As there did not

---

*'Incorrect and sloppy'.

seem to be enough news to fill five minutes a day, the service was curtailed in November 1936 to ten minutes twice a week. As will be seen, when the Welsh Region obtained its own wavelength in 1937, its news service attracted much criticism. Cardiff would have no staff exclusively concerned with the broadcast of news until the Second World War, and decades later its network of local reporters would continue to be woefully inadequate. Yet, although the broadcast news service in Wales was not placed on a satisfactory basis until the 1960s, it was the BBC which invented the concept of all-Wales news and thereby, perhaps, invented Wales.

Like news programmes, other forms of sound broadcasting – among them variety programmes and sports commentaries – did not become well established in Wales in the era of the shared transmitter, and consideration of them would therefore be better postponed. Other forms, particularly religious broadcasting, programmes for children and drama productions, had won recognition almost from the beginning and by the early 1930s they represented a substantial proportion of the output of the BBC's centres in Wales.

Many of the advocates of an improved broadcasting service in Wales considered that one of the chief functions of the new medium was to reflect and sustain the country's religious traditions, for, like Reith, they believed that the most important role of the wireless was to buttress public morality and uphold Christian beliefs. English-language religious services had been provided by Cardiff from the beginning, and 5SX transmitted a full service from St Mary's Church, Swansea, within a few months of the establishment of the station. St Mary's became a favoured source of Anglican services and was the second church in Britain to be permanently wired for broadcast services. (St Martin-in-the-Fields in London was the first.) As has been seen, the Swansea station was also responsible for the first full Welsh-language service to be broadcast – a service from Capel Gomer led by the Revd R. S. Rogers and transmitted on 22 February 1925.[191]

Appleton, who considered himself an authority on religious broadcasting, 'did not think highly of local resources' and was reported in 1928 to be 'glad to have S.B. preachers' from other regions.[192] He was, however, under strong pressure to broadcast religious services of local provenance, particularly those in Welsh. Edgar Jones believed that, as the BBC's Welsh adviser, his chief function was to ensure that the Corporation adequately reflected Welsh religious life. Apart from his work with schools, which proved to be temporary, his main task was to liaise with Welsh religious organizations, and the achievement which gave him greatest pride was his Welsh translation of *New Every Morning*, the service book of the BBC's morning religious services. The BBC's first permanent advisory body in Wales was the Religious Advisory Committee. Both Lloyd George and Reith travelled to Shrewsbury on 8 March 1932 to attend its inaugural meeting. Lloyd George was elected chairman and actively associated himself with the demand for the regular transmission of Welsh religious services. Broadcasts from chapels presented few difficulties, for there was a wide choice of Welsh Nonconformist services within easy reach of Cardiff and Swansea. Anglican services created additional costs for, as Appleton put it: 'In south Wales, the Church in Wales tends to conduct part of the service in English. We have therefore been forced to go to north Wales for our Welsh church services, which is very much more expensive than if they were near Cardiff or Swansea.' Roman Catholic services presented even greater difficulties; in November 1935, a service from Pantasaph Monastery was cancelled because the bishop of Menevia 'was not prepared to omit a prayer which was contrary to the religious policy of the Corporation'.[193]

It is ironic that the form of broadcast most urgently demanded – religious programmes in Welsh – was precisely the offering that was readily available in the country at large. Broadcast services in Welsh were needed, it was said, for the old and the sick, and these were among the main categories for whom, Margaret Mackenzie assumed, broadcasting in Welsh was specifically designed. The other major category was children, for in the 1930s, a high proportion of Welsh-speaking children were unable to follow programmes in English. In the early years, at both Cardiff and Swansea, the children's programmes had been highly successful. Aunts and Uncles were celebrities, and Aunt Lilian was distressed when she was deprived of her aunthood because she was 'intelligent, beautifully dressed [and] rather too hard and cynical for Children's Hour needs'. In 1928, Cardiff's children's programmes were considered less childish than those of many other stations.[194]

In 1929, however, the Control Board expressed its intention of ensuring there should be a 'BBC children's hour [which would be] the same all over the country, [for] except possibly for Scotland, there was not considered to be a true regional outlook'.[195] By the end of 1929, Swansea's *Children's Hour* had been curtailed to fifteen minutes a week, and in 1930 it ceased altogether. Cardiff was also under pressure to reduce its output, and in 1930 it was obliged to restrict production of children's plays following the departure of Arthur Blanche. Welsh-language provision increased in 1934 when Elwyn Evans succeeded Raymond Glendenning as Cardiff's *Children's Hour* organizer. Among the innovations were *Cwrs y Byd*, regular talks on world events given by Alun Oldfield-Davies, a

Cardiff schoolmaster. The demand for increased Welsh-language programming for children led to a call for more children's programmes from Wales in English. The output became somewhat more robust, with fewer of the contributions of the winsome uncles and aunts characteristic of the early years. In the mid 1930s, Cardiff won a wide reputation for its children's plays, particularly the serials written by J. D. Strange, whose death in 1937 was greatly mourned.[196]

The other provision for children was the schools service. By the autumn of 1935, 141 of the 2,000 schools of Wales were regularly listening to the programmes broadcast to Britain as a whole. The low figure is largely explained by the fact that most schools lacked receivers and by the reluctance of Wales's largest education authority – that of Glamorgan – to permit schools to tune in to the broadcasts. Glamorgan reversed its decision in 1934 but felt unable to contribute to the cost of equipping its schools with wireless sets. In that year, the Pembrokeshire and Caernarfonshire education authorities agreed to pay half the costs and in 1936 Meirionnydd paid the full cost of providing each of its schools with receivers, the first education authority in Britain to do so. Opinions of the value of schools broadcasts varied. A member of the Swansea Education Committee welcomed them warmly, for 'if broadcasts become part of the curriculum, we might not need to employ so many teachers'. A Monmouthshire councillor was less enthusiastic. 'In what way', he asked, 'would [wireless lessons] help the children of the working farmer make their way in the world?'[197]

Schools programmes specifically for Wales came to an end in the summer of 1929. They were revived following the establishment of the Welsh subcommittee of the Central Council of Schools Broadcasting in 1932. Chaired by W. J. Gruffydd, the subcommittee was retitled the Welsh Schools Committee in 1937. In order that the programmes should be audible in north Wales, they were also carried by the North regional transmitter, an arrangement which continued even after the opening of Penmon in 1937. Until the Bangor studio was opened, a number of the Welsh schools talks were broadcast from the North Region's studios, for it was easier for a speaker from Bangor to reach Manchester than Cardiff. Ambrose Bebb's volume, *Hil a Hwyl y Cestyll*, was an adaptation of a series of talks he had given from Manchester. Initially, the provision consisted of two weekly programmes in Welsh. In 1934, for example, Thomas Parry presented a series on localities and their historic and literary associations, and T. Rowland Hughes and R. J. Berry dealt with classic stories and Welsh adventurers. In the autumn of 1934, pupils at 55 of the schools of Wales – 33 in the north and 22 in the south – were regular listeners to the Welsh-language broadcasts, a figure which was to rise rapidly in subsequent years. The work was originally the responsibility of Owen Parry, but when he became director of programmes it was undertaken by D. W. Roberts who was also organizer of the Welsh Council for Group Listening. Some of the schools programmes were considered to be stodgy. As a result, there was an increasing tendency to present history, in particular, in dramatic form. Indeed, so prevalent did the historical playlet eventually become that there were complaints that 'everything was being turned into jam'.[198]

The Corporation's desire to concentrate production in London, evident in the matter of children's programmes, was even more evident in drama. Val Gielgud, who was responsible for the Corporation's drama output, wrote in 1929: 'We should aim at complete centralization of drama upon London when we go into Broadcasting House . . . There is no drama which the provinces can do which we cannot do better.' The regions were informed that they would only be allowed to produce dialect plays and adaptations of local novels, but the novels had first to be approved by London and the adaptation had to be carried out in London. Appleton protested, declaring that centralization would 'kill the BBC as a living organism'. He pointed to the number of drama societies in Wales and argued that the country had a wealth of theatrical talent, causing Gielgud to write: 'Radio drama from Cardiff is inconsiderable. This is certainly no sign of the creative intelligence of which Appleton makes so much.' He acknowledged, however, that he invariably left Welsh plays alone because 'I am naturally not particularly competent to deal with them'.[199] Indeed, Head Office's resistance to the expansion of Welsh-language broadcasting was in large part inspired by the fact that such broadcasts could not easily be made subject to their scrutiny and control.

Centralization was relaxed somewhat in 1931 when Cyril Wood, a lively impresario, became the drama producer for the West Region. He left for Bristol in 1934 when he was replaced at Cardiff by Dafydd Gruffydd who became *de facto* the drama producer for Wales. Between them, Wood and Gruffydd introduced the concept of radio drama to Cardiff, for the station's productions in the 1920s had, in the main, been stage performances only slightly modified for the new medium. In the mid 1930s, London again sought to restrict drama productions in the regions. As London had all the necessary resources, argued Gielgud, there was no point in seeking to duplicate them elsewhere. 'At Head Office, I have never been seriously hampered as far as drama is concerned by considerations of finance or staff or accommodation,' he wrote in 1936. 'Conditions in the regions are so astonishingly different.' Appleton again protested. 'No one as metropolitan-minded as [Gielgud]', he wrote, 'could handle purely regional material.' '[Gielgud]', noted Wood, 'has only visited the West once in five years . . . A classic example of centrally controlled territory is the area covered technically by the London region and yet quite unexploited.' A compromise was reached, allowing Cardiff to produce one play a fortnight, which effectively meant twelve Welsh plays and twelve English plays a year. Notable productions included Emlyn Williams's first radio play, *Full Moon*, and the early plays of John Gwilym Jones. In 1935, Cardiff produced *Is y Bannau*, the work of J. D. Jones and the first full-length Welsh play specifically written for radio. Musical dramatic broadcasts included Idwal Jones's *Yr Eosiaid*, the first broadcast Welsh musical, and *Twm Shon Catti*, the first broadcast Welsh pantomime.[200]

Undoubtedly the greatest contribution made to Welsh drama by the Corporation in the 1930s – and probably the most controversial decision made by Welsh broadcasters in that decade – was the result of a commission by Owen Parry. In 1936, he invited Saunders Lewis to write a play for performance on St David's Day 1937. The invitation came after Lewis had been involved in the burning of the Bombing School at Penyberth, an act which led – after a Caernarfon jury had failed to agree on a verdict – to his being sentenced at the Old Bailey to a year's imprisonment. Hopkin Morris gave Parry his full support, causing Lewis to write in 1957: 'A gaf i ddweud . . . fod dewrder ac antur a mawrfrydigrwydd . . . Rhys Hopkin Morris ar y pryd – canys yr oeddwn yn bur ysgymun gan y mwyafrif yng Nghymru – yn rhywbeth na allaf lai na synnu ato hyd yn oed heddiw'*.[201] Cardiff seems to have been deliberately ambiguous in informing London of its plan. Head Office was told that the Welsh Region's St David's Day programme would include a play about St Germanus of Auxerre. 'The script [Hopkin Morris] informed us', noted Tallents, Head Office's public relations director, '[is] wholly uncontentious, dealing only with the life of saints.' The implications of the situation only became apparent when the Cardiff executive officer asked his counterpart in London how a playwright who was in prison should be paid.[202]

Buchedd Garmon ('The Vita of St Germanus') is one of the finest verse plays in the Welsh language. Its most famous passage, with the metaphor of Wales as a vineyard, and with the appeal: 'Deuwch ataf i'r adwy /Sefwch gyda mi yn y bwlch /Fel y cedwir i'r oesoedd a

---

*'May I say . . . that the courage and enterprise and magnanimity . . . of Rhys Hopkin Morris at that time – for I was a pariah among the majority in Wales – is something that cannot but astonish me even today.'

ddel /Y glendid a fu'*,[203] has been interpreted as Saunders Lewis's justification for his action at Penyberth. It may also be his justification for his 'cantankerous' behaviour towards the BBC.

By July 1937, 58 per cent of the households of Wales were licensed to receive broadcasts. The nation had its own wavelength and a talented group of young and enthusiastic producers who were eager to prove their worth. They had twenty-eight months in which to do so. In the month in which the wavelength ceremony was held, Hitler made a lengthy speech in which he demanded *lebensraum* for the Germans, a link in the chain of events which would lead to the Second World War and to the cessation of regional broadcasting in Britain.

---

*'Come to me in the breach/Stand with me in the pass/So that the sanctity of the past/May be preserved for the generations to come.'

3

The Welsh Region, 1937–1945

I The consolidation of the region, 1937–1939

The twenty-eight months between the granting of the separate wavelength and the beginning of the Second World War were an exciting period in the history of broadcasting in Wales. They were the 'heroic years', and such was their promise that 'ni fu'r freuddwyd yn wag na'r delfryd yn ofer'*. The success of the new dispensation caused some surprise. 'The Welsh region', noted the journalist, J. C. Griffith-Jones, in December 1938, 'is slowly but surely establishing itself. Many thought it would break down after a year.'[1] Expectations were high. Describing the hopes that Radio Éireann was expected to fulfil, Maurice Gorham listed aspirations which were wholly relevant in the Welsh context. The service, he wrote, 'was expected not merely to reflect every aspect of national activity, but to create activities that did not yet exist. It was expected to revive the speaking of Irish; to foster a taste for classical music; to revive Irish traditional music; to keep people on the farms . . . to provide a living and a career for writers and musicians . . . to reunite the Irish people at home with those overseas; all this in addition to broadcasting's normal duty to inform, educate and entertain.'[2] On 6 January 1939, the Control Board decided that the *Radio Times* should list the regional service available in Wales under the heading 'Wales' rather than 'The Welsh Region' and that the Welsh regional director should be known as the Welsh director. Henceforth, the word region would be confined to those within England.[3] The decision represented an acknowledgement of the distinctiveness of the non-English parts of the United Kingdom, an acknowledgement which would be taken considerably further in the 1950s.

---

*'The dream was not an empty one, nor was the ideal in vain.'

By 1939 there were 405,945 licence-holders in Wales, representing 64 per cent of Welsh households. Some Welsh licence-holders, particularly in the north-east, were unable to receive the Welsh Service, while in parts of the south-east there was a determined rejection of it. Nevertheless, a substantial majority of the listeners of Wales habitually tuned in to the Welsh Service. As the National Service was considered highbrow, the Welsh Regional Service was, for most of them, their staple listening. Furthermore, that service had hundreds of thousands of listeners outside Wales, and not merely among Welsh emigrés. It could be clearly heard in south-western England, in much of the English Midlands and along the east coast of Ireland. Many of the appreciative letters came from English and Irish listeners, and when Cardiff announced in 1939 that it was going to launch a series for learners of Welsh, almost half the applications for pamphlets came from England. With its regular listeners as many perhaps as two million, the Welsh Regional Service, in the late 1930s, had a larger regular following than had Radio Four throughout the United Kingdom in the 1990s.

The press provides ample proof of the service's mass audience. Leading London newspapers such as the *Observer* and the *Sunday Times* frequently commented upon its programmes. English newspapers with Welsh editions relied heavily on broadcasting to fill their Welsh columns, and the results of broadcast quizzes between Welsh villages were often published in the *News Chronicle*'s Stop Press. The most authoritative discussions of the Welsh Service appeared in the *Liverpool Daily Post*, the work of the veteran Welsh newspaperman E. Morgan Humphreys. In Wales itself, the *Western Mail* was consistently sympathetic to the cause of broadcasting, a fact noted by Reith when commenting upon the presence of Sir Robert Webber, the paper's main proprietor, at the wavelength ceremony in 1937.[4] A debate on housing, in which Councillor Ashton of Wrexham participated, was published almost verbatim in the *Wrexham Leader*; BBC seminars on music and writing for broadcasting were reported in great detail and pamphlets for schools courses were fully commented upon. The Welsh-language press printed the content of entire series; Moses Gruffydd's advice to farmers was widely published *in toto*, as were the sermons of the more popular of the broadcast preachers.

Nest Jenkins, the Welsh publicity officer, delighted in such attention and dreamt up further publicity stunts. In 1937, tourists were offered a reward if they recognized Sam Jones on the promenade at Colwyn Bay – almost as if he were a character in *Brighton Rock*.[5] Welsh broadcasters, however, were concerned at the paucity of considered criticism of their programmes, particularly those in Welsh. A prize of twelve guineas was offered at the National Eisteddfod of 1938 for an informed and detailed discussion of the Corporation's Welsh-language output, but there were no competitors. Hopkin Morris persuaded the educationalist, Dr Gwenan Jones, to write a column in the journal, *Yr Efrydydd*; her articles and those of others, published in the journal, are the first thoughtful comments on Welsh-language programmes.

Apart from press comment, listeners' letters were virtually the only form of reaction available to the BBC. In the mid and late 1930s, Cardiff received several hundred letters a week. Yet, as Nest Jenkins told Stephen Tallents, the Corporation's director of information and publications, those who write letters 'are people of a rather unusual mentality'.[6] Nest Jenkins spent much of her time making her own surveys, and in 1937 she accompanied Hopkin Morris on a visit to Caernarfonshire and Denbighshire when they knocked on the doors of houses bearing aerials.[7] Hopkin Morris saw his directorship largely in terms of public relations. He never broadcast. Instead, he gave innumerable after-dinner speeches and addressed school prize-givings in all parts of Wales. Information on the nature of the audience became more plentiful from 1936 onwards, following the establishment of the BBC's Listener Research Department. Its head, Robert Silvey, began establishing listening panels, on which he acknowledged that the 'Celtic fringe' was markedly under-represented. Nevertheless, he rapidly came to the conclusion that, in terms of taste, there was little regional diversity in Britain apart from the fact that the Welsh and the Scots were more partial to 'vocal recitals' than were the English.[8] The BBC felt the need for more detailed reports on specific areas and in 1938 Jack Jones, the Anglo-Welsh novelist, was given £100 to prepare a report on the social influence of broadcasting in the south Wales coalfield. 'I went into the unemployed clubs', he reported, 'and tried to gather together evidence of the social effects of the coming of broadcasting. They thought I was trying to pull their legs . . . "The thing", as they called it, did no harm . . . People had allowed its going-over voices to drop things into their ears but not into their hearts or minds.'[9]

When the arrangements for the separate wavelength were imminent, there was much exchange of memoranda in London concerning the number of hours Wales should broadcast and the programme allowance it should be granted. In April 1937, the joint transmitter broadcast a total of twenty-four hours' regional material a week, nine of which were West of England productions and fifteen those of Wales – seven hours in Welsh and eight in English. The joint programme allowance was £710 a week, of which Wales received £415 and the West of England £295. Hopkin Morris stated that, when

Wales had its own wavelength, the Region would initially broadcast twenty-two hours a week, a figure which would in due course be increased; he therefore asked for an appropriate increase in programme allowance.[10] Head Office officials were in no mood to accede to his request, fearing a reaction from the other regional directors, particularly the director of the heavily populated North of England Region. Indeed, the regional directors as a group were in a rebellious mood in 1937, attacking London for querying the detailed costing of individual programmes and for insisting that only Head Office could grant leave to regional employees; they were particularly incensed by a ruling that a regional director could not issue a testimonial to one of his staff unless it had been previously checked in London.[11] Part of the rebelliousness was caused by the fact that licence money was being diverted to the television service which had begun on 2 November 1936 and which was only available to a tiny number of London viewers.

Wales's allowance, it was ruled, had to be lower than those of more populous regions. 'If [Hopkin Morris] is proposing to do as many hours as he suggests', wrote Roger Eckersley, the director of regional relations, to Graves, the controller (programmes), on 8 June 1937, 'the actual amount to be spent on individual programmes will be low compared with the other regions . . . [but], because of the political situation, are you prepared to let him try out his twenty-two hours and judge by the results?' Graves answered on 15 June, insisting that twenty-two hours should be the absolute maximum. 'I do feel strongly', he wrote, 'that to exceed what any other region is doing is a wrong policy because one cannot on a limited allowance go for quantity except at the expense of quality.' A weekly allowance of £450 was granted. Cardiff was asking for £550, partly to pay for the increased hours and partly because the new underground Post Office cables, when used for outside broadcasts, involved the expensive deployment of a larger number of repeaters. Without expenditure on repeaters, outside broadcasts would be impossible west of Swansea. 'If we avoid places that are expensive', Cardiff informed Head Office, 'this will create such an outcry that it will become a political matter.'[12]

Head Office refused to yield and Wales sought to produce as many hours as possible on inadequate resources. By September 1937, when Wales was transmitting eighteen hours a week of its own programmes, outside broadcasting had ceased because money to run the van was not available. Yet Hopkin Morris continued to urge his staff to produce more hours, particularly during the winter months. In October 1937, when output was twenty-two hours a week, he was proudly announcing that 'Wales was broadcasting for longer hours than any other region'.[13] London was perturbed. 'I am watching the Welsh situation,' wrote Roger Eckersley in March 1938. Hopkin Morris was prevailed upon to reduce Wales's output during the summer months; by June 1938, the weekly hours had contracted to sixteen, causing complaints that the output was hardly greater than it had been before the coming of the separate transmitter. The hours rose to twenty-seven in December 1938 when Head Office firmly told Hopkin Morris to cut back. He was also faced by resistance from his own staff. 'The quality of our programmes', wrote T. Rowland Hughes in March 1938, 'suffers from our insistence upon a high quota of hours each week. For me to do a feature programme nearly every week is too much. I suggest that Wales would be better served by us if we followed Bristol's example of limiting our output so as to concentrate on bigger and better programmes.'[14]

A further constraint upon Cardiff's ability to increase its production was the lack of studio accommodation. There had been plans in the early 1930s to build a broadcasting centre in Wood Street near Cardiff's General Station, but these were abandoned because the centralization policy assumed that regional productions would be curtailed. In the late 1930s, there were discussions with the Bute estate concerning the lease of a site near the New Theatre where it was proposed to build a Broadcasting House large enough to include television studios. Nothing came of the discussions and Cardiff had to be content with its premises in Park Place. In addition, extensive use was made of Tabernacl, the Welsh Baptist chapel in The Hayes, the setting for many of the BBC's concerts.[15]

Accommodation problems were to some extent relieved by the opening on 1 October 1937 of a new broadcasting centre at Swansea. Swansea's old premises, condemned by Siepmann as 'appalling', were replaced by what the *South Wales Evening Post* proudly described as 'the best studios in Europe outside London'. They were located in the former headquarters of the Swansea Board of Guardians in Alexandra Road, a building leased to the BBC by the County Borough at the very low rent of £425 a year. Converted at a cost of £20,000, the building was furnished with Bryn-mawr furniture; among its resources were a studio capable of holding fifty people and equipped with two ribbon microphones – 'the last word in modernity' – and a drama studio 'in which one notices the unusual effect of being able to "feel" silence'. Following the acquisition of the new Swansea centre, Tom Pickering suggested that it should contribute six of the proposed twenty-two weekly hours. In November 1937, when Pickering was being assisted at Swansea by Geraint Dyfnallt Owen and Wynford Vaughan-Thomas, Alexandra Road was responsible for fifty-one broadcasts, compared with twenty in November 1936. Swansea's sub-region included the Aberystwyth studio; it was only suitable for talks and provided about five items a month. Typical of the concerns of the BBC in the late 1930s were the efforts to ensure that the Aberystwyth studio should be large enough to house a string quartet, efforts which did not come to fruition.[16]

Bangor, with its greater resources, was responsible for somewhat more than the six weekly hours produced by Swansea. Hopkin Morris believed that Sam Jones, the true originator of Welsh-language broadcasting, had been exiled to Bangor in 1935 by a Corporation oblivious of his talents. Jones shared that view. When congratulated on the good fortune of living on the banks of the Menai Straits, he is alleged to have retorted: 'I hate the bloody ditch.' He was transferred to Cardiff as chief producer in 1937 but the experiment was not a success. He returned to Bangor in 1938 where he was assisted by Elwyn Evans and Nan Davies, the Welsh Region's first woman producer. He became reconciled to, indeed enamoured of, his role in Bangor and continued as the north Wales representative until his retirement in 1963. Bangor, eight hours by train from Cardiff, felt itself to be a world apart. Its attitude to Cardiff was not unlike that of Cardiff to London. Asked by Hopkin Morris in 1938 to provide a more lively monthly report, Sam Jones retorted with a Hiawathan ode:

> Then said they to Hopkin Morris
> He the Great Chief of the Region
> He the deputy of the DG
> He the big noise down in Cardiff,
> Cardiff of the many studios
> Cardiff of the numerous workers;
> Say we thus in accents tender
> Accents sweet and accents clear,
> Say we from the Bangor station
> Bangor of the many mountains
> Bangor of the puny studios
> Bangor of the brains and talents,
> That the meeting be more joyous
> That the time may pass more quickly
> And the Board be more contented.[17]

Jones had little interest in producing programmes for network broadcasting, for he deplored the assumption '[fod rhaglenni i'r rhwydwaith] yn haeddu mwy o kudos na chyfathrebu'n effeithiol

106

â'n pobl ein hunain'*.[18] This view was not shared by all the BBC's employees in Wales. Watkin Jones, the chief talks producer, lamented the paucity of productions from Wales broadcast to other parts of the United Kingdom. 'Are we', he asked in November 1937, 'to regard our special demands in Wales . . . as so absorbing as to make it impossible for us to [make programmes] which would be available for inclusion in the general planning of all regions in conjunction with London?' Up to half the region's productions were immediately ruled out because they were in Welsh, but those in English were hardly more successful in securing network transmission. In November 1938, the London Regional Service broadcast 5 hours 40 minutes of music from Wales but no speech programmes at all. Other regions were less concerned to cater specifically for their own listeners. This was particularly the case in the Midland Region where producers concentrated their efforts on programmes suitable for the network. In November 1938, the London Regional Service broadcast twenty-two hours of Midland productions including twelve hours of speech programmes.[19]

The twenty-seven hours a week produced in December 1938 represented Wales's maximum weekly production in the late 1930s. Thus, separate wavelength or no separate wavelength, London continued to dominate the schedule. From the national transmitter at Droitwich, the Welsh received ninety-five hours of programmes a week, almost all of which were London productions. In November 1938, the Welsh Regional Service was on the air for a total of ninety-four hours a week, of which 60 per cent came from London, 30 per cent from Wales and 10 per cent from other parts of the United Kingdom.

When welcoming the appointment of Hopkin Morris in 1936, several newspapers warned that the monoglot English-speaking inhabitants of Wales would react angrily if they came to perceive that Welsh-speakers were excessively favoured. Such angry reaction was rare in the late 1930s, partly perhaps because the linguistic allocation was perceived to be fair, but mainly, it would seem, because most of those who did not want Welsh could easily receive other services. In parts of south-east Wales, there was an assumption that the service provided by the Wales wavelength was the all-Welsh-language service first mooted in 1927. Nest Jenkins, when seeking in 1937 to arouse local interest in an English-language programme on Cefn Mabli, the mansion in the lower Rhymni Valley, was told: 'Nobody will ever think of looking under the Welsh

---

*'That programmes for the network deserve more kudos than effective communication with our own people.'

Region in the *Radio Times* because there is nothing on Welsh Regional for people who do not understand Welsh.' That belief, she discovered, was particularly prevalent among the professional classes. 'This naïve ignorance of what we are doing', she wrote, 'seems almost incredible.'[20]

Maintaining a balance between the two languages was perhaps the most exacting of the tasks of the programme director. When the separate wavelength was granted, the post was held by Owen Parry, a native of Bethel in Caernarfonshire, who, as has been seen, was temporarily appointed to it following the abrupt departure of Hughes Jones in February 1936. Initially he won warm praise. 'Mr Owen Parry so far has done extremely well,' it was noted in April 1936.[21] He was not, however, confirmed in the post, and in April 1938 he ceased to be an employee of the Corporation. He was replaced on 19 April 1938 by John Tudor Jones (John Eilian), a Welsh-speaking Tory of a type that only Anglesey seems to produce. Tudor Jones had been editor of the weekly, *Y Cymro*, and had founded the lively monthly, *Y Ford Gron*. He also had considerable experience of colonial journalism, having edited the *Mesopotamian Times* at Basra and the *Ceylon Times* and the magazine of the Tea-planters' Rifle Club at Colombo. He came to Cardiff full of vigorous ideas. 'At the Welsh BBC', noted the *Daily Herald*, 'brightness started when Tudor Jones settled down as programme director.'[22]

Among his innovations was the establishment of a Welsh Programme Board, the minutes of which provide a valuable insight into the activities of the BBC in Wales in the late 1930s. They portray Welsh-speakers in regular session discussing in English the provision of programmes in Welsh. In the 1930s, and for decades to come, Welsh-speaking members of the middle class rarely used the language amongst themselves, a point seized upon in a jocular article in the BBC's house journal *Ariel* in 1937. 'At Broadcasting House, Cardiff,' noted the article, 'they can all talk [Welsh] at will, but [they] don't do it more often than they can help.' Hopkin Morris, who had a prodigious knowledge of biblical Welsh, rarely conversed in the language; his colleague, Elwyn Evans, never had a conversation with him in Welsh. Unlike their counterparts in Bangor, and to a lesser extent in Swansea, Cardiff producers of Welsh-language programmes felt that they were providing a service for people who lived somewhere else. There was some tendency to view those people as folksy peasants, an attitude which annoyed Saunders Lewis. Welsh, he argued, was one of the major literary languages of Europe and he demanded literary programmes in Welsh which surveyed the entire European literary scene.[23]

It is doubtful whether most of the Welsh staff originally appointed at Cardiff had the capacity to fulfil his demand for, as Thomas Parry pointed out, none of those who joined the staff between 1933 and 1935 had a formal qualification in the language. Matters improved in the late 1930s with the appointment of Alun Llywelyn-Williams and Geraint Dyfnallt Owen, both of whom had first-class honours in Welsh. As has been seen, Llywelyn-Williams was appalled by the standard of broadcast Welsh in Cardiff's news bulletins. He was concerned to ensure a degree of uniformity when broadcasting in Welsh, for the frequent sloppiness of announcers and their lack of agreed Welsh technical terms contrasted painfully with the polished dignity of English announcing. He began a campaign which eventually attracted the attention of Head Office. 'Is there anything we can do', wrote Nicolls in November 1938, 'about standardizing spoken Welsh in the way we have been attempting to do with English?'[24]

Llywelyn-Williams's desire to create a national form of broadcast Welsh, over and above all dialects, was one aspect of the national aspirations of those serving the BBC in Wales in the late 1930s. They were particularly anxious that the Corporation should be the patron of a Welsh national school of music. In 1938, Idris Lewis convened a conference to which forty Welsh composers were invited; he urged them to protest to London that the Welsh orchestra was too small to fulfil its national task. Emphasis was placed on linking north and south, with general knowledge quizzes between southern colliers and northern quarrymen, and debates between young farmers in Caernarfonshire and Cardiganshire. In 1938, the BBC announced the establishment of two annual national lectures, one in English and the other in Welsh, to be given in the first instance by Thomas Jones and W. J. Gruffydd.[25] The war led to the suspension of the lectures, but Welsh and English national lectures on alternate years were introduced in 1951.

While the Welsh broadcasting staff sought to present themselves as innovative, they, like the staff of the Corporation as a whole, fought shy of controversy. In 1937, a feature programme on the 1880s tithe riots in Denbighshire was cancelled, for in that year tithes were a contentious issue in East Anglia. In 1938, the opening of the Ebbw Vale steel works was given very little attention, as it was an occasion that had 'political overtones'. In 1939, an invitation to broadcast part of the South Wales Miners' Federation's May Day pageant was turned down because of its possible political implications. International affairs, which loomed so large in the late 1930s, were only cursorily dealt with by the BBC, a marked contrast with American radio with its wide coverage of Europe's deepening crisis. In 1937, Vansittart, the permanent under-secretary at the Foreign Office, urged Reith to 'lay off Nazism and Fascism for a year or two'. He complied. 'Coatman', he wrote in his diary on 13 July 1937, 'is riding for a fall', because the North of England regional director had broadcast a virulent attack on the German government. Welsh-language programmes were not subject to the same scrutiny. The Spanish Civil War, dealt with by the BBC centrally by giving the rebels three times as much attention as the legitimate government, offered an opportunity. In 1937, John Williams Hughes, an ambulance driver with the Republican forces, broadcast nightly in Welsh from a cellar in Madrid on the Republic's international wavelength. 'They are uncensored', noted the *Daily Herald*, 'for there is no one there who understands them.' The BBC in Wales transmitted some of his highly partisan accounts – the first example (and there would be many more) of the BBC's remarkable ability to find Welsh-speakers in the most unusual places.[26]

The archives contain a detailed analysis of Wales's output in the first six months of 1939. The total amounted to 536 hours, representing almost three hours a day. Music accounted for 208 hours (1 hour 8 minutes a day) and announcing accounted for a further twenty-one hours (seven minutes a day). Of the remaining 307 hours, the percentage in each category was as follows: talks, 29; children's programmes, 23; religion, 15; features and short stories, 10; schools, 7; variety, 6; drama, 5; outside broadcasts, 5. Music programmes contained some element of speech, most of which was in English; of the 307 hours devoted to other forms of programme, 52.6 per cent was in Welsh and 47.4 per cent in English. The two languages were used to broadly the same extent in children's programmes, features and drama; the use of Welsh far exceeded that of English in talks, religion and schools programmes, while the use of English far exceeded that of Welsh in variety and outside broadcasts.[27]

Musical programmes, constituting 39 per cent of the productions of the Welsh Region, were not as dominant as they had been in earlier years. The emphasis varied with the seasons; music could constitute half the output in the summer and less than a third in the winter. Performances by the BBC Welsh Orchestra provided a major part of the region's musical offerings, but other orchestras, in particular the Swansea Festival Orchestra and the Gwynedd Orchestra, were also given considerable airtime. Male voice choirs enjoyed great popularity; the favourite was that of Dowlais, which Idris Lewis considered to be the best in Wales. In 1939, a performance of the Cherubini Mass by the choir of Tabernacl Chapel, Morriston, won wide praise, and particular attention was drawn to the fact that 'most of those who took part were tin-workers'. The music department was particularly proud of its work with children. With the encouragement of the BBC, the schools of Wales were beginning to provide tuition in instrumental music; in parts of the coalfield progress was remarkable, with the Blaenclydach Juvenile String Orchestra winning acclaim as 'probably the best of its kind in Great Britain'.[28]

Talks accounted for over a third of Wales's non-musical output in Welsh and almost a quarter of that in English. There were no specific times for talks. They were fitted into the schedule in what can appear to be a haphazard way, for the notion of tight scheduling, with each programme beginning at its advertised time, and with no gaps between items, was not adopted with any vigour until the war. The *Nine O'Clock News*, launched as the *Third News* on 4 October 1937, rapidly became the fixed point of the evening schedule, but the Welsh-language news – broadcast on four evenings a week and included in the category 'Talks' – had no fixed timing. In the first week of October 1937, for example, it was transmitted at 9.30 on Tuesday, 8.45 on Wednesday, 7.30 on Thursday and 7.05 on Saturday. Despite deficiencies in both language and content, the Welsh news had a wide following, for there was a hunger among Welsh-speakers to hear their language on the air. Nest Jenkins noted that in south Cardiganshire the news was listened to by a family clan of sixteen members who came together as often as possible for that specific purpose.[29]

Commissioned talks by individuals tended to be didactic. Bangor, the source of many of the talks in Welsh, relied heavily on Bangor academics such as Ifor Williams and R. T. Jenkins, while the English-language talks produced at Cardiff drew on the skills of Cardiff academics, especially Gwyn Jones and Brinley Thomas. English talks – indeed, English programmes in general – presented something of a problem. A talk in Welsh, whatever its subject, was indisputably Welsh and therefore suitable for transmission on the Welsh wavelength. Roger Eckersley's dictum that the regions should only produce what London could not supply was not as rigidly enforced in the late 1930s as it had been earlier in the decade. Nevertheless, Head Office continued to expect a broad compliance with the rule that London dealt with the universal and the general, and the regions dealt with the local and the particular. Thus, to justify its transmission on the Welsh wavelength, an English talk was expected to have some Welsh dimension. The Welsh language could deal with the universal; the English language could not, a matter of concern to Watkin Jones, who complained in 1937 that he found it difficult on occasion to give an English talk 'a definite regional character'.[30]

Although there was a bias in favour of talks by well-known public figures, academics in particular, it was less marked in Wales than elsewhere. 'We succeed better than any other region', wrote Watkin Jones in 1937, 'in drawing on a greater variety of talkers, and those for the greater part are "ordinary" listeners.' What Watkin Jones did feel that Wales lacked was 'the type of speaker who does much to pull up the average standard of Talks in other regions. I refer to the effortless, mature, well-informed "essayist" who is often heard on the London programmes.'[31]

The script of a talk had to be sent in well beforehand. It was rigorously checked for its content, its grammar and its felicities of style. The correction of Iorwerth Peate's Welsh by a Corporation underling led to a major confrontation, and a similar confrontation would probably have occurred had Kate Roberts been aware that BBC employees were critical of the standard of her Welsh.[32] Two copies were made of the final script and every page of both was ceremoniously stamped. One copy was read by the speaker, and the announcer used the other to check that the speaker was adhering to the agreed text. If the speaker strayed from it, the announcer had the authority to halt the broadcast, although there seems to be no well-authenticated case of such a halting in the history of the BBC in Wales in the 1930s. The length of a talk could create problems. In March 1939, Clough Williams-Ellis was invited to speak for thirty minutes on *Amenity maketh Man*. His talk was faded out at the stipulated time but he insisted on addressing the studio staff for a further hour. When the broadcast was over, the announcer handed over the fee. In the regions, a fifteen-minute talk earned two to three guineas.[33] (Fees were at least 50 per cent higher in London.) The average male manual wage in 1938 was £3.11s. a week. In any consideration of the lifestyle of Welsh academics, and others, in the 1930s, the BBC's guineas should be borne in mind.

Discussions and interviews were somewhat less rigorously controlled. Nevertheless, what the BBC described as an unscripted discussion or interview was generally a programme in which the contributors were reading a script prepared by the producer, which was agreed to represent a fair distillation of lengthy preliminary conversations. As Alun Llywelyn-Williams discovered, many hours could be uselessly expended if the contributor turned out to be illiterate.[34] The dialogue of such programmes could be arch and winsome, and the patent artificiality of many so-called unscripted discussions led the radio critic of *Yr Efrydydd* to complain that the pretence that the discussions were spontaneous was very foolish. The improvements in recording techniques did, however, permit the Corporation's producers to be somewhat less intrusive. A programme which eavesdropped on the deliberations of the book selection committee of the Tredegar Miners' Library seems to have been genuinely unscripted, as were the *Cross Section* programmes, a series designed for listening groups which sought to broadcast the unvarnished opinions of members of the working class.[35]

Outside broadcasts, although listed as a separate category, were closely associated with talks. They offered a greater degree of genuine spontaneity, especially when they were undertaken by Wynford Vaughan-Thomas who became outside broadcasts assistant on 9 October 1936. 'The outside broadcast', he wrote in 1938, 'is not arranged and stage-managed. [The listener] feels he is being given life itself.' 'Welsh commentators', argued Vaughan-Thomas, 'should use more feeling and more vivid phrasing than English ones. After all, there is no need to worry about "good form" in Wales.' He was eager to put his ideas into practice. On Friday 13 May 1938, he stood under a ladder and asked passers-by for their views on superstitions, thus causing a near riot in Swansea. Earlier in the year, he had accosted shoppers in the New Year sales, a form of broadcasting which had not been attempted outside the United States. Vaughan-Thomas, Cardiff reported proudly, had been conducting street interviews long before London did them on *In Town Tonight*. Outside broadcasters, however, did not always get the material for which they hoped. One attempt in the Rhondda in May 1939 to broadcast miners singing hymns as they finished their shift brought the curt reaction: 'No damn fear'.[36]

While Vaughan-Thomas's outside broadcasts were not 'arranged and stage-managed', outside broadcasts could impose arrangement and stage-management upon occasions which had previously been fairly chaotic. Following the acquisition of its own wavelength, the BBC in Wales felt free to give extensive coverage to the National Eisteddfod; broadcast coverage of the festival rose from five hours in 1937 to eight in 1939. The Corporation sought to insist that the Eisteddfod adhered to its timetable, in order that the highlights should be broadcast during the time the BBC had allocated to them. 'The traditional character of the Eisteddfod,' wrote the *Western Mail*, 'its spontaneity and its elasticity, are being disturbed by BBC interference . . . The chairing was rushed in order to fit in with broadcasting and adjudicators are being obliged to foretell the length of their adjudications.' 'Choirs', wrote the *News Chronicle*, 'so used to eisteddfod unpunctuality were shocked.' Broadcasting the eisteddfod was changing the eisteddfod. The eisteddfod authorities were especially incensed when 'an engineer rushed to the platform and stopped an oratorio because he was not ready'. Financial considerations also soured relations between the Corporation and the eisteddfod. In 1938, the BBC paid £160 to cover the festival and broadcast a total of seven hours of its activities; as the cost of staging the eisteddfod was £14,000, its officials were loud in their condemnation of the Corporation's parsimony.[37]

Similar issues arose with the broadcasting of sporting occasions. In the 1930s, the BBC did not recognize sport as a separate category, and broadcasts dealing with it are listed variously under talks, outside broadcasts, features and children's programmes. As with the eisteddfod, broadcasting tended to impose greater punctuality and formality. Leading sports clubs were suspicious of the Corporation. The Swansea Rugby Club attributed its financial problems to the fact that the BBC was reporting its matches, and in 1934 the Welsh Rugby Union considered banning all broadcasts.[38] The Corporation was as reluctant to pay for giving sound coverage to sporting events as it was to reimburse the eisteddfod. Unlike television coverage, when the event itself is brought before the viewer, sound coverage depends largely on the skill of the commentator; to demand payment under such conditions, it was argued, is hardly different from insisting that newspapermen should pay for the right to compile their reports.

Despite the difficulties, there was growing coverage of sport, although it was slight compared with the provision of the television age. Boxing commentaries were especially popular; the Farr–Louis fight of August 1937, broadcast at 3 a.m., attracted a vast audience at the Cambrian Colliery Institute at Clydach Vale. While at Cardiff, Settle mastered the art of commentating upon a wide variety of sports. After he left, the region tended to rely on outside contributors, but Ernest Jenkins won renown as the man who muttered 'Square One' or 'Square Five' to enable listeners to know in what part of the field the action was taking place. Wales, in 1938, was the first region to offer coverage of a darts match but, despite much pleading, Hopkin Morris refused to allow any mention of greyhound racing.[39] Sports commentaries were almost always in English, although the *mabolgampau* of Urdd Gobaith Cymru were described in Welsh. Gwent ap Glasnant, the Cardiff forward, urged the BBC in 1936 to broadcast eyewitness accounts of major rugby matches in Welsh, but the suggestion was not seriously taken up for decades, largely because, as such accounts would have to be live, a Welsh commentary would have to displace an English one. Anticipating the broadcasting of matches, Eic Davies and others set about providing a full range of terms for a number of sports, rugby and cricket in particular, and they did so with such verve that many of their terms have a vividness lacking in the English originals.[40]

In the regions, all the producers, apart from those specifically concerned with music, were presumed to be capable of producing any kind of programme, a marked contrast with the highly specialized staff in London. The talks and outside broadcast producers were also involved with features, children's programmes and drama. At their best, the feature programmes were 'the great glory' of the pre-war BBC. This was particularly the case in Wales, where features, in the late 1930s, were the particular responsibility of T. Rowland Hughes. Considering that he was already a sick man, his industry was astonishing. Between December 1936 and December 1938, he produced ninety-four feature programmes, averaging over an hour each. (He also won the Chair at the National Eisteddfodau of 1937 and 1940.) Some of them were widely acclaimed. His St David's Day programme of 1938 was described by Joyce Grenfell in the *Observer* as 'one of the most important features heard for a very long time', and months later the *Observer* was still referring to Hughes's 'lovely parable in verse'.[41]

Hughes's parable was broadcast on the network service. That was unusual, for the vast majority of the features produced in Wales were exclusively for home consumption. Among them was a warmly praised series, *In Lonely Places*, in which R. M. Lockley discussed his life on Skokholm Island, and a Ffair Rhos shepherd, in careful, almost biblical, English, described his experiences. In features, even more than in talks, the BBC in Wales was anxious to draw upon the talents of all classes. Reviewing the broadcasts of 1937, Nest Jenkins wrote, 'a large number of speakers who have appeared before the microphone during the year have been peasant people'. This was particularly true of the series *Ein Pentref Ni* ('Our Village'), programmes scripted and presented (with some degree of producer prompting, no doubt) by local communities, a series warmly commended by Frederick Ogilvie.[42]

The great radio crazes of the late 1930s were the Spelling Bees and the General Knowledge Bees, notions borrowed from America; there was much satisfaction in Wales when a participant from Newport won full marks in a Spelling Bee in 1938. Sam Jones was urged to produce a Welsh-language Spelling Bee, but he rejected the idea on the grounds that a phonetic language offered few lexicographic delights. Instead, he designed a Bee based on *cynghanedd*, the intricate system of sound chiming characteristic of Welsh strict-metre poetry. The first was broadcast in April 1938 with R. J. Rowlands ('Meuryn') as adjudicator and Thomas Parry as compère. The *News Chronicle* commented: 'It made English Spelling Bees sound like very tame affairs.' A further example of the grafting of traditional Welsh culture upon broadcasting was the radio eisteddfod held in December 1938, a broadcast which proved to be an important precedent, for it was cited in 1940 when the holding of a conventional National Eisteddfod was deemed to be impractical.[43]

Taken together, talks, features and outside broadcasts accounted in the first six months of 1939 for 44 per cent of Wales's non-musical output. Broadcasts for children – *Children's Hour* and schools programmes – accounted for a further 30 per cent. *Children's Hour*, a somewhat anarchic but greatly appreciated feature of early broad-casting, was a much more formal affair by the late 1930s. In terms of audience reaction, it was by far the most important part of Wales's output; well over half the letters received at Cardiff were written by *Children's Hour* listeners. Wales's share of the programme was formal-ized in 1937. London provided three-quarters of the programme on Monday, Wednesday and Friday and the entire programme on Saturday; Wales's own output amounted to 2.75 hours a week, of which 1.5 hours were in Welsh. Wales's English-language *Children's Hour* programmes, particularly the plays, attracted an audience well beyond the country's borders. Their success depended heavily upon the skills of Lyn Joshua, the son of the revivalist Seth Joshua. The child actors had to live within commuting distance of Cardiff, a restriction which created particular problems where Welsh-language productions were concerned. It was claimed that virtually all the Welsh-speaking teenagers of the Rhondda had appeared on *Children's Hour*, causing northern newspapers such as *Y Cloriannydd* to attack the 'monopoly of the "shonis"'.[44] The criticism led to the production of some children's programmes at Bangor and at Swansea. Thus, the versions of the Welsh language spoken in the north-west and the south-west were broadcast, along with that of the south-east; those of the north-east and of mid Wales were rarely granted air time.

Schools broadcasts increased rapidly in popularity in the post-separate-wavelength era. In 1936, there were 120 primary schools officially equipped with wireless sets; the figure increased to 700 by 1939 and in many of the schools not officially supplied teachers brought their own sets. Trinity College, Carmarthen, was the first college in the United Kingdom to have a lecture room equipped to train teachers in the use of radio lessons. The appeal of schools programmes was not restricted to those for whom they were intended; Nest Jenkins noted in 1938 that housewives were rushing to finish their washing early in order to sit down and listen to them. By then Wales could receive twenty-six series of schools programmes, twenty-three of them London programmes on the National Service and three of them – two in Welsh and one in English – on the Welsh Regional Service. Wales's pioneer series in English was David Williams's *Makers of Modern Wales*, broadcast in 1938–9. It was highly successful; the accompanying pamphlet, costing twopence and containing fifty-nine illustrations, was placed on public sale and three thousand copies were sold in a few days.[45] By 1938, the organizer of schools broadcasts in Wales was Alun Oldfield-Davies, the 6ft 5in-tall son of a Congregational minister from Clydach, near Swansea. He had already come to prominence as the presenter of the children's news programme *Cwrs y Byd*. Head Office was disappointed with the applicants for the post of Welsh schools organizer, for there were no Oxford or Cambridge graduates among them. 'I do not think I am impelled by mere snobbishness', wrote the director of schools broadcasting, 'in singling out people who have been to Oxford or Cambridge. I do so only because I feel we need people with as wide a social experience as possible.' Oldfield-Davies was an Aberystwyth graduate; Hopkin Morris was strongly in favour of his appointment, prophesying that 'he should be a valuable acquisition'.[46] The prophecy was fulfilled, for Oldfield-Davies would, for twenty-two years, be the highly judicious head of broadcasting in Wales.

Of Wales's non-musical output in English, religion constituted 11.5 per cent. In Welsh, programmes categorized as religious loomed much larger. In the first six months of 1939, they represented 18 per cent of the Welsh-language output. The Anglican magazine, *Y Llan*, cast a suspicious eye over the Welsh-language religious programmes of the BBC; the fact that most of the production staff in Wales were Nonconformists, it argued, led to broadcasts in which the Anglican contribution to Welsh history was grossly traduced.[47] In terms of the size of the audience, the most important programme produced in Wales in the late 1930s was the Sunday morning religious service in Welsh – fittingly so, for the demand for regular Welsh religious services had been the primary element in the campaign for a separate Welsh region with its own wavelength. London had laid down a denominational pattern for the broadcast of religious services: in a cycle of six services, three should be Anglican, two Nonconformist and one Roman Catholic. The formula proved to be unsuitable for Welsh-language services; of the eighteen full Welsh-language religious services broadcast in the first six months of 1939, five were provided by the Calvinistic Methodists, four each by the Baptists and the Congregationalists, three by the Church in Wales and two by the Wesleyans. The Corporation confined itself to broadcasting the services of 'mainstream' Christian denominations; where Nonconformists were concerned, this meant those that were members of the Council of Churches. The Unitarians, the leading denomination in parts of south Cardiganshire, were not invited to broadcast. The region did, however, arrange a broadcast of an Islamic service from the Butetown Mosque. Transmitted on the Empire Service, it was conducted by Sheikh Abdulla, who was being sought by the police for performing illegal marriages.[48]

Second in popularity to the Welsh-language Sunday services were programmes of community hymn-singing. 'Some folks are drunk on beer,' wrote one of Park Place's correspondents in 1937, 'but I gets proper drunk on hymn singing.' The programmes, stated the *Liverpool Daily Post*, represented a very distinctive form of broadcasting; unlike

117

a concert, the *cymanfa ganu* was an occasion at which the audience were the performers and the performers were the audience.[49] In addition to the Sunday-morning Welsh service, the BBC broadcast a brief Welsh service every Wednesday morning; it was based upon the English daily service and used *Pob Bore o'r Newydd*, Edgar Jones's translation of *New Every Morning*. Nest Jenkins was delighted to hear that, in the Swansea Valley, old ladies, dressed in their Sunday best, gathered in each other's houses to listen to it. Requests for a Saturday evening religious service, to prepare for 'the worship of the following day', were not, however, acceded to.[50]

In Wales's Welsh-language output, religion extended far beyond the programmes categorized as religious. As often as not, Welsh talks, features and plays dealt with themes that were at least quasi-religious. The play *Crugybar*, which Cardiff considered to be its most popular production of 1937, dealt with the growth of Methodism in northern Carmarthenshire. English-language plays were far more secular. In order to justify them as regional productions, they tended to be peppered with Welsh idioms, and the actors employed Welsh accents which were widely considered to be caricatures. In particular, the plays of Eynon Evans, a Caerffili bus-driver, 'the only real discovery of the Welsh Region', were attacked on these grounds. Following the criticism, accent and idiom were toned down somewhat, and Evans's play *Winning Ways*, broadcast to the whole of the United Kingdom, was praised by the *Manchester Guardian* for its employment of a Welsh accent which was 'intelligible and pleasant to all English listeners'.[51]

Before the coming of the separate wavelength, Wales had sought to produce one Welsh and one English play each month. Even after the wavelength had been conceded, Dafydd Gruffydd doubted the wisdom of exceeding that number. It would be better, he thought, 'to do no more than six plays a quarter (and perhaps only two or three in the summer) and pay really well'. He also doubted the wisdom of seeking to produce an equal number of Welsh and English plays. 'I cannot maintain the necessary standard in Welsh', he wrote, 'unless the percentage is kept 30% Welsh and 70% English because of the paucity of Welsh plays.' (In order to make up for that paucity, Cynan, later a distinguished archdruid, offered a script which was palpably a piece of plagiarism, earning a magisterial rebuke from Hopkin Morris.) The paucity of Welsh plays was not the only constraint, for Dafydd Gruffydd asserted that 'most of my Welsh actors are unfortunately definitely bad . . . The so-called elocutionists have ruined more actors than one cares to think about.' The inevitable consequence was the over-use of those who were competent. By 1938, there were complaints (which would become ever more familiar in subsequent years) that Welsh-language broadcasting was always using the same people. 'Pe digwyddai i Mri Gunstone Jones, Dan Mathews a Mrs Richards gael stroc', wrote *Y Cymro*, 'golygai hynny ddiwedd y BBC.'*[52]

Drama in both English and Welsh could draw upon a tradition of amateur acting which had been gathering strength since the first decade of the century. There was no similar tradition in the field of variety. 'In Wales', noted the *BBC Annual* of 1936, 'the variety tradition as understood elsewhere scarcely exists.' It had been intended to include a variety producer among the new appointees of the mid 1930s, but no such appointment was made, largely because no one seemed to know what Welsh variety was. The obvious candidate was Mai Jones of Newport, 'a brilliant pianist and composer of light items', but there were doubts whether a woman was suitable for such a post. Furthermore, Hopkin Morris found Mai Jones's habit of calling everybody 'darling' profoundly distasteful. Indeed, he found the whole concept of popular entertainment repugnant. Urged by Sam Jones and Elwyn Evans to take an interest in it, he replied: 'What, do you think I have taken on this post to be a sort of clown?' Mai Jones had only a slight knowledge of Welsh but that was not considered a major impediment 'as this is one department in which English work is likely to be predominant'.[53]

Mai Jones did not join the permanent staff at Cardiff until 15 April 1941. The absence of a staff variety producer did not mean that Wales did not produce variety programmes. In August 1938, for example, the Region broadcast a *Llandudno Night*, an ambitious project which was relayed to America and which involved the work of twenty engineers. It was considered to be a legitimate programme for Wales to undertake because Llandudno is in Wales, but it contained little that was specifically Welsh. In 1936, the Corporation urged Wales to produce what Head Office considered to be Welsh humour – performances by 'a good Welsh comedian of the "indeed-to-goodness" kind'. Appleton refused to comply, because 'Welsh people do not like the old-fashioned stage idea of a Welshman, partly because it is unlike anything found in Wales'.[54]

Mai Jones was anxious to produce programmes that reflected Welsh communities and her opportunity came with *Welsh Rarebit*. It was first broadcast on 19 July 1938 and eventually became the only Welsh Region programme to win acclaim throughout the United Kingdom. Mai Jones had already won recognition with her *Souvenirs* ('a medley of song memories'), and her *When the Day is Done*, a

---

*'If Messrs Gunstone Jones, Dan Mathews and Mrs Richards were to have strokes, that would mean the end of the BBC.'

popular musical miscellany. Light entertainment consisted mainly of songs, for the BBC was not to embrace the 'patter' style of comedy show characteristic of American radio until 1939 when *ITMA* was launched. A further restriction upon comedy programmes was the Corporation's refusal to broadcast anything which could be considered even slightly risqué. It issued a ruling listing the subjects about which jokes should not be made. They included clergymen, sick people, mothers-in-law, Scotsmen and Welshmen – but apparently not Irishmen. 'There are only six jokes in the world,' complained John Watt, the head of variety, in 1939, 'and I can assure you that we cannot broadcast three of them.' 'Every gag is scrutinised', noted the *Western Mail*, 'with a care which would make the Lord Chancellor green with envy.'[55]

Concern for propriety was even more marked in Welsh-language light entertainment, for the vigilantes of Welsh-speaking Wales were particularly active. In 1933, the mention of the word *uffern* (hell) was widely criticized and in 1935 the Congregationalists of North Glamorgan passed a motion condemning the use of the word *cythraul* (demon) in a children's programme. Idwal Jones, perhaps the most talented of the contributors to Welsh-language light entertainment, lamented the tendency of listeners 'i wgu a phrotestio am bob bic a bo . . . A ydyw dynion talentog', he asked, 'yn mynd i ysgrifennu i'r BBC os gorfodir hwy i gadw at safon yr hyn a ystyrir yn ddiwylliant gan aelodau ysgol Sul Bethania, Pencnwc?'*[56]

The scrutiny of vigilantes did not prevent the Welsh Region from producing hugely popular Welsh-language light entertainment. The most acclaimed programme was *Y Noson Lawen* ('The Merry Night'), first broadcast on 14 March 1936 and produced at Bangor by Sam Jones. Jones respected the sensitivities of his audience. He would not even allow a reference to *bloneg* (body fat) because 'dach chi ddim eisiau brifo teimladau neb't.[57] His programmes, which were broadcast live in front of an audience, mainly at the Pritchard Jones Hall in Bangor, were occasions 'to which you could safely take your grandmother'. *Y Noson Lawen* consisted of a mixture of catchy songs, dialect monologues and witty verses, the *North Wales Chronicle* in 1937 delighting in its 'rhymsical, whimsical and satirical' scripts. Ironically, in view of the supposedly dour character of Welsh Nonconformity, the programme relied heavily upon Bangor's

---

*'To condemn and protest against every this and that . . . will talented men write for the BBC if they are forced to adhere to the level of what is considered to be culture by the members of the Sunday school of Bethania Chapel, Pencnwc?'
†'You don't want to offend anybody.'

theological students; six of the eight members of its octet were preparing for the Christian ministry. *Y Noson Lawen* was to enjoy even greater success in the immediate post-war years when its appeal owed much to the talents of Meredydd Evans, the 'Bangor Bing'. Its popularity, however, had become firmly established by the late 1930s; council meetings were rearranged so that they did not coincide with the programme, streets – particularly in Gwynedd – were empty while it was on the air and its tunes were constantly whistled by its devoted listeners. In achieving his success, Sam Jones broke all the Corporation's rules and he bore the criticisms of Cardiff and London with equanimity.[58] To his admirers, his work was proof that the struggle for the Welsh Region had not been in vain. And then, in September 1939, everything came to an end.

II The war

Broadcasting in wartime had been discussed in meetings between the BBC and the Imperial Defence Committee since 1935. There were many voices demanding that there should be no wartime broadcasting at all; of the members of the Ullswater Committee, only Clement Davies had dissented from that viewpoint. By July 1938, a compromise had been reached: the National Service would close down but the Regional Service would continue. It would, however, cease to be in any sense regional; a single unified service would be broadcast to the entire kingdom, with the existing transmitters synchronized to broadcast on a single wavelength. When the plan was put into operation, the parliamentary secretary of the Ministry of Information declared that it was not in the public interest to explain the reasons for its adoption. After the war, William Haley, the director-general from 1944 to 1952, gave the impression that he believed that it had been adopted in order to release wavelengths for broadcasts to enemy, allied and occupied countries, and certainly Wales's 373-metre wavelength was extensively used for transmissions to continental Europe. In an off-the-cuff comment in October 1939, Samuel Hoare stated that the cessation of the National Service and the synchronization of the Regional Service were necessary because several wavelengths, each transmitting its own programme, offered wireless beams which could be picked up and used by enemy aircraft.[59] Such fears were undoubtedly central to the Air Ministry's resistance to any wartime regional broadcasting, but the ultimate reason for insisting on a unified service was the urge for centralization which is inherent in states at war. Kenneth Lee, the minister for information, argued in October 1939 that if parts of the

United Kingdom were to receive programmes which were different from the main broadcasts, 'this would give rise to opportunities for disintegrating propaganda'.[60]

The arrangements adopted in July 1939 were given a partial rehearsal during the Munich Crisis of September 1938, when three of Wales's productions were cancelled to allow greater coverage of the unfolding drama. In 1938, also, the Corporation began acquiring property outside London, which it hoped would be secure from German bombing; in particular, it acquired Wood Norton Hall near Evesham, a mansion which had been refurbished in the 1890s for the exiled duke of Orleans. Chamberlain's announcement that Britain was at war was broadcast at 11 a.m. on Sunday, 3 September 1939. The Corporation had already assumed that war was inevitable; on 24 August, a substantial number of the London staff had been transferred to Evesham and the unified service was introduced on Saturday, 2 September. The last programme produced in Wales to be broadcast on the Wales wavelength was *Y Fashiwn* ('The Fashion'), a Sam Jones production transmitted at 9.25 p.m. on 1 September 1939. Among the programmes completed but not broadcast was a celebration of the hundredth anniversary of the opening of Cardiff's West Bute Dock and the series of Welsh lessons which had aroused such interest in England as well as in Wales when it had been announced in the spring of 1939.[61]

Hopkin Morris had been informed of the wartime arrangements on 12 June 1939. Cardiff, he was told, might well become the production centre of some of the BBC's main departments, but it would not initiate any programmes specifically for Wales; the studios at Bangor, Swansea and Aberystwyth would cease operations completely. On 1 August 1939, Park Place tried out its air-raid siren and the entire staff of fifty-one were obliged to sign a statement that they had heard it. Sandbags were delivered and fire-watching arrangements made.[62]

The first few days of wartime broadcasting consisted of little beyond gramophone records relayed from London, together with twenty-three programmes of Sandy Macpherson on the BBC theatre organ. On 4 September, Cardiff was told to compile a daily seven-minute bulletin of announcements which, along with an equivalent bulletin from the West of England, would be broadcast to the whole of the United Kingdom each night between 7 and 7.15 p.m. Hopkin Morris was appointed official censor and the bulletin was to be compiled in conjunction with the regional civil defence commissioners. Nothing was said about announcements in Welsh. The issue, however, had already been raised by Thomas Jones, the South Wales Division food officer, who had asked on 30 August for all food announcements to be translated and broadcast. 'We have', he told Tallents, 'a large number of people in my division, as well as in the North Wales Division, who really do not understand English.' On 7 September, Oldfield-Davies made a strong plea that there should be schools programmes in Welsh; Welsh-speaking children, he claimed, were in danger of being 'swamped by evacuees'.[63]

By the middle of September, the Aberystwyth studio had been closed and the orchestra at Cardiff had been reduced to a quintet. By then the BBC had decided that no major production unit would be moved to Cardiff, largely because of the unsatisfactory land line linking Cardiff with Bristol. From Bristol, material intended for broadcasting was carried on main lines to Gloucester and thence to London and Birmingham; as there was no emergency link between Cardiff and Bristol, any break in the normal line would mean that Cardiff productions could not be broadcast. A further complication was the government's concern over the Athlone Service of the Irish Free State. The service was transmitted on a single wavelength, and could, the Air Ministry believed, be of significant assistance to enemy aircraft. There were plans to broadcast Athlone – a service which had enjoyed wide popularity in Britain in the 1930s – on a synchronized wavelength in the United Kingdom, an arrangement which would make heavy demands upon the land lines linked with the repeater station at Gloucester. On 14 September, the assistant head of engineering urged Nicolls, controller (programmes), to 'rule out Cardiff from the point of view of programme origination . . . Their announcements', he wrote, 'could be done from Bristol . . . and we could move six very valuable men to other work.' At the same time, the Corporation began denuding Swansea of its equipment with the intention of strengthening the production capacity of Bristol, where the studios were intended to be one of the chief centres of wartime broadcasting.[64]

Hopkin Morris reacted sharply. He enlisted the support of Sir Robert Webber of the *Western Mail*, the chief information officer for Wales, and he also ensured that Lloyd George would be involved. On 18 September he wrote to Nicolls:

I was given to understand that before the programmes settled down to a regular war-time basis, I should be given an opportunity of placing my views with regard to broadcasting in Welsh before the Control Board. Today I have received a memo . . . [in which] no provision at all is contained for broadcasting in Welsh at any time. Moreover . . . the Provisional Schools Emergency Programme . . . makes no provision at all . . . for Welsh School Broadcasting. I hope this matter is not going to be definitely settled before I have some

123

opportunity of stating the case fully for some recognition of broad-casts in the Welsh language.[65]

Several Welsh newspapers noted that the BBC on 4 September had launched a daily news service in Afrikaans. By 21 September, the Corporation was prepared to consider a daily news bulletin in Welsh, in addition to the announcements. London, it was believed, was the only possible place to compile it, and if it were broadcast from London the problems caused by Cardiff's deficient lines would be avoided.[66] Frederick Ogilvie, the director-general, was not dis-posed to go beyond granting a daily news bulletin. He will not, wrote Cecil Graves, the deputy director-general, on 24 September, prevent 'Hopkin Morris from making his case', but the Wales director should not be given any 'indication that we were likely to concede anything at all'.[67]

By the end of September, however, there was some change of attitude. Outlining on the 29th the policy 'dictated by the restriction of the single programme', Graves stated that 'all programmes would have to have a general and not a localized appeal'; 'the only possible exception', he wrote, 'might be Welsh broadcasting on 261 metres.'[68] The 261-metre waveband was the former West of England waveband, and it was being used for foreign transmissions. There were doubts in London about the propriety of using it to broadcast one of the indigenous languages of Britain. 'It is an essentially European and non-British service,' noted the Ministry of Information. 'We should keep programmes designed for British listeners on the recognized Home Service wavelength.' Furthermore, if the Welsh programmes were produced in Cardiff, and if the Athlone project eventually materialized, difficulties with land lines would probably mean that the programmes would have to be abandoned. It was argued that if they were put on, and then taken off, more trouble would be caused than if they were not transmitted in the first place.[69]

On 4 October, Hopkin Morris sent Nicolls a 'formal request that we should be permitted to broadcast in the Welsh language: Religion – a full service a month and a fifteen-minute studio service a week; Schools, twenty minutes each week; Children's Hour, either once a week, or at any rate, once a fortnight; a fifteen-minute talk a week.'[70] His request was seen as a bombshell, but Nicolls, who had long been involved with the Welsh issue, proved sympathetic and urged the engineers to tackle the problems of land lines. Head Office informed the Post Office's chief engineer on 11 October:

We are being pressed very strongly . . . to include Welsh items on 261. There is also a demand for occasional contributions from Cardiff on the Home Service routed from London. We could do it if the Post Office could provide us with any sort of circuit for transmitting the Irish programme from Birmingham to Bristol. Will you please consider these proposals because our Programme Division regard the inclusion of some programmes from Wales as of National importance, and we should have to be prepared to make some kind of public statement if it should be impossible to find any solution to the line difficulty.[71]

The Corporation was also under pressure from the Ministry of Information. Lee, despite his misgivings about 'disintegrating propaganda', and his concern about the use of the 261 waveband for Welsh programmes, was much impressed by arguments emanating from Sir Robert Webber's office. They say, he wrote on 12 October, that the lack of Welsh programmes 'will be the cause of complaint from many thousands of Welsh people. [We should seek to counteract] the subversive tendencies of certain sections of the community in Wales . . . Concessions from the BBC would help in defeating [their activities].'[72]

By 12 October, Nicolls had agreed to many of Hopkin Morris's demands. His memorandum 'Broadcasting in Wales' laid down that there should be a thirty-minute Sunday service once a month and a thirty-minute children's programme, a fifteen-minute morning service and a fifteen-minute talk once a week; together with the announcements and the news, the total averaged two hours fifteen minutes a week. Schools broadcasts presented a special problem, for it cost £100 to open waveband 261 during its unused daytime hours. 'Give them it in the Children's Hour slot as homework,' Nicolls advised Hopkin Morris. Nicolls's concession did not enjoy universal support at Head Office. No provision at all was being made for the English regions, and there was particular concern about the likely 'repercussions from Scotland'. As a result of the arrangements for Wales, the Corporation felt obliged to provide programmes in Gaelic; as the number of Gaelic-speakers was one-seventh that of Welsh-speakers, the thirty minutes a week granted to them in 30 November 1939 was considered generous.[73]

Hopkin Morris was convinced that he had wrung from the Corporation the maximum possible concessions. He was also convinced that they were granted because of the personal sympathy and support of Nicolls. To his memorandum acknowledging the new arrangements, he added a hand-written letter to Nicolls: 'I cannot let your memo . . . pass with an expression of official gratitude only . . . I am satisfied from my own experience that without your advocacy the case of Wales would not have been met as it has, and certainly not in as generous a measure. Wales is indebted to you.' It was made clear that if wavelength 261 were needed for more extensive foreign broadcasts, the whole matter would have to be reconsidered. Hopkin Morris promised that he would 'defend the . . . Welsh-language schedule against any pressure from Wales to secure greater concessions'.[74] He did so. Newspaper cuttings reporting his defence of the schedule fill almost an entire volume in the Wales Record Centre. During the war he undertook additional duties as the chairman of the Wales Tribunal dealing with the appeals of conscientious objectors; as chairman, he proved particularly hostile to those who objected to military conscription on Welsh nationalist grounds. Although it would be invidious to suggest that so independent-minded a person would have done so in order to curry favour with the authorities, his comments at tribunals undoubtedly strengthened Head Office's belief that the Wales director was a very sound man indeed.

An additional line between Birmingham and Bristol was provided to enable Athlone to be broadcast. The arrangements made in the first months of the war are proof of the ingenuity of the engineers but, as so often in the history of the BBC, their skills, once they had secured what seemed virtually impossible, were taken for granted. Although the engineers accomplished in an exemplary manner the work necessary to enable Welsh to be broadcast, their correspondence suggests that they did so without enthusiasm. 'Someone', wrote R. T. B. Wynn, the senior superintendent engineer, 'has pulled a fast one.' The Post Office refused to provide an additional line between Cardiff and Bristol and therefore the unsatisfactory link had to be used. 'It is very deficient', it was noted, 'but I suppose it will do for Welsh noises.' 'Before long', wrote Wynn in November 1939, 'we shall have to confine our staffs to jobs which benefit majorities not minorities.'[75]

In December 1939, the concessions granted by Nicolls came under severe attack. The British troops in France, who in the months of the 'phoney' war were largely unoccupied, had virtually abandoned the BBC's unified service in favour of the English-language programmes of Radio Fécamp, a commercial station which also broadcast German programmes. As a result, the Corporation was under pressure to provide an additional service, more popular in style, which would not abide by the Sabbatarian policy which the BBC had continued to operate even after the departure of Reith. Any Forces programme would also be available to the entire home audience. If a popular service were conceded during the war, it could hardly be withdrawn when the war was over. Thus the decision to launch a Forces programme was essentially a rejection of Reith's dictum that the

Corporation's function was not to give people what they thought they wanted, but to provide them with what they would come to want after they had been introduced to richer and more satisfying fare.[76]

The Forces Programme began on 7 January 1940 and became a full service on 18 February. Discussions over its establishment led to a reconsideration of the BBC's entire output. 'In the context of the BEF programme', wrote the director of programme planning on 19 December 1939, 'it should be pointed out that Welsh and Gaelic cannot be broadcast without employing lines which rightly should be held in reserve for other more important services. [Thus] my first recommendation must be a strong one to drop both.' Before submitting his memorandum, he added a further comment: 'Since dictating the above, I have learnt that Germany has now instituted a highly effective propaganda service in both Welsh and Gaelic . . . Much as I believe my recommendations . . . to be right . . . this new factor may clearly have to be taken into consideration.'[77] He noted that the Welsh and Gaelic services were referred to in the reports of the monitoring service. By December 1939, the monitoring service was producing each day transcripts of broadcasts equivalent in length to several substantial novels. They record that on 13 December 1939 Hamburg began broadcasting in Irish. (There are quite well-educated Englishmen who believe that Celtic, Gaelic, Irish and Welsh are all terms for the same language, or for some sort of dialect of English.) On 10 December 1939, an English programme from Hamburg referred to 'the distressed areas of south Wales', and it urged the Welsh not to forget 'how Churchill ordered the military to fire on miners in the coal strike of 1911'.[78] There is, however, no evidence that there were ever broadcasts in Welsh from Germany; nor was there anything equivalent to Germany's Radio Caledonia, which sought to persuade the Scots to sue for a separate peace agreement.

It is difficult to say whether the threat of Welsh-language broadcasts from Germany led to the preservation of the BBC's Welsh-language programmes. But preserved they were. Between September 1939 and February 1940 there were Welsh-language Sunday services on 5 November, 3 December, 7 January and 4 February. A fifteen-minute weekly radio service was transmitted, and thirteen talks were broadcast by leading Welshmen such as Ifor Williams and the blind poet-preacher Elfed. The promise to provide a half-hour in Welsh on *Children's Hour* was honoured; the difficulties over schools broadcasts during daylight hours were overcome, and a weekly series in Welsh was transmitted.[79] In addition, there were the daily Welsh news bulletins. They had originally been conceived of as announcements and were broadcast on the Home Service at 7 a.m.; on 6 November they were moved to the 261 waveband and for the greater part of the war they were broadcast at 5 p.m. The bulletins were launched in London by Sam Jones, who leased a flat in Great Portland Street. Jones soon returned to Bangor, and was replaced by a rota; it consisted of Alun Llywelyn-Williams, Geraint Dyfnallt Owen and Elwyn Evans, who stayed in turn in the flat, which became a major centre for Welsh visitors to wartime London. Llywelyn-Williams's account of the Welsh wartime news unit portrays a group of young men (and young women – the secretaries) devoted to a task that had never been attempted before – the systematic daily presentation of the world's news in the Welsh language. In 1940, London was the place to be, and clearly the Welsh broadcasters enjoyed themselves hugely. The bulletins gave Llywelyn-Williams the opportunity to put into practice his ideas about the dignity of broadcast Welsh, and many of his coinages, particularly those for war terms – the word *awyren* (aeroplane), for example – became incorporated into the language.[80]

The bulletins consisted in the main of a shortened, translated version of the BBC's English news at one o'clock. Yet, as the Welsh unit had full access to the resources of the news centre at Langham Place, use could be made of news items which came in after one o'clock. As a result, the Welsh five o'clock news regularly scooped the English news at six o'clock. During the Finno-Soviet war, for example, non-Welsh-speakers would request their Welsh-speaking friends to be on hand at five o'clock to offer an instantaneous translation of the Welsh bulletin. The Wales Record Centre contains the text of virtually all the bulletins and reading them is a fascinating experience. The justification for them was the perceived need for the monoglot Welsh to be aware of the government's orders and announcements. There were such announcements; on 5 January 1940, for example, farmers were told of new regulations regarding the killing of pigs, and on 9 February all men born in December 1919 were ordered to register for military conscription. Such items, however, constituted a very minor part of the bulletins. Nor did happenings in Wales loom large. Welsh news was difficult to obtain in London, and Llywelyn-Williams and his colleagues had little to report beyond stories about concerts for servicemen held by the London Welsh Association. Essentially, the bulletins are a blow-by-blow account of the Second World War, and their publication *in toto* would be a justifiable venture.[81]

Of the Welsh-language programmes broadcast in the first year of the war, the ones which attracted the greatest attention were those of 5 to 10 August 1940, which offered a substitute for the National Eisteddfod. The Eisteddfod was to have been held at Bridgend, but the difficulties of organizing it and of enabling an adequate number of people to attend seemed insurmountable. Remembering the success of the radio eisteddfod of December 1938, Hopkin Morris suggested that the 1940 National Eisteddfod should take place on the air. In 1940, the National Eisteddfod had not become an exclusively Welsh-medium festival, but Hopkin Morris's plan did assume that the Corporation would allow, for one week at least, a significant increase in programmes from Wales, much of which would be unintelligible to the vast majority of British listeners. Nicolls supported Hopkin Morris and by mid July the arrangements were complete. Apart from the traditional Eisteddfod speech of Lloyd George, which was also carried on the Empire service, the Eisteddfod was to consist of three hours broadcast on the British Home Service. Fifteen minutes apiece were allowed for the crown and chair adjudications; following each, Hopkin Morris opened the envelope containing the name of the winner and announced the name on the air – the only occasions for him to broadcast during his years as Wales director. The name of the winner of the chair was particularly warmly greeted. It was that of T. Rowland Hughes, the main inspiration behind the radio eisteddfod; his *awdl* 'Pererinion' ('Pilgrims') was an adaptation of the 'beautiful parable in verse' praised by the *Observer* in 1938.[82]

The attention given to Wales by the BBC aroused antagonism elsewhere. Melville Dinwiddie, the Scotland director, was particularly critical, arguing in 1940 that 'the political situation in Scotland demands special treatment'. Rather than insisting upon more programmes specifically for Scotland, however, the Scots expended their energies on protesting against the BBC's usage of the word England when it referred to the British state. (The Welsh news unit followed suit and frequently referred to Britain as *Lloegr* (England).) In February 1942, the Corporation issued a ruling that 'England is acceptable if England is really meant ... otherwise Britain should be used except when it sounds absurd'. There were protests too in the English provincial press, causing a Welsh resident in Sheffield to write: 'What prescriptive right have English people to a monopoly of the functions of the BBC? Is the war being fought by English people only and to safeguard their interests only?'[83]

The protests arose in part because of a decision of the Corporation in February 1940 to move the Welsh-language programmes from waveband 261 to the British Home Service, and in part because the time devoted to them had increased. By February, output in Welsh had risen to two hours thirty minutes a week, allowing Hopkin Morris to assert that the amount of time Welsh was on the air was almost half what it had been before war was declared.[84] BBC officials felt that Wales was getting 'a very square deal'. They were particularly incensed by the constant complaint that the thirty minutes allotted to the monthly religious service was insufficient. 'The only argument in favour', wrote the director of religious broadcasting in February 1940, 'is that they like long-winded sermons, and this is an argument that should appal us as broadcasters.'[85]

The emphasis which the advocates of an increased use of Welsh placed upon religious services puzzled those at Head Office. 'These excellent strange-tongued folk', wrote the director of programme planning in January 1940, 'have their own religious organisations working among them and facilities for worship are available.'[86] When the Forces Programme was launched, Hopkin Morris sought assurances that the Welsh language should have at least a token presence on the new service. 'WD wants at least fifteen minutes on the Forces Programme,' noted Nicolls. 'He requires this for political reasons and does not mind if the placing is not a good one . . . A possible solution might be to treat it like the Indian news.' The timing granted was 10.15 to 10.30 a.m., and the programme was *Sut Hwyl?*, a lively quarter of an hour produced in Swansea. There were appreciative letters from soldiers, but there were some complaints that in billets where perhaps a handful of Welshmen wanted to listen to the programme, the radio was switched off on the insistence of the English majority.[87]

The timing of Welsh broadcasts was a constant bone of contention. The Welsh news, it was claimed, had a small audience because at five o'clock most people had not returned from work. There were requests that it should be transmitted immediately after the 9.00 p.m. news. They were turned down out of hand. As that was precisely the time William Joyce (Lord Haw-Haw) broadcast from Hamburg, the BBC took particular care to ensure that it was used for the Corporation's most popular programmes; if the Welsh news were put on at that time, argued Nicolls, it would seem as if the BBC were urging almost the entire British population to listen to German propaganda.[88]

Despite some increase in the number of Welsh-language broadcasts by the early months of 1940, the institution of the single unified service created considerable anxiety in Wales. Watkin Jones, who became Wales director of programmes following Tudor Jones's appointment as head of the BBC's editorial unit in May 1940, was above all concerned to ensure that there should be continuity in Welsh-language broadcasting so that some basis for rebuilding would be available when the war ended. T. I. Ellis, the secretary of Y Genhadledd Genedlaethol er mwyn Diogeli Diwylliant Cymru (The National Conference for the Safeguarding of Welsh Culture – later known as Undeb Cymru Fydd or the New Wales Union), wrote to Ogilvie in February 1940 arguing that the Welsh language had been 'disproportionately penalized by the arrangements introduced since the declaration of war'. Ellis asked for assurances that at least a skeleton staff would be kept and that the pre-war pattern would be restored when hostilities ceased.[89]

In the same month, Bob Owen of Croesor, wrote to Head Office on behalf of Community House, Porthmadog, noting that 'politicians are constantly stating that Britain and France are fighting for the freedom of the world and that they are saving the small nations of Europe from being extinguished; we crave upon you to remember that Wales also wants to be saved from being obliterated.' Maurice Farquharson, the director of home intelligence, was moved by Owen's letter. 'Answer this rather sweet affair from my old friend Bob Owen,' he told S. J. de Lotbiniere, the director of outside broadcasts, 'who is one of those genuine Welshmen who really can hardly speak English.'[90] In March 1940, the Welsh correspondent of the *News Chronicle*, reporting the removal of equipment from Swansea and Cardiff, feared that the pre-war arrangements would never be restored. Hopkin Morris, thought the correspondent, had become such a Corporation man that there 'is little to hope from him'. The magazine *Heddiw* suggested that Welsh-language programmes should be broadcast from the Irish Free State. Watkin Jones took up the idea. 'After all', he wrote, 'British transmitters are used to relay the Athlone programme.' The Irish authorities showed willingness to broadcast forty minutes apiece to Wales and Scotland every fortnight if studio facilities were available; nothing, however, seems to have come from the discussions.[91]

As the exigencies of war had led to the adoption of a single service transmitted to the entire United Kingdom, programmes in Welsh presented problems, if only because England did not want them. English programmes from Wales were an entirely different matter; they were exportable, as Welsh programmes were not. The BBC was resolutely opposed to any wartime transmissions of English programmes specifically for Wales, for the broadcast of such programmes would open up the question of regional broadcasting in England. Thus anything Wales produced in English had to be acceptable to the United Kingdom as a whole. By February 1940, British listeners were hearing up to two hours a week of English-language programmes produced in Wales, a marked contrast with the twelve hours and more a week which Wales had produced in English before the war. With the time and the available resources allotted to fewer programmes, the standard of output rose. Indeed, it could be argued that the Second World War was the golden age of

English sound broadcasting in Wales. Grace Wyndham Goldie, probably the finest radio producer ever employed by the BBC, considered *Home Fires Burning*, a feature on the coal industry produced by T. Rowland Hughes and Jack Jones, to be 'the first breath of reality [since the beginning of the war]'.[92]

Although the production staff at Cardiff had been appointed primarily because of their ability to work through the medium of Welsh, they undoubtedly welcomed the opportunity to make more ambitious programmes in English and delighted in the challenge presented by a far greater audience than that represented by the listeners to the pre-war Welsh wavelength. In paying tribute to T. Rowland Hughes, Alun Oldfield-Davies wrote: '[Bu] cyfyngu ar ei waith yn Gymraeg yn [foddion i] ledu'i orwelion ac ehangu maes ei ddylanwad. Ac rwyf yn lled gredu ei fod yntau'n croesawu hyn ar y pryd.'*[93] While Rowland Hughes was enhancing his reputation as a features writer, Mai Jones was winning plaudits for her variety programmes. On 29 February 1940, *Welsh Rarebit* featured for the first time the song 'We'll keep a welcome', with the words written by Lyn Joshua and the music by Mai Jones. Although to a later generation the song can perhaps sound maudlin, it made a deep impression in 1940 upon those who longed to see their sons 'come home again to Wales'.

The decision abruptly to attenuate the BBC's services in September 1939 was based upon the assumption that once war was declared Britain would be subjected to the full horror of modern warfare. The 'phoney' war in the west, which lasted until the spring of 1940, provided time for adjustment and gave Hopkin Morris the opportunity to state his case for Welsh-language broadcasts. Germany attacked the Low Countries on 10 May 1940, creating an overwhelming and wholly unprecedented hunger for news. With newsprint rationed, the BBC's bulletins became of central importance, and at least half the British population became regular listeners to the *Nine O'Clock News*. France fell in June 1940 and, with the German army at the Channel ports, the invasion of Britain was considered to be imminent. The BBC was put on an emergency basis. By June, guns were in place on the roof of the studio at Swansea, and by November a direct line had been provided linking Cardiff's Broadcasting House in Park Place with the Welsh Regional War Room at 8 Cathedral Road. If invasion threatened, the two centres were to communicate in code, and an ingenious system was evolved, based upon *The Concise Oxford*

---

*'The restriction upon his work in Welsh allowed him to broaden his horizons and to widen the field of his influence. And I tend to feel that he welcomed that at the time.'

Dictionary of Current English. As there were fears that the Luftwaffe would seek to immobilize transmitters such as that at Washford, transmitters working on low power were installed at Cardiff, Swansea and Wrexham, and arrangements were made for BBC messages to be carried to communities beyond their reach by policemen with loud-hailers.[94]

In the dire months of 1940 and 1941, there was much concern about fifth-column activities. 'It should be understood clearly', declared the BBC on 20 December 1941, 'that enemy agents are urging Cardiff citizens to leave the town.' The Corporation ruled on 16 July that no conscientious objector should broadcast. Hopkin Morris wondered what he should do about Iorwerth Peate, who had broadcast frequently after his name had been removed from the blacklist following Appleton's departure from Cardiff; while Peate was not precisely a conscientious objector, he made no secret of his pacificism. Hopkin Morris's quandary was solved on 30 August 1940 when the Corporation ruled that no one who 'has expressed views which are inconsistent with the national effort' should have access to the microphone. The far right had been banned since September 1939; the far left was also under suspicion, for until Hitler's invasion of the Soviet Union in June 1941, the Communist Party maintained that the Germano-British conflict was an imperialist war. David Raymond, a relation of Nest Jenkins and a journalist whose comments on Welsh broadcasting in *Reynolds News* were highly perceptive, was blacklisted on 2 September 1940. 'He has been to Russia', it was noted, 'and he wrote the articles on Wales and the Eisteddfod in the Soviet Encyclopaedia.'[95]

Senior figures at Head Office began to show a close interest in the content of Welsh-language programmes, for there was a widespread belief that they were inherently subversive. The controller of home broadcasting was anxious that they should be carefully scrutinized, in particular to ensure that 'they did not make for national disunity'. He sought to insist that London should be provided beforehand with translations of all Welsh broadcasts, but Nicolls demurred, arguing that there was no danger while Hopkin Morris was at the helm. Particular interest was shown in children's programmes. 'I listened to the Welsh Children's Hour', wrote the West's Children's Hour organizer, 'and picked out the English words.' (One of the English words he cited was Hitler.) An adventure story about pirates was banned because there were fears that it might give the enemy valuable information about inlets in Pembrokeshire. A programme about twelfth-century Glamorgan aroused deep suspicion. 'Who', asked the Children's Hour director, 'is Ifor Bach?'[96]

The heavy bombing of London which accompanied the end of the 'phoney' war led to demands that the movement from London, which had begun with the trek to Evesham in August 1939, should be continued. By 1940, the Children's Hour and Light Music Departments were at Bristol, and the Home Board decided that the Variety Department, which was also temporarily at Bristol, should be moved to Bangor. The move was made in April 1941, and the department's 34-month stay at Bangor is one of the most fascinating episodes in the history of wartime broadcasting. Although the city had experienced the goings-on of undergraduates for almost sixty years, they were as nothing compared with the flamboyant behaviour of many of the variety artists. The whole department was transported from Bristol on a special train which carried 432 people, seventeen dogs and a parrot. 'Bangor, the sedate cathedral and college city of pre-war Wales,' wrote the *Liverpool Daily Post*, 'lost its innocence overnight with one trainful of actors.' Yet, although there were frequent comments about 'painted women' and pained surprise among the citizens on discovering some of the laxer habits of the performers, the sojourn was, on the whole, a happy one. Elizabeth Forster has described the horror of the variety artists when they heard they were to move to north Wales, but many of them, she recalled, came to love it. It was estimated that the presence of the Variety Department contributed a thousand pounds a week to Bangor's economy; the stars gave a number of concerts, the profits of which were donated to local charities and, after most of them had left in 1943, the city council presented the Corporation with a plaque to commemorate their stay. 'The people of Bangor', noted Maurice Gorham, 'turned into an almost permanent studio audience; [the citizens] were the nearest thing we have ever had to the Hollywood radio addicts.' A large number of the artists were accommodated in a holiday colony at Benllech in Anglesey and, when the expected bombing of the Menai Bridge took place, they were to be transported to Bangor Pier by launch. Tommy Handley, the star of *ITMA*, by far the most popular of the wartime variety shows, was housed at Llanfairfechan. He was much taken with the personality of Sam Jones and he included in *ITMA* a hilarious character named Sam Fairfechan.[97]

By April 1941, only about 36 per cent of the Head Office staff were still in London. Of the rest, 29 per cent were at Evesham, 13 per cent at Bristol, 6 per cent each at Oxford and Bangor, 4 per cent each at Manchester and Glasgow and 2 per cent elsewhere. The dispersal of entire departments to locations outside London could lead to difficulties regarding the authority of regional directors. In theory, they were in charge of the BBC production staff within their region. However, the Corporation's heads of department had a higher status than regional directors, causing Coatman to complain that the movement of staff was undermining the power of the directors. The BBC's head of variety, John Watt, had the authority to issue orders to Sam Jones, although Jones was, strictly speaking, responsible to Hopkin Morris in Cardiff. There is some evidence of tension, but overall the system worked well. 'They should work with Sam Jones,' wrote Nicolls; 'he was the uncrowned king of peace-time Bangor and he knows everything there is to know about Bangor and the neighbourhood.' Hopkin Morris agreed. 'Sam Jones created broadcasting in north Wales,' he wrote. 'There is only one Mr Sam Jones in the Corporation. He is first class.'[98]

Although the Variety Department was highly visible at Bangor, the BBC did not acknowledge publicly that it was there. The most the Corporation's officials would say was that the department was 'somewhere in Wales'. Bangor, as Wilfred Pickles put it, was 'the BBC's secret hideout nearly everybody knew about'. The city was chosen because it seemed unlikely to be the target of heavy bombing. It was, however, attacked. A sea mine exploded in Neuadd y Penrhyn in October 1941, an incursion which led to the death of a BBC driver, John Charles Walters.[99] Nevertheless, the multitudinous collection of buildings bought, leased and hired by the Corporation at Bangor survived the war relatively unscathed.

Swansea was not so fortunate. In the severe bombing suffered by the town in February 1941, the premises at Alexandra Road were reduced to rubble. Pickering and his staff moved to Carmarthen, where the Corporation leased the Lyric Theatre. Carmarthen was delighted to be the headquarters of the BBC's west Wales representative, and the borough council and the local newspapers launched a campaign to persuade the Corporation to recognize the town as the permanent centre of its operations in west Wales. 'We fail to see', wrote the *Welshman* in February 1943, 'that Swansea can have a strong claim to the location of a West Wales BBC studio after the war, for the Cardiff station is near enough and the railway facilities so convenient.' There were constant fears that Broadcasting House in Cardiff would be bombed. Hopkin Morris felt the need for an out-station, and in 1941 the Corporation leased the Constitutional Club at Aberdare.[100]

The loss of Swansea was not as devastating as it would have been had it occurred when the BBC in Wales was broadcasting over twenty hours a week of its own material. In February 1941, Wales's output was less than a fifth of that of the late 1930s, although, as all its wartime English-language programmes were produced for the network, they were deemed to be more labour-intensive. Because of the reduction in output, Hopkin Morris was under constant pressure to release his staff for other duties. For the BBC as a whole, the war was a period of massive expansion in the work-force; the Corporation had 4,889 employees in September 1939 and 11,543 in March 1945. Yet in those years regional staffs contracted; furthermore, many in that category were working for Head Office, causing the Midland director to complain that the regions were being turned into 'a species of hidden reserve for London departments'.[101]

Most of the young men appointed in the 1930s became otherwise employed as the war dragged on. Wynford Vaughan-Thomas joined Head Office's Outside Broadcast Unit in April 1940. Using the 'emotionalism and the vital phrasing' which he believed should be the hallmark of the Welsh broadcaster, he became the most distinguished of the BBC's wartime correspondents. Others joined the army, Dafydd Gruffydd, Alun Llywelyn-Williams and Elwyn Evans among them; in 1942 Gruffydd was in Cairo where he recorded impressions which were incorporated into the bulletins of the Welsh news unit. Geraint Dyfnallt Owen joined the Army Intelligence Service and became a leading authority on the culture and history of Romania. With the orchestra disbanded, Cardiff's music department contracted, and Mansel Thomas was seconded to conduct the BBC's Revue Orchestra. J. G. Roberts and Ernest Jenkins went to London, and Alun Oldfield-Davies took over their work as the Wales executive officer. By the later years of the war, Oldfield-Davies was virtually deputy director. 'He is a first class man,' wrote Hopkin Morris, 'and suitable for any responsible post within the Corporation.' The contraction in the staff caused Hopkin Morris grave concern. 'If there are more reductions,' he wrote in January 1943, 'we will have to close down.' That view was not universally shared. 'Cardiff, Carmarthen and Bangor', wrote Gwyn Jones in 1945, '[were] far from denuded. At times indeed there seemed to be too many cooks rather than too few.'[102]

Some of the gaps were filled. Head Office was anxious that men should be replaced by women. Their salary scales were lower, and, if married, they would be obliged to resign when hostilities ended, thus allowing the reappointment of male employees who had undertaken other duties during the war. Nan Davies was promoted to be a features producer, and her work with *Children's Hour* was undertaken by Morfudd Mason Lewis. Another of Wales's wartime female employees was Lorraine Jameson, a native of Glyn-nedd and the young widow of an officer killed in action. On 29 December 1942 Hywel Davies, the 23-year-old son of a Congregational minister from Llandeilo, who had been rejected by the armed services on health grounds, became a BBC employee. He was to be the most outstanding figure in Welsh broadcasting in the post-war years. In August

1942, a permanent position was found for Aneirin Talfan Davies, who had already made numerous programmes on a free-lance basis. Talfan Davies, the son of a Presbyterian minister from Henllan in Carmarthenshire, was a pharmacist whose shop had been destroyed during the blitz on Swansea. A man of wide culture, with 'an Athenian concept of the comprehensive obligations of the citizen', Talfan Davies's contribution to the BBC in Wales, together with that of relations of his to other aspects of Welsh culture, led to the belief that the media in Wales were 'un ymerodraeth fawr Talfanaidd'*.[103]

Staff changes in Wales coincided with greater upheavals in the BBC as a whole. Ogilvie, the director-general since 1938, 'possessed every quality save the ability to run a great corporation'. On the outbreak of war, the BBC ceased to rely upon its licence income; instead it was financed by a grant-in-aid from the government. By the winter of 1941, there were demands that the grant should be reduced on the grounds that the Corporation was handling its money inefficiently. The demands were ill-considered, for, as Asa Briggs pointed out, if the BBC's broadcasts had the capacity to shorten the war by a single day, the Corporation would save the British government £10 million. The total cost of the BBC's wartime operations was about £50 million – less than the cost of a week's fighting – and the expenditure undoubtedly represented the British government's most effective investment in the hostilities. Complaints about the BBC's inefficiency led in October 1941 to the appointment of Robert Foot, the director of the Gas, Light and Coke Company, to investigate the workings of the Corporation. On 27 January 1942 Ogilvie was required to resign and Foot and Cecil Graves became joint directors-general. Reith had wanted Graves as his successor, despite his misgivings over Graves's membership of the Roman Catholic church. By 1942, however, Graves had lost much of his vigour; he resigned in September 1943, leaving Foot as sole director-general. William Haley, an experienced journalist of Channel Island origins, became editor of the BBC in November 1943; Foot resigned in March 1944 and Haley succeeded him as director-general.[104]

The change of leadership was accompanied by a partial dismantling of the cumbersome bureaucracy instituted by Reith and Carpendale in 1933. In 1942, the Control Board was abolished and was replaced by three committees. The rigid division between administration and programme-making came to an end. The Wales executive officer, who under the 1933 arrangements was responsible to the controller (administration) in London, would henceforth be responsible to the Wales director. Foot insisted upon the destruction

---

*'One great Talfanite empire'.

of files containing irrelevant personal details, and he also willingly co-operated with the BBC Staff Association, established in 1940. (Reith had resisted all attempts to unionize the Corporation's staff.) In March 1942, the Regional Board was replaced by regular monthly meetings between the regional directors and the director-general. The new system was not wholly satisfactory; in 1944, the regional directors claimed it was not working, although their frustration sprang more from the virtual absence of regional broadcasting than from hostility to the new arrangements themselves. Coatman was particularly vocal. 'Regional staff', he claimed, 'were permitted to fill up the "bad" listening time with their own material.' The result was 'a false London view on everything'. While he opposed centralization in London, Coatman was even more hostile to the argument that Wales and Scotland, as distinct nations, should have higher status than that of the English regions. 'It means the Balkanisation of Britain,' he wrote in September 1943; Wales and Scotland 'would be driven into politics and twisted and warped away from their primary purpose of broadcasting as parts of the inclusive nation to which they belong, namely the British nation'.[105]

By 1943 the Corporation had become an avid propagandist for the 'British nation'. Early in the war, the BBC had been reluctant to broadcast overt propaganda, but attitudes changed during the baneful years of 1940 to 1942. In 1942, the director of *Children's Hour* asserted that the purpose of his programmes was to make the listeners 'loyal subjects of the Empire'. The BBC in Wales played its part. T. Rowland Hughes's *It might happen here*, broadcast in May 1942, which portrayed the Nazi occupation of a Welsh mining valley, was considered by the *Observer* to represent a 'considerable toughening in BBC propaganda'. Even more effective was *San Demetrio*, a programme devised by P. H. Burton, a Port Talbot schoolmaster, which told the story of a crippled tanker reaching harbour with the help of a school atlas. It was repeated three times on the Home Service and several times on the Overseas Service. *San Demetrio* was made into a film, the first time a radio script was adapted for the screen. Other morale-boosting programmes included *Pride of Britain*, made by Rowland Hughes and Burton to commemorate the second anniversary of Dunkirk, *Service not Self*, a programme celebrating the twenty-first anniversary of the British Legion, and *Silent Village*, an account of the destruction of the Czech mining village of Lidice.[106]

As the tide of war turned, the news programmes became even greater morale boosters than were consciously propaganda programmes. The scripts prepared by the Welsh news unit on the central event of the war – the Battle of Stalingrad (August 1942 to January 1943) – are remarkably intense. On 8 September 1943, the

Welsh-language news was the first of the BBC's bulletins to announce the surrender of Italy. The London *Nine O'Clock News* was the cornerstone of war reporting, and its readers, identified by name, became folk heroes. The news included inserts by war reporters. Wynford Vaughan-Thomas's running commentary on an RAF raid on Berlin on 3 September 1943 was a huge sensation. Vaughan-Thomas covered the landings at Anzio, where he was the first to use the BBC's midget recording machine – although, as the machine with its twelve two-sided records weighed almost half a hundred-weight, its 'midgetness' was relative.[107]

It was the hunger for news, together with the greater spending power of the Welsh working class as a result of wartime prosperity, which made the war a period of considerable expansion in the number of licensed listeners. There were 490,000 licence-holders in Wales in 1945 compared with 405,954 in 1939; the equivalent figures for Britain were 9,940,000 and 8,893,000. But while increasing numbers had the means to buy licences and sets, the availability of sets contracted markedly. In 1938, 1.9 million sets were manu-factured in Britain, a figure which had declined to 50,000 in 1943; there was much buying of the utility set, a disappointment to its purchasers, for the long-wave service, restored after the war, was beyond its reception capacity. In those areas lacking mains electricity, scarcity of batteries meant that listening had to be carefully rationed. Reporting from a remote Welsh farm in 1943, Tom Harrison noted that 'batteries here are too precious to permit the indiscriminate Forces listening of the cities'. There were many who only switched on when Welsh-language programmes were transmitted and, in order to have at least a whisper from their favourite broadcasters, they lovingly warmed their waning batteries in the oven.[108]

While propagandist programmes were dutifully listened to, and news bulletins reporting victories were avidly followed, the greatest broadcasting successes of the war were the programmes which enabled the home audience to have contact with their menfolk overseas. 'Give them more from the boys' was Tudor Jones's advice in 1940.[109] The Second World War was the first in which public sound broadcasting enabled combatants and non-combatants to hear each other. While it cannot compare with the Vietnam or the Gulf Wars, during which mothers sitting at home could watch video recordings of their sons killing people, it did represent a huge advance in the presentation of the actuality of war.

Cairo, where a large number of Welsh servicemen were stationed in 1942 and 1943, provided numerous recordings for home broadcasting. On St David's Day 1943, the BBC broadcast excerpts from the concert of the Cairo Welsh Society, and in October 1943 the proceedings of the Cairo eisteddfod, which attracted an audience of over a thousand, were transmitted on the Home Service. Jerusalem also had a Welsh society and its members recorded talks in places such as the Mount of Olives, much to the delight of Welsh chapel-goers, to whom the topography of Palestine was very familiar. The correspondents drew attention to the absence of a plaque bearing the Lord's Prayer in Welsh in the Pater Noster Church. The BBC took the matter up, and a plaque financed by Urdd Gobaith Cymru was unveiled in the church in 1944. A fortnightly *Welsh Half Hour* from the Middle East was launched in December 1942. In addition, the BBC sent transcripts of its Welsh news bulletin to Cairo for inclusion in Egypt's Welsh magazine, *Seren y Dwyrain* ('Star of the East').[110]

Capel Tabernacl, in The Hayes, was filled to capacity every Sunday night for the service *The Army Sings*. Some of the services were broadcast and included hymns in the languages of the occupied countries; in December 1942, for example, the congregation sang hymns in Danish. Tabernacl's broadcast service in September 1941 proved astonishingly popular, with the deacons obliged to turn away over a thousand servicemen. In September 1943, Cardiff produced *Calling Gibraltar*, and invited relations of servicemen at Gibraltar to broadcast their greetings; of the hundreds who applied, thirty came to Park Place to take part in the programme. *Welsh Rarebit* was a mainstay of the Forces Service and included a highly popular item by Lyn Joshua – 'Dai's letter to the Forces' – a survey in a jocular manner of home news. *Strike a Home Note*, a major Forces programme of 1944, was frequently broadcast from Wales, the programme from Llandudno in May being particularly ambitious.[111]

The entry of the Soviet Union into the war in June 1941 led to the lifting of the ban upon broadcasts by supporters of the far left. The leading Welsh Communist, Arthur Horner, took part in several programmes, and as coal became more scarce a number of left-wing miners' leaders were given opportunities to broadcast. The Welsh news unit proudly reported in 1943 that the London Cymmrodorion St David's Day dinner had been graced by the presence of Ivan Mikhailovich Maiskii, the Soviet ambassador. Several programmes were produced emphasizing the historic links between Wales and Russia; among their revelations was the fact that Gogol mentions a serf called Wil Ifan. The entry of the United States into the war in December 1941 led to the production in Wales of a series of programmes for transmission in North America. *Transatlantic Call*, recorded before an audience of 1,300 at the institute at Rhos-llannerchrugog, was a great success, and a programme from the Rhondda in April 1942 informed Americans that the women of the valley 'appear to thrive on self-denial in these days of rationing'.[112]

With the Soviet Union and the United States at war with Germany, the ultimate victory of the Allies was assured. As the likelihood of invasion receded, demands for more Welsh-language programmes became more vocal. Even in the grim days of 1941, the matter had been raised in the House of Commons in questions from Henry Morris-Jones (National Liberal, Denbigh) and Moelwyn Hughes (Labour, Carmarthen). The reply of Harold Nicolson, the parliamentary secretary to the minister of information, that 'the Corporation cannot increase the time now devoted to programmes in Welsh', caused considerable annoyance. 'If the Welsh Party accepts this, it will accept anything,' wrote the *Western Mail*.[113] Nicolls felt obliged to defend the broadcasts in Welsh. 'The point to realise', he wrote in February 1941, 'is that broadcasts in Welsh [then averaging twenty minutes a day] are the only thing in the day that the monoglot Welsh minority can understand, and if they are deprived of [them] they are deprived of all spoken matter for the day – which is a pity.' In August 1942, he argued that there was a statistical argument in favour of Welsh-language broadcasts. Welsh-speakers represented one sixty-seventh of the population of the United Kingdom; they could therefore claim one sixty-seventh of the 235 hours broadcast each week by the Home and Forces Services – that is, three and a half hours a week. In fact, he noted, they received less than their rightful share. Although Hopkin Morris was adamant publicly that the Welsh language was fairly treated, he was incensed in December 1942 to discover that the Corporation intended to spend an additional 1,600 guineas a week on studying its audience. 'All programmes for Wales', he told the directors-general, 'cost £250 to £600 a week; would it be possible to classify the programmes from Wales as scientific investigation?'[114]

Comparisons were drawn between the 2 hours a week of Welsh and the 7 in Afrikaans, the 16 hours 20 minutes in Portuguese for Brazil and the 2 hours 55 minutes to Albania, a country for which there was no reliable information that any of the inhabitants had wireless sets. The Corporation, it was noted, received over £500 a day in licence revenue from Wales; Welsh licence-holders were two and a half times more numerous than those of the Irish Free State, a country which had its own full service. In July 1942, Caernarfon Borough Council passed a motion demanding more Welsh-language programmes; it sent the resolution to other local authorities, and by October thirty-two of the councils of north Wales had supported it.[115] Earlier in the same year, Plaid Genedlaethol Cymru (or Plaid Cymru, as it was tending increasingly to call itself) organized a petition protesting about the paucity of Welsh-language programmes. Gwynfor Evans, who was to be president of the party from 1945 to

1981, declared: 'Y mae Cymru heddiw yn wynebu argyfwng tostaf ei hanes, ac mae'r radio, a allai fod yn gefn iddi, yn un o'i phrif elynion.'*[116] The petition of Plaid Cymru, wrote Nicolls to Graves, 'has been signed by some 15,000 people . . . I gather from WD that he is not disturbed by [it] . . . although of course, as a Welshman, he would naturally like to see more [programmes in Welsh]. I have agreed with him, by way of concession, to give a second half-hour religious service in Welsh each month.' The additional service was first broadcast in May 1942. 'Alas, more Welsh,' commented the director of programme planning. There was continuing criticism of the brevity of the fortnightly services. They presented, as *Y Cymro* put it, 'Yr Efengyl ar garlam gwyllt't;[117] they were 'rushed through', commented the *Caernarvon and Denbigh Herald*, 'as if they were an affliction on the ether'. As in 1940, there were those who saw the criticism as a comment on the long-windedness of Welsh preachers. A correspondent of *Y Cymro* quoted Thoreau: 'My stories are not long, but it took me a long time to make them short.'[118]

By 1942, the factors which had led to the institution of the single, unified Home Service were widely considered to be no longer valid. In October of that year, the *Western Mail* argued that the pre-war arrangements could be restored, for there had ceased to be a security risk. In England, the Midland and North regional directors used the same argument, asserting, wholly correctly, that in comparison with Wales and Scotland, their regions had suffered disproportionately. The English regions, however, lacked the energizing factor of a different language. That factor manifested itself again in February 1943, when the Ceiriog Rural District Council circularized a motion to the other Welsh local authorities demanding the restoration of the Welsh waveband. Machynlleth Rural District Council raised the matter with Clement Davies, who urged the Welsh Parliamentary Party to seek a meeting with Hopkin Morris. Lloyd George entered the discussions, stressing that he was still the chairman of the Welsh Religious Advisory Committee although the committee had not met since the outbreak of war. At a meeting with the Wales director held in April 1943, Hopkin Morris was able to assure Welsh MPs that henceforth the religious service in Welsh would last for forty-five minutes. He obviously considered that the service was the one essential part of broadcasting in Wales. In February 1944 he advised the Corporation to 'sacrifice [all other programmes] if this were the only means of maintaining the religious programmes in Welsh'. 'If it

---

*'Wales today is facing the severest crisis in her history, and radio, which could be a sustaining force, is one of her chief enemies.'

†'The gospel at a wild gallop'.

is not broadcast,' he stated, 'we will lose the support of moderate people in Wales.'[119]

The length of the Welsh service was one of the two issues raised in the meeting at the House of Commons in April 1943. The other was the use in English programmes of Welsh idioms and the Welsh accent. As has been seen, the matter had been ventilated in the 1920s and 1930s, but concern over the issue was much greater during the war, for then all English-language programmes with a Welsh content were heard throughout the United Kingdom. Sam Fairfechan of *ITMA* was particularly resented, but the idiom of characters from Eynon Evans's plays was also attacked. Evans felt obliged to defend himself. 'I don't use Look You or Indeed To Goodness,' he wrote, 'but I do use Sit You Down and Come You In. Why should we deny our peculiarities of speech? The critics' narrowness would impose restrictions on Anglo-Welsh writers unknown to the writers of any other dialect.'[120] In March 1943, Llantrisant Rural District Council circularized the local authorities, urging them to support a motion that the way the Welsh accent was portrayed on the radio was an insult to Wales. There was some substance to the complaint. David Raymond wrote in *Reynolds News* that accents were exaggerated in order to make English-language plays from Wales sound more genuinely Welsh, and similar criticisms were made by Gwyn Jones in *The Welsh Review*. Yet the item most vigorously attacked was one in which a 'valleys woman talked to her son on a Cairo programme'. The critics assumed that the item was staged, but in fact it was totally genuine. Hopkin Morris promised that in future broadcast accents and idioms would be toned down. The agitation continued after the war, causing Oldfield-Davies to write in January 1946: 'We shall be doing fewer Welsh domestic plays. This omission as far as it relates to plays in English has the advantage of lessening the amount of English spoken with a marked Welsh accent, which comes in for much criticism when broadcast.'[121]

All such worries faded as Britain's campaign moved to its victorious climax. The bulletins of the Welsh news unit became increasingly ebullient. On 23 August 1944, it announced: 'Rhyddhawyd Paris, cipiwyd Grenoble a meddianwyd Jassy. Dyna digon o newyddion cyffrous am un dydd.'*[122] Vaughan-Thomas's adventures were avidly followed. They reached their apogee when he broadcast from Lord Haw-Haw's studio in Hamburg, ruffling as he spoke through papers containing Joyce's comments on him and other British broadcasters. In the last years of the war, the emergency

---

*'Paris has been liberated, Grenoble has been captured and Jassy has been seized. That is enough exciting news for one day.'

arrangements adopted between 1939 and 1941 were gradually abandoned. In July 1942, Hopkin Morris was told that there was no further need for a formal Wales Invasion Committee; most of the variety staff had left Bangor by August 1943; the low power transmitters at Cardiff and Swansea – but not that at Wrexham – had been closed down by the end of 1943. The BBC Warbook at Cardiff, however, was not formally cancelled until 26 September 1945. In that month, there were still three pianos at Aberdare, but the studio there had been virtually closed. Thus the Corporation's only foray into the south Wales coalfield proved to be short-lived.[123]

As the certainty of victory became apparent, interest turned to the form broadcasting would take when hostilities were over. In May 1942, A. R. Burrows was instructed to prepare plans for post-war broadcasting. Almost all options were open, including the expansion or indeed the extinction of regional programmes. When the unified service had been introduced in September 1939, it was stressed that the governors were making no commitment that the regions would ever be restored. T. I. Ellis had requested a promise in 1940 that the Welsh Region would be reconstituted when peace returned, but his request was refused on the grounds that to accede to it would pre-empt arrangements concerning post-war broadcasting. There were at Head Office 'many who had no desire to return to the regional pattern of the 1930s'. On the other hand, Godfrey Adams, the deputy controller of programmes, felt that the Corporation should have a totally open mind and be ready to consider autonomous regions within, or even outside, the BBC. The one option that was excluded from discussion was the possibility of commercial radio; Haley was appalled to find that Robert Silvey had included a question on the matter in his public opinion survey of 1944. Brendan Bracken, the minister of information, floated the idea of a unified service consisting solely of contributions from the regions, but this was rejected on the grounds that such a service was bound to be organized from London and would therefore give only nominal power to the regions.[124]

The regional directors, who had been underemployed during the war, had had plenty of time to consider the future. Coatman brought forward a plan for a Control Board with a majority of its members consisting of regional directors; above all, he wrote, 'we must get away from the notion that the regions produce "kailyard" stuff only'. The senior regional director, Percy Edgar, who had been in charge at Birmingham since the beginning of broadcasting from the city in 1922, prepared a memorandum which was signed by all the regional directors. It protested against a return to the pre-war arrangements when London was a 'programme factory' and when the Corporation 'was [like] a monopoly publishing firm which writes most of its own books in the office'.[125]

In Wales, there were vigorous discussions on the future of post-war broadcasting. *Y Cymro*, which at the time represented the views of Welsh-language loyalists within the Labour Party, demanded at least the restoration of the service which had been available in 1939; it also pressed for new premises at Cardiff and for the establishment of a Welsh orchestra equal in size to those of the other regions. The Welsh MPs, noting that the Charter would expire at the end of 1946, urged that any new charter should make provision for a governor for Wales. Plaid Cymru and Undeb Cymru Fydd put the case for an entirely distinct service for Wales under its own corporation. The *Observer* poured scorn on the idea. 'It would bore the Welsh,' it wrote in September 1944. 'The twelve hours a day demanded by the separatists would cost a million pounds a year.'[126] W. J. Gruffydd, who had been elected Liberal MP for the University of Wales in a celebrated by-election in January 1943, devoted his maiden speech to broadcasting. 'No one will deny', he stated, 'that the BBC has its failings and we in Wales are very particularly conscious of those defects.' In common with many commentators, he noted that the strains of war had led to an increased interest in serious matters among the mass of the British population. Post-war radio, he argued, should build upon that interest. 'Light entertainment', he informed the House of Commons, '. . . regularly under-rates the mentality of the average Briton' – though, as Asa Briggs drily pointed out, 'Professor Gruffydd was hardly the best judge of light entertainment.'[127]

Head Office moved cautiously. In 1943, 60 per cent of the home audience listened to the Forces Service and 40 per cent to the Home Service. The Forces Service was combined with the General Overseas Service in 1944 and the ensuing General Forces Service proved less popular; it had 40 per cent of the home audience compared with 60 per cent for the Home Service. The success of the Forces Service, the likely revival after the war of Radio Luxembourg, or something similar to it, and the possibility that the Conservatives, when they won the post-war election (and that was what almost everybody assumed), would consider the introduction of commercial radio, were all factors which helped to convince Haley that the post-war arrangements would have to include a 'light' programme. Foot, in 1944, had suggested a tripartite service with a 'Light' programme, a 'Home' programme and a programme which would be the equivalent of 'a *Times* of the air'. It was predicted that the first would attract about 50 per cent of the audience, the second 40 per cent and the third 10 per cent. The scheme was accepted by the governors in

April 1944. It represented a major retreat from Reith's concept of public broadcasting.[128]

Haley came to the conclusion, without enthusiasm, that there would have to be a regional component in the tripartite scheme. The plan he adopted was that suggested by G. L. Marshall, the Northern Ireland director, who, for political and practical reasons, was the most ardent advocate among the regional directors of a Home Service containing the greatest possible general British input. Essentially the plan meant the restoration of the pre-war system, but with less emphasis upon requiring the regions to broadcast London programmes. Haley stressed that, apart from the obligation to transmit the London news bulletin, the regional directors would be 'free to do anything they liked', although that ability was rigidly controlled by the programme allowance over which London had almost total control. The creation of a Southern Region, which would also embrace the 'home counties', was discussed, but as it would cost £200,000 a year, and as there appeared to be no appreciable demand for it, the matter was not pursued. The governors and the Cabinet agreed to the merger of the West and Midland Regions, but a vigorous campaign at Bristol led to the abandonment of the plan. Thus, post-war regional broadcasting in the United Kingdom involved the restoration of the six regions which had existed in 1939.[129]

Haley was emphatic that priority should be given to the development of the Light Programme and the basic British element of the Home Service. The Corporation therefore ruled that the numbers employed in the regions should not be larger after the war than they had been in 1939. In January 1945, the ruling was accepted by Hopkin Morris, except where the Music Department was concerned; the same person, he maintained, should not be the head of the department and also the conductor of the orchestra. Haley insisted that, regardless of their duties at the regional centres, the regional directors should be closely involved with the work of Head Office. 'It is impossible', he wrote, 'for the general trend of developments to be understood if the regional directors only come to London for occasional meetings.' He laid down that they should in turn spend a month in London as regional director in residence; this meant that the Wales director would have to spend one month in every six at Head Office. Hopkin Morris was the only regional director to express his opposition to the scheme.[130]

The outline of the BBC's plans was revealed by Haley in a speech to the Radio Industries Fair in November 1944. He provided more details when he addressed the Cardiff Business Club on 15 March 1945. At Cardiff, he made it clear that the planned Home Service would not be a regional service, but rather a service 'capable of regionalisation' – a vital distinction. In addition, he promised that the new structure would be in place ninety days after the cessation of hostilities in Europe.[131]

Germany surrendered unconditionally on 9 May 1945. It was calculated that ninety days from that date would be the August Bank Holiday and therefore the inauguration was brought forward a week. On 29 July 1945, the Light Programme was launched as the direct successor of the General Forces Programme. On the same day, the Welsh Home Service began broadcasting on the 373-metre wavelength, the wavelength that had been used by the Welsh Region until September 1939; its first programme was a concert by the Dowlais Male Voice Choir. By then, Hopkin Morris had resigned as Wales director in order to stand as Liberal candidate at Carmarthen in the general election held on 5 July. Alun Oldfield-Davies, who since September 1944 had been the overseas establishment officer in London, became acting Wales director. He was appointed permanent Wales director on 15 June 1945.[132] Hopkin Morris won Carmarthen, which was the only Labour-held seat apart from Mile End (where a Communist was successful) lost by the Labour Party in the election of 1945. In August, a correspondent of the *South Wales Evening Post* saw the newly elected MP walking from his home at Cyncoed. 'He was smiling', he reported, 'which is a thing I've rarely seen him do since his appointment at Park Place.'[133]

4

From the End of the War to the
Beveridge Committee, 1945–1952

I The aftermath of war

The inauguration of the Welsh Home Service on 29 July 1945 was enthusiastically greeted. There was a particularly warm welcome for the Welsh edition of the *Radio Times*, the initial issue of which is dated 27 July. 'In the first week of the Welsh programme,' wrote the *Liverpool Daily Post*, 'there was much good listening.' Yet, as with all the regions, Wales suffered from the fact that many of its experienced staff had not yet been released from their wartime duties. With the present staffing problems, wrote the *Daily Herald*, it is 'doubtful if any area station can offer more than three or four hours a day'.[1] At first, Wales produced very much less. In July 1945, Oldfield-Davies announced that the aim was to produce nine hours a week for the Welsh Home Service and seventy-five minutes for the Light Programme, well under half the production of the late 1930s. He believed that the new service should concentrate in the first instance upon Welsh-language programmes in order that the language 'should recover ground lost during the war'.[2] By the first week of September the Welsh Home Service was broadcasting eight hours a week of its own programmes, 5.5 in Welsh and 2.5 in English. Despite the emphasis on Welsh, Oldfield-Davies was anxious that the service should not be too closely associated with the language, and in July 1945 he sought unsuccessfully to persuade the Corporation to adopt the title Wales Home Service rather than Welsh Home Service.[3] In parts of south-east Wales there were those who thought that the service had nothing to do with them. 'We do not want you to think of us as Welsh people or treat us as such,' Oldfield-Davies was told when he addressed a dinner at the Newport Mansion House in July 1945.[4] On the other hand, in Wrexham, where the low-power transmitter had been closed down at the end of the

1. Mostyn Thomas singing at Castle Street on the opening night of the Cardiff Station, 13 February 1923. (*All illustrations by permission of BBC Cymru Wales.*)

2. The Cardiff Station Orchestra in 1923.

3. *Children's Hour* at Cardiff in the mid 1920s with Auntie Bettie (Elizabeth Grimwood), Uncle Norman (Norman Settle, the station's executive officer) and Uncle Felix (E. R. Appleton, the station director).

5. An advertisement in the *South Wales Daily Post* on 12 December 1924, the day of the opening of the Swansea Relay Station.

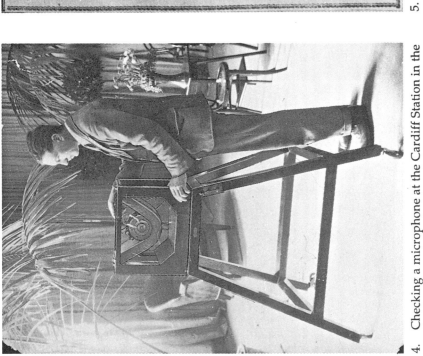

4. Checking a microphone at the Cardiff Station in the mid 1920s.

6. Two members of the Women's Institute – Mabel Russell and Rosina Buckman – taking part in a programme at Cardiff in 1928.

7. The Park Place studios and staff in 1938.

8. Ernest Robert Appleton, Cardiff station director, 1924–1929; West Regional director, 1929–1935; director of the Welsh and the West of England Regions, 1935–1936.

9. Rhys Hopkin Morris, Welsh Regional director, 1936–1939; Welsh director, 1939–1945.

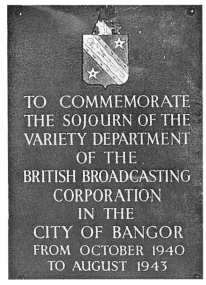

10. The plaque at Bryn Meirion in Bangor presented by the City of Bangor to the BBC.

11. Gunstone Jones and Clydach Thomas taking part in *Sut Hwyl?* in 1942.

12. Sam Jones and the members of 'Triawd y Coleg' discussing songs for *Noson Lawen* in the late 1940s.

13. The children of Cae Top School, Bangor, rehearsing *Wil Six* in 1948. The producer, P. H. Burton, points to the microphone.

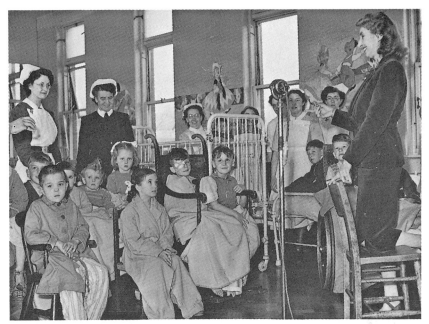

14. Mai Jones recording her programme *Silver Chords* at the Royal Gwent Hospital, Newport, in the early 1950s.

15. A discussion programme at Swansea in the early 1950s. From left to right, G. O. Williams (later the archbishop of Wales), Saunders Lewis, Brinley Thomas and Aneirin Talfan Davies.

16. Alun Williams visiting the Air Sea Rescue Centre at Barry in July 1953, one of the first televised outside broadcasts from Wales.

17. A sketch from *Welsh Rarebit* in 1956; 'The Adventures of Tommy Trouble', featuring Gwenyth Petty, E. Eynon Evans, George David, Tudor Walters and Wyn Calvin.

war, there were demands that it should be reopened to relay the Welsh Home Service. Wrexham also sought a studio linked with Cardiff, while Aberystwyth, which had lost its studio in September 1939, was anxious to see its restitution.

The paucity of the Wales output became a matter of increasing protest. 'No one can truthfully say', wrote the *Caernarvon and Denbigh Herald*, 'that the return of the BBC regional system has opened a new era in Welsh broadcasting . . . Nothing less than a daylong Welsh programme will suffice.' In November 1945, when the 373 wavelength's Wales transmissions were still not exceeding eight hours a week, Emrys Roberts (Liberal, Meirionnydd) raised the issue in the House of Commons.[5] The paucity of programmes was not the only cause of criticism. Welsh-language features – among them *Munudau gyda'r Beirdd*, *Cornel y Llenor*, and *Y Silff Lyfrau* – were attacked as too literary, while discussion programmes were considered to depend excessively on academics. 'The Welsh University', wrote a correspondent in the *Liverpool Daily Post*, 'is not the only facet of our national life.' Programmes in general were attacked for dwelling too much on the past. '[Give us] more of the Wales of today and tomorrow,' wrote David Raymond; 'a little less of Trefecca and a little more of Trealaw.' In the north there were complaints that the Wales output gave the impression that 'everyone in Wales is a collier'.[6]

The whole schedule was perceived to be too rigid, and those responsible for it resentful of outside comment. 'It is the uniqueness of the Welsh Region', wrote Gwyn Jones, himself a distinguished broadcaster, 'to be above criticism . . . [The Region displays an] almost studied lack of zest and vitality [and a] tired pursuit of the ordinary.' The maverick littérateur, Keidrych Rhys, was far more critical. 'Congregations of preachers', he wrote to Barbara Ward, a BBC governor, 'are always intruding their black-coated selves into studios filled with their pompous uncreative sons and daughters . . . and always talking against everything new, good and creative.' Rhys attacked 'Mr R. Hopkin Morris KC MP . . . with his nasty legal stipendiary mind' and declared that he was 'tired of the new Director stumping the country like his predecessor, defending his weak outfit against all criticism'. Ward sent the letter to Haley. Haley sent it to Oldfield-Davies who wrote: 'It is rather difficult to know what Rhys is driving at. He writes toadying letters to our talks producers.'[7]

Matters improved in 1946. By then, most of the Welsh staff who had been otherwise engaged during the war had returned to their posts with the BBC in Wales. The news unit moved from London to Cardiff on 22 January 1946, and news in Welsh from 6.30 to 6.40

became the one fixed daily broadcast in Wales's output.[8] (Initially, Welsh news in English was only broadcast twice a week.) New appointments were made. P. H. Burton became a full-time BBC employee in 1945 and his protégé, Richard Burton, soon became closely involved in Cardiff's broadcasts. Wales received its first full-time religious broadcasting organizer; he was Glyn Parry-Jones, a much respected Calvinistic Methodist minister. His appointment allowed Edgar Jones, who had been organizing religious broadcasts on a part-time basis since July 1931, to go into honourable retirement. Nest Bradney (née Jenkins) joined the staff at Head Office in 1945 where she became responsible for launching *Women's Hour*; she was replaced as public relations officer by Tom Richards, an experienced *Western Mail* reporter.[9] T. Rowland Hughes, whose multiple sclerosis was worsening, resigned in April 1945. The tradition he established of producing ambitious feature programmes was continued in English by P. H. Burton and in Welsh by Aneirin Talfan Davies. In September 1946, Alun Williams, the son of a Calvinistic Methodist minister from Llandeilo, became outside broadcasts organizer; Williams won immediate popularity, and, in subsequent decades, he became to the public the virtual embodiment of the BBC in Wales. The Schools Department was markedly expanded; among the appointees were the historians, A. J. Roderick and A. H. Williams, and also Haydn Davies, Sam Jones's rival in 1932 for the post of Welsh programmes assistant.

The increase in staff led to an increase in programme hours. By August 1946, Wales was producing 20.5 hours a week for the Home Service, 19 hours exclusively for Wales and 1.5 hours for the basic service; of the 19 hours, 10.5 were in English and 9.5 in Welsh. By then, Wales's output was only exceeded by that of the North (22.25 hours) and Scotland (20.75 hours). They contributed 3.25 hours apiece to the basic service, but as up to half Wales's productions were in Welsh and therefore unsuitable for transmission outside Wales, the proportion of the relevant output taken by the basic Home Service from Wales was marginally higher than it was from the North and from Scotland. In addition, Wales contributed up to an hour a week to the Light Programme and occasional items to the Overseas and the European Services.

The Wales output was produced with fewer resources than those available to the other regions. In August 1946, Wales had 29 monthly-paid staff, compared with 43 in Scotland and 41 in the North; its programme allowance was £800 a week while Scotland, the North and the Midlands received £1,250 apiece. John Salt, the North's programme director, argued that a region's programme allowance should be based upon the number of licence-holders within the region. By 1950, there were 600,234 licences in force in Wales compared with 3,667,744 in the North, 1,804,423 in the Midlands and 1,120,968 in Scotland; thus the BBC could claim that it was treating Wales generously.[10]

The Wales allowance was increased to £1,200 in 1947 and to £1,500 in 1949. By 1949, the BBC in Wales had 71 monthly-paid employees, compared with 95 each in Scotland and the North of England and 1,278 in London. 'In each of the "national regions" ', wrote Head Office in 1950, 'the proportion of BBC staff to the population is higher than in any of the English regions.'[11] Gwyn Jones thought the Corporation was guilty of special pleading. The main task of the new director, he wrote in 1945, is 'to stand up to London and, if necessary, make himself thoroughly unpleasant to them there, by demanding more money for his Region and more good listening time'.[12] Oldfield-Davies, a profoundly prudential man whose first concern was the well-being of the Corporation as a whole, disagreed. In 1946 he stated that 'the spending of money will not in itself improve Welsh programmes', and in the same year he authorized Haley to tell the Welsh MPs that 'he had not so far felt any pinch'. In July 1949, he successfully resisted the director-general's attempt to increase the fees paid to contributors to Welsh schools programmes, and in November he informed an audience in Denbigh that 'people in Northern England are asking why they should subsidize the Welsh Home Service'. 'We in Wales', he informed Gwilym Lloyd George in 1950, 'receive . . . an adequate allowance of money to spend on programmes . . . and to be frank, our main problem is to find programmes which are really worth spending money on.'[13]

By the late 1940s, one of the largest single elements in the Corporation's expenditure in Wales was the maintenance of the reconstituted BBC Welsh Orchestra. The disbanding of Cardiff's twenty-member orchestra in September 1939 had been much resented, particularly in view of the fact that those at Birmingham, Manchester and Glasgow continued in existence throughout the war. Adrian Boult, the conductor of the BBC Symphony Orchestra, had taken his orchestra on tour in Wales in February 1943 and had been much impressed by the huge enthusiasm shown by audiences in places such as Treorci and Aberdare. He wrote to the *Western Mail* in October 1943 warmly advocating the creation of an orchestra for Wales.[14] The war years saw a marked growth in interest in serious music. There was a temporary decline in the influence of the members of the Musicians' Union, the fervent opponents of the broadcast of gramophone records ('needle time'). That factor, together with improvements in recording techniques, led to a very considerable increase in the transmission of recorded music; records constituted 40 per cent of the serious music broadcast in 1944, compared with 6 per cent in 1942. The BBC, however, considered that heavy reliance upon records was a feature of the despised American broadcasting system; in 1948, it decreed that no region should broadcast recorded music for more than fifty minutes a week, a decision with which Oldfield-Davies strongly concurred.[15]

Within the Corporation, there was general agreement that pre-war orchestras should be reconstituted. 'There is a moral obligation on us', wrote Nicolls in July 1945, 'to re-form the pre-war Welsh studio orchestra of twenty players.' He was reluctant to increase the number beyond twenty or to give the matter any priority. The situation was complicated by the existence of a committee which was seeking to establish a national Welsh symphony orchestra. Established in November 1944, its members estimated that a 30-player orchestra would cost £35,500 a year. Sales of tickets might produce £18,350; if local authorities contributed £10,000, and if patrons, season-ticket holders and cultural associations subscribed a further £10,000, a national orchestra would be feasible even without the involvement of the BBC. That was Oldfield-Davies's preferred solution, and he was attacked in the press for seeming unenthusiastic about any BBC initiatives.[16]

The situation changed with the establishment of the Arts Council in June 1945. Lord Harlech, the chairman of the Council's Welsh Advisory Committee, suggested to the Corporation a jointly funded orchestra for Wales. The matter was agreed in principle in October 1945 when the Corporation and the Council stated that they were seeking the creation of a 31-member orchestra. No immediate action was taken. Although Nicolls acknowledged in January 1946 that there was 'a local and political need' to establish a Welsh orchestra, he did not consider that the need had to be urgently addressed. In April 1946, Cardiganshire's Music Committee circularized similar bodies throughout Wales asking them to protest against the delay in creating a Welsh orchestra. Many of them did so. 'I am getting tired of this constant stream of protest about the BBC Welsh orchestra,' wrote Haley to Oldfield-Davies in May 1946. 'If we do eventually decide to reinstate it, [it] will look as if we have merely bowed to this engineered storm.' Oldfield-Davies was in something of a quandary. 'What is happening?' he asked Lord Harlech in May 1946. 'We are telling Cardiganshire that we are waiting for you.' In June, Harlech answered stating that the Arts Council's scheme was 'a very long-range project', and urging the BBC 'at present' to proceed alone. Nothing came of the Arts Council's plans, largely because Huw Wheldon, the Council's organizer in Wales, refused to accept the £20,000 offered by the Arts Council centrally because he believed that 'a permanent orchestra would create a monster, always hungry for money'. The BBC decided on 5 July 1946 to advertise for instrumentalists and contracts were issued to the players in October. Mansel Thomas was appointed conductor and the Welsh orchestra of thirty-one players gave its first performance on 5 November 1946. Long after Wheldon had left Cardiff, the notion of BBC co-operation with the Arts Council was successfully revived, and the joint patronage of music-making in Wales by the two bodies was eventually to provide a model which other parts of the United Kingdom would view with envy.[17]

The year 1946 also saw the preparation of plans to establish the BBC Welsh Chorus, plans successfully carried out in 1947. In addition, applications were invited for membership of the Welsh Home Service's Repertory Company of full-time actors. (Before the war, Wales had relied upon the services of part-time actors, such as the highly popular Phillips brothers, the one a Cardiff accountant and the other a Cardiff solicitor.) A total of 220 applications was received, but only three appointments were made. This was largely the consequence of the fact that the BBC sought actors able to perform equally competently in both Welsh and English. Admirable Welsh-language actors were rejected because they sounded unconvincing in English, and the reverse problem arose with admirable English-language actors. Oldfield-Davies reluctantly came to the conclusion that the Repertory Company would have to contain three categories: those totally bilingual, those performing exclusively in English, and those performing almost exclusively in Welsh. By the end of 1946, the Repertory Company had seventeen members; of the eight in the 'largely Welsh' category, three were natives of the Rhondda.[18]

While these developments were occurring, the future of the BBC itself was under discussion. The Charter which had come into operation on 1 January 1937 was due to expire on 31 December 1946. Winston Churchill – never a friend of the BBC – was loud in his demands that there should be no renewal without an exhaustive inquiry, and in Wales he had a vocal supporter in Lady Megan Lloyd George.[19] T. I. Ellis of Undeb Cymru Fydd and Gwynfor Evans of Plaid Cymru also demanded an inquiry, seeing it as an opportunity to put forward their case for an independent corporation for Wales. In Scotland, similar demands were being made by the Church of Scotland and the Saltire Society.

In September 1945, Gwynfor Evans published a pamphlet, *Broadcasting in Wales*, which made much of the ability of Denmark, New Zealand and the Irish Free State to run a full service on revenue less than that contributed by Wales to the BBC. Early in 1946, Undeb Cymru Fydd circularized the Welsh local authorities, seeking their support. Of the thirteen county councils in Wales, five voted in favour of the establishment of a Welsh corporation, a demand which was also endorsed by fifty of the smaller councils. A similar motion was distributed to the local authorities of north Wales by the Caernarfon Borough Council; it was endorsed by three county councils and thirty-five lesser councils. The National Eisteddfod Court was strongly in favour of a corporation for Wales, and it dispatched the academic lawyer, David Hughes-Parry, to discuss the matter with the Welsh MPs. The radio correspondent of the *Liverpool Daily Post* considered the declarations of support to be 'surprisingly encouraging'. 'The bogey of "continuous service" must finally be laid,' he wrote. 'Wales never has, and probably never will, ask for a continuous programme of its own from seven o'clock in the morning until midnight. But we do ask for a continuous evening service of our own.' If fewer resources would in consequence be available, 'it would be open to us', he argued, 'to cut our garment according to our cloth'. A corporation for Wales had considerable support among the Welsh MPs. Several successful Labour candidates had demanded such a corporation in their election manifestos. Emrys Roberts, Liberal MP for Meirionnydd, was active in the House of Commons seeking to discover the precise cost of the BBC's operations in Wales. His fellow Liberal, Rhys Hopkin Morris, poured scorn on the notion of a Welsh corporation, but his efforts were largely negated by the effective way in which T. I. Ellis presented the Undeb Cymru Fydd case to the Welsh Parliamentary Party.[20]

Oldfield-Davies, whose loyalty to the British Corporation was absolute, was deeply concerned. In February 1946, he was invited by John Cecil-Williams, the secretary of the Honourable Society of Cymmrodorion, to advise the society on the matter, 'purely as a member of the Cymmrodorion's Council'. He was glad of the opportunity. 'The Council of the Cymmrodorion', he informed Cecil Williams, 'has done well to pause and consider . . . I take this opportunity to state my views privately . . . The chief limiting factor is not money but the cultural resources of Wales itself . . . Would the Welsh Corporation broadcast BBC programmes? If so, they would have to pay for them. If it [sought to] give a comparable service, it would be bankrupt in a month, culturally as well as financially.'[21] Oldfield-Davies accompanied Haley to a meeting with the Welsh MPs in June 1945 when the director-general stated that 'there is not enough talent in Wales to sustain a full continuous programme'. His comments aroused widespread criticism. 'What nonsense,' retorted Cynan; 'the BBC should devise means of [exploiting the available talent] instead of confining itself to a small pool of actors within cheap rail and bus fares of the Cardiff radio.'[22]

Oldfield-Davies sent the Undeb Cymru Fydd circular to Haley. 'The comparisons with Denmark, Eire and New Zealand', wrote the deeply conservative Haley, 'are completely fallacious. Problems of copyright etc. have not arisen in some of those countries. They would certainly arise in Wales which would be bound to fall in with the practices which, for good or ill, have been agreed to throughout the years by the BBC.' He then indulged in the obligatory offensive remarks about Irish radio. 'If Wales really wants its broadcasting to be compared with Eire, then all I can say is that it is far from the aspiring nation that I have always believed it to be.' He informed Oldfield-Davies: 'Your duty is to make clear that you really are master of your programmes.'[23]

Head Office's constant insistence that the regions were, to all intents and purposes, autonomous was somewhat disingenuous. Within a few months of Haley's letter, the regions sought to pool their resources in order to broadcast one regional play a week. Head Office saw the plan as a conspiracy. 'Regional Directors', wrote Nicolls, 'are permitted to hold a meeting to discuss matters of mutual interest, but with a strong warning against it becoming a hole and corner affair of a cabal.' For regions to plan such plays, wrote Howgill, the acting controller (entertainment), shows 'complete disregard of the Head of the Drama Department's responsibility for the artistic and professional standards of the dramatic output throughout the Corporation.' That regional directors should agree to take each other's programmes without reference to Head Office, wrote Haley 'cannot be said to be exercising judgment', for they were deciding to take a programme 'in advance of knowing what alternative was available [from London]'.[24]

In other areas, also, the autonomy of the regions was severely restricted. Although Oldfield-Davies and Watkin Jones had virtually full discretion in the way they spent their programme allowance, they were totally at London's mercy where any other expenditure was concerned. In 1946, when Oldfield-Davies wished to spend £4.16s. to give a dinner to the West Wales Singers on the occasion of their four-hundredth broadcast, considerable correspondence with London was necessary. There was even more paperwork in 1949 when Watkin Jones went in search of programme material in Ireland; Head Office examined his proposed expenditure rigorously and raised several questions about the cash fund of £31.2s.4d. with which he intended to pay contributors. Capital expenditure in the regions was a matter for Head Office. This rule was slightly relaxed in the late 1940s when the regions were permitted to spend between £5,000 and £10,000 a year on repairs and renovations without reference to London. The heads of the regions, who from 1948 were styled controllers rather than directors, were effusive in their thanks. They informed Haley: 'The Regional Controllers greatly appreciate this proposed delegation of responsibility and the confidence it implies. They hope to prove themselves worthy of it.'[25]

The limitation upon the authority of regional directors was even more marked where the engineers were concerned. They were all London appointments, causing Oldfield-Davies in 1948 to criticize Head Office's failure 'to regard engineers as an essential part of the regional team'. They were allocated to the regions in accordance with the Corporation's convenience, and Welsh engineers working in Wales were rare, especially at the more responsible levels. Tension could arise over the involvement of monoglot English-speaking engineers in the production of Welsh-language programmes, but the overall impression is of a body of men committed to the success of the Welsh Home Service; Sam Hett, who was engineer-in-chief at Bangor from 1935 to 1961, was particularly highly regarded.[26] A greater source of tension was London's insistence that its staff could make programmes in any part of the United Kingdom without reference to the region concerned. 'We [London]', wrote Head Office's director of features in 1946, 'have an unrestricted right to any subject anywhere in the British Isles.' Head Office made several programmes in Wales which betrayed ignorance of Welsh matters. 'Consult us first,' pleaded Watkin Jones, 'for our listeners in Wales hold us in Cardiff responsible for Welsh topics.'[27]

The greatest source of discontent, however, was the substantial differential between London salary scales and those in the regions. In 1945, A1 posts were held by Watkin Jones, the programme director, and Sam Jones, the north Wales representative. Oldfield-Davies argued that others – Elwyn Evans and Talfan Davies among them – should be raised to something similar to the scales generously handed out in London. He was loftily rebuffed. 'Regional producers', noted Head Office, 'say they have a harder job because of the greater range of subjects with which they have to deal, [but] a regional producer carries less responsibility than a similar producer at HQ because the latter has a far greater audience . . . and is expected to achieve a higher standard of excellence because the results of his work are appreciated more widely.'[28]

Despite the very real restrictions upon his much vaunted autonomy, Oldfield-Davies wanted no substantive change in the constitutional relationship between the centre and the regions. 'Our task', he wrote in February 1946, 'is to make the best of the freedom that we enjoy rather than to seek the appearance of complete independence without substance.'[29] In June of that year, Frederick Ogilvie, still smarting from his virtual dismissal in 1942, entered the fray. In a letter to *The Times*, he attacked the whole concept of the BBC's monopoly and gave the impression that he was in favour of full autonomy for Wales and Scotland.[30] Ogilvie was not alone in attacking the Corporation's monopoly. In March 1946, Gwynfor Evans declared: 'Ni ddylai'r BBC barhau fel monopoli.'[*31] In the following month, Peter Eckersley wrote to *The Times* alleging that 'only a small minority want the monopoly renewed', an argument supported by Keidrych Rhys in the same newspaper. While Gwyn Jones did not directly attack the monopoly, criticism of it is implied in his comment: '[Writers are] in the position of peasants who must bring their goods to the lord's market and sell or be refused to sell on the lord's terms.'[32]

In 1946, however, attempts to change fundamentally the constitutional position of the Corporation were unlikely to succeed. The prestige of the BBC was very high, with tributes pouring in from war-exhausted Europe. The Corporation was considered to be the world's model of an impartial truth-telling institution.[33] Furthermore, a Labour government was in power, intent upon placing major industries and utilities under the control of state-sponsored boards and corporations. 'I heard', wrote Harman Grisewood, the controller of the Third Programme, 'Lord Simon [the chairman of the Board of Governors from 1947 to 1952] more than once saying that the BBC was a good example of socialism. Further nationalised monopolies could, he said, learn much from the BBC and he hoped that they would.'[34] The government's White Paper of June 1946 proposed the renewal of the Charter for five years. In 1927 and 1937, the Corporation had been granted ten-year charters, on both occasions after an inquiry had been held. There was to be no inquiry in 1946, for it was widely felt that to subject the BBC to minute scrutiny in the unsettled conditions which prevailed after the war would be injudicious.

In addition to proposing that the Corporation should have a further five years of existence, the White Paper of 1946 recommended that the licence fee be doubled to one pound. This was a reasonable step, for the years 1939 to 1946 had seen an inflation rate of 95 per cent. Furthermore, it laid down that general issues relating to broadcasting would henceforth be the responsibility of the lord president of the Council, thus ensuring – as Reith had wished in the 1920s – that the BBC would be answerable to a minister of Cabinet rank.[35] Of all the postmasters-general since the beginning of British broadcasting, Vernon Hartshorn was the only one to become a member of the Cabinet on his appointment. (Kingsley Wood joined

---

*'The BBC should not continue as a monopoly.'

the Cabinet for part of his postmastership.) Engineering matters, however, remained under the control of the postmaster-general (and his successor in 1969, the minister for posts and telecommunications) until 1974, when the Post Office became a corporation. The White Paper was debated and approved by the House of Commons in July 1946. One of the most forthright speakers was Lady Megan Lloyd George. She wanted broadcasting to be 'an effective instrument for democracy . . . [with] hard-hitting discussions on issues when they were red-hot. The [present] attitude is inhibited, panicky and jittery.' She also demanded that 'whenever an enquiry is set up, the question of a Welsh corporation shall be on the agenda.'[36]

The White Paper's provisions included approval of the BBC's plans concerning television. The matter had been considered by the Hankey Committee, set up in September 1943. Its report, published in March 1945, recommended the re-establishment of a television service in London and its extension to six other populous centres. The matter did not arouse a great deal of interest; *The Times*, for example, only devoted half a column to the committee's report. The London service was re-inaugurated on 7 June 1946 with the same Mickey Mouse cartoon as had been shown immediately before close-down on 1 September 1939.[37] With the cheapest television set costing £70, the equivalent of more than ten times the average weekly wage, few foresaw its eventual popularity. It was attacked by the left as the toy of the rich, while those beyond the reach of London's trans-missions were resentful of the fact that part of the money paid by radio-licence holders throughout the United Kingdom was being spent to provide a service exclusively for the English 'home counties'. Haley was sensitive to such criticism. 'In any BBC publicity', he noted in November 1946, 'it is bad policy to exhibit television photographs in regions which have no hope of receiving television programmes for some years.'[38]

Most of the BBC's senior officials lacked affection for television; it was, argued Haley, a medium which produced passivity. In 1944, he had stated that if television were to be reintroduced, he would not have a set in the house, and he informed a group of senior television staff that 'if you were to do your work properly, people would be watching less not more'. The BBC's television unit was housed in the rat-infested Alexandra Palace; its head was not a member of the Corporation's six-member Board of Management and there was a strong reluctance to allow him adequate funding.[39] Nevertheless, as the London service developed, there was a groundswell of enthusiasm for the new medium. The Aberdare Little Theatre won the British Drama League Cup in 1948 with J. O. Francis's *Birds of a Feather*. The performance was filmed and broadcast from London's transmitter at Alexandra Palace. Emlyn Evans of Aberdare, who was involved in the filming, was enormously impressed. 'One sight of television, even in its present state of imperfection', he stated, 'convinces one that radio is, comparatively, only a minor miracle.'[40]

The White Paper of June 1946 tacitly endorsed the cultural, and indeed the class, assumptions underlying the division between the Home Service and the Light Programme. Those assumptions became more marked with the launching on 29 September 1946 of the Third Programme, '*The Times* of the air' promised in the later years of the war. Rose Macaulay, who had spent her adolescent years at Llanilar near Aberystwyth, was delighted with the new service. Among its productions in its first week was Sartre's *Huis Clos*. 'I hear', she wrote, 'that quite simple people, sitting in the provinces, say they and their maids found it most enjoyable.'[41] Perhaps Sartre's drama of the living dead proved to be too much, for the hope, expressed in 1944, that a highbrow service would attract 10 per cent of listeners was not achieved. In 1947, the percentages of the audience in Britain as a whole listening to the Light, Home and Third Programmes were 53, 40 and 7. By then, the Third's transmitter had been reduced in power because a station in Latvia and Radio Tunis were using the same wavelength; as a result, its broadcasts could be received by no more than 75 per cent of the inhabitants of the United Kingdom.[42]

In Wales, reception was especially poor; only 46 per cent of Welsh households could hear the Third Programme satisfactorily, and its inaudibility in the university towns of Swansea, Aberystwyth and Bangor was particularly criticized. By the late 1940s, its audience had declined to 1 per cent of the listening public. The Third Programme's regular clientele of about a hundred thousand was considerably smaller than the number who made a habit of listening to Welsh-language programmes, a point seized upon by those seeking a fuller Welsh service. In 1947, Haley prophesied that 'in a few years time, the Light Programme will be where the Home Service is now, and the Home will have passed on to other standards' – presumably those of the Third Programme.[43] This did not happen; in fact, a reverse process occurred. Programmes such as *Woman's Hour*, *The Archers* and *Round Britain Quiz*, regarded in the 1990s as staple Home Service (or by then Radio Four) fare, were, in the 1940s and 1950s, broadcast on the Light Programme; they were, however, considered too demanding for Radio Two, the Light's successor. The programmes of Radio One, Britain's most popular service in the 1990s, would, in the 1940s, have been considered by the BBC's officials as unworthy of broadcasting time. It would be kinder not to mention what has happened to the Third Programme. As Robert Silvey put it: 'The BBC wanted evidence that broadcasting was widening public cultural interests. Successive enquiries . . . provided no convincing evidence that this hope was being fulfilled.'[44]

II   The Welsh Advisory Council and its concerns

Among the recommendations of the White Paper of June 1946 was that each region should have an advisory committee appointed by the governors. Wales was to have a council of twenty-one, and in the summer of 1946 Oldfield-Davies gave careful consideration to the drawing up of a representative list of possible members. On 6 September, he sent twenty-four names to Haley. He felt the need to justify the inclusion of some of them; Robert Lloyd ('Llwyd o'r Bryn'), for example, he described as 'the finest type of Welsh peasant'. Nicolls scrutinized the list in detail. 'It would be preferable', he told Haley, 'to have Gwilym Lloyd George [rather than] Megan, as he is more solid and reliable and less apt to make debating points.' The twenty-one members selected by the governors did not include either of the Lloyd Georges; all of them, however, were chosen from Oldfield-Davies's list.[45] T. H. Parry-Williams, the professor of Welsh at Aberystwyth, was appointed chairman, a position which carried with it membership of the BBC's Central Advisory Council. Of the twenty-one, ten were Welsh-speaking. About half the members were Labour activists or considered to be Labour supporters; this was an under-representation in view of the voting habits of the Welsh elect-orate, but the governors queried whether the Council was 'overweighted to Labour'. At the first meeting, held on 13 February 1947, lots were cast to ensure that five of the members would with-draw each year; Gwynfor Evans and Gwilym Davies were among those who were granted only a year's membership.[46]

During its five-year existence (February 1947 to October 1952), the Council met on twenty-five occasions – twenty-three regular quart-erly meetings and two special sessions. Nineteen meetings were held at Cardiff's Park Hotel, three at Bangor, two at Swansea and one at Shrewsbury. Oldfield-Davies and a member of Head Office's management team were in attendance, and most of the members of the Council were content to take their lead from the BBC's officials. The Council had no executive powers and there were complaints that its submissions were ignored by the Corporation.[47] Yet Oldfield-Davies and the Head Office representatives were scrupulous in investigating the matters raised by its members.

Chief among them were the demands for more broadcasts in the Welsh language. Council members were also concerned with the pronunciation of Welsh place-names and with the standard of Welsh used by broadcasters. They requested that 'Hen Wlad fy Nhadau' should be broadcast at close-down and that a Welsh version of *The Listener* should be published. The quality of reception in mid Wales was regularly discussed, as was the expansion of the staff in general and of the orchestra in particular. The shortcomings of the premises at Cardiff were constantly stressed and much was said about the need to rebuild the Swansea studios, to relocate the BBC's operations at Bangor and to provide studios at Wrexham, Aberystwyth, Carmarthen, Monmouth and elsewhere. Its members also expressed concern about allegations of political bias in the Welsh news and argued in favour of party political broadcasts exclusively for Wales. By mid century, with television available in the English Midlands, and shortly to be available in the north of England, its extension to Wales was prominent among the Council's demands. There were requests for the BBC to reveal the total cost of its operations in Wales, a matter which gained increasing importance as the Council came to consider the evidence it would submit to the committee of inquiry (the Beveridge Committee) which began its deliberations in June 1949; the form that evidence would take absorbed much of the energies of the Council in the last two years of its existence.

Pressure for more broadcasts in Welsh came in particular from the Plaid Cymru supporters on the Council, among them Gwynfor Evans, Mrs Morris Williams (Kate Roberts), Enid Parry and Wynne Samuel. They could look to other members of the Council for support; indeed, the most ardent advocate of more Welsh was William Williams, a Labour Party activist from Blaenau Ffestiniog.[48] Although fluent Welsh-speakers were not initially a majority on the Council, those members lacking a knowledge of Welsh acquiesced in the abandonment of the unwritten rule that half the time allotted to spoken-word programmes produced for exclusive transmission in Wales should be in Welsh and half in English. In the first quarter of 1948, the Welsh Home Service broadcast an average of twenty hours a week of its own productions; there were four hours of musical programmes – mainly introduced in English – and sixteen hours devoted to the spoken word, 60 per cent in Welsh and 40 per cent in English. Oldfield-Davies informed Nicolls that the differential had arisen because the provision in Welsh of news and of programmes for schools was greater than it was in English. Furthermore, he stated, the policy had been approved by the Advisory Council. Haley was displeased. 'When', he asked, 'was the half and half policy abandoned? The validity of the Welsh Regional Advisory Council's approval in this matter surely depends upon an examination of the balance of its membership.'[49] In 1945, complaints concerning too little Welsh were as numerous as those concerning too much Welsh. By

1948, this had ceased to be the case, and Haley drew attention to the fact that 'the volume of English complaint against the amount of Welsh content is greater than the reverse'.[50] The radio correspondent of the *South Wales Echo* argued that the dissatisfaction arose, not because of too much Welsh, but because the total amount of time allotted to programmes produced in Wales was insufficient. 'Let me say immediately', he wrote in January 1949, 'that the Welsh-speaking population is entitled to its present ration. They have no alternative choice. But the output in English is inadequate. There should be at least six hours a day of regional programmes.'[51] Others did not see the matter in those terms. In December 1949, R. G. G. Weekes, a Monmouthshire member of the Advisory Council, resigned in order to make way for 'someone with more time at their disposal [to] represent the dissatisfaction which many people in Monmouthshire feel with the Regional Service which they now receive'. In January 1950, the *South Wales Evening Post*, edited by D. H. I. Powell, a member of the Advisory Council, noted that there 'is an increasing agitation among the Anglo-Welsh concerning the number of programmes in Welsh. [Because of the Welsh programmes] many are turning to other regions. [This] is accelerating the disintegration of our people.'[52]

Yet the number of hours in Welsh, even at the 60 per cent formula of the late 1940s, hardly amounted to more than eighty minutes a day, little enough, particularly in view of the fact, as the *Manchester Guardian* put it, that, where broadcasts in Welsh were concerned, 'the whole world must be the province of the BBC, for Welsh programmes must provide elements corresponding to the level and the subjects of all three British services'.[53] Those who were totally dependent for their listening upon the eighty minutes a day were more numerous than official statistics suggest. The Census of 1951 revealed that 41,155 of the inhabitants of Wales had no knowledge of English, but anyone with memories of form-filling in Welsh-speaking Wales on the occasion of that Census will be aware that the figure should in fact have been considerably higher. In the spring of 1951, a smallholder in mid Cardiganshire, who had recently declared herself to be bilingual, acquired her first wireless set. She proudly showed it to a young neighbour. 'Fe gewch chi glywed 'e am hanner awr wedi chwech', she said, 'pan fydd y newyddion ymlaen.' It was six o'clock. 'Mae 'na newyddion ymlaen nawr', said the pushy young neighbour. 'Na,' she answered; 'rhywbeth yn Saesneg sydd ymlaen am chwech o'r gloch.'*

While the Census underestimated the number of Welsh monoglots, it provided no adequate guidance concerning the number capable of

---

*'You will be able to hear it at half past six when the news will be on.' 'There is news on now.' 'No, something in English is on at six o'clock.'

understanding programmes in Welsh. The most recent figures available in the late 1940s were those of the Census of 1931, according to which 36.8 per cent of the inhabitants of Wales could speak Welsh. Oldfield-Davies was convinced that a further 10 to 12 per cent had a sufficient understanding of the language to allow them to follow programmes in Welsh. He was undoubtedly correct, for recent surveys have shown that large numbers of people with some grasp of Welsh are inhibited from revealing the fact because of the official nature of the Census. In the late 1940s, audience research indicated that the proportion of the inhabitants of Wales listening to the more popular Welsh-language programmes could exceed the proportion claiming a knowledge of Welsh. Oldfield-Davies requested Huw T. Edwards, the chairman of the Council of Wales, to urge the Census authorities to include among the questions relating to the Welsh language one enquiring about the ability to understand it. Edwards refused on the grounds that such a question could 'depress the numbers stating that they spoke it'. Oldfield-Davies was also concerned about the hundreds of thousands of people in England capable of following Welsh-language programmes, and he suggested to Edwards that some way should be found of enabling them to reveal that capacity. The suggestion was rejected because such revelations would necessarily be voluntary; there was nothing voluntary about Census form-filling.[54]

The demand for more programmes in Welsh led to less controversy than did the Council's request in September 1947 for Welsh place-names to be pronounced according to Welsh-language usage. Oldfield-Davies acceded to the request. Thus broadcasters who had previously said 'Mirth-eh' and 'Pôth-call' were required to say Merthyr and Porth-cawl. The innovation was widely disliked. It was relaxed in 1949, initially in programmes giving sports results. In September 1951, the Council decided unanimously that pronunciation should follow 'generally accepted usage'. It was by no means clear what 'generally accepted usage' was for, as Oldfield-Davies commented: 'I find Penâth and Pôth-call acceptable, but I dislike Bang-uh and Caw-wen.' Nevertheless, a broadly acceptable compromise was found – in Wales at least. London announcers and newsreaders, however, proved totally incapable of mastering the simple rules of Welsh pronunciation, much to the surprise of Michael Aspel, who began his broadcasting career as a member of the Welsh Home Service's Repertory Company. '[They] make brave tries at Russian and Arabic titles,' he wrote in his autobiography, 'but give a laugh and a shrug at simple names like Ynysybwl and Pwllheli.'[55]

A cognate issue, and one frequently discussed by the Council, was the standard of Welsh used by broadcasters, especially newsreaders.

Kate Roberts was particularly vocal on the matter. The problem arose, argued the radio critic of the *North Wales Chronicle*, because Welsh newsreaders 'did not use the language as an everyday medium'. Controversy over grammar and vocabulary (but not over diction) loomed larger in Welsh broadcasting than in English, and the issues raised by Kate Roberts would still be much debated in the 1990s. The explanation offered by the *North Wales Chronicle*, however, became less valid following the increasing recruitment of Welsh announcers from among language loyalists.[56]

The request that the national anthem be played at close-down proved to be uncontroversial. 'Hen Wlad fy Nhadau' (followed by 'God Save the King') was first broadcast at close-down on 31 July 1949. It was a costly concession. As the Welsh Home Service rarely transmitted its own programme after 9.30 p.m., a presenter was obliged to remain on duty at Park Place until the basic Home Service came to an end (generally at 11.03 p.m.) in order to activate the records of the anthems. The demand for a Welsh-language *Listener* proved more difficult to satisfy. The matter had been raised by Appleton in 1935, but fear of opposition from existing Welsh periodicals had led to the abandonment of the project. Several volumes of Welsh-language radio talks had been published in the 1930s and during the war. Despite the urging of the Advisory Council, the Corporation refused to publish a periodical which was unlikely to make a profit, and in 1948 the Council suggested that Welsh-language talks should be printed in *The Listener*. The suggestion was rejected; indeed, reluctance to include Welsh-language material in the BBC's journals extended to the *Radio Times*, which in the first thirty-five years of its existence contained no Welsh at all apart from the titles of programmes. As a result of the uncooperative attitude of the Corporation, the publication of Welsh radio talks was left to private enterprise, particularly that of Aneirin Talfan Davies and his brother Alun, the owner of Gwasg y Dryw.[57]

No meeting of the Advisory Council passed without discussion of problems of reception. Industrial Denbighshire was particularly poorly served by the Welsh Home Service. The problem was partially solved by the installation at Wrexham in February 1946 of a transmitter with a ten-mile radius. There were populous areas – parts of Swansea and its vicinity in particular – where both the Light and the Third were barely audible, a major reason why west Glamorgan was the source of many of the complaints against Welsh-language programmes. Transmissions from Washford were patchily received in the south Wales coalfield and there the reliance upon relay companies, already apparent in the 1930s, continued. Reception problems were at their worst in mid Wales where there had been a 'mush' area ever since the synchronization of Washford and Penmon in 1937. The Welsh Home Service was inaudible in the Wyre valley; Evan Griffiths of Llangwyryfon was fined in 1949 for refusing to pay for a licence on the grounds that the only services he could receive came from England. Mid Wales was too sparsely inhabited to attract the relay companies. A report in March 1949 noted: 'Radio relay is available throughout the Cardiff Rural District. It is ironic that the facility is available where radio reception is excellent, while central Wales, which suffers from poor radio reception is . . . an unprofitable field for radio relay enterprise . . . Nothing will induce [the companies] to go to remote country districts. The town authorities who complain could consider operating municipal radio relay services.'[58]

The BBC was also reluctant to invest in remote country districts. The Copenhagen Agreement on the use of wavelengths, signed in 1948, made provision for the erection of low-power transmitters at Pwllheli and Aberystwyth, 'but this does not necessarily mean', wrote Noel Ashbridge, controller (engineering), 'that we shall build them . . . The population density [in mid Wales] is very low'.[59] A new problem arose in the late 1940s when the Welsh Home Service began suffering interference from an American Forces Network station in Austria. The Copenhagen Agreement only applied to European states and therefore the Americans did not consider that it was binding upon them. The problem of interference, first discussed by the Advisory Council in December 1950, was to become a dominant issue in Welsh broadcasting in the 1950s. The BBC considered that Welsh listeners could do much to help themselves by buying new sets and installing effective earths and aerials. Antiquated receivers were certainly part of the problem, a report in 1948 noting that 43.5 per cent of listeners had radio sets that were over ten years old.[60]

The only complete solution, stated Ashbridge, was to broadcast the Welsh Home Service on long wave, but as Britain only had one long wave, and as it was used for the Light Programme, that solution was not an option. In September 1948, however, a new possibility emerged. Ian Jacob, the director of the Overseas Service, who was shortly to meet the Welsh Advisory Council, asked Ashbridge whether he could give the Council any encouraging message about reception. Ashbridge answered: 'We are trying VHF at Wrotham; you could refer to that.' As transmission bands on VHF (very high frequency) are virtually limitless, the Wrotham experiment opened the way to the solution of the problem of the scarcity of wavelengths which had plagued the BBC almost from its inception. The Council was told of the possibilities of VHF. Jacob's statement received no publicity at the time but implicit in it was a total transformation of sound broadcasting.[61]

To Oldfield-Davies, the prospect of VHF was less immediately important than the need to expand his staff. He considered that Wales's Religious Broadcasting Department, which produced far more hours of programmes than equivalent departments elsewhere, was seriously overworked. On the urging of the Advisory Council, he persuaded Head Office to provide Parry-Jones with an assistant. Oldfield-Davies would have preferred a member of the Church in Wales, but the man appointed was a Wesleyan minister, J. O. Jones. Oldfield-Davies believed that the Bangor studios were understaffed, a view strongly supported by the Advisory Council. In 1949, John Gwilym Jones, who later won distinction as a playwright, was appointed drama producer at Bangor, where by 1950 the studios were contributing five to six hours a week to the Welsh Home Service.[62]

Oldfield-Davies was less enthusiastic about expanding the orchestra to full symphonic strength, a matter regularly raised by members of the Advisory Council, who drew attention to the fact that Scotland's BBC orchestra had fifty-seven players compared with the thirty-one in Wales. 'The first aim to be realized', declared the composer, Daniel Jones, 'must be a national orchestra.' Haley had no sympathy for the agitation. The BBC Welsh Orchestra, he noted, 'is not intended to be a national orchestra'. Oldfield-Davies agreed. 'O safbwynt y BBC', he stated in 1963, 'prin iawn yw'r angen am gerddorfa fawr arall.'*[63]

More urgent, according to Oldfield-Davies, was the need to rehouse the BBC's operations at Cardiff. By the late 1940s, the Corporation occupied numbers 38, 39, 40 and 57 Park Place, a group of late-nineteenth-century houses on one of Cardiff's busiest thoroughfares. Adaptation and re-adaptation had turned the buildings into a warren of corridors, offices and studios. There was virtually no parking space and, as most of the surrounding buildings were occupied by the University College, there was little likelihood of acquiring adjoining premises. In 1948, Oldfield-Davies recommended that the Corporation should seek to acquire a six-acre site in the centre of Cardiff. Tentative discussions were held with the city, which in 1947 had received the castle and its park as a gift from the marquess of Bute. By March 1949, however, it had become apparent that 'it is impossible to find [six] acres within convenient distance of the civic centre; a two-acre site may become available in bits over ten years; a three-and-a-half acre site in Llandaf is a possibility.' In September 1951, the Corporation acquired a larger Llandaf site, the ten acres surrounding Baynton House, a quarter of a mile north of the cathedral. The provision of a new Broadcasting House at Cardiff was

---

*'From the BBC's point of view, there is little need for another large orchestra.'

acknowledged to be a lengthy process, Haley informing the Welsh Advisory Council in September 1949 that it would not be available for at least ten years. In the mean time, Oldfield-Davies was told to lease temporary premises, a process which had begun with the acquisition of 48 Charles Street in 1943.[64]

The restoration of Broadcasting House in Swansea also proved protracted. As Swansea and Cardiff were 'in close proximity', there were strong doubts at Head Office whether a studio was needed at Swansea. (A similar argument was used where Edinburgh was concerned.) Doubts continued to be expressed even after rebuilding work on the bombed premises at Alexandra Road was well advanced. They were not fully cast aside until January 1952 when the Corporation's Efficiency Committee noted: 'Although the Cardiff/ Swansea and the Glasgow/Edinburgh pairs were founded and maintained mainly for political reasons, these reasons are so strong that no considerations of economy could override them without trouble and ill will wholly uncommensurate with the money saved.'[65] The BBC had no intention of staying in Carmarthen, despite the strong advocacy of Keidrych Rhys and the spirited campaign of Lottie Rees, a leading Carmarthenshire Labour activist. The efforts to ensure that Carmarthen would become the permanent centre for the Corporation's activities in west Wales were condemned by the *South Wales Evening Post* as a mean-minded attempt 'to seek to retain an advantage gained by the disaster which befell a neighbouring town'.[66] The last programme produced at Carmarthen's Lyric Theatre was broadcast on 9 August 1947. By then the Corporation had leased temporary accommodation at St Gabriel's Hall in Swansea, from whence it moved on 15 December 1947 to a studio at the Grove in Uplands. The Welsh Advisory Council pressed the Corporation to proceed with the restoration of the Alexandra Road premises, but in January 1951 the building was still roofless and there were fears that it was beyond renovation. In the spring of 1952, however, with building materials more readily available, work proceeded rapidly and Swansea's restored Broadcasting House was opened on 1 May 1952. The opening ceremony, performed by Lord Tedder, the vice-chairman of the governors, was a melancholy occasion, for Tom Pickering, the west Wales representative, had died a few weeks earlier. His successor, Aneirin Talfan Davies, took up his duties on 1 July 1952.[67]

At Bangor, network programmes under the auspices of Head Office ceased to be produced in March 1946 when Sandy Macpherson and the ten-ton BBC theatre organ were dispatched to London. The Corporation divested itself of most of its premises in the city and by 1947 the buildings available to Sam Jones consisted only of Bryn Meirion and Bron Castell. Members of the Welsh

Advisory Committee strongly advocated better facilities at Bangor. In particular, they were concerned at its drawbacks as a centre for radio drama; the cast of a play which had been rehearsed at Bangor were obliged to travel to Cardiff to enable the play to be broadcast. The BBC sought premises near Bryn Meirion and attempted to exchange Bron Castell for a building belonging to Bangor's Normal College. Nothing came of the scheme, nor of efforts to buy the vicarage adjoining Bryn Meirion, and by the late 1940s the Corporation was considering acquiring a site outside the city where a new broadcasting centre could be built.[68]

The Advisory Council's request for studio facilities at Wrexham was acceded to, with the installation of an open microphone at Salisbury Park Chapel. Oldfield-Davies saw no need for further provision for he believed that 'the number of people in Denbighshire who had anything to contribute to broadcasting had little difficulty in travelling to Bangor or Cardiff'.[69] Neither did he believe that there was any pressing necessity to yield to the Council's demand for studios at Aberystwyth, Carmarthen and Monmouth. By mid century, there were calls for the creation of a network of studios which would ensure that no one in Wales was more than an hour's car journey from a BBC microphone, but such a network was not fully established until the 1980s.

In recommending members of the Welsh Advisory Council, Oldfield-Davies was concerned to ensure a broad political balance. He tended, however, to suggest the names of the more consciously Welsh supporters of the main political parties. For example, he urged the appointment of the patriot industrialist Kenneth Davies and the patriot trade unionist Huw T. Edwards. In the 1940s the Labour Party's officials were strongly centralist, with Morgan Phillips in London and Cliff Prothero in Cardiff deeply hostile to any developments which could be construed as concessions to Welsh nationalism. In 1950, the members of the Welsh Advisory Council were perturbed by accusations that the Welsh radio news service was biased against the Labour Party and in favour of Plaid Cymru. In 1948, the Labour Party in Scotland had accused the Gaelic news and the programme *Scottish Opinion* of favouring the Scottish National Party, and the appointment of Wynne Samuel to the Welsh Advisory Council in 1949 led the Aberdare Labour Party to claim that 'the BBC in Cardiff is almost a branch of [Plaid Cymru]'.[70] In 1950, the bone of contention was the decision of Ifan Pugh, the news editor of the Welsh Home Service, to send a recording van to a Plaid Cymru rally at Llandrindod on 1 July 1950, while, on the same day, a more widely attended Labour rally at Newtown was covered only by a reporter. Labour supporters were further incensed by Pugh's use of reports supplied by Wynne Samuel and J. E. Jones, both of whom were full-time Plaid Cymru officials. Following a complaint by the Welsh Regional Council of Labour, the scripts of all the news bulletins broadcast in the first six months of 1950 were scrutinized by Head Office officials. T. R. P. Hole, the Corporation's editor (news), spent two days at Cardiff examining the work of the Wales newsroom, and Pugh was obliged to undergo further training in London.[71]

Hole found no evidence of bias at Cardiff. Although he deprecated the use of Plaid Cymru officials as reporters, he considered that the greater attention given to the Llandrindod rally compared with that at Newtown was justified and was in line with the coverage of the two events by the press. Cliff Prothero, the secretary of the Welsh Regional Council of Labour, brought the matter to the attention of the lord president of the Council. Prothero was much annoyed when the BBC governors, at their meeting on 9 November 1950, confirmed that no evidence of 'bias . . . in favour of the Welsh Nationalist Party could be found', and rejected demands for a full inquiry. '[The Welsh Regional Council of Labour]', wrote Prothero, 'does not consider that Sir William Haley and Editor (News) London, neither of whom possess an intimate knowledge of Welsh affairs, are fully competent to judge whether or not bias has been shown purely on the basis of textual evidence.' The veteran Labour leader, Huw T. Edwards, a member of the Advisory Council, urged Prothero to abandon his campaign 'in the interest of the Movement itself . . . Whenever we have had news [Ifan Pugh] has done his best to give it publicity.' Pugh himself asserted 'nid oes gan Mr Cliff Prothero y syniad lleiaf am werth newyddion gwleidyddol fel newyddion'*[72], an assertion supported by the *Liverpool Daily Post*, which noted that all Labour publicity came from London; 'they don't bother in Wales'. Hole put forward a similar argument. 'A relatively small but energetic political organisation', he wrote, 'might exceed in items a much larger but less publicity-minded one. Items might be broadcast which might never have got there had there been an opportunity to judge them against items of equal or better value. False values can spring from that . . . and to the untutored, false values may easily suggest bias.'[73] The controversy had died down by the end of 1950, but memories of it served to fuel a far more strenuous attack upon the news bulletins of the Welsh Home Service in 1956. In 1951, Pugh punctiliously sent a recording van to the Labour Party Welsh Rally, but Attlee, who was the main speaker, refused to allow his speech to be broadcast.

Labour suspicions of the BBC in Wales arose in part from the Welsh

---

*'Mr Cliff Prothero has not the slightest idea about the value of political news as news.'

Advisory Council's dogged interest in party political broadcasts. That interest involved two overlapping issues. The Council was anxious that Wales should have its own party political broadcasts in order to enable political questions specific to Wales to be ventilated and to allow politics in general to be discussed in the Welsh language. It was also concerned to provide Plaid Cymru with an opportunity to broadcast to the electorate. Ever since their institution in the mid 1920s, the allocation of party political broadcasts had been the responsibility, not of the BBC, but of the party whips. Commenting in February 1948 upon the Council's demand for specific broadcasts for Wales, Haley noted: 'There is nothing to prevent the parties, within the scope of the present agreement, from devoting any of their broadcasts to Welsh affairs.' The two major parties, however, had no desire to sacrifice a Britain-wide broadcast in order to address a regional audience. 'The only basis for political broadcasting', asserted Attlee, 'is a broad national United Kingdom basis.' The leading Conservative Harry Crookshank agreed. 'National politics,' he declared, 'are national politics.'[74] The *Liverpool Daily Post*'s radio critic had a more cynical explanation. The Labour and Conservative Parties resisted party political broadcasts for Wales, he argued, because 'they lack confidence in their Welsh message'. The BBC's General Advisory Council had a more practical objection. Party political broadcasts, it noted, 'were unpopular with the public and there would be criticism if their number were increased'.[75] The Liberals were strong supporters of party political broadcasts specifically for Wales; so also were the Communists, who were virtually banned from broadcasting in the wake of the deepening of the Cold War. Indeed, opposition to demands that political organizations other than the three major British parties should have air time were primarily motivated by the determination to exclude the Communists.

Broadcasts by Plaid Cymru in addition to the Britain-wide broadcasts by the three main parties were a somewhat different matter. In the general election of 1945, the Common Wealth party had been granted ten minutes in which to address the electorate, but a similar concession was not granted to 'splinter parties' such as Plaid Cymru and the Scottish National Party, despite the advocacy of the Welsh and Scottish regional directors.[76] Plaid Cymru had seven official parliamentary candidates in 1945, seven in 1950 and four in 1951. Its demand for air time perturbed Head Office. The party paid £600 in lost deposits in 1951 (four times £150); if it were granted a party political broadcast, Corporation officials feared that there would be allegations that broadcast time could be bought for £600. In its discussions of party political broadcasts, the Advisory Council made no mention of Plaid Cymru. To Huw T. Edwards, the most forceful of the Council's members, the issue was one of autonomy for Wales; his major concern was to oblige his own party, the Labour Party, to broadcast specifically to the people of Wales, a step which would put pressure upon it to bring forward specific Welsh policies. Those opposed to such policies saw the issue in terms of providing a platform for Plaid Cymru; they believed that the Welsh Advisory Council had an obsessive interest in the subject, a belief which confirmed their suspicions of the operations in Wales of the BBC and its associated bodies. The Advisory Council made no progress in its demands for party political broadcasts for Wales; the matter, however, remained on the agenda and would loom large in the discussions of the Council's successor, the Broadcasting Council for Wales.

III The coming of television

By the late 1940s, the Advisory Council was increasingly concerned to ensure that television should be available in Wales, and specifically from a transmitter situated on Welsh soil. The Hankey Committee's report had asserted that most of Britain could be covered from six sites, and there was no suggestion that any one of them would be in Wales. No part of the country could be reached by the transmissions of Alexandra Palace, but many Welsh households were able to receive television following the opening of Sutton Coldfield, the transmitter serving the English Midlands, on 17 December 1949. There was much excitement at Welshpool, where there was admirable reception even on the cheapest sets. Sutton Coldfield could also be received in parts of northern Monmouthshire and Glamorgan, along the borders of Breconshire and Radnorshire, in extensive areas of Flintshire and Denbighshire and in coastal Caernarfonshire. Although television licences were not yet on sale in Wales, the country had by May 1950 over a thousand licence-holders, people who had, presumably, crossed the border in order to pay the £2 combined television and radio licence demanded of conscientious citizens. They included 520 in Denbighshire, 144 in Flintshire, 110 in Glamorgan and 67 in Caernarfonshire.[77]

Reception in north Wales improved markedly following the opening on 12 October 1951 of Holme Moss, the transmitter for northern England. Located at 1,700 feet above sea-level on the Pennines, with a 750-foot mast, its signal was available from the coast of Yorkshire to the coast of Anglesey. Splendid pictures were available at Colwyn Bay, although the town was eight miles west of the presumed reach of the transmitter. By May 1952, there were 10,048 licences in Wales:

Denbighshire headed the list with 3,497 licence-holders, followed by Monmouthshire (2,095), Flintshire (1,926), Caernarfonshire (1,569) and Glamorgan (725).[78]

In the early days of sound radio, every transmitter broadcast its own exclusive programme. Television, however, was centrist from its beginnings. The programmes broadcast from Sutton Coldfield and Holme Moss were identical with those transmitted from Alexandra Palace. The north of England, it was stated in November 1951, 'is likely to be drowned in South of England milk-and-water soppiness'. The unified service did not preclude the possibility of inputs from the regions. Indeed, Wales made a contribution to television several years before the country had the capability of transmitting the service. As has been noted, *Birds of a Feather* was televised in 1948; in 1949, Cliff Gordon's *Choir Practice*, featuring Donald Houston and Stanley Baker, was rehearsed in Wales and televised from Alexandra Palace for the delectation of viewers in the English 'home counties'. The play included at least background mutterings in Welsh and was introduced bilingually. Thus 2 August 1949 was the first occasion on which the Welsh language emanated from the cathode tube.[79]

By the late 1940s, there was a general assumption that the BBC in Wales would soon be making regular contributions to the output of the television service. In 1949, several members of the Cardiff staff, Alun Williams among them, were seconded to London to learn television techniques. In seeking a six-acre site for a new Broadcasting House at Cardiff, Oldfield-Davies maintained that 3.5 of the acres would be needed for television studios. He was emphatic that the programmes produced on those acres would be contributions to the general British service, for he believed that the cost of television productions was such that many years would pass before there would be programmes exclusively for Wales. 'As to when Wales will have its own television programmes,' he stated in 1949, 'your guess is as good as mine. Apart from the technical difficulties, the costs of [bringing] television to you are fantastic.' His close associate, Powell of the *South Wales Evening Post*, was even more emphatic. 'We cannot hope', he wrote in June 1949, 'for the development of regional television for at least fifteen years. It would need a new building at Cardiff . . . Eleven times as much money is needed to make a television rather than a radio programme.'[80]

By 1949, there were increasing complaints that the BBC was dragging its feet over the installation of a transmitter to serve Wales. 'Television will be old before it reaches Wales,' stated the *South Wales Evening Post*, and the *Liverpool Daily Post* claimed that 'Wales [is] the neglected sister where television is [concerned]'. Enthusiasts for sound radio, however, were not anxious to hasten the coming of television, 'radio's possibly matricidal child', as the *Liverpool Daily Post* put it. 'Television', noted the paper, 'will kill off "steam radio", and the departments at Bangor, Swansea and Cardiff will before long be [broadcasting in] the medium of the past.'[81] Saunders Lewis's objections to television were more fundamental. He was much impressed by Alistair Cooke's description of its dire effects on American society. 'Y mae dod â'r cinema i'r tŷ . . . bob dydd o'r wythnos', he wrote in 1951, 'yn berygl moesol . . . Fe all lwyr ddinistrio pob diwylliant.'*[82] Those worried about the future of the Welsh language saw the spread of television as a threat. John Tudor Jones (John Eilian), who had been the Welsh Region's director of programmes in the late 1930s, wrote a vituperative article in *Y Llenor* in 1950 in which he stated: 'Braw i mi yw gweled Cyngor Cymreig y BBC ac eraill yn galw mor anghyfrifol am orsafoedd telefisiwn i Gymru . . . [Dylai'r Cymry] wrthwynebu datblygiad telefisiwn neu weithio dros ei ohirio.'†[83] The opening of Sutton Coldfield in 1949 allowed the inhabitants of some of the strongholds of the language to receive a wholly English service; the fears that had been raised in 1927 about the impact of sound radio upon Welsh-speaking communities resurfaced, but in a more urgent form, for the 'matricidal child' was perceived to be more insidious than its parent.

Concern over television provision for Wales increased following a speech by Haley at Scarborough in May 1949 in which he referred to a transmitter which would be built to serve both Wales and south-western England. 'There is much questioning and . . . adverse comment', noted the meeting of the director of home sound broadcasting. '[The announcement] stirred up the embers of the controversy over the old West Region.' Oldfield-Davies loyally defended the Corporation's decision. The decision meant that television would not be available in mid Wales, in much of west Wales and in those parts of north Wales outside the reach of Sutton Coldfield and Holme Moss. 'Is Wales so impossible to provide with television?' asked an editorial in the *Western Mail*. 'An expert has given as his opinion that a high-power station in south Wales with a booster in the north would serve the whole of the Principality. This contrasts with the pessimistic attitude of . . . Controller Wales.'[84]

Having accepted that a single transmitter serving both sides of the

---

*'Bringing the cinema into the home every day of the week is a moral danger . . . It could totally destroy all culture.'

†'It frightens me to see the BBC's Welsh Council and others calling so irresponsibly for television stations in Wales . . . The Welsh should oppose the development of television or work to postpone it.'

Severn Estuary was inevitable, Oldfield-Davies devoted his energies to ensuring that the transmitter should be sited in Wales. His efforts were strongly supported by the Advisory Council. 'A television transmitter on Welsh soil', noted the meeting of the director of home sound broadcasting in November 1949, 'if at all practicable, will have great political advantages.' The Welsh MPs were also involved. S. O. Davies (Labour, Merthyr Tydfil) informed the House of Commons that 'Welsh people would take exception to a service coming to Wales from outside Wales', and D. A. Price-White (Conservative, Caernarfon Boroughs) declared that 'to associate south Wales with . . . Bristol is like showing a red rag to a bull'.[85]

In April 1950, Ashbridge prepared a report on sites suitable for the transmitter. He considered three: Brendon near Minehead, the Mendip Hills and St Nicholas in the Vale of Glamorgan. The Mendips, he concluded, 'would provide reception for the greatest number of people [4.1 million] but it overlaps severely with Sutton Coldfield'. A transmitter at either St Nicholas or Brendon would serve about three million people, but if St Nicholas were chosen, television would not be available in south Devon. Brendon would provide a better signal to Swansea and Port Talbot than would St Nicholas, but reception at Bristol would be so poor that a booster station for the city would be necessary. 'From a technical point of view', wrote Ashbridge, 'Brendon together with a Bristol booster would be the best solution [but] the ultimate decision must be arrived at partly by considerations other than the purely technical.' Among such considerations were the additional cost of a Bristol station and 'the political difficulty of not putting the station in Wales'. He therefore recommended that a single station should be built at St Nicholas, a recommendation endorsed by Ness Edwards, the postmaster-general. The members of the Advisory Committee were told of the decision on 30 June 1950 and Ness Edwards met his fellow Welsh MPs to discuss its implications on 19 July 1950. At the meeting he stated that transmission from St Nicholas would not reach west and central Wales, but he emphasized that the populous areas of north Wales would be adequately served from Sutton Coldfield and Holme Moss.[86]

Permission to erect a transmitter at St Nicholas was readily granted by the Glamorgan County Council, but the plan was opposed by the St Nicholas Parish Council. Haley insisted that local opposition should be heeded and a new site was chosen at Wenvoe. The Wenvoe transmitter, rearing up 1,175 feet above sea-level, was, at the time of its opening, the tallest man-made structure in the world; when on full power, it was, along with Kirk o' Shotts in Scotland, the most powerful television station in the world. Oldfield-Davies emphasized that, although the new station was to be in Wales, it should not be considered a Welsh station; he was, however, at more pains to stress that 'the fact that it [would be] on Welsh soil has important long-term possibilities'. Haley was rather less forthcoming. On 8 December 1950, he informed the Advisory Council: 'It would be possible, say on special occasions, for Wenvoe to opt out of the main programme, but there would have to be consideration for the West of England viewers who were also part of the transmitter's audience.'[87]

The Wenvoe transmitter was officially opened on 15 August 1952 in a ceremony which gave equal prominence to Wales and to south-western England. The Welsh Dragon and the Wessex Wyvern were flown, and the guests, who included leading civic dignitaries from both sides of the Severn Estuary, were entertained by the Bryn-mawr Dancers and by a south-western England regimental band. *Y Faner* saw the opening of Wenvoe as ushering in tensions similar to those of the early 1930s. 'Proffwydaf', wrote the paper's editor, 'y cawn weld ailadrodd o'r hen gynnen rhwng trwyddedwyr Cymru a thrwyddedwyr Gorllewin Lloegr.'*[88] The *Western Mail* also recalled the 'uneasy wedlock with radio' and urged that 'the marriage of convenience with South West England [should] not last'. Ernest Hughes, a veteran of the struggle for a wavelength for sound broadcasting in Wales, predicted trouble. 'We are told', he wrote in the *Western Mail* in May 1952, 'that television has created a social revolution in England, but that is nothing like the conflict which will come from this new medium in Wales.' Lady Megan Lloyd George, who addressed viewers on the evening of 15 August, stated that 'Wales and the West of England have come together in order to separate'. 'We should not rest', she declared, 'until each separate nation [in the United Kingdom] has a television station of its own.'[89]

IV   The Beveridge Report

Megan Lloyd George's comments in August 1952 were those of a public figure whose recent experience had included a close involvement in the deliberations concerning the future of broadcasting in Britain. The BBC's Charter, renewed for five years in 1946, was due to expire on 31 December 1952. In May 1949, the government appointed a committee 'to examine every aspect of home broadcasting in the United Kingdom'. Chaired by Lord Beveridge, its eleven members included Megan Lloyd George, the committee's

---

*'I prophesy that we shall see the repeat of the old quarrel between the licence-holders of Wales and those of the west of England.'

only experienced broadcaster. Beveridge had an instinctive dislike of monopoly and centralization, and sought evidence to confirm his instincts. During his visit to Cardiff on 3 May 1950, he 'expected an anti-London bias and seemed surprised', according to Oldfield-Davies, 'not to find one'. He did find confirmation of his belief that the Corporation's administrators saw themselves as an élite. His question to Oldfield-Davies: 'Do you consult experts?' elicited the reply: 'We are the experts.' 'That', commented Beveridge, 'is the spirit of the BBC that I find quite dangerous.' He also found confirmation for his belief that centralization meant that the governors had insufficient contact with broadcasting activities outside London. He was particularly concerned to discover that Oldfield-Davies, in his five years as head of broadcasting in Wales, had only met the governors on two occasions. Beveridge's somewhat obsessive interest in the constitutional relationships between the various sectors of the Corporation led him to be curiously unmindful of the main feature of mid-twentieth-century British broadcasting – the rapid advance of television. The Beveridge Committee held a total of sixty-two meetings, but televison was not discussed with the BBC representatives until the thirty-first meeting.[90]

Concern about the power enjoyed by Head Office became a central feature of the Beveridge inquiry. Pressure groups seeking to modify that power were more active in Wales than in any other part of the United Kingdom. On the committee itself, Megan Lloyd George, who had been appointed to represent Welsh and feminist interests, was the most ardent of the devolutionists. 'Mr Attlee's government', wrote Mary Stocks, a member of the Beveridge Committee, 'for some reason shilly-shallied over the implementation of the Report [thus handing] the issue over to the Conservative Party which assumed power in 1951.'[91] The main reason for the shilly-shallying was the complexity of the Committee's recommendations concerning devolution. The terms of the BBC's fourth Charter and of the new licence were to be those of a Conservative government and they included the abrogation of the Corporation's television monopoly. The devolution recommendations were specifically the result of demands from Wales, demands which were mainly motivated by devotion to the Welsh language. As the course of charter renewal was discomposed by the recommendations, it could be argued – somewhat tortuously perhaps – that commercial television came into existence in Britain at the time it did because of the activities of the devotees of the Welsh language.

Within Wales, demands for changes in the constitutional position of Welsh broadcasting came from four sources: Undeb Cymru Fydd, Plaid Cymru, the Welsh MPs and the Welsh Advisory Council.

Undeb Cymru Fydd and Plaid Cymru sought a corporation for Wales with its own board of governors and they reiterated the arguments put forward in 1945–6 by T. I. Ellis and Gwynfor Evans. Ellis circularized the Welsh local authorities and by January 1950 four county councils and twenty-nine lesser councils had endorsed the call for a Welsh corporation. S. O. Davies, in a memorandum he prepared at the request of the Welsh MPs, made similar demands. Davies made much of the reluctance of the Corporation to provide full details of its expenditure in Wales, an issue which had been raised by Gwynfor Evans during his brief membership of the Welsh Advisory Council in 1947. The memorandum attacked 'the excessively narrow limitations now inflicted upon the Welsh Region of the BBC' and stated that the London programmes available in Wales were 'more often than not foreign to our traditional reactions, our literature and our cultural interests'. The memorandum was submitted to the Beveridge Committee in the name of the Welsh Parliamentary Party; the Corporation, in its submission, expressed doubts whether the views it contained were 'shared by the MPs from all the constituencies of Wales'.[92]

Members of the Welsh Advisory Council ranged from supporters of the status quo to advocates of complete independence. On 9 December 1949, the Council appointed a subcommittee to prepare a memorandum for Beveridge. Of its members, Kate Roberts supported a Welsh corporation, a proposal for which Huw T. Edwards also expressed sympathy, while Wynne Wheldon ridiculed the idea and also opposed the suggestion that there should be a devolved commission responsible for the Welsh Home Service. 'Dual control', he wrote to Oldfield-Davies, 'would be very bad for you and your colleagues, who really must keep the whole thing going without constant interference. You have read Reith's book. Are there not still plenty of Mrs Snowdens about?'[93] The notion of an executive body was brought before the full Council, but as it was equally divided on the issue, it was omitted from the submission to Beveridge. Instead, a brief document was prepared urging that 'Wales should not be considered as a region of the BBC . . . [but] as a national broadcasting unit within the pattern of British broadcasting'.[94]

Although Beveridge considered the BBC to be 'one witness among others', Haley decided that the Corporation should deluge the committee with written and spoken evidence – 620,000 words in all. It commented upon all the recommendations from Wales and was more informative than hitherto about its expenditure on Welsh broadcasting. The information was provided in the context of the BBC's attack upon the notion of a Welsh corporation. It was claimed that in the year ending 31 March 1949, Wales produced £287,000 in income available for revenue expenditure; £372,000 was spent on operations in Wales, while the cost of shared services (Wales's share of the outlay on the basic Home Service and the Light and Third Programmes) amounted to £164,000. Thus Welsh listeners received a subsidy of £249,000, largely from the substantial surpluses of the London and Northern Regions. Doubt was cast on the accuracy of the figures, but the Corporation considered them to be conclusive proof that a separate Welsh corporation would not be able 'to support an equivalent service'. There were suggestions in Wales that Welsh listeners who wanted the shared radio services would be able to receive them without contributing to their cost, as could listeners in parts of the Irish Republic, France and the Low Countries – or, indeed, where the General Overseas Service was concerned, listeners throughout the world. Beveridge investigated the suggestion. He asked the BBC's representatives: 'If there were separate corporations in Wales and Scotland, could Welsh and Scottish listeners be prevented from enjoying English programmes free?' He was told that they could hear them from transmitters in England, 'but in all future dispositions of English transmitters, the interests of Wales and Scotland would be disregarded'.[95]

The press followed the deliberations of the Beveridge Committee with close attention. Among Welsh-language newspapers, *Y Faner* was strongly in favour of a Welsh corporation, while John Aelod Jones (John Roberts Williams) in *Y Cymro*, advocated a moderate federalist approach. The *Liverpool Daily Post*, which in March 1949 had stressed the need 'to campaign for radio home rule', argued that the 'BBC gets a fat windfall from Wales' and accused 'Portland Place of clutching the purse-strings with miserly tenacity'. D. H. I. Powell of the *South Wales Evening Post* was disturbed by the apparent endorsement of a separate corporation by the Welsh MPs. The idea was put forward, he claimed, by 'theorists out of touch with reality who say they speak for the majority of the Welsh people'. 'We are the only paper', he wrote on 17 January 1950, 'protesting against a Welsh Broadcasting Corporation.' Ten days later the *South Wales Echo* took up the matter. 'Until recently', wrote its radio correspondent, 'I thought the affair so ridiculous that I paid little attention to it [but now] the Welsh Parliamentary Party seems to have virtually approved the case.'[96] Oldfield-Davies was discreetly active in disseminating arguments against a Welsh corporation. The memorandum submitted to the Beveridge Committee by the Association of Welsh Local Authorities incorporated large sections of a letter which he had sent to the association's secretary, and controller Wales also sought to persuade MPs such as Gwilym Lloyd George to distance themselves from S. O. Davies's memorandum.[97]

The Beveridge Committee sat for eighteen months. It had members other than the chairman who were suspicious of the Corporation's monopoly and its size, but the BBC's well-organized presentation of its case and its undoubted programming achievements served to allay the fears of almost all of them. In the report, published in January 1951, ten of the eleven endorsed the recommendation that the BBC, after the expiration of its current licence, 'should continue as the authority responsible for all broadcasting in the United Kingdom including Television and the Overseas Services'. The dissentient was Selwyn Lloyd, who called for the abolition of the monopoly and the creation of a competing commercial service. Three of the other com-mittee members – Beveridge, Mary Stocks and Megan Lloyd George – recommended that there should be a limited amount of advertising, but on the BBC's own wavelengths rather than upon those of any rival.[98]

Where devolution was concerned, the committee sought 'federal harmony' rather than centralization. It recommended that Wales, Scotland and Northern Ireland should have separate commissions, each of which 'should initiate and decide upon a Home Service pro-gramme in its region and should have powers in relation to finance, accommodation and staff'. Television, noted the committee, 'would for some time presumably remain a central activity though here, too, the commissioners would take growing responsibilities'. The com-mittee was, however, content to leave the detailed definition of the authority of the commissioners to the BBC. The powers of the Board of Governors should be enhanced and its membership increased from six to nine by the addition of governors with special knowledge of Wales, Scotland and Northern Ireland. The recommendations were generally welcomed by the Welsh press, with *Y Cymro* expressing its satisfaction and the *South Wales Evening Post* asserting that the report was 'a triumph for the moderate and practical advice of the Welsh Advisory Council'. The other 'national regions' were less enthusiastic. The Scottish Advisory Council believed that the existing degree of autonomy was adequate and saw no point in establishing a commission until more wavelengths and resources were available; that of Northern Ireland welcomed the notion of an 'Ulsterman governor' but declared that it did not want a commission under any circumstances.[99]

The BBC's governors and and senior officials viewed the devolution proposals with hostility. They meant, wrote Lord Simon, that there would be on the Board of Governors 'three members who knew a section of the BBC more intimately than [did] the Director-General'. The proposed commissions, wrote Nicolls, 'will counter the present unwritten and unspoken influence of the centre, which causes the Regional Controller to exercise his autonomy sensibly . . .

[The proposals] involve the spiritual disruption of the BBC.' A chairman of a National Commission, wrote Haley, 'might come to think that being chairman was as important . . . as being a governor of the BBC. This would be a wrong sense of values.' Addressing the Welsh Advisory Council on 9 March 1951, he stated that the BBC welcomed the proposals in Beveridge that Wales, Scotland and Northern Ireland 'should be national units within the pattern of British broadcasting', but he concurred with Oldfield-Davies's view that the dual control implicit in the scheme for commissions was 'completely unworkable'. The Advisory Council set up a subcommittee to examine the Beveridge proposals. Reporting to the Council on 2 April 1951, it called for a commission of twenty-five members. The Commission's chairman should be a BBC governor; programme policy, staff accommodation and finance should all come within its purview but the freedom of broadcasting staff to initiate and frame programmes should be safeguarded. The Council accepted the subcommittee's report, although Wheldon reiterated his total opposition to any suggestion of dual control.[100]

The government had aimed at issuing a White Paper in February 1951, but 'with the discussion of regionalism dominating the timetable for considering the whole report', it was not published until July. 'The Cabinet', wrote the *New Statesman*, 'convinced itself that the [Welsh] nationalists, whose chief strength is in professional and artistic circles, would muscle in on any nominated council.' Its fears were fanned by Welsh Labour MPs under the leadership of Ness Edwards, the postmaster-general. He suggested a commission wholly drawn from the local authorities of Wales on the basis of one member for each 120,000 of the population. 'The aldermen and councillors of Wales', declared Edwards, 'would be the best people to run the Welsh broadcasting service.' The Board of Governors reacted sharply, criticizing 'a system of control based upon a membership qualified by political election'. The government's White Paper was discussed in both Houses of Parliament in late July when the proposals concerning the composition of the commissions dominated the debate. Edwards campaigned vigorously in favour of his scheme but by October 1951 Nicolls was relieved that Edwards was the only public figure actively advocating it.[101]

By then, the election campaign was in full swing. The general election of 25 October 1951 led to the return of a Conservative government. With the Corporation's Charter due to expire in sixty-seven days, a six-month extension of the Charter was granted to allow the new government to consider its broadcasting policy. A second White Paper was published on 15 May 1952. It mentioned the possibility of commercialism and recommended the renewal of the

BBC's Charter – without guarantees on monopoly – for ten years from 30 June 1952. It also recommended that Wales should have a Broadcasting Council which would be responsible for the policy and content of the Welsh Home Service, and would have advisory powers where television was concerned. It would consist of a chairman, who would be a member of the Board of Governors, and eight members drawn from various spheres of Welsh public life, local government among them. The White Paper was implemented and Article Ten of the 1952 Charter authorized the appointment of national governors and the establishment of national regions. Reith was 'sickened and infuriated' by the decision, but a later director-general believed that the new arrangements had great merit. Writing in 1979, Charles Curran argued that the national regions, 'although they appeared to be much in advance of the needs of the day, represented . . . an accurate foreshadowing of the devolutionary tendencies which were to become very evident by the end of the 1960s. Had there not been a constitutional framework of the kind provided by Article Ten . . . it is very likely that a good deal more tension would have developed in the internal affairs of the BBC over the nationalist problem than in fact occurred.'[102]

The Welsh Advisory Council met on 23 May 1952 to discuss the White Paper. Its members were generally enthusiastic, but the statement that the proposed Welsh Broadcasting Council's responsibility for appointments would be confined to 'staff wholly employed in connection with the [Welsh] Home Service programmes' was considered to be vague and misleading. In July 1952, it was announced that Lord Macdonald of Gwaunysgor, the paymaster-general in the post-war Labour government and from 1946 to 1949 the governor of Newfoundland, would be the Welsh national governor. A Welsh-speaker, a leading Wesleyan lay preacher and an ardent teetotaller, his appointment won widespread approval. On 24 October 1952, he attended the last meeting of the Welsh Advisory Council where he met the 84-year-old Edgar Jones, whose appointment as advisor twenty-one years previously had been the BBC's first acknowledgement that broadcasting had a Welsh dimension. The Advisory Council 'broke up in a very happy spirit' and its members, their task completed, were taken to Wenvoe 'where tea was served'.[103]

V   Listeners and programmes, 1945–1952

Following the opening of the Wenvoe transmitter, almost all the populous areas of Wales were within reach of television. Thus, 1952 marks the beginning of the television era in Wales. It also marks the apogee of the sound radio era, for it was in the immediate post-war years that sound broadcasting became an integral part of the lives of the vast majority of the Welsh people. The country had 490,000 radio licences in 1945, representing 65 per cent of Welsh households; the equivalent figures in 1952 were 603,473 and 82 per cent.[104]

The marked growth in the Welsh audience coincided with a fuller understanding of its nature and tastes. The BBC's research into its audience, initiated in 1936, made little attempt to examine listening habits region by region, and, as has been seen, its original panel of volunteers markedly under-represented the 'Celtic fringe'. When plans for listener research were first discussed, Nest Jenkins suggested that a Welsh questionnaire should be devised, but no action was taken until December 1945 when a Welsh section of the listening panel was established. By 1948, the panel consisted of 585 members, 29 per cent of whom were fluent in Welsh with a further 15 per cent having some knowledge of the language. Their primary task was to keep a record of their listening habits. The Corporation, however, was not content merely to discover how popular its output was; it sought to measure reaction to programmes, for Robert Silvey, the head of audience research, feared that if size alone were investigated, the argument that 'bigger means better would win by default'. Panel members were therefore asked to award points to selected programmes in order that an appreciation index could be compiled. Silvey was fascinated to find that 'appreciation indices and audience sizes moved quite independently'. Panel members were largely self-selected and, fearing that they were not fully representative of the public at large, Silvey also organized extensive random sampling. By 1949, Wales had 150 field workers who received out-of-pocket expenses for interviewing 500 listeners a day.[105]

Audience research revealed that in the late 1940s the three British radio services had between them an evening audience of about 25 per cent of the inhabitants of the United Kingdom in the summer months, a figure which could rise to 35 per cent and more in the winter months. Of those listening, an average of 61 per cent were tuned to the Light Programme, 38 per cent to the Home Service and less than 1 per cent to the Third Programme. The pattern was somewhat different in Wales, where loyalty to the Home Service was greater than it was in any other part of the United Kingdom. A higher proportion of the Welsh listened to nothing but the Home Service, and in Wales the service's audience was not much smaller than that of the Light Programme. Indeed, in week 33 of 1948, 53 per cent of Welsh listeners were tuned to the Home Service, a percentage never recorded in any of the English regions and only once in

Scotland. The appeal of the Light Programme was greatest during peak hours. In 1949, no region had a majority of listeners tuned to the Home Service between 6 and 10 p.m.; its peak-time programmes enjoyed their greatest popularity in Wales, where 49 per cent of those listening to the radio were tuned to the Home Service during the evenings of week 17.[106]

Loyalty to the Home Service did not necessarily mean loyalty to the Welsh Home Service. Listeners in Scotland could rarely satis-factorily receive a Home Service except their own, and it was noted in 1948 that 82 per cent of the Scots never listened to other Home Services. In Wales, there was satisfactory reception of the West of England Service in south-east Glamorgan and in the whole of Monmouthshire, of the North of England Service in eastern Den-bighshire and in the whole of Flintshire and of the Midland Service in a broad swathe along the border. Thus over half the Welsh population had a Home Service alternative. A survey in 1948 showed that 57 per cent of the Welsh never listened to a Home Service other than their own; 14 per cent did so regularly and 29 per cent fairly frequently. Further evidence is provided by the sales of the various editions of the *Radio Times*. In 1950, listeners in south Wales bought 279,591 copies of the Welsh edition and 23,522 copies of others, 15,338 of which were Midland and 7,205 were West of England editions. Listeners in north Wales bought 67,730 copies of the Welsh edition and 26,723 copies of others, 26,286 of which were the North of England edition. Purchasers of non-Welsh editions were most numerous in the north-east, the *Wrexham Leader* noting in 1949 that Wrexham had as many subscribers to the North of England as to the Welsh edition of the *Radio Times*.[107]

Compared with listeners in other parts of the United Kingdom, those in Wales were more prone to stray from their own Home Service; yet, paradoxically, they led the field as enthusiasts for their own programmes. An inquiry in 1948 seeking to discover whether listeners were 'usually interested if a programme comes from your own region' elicited an affirmative response of 59 per cent in Wales and of 58 per cent in Scotland, the only parts of the United Kingdom to register over 50 per cent. The Welsh and the Scots, noted the inquiry, were far more aware of their own services.[108] In that aware-ness, accent was a major factor. Although it attracted considerable criticism, Welsh-accented English was the norm on the Welsh Home Service. English Home Services (the North was to some extent an exception) avoided regional accents except in dialect plays, opting instead for the 'neutral' accent beloved of Head Office.

There were audiences in Wales for services other than those of the BBC. Much to the astonishment of the Corporation, Radio Éireann had numerous Welsh listeners. The American Forces Network was appreciated by the young who considered its programmes to be 'more matey'. To some extent that was also true of the Forces Network serving the British Army of the Rhine. Radio Luxembourg, however, attracted the greater part of the cross-frontier listening. The service had closed down in 1939 but was restarted under the original company in 1945. It transmitted about nineteen hours of programmes in English each week, a third of which were broadcast on Sunday, when its output successfully competed with the BBC's sombre Sabbath offerings. Its broadcasts included reports on the south Wales football pools dividends and religious programmes of a 'strong American Armageddon character' which were particularly well received in Glamorgan. As the station used a pirated wavelength, the post-war Labour government took 'all steps in its power to get rid of it', but its existence was supported by libertarians and by those among the Conservatives who were anxious to familiarize British listeners with commercial radio. In the 1930s, the BBC had banned artists who participated in Radio Luxembourg's broadcasts; the ban was not reimposed after the war but such participation was discouraged 'in the artists' own interests'. Radio Luxembourg's performers included several distinguished British broadcasters, with Richard Attenborough presenting a programme for Pin-Up Home Permanent Wave, Ted Kavanagh for Horlicks, Sam Costa for Rowntree and John Mills for Cadburys.[109]

Cross-frontier listening, although significant, constituted a small part of the radio experience of the people of Wales. While Home Service listening was more prevalent in Wales than in the rest of Britain, the Welsh, like the other peoples of the United Kingdom, were above all listeners to the Light Programme. In the immediate post-war years, the popularity of the Light Programme was astounding, with its best-known broadcasts attracting an audience of well over half the entire British population. Its most phenomenal success was *Have a Go*, a travelling 'chat' show featuring ordinary people and saved from banality by the unforced conviviality of its presenter, Wilfred Pickles. When *Have a Go* visited Ebbw Vale in January 1948, a participant said she would like a pair of nylons; hundreds of pairs were sent to her. Another participant said he would like his son to be able to leave the steelworks in order to pursue a career in art; the son received £50 from a well-wisher. In April 1948, 500 people gathered to hear *Have a Go* at Penygroes (Caernarfonshire), and when the programme visited Blaenau Ffestiniog in September 1949, preference in allotting seats was given to those who 'had bought tickets for the Orchestral Concert in August'. Other highly popular offerings of the Light Programme included the comedy shows *ITMA, Take It From Here* and *Much Binding In The Marsh,* the quiz game, *Twenty Questions,* and the young people's serial *Dick Barton.* On 1 January 1951, *Dick Barton* yielded its 6.45 p.m. slot to *The Archers,* a farming serial which won such rapid popularity that it was prophesied in 1951 that it might one day rival the astoundingly popular *Mrs Dale's Diary.*[110]

The Archers was a Midland production and *Have a Go* originated in the north of England. Wales too made a much acclaimed contribution to the Light Programme. As has been seen, *Welsh Rarebit* began as a programme on the old Welsh Regional Service and won great popularity when it was featured on the basic wartime Home Service. It was the creation of the highly talented Mai Jones and, like its creator, most of its cast were natives of Monmouthshire. With the restoration of regional broadcasting in 1945, it was transmitted on the Welsh Home Service where it broke all Listener Barometer Records by winning an estimated audience of 59 per cent. *Welsh Rarebit* was transferred to the Light Programme for a season in March 1948 and again in February 1949. Among British audiences generally, it won more listeners than *Take It From Here.* 'Welsh Rarebit is a palpable hit,' announced the *Daily Mail.* '[It] is the darling of the Light,' enthused the *Manchester Guardian.* 'It is the most popular variety show on the Light,' reported the *Daily Herald.*[111]

In addition to *Welsh Rarebit,* Welsh productions for transmission outside Wales included further items for the Light Programme and contributions to the basic Home Service, the Third Programme, the BBC's overseas broadcasts and the output of other radio services. Some of these also enjoyed great popularity, especially Mai Jones's *Silver Chords,* a 'semi-sacred' programme of Sunday music. In terms of programme time, Wales made its chief contribution to British broadcasting in general through its orchestra, which in the late 1940s provided a 30-minute programme weekly on the basic Home Service and occasional performances for the Light and the Third. Drama from Wales was much scarcer; in 1948, for example, Cardiff was responsible for only two of the plays broadcast in the *Saturday Night Theatre* series. Wales was considered to be the natural centre for the production of programmes on the coal industry. In 1946, P. H. Burton produced *The Battle for Coal,* a 'frankly propaganda feature' which won the enthusiastic endorsement of the minister of fuel and power. In 1948, Burton was responsible for a series aiming at 'improving the atmosphere in the industry', and details of the programmes were posted at pitheads. Cardiff planned further network features on coal but was told by Head Office: 'The governors think we should damp down on miners. We have praised them a little too much.' Among other Welsh productions on the Home Service were plays for *Children's Hour* (*Fifth Form at St Dominic's* in 1947, for example – a rather curious choice) and a monthly programme for the series *Festival Review* broadcast in 1951. Basic Home Service productions featuring Welsh contributors attracted much attention, and pleasure was expressed in 1947 when Ernest Hughes and Wyn Griffith, the Welsh team of *Round Britain Quiz* – then one of the BBC's most popular programmes – became the first to beat the London team. London outside productions broadcast from Welsh locations aroused great enthusiasm; following a visit by *Down Your Way* to Carmarthen in 1949, the *Carmarthen Journal* published each interview in full.[112]

Welsh contributions to the Third Programme consisted of little beyond occasional performances by the orchestra. In the last three months of 1950, Wales provided thirty-nine hours for the Light and five and a half hours for the Overseas Services, but only twenty minutes for the Third. For the services broadcast outside Britain, Wales provided a monthly newsletter in Welsh for the Dominions and, by 1950, it was producing a *Welsh Magazine* which was broadcast three times a month on the General Overseas Service. The most intriguing overseas programme was the religious service broadcast four times a year to the Welsh colony in Patagonia. The first was transmitted on 15 August 1947, and in March 1948 the BBC in Cardiff received a letter of appreciation signed by 204 residents of 'Y Wladfa'. Radio Éireann broadcast some Welsh programmes, including a performance of the opera *Tir na Nog* in 1948, and in 1949 Wales produced a series on the anthracite coalfield for transmission on the Romanian, Serbo-Croat and Bulgarian services of the BBC.[113]

Although it was through the Light Programme that the Welsh people had the greater part of their experience of radio, a study of broadcasting in Wales in the immediate post-war years must of necessity concentrate upon the output of the Home Service. Among the Home Service programmes from London and elsewhere which enjoyed a wide following in Wales were *Saturday Night Theatre* and the West of England's *Any Questions*, which was transferred to the Light in 1950. Above all, there was the *Nine O'Clock News* which had an almost ritual significance, although its listeners were far less numerous than they had been during the recurrent crises of the Second World War.

In the daytime, London productions were wholly dominant. Programmes produced in Wales were mainly broadcast between 5 and 9.30 p.m.; thus most of the output of the BBC in Wales was transmitted during peak listening hours. The late 1940s, the last years of the dominance of broadcasting by sound radio, were a period of much achievement in Wales. Advocates of innovative radio in the 1990s will discover that many of their ideas were implemented by Welsh broadcasters in the years around the mid century. The Reithian ideal that broadcasting should elevate public taste and buttress public morality – although frayed elsewhere – certainly held sway in Wales. Broadcasters such as Aneirin Talfan Davies sought 'not only to reflect Welsh life but to open windows . . . to the world and thus broaden the ideas of Welsh listeners'.[114]

Broadcasting in the Welsh language was especially Reithian.[115] Reith had opposed the use of wavelengths to target specific listener categories, advocating instead mixed scheduling which would allow the devotee of a particular service to be stimulated by a wide variety of broadcasting experiences. That principle was abandoned in 1945–6 with the introduction of the Home Service and the Light and Third Programmes. Welsh-language broadcasting with its considerable religious content and with the transmission of everything – from the lightest of variety to lectures on philosophy and performances of Greek plays – on the same wavelength was the sole example in British broadcasting of the Reithian principle of mixed scheduling continuing into the second half of the twentieth century. And, judging by the figures produced by audience research, it worked.

Broadcasters in Wales were proud of the mass interest in their productions: the thousands of letters received at Cardiff, Bangor and Swansea, the 320,000 regularly listening to the Welsh Sunday morning service, the 150,000 following broadcast Welsh lessons, the 2,000 at Liverpool who attended a broadcast Welsh variety concert, the 300 who queued at Llanelli to hear a broadcast discussion on gambling. In 1949, BBC officials were delighted that two Welsh Home Service programmes were cited by witnesses in court cases. Producers sought fresh contributors and it was proudly announced in 1948 that over the previous year Wales had broadcast 656 new voices. The country was scoured for material, with BBC officials anxious to ensure that 'all Welsh sources have been tapped'.[116] Appreciation indexes of 80 per cent and more were frequently recorded, causing the Welsh correspondent of the *News Chronicle* to declare that 'the BBC in Wales is going from triumph to triumph'. Even Saunders Lewis, long the scourge of Welsh broadcasting, was, by 1949, effusive in his praise. There was some evidence that the BBC was a force in uniting the Welsh-speaking community. In 1947, Aneirin Talfan Davies noted that a southern dialect play 'has been enthusiastically welcomed in the north, and "Hedd Wyn" has proved acceptable in the south . . . which perhaps indicates that radio may be the means of breaking down barriers of dialect'. Oldfield-Davies hoped that broadcasting would unite Welsh people of all descriptions. 'The basic job of the BBC in Wales', he stated in 1949, 'is to nourish and encourage national unity and to add wealth, depth and value to all aspects of national life.'[117]

In the twenty-six weeks, October 1949 to March 1950, the Welsh Home Service broadcast 592 hours of its own productions. Music accounted for 104 hours. Of the remaining programmes (many of which also contained a musical element), 245 hours were in Welsh and 243 in English, indicating the abandonment of the 60/40 formula adopted in 1948. The various categories of programmes had the following percentages of the 592 hours: music 17, talks and discussions 14, news 12, *Children's Hour* 12, schools programmes 10, religion 10, variety 9, sport 6, features 5, drama 4, outside broadcasts 1. Where *Children's Hour* and features were concerned, the two languages had roughly the same amount of air time. Welsh was more extensively used in talks, news, schools programmes and religion, and English was more extensively used in variety, sport, drama and outside broadcasts.[118]

Music, at 17 per cent of the Wales output, had slumped from the overwhelmingly dominant position it had enjoyed in the early days of broadcasting. Nevertheless, it remained the largest single element. Opposition to gramophone records declined and, by 1948–9, the Home Broadcasting Services were jointly transmitting thirty hours of records a week. Wales made little use of records, for an indigenous record industry had hardly yet come into existence. Popular music was attracting an increasingly frenzied following; in 1950, eight thousand people attended a concert broadcast from Swansea, featuring the Ammanford-born crooner, Donald Peers.[119] Traditional music received considerable air time and the superb broadcaster, David Davies, was enthusiastic in praise of the 'exquisite singing' of Shân Emlyn. Welsh choral societies were perceived to be 'not as flourishing as they used to be', but when Cardiff, in 1949, was invited to exchange programmes with Strasbourg, its offering was the Dowlais United Choir. The BBC took pride in its belief that it had saved the Three Valleys Festival – the festival of choirs from the Cynon, Taff and Rhondda Valleys held annually at Abercynon. Among Welsh audiences, singing was far more popular than instrumental music. The first performance of the BBC Welsh Orchestra – which competed with a boxing commentary on the Light Programme – attracted an audience of 3 per cent. A programme of the songs of David Vaughan-Thomas had an audience of 14 per cent, while there were occasions when 28 per cent tuned in to the series *Cenwch im' yr hen ganiadau* ('Sing to me the old songs').[120]

Although instrumental music failed to find a mass audience, the Corporation considered that it was duty bound to maintain the BBC

Welsh Orchestra – although, as has been seen, suggestions that it should be expanded were resisted. Its members faced considerable difficulties; as the BBC was virtually the only employer of instrumentalists in Wales, there were no opportunities for Cardiff-based performers to augment their income. Their problems were exacerbated by tensions within Cardiff's music department. As he neared retirement, Idris Lewis, the head of music, became increasingly irascible, and conflict between him and Mansel Thomas, the orchestra's conductor, led to 'a detriment in the orchestra's morale'. Lewis retired in 1950, when Mansel Thomas became acting head of the Music Department. Head Office, justifiably proud of the excellence of the BBC Symphony Orchestra, was condescending towards all regional orchestras. Annoyed by a particularly critical report in 1951, the North of England's head of music retorted: 'If the BBC only broadcast the best, it would always have the Philadelphia with Toscanini.' 'The Welsh Orchestra', London's head of music noted in 1951, 'does much good on the Welsh Home Service in its programmes . . . by Welsh composers [but] it is by no means easy to persuade the Home and Light to take their full allocation of [its performances].'[121]

Others were less dismissive. In 1951, the great horn-player, Denis Braine, declared that, in their ability to sight-read, the members of the BBC Welsh Symphony Orchestra were superior to those of the Vienna Philharmonic. A performance by the BBC Welsh Singers and Orchestra of Schubert's Mass in B flat in 1948 was hailed as 'the best thing of its kind ever done by the BBC in Wales'. The orchestra's industriousness was remarkable; in 1949, it was responsible for a total of 300 broadcasts. As Head Office noted, without it Welsh composers would have been totally bereft. Temporarily augmented to fifty players, it gave the first performance of Daniel Jones's First Symphony in 1948 and of his second in 1951. In 1949, twenty living Welsh composers had separate programmes devoted to their work, and in 1951 there was much praise for the orchestra's performance in a special Festival of Britain concert on the Third Programme consisting exclusively of the recent works of Welsh composers.[122]

Talks and discussion were the second largest category in the output of the Welsh Home Service. Talks, it was reported in 1949, enjoyed a greater following in Wales than in any other part of the United Kingdom. There was a widespread belief that the Welsh, paticularly those with a Nonconformist background, were natural radio talkers. 'As a chapel regular,' wrote I. B. Griffith, 'I was no stranger to conversations with the unseen.' Talks of an academic nature could attract very considerable audiences. Professor Aaron's introduction to Greek philosophy, given in English in January 1946, had a listening index of 12 per cent, and a description of the travels of Giraldus Cambrensis in December of the same year had one of 17 per cent.[123]

On the Welsh Home Service, talks in Welsh exceeded in number those in English by 30 per cent and, considering that they were accessible to less than two-fifths of the population of Wales, their listening indexes were high. In 1946, 8 per cent heard T. J. Morgan discussing *Crefft Geiriau* ('The Craft of Words') and 6 per cent tuned into W. J. Gruffydd's *Hen Atgofion* ('Old Memories') despite the fact that it coincided with *ITMA*. The themes of Welsh-language talks tended to be somewhat restricted. An attempt in 1948 to provide 'a science magazine was a gallant but not entirely successful venture'. 'It is difficult', wrote Oldfield-Davies, 'to find speakers fluent in Welsh who have the necessary knowledge to discuss industrial and commercial matters. For that reason the output in Welsh still tends to be predominantly literary and theological.' In both languages, broadcasts on industrial communities tended to dwell on the past: a programme featuring tinplate workers in 1951 was 'a series of reminiscences rather than a survey of the present day'.[124] Interviews continued to be scripted despite Megan Lloyd George's campaign to open up the microphone to spontaneous discussion. The dialogue in the programme *Country Magazine*, stated the *Liverpool Daily Post*, 'lacked homeliness. Some of the speakers knew full well the meaning of the long words they were made to use [but] it took all their time to pronounce them. Words . . . should match the characters.' *Seiat Holi* (the Welsh *Brains Trust*) was considered to be particularly stilted, with academics excessively represented. However some university figures – Ifor Williams of Bangor in particular – were very highly regarded, and Stephen J. Williams of Swansea was praised 'because he does not sound like a professor on the microphone'.[125]

Political discussions continued to be handled very cautiously. As within the Corporation as a whole, Welsh broadcasters gave no coverage to elections. Discussion of current events was prohibited by the Fourteen-Day Rule adopted in September 1948, which sought 'to ensure that the BBC did not become an alternative debating forum to Parliament'. Issues to be debated at Westminster could not be discussed on the air during the fourteen days preceding the debate, and MPs were not permitted to take part in broadcasts on subjects of legislation from the First Reading to the Royal Assent. A close check was kept upon participation by politicians. Following the general election of 1945, the Welsh were represented by twenty-five Labour, seven Liberal and four Conservative members, but in inviting MPs to appear before the microphone, the BBC in Wales was expected to adhere to the British allocation of six Labour broadcasts to five Conservative to one Liberal. Accounts of the activities of Parliament given by MPs had a considerable following, with both *Wales in Westminster* and *Y Mis yn y Senedd* ('The Month in Parliament') regularly receiving listening indexes of 10 per cent. Oldfield-Davies, however, considered that 'some MPs do the work rather casually although they are well-paid for [it]'.[126]

Those outside the main British parties were not invited to participate in political discussions, although Plaid Cymru members were prominent in programmes dealing with cultural topics. On the far Right, it was widely believed that the BBC was riddled with Communists, and Wing Commander Geoffrey Cooper considered P. H. Burton's series on coal to be typical of the 'Communist-dominated BBC'. A secret memorandum, drawn up by the director of the spoken word in 1948, obliged regional controllers to supply monthly lists of proposed talks by known members of the Communist Party. The BBC, stated the memorandum, did not intend to ban Communists, but 'in present circumstances vigilance should be exercised to preserve proper proportions'. Cardiff's reports – copies of which controller Wales was requested to destroy – note broadcasts by, among others, William Eames and Idris Cox. T. E. Nicholas, among the most distinguished of Welsh Communists, was invited to broadcast in 1947; his commission was to pay tribute to his three favourite hymn-writers.[127]

News programmes, which represented 12 per cent of the output of the Welsh Home Service, were conceived of as primarily a Welsh-language service. 'In giving news in Welsh of world and local events,' wrote Watkin Jones, 'we continue to meet a need which otherwise would not be met at all. [From September 1939] "Newyddion" ... a national news service [was] the sole basis of our existence as broadcasters in the Welsh language.' Despite the accolades won by the BBC's news coverage during the war, the Corporation, after the war, 'began a quick march backwards into the unimaginative warp of the Thirties'. T. R. P. Hole, the Head Office news editor, sought safe, double-checked – and therefore rather stale – items, preferably about the royal family, eschewing human interest stories, the pursuit of scoops and the projection of the personality of newsreaders and reporters.[128] Wales followed the lead of Head Office. The twice-weekly English bulletin, *News from Wales* (the choice of preposition is interesting), became a nightly ten-minute broadcast on 29 September 1947; it was followed by a fifteen-minute bulletin in Welsh, containing some news from outside Wales but consisting in the main of a translation of the previous programme. As the BBC in Wales employed no reporters, the Welsh news was compiled from material submitted by journalists on local papers who received ten shillings for every item used. Oldfield-Davies noted in 1950 that 'as there is an inadequate flow of copy into the Welsh newsroom day by day, trivial items . . . are sometimes included to fill the time'. The bulletin, he argued, 'should vary in length according to the supply of news items which are really worth including'. However, Cardiff never emulated the celebrated statement broadcast from London on Good Friday 1930 announcing that 'there is no news today'.[129]

Following the complaints of the Welsh Regional Council of Labour, a Head Office emissary made a study of the BBC's news-gathering operation in Wales. The bulletins, he reported, 'had too much of an evening-newspaper air'. Local correspondents should be urged to specialize, and accounts of speeches by MPs should be curtailed. The world news element in the Welsh-language bulletin, which hitherto had been culled from the one o'clock news of the basic Home Service, should be provided with a late afternoon update from London. Ifan Pugh – a conscientious objector during the war and a campaigner for an amnesty for Breton nationalists – was deemed to be unsuitable as the Wales news editor. Oldfield-Davies was, however, unwilling to remove him from the post in 1950 in the wake of Labour Party complaints, lest it should seem 'that the one event was connected with the other'. 'It was expedient', wrote controller Wales, 'to allow an interval of time to elapse between the Welsh Regional Council of Labour's complaint . . . and Ifan Pugh's removal.' Pugh's contract as news editor was terminated in June 1952 and his place was taken by Tom Richards, previously the BBC's publicity officer in Wales. Despite the much discussed weaknesses of the news service of the BBC in Wales, it proved popular with its audience. An average of 11 per cent listened to *News from Wales* and the Welsh-language bulletin attracted 6 per cent, the equivalent of 20 per cent of the listeners capable of following Welsh-language broadcasts.[130]

With *Children's Hour* at 12 per cent and schools programmes at 10 per cent, programmes for children represented nearly a quarter of the total output of the BBC in Wales. In the late 1940s, Welsh-speaking children were rare in Cardiff, for the movement to establish Welsh-medium schools was then in its infancy. 'The planning of Welsh [language] programmes', wrote Lorraine Davies, the *Children's Hour* producer, in 1948, 'is a miserable hand-to-mouth business . . . In Glamorgan, the problem of finding young [contributors] gets worse week by week. As far as Children's Hour . . . programmes are concerned, the sooner we move west the better.' Despite the dearth of Cardiff-based contributors, the late 1940s was a period of much achievement in Welsh-language children's programmes. In 1948, the serial *Wil Six*, written by Hugh K. Evans, a Wrexham schoolmaster, and produced at Bangor, won wide acclaim. 'It can never be hinted again', wrote the *Liverpool Daily Post*, 'that it is not possible to broadcast first-rate features and drama from the north.' *Gari Tryfan*, a detective serial written by the Llanrwst minister, Idwal Jones, and others, was even more popular. Cardiff's Monthly Report in February 1949 noted that Gari Tryfan 'almost rivals Dick Barton'.[131] English-language serials also enjoyed a wide audience. Distinguished broadcasters in both languages – Hywel Gwynfryn and John Darren, for example – began their careers as child actors, and Michael Aspel recalled with admiration how Lorraine Davies 'bullied, cajoled and gently drew the best from [us]'.[132]

Child actors were also prominent in schools programmes, for the practice of conveying information through drama, already apparent in the 1930s, became increasingly dominant. Cardiff had been successful during the war in pressing for schools broadcasts in Welsh; one a week was provided in January 1940 and the number rose to three in September 1942. Provision doubled following the inauguration of the Welsh Home Service in July 1945. The Welsh Committee for Schools Broadcasting, established in 1933, gave way to a more autonomous body, the Schools Broadcasting Council for Wales, in October 1947. Chaired by Wynn Wheldon, the secretary of the Welsh Board of Education, and consisting of twenty-five members, it advised on the expenditure of the funds (£7,000 in 1950) granted by the Corporation to finance the schools programmes. By 1950, Wales was producing six programmes a week for schools, four in Welsh and two in English. (Schools programmes broadcast to the whole of the United Kingdom averaged twenty-five a week.) The English-language programmes dealt in the main with the history and topography of Wales, but in 1947 the BBC began providing Welsh lessons for monoglot English-speaking pupils. In 1948, 1,047 of the schools of Wales were receiving the programmes; the figure had risen to 1,633 by 1952, partly because of the increasing availability of mains electricity in rural schools.[133]

Among the BBC's Home Services, that of Wales had two main distinguishing features: its numerous broadcasts in a language other than English and its substantial output of religious programmes. In 1949, 120 hours were devoted to religion by Wales, a far higher figure even than that of Scotland. The difference is largely explained by the need to provide religious services in both Welsh and English. Provision in Welsh was far greater than in English; of the 120 hours, 84 were in Welsh and 36 in English. 'By present day standards,' wrote Lucas in 1981, 'religious broadcasting in the immediate post-war years was singularly restricted and unadventurous.' Beliefs other than those of mainstream Christians were ignored, and nothing was broadcast which might suggest that there were among the Welsh many who doubted the truth of the Christian message. Oldfield-Davies, a devout Congregationalist and Sunday school teacher, informed the Beveridge Committee that 'Welsh listeners would object to an anti-Christian talk'.[134]

The Welsh Religious Advisory Committee, the first Welsh organization in the history of the BBC, had been established under the chairmanship of David Lloyd George in 1928. It had suspended its meetings in 1939, but was re-formed in 1944. Chaired by John Roberts, the secretary of the Presbyterian Church of Wales, it had fourteen members representing all the main Trinitarian denominations apart from the Roman Catholics, together with a lay subcommittee. The Committee conceived of religious broadcasting almost wholly in terms of providing believers with religious services, a view shared by Glyn Parry-Jones, the religious broadcasts organizer. 'Religious convictions', he stated in 1950, 'are still the main basis of thought and practice.' In Welsh there was a morning and an evening service and a programme of hymn-singing every Sunday and a studio service on two weekday mornings. There were regular reports from denominational conferences, and in 1946–7 two series of programmes for Sunday schools were produced, a form of broadcasting undertaken by no other section of the Corporation. Output in English consisted mainly of an occasional Sunday service and a weekly morning studio service. Religious programmes attracted large audiences, with a third of a million people regularly listening to the Sunday morning service. 'The service', it was noted, 'is the "top of the pops".' Religious themes extended well beyond the confines of specifically religious programmes. *Wedi'r Oedfa* ('After the Service'), a Sunday-night talk programme, contained much piety, and a feature on the Labour leader, Mabon, was, argued one critic, over-concerned with hymn-singing.[135]

Of the time allotted to religious programmes, 70 per cent was devoted to output in Welsh and 30 per cent to output in English. With variety, the percentages were exactly reversed. In the half-year October 1949 to March 1950, the Welsh Home Service broadcast thirty-six hours of English variety and fifteen hours of Welsh. *Welsh Rarebit* was the main English-language offering, but there were devotees of other programmes, among them *Welsh Half Hour*, another of the productions of the indefatigable Mai Jones. Sam Jones's Welsh-language variety programmes had an even more enthusiastic following, for the late 1940s was the golden age of radio variety in Welsh. His *Noson Lawen*, a development of a formula he had pioneered in the 1930s, was a phenomenal success. With a listening index of up to 22 per cent (the equivalent of 66 per cent of those claiming to speak Welsh) and with appreciation indexes in the high eighties, *Noson Lawen* was the most popular programme in the history of Welsh-language sound broadcasting. A monthly series, it depended heavily upon the talents of 'Triawd y Coleg' (The College Trio), in particular those of Meredydd Evans, whose accolade, 'the Bangor Bing', has already been noted. Sam Jones's light entertainment programmes also included *Smalio, Cymru Fodern, Pawb yn ei Dro, Raligamps* and *Camgymeriadau*. His remarkable personality, combined with a natural desire among northerners to stress the popularity of the programmes emanating from Bangor – most of which were, in fact, produced by southerners – led to the belief that Bangor was the only source of Welsh variety in the heyday of sound radio. The belief was mistaken, for *Sut Hwyl?*, produced in Swansea, and several Cardiff programmes also attracted substantial audiences.[136]

Sport, one of the mainstays of broadcasting in the 1990s, represented a very small proportion of transmissions in the 1940s. In 1945, it accounted for 1.9 per cent of the output of the Light Programme, a percentage which rose to 3 in 1948. The Welsh Home Service, 6 per cent of whose air-time was devoted to sport in 1950, gave it rather more prominence. A predilection in Wales for rugby was the only factor which distinguished the Welsh taste for sport; a survey in 1947 showed that 10 per cent of the listeners of the United Kingdom enjoyed commentaries on rugby union matches; the figure in Wales was 22 per cent. Coverage of sport essentially meant commentaries on rugby, association football and cricket, although, during the Olympics in London in 1948, Welsh broadcasters reported on a wide variety of sports. The Welsh Home Service was proud of Alun Williams's coverage of cricket and G. V. Wynne-Jones's coverage of rugby, but there were laments in 1949 that 'a good association football commentator has yet to be found'. The lament was soon to become irrelevant, for in 1949 the Football League refused to allow the broadcasting of League games on regional wavelengths. There were difficulties with the rugby authorities also. The Welsh Rugby Union refused to seat the BBC's reporters in the grandstand at Cardiff Arms Park, obliging them to give their commentaries from highly inconvenient locations. In 1951, the Union banned Wynne-Jones from commenting on their games because he had published a book in which he cast doubt on the amateur status of some of the members of the national team. The Welsh Home Service chose another commentator, giving rise to attacks upon the 'meekness' of the BBC. Coverage of sport was almost entirely in English; the 33 hours 40 minutes devoted to the subject between October 1949 and March

1950 included no Welsh-language output at all. On 14 September 1951, however, the first Welsh commentary of a complete rugby match was broadcast, a precedent for extensive Welsh-language coverage of sport in the future.[137]

Features, constituting 5 per cent of the output of the Welsh Home Service, were the most highly prized of the service's productions. Features in Welsh were particularly ambitious. 'Welsh features', wrote Elwyn Evans, 'should be wide, indeed wider than English features, since English features emanating from Wales are confined to subjects of Welsh interest, whereas Welsh features should, as far as possible, represent trends in thought of general interest.' Evans and his colleagues were appalled by a suggestion in 1946 that the features department should be moved from Cardiff to Bangor. 'A man based at Bangor', wrote Aneirin Talfan Davies, 'will inevitably fall into the habit of writing material most suited for the ethos of the Welsh countryside, and avoid the difficult task of cosmopolitanising Welsh Features. (By this I do not mean that they should be less Welsh, but that the Welsh should cease from endlessly contemplating their innards.)'[138]

Features in English fell into three broad categories: Welsh history and topography, cultural developments in Wales and investigations into issues of current concern. Typical of the output were programmes such as *The Seven Wonders of Wales, Swansea and the Arts* and a discussion on tree-planting in the upper Tywi Valley, a programme which the Forestry Commission attempted to censor. A significant innovation was the *Arts Magazine* launched in 1949; it sought to provide a platform for Anglo-Welsh writers and among its early contributors were Dylan Thomas and Vernon Watkins. Despite the care lavished upon features, their listening index was not high. The 5 per cent who in 1950 heard *Y Dewraf o'n Hawduron*, an account of the work of T. Rowland Hughes, was considered satisfactory, but a programme on Richard Wilson, broadcast in 1949, had an audience of less than 1 per cent. With features, as with all programmes, audience size was profoundly affected by what was on offer on other wavelengths, and what was broadcast before and after. John Gwilym Jones's first production, a programme on sixteenth-century morality plays, coincided with the Light Programme's commentary on the Mills–Maxim boxing match. 'It is feared', stated the Welsh Home Service's Monthly Report, 'that [its] audience was very small.' *Swansea and the Arts* won an audience of 10 per cent, but it was pointed out that it was followed by a special prime ministerial broadcast.[139]

Drama had a far more substantial following. The drama producer, Dafydd Gruffydd, believed that listeners in Wales fell into three categories broadly equal in size: 'the purely English audience which prefers plays of a normal metropolitan character'; 'the Anglo-Welsh audience which likes a Welsh dialect play with a strong bias in favour of comedy'; the Welsh-language audience which 'wants plays about Wales with well-known obvious themes and containing strong religious and sentimental backgrounds'.[140] The first category, believed Oldfield-Davies, was of no concern to the Welsh Home Service, for its needs could be far better supplied by London. The second category was provided with a monthly offering by play-wrights such as Eynon Evans, Leyshon Thomas and Idris Williams. Eynon Evans's work regularly scored listening indexes of 25 per cent and more, while Idris Williams's *The Rescuers*, with Richard Burton in the leading role, won an appreciation index of 85. 'Richard Burton', wrote the *South Wales Evening Post*, 'is in danger of becoming a great actor.'[141]

Although the perceived tastes of Welsh-language listeners were occasionally catered for, Oldfield-Davies and his colleagues con-sidered that radio offered an opportunity to present the works of the world's greatest dramatists in Welsh, and translations were commissioned of plays by, among others, Sophocles, Aristophanes, Shakespeare, Molière, Ibsen and Eliot. Ibsen was particularly favoured, with Welsh-language performances of *Pillars of Society, A Doll's House, Ghosts, An Enemy of the People, The Wild Duck* and *Hedda Gabler*. *Pillars of Society*, noted the Monthly Report of April 1949, portrays 'a local scene in Norway which corresponds with what our listeners are familiar with in country places in Wales'. *Y Brenin Llŷr* ('King Lear'), Dafydd Gruffydd's production of the translation by his father, W. J. Gruffydd, was hailed as 'probably the most important and significant dramatic performance ever broadcast in Welsh'. In addition to the translations, five of the plays of Saunders Lewis were broadcast between 1947 and 1952, among them *Blodeuwedd*, with Huw Griffith, Lorraine Davies and Meredith Edwards. Listening indexes were respectable, with 11 per cent for *Y Brenin Llŷr*, 7 per cent for *Lladd wrth yr Allor* ('Murder in the Cathedral') and 6 per cent for *Antigone*. 'Plays in Welsh', noted the BBC in its evidence to the Beveridge Committee, 'are very solid fare.'[142]

There was a feeling that the offerings were rather too solid. Commenting upon the production of *Hedda Gabler*, Dafydd Gruffydd argued that 'it is not wise from the entertainment point of view to broadcast anything at all advanced in the Welsh language'. The Monthly Report of June 1951 felt misgivings about 'translations of the classics and rather highbrow verse plays that tend to loom large in the dramatic productions in Welsh . . . There is a need to cater for the Light Programme audience in the Welsh language. A daily programme on the lines of *Mrs Dale's Diary* [is being considered].' *Teulu Tŷ Coch*, a daily serial portraying the life of a Swansea Valley schoolmaster and his family, was launched on 1 October 1951. Broadcast at 6.45 p.m., it coincided with *The Archers*, a matter of some complaint. It achieved a listening index of 4 per cent and by the end of 1951 there were reports that the audience felt that 'the series was growing on them'.[143]

In the six months, October 1949 to March 1950, outside broadcasts, other than sports commentaries, amounted to 7 hours 20 minutes of the productions of the Welsh Home Service. The winter output was largely in English, but in the summer a number of OBs in Welsh were broadcast, in particular from the National Eisteddfod. In 1948, for example, there were four afternoon eisteddfod broadcasts, with an average listening index of 13.5 per cent. Under the leadership of Hywel Davies – the one truly innovative figure in Welsh broadcasting in the years following the Second World War – OBs became increasingly sophisticated. At a debate in Aberystwyth in 1949, he made use of a roving microphone in a live broadcast, a practice which Head Office viewed with trepidation.[144] In 1949, Davies had not yet reached his thirtieth year and the belief that his talents would be available to Welsh broadcasting for decades to come was the cause of much satisfaction. Alas, it was a hope that was not fulfilled.

5

The Era of the Fourth Charter:
Broadcasting in Wales, 1952–1964

I The early television age

In May 1952, three months before the opening of the Wenvoe trans-mitter on 15 August, 10,548 Welsh households had combined radio and television licences, the majority of them held by viewers receiving the transmissions of Holme Moss. Between 15 and 18 August, a further 5,000 licences were bought, and by the end of 1952 there were 38,236 in force – one for every twenty-one of the households of Wales. The number had risen to 82,324 by September 1953, an increase partly attributable to a surge of buying in time for the coronation of Elizabeth II. By then, there were more licences in Wales than in Scotland, although Scotland was twice as populous and its station had been in operation for eight months before the opening of Wenvoe. Of the 82,234 licensed households, almost 60,000 received the Wenvoe transmissions, 13,000 those of Holme Moss and 10,000 those of Sutton Coldfield. Between September 1953 and March 1955, Wales's licences more than doubled to 197,726, a figure which represented nearly 25 per cent of the country's households. By March 1958, half the households of the United Kingdom were licensed to view television, with 8,090,003 licences in force, the equivalent of 50.31 per cent of the 14,646,350 households. At that time, Wales had 378,491 licences, representing 46.24 per cent of Welsh households. By 1959, however, Wales had also reached 50 per cent, with 450,720 of its households licensed to view. In the ensuing years, the figure continued to rise and by March 1964 it had reached 638,182. In addition, there were undoubtedly large numbers who viewed without a licence. This was particularly true in the early years, before the Post Office began taking serious punitive action; indeed, the *Daily Mail* estimated in 1952 that in Wales and south-western England there was one unlicensed viewing household for every two licensed ones.[1]

Several factors inhibited the spread of television. Chief among them was the cost. In the 1950s, equipping a household to receive television was five times as expensive, in comparative terms, as it had been to equip a household to receive radio in the 1920s. In 1952, a workmanlike twelve-inch set cost about £70, two-fifths of which was purchase tax. More elaborate sets cost £200 and more, and those who wished to flaunt their prosperity bought a television combined with a radiogram, representing an outlay of up to £400. Prices fell rapidly in the late 1950s, and the average male manual wage, which was £4.16s.5d. (£4.82) a week in 1952, had risen to £8.16s.4d. (£8.81) by 1964. Those unable to afford a set were not necessarily debarred from viewing. In 1952, the *South Wales Argus* noted a new phenomenon – the pavement viewers who spent the whole evening staring at the windows of television shops. There was considerable viewing at the homes of neighbours; 8 per cent of those watching television at any given time were estimated to be guest viewers, and the *Manchester Evening Chronicle* commented: 'Put a television aerial up over your house and you will be astonished to find how many friends you have.'[2]

A further inhibiting factor was the unavailability of sets. There were long waiting lists at retailers in 1952 but the situation soon improved, and in 1953 the production of television sets exceeded that of radio sets for the first time. The Phillips factory at Hirwaun was a particularly important source; the five hundred who had been made redundant at the radio factory there in 1951 were re-employed in 1952 to construct television sets.[3] Some did not acquire a television because they had no electricity. In 1952 many of the rural areas of Wales lacked a mains supply and satisfactory battery-driven television sets were not available until the 1970s. Those determined to view installed generators, and the thump of the generator frequently drowned the output of the set.

For the inhabitants of some parts of Wales, there was no point in acquiring a television because they were beyond the reach of the service. Following the opening of Wenvoe – or more specifically, following the transmitter's switch to full power in December 1952 – satisfactory reception was available to about 2,330,000 of the 2,610,000 people of Wales. Of those, 1,866,000 were served by Wenvoe and 464,000 by Holme Moss and Sutton Coldfield, with the former providing a service to a far larger number than the latter. The opening of the Blaenplwyf transmitter near Aberystwyth on 29 April 1957 added a further 71,000 viewers, but there still remained 209,000 who lacked the service. By 1958, it was within the reach of 98.8 per cent of the inhabitants of England, 94.7 per cent of those of Northern Ireland, 93.5 per cent of those of Scotland and 92.4 per cent of those of Wales. In that year, the number unable to receive television was highest in Pembrokeshire (67,400), followed by Caernarfonshire (40,000), Meirionnydd (27,000), Carmarthenshire (24,000) and Radnorshire (17,100). Indeed, in 1958 Pembrokeshire, Meirionnydd and Radnorshire were the only counties in Britain in which more than half the population was beyond the reach of transmissions. The deprivation was relieved to some extent by the opening of the Llandrindod transmitter in December 1961 and of that at Llanddona in Anglesey in May 1962; in addition, there were by 1964 low-power relays at Haverfordwest, Carmarthen and Holyhead. Yet the BBC was still, in the 1980s, tackling the problems of isolated pockets. Bringing television to the urban multitudes was cheap – the cost of providing a service for the Sutton Coldfield viewers was 10*d*. (4p) a head – but ensuring that small communities in mountainous areas had adequate reception could be astronomically expensive.[4]

An additional – although minor – factor in inhibiting the spread of television was the resistance of intellectuals. As with radio, the educated élite did not warm to the new device, regarding it as a goggle-box and an idiots' lantern. When he succeeded Lord Simon as chairman of the BBC's Board of Governors in 1952, Sir Alexander Cadogan had never seen television. 'In the 1950s', noted Robert Silvey, 'of two middle-class families of similar income, the one with the lower educational level would be the one most likely to own a television.'[5] As television owners spent at least half their leisure time viewing, acquiring a set was regarded by intellectuals as publicly confessing – and it was necessarily public, for early aerials were very obtrusive – an inability to fill one's leisure hours with worthwhile pursuits. There were other reasons too why some of those able to afford a set refrained from buying one; they included concern for the quality of family life, fear of the hostility of offspring if their viewing hours were curtailed, and – among Welsh-speakers – a reluctance to install an anglicizing device in the home.

Yet the inhibiting factors proved to be only a slight brake upon the remorseless spread of television. It had taken thirteen years (1923 to 1936) for half the households of Wales to be legally entitled to receive radio broadcasts; it took seven years for that to occur in the case of television. The difference can be attributed to the fact that television coverage was achieved more rapidly than had been the case with radio, to the greater appeal of the new medium and to the relative prosperity of Welsh people in the 1950s.

When television was revived after the war, it initially consisted of production facilities in London and a transmitter for London. The subsequent installation of transmitters elsewhere did not imply the provision of production facilities elsewhere. Yet Head Office recognized that there were events in the regions of sufficient interest to merit the attention of the entire body of viewers, and, to that end, the regional centres were provided with television outside broadcast units. The unit for the region served by Wenvoe was based at Bristol; it did not arrive until February 1953 and Wales was not to have one of its own until May 1954. Originally, there was no intention of building regional television studios nor of producing regional alternatives to the main output. The hours during which television was permitted were laid down by the government, for Christopher Chattaway, who was minister of posts and telecommunications from 1970 to 1972, was the first minister responsible for the Post Office not to believe that television was 'a drug which the patient should only be allowed in prescribed doses'.[6] Initially, thirty-five hours a week were permitted, a figure which was increased to fifty in 1955. Nothing could be transmitted between 2 and 4 p.m. on a Sunday, lest children should be discouraged from attending Sunday school, nor between 6.15 and 7.30 p.m., 'to protect Evensong'. On weekdays, there was a closed period between 6 and 7 p.m. to ensure that infants were not distracted at bedtime.

Oldfield-Davies considered that the 'Toddlers' Truce' offered an opportunity, for he was determined that the Welsh language should have at least a token presence on the new medium. Although he was at pains to stress that Wenvoe was not a Welsh station but rather a British station on Welsh soil, he extracted a promise from the Corporation that the transmitter should be allowed to broadcast occasional Welsh-language programmes outside network hours and it was the period from 6 to 7 p.m. that he had in mind. Welsh programmes in English were a different matter. They would have to be on the network. 'By the spring of 1953', Oldfield-Davies informed Welsh Home Service listeners in August 1952, 'the single network will offer a programme from Wales perhaps twice or three times a month.' That means, commented the broadcasting correspondent of the *Liverpool Daily Post*, 'that we will not get anything which will not be of interest in England or Scotland'. In the early months, there were no production facilities at all in the area served by Wenvoe, and therefore all the television programmes planned in Wales were filmed by outside broadcast units based in London. They were the responsibility of D. J. Thomas, who until March 1954 was Wales's sole television producer. In 1952, Wales's television establishment cost the Corporation £2,170, with an additional £160 for telephones and other charges.[7]

The BBC's policy of not permitting opt-outs during network hours was reviewed in the autumn of 1952, partly because of pressure from the regions, but chiefly because the rise in licence income was more rapid than the Corporation had expected. 'Kirk O'Shotts is not transmitting the composite edition of children's newsreel every Saturday morning', noted the *Liverpool Daily Post* on 9 September, 'and the North will transmit some programmes from Holme Moss alone. But it is hopeless for Wales to consider doing so because the country is split between Holme Moss and Wenvoe, and Wenvoe also supplies the West Country.' Indeed, Wenvoe was the last of Britain's five main television transmitters to undertake network opt-outs on any considerable scale. In the early months of the transmitter's existence, however, Wales did produce some network programmes. Two were broadcast on the day Wenvoe was opened – the opening ceremony and a discussion in the evening. Wynford Vaughan-Thomas, in describing the opening, spoke a few sentences in Welsh, as did Lady Megan Lloyd George, a contributor to the discussion programme. Before the end of August, the transmitter had broadcast some Welsh in two other programmes – in a televised service from Llandaf Cathedral and in a review of the 1952 National Eisteddfod superbly introduced by Hywel Davies. Also during August, a televised version of *Welsh Rarebit* was broadcast. It was presented by Alun Williams and was considered to be not wholly successful.[8]

Wales's output over the following five months was rather sparser. Richard Dimbleby presented a programme from Snowdonia on 26 September and an Emlyn Williams play was broadcast on 9 November, but in the last four months of 1952 the only television programme involving the BBC in Wales was one portraying the Melingriffith tinworks transmitted on 1 December. By January 1953, the paucity of Welsh-originated programmes was the cause of increasing comment. 'Television', wrote the *Liverpool Daily Post*'s broadcasting correspondent, 'visited Melingriffith some weeks ago. When are we to get another programme on a Welsh subject? There is much more from Scotland.' The Corporation seized the opportunity offered by St David's Day 1953 to broadcast a number of Welsh productions, among them the first television programme entirely in Welsh. It was a religious service from Cardiff's Tabernacl Baptist Chapel. On 6 March, the first Welsh-language feature programme was broadcast. Filmed at the National Museum and transmitted between 7.40 and 8.0 p.m., it was carried by Holme Moss and Sutton Coldfield as well as by Wenvoe. The programme was a portrait of the remarkable bibliophile, Bob Owen of Croesor, Meirionnydd. There were protests from England, although all that the broadcast replaced was the test card. 'I hope the English will cry with pain,' wrote the *Western Mail*'s broadcasting correspondent. 'The louder they cry, the sooner Wales will have its own television service.' Other programmes broadcast in the first week of March included a discussion chaired by Hywel Davies, Welsh songs from the Albert Hall and a poetry reading by Dylan Thomas; in addition, there was much interest in the fact that three Welsh people appeared on the hugely popular guessing game, *What's My Line.* 'Television has come to . . . Wales in a rush,' stated the *News Chronicle.* 'Welsh viewers', declared Oldfield-Davies, 'are being treated far more generously by television than was anticipated.'[9]

The upsurge in production coincided with a search for a generally acceptable Welsh word for television. *Radlunio, radiolwg* and *telefisiwn* were in use, but none of these had won affection. A competition was launched and over a thousand words were suggested, some of them weird and wonderful. In May 1953, the word *teledu* was selected, although it was noted that it is the name of the stinking badger of Sumatra. The word had the merit of being usable as a noun or a verb, and, with affixes, offered words for one who televises and for a television production. T. H. Parry-Williams, the chief judge of the competition, admitted that it was very much a coinage, but he noted that the word television is a mongrel too.[10]

The momentum of early March 1953 was not fully maintained. Nevertheless, when the Corporation reviewed the first year of Wenvoe's transmissions in July 1953, it felt it had cause for pride. The promise of an average of two broadcasts a month from Wales had been fulfilled. They included a televised version of *Pawb yn ei Dro* – a popular radio programme – and also *Stori a Chân*, the first light entertainment television series in Welsh. The latter appealed to non-Welsh as well as Welsh-speakers, for, as the *South Wales Echo* argued, 'unlike sound radio, a viewer can enjoy a televised performance regardless of language'. The major broadcasting event of the summer of 1953 was the televising of the coronation and the commentators included Wynford Vaughan-Thomas and Alun Williams. The *Western Mail* was somewhat scornful of the Corporation's pride in its television achievements in Wales. 'After the royal splash', it stated on 20 July 1953, 'we will have to be content with infrequent and desultory television programmes from Wales. As in the early days of radio, the BBC hierarchy in London is retarding regional development until it has secured a close grip on the whole television service.'[11]

The comment was not wholly fair, for in 1953 the hierarchy was actively seeking to solve the problem of providing Wales with its own exclusive service, particularly with a view to increasing the number of Welsh-language programmes. Of the population of Wales in that year, 10 per cent could not receive any programmes at all and the deprived areas included much of Welsh-speaking Wales; 20 per cent received their broadcasts from transmitters sited in England, a percentage which also included a large number of Welsh-speakers; 70 per cent were served by Wenvoe, but that transmitter broadcast to as many viewers in south-western England as in Wales. The situation which had arisen in the early years of sound radio had been almost exactly replicated. In the 1950s, however, the Corporation reacted with far more sympathy than it had done in the 1930s, partly because Ian Jacob, who replaced Haley as director-general on 1 December 1952, was far more interested than Reith had been in the possibilities of regional broadcasting. A former defence adviser to the Cabinet, Jacob's experience of the BBC had come through his work with the Overseas Service at Bush House rather than through the domestic services at Broadcasting House, and broadcasts in languages other than English were wholly familiar to him. Furthermore, Oldfield-Davies was incomparably more concerned to serve Wales than Appleton had been, and in his efforts he was supported by the Broadcasting Council for Wales (henceforth referred to as the BCW), a body enjoying charter status, which began its deliberations in January 1953. Although the Council only had an advisory role where television was concerned, its arguments on the subject, put to the Board of Governors by Macdonald in a genial but tenacious fashion, received a fair hearing. Of relevance too was the fact that, in 1953, the threat of a commercial alternative to BBC television was hardening, and the Corporation was anxious to prove that it was more capable than any possible rival body of providing Wales with an adequate television service. In the 1950s, there were no articles in the *BBC Yearbook* calling for more dead languages and no trumpeting about the re-creation of the kingdom of King Arthur. Indeed, BBC officials sought punctiliously to ensure that there was no suggestion in its publications that – where television was concerned – Wales and south-western England were subordinate elements in some reconstituted West Region.[12] In the history of BBC broadcasting in Wales, the importance of the victory won in sound radio in the mid 1930s can scarcely be exaggerated. All the subsequent recognition of Wales in the field of broadcasting (and, it could be argued, in other fields also) stemmed from that victory.

The Corporation believed that the only answer to Wales's problems was to provide the country with a new series of transmitters employing hitherto unused frequencies. The Wenvoe transmitter had been built as part of a plan to provide the largest possible number of people with television in the shortest possible time, but the difficulties inherent in that plan justified its reconsideration. The Stockholm Conference of 1952 had granted the United Kingdom five frequencies in Band I and further channels in Band III. The Band I frequencies were all in use, but some of those in Band III could be employed to provide the whole of Wales with its own service through the construction of five new transmitters. As the BBC intended to apply to the Post Office for the Band III channels in any case, the solution the channels would provide in Wales was seen as a useful addition to the Corporation's armoury of arguments. In the summer of 1953, it urged the postmaster-general, Earl de la Warr, to release the Band III channels to the BBC, but by then the discussion over the use which should be made of additional channels had become subsumed into the debate over commercial television.[13]

The government's White Paper of 15 November 1953 proposed the establishment of an independent television authority to which channels in Band III would be allocated. Legislation enacting the main provisions of the White Paper reached the Statute Book on 31 July 1954, thus negating the BBC's 1953 plan for Wales. A number of Welsh patriots supported the coming of commercial television and several would be actively involved in commercial companies. Their activities distressed Oldfield-Davies, who, like Reith, considered commercial television to be not merely ill-advised but evil. He stated: 'Yr oedd 'na gynlluniau ar y gweill i gael gwasanaeth teilwng i Gymru a chael sianel ar wahân. Ond . . . fe chwalwyd y gobeithion hyn gan y Llywodraeth Doriaidd yn 1951 ac yr o'n ni'n synnu braidd bod arweinwyr amlwg, yn Cymry Cymraeg, yn ymfalchïo yn y ffaith fod 'na gystadlu i fod â'r BBC.'*[14]

With Band III denied to it, the Corporation saw no satisfactory answer to the problems of television coverage in Wales. For the rest of the 1950s, all Welsh complaints were answered with the statement that no channel was available – an exact echo of the BBC's reaction in the 1930s. Jacob was anxious to find some solution, however inadequate, and he ruled that the hitherto *ad hoc* practice whereby Holme Moss and Sutton Coldfield carried Wenvoe's ex-network Welsh-language programmes should become a fully recognized arrangement. 'Until something can be done for Welsh television', he stated, 'it would be necessary for English regions to make sacrifices to provide pre-network facilities.' He also sought from the postmaster-general a formal recognition that such Welsh-language programmes were not to be considered part of the maximum permitted hours. The matter was the subject of a ruling published by the Post Office on 3 July 1955. Television hours were restricted to a maximum of thirty-five between Monday and Friday and there

---

*'There were plans afoot to have a satisfactory service for Wales and a separate channel. But . . . these plans were dashed by the Tory government in 1951, and I was surprised that prominent leaders, Welsh-speakers, were pleased by the fact that there was to be competition with the BBC.'

could be no broadcasts before 9 a.m. or after 11 p.m. or between 6 and 7 p.m. On Saturday and Sunday, the maximum was fifteen hours and the Sunday closed periods were confirmed. The only exception to the ruling was that Welsh-language programmes for adults could be broadcast between 6 and 6.45 p.m. on weekdays and between 6.15 and 7.15 p.m. on Sundays, but 'there should be no more than one such programme . . . during these periods in any one week'. Oldfield-Davies was disturbed by the reference to adult programmes. 'If there is no Welsh children's television,' he wrote, 'there will be an outcry.' In September and again in October, the BCW minuted its concern that 'no time has yet been allocated for children's programmes', and in November 'token Welsh programmes for children were permitted monthly on Sunday morning'.[15]

These developments coincided with a further relaxation of the network-only policy. 'In 1955', noted a Corporation memorandum in 1958, 'small financial contributions [were] made to each region to broadcast occasional programmes for local audiences . . . and the BBC decided that the regions should also be provided with properly equipped studios for the production of plays, entertainment programmes etc.' The regional controllers were not wholly satisfied, for, as controller North pointed out, 'the allowance, which was intended for regional work, [is] mainly absorbed by the additional cost of network items'.[16] A major constraint upon the development of regional opt-outs was the fact that, whatever the regions put out, there still had to be a flagship, and therefore a costly, 'national' broadcast from London. As the London region was a fiction, there were no plans for it to have regional broadcasts which could be transmitted at the same time as the other regions transmitted their own programmes. Ironically, although all broadcasting innovations were first launched in south-eastern England, its culture as a region (assuming, as one should, that it had a regional culture apart from the metropolitan culture of London) was worse served by the BBC than were the cultures of the other regions of the United Kingdom.

These decisions were reflected in the increasing number of television programmes produced by the BBC in Wales. Between 1953 and 1955, they rose from two to seven a month. Of the twenty-one programmes produced in Wales in the second quarter of 1955, twelve were English-language contributions to the network and nine were Welsh-language programmes transmitted outside the prescribed hours. In addition, Wales was providing at least two items a week to the network news. (In the 1950s, Wales's television output in English consistently exceeded its output in Welsh, a fact not immediately apparent to a reader of the archive.) Small though the output was, it was beyond the capacity of D. J. Thomas, originally Wales's only TV producer. The veteran radio man, Dafydd Gruffydd, switched to television in February 1954, and in October of that year Selwyn Roderick, who had begun in sound, became Britain's youngest television producer. The BBC's practice of recruiting its television personnel from its radio staff reflected the Corporation's belief that television was nothing more than an extension of sound broadcasting and was subordinate to the senior service. The practice was denounced in the press. 'Regional television', stated the *South Wales Evening Post*, 'is a closed-shop for the sound-radio man. Outsiders, whatever their experience in the visual medium of films, or the theatre, are barred.' By the mid 1950s, television was beginning to resent its radio ancestry and the readiness of BBC television staff to join commercial companies can be explained in part by the fact that those companies were not encumbered by the radio tradition.[17]

The increase in television output needed additional accommodation as well as more producers. The *Western Mail* noted in August 1954: 'The North has a television studio and the West and Midlands are on the way to having them. Glasgow is pressing ahead. Is anything happening here?' In 1955, Broadway Methodist Chapel was converted into a drive-in studio and was first used on 11 October. Cardiff, however, was the last major regional production centre to have full facilities; that did not occur until 1959, when further premises were acquired near Broadway, enabling programmes not only to be filmed in Wales but also to be edited there. The Corporation had acquired Baynton House and its ten acres in 1952, with the intention that the site should accommodate all the BBC's radio and television activities in Cardiff. In considering names for the proposed headquarters, Oldfield-Davies noted that broadcasting appeals to both the eye (*llygad*) and the ear (*clust*). He coined the word *llust* and suggested that the Baynton buildings should be known as Tŷ Llust. (As the name would almost certainly have been anglicized into Lust House, the idea was not pursued.) Baynton House began to be used as office accommodation in 1955, but the Corporation was reluctant to build on the site despite the fact that the University College was pressing it to give up its premises in Park Place. On several occasions the building projects were postponed on cost grounds and there were accusations that Cardiff's plans were too grandiose.[18] In 1963, however, the foundations of a building designed by Percy Thomas were laid. Radio studios came into use in 1966, but the site did not acquire an adequate television studio until 1974. In 1975, Baynton House was demolished, an act which was widely criticized.

The mid 1950s saw a number of firsts in the history of television in

Wales. They included the first programme filmed before a live audience (February 1953), the first elaborate outdoor programme (a portrayal of coracle-men broadcast in April 1954), the first televising of a rugby match played in Wales (January 1955), the first Welsh-language television play (*Cap Wil Tomos*, transmitted in January 1955) and Wales's first televised play in English (*Wind of Heaven*, broadcast in June 1956). Yet the increase in output should not be exaggerated. In the last quarter of 1954, a monthly average of 1 hour 52 minutes in English and 1 hour 10 minutes in Welsh was broadcast, figures which had risen to 2 hours 40 minutes and 1 hour 25 minutes by the last quarter of 1955. 'We have still not achieved the aim', it was noted in December 1955, 'of having one programme a week for adults in Welsh.'[19] In February 1957, the *Radio Times* noted that, with the imminent abolition of the 'Toddlers' Truce', the only periods available for Welsh-language programmes would be 'before 2.30 p.m., 6–7 p.m. on Sundays, 4–5 p.m., Mondays to Fridays, and up to 3.0 p.m. on Saturdays'. A slot on Sunday seemed the obvious choice and the *Radio Times* expressed the hope that 'one p.m. on Sunday will become a fixed point in the minds of Welsh viewers'. From 24 February 1957, a regular Welsh-language programme was broadcast at that time. Among the offerings was the topical magazine, *Cefndir* ('Background'), first broadcast on 10 March; it was an expansion of the programme *Telenewyddion* ('Telenews') which had been been broadcast as one of the sporadic Sunday offerings transmitted before February 1957. *Cefndir* was introduced by Wyn Roberts and filmed by Wales's outside broadcast unit; its editing – the work of John Ormond Thomas – was carried out in London where the staff referred to the programme as 'Radio "Look You"'.[20]

As *Cefndir* was transmitted by Holme Moss and Sutton Coldfield as well as by Wenvoe, it was available to Welsh-speakers in most of the north and the midlands of England, a fact which aroused envy among the London Welsh. The possibility that they could have Welsh television programmes had been mooted in 1954. The matter had been raised by Alban Davies, a London-Welsh philanthropist with strong Cardiganshire connections, and had been taken up by Thomas Jones, who, in 1929, had been the first to intimate to Reith that broadcasting had a Welsh dimension. Oldfield-Davies viewed the request with suspicion. 'The intention of the broadcasts [from the transmitters in England]', he informed Head Office, 'is to serve Wales and that is all that can reasonably be expected of the BBC . . . The clear duty of the BBC is to ensure a service in Wales and that is much more urgent than to satisfy Welshmen in other parts of the United Kingdom.' With the launching of a regular programme, there were further demands. Oldfield-Davies remained unenthusiastic. 'It is merely incidental', he informed a resident of Wimbledon, 'that Welsh programmes are available in places like Birmingham . . . What I want to protect are those in Wales who view Holme Moss and Sutton Coldfield . . . To raise the matter might well result in the programmes being lost altogether.' In the spring of 1957, there was an organized campaign led by the Cymmrodorion, and Oldfield-Davies reluctantly made a formal application to Head Office. 'It would be better to grant the facility freely', he argued, 'than to be forced into it unwillingly . . . All it means is opening the Crystal Palace transmitter on Sundays [a little] earlier than usual.' Beadle, the director of television broadcasting, and Bishop, the director of engineering, were strongly opposed, arguing that it was difficult to justify the cost as the viewers were very few. Oldfield-Davies argued that there were 300,000 Welsh people in London, and Jacob proved sympathetic. The Sunday programme became available in the south-east of England from 23 February 1958. In subsequent years, other Welsh-language programmes were transmitted from Crystal Palace and in 1959 the London Welsh presented the Corporation with a plaque as a token of their appreciation. Requests from Welsh societies in north-eastern England that Welsh-language programmes should be broadcast from the Pontop Pike transmitter were, however, not acceded to. Many English people viewed the Welsh programmes, partly in order to play the game of spotting the English word. The religious broadcasting organizer, C. H. Beales, listened to a Welsh radio service in 1954, and the only two words he understood were Gandhi and Mickey Mouse. 'I do not know why these two characters were included,' he commented.[21]

Oldfield-Davies was convinced that only a non-commercial, quasi-state enterprise could provide a satisfactory service for Wales and he viewed with scepticism claims by the anti-monopolists that commercial television could provide Wales with its own service. The Popular Television Association held a rally in Cardiff in 1953, when that claim was given great prominence. Led by the earl of Derby, and including among its vice-presidents Sir Godfrey Llewellyn, the chairman of the Conservative Association in Wales, the association could appear to be a right-wing pressure group. Yet Tory grandees had no sympathy for commercial television and, although the Labour leaders were opposed to it, it was supported by a higher percentage of Labour MPs than by those of other parties. When commercial television eventually materialized, it found greater approval among Labour than among Conservative voters. The anti-monopolists wisely concentrated their efforts upon television, which did not have the prestige won by BBC sound broadcasting during the war, and the Corporation's service could be convincingly attacked as over-regulated and as lacking in the resources to develop the new medium. Furthermore, television advertisements were perceived to be more effective and profitable than sound radio advertisements, and commercial television was fortunate to come into existence at the opening phase of a long consumer boom and of an increasing desire to win recognition for branded goods. The small majority of the Conservative government of 1951 to 1955 made it vulnerable to a vigorous campaign largely conducted by its own supporters. And vigorous the campaign certainly was. The National Television Association, established to fight for the continuance of the BBC's monopoly and including fourteen university vice-chancellors among its members, proved no match for it. As Christopher Mayhew put it, the anti-monopolist lobby 'was populist, mendacious, mercenary and rich; its opponents were weighty, honest, public-spirited and poor'.[22]

Among Welsh patriots, there were suspicions of the BBC which dated back to the days of Appleton. The Corporation's hope of using Band III to create a full Welsh service was not made public, and there was a willingness to believe the claims of the Popular Television Association. 'The BBC will only have limited money for a regional service,' declared the broadcasting correspondent of the *Liverpool Daily Post*. 'Is it not better to have programmes with a Welsh slant, even if they are advertising someone else's products, than to be tied hand and foot to the London programme?' John Eilian of the Herald newspaper group, who had no love for the BBC following his abrupt departure from the service in 1943, was a particularly vocal advocate of the breaking of the monopoly. He was among a number of ex-Corporation employees who took that view; they included Coatman, and more particularly Norman Collins, who had been shabbily treated when head of BBC Television between 1947 and 1950, and who was the true begetter of the commercial television service.[23]

The government's commercial television bill made no mention of any responsibility a company might have towards the community it served. An amendment, however, was carried which obliged the companies 'to appeal specially to the tastes and outlook of the persons served'. Much was made in the House of Commons of the duty of the companies serving Wales to provide Welsh-language programmes, causing the *South Wales Echo* to express its opposition to 'the proposals of some MPs to hamstring commercial television by making it serve the scattered Welsh- and Gaelic-speaking communities'. The Act did not stipulate that Welsh-language programmes had to be provided, but it was argued that the obligation to do so was implied in the clause concerning tastes and outlook. The legislation gave wide powers to the Independent Television

211

Authority (the ITA) and it was the Authority, not the government, which decided that franchises should be allotted region by region. The decision meant that commercial television was regional in a far more fundamental sense than was the BBC. Commercial television, noted a Corporation memorandum in 1958, 'does not provide a national service [although] it has been obliged, by good business reasons, to adopt networking on an extensive scale . . . The BBC is unlikely to fragment its output regionally to the extent that is obligatory on commercial television.'[24] The providers of BBC broadcasts were all employees of the Corporation, which had its headquarters in London. The providers of the commercial programmes were the employees, not of the ITA, but of the contract companies, most of which had their headquarters outside London.

The new service started in London on 22 September 1955 with an advertisement for toothpaste. Birmingham followed on 17 February 1956. Birmingham's offerings could be received along the fringes of mid Wales, but commercial television did not substantially impinge on Wales until the inauguration of the Granada service from Manchester on 3 May 1956. Granada's service could be received by most of the inhabitants of north-east Wales and by many in the north-west – at least if they had bought a set capable of receiving two channels or had paid £15 or so to adapt their set to pick up a second channel. With the opening of Granada, the four companies serving the greater part of England – two in London and one apiece in Birmingham and Manchester – had all begun operations. They established Independent Television News, a non-profit-making concern charged with the duty of supplying all the companies with news programmes. The four companies became known as the main contractors or the parent companies and the eleven companies established later revolved around them like planets round the sun. The main contractors produced over 80 per cent of British commercial television programmes, and the other eleven companies – although most of them acquired elaborate facilities – failed to break the stranglehold. Granada was particularly productive, responsible as it was for 25 per cent of the commercial programmes.[25]

The threat posed by the regional structure of commercial television was of acute concern to the BBC. Controller North wrote in December 1954: 'The Opposition will make its first big drive in the provinces rather than London . . . There is the sheer material strength of the established BBC defences in London [whereas] . . . in comparison, the provinces may appear ill-equipped and ill-defended by us . . . Provincial audiences are less sophisticated and therefore are much easier to satisfy.' He then proceeded to ask for additional resources for BBC television in the North of England Region.[26]

Controller North's letter is the first indication that regional controllers would use the threat of commercial television to pressurize London. (The BBC's television staff in London also found the argument useful, for Head Office was still giving priority to radio.) Controller Wales, his hostility to commercial television notwithstanding, became adept at using the threat. He stated in September 1956 that he thought it unlikely that the commercial companies would do as many programmes of Welsh interest as the BBC. He was therefore flabbergasted when on 19 September 1957 Granada launched a series of hour-long Welsh-language programmes twice a week. Inaugurated by Lady Megan Lloyd George, the decision was 'bold and unheralded'. The programmes, wrote Oldfield-Davies, 'are hastily put together and under-rehearsed, but the presentation is lively and they are making an impression'. Jacob was concerned. He believed that Granada 'was exceeding its brief'; he raised the matter with Ernest Marples, the postmaster-general, but there is no evidence that Marples took any action.[27]

As the BBC, in September 1957, was broadcasting half an hour a week of programmes in Welsh, Oldfield-Davies seized upon Granada's initiative. 'It is necessary', he informed Beadle in October 1957, 'for the BBC to increase its output of Welsh-language programmes. As can well be imagined, the two hours a week in Welsh televised by Granada . . . has added point and force to complaints that there is too little in Welsh done by the BBC.'[28] Beadle, who had been a regional controller for twenty-five years, first in Northern Ireland and then in the West of England, and therefore had much sympathy with regional broadcasting, was nevertheless perturbed by the financial implications for the BBC of Granada's initiative. To compete would be expensive, for the Corporation could not augment its income by augmenting its hours of output. The commercial companies could do so. The only programmes permissible outside the prescribed hours were programmes in Welsh, and by broadcasting Welsh programmes, Granada was increasing its hours on air. As the time allowed for advertisements was a percentage of the total air time, the company could add to the minutes it devoted to advertisements at peak hours (and thereby significantly add to its income) because of its Welsh-language programmes. Bernstein, wrote Beadle to Oldfield-Davies, is putting out the Welsh programmes 'in order to build up some additional advertising time for the evening programmes'. 'Competition in this field', he continued, 'is most unfortunate and unprofitable, and some sort of co-operative agreement would be in everyone's interest in the long run . . . [A] concordat between the BBC and the programme companies on this issue would be a good thing.' The ITA, noted Beadle, 'might be prepared to come to some limiting agreement with the BBC'. Jacob expressed sympathy with the idea, but controller Wales made it clear that if a limiting agreement were a secret, it would be a conspiracy, and if it were made public 'it would be difficult to justify to Welsh public opinion'.[29]

Competition became a more acute matter following the opening of the ITA's transmitter at St Hilary in the Vale of Glamorgan on 14 January 1958. The area it served was roughly the same as that served by Wenvoe, for the Authority had decided that south Wales and south-western England should constitute a single franchise territory, presumably on the grounds that, as the mistake had been made twice, there was no reason why it should not be made a third time. The contract was given to the Television Wales and West Company (TWW), the main shareholders in which were the earl of Derby and his associate, the impresario Jack Hylton (25 per cent), and the *News of the World* (20.5 per cent); the *Liverpool Daily Post* later acquired 14 per cent. Little of the original investment came from Wales or south-western England, but prominent Welsh people were eager to serve on the company's board, a marked contrast with Scotland, where the élite held aloof from Roy Thomson's Scottish Television Company. Although the ITA's prospectus had not stipulated that the contractor would be obliged to provide Welsh-language programmes, TWW agreed to a contractual provision that 'so far as was economically possible, it would supply a certain amount of broadcasting in the Welsh language'. The clause was included at the request of Alban Davies, the ITA's member for Wales.[30]

Robert Fraser, the director-general of the ITA, an Australian by birth, was a Labour Party activist and a Benthamite. He thus belonged to that branch of Utilitarianism which believes that the principle of 'the greatest happiness of the greatest number' need not be tempered by J. S. Mill's warning that the principle could lead people to become addicted to inferior pleasures. Benthamism was the prevailing creed of commercial television, in contrast with the platonist ideals of the BBC. The impact of Benthamism soon became apparent. By the late 1950s, about 12 per cent of the peak-time output of the commercial companies was classed as 'serious television', compared with 36 per cent in the case of the BBC. Those most eager to obtain the commercial programmes were the first to adapt their sets or to buy a two-channel television. This was reflected in the fact that by the summer of 1957, of those able to receive both ITV and BBC programmes, 72 per cent were viewing the commercial programmes and 28 per cent those of the BBC. The Corporation was perturbed, for if its viewers were to become a small minority, the case for obliging all television-owners to buy a licence would be seriously undermined. Furthermore, in the mid 1950s, the inflation so characteristic of the late twentieth century was becoming increasingly apparent. When licence-buying peaked – as it inevitably would – the Corporation would be obliged to seek a higher licence fee merely to maintain its income. To ask for more money to provide a service for a declining number of viewers seemed impolitic. Indeed, it was the inflation factor above all which made the BBC sensitive to the charge that it was becoming a minority service. Jacob believed that to hold 35 per cent of the viewers was sufficient to justify the licence fee. An equal share, he argued, might even be considered to be undesirable, for that might imply that the BBC was no different from ITV; in that case, what was the purpose of having the BBC?[31]

The Corporation's ratings improved in the early 1960s, in part because an increasing number who were not particularly determined to watch commercial programmes acquired two-channel television sets, but largely because of the break-up of the Reithian ethos and the change in the BBC's output as a result of competition. It became less ponderous and condescending, causing even that determined opponent of commercial television, Christopher Mayhew, to admit that 'the breaking of the BBC's monopoly did blow away some cobwebs'. Above all, ITV taught the BBC that it had to be more entertaining. The news in particular became more exciting and innovative, especially following the replacement of the staid Hole as director of news and current affairs by the flamboyant Hugh Carleton Greene in August 1958. Greene believed that the BBC should seek to secure at least 50 per cent of the viewers and, after he succeeded Jacob as director-general in 1960, winning the ratings battle became one of the Corporation's chief concerns.[32] These developments were first apparent in London, but they spread elsewhere and by the 1960s the BBC's television output in Wales had a distinctly lighter touch. Oldfield-Davies's comment that the Granada programmes were under-rehearsed is particularly revealing. The BBC's early television output tended to be over-rehearsed, with participants acting a part they had learnt by heart rather than communicating naturally.

The rise of commercial television had other implications too. As the BBC had the only body of trained television personnel in Britain, the commercial companies had either to train their own employees or to poach those of the Corporation. They did both, and the influx of BBC staff into ITV served to graft something of the ethos of public service broadcasting upon the new concerns. The Corporation lost some dead wood, allowing the more rapid advancement of its younger, bolder spirits. It also lost some highly talented employees; in 1957, for example, Cardiff noted with regret that Wyn Roberts, a young man of great promise, had left for TWW. With posts available in more than one organization, those employed or seeking employment in broadcasting had a field to play, and they played it. Salaries rose considerably, and as commercial companies were eager to build up their staffs as quickly as possible, they were ill-placed to resist the demands of the unions. This was particularly the case with the technical and engineering unions, many of whose members had notions on pay and conditions which they had acquired in the film industry. ITV's capitulation to the unions obliged the BBC to follow suit. Until the 1950s, the Corporation had experienced very little industrial conflict; matters would be very different in subsequent decades.[33]

Where Welsh-language television was concerned, commercial television was a two-edged sword. It gave Oldfield-Davies much leverage when seeking resources, and its arrival also meant that there was television on two channels. With an alternative available, it was possible to argue that Welsh-language programmes could be transmitted in network hours, assuming that care was taken to ensure that both channels did not do so simultaneously. On the other hand, as the ratings battle was teaching the Corporation to be concerned about maximizing its viewing figures, especially at peak times, it was reluctant to sanction such network programmes, for by definition they could not expect to attract high ratings. Welsh-language programmes therefore continued to be transmitted in non-network periods, but the timings were likely to become increasingly inconvenient for viewers because the ITA was determined to undermine the whole notion of prescribed hours. Its first victory came in March 1957 when the 'Toddlers' Truce' was abandoned. The BBC did not seriously believe in that somewhat preposterous concept, but, as it could not increase its income at will, it strongly supported the limitation of broadcasting hours. Had the 'Toddlers' Truce' not come to an end, a Welsh-language service could have developed in a period verging upon peak time (6 to 7 p.m.) without displacing English programmes, and thus much of the bitterness expressed in subsequent years would have been avoided. The ITA argued that limiting broadcast hours made it difficult for the companies to develop regional broadcasting, and that the period 6 to 7 p.m. was specially suitable for regional programmes. There was substance to the argument, but applying it to Welsh-language programmes invited conflict.

It was under these circumstances that Oldfield-Davies argued his case, particularly the case for programmes in Welsh. In the entire history of the advocacy of the Welsh language, there can be few things comparable with his correspondence with Head Office in the late 1950s and early 1960s. The archive reveals him to have been meticulously courteous, eminently reasonable and, above all, tenacious. Younger (and lesser) Welsh patriots saw him, with his royalism and puritanism, as a somewhat *passé* figure, more concerned with justifying the Corporation to Wales than in justifying Wales to the Corporation. They were wrong. If there was a single creator of Welsh-language television, it is Alun Oldfield-Davies. (Reading an archive can be a humbling experience.) In his efforts, he was much assisted by the fact that, from 1957 until his retirement in 1967, he was the senior regional controller and thus the main spokesman of the BBC's regions as a whole. At Cardiff, he had the whole-hearted support of Wales's head of programmes, Watkin Jones, and that of the deputy head, Hywel Davies. Indeed, by the late 1950s, the cause of Welsh broadcasting in general was greatly enhanced by the increasing recognition of Hywel Davies's brilliance. His superb voice, his intuitive sympathy for those he interviewed, his skills as a producer and his ability to project an intoxicating mixture of power and charm caused him to be much in demand beyond the borders of Wales. Oldfield-Davies, who was clearly grooming him for the succession, wanted Hywel Davies's talents to have fuller expression. The opportunity came in 1957 when Ernest Jenkins, who had been Parsons's deputy at Swansea in 1925, retired from the post of Welsh executive. Watkin Jones was prevailed upon to accept the post, thus releasing the headship of programmes to Hywel Davies. Aneirin Talfan Davies became deputy head and was replaced as west Wales representative by W. R. Owen. The three Davieses were a remarkable team and, in the late 1950s, the BBC in Wales undoubtedly had as talented a leadership as had any section of the Corporation.[34]

Although Oldfield-Davies had been actively seeking to expand Welsh-language television output since 1952, his efforts became far more vigorous in the wake of the growth of commercial television. They coincided with a mounting campaign among Welsh-language loyalists. Sir John Cecil-Williams, the secretary of the Cymmrodorion, sent numerous letters to the postmaster-general, pleading for more Welsh on television. (The letters were signed by Cecil-Williams, but it is likely that they were actually written by Oldfield-Davies.) In 1953, a report to the Ministry of Education, *Welsh and English in the Schools of Wales*, sought assurances that Welsh would be used in television school broadcasts, an issue persistently raised in subsequent years by leading educationalists. In December 1957, Gwynfor Evans joined the BCW and doggedly pursued the issue of Welsh on television. Plaid Cymru organized protests, including one from the International League on the Rights of Man in New York. In 1958, a Television Action Committee was established which sent a high-powered delegation to put the case before the BCW. With its success in the 1930s as a precedent, the University of Wales set up a committee in 1958 to inquire into the Welsh television service. The Welsh Parliamentary Party discussed the matter with the postmaster-general in January 1959 and, in November of that year, the lord mayor of Cardiff convened a conference to discuss ways of solving the 'intractable problem' of providing Wales with a satisfactory television service.[35]

Oldfield-Davies did not welcome every one of these pressures. In particular, he did not care for Gwynfor Evans's contributions to the BCW's discussions. He informed Head Office:

> I question . . . the propriety of having the leader of a political party as a member of the Council . . . [Evans] brushes aside technical difficulties, supposing them to be easily surmountable given the will; he is concerned to nourish and develop political energy in Wales that will produce the will . . . I find myself unsympathetic to his political approach to a question which seems to me to be one of constantly balancing competing tastes and demands in relation to available resources.[36]

Oldfield-Davies's approach was to submit a substantial claim year after year and to use the fulfilment of the one claim as the basis for the next. Thus in 1957 he was praising the Corporation for making it possible to broadcast one Welsh-language programme a week, but in 1958 he was seeking one such programme a day and by the end of the decade he was arguing for considerably more extensive provision. Constantly, he used the spur of commercial television, urging that for the BBC to be upstaged by an upstart would be to undermine its role as the national service. Following the launching of the Granada Welsh-language programmes in September 1957, he requested an additional £30,000 (at least £500,000 at 1994 values) to employ twelve extra staff and to increase the BBC's regular Welsh-language output from half an hour to two and three-quarter hours a week, in particular by providing a daily news programme. Head Office demurred, arguing that Granada's programmes would be likely to be a temporary feature of its output. 'It would be unwise of us', controller Wales was informed, 'to spend a lot of money to counteract something that cannot last.' Oldfield-Davies retorted that TWW would soon be on the air. The company 'is boasting of its well-equipped studios at Pontcanna'; it had made extensive promises about its Welsh-language productions and they were likely to be a permanent feature of its output. A fifteen-minute daily bulletin at 1.15 p.m. was authorized. It began on 30 December 1957, raising the BBC's regular weekly output in Welsh from half an hour to two hours. Beadle, however, stressed that 'no further increase in Welsh-language output could be considered for some time to come . . . for [I] am concerned that the BBC's revenue should [not] be diverted solely for the purpose of competing with ITV in this field'.[37]

Oldfield-Davies was also anxious that the BBC should not be upstaged by ITV where English-language Welsh programmes were concerned. With Granada opening in May 1956, the Wales outside broadcasting unit concentrated its attention in the second quarter of the year upon making English-language programmes in north Wales 'to counter the impact of commercial television'.[38] With the relaxation of the network-only policy, English-language broadcasts displacing the 'national' programme and transmitted solely by Wenvoe became possible. In Scotland, the change of policy was seized upon as an opportunity to create the beginnings of a national Scottish television service. That option was not open to Wales, for Wenvoe's output was beyond the reach of the inhabitants of west, mid and north Wales and over half its viewers lived in south-western England. Indeed, in terms of providing it with a national broadcasting service, Wales seems geographically to be almost wilfully designed.

In the early years, Wenvoe's opt-outs were very rare indeed. In the first three months of 1955 there were only three – two broadcasts of *Westward Ho!* (a south-western England miscellany), and one of *Outlook* (a Welsh miscellany). Jacob was anxious that the Wenvoe opt-outs should be less numerous than those of other major transmitters, 'for increasing the frequency of programmes of local interest [from Wenvoe] would remind viewers more frequently of the inconvenience of the shared wavelength'. The problem became more acute when regional television news was launched following the abolition of the 'Toddlers' Truce' in February 1957. Most of the period 6 to 7 p.m. was filled by the lively network programme *Tonight*, presented by Cliff Michelmore and produced by Donald Baverstock, a native of Merthyr and one of the most promising of the protégés of the remarkable Grace Wyndham Goldie. Five minutes, however, were set aside for regional news and Head Office expressed willingness to grant each region £18,000 a year to pay for their bulletins. 'Regional news', stated Jacob, '[is] the prime justification for the policy of supporting television production facilities in the regions.' The service was launched in the North of England Region on 18 February 1957 and by the spring Scotland and the Midland Region also had their bulletins. Controller Wales and controller West opposed the notion of a joint bulletin, causing Beadle to state that 'as it would not be practicable for the West and Wales to have ten minutes . . . and the other regions five . . . [they would] be asked to stand down for the time being'. 'That would be unacceptable', wrote Oldfield-Davies, a comment which led Beadle to suggest that Wales and the West of England should have two and a half minutes each. The issue remained unresolved throughout the summer of 1957, with Oldfield-Davies pressing Head Office to remember that 'it is important to start a five-minute topical programme [as soon as possible] before the local commercial contractor starts in south Wales'. The bulletin – read by Michael Aspel – began on 30 September, and was made possible by the retiming of *Tonight*, but later it became an opt-out from that programme, an arrangement fraught with difficulties. 'The news is going well', reported Oldfield-Davies at the end of the year, 'but mid and north Wales get Midland and North of England respectively.'[39]

The launching of TWW's service on 14 January 1958 gave controller Wales additional ammunition in his battle to expand Welsh-language broadcasting. TWW and Granada broadcast each other's Welsh programmes, providing 3 hours 20 minutes in Welsh each week compared with the 2 hours 15 minutes provided by the BBC. Among TWW's productions was *Gwlad y Gân* ('Land of Song'). It was broadcast during the Sunday closed period on all the ITA's transmitters and was widely appreciated in other parts of the United Kingdom, particularly in Scotland. Although introduced in Welsh, it was designed also to appeal to those who did not understand the language. The BBC believed that TWW was breaking the gentlemen's agreement on Welsh programmes and Jacob made a formal protest to Fraser, the director-general of the ITA:

> A public broadcasting system is bound to recognize, even by only a token number of broadcasts, the minority whose principal or only language is Welsh . . . [The BBC] publishes its programmes in Welsh and no English is used by word or caption . . . But Land of Song is avowedly seeking to attract a non-Welsh audience . . . [The Sunday closed period] was instituted to safeguard periods of religious observance from competition [and] should not be used to attract large audiences.

The last action of Kenneth Clark as chairman of the ITA was to chastise TWW for broadcasting Welsh-language programmes which were attractive to those who had no knowledge of the language. The ITA ruled that for a programme 'to qualify as being in the Welsh language, it must be Welsh in performance and exclusively Welsh in language'.[40]

As a totally loyal BBC man, Oldfield-Davies was disturbed that commercial television was being seen as a more effective provider of a service for Wales. In June 1958, he wrote a lengthy letter to Jacob.

'It is of supreme importance to Wales', he informed the director-general, 'that, in addition to network programmes, it should have a regular television service which it could regard as its own . . . If the BBC does not claim the right to provide it, there are signs that other interested parties will do so. It would seem to be the natural obligation of a public service Corporation to meet the legitimate national needs of Wales and it is to be devoutly hoped that the Corporation will do so.' Noting that discussion had begun concerning the allocation of the remaining channels in Band III, he urged that frequencies should be allotted to Wales to enable the country to have 'a regular Welsh television programme . . . Viewers would then have a choice of BBC network programmes and, for part of each evening, programmes of particular interest to Wales.' The Corporation was hoping to receive the remaining channels in order to provide a second BBC television service, and, as in 1953, the demands from Wales were seen as 'a valuable argument in the case for a second service'. The BBC wanted another service partly in order to have a separate outlet for its more serious productions; that would allow the programmes of the original channel to be lighter, thus enabling the Corporation to fight the ratings battle more effectively. The commercial interests also wanted their own second service, arguing that only then would the principle of competition in broadcasting have real substance. The ending of the BBC's monopoly had not created a free market in television; the establishment of a series of companies, each with its own territory, had served to convert the monopoly into a duopoly. Additional channels for the commercial sector would allow an increased number of companies and thus permit meaningful competition.[41]

In seeking additional frequencies for Wales, Oldfield-Davies was hoping that they could be provided quickly, without waiting for the necessarily lengthy discussions which would precede their use in Britain as a whole. The Corporation's director of engineering commented upon Oldfield-Davies's plan in July 1958. It would be possible to expand Band III, he thought, thus allowing Wales and south-western England to have distinct services, but 'other regions have claims and so it seems to me that the possibility of a separate channel for Wales is very remote'. In October 1958, the BCW submitted a formal request that Oldfield-Davies's plan be implemented and the report was supported by detailed arguments and costings.[42] In November it was rejected by the governors on the grounds that the cost would be substantial, and that the plan, if implemented, could deprive the rest of the United Kingdom of frequencies. 'It would be wrong', they stated, 'to hold out hopes that cannot be realised.' The issue was complicated by the fact that

221

Undeb Cymru Fydd was arguing that, as there was not enough Welsh material to maintain two services, the BBC and ITV should jointly provide a single Welsh-language service, a scheme which was strongly advocated by Huw T. Edwards, one of TWW's directors. Beadle, in 1957, had suggested that the BBC and ITV should share each other's Welsh-language programmes, and the matter was broached in the BCW's submission of October 1958. Corporation officials were not enthusiastic. Such a scheme, it was noted, 'would lead to formidable difficulties of programme planning'. More important, however, was their belief that the entire plan was a ploy to allow a commercial company to muscle in on frequencies which loyal BBC employees considered rightly belonged to the Corporation.[43] The issue did not go away. Indeed, in subsequent years, channel sharing would be increasingly seen as the solution to the problem of providing an adequate Welsh-language television service.

Welsh requests for additional frequencies were also complicated by the fact that, by 1959, the government was considering appointing a committee to examine the entire future of broadcasting in the United Kingdom. In 1952, the BBC had received its third Charter; granted for ten years, it would expire in 1962. In 1954, the IBA was licensed to operate for ten years, a licence which would expire in 1964. (The former owed its existence to a royal charter, the latter to an act of Parliament; BBC governors were appointed by the Crown, the members of the IBA by the government – a subtle way of emphasizing that the older service was more establishmentarian than the young upstart.) The Corporation's Charter was extended by two years in order that future dispositions relating to both public-service and commercial broadcasting should be considered together. The committee of inquiry, set up in July 1960, was chaired by Harry Pilkington, the glass manufacturer; it submitted its report in 1962. The Pilkington Committee was the first broadcasting inquiry to be concerned mainly with television. When Beveridge was set up, there were 11.684 million sound-only licences and 586,000 combined licences; the equivalent figures when Pilkington was set up were 4.535 million and 10.469 million.

Oldfield-Davies considered that the existence of the committee offered an opportunity to mount a public campaign to secure additional frequencies for Wales. 'It would be tragic', he informed an audience at Aberystwyth in August 1960, 'if the people of Wales were content with anything less than a Welsh network to be provided by the BBC and involving the allocation to the BBC of a Band III frequency.' By then, Head Office agreed with him. It had also come to accept Oldfield-Davies's view that a network of transmitters linked with Wenvoe and covering the whole of Wales should be completed as soon as possible, without prejudice to any final post-Pilkington solution. This, it was considered, was an 'inadequate substitute', indeed a 'truncated plan', but it was one which could be undertaken at once, given Post Office permission. In December 1960, Arthur fforde, who had succeeded Cadogan as chairman of the governors on 1 December 1957, asked Bevins, the postmaster-general, for permission to implement the plan. Bevins considered the request for seven months and then rejected it, citing the need not to 'prejudice developments in the United Kingdom as a whole'. The ITA had been given permission to enable the whole of Wales to receive commercial programmes from Welsh-based transmitters and the Post Office's refusal to allow the BBC to do the same caused fforde to accuse Bevins of putting the BBC in an 'unacceptable situation'. His protest was of no avail.[44]

The Post Office's attitude was not unexpected. Indeed, although Oldfield-Davies was insistent that new frequencies were the only answer, he was aware in the late 1950s that he would have to operate for some years to come within the existing transmission system. As senior regional controller, he was actively concerned with his fellow controllers in seeking to obtain more resources for the regions as a whole. With the Pilkington Committee sitting, Head Office was anxious that the Corporation should maintain a united front. In September 1960, Carleton Greene, the director-general since January 1960, discussed with the regional controllers the evidence that the BBC should submit on regional broadcasting. They informed him that 'all [of them] felt that some bias against the Regions existed in London, but [they] agreed it would be most undesirable if any such attitude should reveal itself while the committee of inquiry was in progress'. This conciliatory demeanour was much assisted by significant developments in Head Office's regional policy in the months immediately preceding the establishment of the Pilkington Committee. In July 1959, it announced that £500,000 (£10 million at 1994 values) would be available for additional regional programmes, with £300,000 allotted to opt-outs and £200,000 to network contributions. There were to be thirty-two centres in Britain capable of undertaking at least some television work: six in category one (the main regional centres, Cardiff among them), five in category two (none of which were in Wales) and twenty-one in category three. The third category included Swansea, Bangor and Aberystwyth, which were to be equipped with small studios and effective links with Cardiff. Audience research on opt-out television would be instituted and, if the results were encouraging and if resources permitted, the regions would eventually be allowed to opt out at will.[45]

With English-language programmes, the concerns of controller Wales were similar to those of his fellow controllers and his successes in that field paralleled theirs. What made his position unique was that he was also pressing for more resources for television programmes in a language other than English. (Gaelic television was minimal and the BBC in Northern Ireland had decided in 1936 to broadcast no spoken Irish.) By mid 1958, the BBC's regular Welsh-language output consisted of a fifteen-minute regional programme at 1 p.m. on weekdays, together with a forty-five-minute programme between 1 and 1.45 p.m. on Sundays. 'There is an immediate need', Oldfield-Davies informed Head Office in June 1958, 'for an additional weekly programme of thirty minutes.' The £20,000 needed to finance it was promised in November and the programme was launched in June 1959. Transmitted after the network closed down, it initiated the practice of late-night broadcasting to a people with a tradition of going to bed early. The programme rarely started on time, for over-running was a common feature of the BBC's output in the late evening. 'The Welsh programme', complained Hywel Davies in February 1962, 'was billed for 10.50; football caused it to be delayed until 11.20 but it did not start until 11.31.' 'Wales must accept', wrote Head Office's presentation director, 'that any programme billed to start . . . [late] must inevitably be affected by the timing of earlier programmes, [for] a fade to time would obviously [be] a disservice to the majority audience.'[46]

Having won permission to broadcast an extra half-hour a week for adults, Oldfield-Davies turned his attention to children's programmes. The commercial companies had, in May 1957, been the first to broadcast television schools programmes. The BBC followed in 1958, and the first schools broadcast in Welsh was transmitted on 22 April 1959. All that Oldfield-Davies had originally sought had been an experimental series of five programmes in the summer term of 1959, but by October he was seeking one programme a fortnight. Beadle was concerned. 'I know very well', he told Jacob, 'that the Welsh [meaning Oldfield-Davies, no doubt] will go on pressing until they get one a week, which is thirty a year.' 'I hope that the ultimate cost', wrote Oldfield-Davies, 'will not deter steps being taken quite soon to move from the present almost negligible output. Unfortunately it is no good saying in Wales: "Look how much the BBC is to spend on television for schools in the United Kingdom." The reply to that is: "That is all the more reason why the BBC should spend more on broadcasts to schools in Wales".' By 1962, there were ten Welsh-language schools programmes a term and Beadle's fears had been realized. Others shared Beadle's concern over the successive applications from Wales. 'Last year', the controller of television administration informed Oldfield-Davies in March 1961, 'we did a general tidying-up operation on all the Regions so that they would be adequately staffed . . . It is difficult to make continued additions to the Establishment and disconcerting to find that further requests are coming along.'[47]

The Welsh-language schools programmes were outside network hours, as was the case with the adult programmes also. In March 1961, however, Oldfield-Davies sought permission to broadcast in Welsh once a week between 6.20 and 6.50 p.m., a period which had been part of the Toddlers' Truce but which had not been used for Welsh-language programmes since the demise of the truce in 1957. Greene demurred, arguing that 'too many non Welsh-speaking people would be deprived of a programme in consequence'.[48]

Oldfield-Davies's request for Welsh-language opt-outs, a request he had not made before, was motivated in part by the knowledge that commercial television would shortly be available in west and north-west Wales. TWW was anxious to extend its operations to those areas, in particular because the opening of Westward Television at Plymouth in May 1961 raised the possibility that it might lose many of its viewers in south-western England. Yet, although TWW's financial success made it one of the ITA's 'golden boys', there were doubts about the strength of its commitment to its territory. Unlike the other non-metropolitan companies, its head office was in London. That decision had been made, stated its senior executives, to avoid the invidious task of choosing between Cardiff and Bristol, but the company's critics considered that the decision was symptomatic of the attitude of the company as a whole. Writing of TWW, Clive Jenkins argued that 'in Wales more than anywhere else, the deplorable impact of a profits drive upon a national cultural situation can be seen'. The company made very few English-language programmes of regional interest, partly because of the nature of its territory. Programmes of interest to south-western England would have little appeal in Wales – and vice versa, *a fortiore*, probably. More significant to so mercenary-minded a company was the fact that extensive expenditure on regional programmes would reduce its profits. Most of its network-hours output was obtained from the main contractors at discounted rates. English-language regional programmes would have to be opt-outs from the network and paid for by TWW itself. Opt-outs tended to attract smaller audiences and therefore brought in less advertising revenue. These considerations did not apply to Welsh-language programmes because they were the only broadcasts permitted outside the pre-scribed hours. Furthermore, the Welsh members of TWW's board were far more interested in expanding the company's Welsh-language output than in pressing the company to increase the number of its English-language programmes of particular interest to Welsh viewers. The financial drawbacks inherent in producing regional opt-outs were relevant to the commercial companies as a whole, and, with the exception of Granada, they all interpreted the clause on 'tastes and opinions' in a somewhat cavalier manner. Nevertheless, TWW was considered to be particularly delinquent. In June1959, C. D. Shaw of the Corporation's Secretariat informed controller Wales of a private conversation he had had with a member of the ITA. 'TWW', wrote Shaw, 'is the ITA's problem child. The Authority is doing all it can to inculcate a greater sense of public responsibility . . . The fly in the ointment is Jack Hylton . . . The ITA proposes to offer a contract for a station at Aberystwyth to an all-Welsh group if such a group can be found.'[49]

Alban Davies, Wales's representative on the ITA, was strongly opposed to any extension of TWW's territory. 'The contract', he informed the Authority, 'should go to a company owned and controlled by Welshmen.' '[He] told me privately at the Cardiff National Eisteddfod', Oldfield-Davies told Beadle in August 1960, 'that an independent Welsh company dedicated primarily to Welsh-language television will be formed in October.' By October, Oldfield-Davies was setting out his long-term plans for BBC television production in Wales. Welsh-language transmissions should be increased from three and a half to eight hours a week and English-language opt-outs from one and a half to four hours a week. In addition, he urged that, as long as Wenvoe also served south-western England, links between Cardiff and the BBC's Welsh transmitters other than Wenvoe should be strengthened to allow them to opt out of Wenvoe in order to broadcast Welsh-language programmes at peak periods. If these plans are not carried out, he informed Greene in September 1960, 'I think the claim of the BBC to be the national institution of broadcasting in Wales will be seriously weakened'.[50]

Invitations to apply for the contract to provide commercial television to west and north Wales – the fifteenth and last contract to be granted during the first phase of the ITA's existence – appeared in the press in April 1961. The territory on offer consisted of those parts of Wales not considered to be covered by any other commercial company. It was to be served by a transmitter on the Preseli Mountains and another in the Llŷn peninsula. The Post Office, however, was prepared to allow the ITA to provide the contractor with an additional transmitter in north-east Wales – a part of Granadaland – on the understanding that its broadcasts would be markedly different from those of the Manchester company. With the north-eastern addition, the territory contained almost a million inhabitants, but well over half of them could receive a service, of varying degrees of viewability, from other commercial companies. Furthermore, the relay companies, who were almost as influential in supplying Wales with television as they had been with radio, were likely to be unsympathetic towards the proposed service. Bevins was somewhat embarrassed that he had authorized an additional ITA transmitter in north-east Wales while refusing a similar concession to the BBC. Perhaps in order to justify an apparent act of discrimination, he initially insisted that 50 per cent of the contractor's transmissions should be distinct from the network. Fraser protested, pointing out that STV, with four million people totally dependent upon it for their commercial programmes and with a massively secure financial base, only initiated 9.5 hours a week of its transmissions. The Post Office relaxed its demands somewhat, but still insisted that the contractor should broadcast ten hours a week of Welsh and Welsh-related material, and, with 'bleak rigidity', laid down that children's programmes in Welsh should not count towards the ten hours.[51]

As any company winning the franchise would clearly not be in the television business primarily to make money, Oldfield-Davies was inclined to consider a potential competitor in west and north Wales as veering upon being a public-service broadcasting organization and therefore akin to the BBC. In May 1961, the regional controllers' meeting discussed the BCW's suggestion that there should be co-operation between the BBC and ITV in the provision of a Welsh-language service. Reporting the views of the Board of Governors, Greene stated that as the organizations were 'two different animals, [they] could not co-operate effectively except on a very limited operational basis'. Controller Wales disagreed, arguing that if the contract went to 'a group . . . proposing to operate on a non-profit basis . . . [the governors'] attitude may be difficult to maintain'. The governors were not disposed to change their policy and in June 1961 the BCW minuted that 'it had accepted the Board's view that no offer of co-operation with commercial television should be made at this stage'. The issue remained on the agenda, however, and would be vigorously revived by the ITA.[52]

Four groups bid for the west and north contract. It was won by a group led by Haydn Williams, the director of education for Flintshire, and Cennydd Traherne, the lord lieutenant of Glamorgan. Among the group's other members were Gwynfor Evans of Plaid Cymru, Llewellyn Heycock, the chairman of the Glamorgan Education Committee, Miles Thomas, a leading industrialist, and

David Vaughan of Barclays Bank. The ITA granted the contract on the condition that Eric Thomas of Woodalls Press, a member of a group making a rival bid, should join the board, and that shareholders should be informed that dividends were a secondary consideration. The new company originally called itself Wales TV Ltd., with the implied claim that it was serving the entire country. The ITA ruled that the title should be changed to Television Wales (West and North) Ltd. (TWWN), but Haydn Williams, the chairman of the directors, was not always punctilious in obeying the ruling. Its Welsh title, Teledu Cymru (Wales Television) annoyed TWW, as did the title of its magazine (*Wales TV Weekly*), but these remained unchanged. The company acquired premises on Western Avenue in Cardiff and began broadcasting on 14 September 1962, when only the Preseli transmitter was available to it. The Llŷn transmitter was opened in November 1962 and that at Moel-y-parc serving the north-east came into operation in January 1963.[53]

In its initial months TWWN broadcast nearly eleven hours of Welsh and Welsh-interest programmes a week, most of which were transmitted at peak hours. A half were its own productions and a half those of TWW. (Granada ceased to produce programmes in Welsh when the new company began.) 'It really was', noted Robert Sendall, the deputy director-general of the ITA, 'a very creditable achievement.' Realizing TWWN's difficulties, the ITA treated it generously. Its transmission costs were £200,000 a year, but the Authority only charged £50,000, thus providing a subsidy of £150,000. TWW was also generous, particularly in view of the fact that its own ambitions had been thwarted, for it allowed TWWN to broadcast its programmes virtually free of charge. Yet all was not well. As Sendall put it: 'Bevins and his officials had, by their unreasonable demands, done all they could to put the infant company's chances of survival in jeopardy . . . [There was also]', he continued, 'a lack of prudent foresight and an impetuous excess of zeal [together with] occasional failures of tact and public-relations sense common to men who are convinced of the righteousness of their cause.' Miles Thomas and David Vaughan resigned from the board within a few months of the foundation of the company, probably because, as successful businessmen, they felt out of their depth in an organization in which dividends were a secondary consideration. Haydn Williams was not always easy to deal with, and Harvard Gregory, the company's head of programmes, remembers his relationship with Williams with some bitterness. Oldfield-Davies did not believe 'fod dechrau pethau'n hollol iach . . . Gormod o uchelgais a thipyn bach o ddicter.'*[54] His

---

*'that matters were wholly healthy . . . Too much ambition and some bitterness.'

colleague, Talfan Davies, was more explicit. He wrote a pamplet, *Teledu Mamon* ('The Television of Mammon') in which he lamented that some of the members of the continuing committee, established at the conference convened by the lord mayor of Cardiff, had devoted 'eu holl egni, nid i gynnal y frwydr dros gwasanaeth teledu i Gymru gyfan, ond i ffurfio cwmni masnachol preifat . . . Tynged Cymru ar hyd y canrifoedd yw gweld carfan o'i thylwyth hi ei hun yn encilio o'r frwydr i gynnal ei brwydr fach breifat ei hun . . . Y mae'r cwmni hwn yn cychwyn ei yrfa trwy ildio i arianwyr Llundain.'*[55]

Fraser and Sendall were insistent that the company's difficulties were the result of the Post Office's unreasonableness. TWWN, thought Fraser, had many merits and the deficit of £290,000 it had accumulated by March 1963 was not, in his opinion, the result of improvident expenditure. The company's rental was reduced to £100 a year and its staff reduced from 140 to 60; TWW and the main contractors agreed to supply it with programmes free of charge and Haydn Williams was replaced as chairman by Eric Thomas. The postmaster-general released TWWN from its commitment to ten hours a week on 28 March 1963, but by then the company had ceased to make its own programmes. With pressure from creditors, bankruptcy loomed. As there was no recognized way for a television company to go into liquidation, the ITA was relieved when, in September 1963, TWWN was bought by TWW. The output of the two companies was merged on 1 January 1964, but TWWN remained in existence as a subsidiary of TWW until contracts came to an end. The purchase occurred at a time when TWW was under voracious pressure from Westward Television and it was glad of the opportunity to expand its territory in Wales. Indeed, there were suggestions that, as TWW was taking over virtually the whole of Wales, it should become an exclusively Welsh company and release its English territory to other interests. That it was not prepared to do, for its activities in Bristol were highly profitable and, unlike those in Wales, largely protest-free. Taking over TWWN had another advantage for TWW. Aware of the ITA's low regard for its record, and with contracts up for renewal in 1964, it could feel confident that, as it had saved the commercial sector from a potentially embarrassing situation, its future was assured. As Fraser put it to Charles Hill, the chairman of the ITA from 1963 to 1967: 'They can hardly expect to buy TWWN one day and be dismissed from TV the next.'[56]

---

*'all their energy, not to the struggle for a television service for the whole of Wales, but to form a private commercial company . . . the fate of Wales throughout the centuries is to see a faction of its own kin retiring from the struggle to maintain its own private battle . . . This company starts its career through yielding to the financiers of London.'

The entire episode, thought Sendall, was proof of the crassness of the Post Office. But, more importantly, it proved the futility of seeking to create a Welsh institution, purporting to be national, which did not include the industrial south. TWW, in its determination to be TWWN's legatee, was affirming that the reverse is true also.

While preparations were being made in the summer of 1962 for the launching of the new but doomed service in west and north Wales, the prospects of BBC television in Wales as a whole were transformed by the White Paper of 4 July. The White Paper was the government's response to the report of the Pilkington Committee, which was published on 27 June. The committee of eleven included a Welsh member, Elwyn Davies, the secretary of the Council of the University of Wales and the brother of Hywel Davies. It also included the actress Joyce Grenfell, and more importantly the social commentator, Richard Hoggart. On its appointment on 13 July 1960, it had been charged with the duty of considering the future of the BBC and commercial television – the continuance of both forms of broadcasting having been taken for granted. As with Beveridge, the Corporation deluged Pilkington with evidence; in all, seven times as many words were addressed to it as are contained in *War and Peace*. In preparing for Pilkington, Greene was naturally concerned to 'sell the BBC', but he also sought 'to unsell ITV'. Evidence was submitted by ten Welsh bodies. Most of it was concerned with securing a television service exclusively for Wales and available throughout Wales, an aim also supported in the Corporation's own submissions. The issue of a separate Welsh corporation, which had loomed large during the Beveridge deliberations, was hardly raised at all, but most of the Welsh bodies making submissions wanted the BCW to have the same responsibility for television as it had for radio, a recommendation also made by the Council itself.[57] Among the most effective pieces of writing directed at the Pilkington Committee was a pamphlet written by Alwyn D. Rees, the director of the Extra-Mural Department at Aberystwyth. The committee, he declared, represented 'Wales's last chance to obtain broadcasting justice through democratic means'. Presenting his argument as a parable, he pleaded with Pilkington 'not to give to Wales what you would be ashamed to give to England'.[58]

The committee recommended that a television service for Wales should be provided in Band III, and that the BBC, whose record it praised almost without reservation, should be allowed to launch a second television service. It was less enthusiastic about the commercial sector. Hoggart, whose book, *The Uses of Literacy*, is a landmark in the history of the study of popular culture, was much concerned with the uses or purposes of broadcasting, a concern which dominated the Pilkington Report, giving it a somewhat Reithian air. Much of ITV's output, declared the report, was 'vapid and puerile'. The ITA had too negative a view of the purposes of broadcasting. 'Winning the largest number of viewers . . . is not the only, and by no means the most important, test of a good broadcasting service.' The committee was emphatic that the commercial sector should not be permitted to provide a second television service until it had put its house in order. The ITA should have stronger powers to enable it to oblige the companies to fulfil 'the purposes of broadcasting'. Unfairly perhaps, Pilkington had nothing positive to say about the undoubted achievements of the companies in providing regional broadcasting – the fact, for example, that in 1960 they produced 3,750 hours of programmes outside London compared with the 1,220 hours produced by the BBC. Admittedly the companies had far greater resources with which to produce them. The BBC's expenditure on television rose from £9 million in 1956 to £16 million in 1960; ITV's advertising revenue increased from £10 million in 1956 to £60 million in 1960. Over half the revenue was paid out to shareholders – in 1959, for example, TWW paid a dividend of 110 per cent – but some of the larger companies, Granada in particular, invested extensively and commendably in programme-making. As Sendall put it: 'The ITV companies did not realize the extent to which the BBC could marshal middle-class prejudice against them.'[59]

The White Paper of July 1962 endorsed many of the recommendations of the Pilkington Committee, thus giving the BBC almost everything it had asked for. In addition to the second channel, it approved of the Corporation's plans for colour television and for changing from 405 lines to 625, a change which would bring it into line with the rest of Europe, thus improving the export prospects of British television manufacturers. Where Wales was concerned, the White Paper recommended that the BBC should have the facilities to allow it to provide an all-Wales service and that the input into that service which was produced in Wales should be the responsibility of the BCW. This provision was included in the fifth Charter, thus further differentiating Wales's position within the Corporation from that of the English regions. Indeed, unlike the fourth Charter, which laid down that, in England, 'responsibility should be devolved upon the Controller of each region', the fifth contained no such provision, the cause of great annoyance, especially in northern England.[60]

A second White Paper was published in December 1962. It advocated greater powers for the ITA and also endorsed Pilkington's suggestion that Wales should have a statutory ITA advisory council, on the lines of those already in existence in Scotland and Northern Ireland. (Hitherto, there had only been TWW's *ad hoc* Welsh committee.) An act of Parliament legislating on the changes in commercial television and authorizing the ITA to remain in existence for a further twelve years from 30 July 1964 reached the statute book on 31 July 1963. During the debate on the bill the Authority's approach to the designation of contract areas, particularly where Wales was concerned, came under attack. It was absurd, Ness Edwards believed, to have two Welsh companies, one of which needed a slice of south-western England to have a viable population and the other unable to survive because of the smallness of its audience. An amendment was brought before the House of Lords requiring that programme areas should be of adequate size, and one of its supporters, Lord Champion, stated that its main objective was to ensure that 'Wales should be treated as a contract area . . . [enabling] it to have a commercial service capable of expressing its own culture . . . and characteristics'. The amendment was defeated by forty-two votes to thirty-eight, but Bevins did announce that the ITA 'was looking again at the situation in Wales'.[61] Yet, in September 1963, when the Authority advertised the new contracts, it retained the Wales and south-western England territory. The franchises on offer were to last for three years, but they would be terminated earlier if a second commercial television channel started during that period; if there were no such channel by July 1967, contracts could be extended for a further six years. All the fourteen existing companies applied for the renewal of their contracts, and eleven of them faced rival bids. TWW was challenged by a consortium led by Edward Martell, whose Freedom Group put in bids for five of the proffered contracts. Every one of the existing companies had their contracts renewed, and although TWW had not faced very serious competition, Lord Derby and his company could feel that their rescue operation in west and north Wales had been amply rewarded.[62]

As the BBC operated under a royal charter, no legislation was necessary in its case. It received its fifth Charter, which took into account the recommendations of the White Paper of July 1962, and the Corporation was assured of its existence until 29 July 1976. The ITA obtained similar assurance through the Broadcasting Act of 1963. That act included clauses giving the ITA more powers to discipline the contractors, but little use was made of them. 'There has been no obvious improvement', wrote Anthony Sampson in 1965, 'in the meanness and philistinism of the companies.'[63] Under the BBC's new Charter, the United Kingdom would henceforth have three BBC television services: BBC1, BBC2 and BBC Wales. Transmitters were to be provided to ensure that all parts of Wales received BBC2 and BBC Wales; BBC1 – with its West of England or Midland or North of England opt-outs – would be fortuitously available in those parts of Wales which could receive broadcasts from transmitters sited in England.

As BBC Wales would be the only television service unique to Wales, the idea was mooted that it should carry the commercial sector's Welsh-language programmes as well as those of the Corporation. The notion of channel-sharing was therefore revived, a notion strongly advocated by the TWW directors, Huw T. Edwards and Alun Talfan Davies (the brother of Aneirin). The issue had been raised by the Pilkington Committee during its visit to Cardiff in April 1961. On that occasion, Oldfield-Davies advised the BCW to inform the committee that channel-sharing was possible but that a full 'joint working agreement in the planning and provision of programmes was out of the question'. Greene – who unlike his predecessor did not regret the ending of the Corporation's monopoly – was interested in the possibility, but in June 1961 he joined Oldfield-Davies in informing the BCW that an offer of channel-sharing would weaken the BBC's claim for a separate television service for Wales.[64]

In the autumn of 1962, with a BBC service for Wales having been endorsed by the White Paper and in view of the likely difficulties of TWWN, the ITA made a formal proposal that the all-Wales channel be shared, with the BBC and the commercial sector providing programmes consecutively. Oldfield-Davies argued that such an arrangement would be difficult 'without recourse to some external authority for the purpose of settling disagreements', and an external authority would be unacceptable to the Corporation. Furthermore, if BBC programmes were linked with those of ITV, there was a possibility that the Corporation's output could be flanked by advertisements. The BCW therefore opposed the scheme. Bevins pressed the BBC on the matter, but in Cardiff and in London the prevailing feeling was that, as the Corporation had been victorious in its bid to provide an all-Wales service, to share the victory with the opposition bordered upon the perverse. The postmaster-general therefore confined himself to issuing a directive instructing the BBC and ITV 'to co-operate as far as possible in respect of programmes where competition would be inappropriate', and he cited Welsh-language programmes in particular. The key words, Greene commented, were 'as far as possible'. The BBC and ITV agreed to exchange programme schedules in order to ensure that the two services did not both broadcast in Welsh at the same time. The arrangement did not always work smoothly and 'overlapping' became the cause of much acrimony following the launching of BBC Wales on 9 February 1964.[65]

II   The Welsh Home Service and the Broadcasting Council for Wales

The vigorous debate over commercial television – the atmosphere of holy war in the House of Lords and the utterance of more words on the matter in Parliament than are contained in the entire Old Testament – suggests that the central event in the history of broadcasting in the United Kingdom in the 1950s was the ending of the BBC's television monopoly. That was not so. The central event was the upstaging of sound radio by television. The Light Programme's celebrated enactment of Grace Archer's death by fire on the night commercial television was launched in London was not the BBC's spoiling tactic against its rival; it was sound radio's spoiling tactic against television in general. But there was no stopping the spread of the new medium. Sound-only licences peaked in Wales and in the United Kingdom as a whole in 1955. By 1958, less than half the Welsh households licensed to receive BBC programmes were sound-only households. Thereafter, sales of sound-only licences declined rapidly until, by the late 1960s, it was uneconomical to sell them. Following the abolition of the sound-only licence in 1971, those with a radio but no television received the BBC's broadcasts free of charge.[66]

The 1950s offer several landmarks in the upstaging of sound radio. The coronation in 1953 was the first event which more people experienced through television than through radio. Receipts from the combined licences exceeded those from sound-only in 1958; the BBC's expenditure on television surpassed that on radio in 1959. From September 1957 onwards, the *Radio Times*, which hitherto had given precedence to the listing of radio broadcasts, began devoting the bulk of its space to television. As electricity had displaced steam power, so pictures and sound displaced sound only, a change symbolized by the popularity of the term 'steam radio'. 'In two or three years time', prophesied the *Western Mail* in 1952, 'only the over-seventies will be listening to radio.'[67] The prophecy was not fulfilled, for sound broadcasting proved adaptable. It yielded the peak hours, 7 to 10 p.m., to television, but it discovered new peak hours – at breakfast time, midday and in the late afternoon. It changed from being a service expecting an intent audience to one to which people listened when they were doing something else, a change facilitated by the availability of portable sets and, particularly, by the proliferation of car radios. The 'tap listeners', contemptuously dismissed by Graves in 1936, came into their own. Cheaper sets meant that households could buy more than one; household listening became individual listening and a distinct teenage audience emerged. These factors led to a demand for sound-radio programmes less substantial in content than those traditionally provided by the BBC. By 1955, Radio Luxembourg was attracting a quarter of the British audience. 'They are listeners', noted Head Office, 'that the BBC had never had', and – it was implied – had never sought.

Among the Welsh people in the 1950s, as in previous decades, listening to the radio meant, in the main, listening to London's output. Audience research showed that the Third Programme had proportionately more listeners in Wales than in any other part of the United Kingdom, and its controller, aware that his service had a very small audience, was delighted when Swansea's intelligentsia, led by Daniel Jones and Kingsley Amis, established a committee to demand that it should be adequately audible in the town. Despite its comparative popularity in Wales, the numbers listening to the Third Programme were minute compared with the legions of the Light Programme's devotees. *The Archers*, which until the ending of the 'Toddlers' Truce', had no television competitor, attracted virtually half the population and at occasions like the Abergavenny Annual Show cast members such as Tom Forest were cult figures. To those growing up in the 1950s, the most abiding memory of BBC radio is that of teenagers (almost all male) who talked in the strangulated accents of *The Goons*, a zany Light Programme offering which lasted from 1952 to 1961. *The Goons* included Harry Secombe, one of Mai Jones's discoveries; Secombe, along with Wynford Vaughan-Thomas, could be claimed as the most widely known of all Wales's radio performers.

The Home Service too had its devotees, although, curiously, they contracted more rapidly following the coming of television than did those of the Light Programme. Programmes produced in Wales constituted about 22 per cent of the Home Service output broadcast from Welsh transmitters. Of the Corporation's total output audible in Wales, the proportion produced there – the twenty-six hours a week for the Home Service, together with occasional productions for the Light and the Third – was about 8 per cent, or rather less in view of the fact that other Home Services were available over much of the country. In accordance with the fourth Charter, the content of that 8 per cent and the staff producing it were the responsibility of the BCW. In the following pages, the way that responsibility was exercised will be discussed in some detail. As the BCW had authority over only a very small part of the radio experience of the Welsh people, such detail may seem excessive. Yet, as the subject of this study is BBC broadcasting in Wales, not BBC broadcasting to Wales, the Council must necessarily receive greater attention than the attention given by Welsh listeners to the output for which it was responsible.

As has been seen, the appointment of Lord Macdonald to the chairmanship of the BCW was announced in July 1952. Six months went by before the composition of the Council was made public. 'Four months have passed since the granting of the new Charter', noted the *South Wales Echo* in October, 'but there is still no sign of the promised independence and Lord Macdonald still has no Council.' The delay was caused mainly by a readiness to accept the argument of Ness Edwards and others that the BCW could become a creature of the Nationalists unless great care were taken in selecting its members. That fear led the Corporation to be diligent in seeking a balanced appointing panel. Consisting of Henry Brooke, Elspeth Huxley, James Griffiths, Lewis Jones and Megan Lloyd George, it laboriously worked through a list of over a hundred names. (Among the highlights of the archives are Elspeth Huxley's letters to Oldfield-Davies. 'How young is Glanmor Williams?' is one of the most intriguing of her questions.) On 29 December 1952, the names of the eight members were announced. In addition to Macdonald, they included three Labour Party members (Huw T. Edwards, W. H. Crews, the deputy president of the south Wales area of the NUM, and T. J. Evans, the mayor of Merthyr Tydfil), one avowed Conservative (Sir Hugo Boothby, a Vale of Glamorgan landowner), and one known Liberal (Miss Magdalen Morgan, the principal of Wrexham Training College). The political convictions of the other three (T. H. Parry-Williams, Bennet Evans, a Montgomeryshire farmer, and Mervyn Jones, the chairman of the Wales Gas Board) were unknown, but they all probably inclined to Liberalism. (To be a Liberal in Wales in the 1950s was virtually to be apolitical.) Of the nine (including the chairman), four – Macdonald, Edwards, Parry-Williams and Magdalen Morgan – were Welsh-speakers.[68] The BCW did not include a Plaid Cymru supporter until 1954 when Thomas Parry, the professor of Welsh at Bangor, became a member, and the first Plaid Cymru activist on the Council was Gwynfor Evans, who joined it in 1958. Nevertheless, from the beginning, many of the BCW's statements sound as if they could have been drafted in the Plaid Cymru headquarters, proof perhaps of the dictum that, in order to justify its existence, an all-Wales body, however constituted, inevitably makes at least quasi-nationalist noises.

The Council held its first meeting on 6 January 1953. It met monthly, except in August, and although Cardiff's Park Hotel was its chief meeting-place, it did hold sessions elsewhere. In 1954, for example, it met six times at Cardiff and once apiece in Wrexham, Llandrindod, Beaumaris, Aberystwyth and London. Jacob expected the Welsh and Scottish controllers to keep a firm rein on their councils. 'If and when the Councils desire you to do something which you know to be against BBC policy', he informed them in January 1953, 'it will be incumbent upon you to make sure that they understand this.' In particular, Jacob was disturbed by the fact that the staff producing the Welsh and Scottish Home Service programmes would henceforth be the responsibility of the respective councils. The controllers, he believed, should be specially concerned to ensure that the BBC's employees 'will continue to feel and to be a united body of men and women as before'.[69]

The first issue facing the BCW was the possibility that it would have nothing for which to be responsible, for its establishment coincided with a severe crisis in the history of the Welsh Home Service. At the Copenhagen Wavelength Conference in 1948, the United Kingdom had been granted eleven medium wavelengths, a generous allocation which reflected Britain's status as a victorious power. The conference had calculated that Europe, North Africa and the Near East could sustain 246 stations, but by 1954 there were 412 in operation. The United States was not involved in the Copenhagen decisions, and some Communist states, East Germany in particular, did not consider themselves bound by them. As has been seen, the first mention of interference by the American Forces Network appeared in April 1952. Two stations were involved: that at Frankfurt and the Blue Danube station at Linz. Their broadcasts overlaid those of the Welsh Home Service on 341 metres, particularly during the winter when darkness enhanced the range of the transmitters. By December 1952, there was talk in Montgomeryshire of a campaign to refuse to pay the licence fee and sad pictures were published of children deprived of their favourite programmes. Even without the interference, mid Wales was poorly served, and in January 1953 a temporary transmitter was installed at Tywyn, raising the number of transmitters serving Wales to four. The Tywyn transmitter worsened matters for listeners in Cardiganshire, and in March 1953 there were plans for a licence strike at Cardigan. At the request of the Council, R. T. B. Wynn, who had succeeded Ashbridge as the BBC's head of engineering in 1952, gave a talk on reception on the Welsh Home Service in February 1953, but he had little comfort to offer.[70]

Representations were made to the American authorities in Germany and Austria by the BBC and the English-speaking Union, and in November 1953 the Frankfurt station moved to another wavelength. The American ambassador visited Cardiff in March 1954 and was perturbed by the problems created by his country. The rural dean of Edeirnion wrote to Yale University, where the American secretary of defence had been educated, and claimed that he had been successful when more powerful forces had failed. His claims were doubted but, by the late spring of 1954, complaints about the American Forces Network had virtually come to an end. Then, in September 1954, concern began to be expressed about interference from Berlin Eins in East Germany. The station had begun on 341 metres in April, but its impact only became apparent as the days shortened. The saga of the Berlin station lasted for four years. Complaints were at their height in the autumn and winter of 1954–5, when they wholly dominated press comment on broadcasting in Wales. In October, the *Western Mail* wrote of the 'grave crisis of the Welsh Home Service', and *Y Cymro* urged the BCW's members to resign *en bloc* in protest. 'The time is fast approaching', declared Gwyn Griffiths, the perceptive correspondent of the *Wrexham Leader*, 'when [the Welsh Home Service] might as well be shut down.' 'It is seriously questioned', Watkin Jones informed the BCW on 18 October, 'whether it was worthwhile transmitting any Welsh broadcasts after dark.'[71]

Head Office informed the Council that the only way Wales could have interference-free radio was to provide the country with transmitters broadcasting on Very High Frequencies (VHF). Yet, as the BBC's initial plan for VHF did not include any transmitters in Wales, and as VHF sets had not yet reached the shops, the solution seemed a long way away. Furthermore, such sets were believed to be prohibitively expensive – prices between £22 and £30 were mentioned – and in the mid 1950s the government placed severe restrictions upon hire purchase. Other solutions were therefore sought. Head Office sent a senior official to Berlin in November 1954 but his journey proved fruitless. Approaches by leading Welsh left-wingers to the Pankow government and to the Soviet authorities were equally unsuccessful. In January 1955, Wynn visited Finland, a state which had not used all the wavelengths allotted to it at Copenhagen, but the Finns were not prepared to lend a frequency to Wales. Macdonald requested the other regions to broadcast some of Wales's output during hours of darkness, but they were unwilling to do so, and suggestions that the Welsh Home Service should be transmitted on the sound channel of the television service when television programmes were not broadcast proved technically impossible. In the winter of 1954–5, the BBC repeated some of the more popular night-time broadcasts during the day, but the arrangement was expensive and inconvenient.[72]

In November 1954, Wenvoe, Penmon, Wrexham and Tywyn were provided with low-powered transmitters working on the 202-metre shared international wavelength, but as their maximum range was only eleven miles, they proved wholly inadequate. John Eilian, continuing his feud with the BBC, suggested that such transmitters could be erected in all the towns of Wales, thus providing a genuine local service. A station at Caernarfon, he alleged, would cost no more than £1,500 to build and would only need to employ an engineer and a programme director, for performers would gladly give their services free. The Caernarfon Borough Council took the matter up and applied for a licence. Its action won widespread publicity, with Haley in *The Times* giving it sympathetic consideration. The radio correspondent of the *Western Mail*, however, considered the idea appalling. 'It would make us more provincial than ever,' he wrote. The BBC's governors were concerned. 'There can be no question of granting such a licence', they declared, '[for] it would be a breach of the BBC's [sound] monopoly.'[73]

The appalling reception was particularly resented in the countryside of north Wales, where rural district councils and branches of the Women's Institute were highly vocal. 'We have no service at all', stated the chairwoman of the Cerrigydrudion Women's Institute, for she claimed that in her community 75 per cent tuned in to nothing but the Home Service's Welsh-language programmes. The Gwyrfai Rural District argued that in Wales radio licences should be halved, because the Welsh only received half a service. In January 1955, Plaid Cymru established a Listeners' Association and in February the association submitted to the Post Office a list of a hundred radio-owners who had pledged to withhold the licence money. Fining two of them at Mold in June, the magistrates declared that 'our sympathies are with the defendants'. The magistrates at Llanrwst were less conciliatory; on being fined, the playwright and minister R. J. Berry was informed: 'If you take out a fishing licence, it does not guarantee that you will catch fish.' The distinguished journalist, John Roberts Williams, was near despair. 'Os peri'r ymyrraeth am ddwy flynedd eto,' he wrote in *Y Cymro*, 'bydd pobl nid yn unig wedi peidio â cheisio gwrando ar Radio Cymru, ond wedi anghofio fod yna'r fath beth.'*[74]

Complaints from Wales caused Jacob to amend the original plan of confining initial VHF stations to England. He announced that of the nine to be built, one would be in Wales, but it was fifth in order of

---

*'If this interference continues for another two years, people will not only have ceased to listen to Radio Cymru, they will have forgotten that there is such a thing.'

priority. The experimental station at Wrotham became a regular service in June 1955 and in that month Head Office decided that, because Wales's medium-wave service was so dreadful, the country should have Britain's second VHF station. Opened at Penmon on an emergency basis in October 1955, it offered a service to most of north-west Wales. Wenvoe followed in December 1955 and Blaenplwyf in October 1956; the Penmon transmitter was moved to Llanddona in December 1958, and in that month also Llangollen's VHF transmitter began broadcasting. By the end of 1957, 96 per cent of the inhabitants of Wales were within the reach of VHF transmissions, a figure which was not reached in Britain as a whole until 1959. Sales of VHF sets did not boom. They were twice as expensive as ordinary sets and, with the relaxation of hire-purchase restrictions in the late 1950s, buyers gave priority to the acquisition of a television. In 1971, only 41 per cent of the United Kingdom's radio-owners had a VHF set; indeed, as Charles Curran, the director-general of the BBC from 1969 to 1977, put it: 'The British audience for broadcasting is the greatest collective connoisseur of the obsolete in the world.' Nevertheless, those in the worst affected areas of Wales undoubtedly acquired VHF sets, for by 1958 complaints of poor reception were in rapid decline and by 1959 they had ceased altogether.[75]

Apart from providing a lifeline for the Welsh Home Service – and it must be stressed that by January 1955 that service was perilously close to oblivion – VHF offered other possibilities. Broadcasting in Britain had begun as local radio, but had been converted into regional radio because medium wavebands are a scarce commodity. With its almost limitless frequencies, VHF made local radio practicable on a far greater scale than had been undertaken in the 1920s, enabling it either to co-exist with regional radio or to replace it. Initially, the BBC advocated co-existence, but, where England was concerned, it increasingly favoured replacement. Head Office had always argued that the radio regions of England were artificial, but it was also suspicious of them (particularly of the North of England) as rival centres of power. VHF, by allowing the rise of local radio, provided an opportunity to break up the English sound regions, thus vastly enhancing London's position within sound broadcasting in England. There were undoubtedly at Head Office those who wished to break up the 'national regions' also, and replace them with an agglomeration of districts served by local radio, but that was not an option for the status of the Home Services of the 'national regions' was safeguarded by the Charter. Local radio, however, belonged to the future, for in the 1950s the BBC acknowledged that to provide it was beyond its means. The Corporation recognized that commercial interests could afford to do so, but emphasized that they would be bent upon creating a service wholly different from that contemplated by the BBC. Some limited experiments were undertaken. In the late 1950s, Wenvoe and Blaenplwyf opted out for brief periods to provide local news bulletins, and the practice was extended in subsequent decades. The BBC's Welsh staff, however, were not eager to fragment the audience of the Welsh Home Service. 'A service for the whole of Wales', wrote Oldfield-Davies in 1958, 'acts as one of the very important and effective unifying influences in Welsh society.'[76]

Far more significant in the Welsh context was the fact that transmitting the Welsh Home Service on VHF meant that the service was available over most of Wales on two channels. Thus, by the mid 1950s, the possibility existed of providing Welsh listeners with two distinct services, one in English and one in Welsh. The arrangement was advocated in 1954 by Urien Wiliam (the winner of the *teledu* competition) and, by the late 1950s, it had won extensive support. Yet two decades went by before it was implemented. During those decades, Wales's input into the Welsh Home Service continued to be bilingual and followed the 50/50 formula established in the late 1940s. Before the establishment of the BCW, the linguistic balance was a matter on which the director-general could rule, and, as has been seen, Haley in 1948 intervened to stop the drift towards a higher proportion of Welsh. Under the fourth Charter, the balance was a matter for the Council. Although the Corporation's senior officials in London had opposed the granting of autonomy to 'national regions', it would seem that they were glad that there was a shield between them and the complaints from Wales. Letters received at Head Office complaining about too much or too little Welsh were sent to Cardiff and complainants were told to address themselves to the BCW. Jacob, ardent advocate of regional broadcasting though he was, sometimes felt it politic to agree with a protester and then to admit his powerlessness. In January 1953, for example, he told an opponent of Welsh-language programmes that 'I very much sympathise with your feelings . . . Unfortunately, the Welsh-speaking citizens of your country are most vocal and insistent and over the years have steadily forced their views on us . . . However, all this is now of academic interest as far as we in London are concerned, because the government has assigned full responsibility for the policy and content of the Welsh Home Service to the new Broadcasting Council for Wales.' He informed another protester in May 1953: 'It is perfectly true that the tail wags the dog in Wales as far as the Welsh Home Service is concerned. The fact remains that the Welsh Council [has the authority] . . . and will only pay attention if enough of their English-speaking listeners in Wales make their views known to them.'[77]

The Council carefully monitored listeners' letters, particularly those attacking programmes in Welsh. In the 1950s, they averaged two a month and were almost invariably written by immigrants to Wales, for the indigenous English-speakers seemed content with the service they received. Some of the letters were highly offensive. A particularly abusive one from Carmarthenshire written by 'an English resident in Wales since 1913' provoked from Oldfield-Davies the reply: 'One of the more praiseworthy and likeable qualities in an Englishman is his active tolerance.' A Gower resident in 1954 informed him that 'Wales has no culture as such' and several letters emphasized that 'the United Kingdom exists and English is its official language'. Most of the replies were written by Rowland Lucas, who had succeeded Tom Richards as publicity officer in 1952. Lucas, a native of the Forest of Dean, had learned Welsh as a schoolboy in Cardiff but, as his name was English, correspondents tended to assume that he was in agreement with them. Part of the antagonism arose from the abandonment of the practice – which prevailed under Hopkin Morris – of not speaking Welsh at work. 'Erbyn hyn', wrote Oldfield-Davies in 1953, 'y mae mwy o Gymraeg nag o Saesneg i'w glywed yng nghanolfannau'r BBC yng Nghymru.'*[78] Thus monoglot English-speaking visitors to those centres could feel that they had entered an alien world. Press comment on the matter was more subdued than it was to be when Welsh-language television programmes became a major issue. Indeed, in 1953 the *South Wales Echo* claimed that the fact that there were complaints about too much Welsh and about too little Welsh was 'a sure sign of BBC impartiality'. On the other hand, the *Western Mail* in the same year wondered whether BBC officials had 'qualms over the numbers listening in the south to West of England and in the north to the Northern or Northern Ireland services'.[79]

Those seeking evidence of the BBC's partiality towards minority interests could point to the BCW's determined campaign to secure party political broadcasts for Wales, a matter which had also been of concern to the Welsh Advisory Council. The issue was the second item on the agenda of the BCW's first meeting in January 1953 and, in the archival material relating to the BCW's activities in the 1950s, it looms larger than any other subject. It was perhaps perverse for the Council to devote so much of its attention to a form of broadcasting that was among the least popular. Admittedly, in 1945 party political broadcasts had listening indexes of 40 per cent or more, but

---

*'By now, more Welsh than English is heard in the BBC's centres in Wales.'

in the history of democratic politics 1945 was an exceptional year. By the 1950s, the twelve broadcasts a year transmitted by the BBC – five Labour, five Conservative and two Liberal – were considered to be very tedious. It should be borne in mind, however, that until the mid 1960s the BBC transmitted nothing of a political nature during election campaigns apart from the party broadcasts. The broadcasts therefore had in the 1950s a far greater significance than they would have in the 1990s.[80]

As the BCW was empowered by the Charter to control the content of the Welsh Home Service, it assumed that it had the authority to organize party political broadcasts for Wales without reference to other bodies. For Macdonald, the issue became central to his concept of the Council's dignity. To Huw T. Edwards, who raised the matter at the January meeting, and also to Macdonald, the principle at stake was the right of Wales to have autonomous discourse on politics. Nevertheless, it rapidly became focused upon whether or not Plaid Cymru should have its own party political broadcasts.

Initially Jacob had 'no objection to pre-election broadcasts from Wales and Scotland provided they are confined to matters of special interest to those countries'. Harman Grisewood, the director of the spoken word, was more circumspect. 'The ratio of party represent-ation in Wales', he noted, 'is very different from that of the United Kingdom.' He was present at the BCW's meeting of 5 April 1953 when its members unanimously agreed to invite representatives of the parties to discuss the matter with Macdonald. 'It is', declared Head Office, 'a dangerous idea.' At the discussion, held in July 1953, the Liberal and Plaid Cymru representatives stated that they would participate in the proposed scheme. Those from the Labour and Conservative Parties stressed that their presence was exploratory only, and in September the BCW was informed that the two major parties had rejected the invitation to participate. Their decision, declared Huw T. Edwards, 'is a challenge to the Council to stand up for the rights of minority parties'.[81]

The Board of Governors refused to become involved, declaring that 'it is entirely a matter for the Welsh Council and one for which under the Charter the governors had no responsibility'. The BCW decided to press ahead with those parties prepared to participate, Macdonald informing Oldfield-Davies that he believed 'na fyddai'r llywodraethwyr yn caniatáu i blaid sy'n gwrthod manteisio ar y cyfle i amddifadu plaid arall o'r cyfle'.*[82] Grisewood and Beadle, however, let it be known that they 'greatly regretted the decision of

---

*'that the governors would not permit a party which refused to take advantage of the opportunity to deprive another party of the opportunity.'

the Welsh Council to go ahead without agreement between the parties. It would endanger the BBC's impartiality, and as broadcasts affected the composition of the National Parliament, the Council should consider the attitude of the parties at the centre'. By November Jacob was becoming concerned. He sought the opinion of the BBC solicitor, who stated that 'the Corporation could forbid the Council from transmitting special Welsh broadcasts *in substitution* for the party political broadcasts arranged for the Corporation, but I think it doubtful if the Corporation could prohibit the Council from transmitting such broadcasts *in addition* to those organized by the Corporation'.[83]

By January 1954, the attitude of the two major parties had stiffened and their chief whips refused an invitation to meet the BCW. Macdonald was incensed and considered publishing the entire correspondence. He pressed for a meeting with the party leaders; it was held in June 1954 and in it Attlee proved particularly uncooperative, especially on the issue of regional broadcasts between nomination day and polling day. On that point the BCW yielded, stating in September that 'as it has been the established practice of the BBC that election broadcasts are arranged by agreement with the political parties . . . the Council has regretfully decided, in the absence of such an agreement, not to proceed with Party Political Broadcasts during General Elections'.[84]

The statement was widely criticized. 'It has been condemned by newspapers almost without exception,' stated the *Liverpool Daily Post*. 'The Broadcasting Council has failed lamentably. They must shed their timidity.' The *Western Mail* published a leading article defending the right of Plaid Cymru to have party political broadcasts, and David Llewellyn, the Conservative MP for Cardiff North, declared that 'although I dislike Welsh Nationalism intensely, I loathe the restriction of liberty more'. Local authorities, particularly those containing a strong Liberal element, passed resolutions urging the BCW to reverse its decision. The agreement between the Corporation and the major political parties stipulated that party political broadcasts would only be given by parties fielding at least fifty candidates and that such broadcasts should be restricted to parties whose ultimate aim was to achieve a majority in the House of Commons. However, the BBC had not adhered rigidly to the agreement, for it had offered broadcasts to the Northern Ireland parties in 1953. Furthermore, it had not consistently denied facilities to one party when they had been refused by another. In 1954, for example, it televised the Conservative Party's annual conference, although the Labour Party had refused to allow BBC cameras to film its conference.[85]

Encouraged by press and local authority support, the BCW resolved to provide party political broadcasts outside general election periods. Its plan became known to Jacob in November 1954. 'The Council intends', he informed Cadogan, 'to have sixteen broadcasts a year shared equally between parties that have more than three candidates, with no attention paid to party strength. The party may choose whether to use Welsh or English . . . We should counsel moderation; sixteen on top of the twelve national broadcasts which the Welsh Home Service have to carry seem a considerable overdose.' (In fact the Council planned eight programmes a year of fifteen minutes each, with the four parties having a programme apiece every six months.) Jacob was particularly concerned about the impact on Scotland. The Scottish Council was consistently more pusillanimous than the Welsh, but it was also considering organizing some form of political broadcasting.[86]

The BCW instructed Oldfield-Davies to write to the parties 'not to invite their views', but to inform them of what was being planned and to ask them if they wished to take part. 'My guess is', he informed Grisewood, 'that the parties in Wales will accept.' Grisewood, who was disturbed by the 'fait accompli element in the decision of the Council', sought to ensure that the programmes would be restricted to Welsh affairs. 'The limits', he wrote, 'should be those of Welsh Day Debates' and he asked the BBC's parliamentary correspondent what those limits were. The correspondent was not reassuring. 'The chair has wide discretion,' he wrote. 'The House has been compelled to manufacture opportunities to consider Welsh business and the machinery for doing so bears, by contrast with that of Scotland, a distinctly improvised look.'[87]

As Plaid Cymru had put up four candidates in the general election of 1951, the choice of a minimum of three candidates was seen as a deliberate attempt by the BCW to ensure that it could broadcast. That was not so, stated the Council. As a minimum of fifty seats applied to the United Kingdom as a whole, and as fifty represented a twelfth of the membership of the House of Commons, the same principle had been applied in Wales, for three represented one-twelfth of the thirty-six Welsh seats. The Labour Party, which initially had not been wholly hostile to the BCW's plan, became antagonistic when it realized that it would have the same airtime as Plaid Cymru. As it received over half the Welsh vote, it considered itself to be the true Plaid Cymru (Party of Wales); indeed, on occasion it gave the impression that it saw activity in Wales by any other political grouping as an unwarranted intrusion upon its fiefdom. It demanded that broadcasts should be shared out in accordance with the votes gained by the four parties in the general election of 1951. On that occasion, for every vote cast for Plaid Cymru, the Liberals received 10, the Conservatives 43 and the Labour Party 87. Thus, on a strictly statistical basis, 140 broadcasts would have to be organized for Plaid Cymru to have one. The Council's adherence to the equal sharing of airtime led the Labour Party in January 1953 to refuse to participate in the scheme. The Conservatives also refused, for 'they took a serious view of a decision taken by a National Council without consultation with party leaders . . . [and because] they were impressed by the desirability of dealing centrally with the BBC over all political matters'.[88] More basic to the objections of the two main parties, however, was the fact that they had little in the way of specific Welsh policies. Party political broadcasts for Wales would be a recognition of the autonomy of Welsh politics and would play into the hands of Plaid Cymru and the Liberal Party, both of which had detailed blueprints for the future of Wales.

Macdonald was unmoved. He informed the Board of Governors in January 1955 that the BCW intended to go ahead with those parties which were prepared to participate. The Conservative chief whip sought advice on the correct interpretation of the BBC's Charter and the government's law officers provided him with an opinion similar to that of the BBC's solicitor. They did point out, however, that clause 15(4) of the BBC's licence gave the postmaster-general the right to forbid any broadcast, 'but that power is not one he would wish to exercise if the Corporation has the power'. As the Corporation did not have the power, the broadcasts could only be stopped by a specific directive from the postmaster-general. Charles Hill, the holder of the office, was reluctant to exercise his authority, and believed an amendment to the Charter would be preferable, for that would appear 'less high-handed, and less of a personal act of the Postmaster General than would a notice issued by him'.[89]

No postmaster-general had ever given a directive of the kind, largely perhaps because the BBC had exercised self-censorship. The Corporation was anxious that such a directive should never be issued and in the early months of 1955 its senior officials placed intense pressure upon Macdonald. 'The governors', Jacob stated on 1 March 1955, 'would not wish to jeopardize the understanding built up over many years between the BBC and the main parties with regard to party political broadcasts. If the parties were to lose confidence in the way matters were being handled, the result might well be to bring about a more stringent and undesirable type of control.' Meetings were held with Hill, who informed the BCW that, if it did not reconsider its decision, 'he would have no alternative but to issue a directive to ensure that the principle continues to be observed that party political broadcasts should be made only in respect of the United Kingdom as a whole'. Undeterred, the Council on 20 April 1955 reaffirmed its intention of arranging party political broadcasts between elections.[90]

The directive forbidding the BCW to organize party political broadcasts was issued on 27 July 1955. In a covering letter to Cadogan, Hill noted that, although the Charter 'does give power to National Broadcasting Councils to put on regional broadcasts, [the Charter framers] surely did not have this intention . . . If the Welsh Council succeeds, any group of three could get fifteen minutes twice a year at the cost of £450.' 'I am taking this action', he added, 'with the approval of the Opposition.'[91]

Plaid Cymru was outraged by the ban, and much pamphleteering and slogan-painting followed. It believed that the directive was specifically aimed at itself, and indeed Ness Edwards acknowledged that that was the case. *The Times* thought the ban was justified, but believed that it would be preferable to abolish party political broadcasts in their entirety. By the mid 1950s, several leading BBC officials agreed. 'If the parties', commented Grace Wyndham Goldie, 'wanted to say something too complex and they failed, the BBC was blamed. The broadcasts always have an air of falsity and half truth.' The alternative, argued the abolitionists, would be to broadcast parliamentary debates, but that was a step most MPs were not then prepared to take. David Llewellyn's concern that Plaid Cymru was denied the opportunity to put its case was shared by other Conservative MPs. 'I am quite satisfied', Raymond Gower (Barry) informed the House of Commons, 'that this ban . . . is contrary to the considered opinion of the adherents of the Labour, Conservative and Liberal Parties in Wales. If anything is calculated to encourage extremism, it is the appearance of discrimination against a political group.'[92]

The BCW protested strongly against the directive and was to repeat the protest annually. Ways were sought to circumvent the ban. Cardiff launched a series of political discussions and Head Office was informed in September 1955 that 'members of minority parties (including the Communists) would be given a chance in turn'. The Council monitored the activities of the commercial companies, noting occasions when Granada and TWW gave 'an outlet to Welsh nationalist opinion'. On 18 December 1957, it minuted the fact that Plaid Cymru officials had stated in a Granada interview that they had never been interviewed by the BBC. The commercial companies proved more enterprising than the Corporation in dealing with party politics, and in 1958 Granada's reporting of the Rochdale by-election was particularly innovative. The governors declared themselves 'reluctant to embark on a new policy . . . in the circumstances of the Rochdale by-election [because] certain types of by-election broadcasting, including news coverage, are perhaps inadmissible under the Representation of the People Act'. They did, however, maintain a dialogue with the parties on all aspects of political broadcasting, including the ban. In October 1958, the regional controllers were informed that 'the Whips were working out a scheme'. The scheme, which was adopted in time for the general election of 1959, retained the fifty-candidate rule but per-mitted 'regional hustings broadcasts open to those parties contesting at least a fifth of the seats in the area concerned'. As Plaid Cymru fielded twenty candidates in 1959, it did not qualify for its own election broadcasts – it would have to have contested fourteen seats outside Wales in order to do so – but it was permitted to take part in four hustings programmes, two in English and two in Welsh. The BBC promised to review the whole matter with the parties after the election, but by 1960 the issue became subsumed in discussion concerning the Pilkington Committee and the renewal of the Charter.[93]

The BCW's campaign to secure party political broadcasts for Wales – widely viewed as an attempt to succour Plaid Cymru – helped to nurture the belief that the BBC in Wales was biased towards the Nationalists. That belief was extensively aired at the Welsh Day Debate held on 30 January 1956 under the chairmanship of Rhys Hopkin Morris, the deputy speaker. David Llewellyn used the occasion

> to make the direct charge . . . that there is a distinct bias in the Welsh Region of the BBC in favour of Welsh Nationalism and Plaid Cymru, in favour of the Parliament for Wales Campaign and in favour of the individuals who support these movements . . . In the news and broadcasting from Wales there is evidence of a corruption of power . . . By suppression, selection and distortion, the strength of Welsh Nationalism is exaggerated day in and day out . . . It is monstrous that the wells of information . . . should be poisoned at their source.

He cited two cases in particular: the omission of any reference to a speech by the Labour candidate for Montgomeryshire attacking the notion of a Welsh parliament, and a report by W. J. Morgan which, argued Llewellyn, was undiluted Welsh Nationalist propaganda. He made a bid for the support of the Opposition. 'The Welsh Region', he declared, 'is hostile to the Conservative Party and [even] more hostile to the Labour Party.'[94]

Nineteen of the thirty-six Welsh MPs spoke in the debate. Garner Evans (National Liberal and Conservative, Denbigh) declared that the reaction of the House showed that 'nearly every Honourable Member agreed wholeheartedly with [Llewellyn]', a view also expressed by Ness Edwards (Labour, Caerffili). In fact, the majority of the speakers said little beyond noting that, as serious allegations had been made, an inquiry should be instituted. Six endorsed the accusations to varying degrees. George Thomas (Labour, Cardiff West) accused the BBC of 'corrupting the minds of the Welsh people' and demanded a royal commission on the Welsh Home Service. Edwards declared that 'the monopolisation of the BBC in Wales for a special political purpose [was the] mis-spending of public money'. Winding up, Gwilym Lloyd George, the home secretary and minister for Welsh affairs, promised to pursue the matter with Charles Hill, the postmaster-general. During the debate, the BBC in Cardiff released a statement denying the charges, an action which Jacob considered ill-advised and one which incensed Edwards. 'This is really going too far,' he stated. 'It is about time the government put the BBC in its place.' Thomas suggested that the denial sprang from guilty concern, causing Hopkin Morris to remark: 'The Honourable Gentleman's intervention was not justifiable.'[95]

The BBC was used to attacks by MPs and tended to dismiss them as ill-informed. As the General Advisory Council commented in 1955: 'MPs cannot be great listeners or viewers [but] they are subject to much second-hand advice about the BBC from interested parties.' The usual attacks were accusations of left-wing bias by the right, or (somewhat less often) of right-wing bias by the left. Condemnation from both sides of the House was an unusual phenomenon and one which, it was felt, called for immediate action. On 2 February, Hill informed Jacob and Macdonald that he was setting up a committee. His letter crossed with one by Macdonald informing Hill that the BCW was instituting an inquiry. Hill's action annoyed the Corporation. Its Liaison Committee expressed the view that the post-master-general 'had no real power . . . to set up an enquiry of this kind', and the General Advisory Committee recorded its concern 'about the procedure that had been adopted'. The press was also critical. 'The Postmaster-General', declared *The Times*, 'should have left the matter to the Governors or the General Advisory Council. [His] action is bad in itself and bad as a precedent.'[96]

Oldfield-Davies was much perturbed by the allegations. He had been given some warning. Llewellyn had written three letters to him in January, one of which stated that 'I am hoping to raise various matters relating to Welsh broadcasting on the next Welsh Day'. Copies of a number of scripts had been requested, but their contents were so innocuous that Oldfield-Davies felt no cause to be deeply concerned. 'There is nothing very interesting in the pieces David

Llewellyn has asked for,' Tom Richards informed him on 10 January. The ferocity of the attack was therefore unexpected. 'I was very surprised and disappointed', he wrote to Huw T. Edwards, 'at the irresponsible way in which charges were flung about.' 'I know from contact with them', Edwards told him, 'that [some of those making the allegations], immediately they hear the Welsh language spoken over the air, assume it to be the contribution of some Nationalist or other . . . Will you please convey to your staff . . . my faith in their impartiality and indeed my pride in the grand way in which they are serving Wales.'[97]

Edwards was not wholly representative of Welsh Labour activists. As has been seen, the Welsh Regional Council of Labour had sought an inquiry in 1950. In 1953, the Council had complained because a protest by thirty thousand miners had received less attention than a far more thinly attended demonstration organized by Plaid Cymru. In 1954, Welsh Labour MPs let it be known that 'they had sufficient evidence to prove that the Welsh BBC is heavily biased in favour of Nationalist elements', and the BCW's plan to distribute its political broadcasts equally among the parties seemed to be further evidence of that bias. The belief that the BBC in Wales was anti-Labour was fuelled by its practice of giving disproportionate attention to Welsh Conservative MPs. It did so because, as Oldfield-Davies explained to Tudor Watkins (Labour, Brecon and Radnor), 'we are obliged to observe in the Welsh Home Service a balance of parties as it exists over the country as a whole'. The ability to speak Welsh was rare among Conservative MPs, and less rare among Labour MPs, and therefore Conservatives were particularly over-represented on the more widely heard English-language broadcasts. 'English-speaking Labour MPs', Eirene White (Labour, East Flint) informed the House of Commons, 'have less of a chance to speak on *The Week in Westminster* because Tories hogged the English broadcasts because they could not take part in the Welsh ones.' Although the issue had been raised by a Conservative MP, the resentment was more widely felt on the Labour side, and the Welsh Regional Council of Labour was the only body to prepare evidence for the committee of inquiry.[98]

Among the Conservatives, Llewellyn was an isolated figure. His colleague, Raymond Gower, believed that the whole thing was a nonsense. Llewellyn's cousin, Sir Godfrey Llewellyn, the chairman of the Conservative Association in Wales, agreed. 'I had no idea', he informed Oldfield-Davies, 'that [the attack] was contemplated . . . and the Conservative Central Office was equally ignorant . . . I was furious when [it] occurred . . . I cannot go into active opposition [but] personally I feel that the BBC will come through this in a very satisfactory manner and I can assure you that is my wish . . . As for the Office, we have no complaints.'[99]

Oldfield-Davies received a number of similarly reassuring letters in the early months of 1956. Nevertheless, he left nothing to chance. He put his staff on a war footing. Under the leadership of the news department, which consisted of Tom Richards and his assistants Wyn Roberts, Wyn Williams and John Ormond Thomas, they worked through millions of words and prepared a mass of material relating to the incidence of references to Plaid Cymru, Nationalist activists and the Parliament for Wales Campaign. In particular, they were concerned to compare BBC coverage with that of the press. As the mid 1950s were a crucial period in the history of broadcasting in Wales, the diversion of so much energy to such a task was not without significance. Cardiff's research revealed that of the 360 speakers taking part in talks and discussions in 1955, fifteen were known to be members of Plaid Cymru. The party was totally ignored by the entire BBC output apart from the programmes produced in Wales. Indeed, some Plaid Cymru supporters felt that if those programmes – constituting as they did a mere 8 per cent of the sound broadcasting audible in Wales – showed some partiality towards their party, that served to even out the balance somewhat.[100]

Macdonald maintained that Hill's inquiry 'should be confined to the charges made in the debate'. Hill insisted that, as those charges were imprecise, they offered no basis for an inquiry. 'The Post Office', Jacob informed Oldfield-Davies in February 1956, 'has told David Llewellyn and the other Welsh MPs that they have to formulate their allegations and they cannot simply leave the words they used in the House to stand as their case.' The inquiry, which began its deliberations on 12 March 1956, was chaired by Godfrey Ince, the chairman of the Cable and Wireless Company, who had in the course of his career been permanent secretary to the Ministry of Labour and London editor of the *Manchester Guardian*. Assisted by two other members and a secretary, Ince hoped that the inquiry could rapidly be completed. The hope was not fulfilled. Hill's request that allegations be formulated led Llewellyn to demand that copies of all the the Welsh Home Service news bulletins – English and Welsh – broadcast since 1945, and the scripts of all the English-language talks produced in Wales since 1945 should be deposited in the House of Commons library. '[It is] an extraordinary list,' wrote Jacob to Oldfield-Davies. The total, it was estimated, would represent a three-foot-high pile on a table six foot square. Oldfield-Davies was reluctant to allow the scripts to leave Cardiff but stressed that Llewellyn was welcome to visit Park Place to examine them. But, as Cadbury, the inquiry's secretary, put it: 'It is a matter of pride with

Mr Llewellyn not to go cap-in-hand to the BBC.' Nothing therefore happened for months. On 10 April, the Liaison Committee noted that 'Sir Godfrey has not started his enquiry because the author of the charges has not yet framed evidence'. On 17 April the Association of Broadcasting Staffs demanded that 'the accusers should draw up a properly constituted indictment', but on 27 April Cadbury reported that 'we have reached an impasse with Mr Llewellyn'.[101]

In May, the BCW agreed to deposit the scripts relating to the years 1952 to 1955 in the National Museum and Ince sent Llewellyn an ultimatum. 'You must send us a really full memorandum by 2 June,' he wrote. 'We want to have something substantial to bite on from you.' Llewellyn submitted memoranda on 1 and 6 June but stated that he had further enquiries to make. He submitted a third memorandum on 1 September. 'I am afraid', wrote Cadbury, 'that he is being particularly tiresome.' By the end of September, all the evidence had been received. Apart from submissions by BBC staff, they consisted of Llewellyn's memoranda, a series of complaints from the Welsh Regional Council of Labour and a statement from George Thomas – although Thomas acknowledged 'that we now find that we have to scrape the barrel to substantiate our charges'.[102]

The Ince *Report*, which was published on 6 December 1956, came to the conclusion that, although a number of the allegations were irrelevant or inaccurate, 'some criticism of a lack of balance over the last six years is justified, particularly in the earlier part of the period'. Yet 'in view of the considerable output of the BBC staff in Wales . . . and the pressure under which they work, we would have been much more surprised to find that there had been no lapses of judgment'. 'If Nationalism in the widest sense [is considered]', argued Ince, 'then it is difficult for the Broadcasting Council in Wales to avoid possible charges . . . as it has the duty "to pay full regard to the distinctive cultural interests of Our People in Wales".' The *Report* asserted that some of the complaints of the Welsh Regional Council of Labour were valid, but 'four fifths of them relate to 1950 before the setting up of the [BCW, and] . . . they were errors that had been admitted and improved upon'. Virtually all Llewellyn's allegations were dismissed. In his last memorandum, he accused the BBC in Wales of treating Welsh-language culture as if it were the country's majority culture. Ince believed that the examples that he offered were 'not very powerful'. Llewellyn had included the comment as an after-thought, but it is interesting and not without substance. Indeed, it could be argued that the somewhat unfocused unease with which many of Wales's monoglot English-speakers viewed the BBC's activities in Wales was articulated in that comment.[103]

The Ince *Report*, stated the *Western Mail*, 'completely vindicated the honour of Welsh broadcasters', and the paper regretted that Llewellyn was not willing to withdraw his allegations. *The Times* argued that 'the idea that impartiality can be weighed statistically is based on ignorance of the nature of news'. 'The BBC', commented Plaid Cymru, 'did not overstate us; it understated us.' 'We fear', declared the party, 'that the Corporation in Wales will defend itself from future criticism by applying a political test to those invited to take part in its programmes . . . There are fears for the Welsh programmes themselves . . . A witch hunt might lead the BBC to suppose that broadcasting in the Welsh language is in itself proof of political delinquency.' The BBC's own internal inquiry led to improvements in the Cardiff news department. T. P. R. Hole, who spent some days at Cardiff in February 1956, argued that 'news values could be endangered when the total amount of material received daily left scarcely any margin of newsworthy items over and above those required to fill the bulletins'. The BCW was determined not to curtail the bulletins. Instead it successfully pressed for an additional member of staff and the grading and provision of further training for local correspondents. The new appointee was the poet, novelist and boon companion, the inimitable T. Glynne Davies. David Llewellyn's links with the Welsh Home Service did not cease with the publication of the Ince *Report*. In 1961 he became a member of the BCW. He was present at the meeting of 14 April 1961 which decided unanimously that Saunders Lewis should be given complete freedom in selecting his subject for the BBC Annual Lecture of 1962, a lecture which became the most famous of all the broadcasts of the BBC in Wales.[104]

The meeting which endorsed Saunders Lewis's request to be free to choose his subject was not chaired by Lord Macdonald. It was chaired by Mrs Rachel Jones, the BBC's Welsh governor from 1 July 1960 to 30 June 1965. On his appointment in 1952, Macdonald was given a five-year term of office. His tenure was renewed for two years in 1957; he was offered a further two years in 1959, but as he was then seventy-one he contented himself with one year. The BBC's Charter laid down that the Welsh governor was to be selected 'in virtue of his (*sic*) knowledge of the culture, characteristics and affairs of Our People in Wales and his close touch with Welsh opinion'. The appointment of Mrs Jones as Macdonald's successor caused consternation. She had been born in Brecon, but from her teens to her middle age she had lived outside Wales, mainly in Australia. The wife of the dean of Brecon, she was respected in the city but virtually unknown outside it, and furthermore she had hardly any knowledge of the Welsh language. She was, however, a close friend of Vivian

Lewis, who in 1957 had been appointed under-secretary for Welsh affairs and elevated to the peerage as Lord Brecon. When her appointment became known in June 1960, the Council members (with one dissentient vote – that of David Llewellyn) announced publicly that it was unacceptable. They stated:

> She is unknown outside Brecon. This does not indicate that she has [the qualifications listed in the Charter] . . . A comparable appointment in England would be unthinkable. There are great decisions to be made . . . [and in the making of them] the key figure is the National Governor for Wales . . . We have offered names. We receive with incredulity the statement of the Minister for Welsh Affairs [Henry Brooke, who combined the post with that of minister for housing and local government] that none of those would have the time to undertake the duties of this office . . . We ask for the appointment to be reconsidered.[105]

Macdonald issued a statement to the press, which as an example of an office-holder condemning his successor must have few competitors. He declared:

> In every case the person appointed to the Board of Governors has been a person of proved worth, who had rendered vast public service and who was a person of national stature and eminence . . . Is it surprising that people in Wales should ask why Wales should not receive the same consideration, or is it a case of anything being good enough for the Welsh? . . . I should have been handicapped on various important occasions had it not been that I was able to speak and understand both English and Welsh . . . If full justice is to be done to all the requirements of this important post, both languages are equally necessary . . . [In 1959] I agreed to a final year . . . but I am willing to stay on for a short time . . . to clear up this situation.

He clearly meant that he would remain as governor until Mrs Jones withdrew her acceptance and was replaced by someone with qualifications more in keeping with the stipulations of the Charter. She did not withdraw, and two members of the Council – Gwynfor Evans and Huw Morris Jones – resigned in protest.[106]

In her decision to remain as governor, Mrs Jones was supported by Henry Brooke and Arthur fforde, the chairman of the Board of Governors, and also by Oldfield-Davies. Brooke was informed by fforde:

> She has asked me twice whether she ought to resign and I have on

each occasion said certainly not . . . I myself don't pretend to understand the interplay of personalities in Wales [but] . . . I have absolutely no doubt whatsoever about the sincerity, capacity and wisdom of Alun Oldfield-Davies . . . The line we are taking is that she is wholly welcome as a colleague . . . [although] Macdonald does not agree with the appointment . . . and [Lord] Aberdare [a member of the BBC's General Advisory Council] retains doubts about [its] viability.

Oldfield-Davies wrote to fforde:

I was interested to know that Mrs Jones had asked you whether she ought to resign. Had she asked me my answer would have been the same as yours. Whether she was wise to accept in the first place is a different matter . . . I gather from the tone of your letter to Mr Brooke that he feels rather uneasy about the situation in Wales over the appointment . . . and I think he should realize that the opposition is only partly due to her lack of Welsh. The main objection is that she was relatively unknown and has much to learn about Welsh affairs and it is widely believed that she owes her appointment to her friendship with Lord and Lady Brecon. The current jibe is that the BBC in Wales now stands for the Brooke, Brecon Club . . . I am sure Mrs Jones fully realizes the importance of not appearing to be in any way a 'creature' of Brooke, Brecon and Blaise Gillie, the permanent head of the Ministry of Housing and Local Government in Wales, who is also a personal friend of hers . . . She need not worry at all about the attitude of the staff. Whether or not some, if not most, consider the appointment a mistake, it is the conviction of the staff throughout the service that, once appointed, the chairman must be served loyally and well . . . [With the resignation of Evans and Morris-Jones] we should get the panel to agree on a number of alternative names of people who represent a strong Welsh viewpoint . . . People of Nationalist sympathies, if invited to serve, may feel compelled, out of loyalty to Gwynfor Evans, to refuse [although] Gwynfor himself assured me that he would not do or say anything that would lead anyone to think that he expected such loyalty.[107]

Although Mrs Jones had an inadequate knowledge of Wales, no distinguished record of public service and only a slight acquaintance with the Welsh language, these considerations proved less of a handicap to her than many of the critics of her appointment had feared. Despite the fact that she could not understand up to half the output for which her Council was responsible, Corporation officials often found it useful, when countering accusations that the BBC in

Wales was a closed shop for Welsh-speakers, to point out that the Welsh governor herself had little knowledge of the language. Furthermore Mrs Jones, a woman of courage, intelligence and tenacity, was determined to prove that her critics were mistaken. Her term of office coincided with a major expansion in television production in Wales and with the extension of the responsibility of the BCW to include television as well as radio. Considerably younger and more vigorous than her predecessor, and unburdened by the heavy professional commitments of most of her successors, Mrs Jones was able to play a full and constructive part in these developments. Indeed, she has been described by informed commentators as the best chairman the BCW has ever had. Proof of her success in disarming her critics is the fact that when her governorship was renewed for a year in 1964, her fellow Council members received the news with great pleasure. On her retirement in June 1965, she was warmly congratulated on her 'very successful term of office'.[108]

Among the first tasks of the Council under Mrs Jones's chairmanship was to prepare its evidence for the Pilkington Committee. As has been seen, the main concern of the members was to secure an all-Wales television service and to ensure that the Council had responsibility for television as well as radio. The appointment of Mrs Jones led her fellow members to seek an amendment to the Charter laying down more specifically the qualifications expected in a Welsh governor, in particular an ability to understand the entire output of the BBC in Wales. Under the circumstances, it was a somewhat embarrassing discussion, but Mrs Jones chaired it skilfully. Arthur fforde argued against 'limiting potential chairmen . . . to those able to speak Welsh', and the Scottish Council was disturbed by the possibility that demands might arise for the Scottish governor to have a knowledge of Gaelic. The fourth Charter had stated that the BCW should carry out its duties 'with full regard to the distinctive culture, interests and tastes' of the people of Wales. Following representations from the BCW, the BBC's fifth Charter included the word 'language' in addition to the words 'culture, interests and tastes'.[109]

In its evidence to the Pilkington Committee, the BCW also sought the authority to arrange party political broadcasts specifically for Wales. It suggested that each year Wales should have a hundred minutes of its own political broadcasts, with fifty minutes for the Labour Party, thirty for the Conservatives and ten apiece for the Liberals and Plaid Cymru, the time to be divided equally between radio and television. The Pilkington Committee recommended that Wales should have its own party political broadcasts and the White Paper of July 1962 stated that the government 'proposed to discuss the Pilkington recommendation with the political parties'. After much wrangling with the postmaster-general, regional broadcasts were permitted following the general election of 1964 and Plaid Cymru's first party political broadcast was transmitted on 29 September 1965.[110]

Among the Corporation's submissions to the Pilkington Committee was a request that the BBC should undertake local broadcasting on a large scale and plans were drawn up to establish stations in over a hundred of the towns of the United Kingdom. 'In other countries', stated Head Office, 'local radio has become sadly debased, dealing only in pop records and advertisers' announcements. Such a service would hardly find favour in Britain. The BBC's concept is vastly different . . . News would be a key service. Up to half a dozen local bulletins would be provided every day . . . catching local life on the wing . . . Many a university might set up its own studio and contribute directly into the local . . . service.' Where Wales was concerned, the BBC was thinking in terms of eleven town stations broadcasting almost exclusively in English and four area stations broadcasting mainly in Welsh. Each station would need a minimum staff of fifteen and an increase in the licence fee would be necessary. The Corporation considered it unwise to be precipitate in the matter. As the local services would be transmitted on VHF, and 'as few households had VHF receivers, [local broadcasting would] be jeopardized by lack of listeners. It is necessary to get VHF itself reasonably well-established before it could safely be used to carry a complete new service.' Oldfield-Davies was not anxious to pursue the matter. Lewis Jones, a member of the Corporation's General Advisory Council, asked him in 1960 what he should say in the Council about local broadcasting. Oldfield-Davies told him to say that 'he welcomed local broadcasting in Wales as a supplement to the main BBC service but it should not be developed to the detriment of programmes serving the whole of Wales'. Jones dutifully said exactly that. In 1960–1, the BBC conducted eighteen closed-circuit experiments in local broadcasting, including one at Swansea in October 1961 and one at Wrexham in November. They proved successful, with the *Wrexham Leader* in particular expressing great enthusiasm. The Pilkington Committee recommended that the BBC should undertake local radio but the recommendation was not included in the government's White Paper. The Corporation was not to have permanent local radio stations until the late 1960s and, where Wales was concerned, local radio would be developed almost exclusively by the commercial sector.[111]

III   *Programmes, viewers and listeners, 1952–1964*

Watching television, to a degree far greater than listening to the radio, is a substitute activity. In 1948, over 90 per cent of sets were switched on each evening, and anyone with memories of the 1950s will remember the cups of tea hastily made between programmes and the sandwiches handed round in the semi-darkness. There was an assumption that viewing took the place of other, more worth-while, activities, although it may have filled a leisure gap which existed already. Until the arrival of ITV, when a choice became available, viewers watched far more demanding programmes than they subsequently would. Classical plays had an eager following and it would be difficult in the 1990s to envisage the equivalent of the distinguished archaeologists, Mortimer Wheeler and Glyn Daniel, enjoying the status of household names. Nevertheless, many cultural and social activities withered when faced with the com-petition of the box. 'Will television', asked a Cynon Valley enthusiast for amateur drama, 'kill the Aberdare Little Theatre?'[112] It did. It also contributed to the attenuation of male-voice choirs, the disappear-ance of whist drives and the decline in a host of chapel-based activities. Yet the direct causes and effects are very difficult to establish, and it is possible that family life received a boost as the entire family sat down together to view. Television certainly had an impact upon the layout of houses, for the demolition of the partition between the front room and the middle room, carried out in thousands of the terraced houses of the south Wales valleys in the 1950s and 1960s, was mainly motivated by the desire to have a lounge worthy of the in-house movie theatre.

While television remained a novelty, its devotees watched in reverential silence, and surveys indicated that, compared with radio-listeners, twice as many television-viewers gave the broadcasts their full attention. As the eye is surfeited more rapidly than the ear, the succession of stimuli had to be much greater than had been the case with the older medium. Educationalists, who had long lamented the impact of the cinema on pupils, considered television to be an even more dire danger. 'Schoolchildren', declared the headmaster of Cardiff's Cathays High School, 'should see as little television as possible.' Whereas those who had been involved with television in the 1940s had considered the new service to be little more than radio with pictures – and not always with pictures, for early television news was sound only – younger producers at the BBC in the 1950s were eager to emphasize the differences between it and 'steam' radio. They stressed that television is primarily a matter of pictorial images. Where there is nothing that can be visually presented, there is no valid television. Such an attitude can lead to the eschewing of the complicated and the abstract and, where news is concerned, can give rise to the belief that, if pictures are not available, there is nothing to report. 'You cannot', stated George Barnes, the BBC's first director of television, 'put thought on television.' 'Television', argued Anthony Sampson, 'drains subjects of their meaning, leaving faces remembered but not what they said.' The public's remembrance of faces meant that the new medium was a mass producer of celebrities. Radio broadcasters can mix with their listeners unrecognized; television broadcasters cannot. For many viewers, a person's picture is more real than the actual self. Emyr Daniel, one of Wales's best-known broadcasters in the later twentieth century, was told on being met in the flesh: 'You do look like yourself.' On ceasing to be on view, performers were presumed to have ceased to exist. Jeffrey Iverson, at one time the most active television newsman of the BBC in Wales, was asked after he had given up being a correspondent: 'Didn't you use to be Jeffrey Iverson?' While viewers were above all struck by the pictorial presentation of personalities, broadcasters themselves were above all impressed by 'television's terrifying capacity to devour'. 'Even more than sound radio', wrote Val Gielgud, 'television is a Moloch.'[113]

Those responsible for feeding the Moloch were assisted in their task by a succession of technical innovations, including the zoom lens (1949), the button microphone (1955), videotape (1958) and vastly improved cameras. Videotape, which released programme-makers from the need to develop their film, was revolutionary in its impact, although more traditional producers, who considered film to be more elegant, would still, in the 1990s, be reluctant to use it. Some of the innovations reinforced the unreality of television. In the early days, 'pieces to camera' were either memorized or improvised but, with the coming of the teleprompter in 1957, a broadcaster was able to read a script while giving the impression of spontaneous speech. The use of the monitor in outside broadcasts, a practice which dates from 1963, was another visual lie, for henceforth the commentator would be describing, not the event itself, but the view of it displayed on the monitor. Two developments in the early 1960s presaged major changes which would occur in the later twentieth century. Colour television went on public display in Wales for the first time at the Royal Welsh Show in 1961. In 1962, Telstar was launched, the first step towards the multiplicity of satellite channels which would, by the 1990s, transform the context in which the BBC operated. Changes in Welsh society as a whole also eased matters for broadcasters. Between 1952 and 1964, private car ownership in Wales increased from 115,000 to 410,000, thus helping to release BBC staff and contributors from reliance upon Wales's inadequate public transport system. The electrification of rural Wales was virtually complete by 1960, enabling television crews to gather material unencumbered by generators. The number of Welsh households with a telephone increased markedly in the 1950s and 1960s, and as a result the task of contacting performers and arranging outside broadcasts was greatly simplified.

Despite the success of Oldfield-Davies and his colleagues in ensuring that programmes produced in Wales had first a toehold and then a foothold in the Corporation's television output, viewing in Wales in the era of the fourth Charter – and subsequently – overwhelmingly meant the viewing of non-Welsh productions. In the early 1950s, that meant watching quiz programmes such as *What's My Line?* and *Animal, Vegetable, Mineral*, programmes on cooking with Philip Harben and occasional American imports including *The Perry Como Show*. 'There were', recalled Alasdair Milne, the director-general from 1981 to 1987, 'some bold dramatic ventures – the marvellous adaptation of George Orwell's *1984* [and] the first *Quatermass* series . . . But there was a great deal of dross . . . And the news was a joke.' In the late 1950s, under the spur of competition and with the recruitment of producers who actually liked television, there were vast improvements. By the end of the fourth Charter era, viewers had been offered a rich array, including *Panorama* (1953), *Tonight* (1957), *Monitor* (1958), *Grandstand* (1958), *Face to Face* (1959), and the Wednesday play series (1962). Young radicals such as Donald Baverstock were eager not to be rigid in carrying out what the Charter laid down, but rather to ask: 'What does the Charter not prevent us doing?' Hugh Carleton Greene, who became director of news and current affairs in 1958, set about transforming news programmes. Among his rulings was one laying down that a royal story need not automatically have precedence. Obsequiousness towards politicians – the BBC's practice of asking Cabinet ministers: 'Have you anything to tell us, sir?' – gave way to more vigorous investigative reporting.[114]

Deference received a serious blow with the broadcast of the most famous of the programmes of the early television age. *That Was the Week That Was* (TW3) was launched in November 1962 and its biting satire and savage wit made it cult viewing. More than anything else, TW3 created the paradox – which became more evident in subsequent decades – that the BBC, although emphatically of the establishment, was also anti-establishment. With its lampooning of the government – which happened to be Conservative – the programme helped to reinforce the widespread view among Tories that the Corporation was biased against them. TW3 was also useful in the ratings battle, particularly in view of the fact that the commercial companies were barred from making such programmes, for the ITA's licence specifically obliged the commercial sector to refrain from lampooning living persons. Greene, director-general from 1960 to 1969, eventually yielded to the pressure of the Board of Governors and brought the series to an end in December 1963, but the fact that he had allowed it to be transmitted in the first place gave substance to the belief 'that he was just out to shock the bourgeoisie'.[115]

Producing television programmes was expensive. In 1961, the average cost was £4,000 an hour, compared with £560 for sound radio. The combined television and sound licence fee, which had been set at £2 in 1946, was increased to £3 in 1954 and to £4 in 1957; of the £4, the government took £1 in excise duty and the Post Office took 4*s*.6*d*. (22.5p) as a collection charge. The rise in licence-buying caused the net income of the Corporation to rise from £12.94 million in 1952 to £33.52 million in 1960, but inflation, the enhanced salaries caused by commercial competition, the huge expenditure on London's obsolescent Broadcasting House and the costs attendant upon the BBC's determination to produce more and better programmes – not to mention demands from the regions – led the Corporation in the early 1960s to seek an end to the excise duty and an increase in the overall fee. It was then that the level of the licence fee became a central concern of the BBC, and it would remain so until the decision in 1988 to link the fee with the retail price index. From October 1963 the duty was rescinded, allowing the BBC to have the full £4, except for the Post Office's collection charge. The Corporation considered it needed £5, but Bevins refused to increase the fee and he boasted of his refusal in his 1964 election campaign. (He lost his seat.) 'I forced the [Corporation] to borrow,' he stated in his autobiography, 'hoping it would make them cut out extravagance . . . There is no doubt whatsoever that the BBC lives on the fat of the land.'[116]

That the BBC was profligate was a belief which became firmly implanted in the minds of politicians. If the accusation had substance, it was largely caused by the need to give in to union demands in the face of commercial competition. Admittedly Tom Burns, who interviewed 200 of the BBC's employees in 1963, reported that all of them had stories of wastefulness, but that would probably be the case with any large corporation. Much of the BBC's expenditure arose from its determination to do everything properly. Before choosing sites for transmitters, for example, it conducted exhaustive and expensive trials. Teilifís Éireann, which began in 1961, could not afford such meticulousness, and Gorham described how its chief engineer borrowed a relief map of Ireland from the

National Museum, placed lights on the tops of the mountains and observed where the shadows fell. The work took an afternoon, cost virtually nothing and proved highly effective.[117]

Within two years of the launching of Teilifís Éireann, the service was broadcasting for forty-two hours a week, of which eighteen hours were its own productions. By then the BBC in Wales was producing three hours of television specifically intended for Welsh audiences and in addition was providing occasional programmes for the network. In 1963, its main output was a weekday news bulletin in Welsh together with the topical programme *Heddiw* ('Today'), broadcast from 1 to 1.25 p.m., and *Wales Today*, broadcast between 6.10 and 6.25 p.m. TWW also provided a daily Welsh-language topical programme – *Y Dydd* ('The Day') – which proved to be more innovative than *Heddiw*. Yet, as the news stories specific to Welsh-speaking Wales were limited, versions of the same happenings tended to be broadcast on both programmes, a factor which gave substance to the argument that the Welsh-language output of the BBC and TWW should be transmitted on a shared channel. In addition, TWW transmitted several 'give away' programmes, and series such as *Siôn a Siân*, *Taro Deg* and *Seddau Cadw* are remembered with affection by those who profited from them. The BBC's Welsh-language general programmes were more highbrow. In April 1964, for example, its broadcasts included a series investigating the future of the University of Wales, several short plays, a survey of scientific innovations, a church service and a discussion of Welsh religious traditions.[118]

Because of the Welsh-language output, the television hours produced by Wales specifically for its own viewers exceeded those produced by any other region. Of the total of 222 hours of such programmes broadcast in 1958, Wales was responsible for a third, its 75 hours comparing with between 21 and 23 hours apiece for the Midland, Northern Ireland, West and North regions and 60 for Scotland. Virtually all the 60 hours produced by Scotland in 1958 were in English. Of the 75 non-network hours produced by Wales, about a half were in English.[119] It could therefore be argued that the provision of Welsh-language programmes caused the English-speaking Welsh to be worse served by BBC television than were the English-speaking Scots. It could also be argued that, had not the existence of the Welsh language energized Welsh patriots to secure a broadcasting service for Wales, there might not have been any English-language Welsh programmes at all.

Where network television programmes were concerned, Wales, in 1958, produced fewer hours than any other region except Northern Ireland; they amounted to 56, compared with the Midland's 131. Rare though they were, they included programmes of high distinction.

Between 1957 and 1959, Dafydd Gruffydd and Emyr Humphreys produced 37 network plays, causing Cardiff to be the largest centre of BBC drama production outside London. Among other acclaimed programmes produced in Wales were Hywel Davies's *Out of this World*, a portrait of a community of Carmelite nuns at Presteigne, which won a prize at the World International Festival of Catholic Radio and Television, and *Borrowed Pastures*, also the work of Hywel Davies, a poignant study of Polish refugee farmers in Wales.[120]

While the 1950s and 1960s in Britain were the era of the victory of television, in the world as a whole they were emphatically the era of sound broadcasting, for it was in those years that the radio came to be heard by the majority of the world's population. Transistor sets became available in 1958 and by the 1960s cheap and reliable radios were flooding from Third World factories to all corners of the earth. Most of the revolutionary pressures and many of the social changes of the 1950s and 1960s were radio-led, and to describe those years as the television era is perhaps to take a very partial view of the experience of mankind.[121]

Even in Britain, where the percentage of the population addicted to television was higher than anywhere except the United States, sound broadcasting was by no means totally eclipsed. Significant sections – those with impaired sight, evening shift workers and households which could not afford television or were unable to receive the service – were totally dependent upon it. Although evening audiences slumped dramatically, they did not become negligible, for, as Robert Silvey pointed out, if listeners only heard ten minutes apiece, that represented a constant audience of one and a half million people. The impact of television, the competition of Radio Luxembourg and the increasing study of society (academic sociology in Britain began in the 1950s) led to a questioning of the tripartite division of radio created by Haley after the war. Haley had conceived of the BBC's audience as a pyramid with the Light Programme as the broad base and the Third Programme as the apex. 'The concept', argued controller North in 1956, 'of three clearly demarcated intelligence groups . . . is extremely demagogic . . . We may have contributed considerably to the perpetuation of class prejudices.' As it came to be realized that devotees of the Third Programme also listened to the Home and the Light, the pyramid theory gave way to a more complex view of the audience.[122]

The demand for regional television led Head Office to scrutinize the radio output of the regions with the intention of reducing the numbers producing it in order to transfer staff to television. Regional controllers were asked in June 1956 whether 'they were . . . doing too much of an ordinary nature' – meaning, presumably, programmes that could be done in London. A policy of integration was instituted which involved restricting the rights of the regions to opt out at will and obliging them to concentrate on the type of programme which Coatman had dismissed in 1943 as 'kailyard stuff'. The Welsh and Scottish controllers protested vigorously and 'integration' was only fully implemented in the English regions. 'It has been necessary', it was noted in 1958, 'to limit to some degree the freedom enjoyed by the regions to plan their own programmes independently of each other and of the centre. Programme planning [has been] more closely co-ordinated [and thus] the regions (excluding Wales and Scotland) have lost a small measure of independence.'[123]

More worrying were the inroads made by Radio Luxembourg. 'The BBC', commented controller North, 'has not really got a sound monopoly.' A working party on the tripartite division was set up in 1950. It came to the conclusion that 'the Home and the Light are too similar; some categories of listener are fed twice over [while] others have been underfed'. The Third Programme was 'directed at types of people less dependent on broadcasting for their mental and intellectual food than anyone else . . . [Its output] was not bread but only a scraping of caviar for the appetites of those least in need of supplementary titbits.' Oldfield-Davies agreed that 'the Light is not light enough. If [it] stuck to its brief, it could take listeners from Luxembourg and release some to the Home and the Third.' Head Office was determined that, if there were to be changes, they should not cost money, for it ruled in April 1957 that sound broadcasting should have no additional funds for at least three years. The changes suggested by the working party were implemented in September 1957. The Light lost all programmes which 'demand sustained attention'. The path which would lead to Radio Two, if not Radio One, had been taken. The Third Programme was restricted to three hours a day, and a new service – Network Three – was created to take over the rest of the Third's timings. The changes to the Light Programme aroused little opposition, but those to the Third led to the establishment of the Third Programme Defence Committee (later the Sound Broadcasting Defence Society), which claimed that the BBC was turning its back upon culture.[124]

The charge was somewhat exaggerated, for although the changes of 1957 represented a significant shift away from the pattern of sound broadcasting created after the war, the BBC's overall radio output remained much as before. Although their places on the different services changed, London's programmes – still the staple listening of the Welsh audience – had broadly the same character as they had had in the late 1940s. The challenge of Luxembourg was recognized, but Luxembourg did not have the same impact upon BBC radio as did the challenge of the commercial companies upon BBC television. Yet it would be misleading to suggest that, during the era of the fourth Charter, the Corporation's sound output underwent no development. As with television, technological advance was highly significant. The tape recorder, which first came into use in 1948, allowed ninety minutes to be recorded at a stretch, compared with four and a half minutes on a wax disc. The process was cheap and became cheaper, and the machines became ever lighter. They worked on ordinary batteries, and the *Montgomeryshire Express* noted with astonishment in 1953 that a BBC producer, unaccompanied by lorryloads of equipment, had made a programme in the still electricity-less village of Pant-y-dŵr.[125] Tape could be cut and stuck together, allowing for more rapid editing and opening up the possibility of programmes in which contributors' comments were a series of complementary or contrasting sound bites.

Inexpensive and convenient recording equipment reduced the need for elaborate scripting, as misinformation, libel, swear words and other sins could easily be edited out before transmission. Indeed, perhaps the chief change in BBC sound broadcasting in the third quarter of the twentieth century was the wholesale abandonment of the script in talks and discussions. The change was encouraged by the advent of television, for as a discussion in which scripts were visibly read would be absurd, the same sense of absurdity came to be felt over radio discussions. Sam Jones at Bangor experimented with an unscripted talk in 1952. 'The speaker [Waldo Williams]', reported the *South Wales Evening Post*, 'stumbled and stammered, but the result was the most natural broadcast I have ever heard.'[126] The single speaker – with or without a script – addressing listeners unchallenged came to be looked at with increasing disfavour. The Department of the Spoken Word, the rather pompously named department created by Haley in 1948, was abolished in 1955 and the Talks Department followed it into oblivion in 1964. Hostility to the single voice speaking for fifteen minutes or more spread to the news bulletin. The newsreader became the anchor man or woman. He (or much more rarely, she) read the headlines and then presented the details of the news through a series of interviews or reporters' inserts, as with *The World at One*, launched in 1965. This practice, together with the collapse of radio's evening audience, led Greene to discontinue the BBC's great flagship, *The Nine O'Clock News*. It was last broadcast on 17 September 1960 and its demise was angrily denounced by its dwindling band of devotees.

The increasing readiness of the BBC to broadcast comment rather than merely providing an unvarnished account of events – a readiness more apparent in radio than in television – indicated that in the 1950s the Corporation was moving away from the rigidities imposed by Reith and largely maintained by Haley. Among Haley's decisions in 1952, a few months before he left the BBC for the editorship of *The Times*, was to scrap virtually the entire radio and television schedules over the nine days between the death and the funeral of George VI, an act which Lindsay Wellington saw as an indication that the Corporation was lagging behind public opinion. The rule that morals and religion should only be presented in the context of orthodox Christianity was abandoned in 1954, when an avowed atheist, Margaret Knight, gave three talks, the first two broadcast only to south-eastern England listeners and the last sent out on all the BBC's transmitters. The talks were fiercely attacked, and Mrs Knight had to be smuggled out of Broadcasting House lest she be molested by a mob. More significant was Jacob's decision in 1956 to allow the leader of the opposition to reply to Eden's broadcast justifying Britain's invasion of Suez. In his speech, Gaitskell appealed to Conservative MPs to remove Eden from the premiership, and his comments, and the widespread hostility to the invasion, were reported on the BBC's overseas programmes, including those in Arabic. In permitting Gaitskell to broadcast, Jacob was fully supported by Cadogan, a personal friend of Eden. For many Conservatives, the Corporation's decision to announce to the world that Britain was deeply divided, and to do so while British forces were in action, was proof that the BBC was a traitorous institution. Eden instructed the lord chancellor to prepare a plan to take over the Corporation, and it would probably have been implemented had not the Suez crisis come to a rapid end. Jacob was also anxious that the BBC should shed the pusillanimity which, ever since 1926, it had shown concerning industrial conflict. He urged all the regions to appoint industrial correspondents.[127] The first to hold the post in Wales was Alan Protheroe, previously of the *Glamorgan Gazette*, the beginning of a BBC career which would end with Protheroe as the Corporation's assistant director-general. With his appointment, strikes and the threat of strikes became a central feature of the Welsh Home Service's news bulletins.

Such developments indicate that the BBC in Wales, as in the rest of Britain, was increasingly prepared to face reality. In 1952, the *Western Mail* was astonished by a programme on silicosis in which 'we heard the cough of victims, the anguish of families and the burning zeal of crusading doctors . . . Ten years ago it is doubtful whether the BBC would have risked such frankness.' Nevertheless, the sound output of the BBC in the era of the fourth Charter was broadly similar to that which it had been in the late 1940s and therefore does not call for further close analysis. Througout the 1950s and early 1960s, Wales's input to the Welsh Home Service averaged around 23 hours a week, rising to 27 in winter and declining to 18 in summer. In 1951, when the Midland, North and Scottish Regions were receiving programme allowances of £2,000 a week, Wales's allowance was £1,500. It was the same as that for the West of England, although Wales produced five hours a week more than did the West. 'An excessive amount of our time and energy', complained Oldfield-Davies, 'goes on cheese-paring.' Following the establishment of the BCW, Wales's allowance rose to £1,800 and it was further increased to £2,000 in 1956. 'There was a tendency in the past', wrote Oldfield-Davies in 1955, '. . . to regard Scotland, North and Midland as top-grade regions, Wales and the West of England as second class and Northern Ireland at the end of the queue . . . However, by now, it is fair to state that the BBC spends money in proportion to the revenues available and the needs of listeners.' In 1957, in the wake of the integration policy, the allowances of the English regions were reduced by 10 per cent, while those of Wales and Scotland were only reduced by 5 per cent. The differential marked a further stage in the process which had begun with the establishment of the Welsh and Scottish Councils of giving more favourable treatment to the two nations than to the regions of England. (Northern Ireland, 'that most contrary region', with its BBC governor but no council, remained at the end of the queue.)[128]

Head Office, in opposing the proposal for National Councils, had been partly motivated by concern that autonomy would lead to a reduction in the network contributions of the 'national regions'. In the mid 1950s, its fears seemed to have been confirmed. Asked for Wales's network offerings in February 1955, Watkin Jones answered: 'It is only half of our spoken word content that we can even begin to think of offering to you, and it so happens that this year . . . we are living rather more than usual to ourselves.' 'This is interesting', commented the controller of the Home Service. 'I suppose that by now the National Council has picked up the threads and is in a position to undertake its Charter duty . . . I must say I anticipated this kind of effect.'[129] Nevertheless, in the late 1950s and early 1960s, Wales did contribute about one and a half hours a week to the basic Home Service and some two hours to the Light, although none of its contributions to the two services achieved the acclaim won by *Welsh Rarebit* in the 1940s.

It was otherwise with the Third Programme. In 1953, the Third's most successful feature was *Gazooka*, 'a work of real originality, full of wit and fancy', written by Gwyn Thomas. First broadcast in May 1953, it had been repeated seven times by September. Another Thomas extravaganza, *Vive l'Oompa*, was broadcast in September 1955, causing other regions to be jealous of the comic genius available to the Welsh Home Service. Other successes on the Third included R. S. Thomas's *The Minister*, first broadcast in September 1952, and the liturgy from David Jones's *Anathemata*, specially produced by Wales for transmission during coronation week. Cardiff was also responsible for a series of highly praised programmes based on early Welsh literature, including *Men went to Catraeth*, *The Story of Llywarch Hen*, *The Misfortunes of Princess Heledd*, *Saith Doethion Rhufain* and *Hywel ab Owain Gwynedd*. The BBC won the Italia Prize in 1954 with *Under Milk Wood*, a Third Programme commission. It was produced in London, but the cast was assembled by Cardiff. Dylan Thomas was also partly responsible for the Welsh Home Service's first international 'hit' song. Taken by Talfan Davies to the Llangollen International Folk Eisteddfod in 1953, his radio account of his visit, 'full of resounding superlatives and chromatic images', included a reference to the Obenkirchen Girls Choir – 'the angels in pigtails'. Their song, 'The Happy Wanderer' – which failed to reach even third place at Llangollen – won immense popularity. Thomas's Llangollen talk was among the last things he did for the Welsh Home Service. His death in New York at the age of thirty-nine on 9 November 1953 was as much a loss to broadcasting as it was to poetry.[130]

Cardiff was very proud of its Third Programme successes. They were the work of Elwyn Evans, 'our star producer', as Oldfield-Davies called him.[131] In January 1957, however, Evans accepted a three-year contract as programme director of Nigerian Broadcasting. On leaving Nigeria, he did not return to Wales; Head Office claimed him, and he ended his career as chief instructor (sound). Watkin Jones retired in 1961 and Dafydd Gruffydd and Nan Davies in 1969, which meant that by the end of the 1960s none of the 1930s pioneers among the production staff were left. There were other important staff changes. The major reshuffle of 1957, with Hywel Davies and Talfan Davies taking charge of output, has already been mentioned. Mai Jones retired in 1958 and Sam Jones in 1963. On retirement, Sam was honoured with a D.Litt. by the University of Wales; Mai, whose contribution had been equally important, did not get a D.Mus. The post of north Wales representative went to W. R. Owen, who since 1957 had been in charge at Swansea. Owen was replaced as west Wales representative by Tom Richards. Alan Protheroe, the industrial correspondent, succeeded Richards as head of news, and Protheroe was succeeded in turn by Jeffrey Iverson. Cliff Morgan, Wales's sports editor, became editor of *Grandstand* in 1963 and was eventually replaced by Onllwyn Brace.

Most of the changes occurred without controversy. One did not. Dafydd Gruffydd's move from radio to television in 1954 left vacant the post of radio drama producer. By far the strongest candidate was Lorraine Davies, with her years of experience producing *Children's Hour* plays. The BBC had abandoned its opposition to the employment of married women and permitted a woman to continue in her existing post even if she married a fellow Corporation employee. It was not, however, prepared to offer a new appointment to a woman whose husband was on the BBC staff. Lorraine Davies was married to Hywel Davies. The BCW, in defiance of the Corporation's rule, urged that she should be offered the post of radio drama producer. Head Office refused to agree, and after a delay of eight months the post went to the novelist, Emyr Humphreys. Humphreys's novel, *The Toy Epic*, won the Hawthornden Prize in 1959; in its original form – *Y Tri Llais* ('The Three Voices') – it was a radio script commissioned by the Welsh Home Service.[132]

Music, the staple of sound broadcasting from the beginning, nestled between the Welsh Home Service's English and Welsh output. There were programmes of songs in both English and Welsh, but instrumental music was almost invariably introduced in English. By the 1950s, music represented 40 per cent of the BBC's sound transmissions, a marked contrast with its television service, on which musical programmes, strictly defined, constituted less than 5 per cent. The BBC Welsh Orchestra continued to be central to Wales's musical output and the salaries of its members represented 44 per cent of the salaries bill of the Welsh Home Service. The orchestra enjoyed a high reputation, with Hubert Clifford, the BBC's head of music, declaring in 1955 that its conductor, Rae Jenkins, was 'the most gifted and experienced conductor of light music in the country'.[133] His orchestra, with its thirty-one members, could not adequately perform full symphonic works, but, as has been seen, Oldfield-Davies was reluctant to seek its expansion, for he believed that the Corporation was already supporting more orchestras than it needed. In October 1963, however, the BCW discussed the possibility that the orchestra might form the nucleus of a Symphony Orchestra for Wales with Arts Council support, a notion suggested by the Council for Wales. The idea had been mooted in 1946 and it was not immediately to bear fruit in 1963, but the creation of a jointly supported symphony orchestra would be one of Wales's greatest cultural achievements in subsequent decades.

The production of programmes in the Welsh language was the outstanding differentiating feature of the Welsh Home Service. Following the introduction of integration in 1956, Oldfield-Davies and his colleagues decided to consolidate their Welsh output into a nightly hour between 6.30 and 7.30 p.m. 'Yr Awr Gymraeg' ('the Welsh Hour') had its critics, partly because the advent of television meant that daytime programmes enjoyed a larger audience than those transmitted in the evening. The movement away from the evening began in 1960, with the introduction of *Trem* ('Viewpoint'), a Swansea-produced programme broadcast at 8.15 a.m. and an acknowledgement that breakfast-time was emerging as the peak listening period. Weekday audiences for Welsh-language programmes were small compared with the phalanx listening on Sunday. The morning service, broadcast between 11.45 and 12.30, regularly had an audience of 300,000. (The sermons could lack zest; after hearing a particularly mournful radio preacher, the *Liverpool Daily Post* commented: 'Cheer up, old man, you'll soon be dead'.) *Caniadaeth y Cysegr* ('The Songs of the Sanctuary'), the late Sunday afternoon hymn-singing programme, was almost as popular, and the evening miscellany, *Rhwng Gŵyl a Gwaith* ('Between Holiday and Work'), introduced by the inimitable I. B. Griffith, won a devoted following. As in earlier decades, much of the Welsh-language output had a pietistic air, a cause of annoyance to younger, more secular, listeners. Commenting on a programme portraying a leading Congregational minister, the broadcasting correspondent of the *South Wales Evening Post* wrote: 'There is an essentially Welsh audience for whom [such a programme] means a great deal . . . It is we divided souls who are dissatisfied . . . [We are trying] to impose the pattern of one culture on another.'[134]

The values of Nonconformity extended into light entertainment. Listing the seven leading script-writers of Welsh variety shows in 1953, the *Western Mail* noted that only one of them was not a minister, and the exception (the schoolmaster, R. E. Jones) was the author of a book on St Mark's Gospel. *Yr Herald Gymraeg* expressed astonishment. 'Flynyddoedd yn ôl', it commented, 'fe fyddai'n ddigon i gael eich hel o'r Seiat.'*[135] Comments that Welsh light entertainment did not conform to true Welsh tradition annoyed Islwyn Ffowc Elis, one of the minister script-writers. 'Gellid meddwl', he wrote in *Y Faner*, 'mai gan Loegr yn unig y mae'r hawlfraint ar bob math ar raglen ysgafn . . . Anwybodaeth sy'n haeru hynny. [Y mae'r fath beth â] ffrwd gydgenedlaethol . . . Ni fyddai caneuon fel y Blues i'w clywed gan y Saeson ychwaith oni bai eu bod wedi dynwared y Brasiliaid a'r Ffrancod a'r Negroaid.'†[136] Yet the search for an

---

*'Years ago it would have been enough to have you driven out of the *seiat* [the fellowship meeting of the Calvinistic Methodists].'

†'One might think that England alone has the copyright on all forms of light entertainment. That is an ill-informed view. [There is such a thing as] an international stream . . . Songs like the Blues would not be heard among the English had they not imitated the Brazilians and the French and the Negroes.'

authentically Welsh pattern of light entertainment was a matter of concern, particularly to Meredydd Evans, who became head of light entertainment in 1963. The 'Bangor Bing' of the 1940s, Evans spent several years as an academic in the United States where he gained an encyclopaedic knowledge of American folk-singing. On returning to Wales, he and his American-born wife, Phyllis Kinney, became the leading authorities on Welsh folk songs, a tradition preserved and popularized by the Welsh Home Service.

In Welsh-language radio drama, high culture had been the norm but, as has been seen, Dafydd Gruffydd was anxious to offer some more popular programmes. By 1952 the nightly serial, *Teulu Tŷ Coch*, was absorbing all his energies. After 195 episodes, Gruffydd was bored with it and sought to kill it off. Its loyal listeners protested and in 1953 the operation moved to Swansea, much to the delight of the *Herald of Wales*. It lasted for another 105 episodes and finally came to an end on 25 June 1954. Among the serial's leading participants was Siân Phillips, who was later to undertake rather more exacting roles. *Teulu Tŷ Coch*, rooted in Glamorgan, was succeeded by runs of weekly series, among them *Teulu'r Siop* and *Teulu'r Mans*, programmes more orientated to the dialect of Gwynedd. The adult series enjoyed considerable success, but the Welsh Home Service's most memorable broadcasts of the early 1950s were further episodes of the children's serial *Galw Gari Tryfan*. *Gari Tryfan* convinced many of those in their young teens who were on the fringes of Welsh-speaking Wales that Welsh – and indeed Wales – had something to offer them. Lorraine Davies, the serial's producer, was dismayed by the need to find an endless stream of Welsh-language children's plays. The *Gari Tryfan* scripts were heartening, and even more encouraging was the work of the talented and productive Cardiganshire schoolmaster, T. Llew Jones.[137] *Children's Hour*, as a formal slot in the schedule, came to an end in April 1961, but children's radio programmes continued to be broadcast until the late 1960s, when it was realized that a new generation had arisen, so soaked in visual images that its members were incapable of appreciating the joys of 'steam' radio.

The retreat from high culture, advocated by Dafydd Gruffydd, was not complete. Talfan Davies, in particular, continued to argue that the Welsh Home Service should continue to offer the best of world drama. Audience response was not always enthusiastic, *Yr Herald Gymraeg* complaining in 1955 that *Yr Iarlles Cathleen* ('Countess Cathleen') was an excessively highbrow exercise. Well-crafted plays with a contemporary message were broadcast, *Glo Caled*, a sensitive drama set in the anthracite coalfield, being a particularly good example. Talfan Davies was determined to foster native Welsh playwrights and sought above all to encourage the talents of Saunders Lewis. After much badgering, Lewis delivered the text of *Siwan*, a play portraying Joan, the wife of Llywelyn the Great and the daughter of King John. First broadcast on St David's Day 1954, it won high praise. In 1961, Lewis offered the BBC a play on a contemporary Welsh theme. *Excelsior*, broadcast on 1 March 1962, told the story of a young Nationalist whose political ambitions led him to marry the daughter of a Labour peer, a marriage which assisted him to gain a safe Labour seat. The story bore an uncanny resemblance to the career of Llywelyn Williams, the MP for Abertyleri and the son-in-law of Lord Macdonald. Threats of a libel action caused the Corporation to cancel the play's repeat broadcast, and when the BBC deposited its scripts in the National Library, an embargo was placed on the script of *Excelsior*. 'Welsh culture is remarkable,' commented the *Manchester Guardian*; 'there is still a lot of bite in it.'[138]

Shortly before the broadcast of *Excelsior*, Lewis had made an even more significant contribution to the output of the Welsh Home Service. Rachel Jones, David Llewellyn and others had agreed in 1961 to permit him to be totally free in choosing his subject for the Service's National Lecture of 1962. He chose to discuss the future of the Welsh language. In *Tynged yr Iaith* ('The Fate of the Language'), broadcast on 13 February 1962, he declared that revolutionary methods alone could ensure the language's future. His challenge was taken up by Cymdeithas yr Iaith Gymraeg (the Welsh Language Society), which in 1963 began a campaign of law-breaking aimed at forcing the authorities to give official status to the Welsh language.[139] In advocating revolutionary methods, Lewis did not argue that they should be used in the context of broadcasting. But they were, for in the 1970s the activities of the society subjected broadcasting in Wales to revolutionary pressures.

6

From BBC Wales to the Crawford Report: BBC Broadcasting in Wales, 1964–1974

I BBC Wales

In 1937, the BBC in Wales received its own wavelength for sound broadcasting; in 1964, the BBC in Wales received its own wavelength for television broadcasting. The campaign to obtain the former, initiated in 1927, had taken ten years; the campaign to obtain the latter, initiated with the opening of Wenvoe, took twelve years. The substance of the two campaigns was very different, largely because the victory of 1937 had ensured that there could be no serious questioning of the notion that, whatever the difficulties – and they were great – the nation of Wales had an inalienable right to be a broadcasting unit. Lady Megan Lloyd George's invention of 'national regions' – by far the most important achievement of her career – sealed the victory of 1937. The Broadcasting Council for Wales, the fruit of her invention, became responsible in 1964 for Wales's input into BBC Wales on Channel 13, the BBC's second television service. Scotland, Northern Ireland and the English regions had the BBC's basic service with opt-outs. Wales had BBC Wales – a famous victory indeed. The architect of victory was undoubtedly Oldfield-Davies, who remained as controller Wales to oversee the inauguration of BBC Wales. An associate architect was Mrs Rachel Jones, who accepted an additional year as national governor in order to have a role in the inauguration. There was much excitement at Cardiff as the opening day approached. The mast which would carry the service, erected at Wenvoe 160 feet away from the 750-foot mast of 1952, and 170 foot shorter, was put up in ten months. Twenty new posts were on offer and there were 830 applicants. Head Office provided £348,000 for capital development and £550,000 a year for current expenditure. When BBC Wales was launched on 9 February 1964, the Broadcasting Council for

Scotland sent Cardiff a congratulatory telegram in Gaelic.[1] (Could it be that its members were acknowledging that they had failed to exploit the possibilities of an autochthonous language?)

The BCW closely monitored the reaction to the new service and noted with interest in March 1964 that there was a two-week waiting period at Cardiff for sets to be converted to receive Channel 13, the BBC's only service in Band III.[2] Most of the comment concerned the Channel's Welsh-language output. It was the intention of the BCW that BBC Wales should opt out of the basic service for twelve hours a week, seven in Welsh and five in English. The intention was not fulfilled until 1972; in the spring of 1964, BBC Wales broadcast 8.9 hours of programmes produced in Wales, a figure only marginally higher than had been broadcast when Wales shared the original Wenvoe transmitter with south-western England. There was one major difference, however. Before 1964, all Welsh-language programmes were transmitted outside the prescribed hours and therefore did not replace programmes in English; after February 1964, they were broadcast during network hours, with the Welsh news and the daily magazine *Heddiw* occupying the prime time of 6.35 to 7.00 p.m.

Initially, the most vocal reaction came from those outside the range of the new service. With BBC Wales available from Wenvoe Two and its associated transmitters at Blaenplwyf, Llanddona and Llandrindod, the ex-network transmission of Welsh-language programmes by Wenvoe One, Sutton Coldfield, Holme Moss and Crystal Palace came to an end. There were vigorous protests from Carmarthenshire and parts of west Glamorgan, districts which could receive the output of the more powerful Wenvoe One transmitter, but not those of Wenvoe Two. Complaints also came from north-east Wales, where the Moel-y-parc transmitter was not yet equipped to broadcast BBC programmes. Welsh people in England felt deprived, and the issue was taken up by MPs, John Morris (Aberafan) in particular. Oldfield-Davies did not want to press that Wenvoe One should resume broadcasting Welsh-language programmes on an ex-network basis, for he was anxious that viewers within the reach of Wenvoe Two should convert their sets to receive BBC Wales. This consideration did not apply in the case of the other transmitters and in April 1964 programmes in Welsh were once again broadcast by Sutton Coldfield, Holme Moss and Crystal Palace. The decision angered Donald Baverstock, the Corporation's assistant controller of programmes. 'I am concerned', he wrote, 'about the continued tolerance of the Welsh by the English citizenry. Not being a member of this minority living in a neighbouring country, [Oldfield-Davies] is perhaps unaware how careful we Welsh have to be not to provoke the hostility of our hosts.'[3]

Annoyance at being deprived of the BBC's Welsh-language output was soon more than counterbalanced by annoyance at what was seen as their imposition during network hours. In March 1964, there were meetings at Builth and Llandrindod in which resolutions were passed calling for the Llandrindod transmitter to broadcast the basic BBC service, and after the Pembrokeshire transmitter came into operation in January 1965, similar demands came regularly from Haverfordwest and Milford Haven. Cardiff sought to disarm the opposition by commissioning English-language programmes of special interest to the protesters, and in June 1964 the clerk of the Llandrindod Urban District wrote to express his appreciation that the town 'has recently featured in three television broadcasts'. Nevertheless, in 1966, the Llandrindod Chamber of Trade, through what Oldfield-Davies considered to be a highly loaded plebiscite, offered evidence to show that the vast majority of the town's inhabitants were opposed to what they saw as the imposition of BBC Wales.[4]

A more unexpected protest was that from Aberystwyth, a town which Cardiff considered to be very much part of the Welsh-speaking heartland. Shortly after Blaenplwyf began transmitting BBC Wales, a group of townspeople raised a petition complaining that they were denied the choice of BBC services available in much of southern Wales, and another group protested that Blaenplwyf was broadcasting too much Welsh. In January 1964, Oldfield-Davies travelled to Aberystwyth and addressed a packed meeting. He informed the meeting:

There will be a maximum of seven hours in Welsh. No more than three and a half hours would be in the evening, and at a time when minority interest programmes were being shown on the general network . . . I cannot understand how any reasonable person can possibly imagine that, out a total of fifty viewing hours a week, seven hours of Welsh programmes constitutes an 'outrage', an injustice or a form of dictatorship . . . English people in Wales have exhibited a degree of intolerance that is not usually associated with English people not living in their own country.[5]

By the autumn of 1964, 68 per cent of the Welsh people could receive the broadcasts of transmitters offering BBC Wales and 75 per cent could receive those of transmitters offering BBC1. In addition, a large number of Welsh households were dependent upon relay companies which were generally indifferent, if not hostile, towards the output of BBC Wales. Indeed, it would seem that if subscribers did not insist that they wanted the service, they were automatically supplied with BBC1. The Welsh edition of the *Radio Times* (renamed the Wales edition in 1965) naturally gave prominence to the programmes of BBC Wales and was therefore less relevant than were English editions to the large number of Welsh households which could not receive the programmes. In 1950, 87 per cent of the Welsh subscribers to the *Radio Times* bought the Welsh edition. In June 1964, the BCW was concerned to hear that the edition's circulation had slumped, although the circulation manager insisted that the decline was 'connected mostly with reception difficulties [rather than] with the nature of the programmes on BBC Wales'.[6]

The answer, it was felt, was to ensure that BBC Wales was more widely available, an issue which was in the forefront of the BCW's deliberations in subsequent years. The Moel-y-parc transmitter, originally built for TWWN, began broadcasting BBC Wales in 1969, bringing in a potential additional 350,000 viewers in the north-east. The problems of bringing the service to isolated pockets in mountainous country were great. In order to complete the coverage of Meirionnydd and Montgomeryshire, twelve small-scale relays would be needed, but they would only increase the total number of viewers by 1 per cent. To ensure reception for the 1,600 inhabitants of Bala cost five times as much as it cost to serve 30,000 at Llanelli. The BCW discovered that the Highlands and Islands Development Board paid for relays in the remoter parts of Scotland, and it sought, with some degree of success, to persuade the Mid Wales Development Board to provide similar help. TWW obtained an additional Band III channel in February 1965, allowing it to separate its service for Wales from that for south-western England. In covering Wales, the company had problems similar to those of the Corporation and it became common practice for the BBC and the ITA to build masts jointly. A total of nineteen new masts had been erected by June 1970, when BBC Wales was available to 75 per cent of Welsh households. In that month, the campaign to extend the coverage of Channel 13 in Band III came to an end. Channel 13 offered a Very High Frequency (VHF) service, a service which the Corporation was planning to abandon in favour of Ultra High Frequency (UHF) services in Bands IV and V.[7]

The Corporation's first service on UHF was BBC2, which began in south-east England on 20 April 1964. It was extended to the English Midlands on 6 December 1964, when it became available along the borderlands of Wales. The Winter Hill transmitter in Lancashire offered BBC2 from 31 October 1965, enabling the service to be viewed in extensive areas of Denbighshire and Flintshire. Wenvoe began transmitting it on 12 September 1965, and by the early 1970s it was also available from Llanddona, Moel-y-parc, Carmel

(Carmarthenshire), Preseli and Blaenplwyf. By then, BBC2 was available to 90 per cent of the inhabitants of Wales. Its transmission system was wholly determined by technological factors, for it was not intended that it should serve specific communities through opt-outs. Designed to carry heavier programmes than BBC1, the public did not rush to avail themselves of it. Three years after it had been launched, 13 per cent of those capable of receiving it had adapted their sets in order to do so; after six years the proportion was 60 per cent. The equivalent figures in the case of ITV were 45 and 90 per cent.[8] By 1970, it was attracting about 10 per cent of the viewing public, thus allowing BBC1 to lag behind ITV in popularity while still enabling the Corporation to claim a majority of viewers.

As BBC2 permitted BBC1 to offload some of its more serious programmes, it exacerbated the problem of regional opt-outs. 'The blatant aim of this new network', wrote Hywel Davies in June 1965, 'is to attract larger audiences to BBC1 . . . It makes our planning job of choice and rejection much more difficult.' It had other implications too. From 1964, the Corporation was maintaining two television services (three if BBC Wales is considered to be a separate service) together with three radio services. The Labour government elected in 1964 increased the combined licence fee from £4 to £5 and the sound-only licence from £1 to £1.25. The Corporation's income thus rose by 25 per cent but the costs of BBC2 and inflationary pressures caused its fiscal needs to rise by 75 per cent. By 1965, the Corporation's deficit was increasing by a million pounds a month and in 1966 Lord Normanbrook, who had succeeded fforde as chairman of the governors in April 1964, called a news conference to announce that the BBC was seriously underfunded. Anthony Wedgwood Benn, the postmaster-general from 1964 to 1966, reacted by suggesting that both the BBC and ITV should be taken over by the government, a notion which horrified the governors and offered proof of Benn's maverick attitude towards broadcasting. The Corporation's financial problems caused it to delay many capital projects, including developments at Baynton House. The administrative staff and all Cardiff's sound broadcasting operations had been transferred to the Llandaf site by the autumn of 1966, and the new Broadcasting House was officially opened by Princess Margaret on 1 March 1967. The budget for accommodating sound at Llandaf was £244,000 but the total sum spent was £534,000, the over-run of £290,000 causing deep concern to senior Corporation officials. They showed marked reluctance to finance further developments at Llandaf and thus BBC television production in Wales continued to be centred on and around Broadway on the other side of Cardiff from Llandaf. Thirteen buildings, including hired halls, redundant chapels and terraced houses were in use; parking facilities were minimal and, by the late 1960s, the hook road planned for Cardiff threatened virtually the entire complex with demolition.[9]

Among the tasks of the Labour government of 1964 to 1966 was the selection of a new national governor for Wales. It chose one of the country's most distinguished academics. He was Glanmor Williams, whose youth had been questioned by Elspeth Huxley in 1952. Professor of history at Swansea, a Welsh-speaker, a Labour sympathizer and a leading figure in Welsh Nonconformist, cultural and judicial circles, he was a man of extraordinary industriousness and a master of cogent argument. Williams was the first ex-BBC employee to become a governor; as a student, he had been employed during vacations as a cleaner at the Swansea studio. Virtually his first duty as governor was to pay tribute to Hywel Davies, whose death on 16 September 1965 at the age of forty-four was a calamitous loss to broadcasting in Wales. Hywel Davies, as Tom Richards put it, 'was the first truly dedicated and creative mind working wholly in radio and television in Wales'. Williams's tribute was widely admired. 'What a splendid person the new National Governor seems to be,' wrote Hugh Carleton Greene to Oldfield-Davies. 'His touch was very sure.'[10]

Hywel Davies was controller Wales designate, for Oldfield-Davies was due to retire in the autumn of 1965. He agreed to stay on for two years to give the governors time to select a new successor. Hywel Davies's post of head of programmes went to his deputy Talfan Davies, who would have made an admirable controller – indeed, as his literary activities caused him to have a higher profile than Oldfield-Davies, many in Wales believed that he had long held the post. As he would be retiring in 1970, however, his age precluded him from consideration. London thought that the controllership should go to a Welshman well versed in the ways of Head Office, partly because it was believed that Cardiff was tending to become too independent. An example of that tendency in January 1965 – the decision to opt out of *The Valiant Years*, broadcast by BBC1 following the death of Winston Churchill – was strongly deplored in London. 'We need', wrote the director of television, 'to have a *British* policy over such matters. What is going to happen if we arrive at a state of acute international crisis, where the same need to be together might have more than reasons of deep national sentiment?'[11]

London was also prone to consider that an appointment to a regional controllership was a useful way of ridding Head Office of an able but awkward employee. In 1962, Leonard Miall, whose colleagues found him difficult, was told that the only BBC post open to him was that of controller Scotland. In 1965, Head Office had an able but awkward Welshman who was jockeying for position with an able and less awkward Welshman. The latter was Huw Wheldon, who had all the qualities needed in a Welsh controller. He was a member of a distinguished Welsh family – his father, Wynn Wheldon, had been prominent on the University of Wales broadcasting committee in the 1930s – a Welsh-speaker and a man of great charm and authority, but his eyes were firmly fixed upon promotion in London. The former was Donald Baverstock, whose abrasiveness led Greene to believe that exiling him to Cardiff was a very good idea. Baverstock attended the interview for the Welsh controllership convinced that he had already been promised the post, though Arkell, the director of administration, believed that he would immediately alienate the entire Cardiff staff and prove to be a disastrous appointment. At the interview, Glanmor Williams, who, like Baverstock, was a native of Merthyr Tydfil, asked questions which the interviewee considered to be banal. Baverstock retorted that he would not subject himself to such treatment and sealed his fate. 'I dug my toes in,' wrote Williams.[12]

Eventually a suitable controller Wales was discovered. He was John Rowley, Head Office's controller, staff administration. Born in the north of England, Rowley had been brought up in Llanfyllin, Montgomeryshire, where he had acquired a sufficient command of Welsh to win the crown at the University of Wales Eisteddfod. He had served as a district commissioner in India and one of his favourite anecdotes concerned the difficulties which could arise when seeking to tax yaks. A man of great humanity and innate democracy, it was his invariable habit at the Llandaf canteen to sit wherever there was room and to enter into immediate conversation with the most lowly of his colleagues.[13] He became controller Wales in April 1967 and held the post until June 1974. Where broadcasting in Wales was concerned, those were years of increasing agitation and mounting polarization, the cause of much distress to the conscientious and sensitive controller.

Rowley's appointment coincided with increasing strains within the Corporation as a whole. The BBC suffered its first work-to-rule in 1967 and was subjected to strike action in 1969. Greene's libertarianism and the lightening of the output of BBC1 following the launching of BBC2 aroused strong passions. Reith believed that programmes such as *Juke Box Jury* represented absolute evil. '[Greene],' he wrote, 'follows the mob in every disgusting manifestation of the age. . . . The BBC is no longer on the Lord's side.' Realistic drama with more than a hint of sex outraged the prurient. In 1966, Mrs Mary Whitehouse began her Clean Up TV movement, which later became known as the National Viewers' and Listeners' Association.

Its members considered Greene to be villainous. 'He is responsible', declared Mrs Whitehouse, 'for the moral collapse of the country.' He considered her, with her connections with Moral Rearmament, to be a quasi-fascist and refused to have any communication with her.[14]

More significant was the increasingly strained relationship between the BBC and Harold Wilson's government. The lampooning of the Conservative government in the early 1960s had convinced Labour leaders that the BBC under Greene leaned to the left. On assuming office, however, they discovered that the Corporation was not prepared to allow them any special privileges, and Wilson in particular came to the conclusion that Greene was personally hostile to him. When Lord Normanbrook died in June 1967, the prime minister appointed Charles Hill as his successor as chairman, specifically charging Hill with the task of reasserting the authority of the governors. Hill had a long association with broadcasting. During the war he had been the radio doctor, 'informing people about their bowels in his rich, gravelly voice'. In the late 1940s, as secretary of the BMA, he had organized the opposition to Aneurin Bevan's health proposals, an experience which gave him a taste for aggressive action. Postmaster-general from 1955 to 1957, he became chairman of the ITA in 1963. He left the ITA chairmanship to become chairman of the BBC, the main reason why the governors received the news of his appointment with incredulity. 'It was like appointing Rommel to lead the Eighth Army,' commented David Attenborough. While previous holders of the office – fforde in particular – had conceived of the chairman as being analogous to the chancellor of a university, with the director-general as vice-chancellor, Hill saw the relationship as similar to that between a government minister and the permanent secretary of the department. He demanded a suite of rooms at London's Broadcasting House and refused to support a request for an increase in the licence fee until the Corporation had been subjected to an outside inquiry regarding the efficiency of its operations. Hill's relationship with Greene was not cordial and, soured by the experience of working with such a chairman, Greene resigned on March 1969. He was succeeded by Charles Curran, the BBC's director of external broadcasting.[15]

Before leaving the ITA for the BBC, Hill had been responsible for a decision which had an impact upon the context in which BBC Wales operated. With no immediate prospect of a second ITV channel, the ITA decided in 1966 that the contracts of the companies should terminate in July 1968. Huw Wheldon had suggested to the distinguished broadcaster, John Morgan, that he might consider becoming controller Wales. Morgan replied that he was congenitally incapable of having a regular job, but the suggestion turned his thoughts back to his native country. He decided to challenge TWW for the Wales and West of England franchise. Getting together a galaxy of Welsh stars including Richard Burton, Geraint Evans, Stanley Baker and Harry Secombe, Morgan set up a group headed by Lord Harlech, at one time the British ambassador to the United States and a confidant of President Kennedy. The Harlech group prepared its submission with care and Sendall considered that Lord Harlech's speech in support of the submission was the finest piece of prose addressed to the ITA. TWW was vulnerable. Its head office was in London. Ten of its seventeen directors lived outside the area served by the company and six of them were over seventy. Its record in programme-making was not as poor as its opponents suggested but, as Hill put it: 'If promise is never preferred to performance, then every television company will go on forever.' The Harlech group, which stated that it would have its headquarters in Cardiff, was awarded the franchise, causing TWW to be the first company in Britain to be dismissed from television. The new company (HTV) was required to buy TWW's studios and was licensed to start operations on 30 July 1968. TWW, however, decided to bow out early and sold the last twenty weeks of its contract to the interloper. HTV took over at 2.00 a.m. on 15 March 1968. The previous night TWW broadcast an elaborate show entitled *All Good Things Come to an End*. The BBC filmed Lord Derby leaving TWW's headquarters in London spluttering with rage. 'The thing is an absolute disgrace,' he declared. 'No one has ever told us why we were dismissed.'[16]

The BCW followed these developments with some alarm. Noting the new company's promises, Glanmor Williams commented that HTV represented a much greater challenge than TWW, especially in the fields of drama and current affairs. There were fears also that the company would poach BBC staff. In the event, HTV kept on most of TWW's employees, although some were demoted. Others chose to leave. Wyn Roberts, for example, decided that it was time for a career change; in 1970, he was elected Conservative MP for Conwy, and in 1979 became the minister of state at the Welsh Office, a post he held for fifteen years. HTV enticed the able BBC producer, Aled Vaughan, to become its Welsh head of programmes, but the loss of BBC staff was less than had been feared, initially at least. Neither did HTV fulfil the promises of its prospectus. As Sendall put it: 'After a shaky start, [Harlech] became a sound and workmanlike company providing an enterprising programme service which was none the worse for bearing no very marked resemblance to the one so elegantly described in [its] application.'[17]

For both the BBC and the commercial companies, the chief development of the late 1960s was the coming of colour television. In authorizing colour transmissions, the government laid down that they should be confined to UHF channels. BBC2, which from its inception had been transmitted on UHF, began broadcasting in colour on 21 August 1967. Initially it offered five hours a week but by 1968 it was providing a full colour service, the first such service in Europe. The implications of the innovation were far-reaching. The making of programmes in colour is much more expensive than making them in monochrome but, as a colour service could be considered a luxury, there was a case for imposing a surcharge upon those with colour sets. On 1 January 1968, the colour licence was set at £10; it was increased to £11 on 1 January 1969 and to £12 on 1 July 1971. The monochrome fee, £4 in 1963, was increased to £5 in 1965, to £6 in 1969 and to £7 in 1971. In subsequent years, the differential would widen and in the 1970s and early 1980s the colour surcharge proved to be the Corporation's salvation. As there was to be no colour on VHF, BBC1, BBC Wales and the ITV services would have to be transmitted on UHF if their viewers were not to be confined to monochrome. In February 1967, Edward Short, the postmaster-general, authorized the VHF services to be duplicated on UHF channels. The duplication, which cost the Corporation £350,000 a year, was intended to continue until most viewers had acquired UHF sets; believing that that would take seven years, Short presumed that the VHF services would come to an end in 1974. By September 1969, BBC Wales was originating all its programmes on UHF, but only the Wenvoe transmitter was broadcasting on that waveband. The other Welsh transmitters would not do so until the early 1970s. The first colour programme made by BBC Wales was a report on the Llangollen Eisteddfod, transmitted on 9 July 1970. By then BBC1 and the commercial companies were broadcasting extensively in colour and members of the BCW were aware that most of the output for which they were responsible looked drab in comparison. In September 1972, the Council concurred with Rowley's decision to cease producing opt-ins for *Match of the Day* because Wales's contributions to the progamme contrasted painfully with those of the network.[18]

The main constraints upon the development of colour were the expense and the lack of premises. *Heddiw* began using colour on 30 October 1972, but the programme frequently had to revert to monochrome because colour film was so expensive. The facilities at Broadway were inadequate and, with the hook road threat looming, there was a reluctance to invest in an area suffering from urban blight. In 1970, it became apparent that the small colour studio at Llandaf would not be ready until 1974 and that no date was available for the completion of the larger one. Birmingham offered the use of its Pebble Mill studios, but the offer was strongly resisted by the Association of Broadcasting Staff. The association feared job losses and considered that the use of Pebble Mill by BBC Wales was 'an indication of the BBC's lack of willingness to develop its services in Wales'. It was also opposed by Nationalists such as the folk group *Y Tebot Piws*, whose song 'Dy ni ddim yn mynd i Birmingham' ('We're not going to Birmingham') enjoyed considerable popularity. Some BBC Wales programmes were made at Pebble Mill (Y Felin Graean) and also at studios in London, but in 1972 Rowley acknowledged that BBC Wales could not compete with HTV's Welsh output, all of which was in colour. 'My colleagues and I', he informed the BCW on 19 May 1972, 'are finding our task increasingly more daunting and depressing.'[19]

Where Wales was concerned, there were other consequences of the adoption of UHF which were even more daunting. The early viewers of BBC2 had acquired dual-standard sets which could receive both VHF and UHF. With duplication there was no reason to buy such sets and their manufacture had been phased out by the mid 1970s. As the number of viewers exclusively reliant upon UHF increased, the pattern of transmission in Wales underwent fundamental change. Compared with VHF transmitters, those broadcasting UHF have a much shorter range. Wenvoe Two, five major relays and some sixteen minor ones enabled 75 per cent of Welsh households to receive BBC Wales on VHF. To achieve similar coverage on UHF called for at least ninety transmitters. Wales, with one-twentieth of Britain's population, needed one-fifth of the Corporation's UHF transmitters in order to be adequately served. On VHF, 70 per cent of the inhabitants of Wales could receive the BBC1 alternative to BBC Wales, because they were within reach of transmitters intended for viewers in England; chief among them was Wenvoe One – the West of England service – but there was also much viewing of the transmissions of Holme Moss and Sutton Coldfield. The West of England UHF service came from a transmitter sited on the Mendip Hills which came into operation in 1969. The change of site, the shorter range of the UHF Mendip transmitter and the phasing-out of the dual-standard sets drastically reduced the availability in south Wales of services intended for England. Similar factors reduced their availability in mid and north Wales. The proportion of Welsh households with a BBC1 alternative to BBC Wales declined from 70 per cent in the mid 1960s to less than 50 per cent in the mid 1970s. BBC1 ceased to be available in places like Neath where the town clerk was instructed to protest to the Corporation in the strongest terms. The degree of deprivation suffered by monoglot English-speaking viewers should not be exaggerated. When Welsh was broadcast at prime time on BBC Wales, there was always an English-language alternative on BBC2 and also on HTV, for arrangements to avoid 'overlapping' were working well by the 1970s. There were hopes that subtitles would make programmes in Welsh acceptable to those who lacked a knowledge of the language and the first subtitled Welsh play, *Y Drwmwr Bach*, was broadcast in May 1968. The BCW, however, was only prepared to permit subtitles on the second showing of a programme, otherwise 'it would seem as if Welsh was a foreign language' in Wales.[20] (The situation changed when technology allowed a viewer to choose whether or not to have subtitles.)

The phasing out of dual-standard sets also had other implications. In the most populous areas of southern Wales, those with such sets needed only one aerial in order to receive five services – BBC Wales, BBC1 (West of England), BBC2, HTV Wales and HTV (West of England). A single aerial of an exclusively UHF set provided three services. A viewer at Cardiff could have an aerial offering BBC Wales, BBC2 and HTV Wales, or one offering BBC1 (West of England), BBC2 and HTV (West of England). Similarly a viewer in Wrexham could have BBC Wales, BBC2 and HTV Wales or BBC1 (North of England), BBC2 and Granada. Along the southern coastlands and in much of north-east Wales – the main areas where a choice existed – fewer than 10 per cent of the inhabitants understood Welsh. The vast majority of those lacking a knowledge of Welsh chose aerials which did not receive programmes produced in Wales, thus depriving themselves of BBC Wales's output in English as well as in Welsh. 'The disintegration of our people' feared by D. H. I. Phillips in 1950 seemed to be gathering pace.

In 1968, controller North wrote to Rowley, noting that most of the viewers on 'your bank of the Dee' chose to receive their broadcasts from northern England and suggesting that the North of England Region should offer them regular programmes. 'What we must avoid at *all costs*', commented Talfan Davies, 'is the appearance of a "takeover" by the North of this strip of Welsh Country . . . It will weaken our claim that the BBC considers Wales to be an auto-nomous national region.' Rowley informed controller North:

A whole series of factors are involved. They range from the clearly rational to what can appear to those not directly involved as highly irrational, [but] in the present situation in Wales, the factors which may appear to some as 'irrational' have an inescapable validity and importance . . . Occasional uncoordinated items of interest to Wales would not be objectionable, but a programme aimed at [Wales] would . . . Your sorties into Flintshire should only occur with our prior knowledge and agreement. Do it slowly and quietly with no pronouncements.[21]

Protests such as that from the town clerk of Neath rose to about six a month by the early 1970s, causing one member of the BCW to urge that the Council should reconsider its firm rule that all the Corporation's masts sited on Welsh soil should transmit BBC Wales. Could not masts in English-speaking areas transmit BBC1 and those in Welsh-speaking areas transmit BBC Wales? The matter was not pursued, partly because even those members critical of BBC Wales's commitment to the Welsh language did not wish to see the Council depriving itself of any role where the majority of the Welsh people was concerned, and partly because the scheme was impractical. English-speaking and Welsh-speaking Wales are not two discrete blocks. By the 1970s, the majority of Welsh-speakers lived in communities in which they were outnumbered by their monoglot English-speaking neighbours. Furthermore, as the petition from Aberystwyth had shown, some inhabitants of traditionally Welsh-speaking areas resented BBC Wales. Indeed, Aberystwyth – where tensions on Welsh-language issues were high during the late 1960s and early 1970s – had among its inhabitants those who did not want the English-language programmes of BBC Wales either. Enraged that he had lost a historical programme from London because BBC Wales was broadcasting its weekly news survey, one of the lecturers at the University College berated Cardiff for imposing upon him 'the parochial banalities of *Week In Week Out*. It raises doubts', he wrote, 'about the ability and . . . the perception of the people who . . . make these choices.'[22]

Issues relating to broadcasting in Wales were of increasing concern to Welsh MPs, particularly those representing constituencies within reach of the Mendip transmitter. They were glad of the opportunity to appear on BBC Wales but were annoyed that the great majority of their constituents were not equipped to view them. They also complained that their monoglot English-speaking constituents were barred from employment by the BBC, for there was a widespread belief that in Wales the Corporation only appointed Welsh-speakers. In 1974, figures were released showing that a knowledge of Welsh was required for 34.3 per cent of the non-manual posts of the BBC in Wales. The disclosure was somewhat disingenuous. About half the non-manual posts were in engineering, a department containing very few Welsh-speakers. Thus about two-thirds of the production staff were required to have a knowledge of Welsh, and at the higher levels the requirement was virtually 100 per cent. Some of the members of the BCW came to see themselves as the champions of

English-speaking Wales, a marked contrast with the cosy consensus of the Council's early years. In 1970, after Protheroe had left for London, there was resistance among the Council's members to the demand that his successor as head of news and current affairs should be required to speak Welsh. The resistance was unsuccessful; the post went to Owen Roberts, who had distinguished himself in a similar post at HTV. In 1972, some of the members of the BCW sought an assurance that the advertisement for the post of deputy head of programmes should not ask for a knowledge of Welsh. Rowley insisted that it was a post in which Welsh was essential, but he promised to look into the possibility of appointing two deputy heads with a knowledge of Welsh required by only one of them. By the 1970s, several non-Welsh-speakers had been appointed to senior posts. They included Jeffrey Iverson (industrial correspondent, 1969), Patrick Hannan (political correspondent, 1970), George Salter (head of programme services and engineering, 1970) and Michael Brooke (chief assistant (general), 1973). In 1970, the BBC began to release staff to attend Welsh classes and in subsequent decades those who had learnt the language in adulthood would constitute a significant proportion of the Corporation's employees.[23]

In the 1950s, the Welsh MPs had accused the Welsh Home Service of being biased in favour of Plaid Cymru. In the late 1960s and early 1970s they made the same accusation against BBC Wales. In the mid 1960s, however, they had other complaints. The Labour Party won 28 of the 36 seats of Wales in 1964 and 32 in 1966. The party's success posed problems for the BBC, for in its political programmes for Wales it was obliged to reflect the general British party balance. With Welsh representation so different from that of Britain as a whole, BBC Wales did not follow the Welsh Home Service's practice of inviting MPs to comment on Westminster affairs. Instead it began thinking of appointing its own parliamentary correspondent and in the meantime it made considerable use of David Rosser, the parliamentary correspondent of the Tory *Western Mail*. That led to accusations of pro-Conservative bias and the Welsh Labour MPs were successful in banning Rosser as a broadcasting commentator on Westminster. By the late 1960s, however, they were much more concerned about Plaid Cymru. Gwynfor Evans's victory in the Carmarthen by-election of July 1966 and the party's near misses in Rhondda West in 1967 and in Caerffili in 1968 caused Welsh Labour MPs to feel vulnerable. The late 1960s also witnessed increased activity by Cymdeithas yr Iaith Gymraeg, in particular its roadsigns campaign and its protests against the investiture of Prince Charles as prince of Wales. The public did not distinguish between the Society and Plaid Cymru and neither did most MPs. The Society's campaign spawned a mass of protest songs, in particular those of its leader, Dafydd Iwan. By 1970 they had taken over the entire Welsh-language pop scene, and George Thomas accused the young people's programme, *Disc a Dawn*, of being a weekly half-hour plug for Plaid Cymru. BBC Wales was considered to give too much attention to the Society's activities and Mansel Davies, the professor of chemistry at Aberystwyth, wrote to James Callaghan attacking what he called 'the sickening excess of public attention given by the BBC to the Welsh language cum nationalist fanatics'. Callaghan, who stated that he had received several letters similar to that of Mansel Davies, raised the matter with Curran, causing near panic at Cardiff. 'Emotional outbursts [like that of Mansel Davies],' wrote Talfan Davies, 'if repeated in the Commons, could give rise to another Llewellyn Inquiry. We should do everything possible to scotch this at once.' The record was checked and it was found that of the 900 news stories broadcast in Welsh in 1969–70, 19 referred to Cymdeithas yr Iaith Gymraeg. George Thomas, who could not follow programmes in Welsh, was not satisfied by the Corporation's assurances about the content of its Welsh-language news bulletins and in 1971 he sought a guarantee that no news item should be broadcast in Welsh unless it were also broadcast in English. In 1972, BBC Wales was embarrassed by the fact that Mici Plwm, an artist on contract, had refused to buy a licence as a protest against the paucity of Welsh-language programmes. Wheldon was perturbed and corresponded energetically about what he called 'l'Affaire Plwm'. 'It is inconsistent if not dishonest', wrote Head Office, 'to take money from the BBC and not help to finance it.'[24]

Despite the barrage of complaint, BBC Wales was in fact somewhat pusillanimous in dealing with nationalist protest. It made a brief reference to the invasion of a sitting of the High Court by members of Cymdeithas yr Iaith Gymraeg, an episode covered in detail by *The Times* and one to which HTV devoted an entire programme. The activities of the Free Wales Army and the lengthy trial of its members were handled very gingerly by Cardiff, but London devoted a programme to the matter, much to the anger of Glanmor Williams. Dafydd Iwan, who had come to prominence through his appearances on TWW, was rarely featured by the BBC. 'It would indeed make our life much easier', wrote Rowley to Arthur Probert, the MP for Aberdare, 'if there were equally successful pop groups in Wales expressing all sorts of other viewpoints by means of popular songs but they don't exist at present.' Cardiff was particularly careful in its dealings with Plaid Cymru. It refused to support the party's request for party political broadcasts longer than five minutes; even to raise the matter, argued a member of the BCW, might be construed as evidence of bias. A major rally organized by the party in 1971 was ignored, as were appeals to cover its annual conference. On three occasions Head Office asked Cardiff whether it was giving Plaid Cymru sufficient attention in view of its increasing significance in Welsh life, and it was pressure from the director-general which led the BCW to decide that cameras should be sent to the party's annual conference.[25]

While George Thomas and others thought that BBC Wales was in hock to Welsh fanatics, and while Mendip-watchers ignored its output completely, devotees of the Welsh language considered that the service was failing lamentably in its duty. They had a case. The Census of 1971 showed that one in five of the inhabitants of Wales spoke Welsh, but only one in eighteen of the hours of television beamed to the households of Wales from transmitters sited on Welsh soil spoke to Welsh-speakers in their own language. When BBC Wales was launched, the Corporation had promised to broadcast seven hours a week in Welsh. Mrs W. E. Jones, a member of the BCW from 1968 to 1972, regularly demanded that the commitment should be honoured but the figure was not reached until the last few months of her membership. The Council insisted that *Heddiw* and the nightly Welsh news bulletin should be transmitted during prime time. There was a tendency, however, for other programmes to be relegated to ex-network hours. The whole concept of network hours was dispensed with in 1972, when Christopher Chattaway, the minister for posts and telecommunications, announced that the Post Office would no longer prescribe hours of broadcasting. Henceforth the BBC and the commercial companies could be broadcast whenever they liked, causing one wag to comment facetiously and unfairly that after 1972 television was certainly a medium, for it was neither rare nor well done. The end of prescribed hours threatened the ex-network broadcasts of Welsh-language programmes by transmitters in England. They had been curtailed in 1970 and in 1976 there were attempts to get rid of them altogether. The 1972 decision also posed a threat to Welsh-language broadcasts in Wales, for if popular English programmes were scheduled for previously ex-network hours, Welsh was likely to be pushed to even remoter edges of the timetable.[26]

In the early months of 1968, Mrs W. E. Jones believed that in seeking more Welsh on television hers was a lonely voice. That would soon not be the case. In May 1968, two hundred members of Cymdeithas yr Iaith Gymraeg marched to Llandaf bearing a petition calling for a substantial increase in Welsh-language broadcasts. Glanmor Williams, who was considered 'a formidable fighter for his nation's interests', believed that his main task as governor was to ensure adequate resources to allow BBC Wales to improve its existing output and he feared that more hours would result in quantity at the expense of quality. In response to the Society's petition he commented that 'Wales was already more fortunate than other regions in that it did have a separate broadcasting system'. In September 1968, the Society announced that it considered the BBC's reply to be inadequate and that it was planning 'controlled forms of violence involving damage to buildings only'. It organized a sit-in at Bangor and one at Cardiff on 29 November, leaving the premises 'in a severe state of disorder'. The BBC decided not to prosecute, for as Rowley put it: 'What the Welsh Language Society wants is to produce martyrs.'[27]

Early in 1969, the Society published a pamphlet calling for separate Welsh-language television and radio networks but the BBC declined to comment on it as the scheme was considered wholly impractical. The Society staged another sit-in on 9 December 1969 but on that occasion its members committed no damage. In January 1970, Plaid Cymru organized a 'non-political' conference on broadcasting in Wales. Addressing the conference, Emyr Humphreys, after noting that many Welsh households received their television from England, pointed out that when satellite television became common, all countries would get 'pepsi cola programmes from the sky'. 'Our problem in Wales today', he declared, 'is England's problem tomorrow.' Cymdeithas yr Iaith Gymraeg became more aggressive in the spring of 1970. In May, three of its members interrupted a programme broadcast from Bangor and were subject to heavy fines. 'I am glad', stated Rowley, 'that the magistrates took severe notice of the incident.' By the autumn of 1970, the Society's call for separate Welsh-language television and radio services was winning increasing support. It was adopted by Yr Academi Gymreig and was advocated by the journal *Planet*. The Cymmrodorion Society was asked for its views. Wheldon, a Cymmrodorion member, was totally dismissive. 'The thing is a nonsense,' he wrote to Rowley. 'What we have in Wales already is very good indeed. I hope Oldfield-Davies and Glanmor will be at the meeting [to oppose the scheme].'[28]

In December 1970, Cymdeithas yr Iaith Gymraeg submitted a lengthy document to the BCW. Where television was concerned, the Society's ultimate aim was to have two full services, one in Welsh and one in English, under the control of a Welsh Broadcasting Corporation and financed partly by a licence fee and partly by advertisements. The Society also put forward an interim scheme whereby the still unallotted fourth UHF channel should be used in Wales for the broadcast of twenty-five hours of Welsh-language programmes a week, the channel to be administered by a joint committee of BBC Wales and HTV. The interim scheme also proposed that there should be twenty-five hours of Welsh-originated English programmes, half on the BBC's channels and half on that of HTV.

Having read the proposals, the BCW requested a meeting with the leaders of Cymdeithas yr Iaith Gymraeg. At the meeting, which took place on 19 February 1971, the Society requested the Council to approve in principle at least its interim plan. The Council declined to do so but agreed to seek detailed costings of both the interim and the ultimate proposals. Rowley was anxious that the costings should stand up to detailed scrutiny, for he believed that the exercise was not merely a matter of mollifying a group of young agitators. 'There are', he informed Adams, the director of public affairs, 'others involved – the University of Wales, for example, and the Welsh Academy – and therefore the answer to the Welsh Language Society has a wider significance . . . As [our] reply in this matter will be carefully studied in Wales by experts outside the BBC, the Council is most anxious that they should be as clear and as authoritative as possible.'[29]

Work on the costings proved long and intricate, partly because Rowley insisted on checking and rechecking them and partly because the ITA and HTV were also involved. Initial figures were placed before the BCW in September 1971 but Cymdeithas yr Iaith Gymraeg did not receive a reply until February 1972. While work on the costings was being undertaken, the Society continued its campaign with a rash of mast-climbing and the infliction of extensive damage on the Granada studios at Manchester. Security precautions were introduced and Rowley pointed out that, as they were expensive, there was less money to spend on programmes. Several Council members demanded that if the cost of precautions led to cuts, it was Welsh-language programmes that should be cut. In the summer of 1971, the Welsh Schools Parents' Union, the Presbyterian Church of Wales and the Union of Welsh Independents declared their support for the Society's interim plan, and it was also viewed favourably by some Welsh MPs, those with little sympathy for the Welsh language among them. 'It is interesting', noted Rowley in December 1971, 'that the current demands of the Welsh Language Society have gained appreciable support from people who would not normally be expected to subscribe to them.' In his correspondence with Adams over costings, it is apparent that Rowley also saw virtue in the demands. He wrote in 1971:

The ideal would be to have Welsh-language programmes on a separate network. For the BBC and ITV to share a Welsh-language

290

network would involve a radical departure in principle and practice but there is a similar scheme in Finland and the present co-operation with HTV over timings has worked smoothly . . . I would want to tell the Welsh Language Society of the many practical difficulties, but I would also want to say that the BBC would be willing to try its utmost to work out acceptable answers to such difficulties . . . Any less positive answer than this would be seriously to the BBC's disadvantage in the present situation in Wales.[30]

The initial costings presented to the BCW in September 1971 indicated that the Society's interim television scheme would involve a capital expenditure of between £5 and £8 million and an annual expenditure of £4 million. The figures for the ultimate scheme were £30 million and £14 million. Rowley, who thought the ultimate scheme was hardly worth discussing, stated that when publishing the costings of the interim scheme, 'it was important that the Council should not seem to be pricing the proposals out of court'. Glanmor Wiliams, who believed that 'the BBC would not accept that its output should be linked with HTV', was sceptical about the whole exercise. Williams stressed that the BBC services available in Wales already cost £2.2 million a year more than the country's licence revenue. Even to put the interim scheme into operation would 'not be possible without an enormous grant from the government'. He emphasized in particular the severe problems inherent in the ultimate plan. As it involved the replacement of the BBC and ITV by a Welsh Broadcasting Corporation, there were other vast costs, for it was not conceivable, argued Williams, that the BBC premises and its transmitters 'would be handed over on a plate'. He was also concerned about the content of a Welsh-language channel. 'Was the talent there?', he asked. This was a matter which also worried experienced broadcasters. 'O gael Sianel Gymraeg', wrote Talfan Davies in 1972, 'fe fyddai y jam wedi'i wasgaru mor denau ar y bara nes creu syrffed ymhlith y mwyaf brwdfrydig o garedigion yr iaith.'*[31]

The meeting of September 1971 was the last to be chaired by Glanmor Williams. His successor was Dr Glyn Tegai Hughes, the warden of the University of Wales residential centre at Gregynog. (Gregynog is in the depths of northern Powys, and the Corporation was embarrassed on discovering that the new governor was unable to receive any BBC services on UHF.) A German scholar and a man

---

*'If a Welsh Channel were established, the jam would be spread so thinly on the bread that even the greatest enthusiasts for the language would be surfeited.'

of wide culture, Tegai Hughes was active in Liberal politics and in the affairs of the Wesleyan Methodist Church. He was chairman of the BCW and Welsh governor from November 1971 until July 1979, a period of great turbulence in the history of broadcasting politics in Wales. He proved to be more sympathetic than his predecessor to the concept of a fourth channel carrying the Welsh-language output of the BBC and the commercial sector. At the first Council meeting he chaired, he urged the setting up of a committee to examine the technical issues involved in providing such a service. In January 1972, he commissioned a paper on the television services of others of the bilingual countries of Europe, and he may have been responsible for the fact that on 14 December 1971 his close associate, Emlyn Hooson, the Liberal MP for Montgomeryshire, asked a parliamentary question about the posibility of devoting a wavelength to Welsh-language broadcasts. In February 1972, Tegai Hughes contacted the IBA's Welsh officials, suggesting there should be a joint link between the BCW and the IBA's Welsh Advisory Committee.[32]

The ITA had made a formal submission to the Post Office in December 1971, asking for the fourth channel to be used to transmit a second ITV service, and in its submission it suggested that all commercial programmes in Welsh should be broadcast on ITV2. Yet, as advertising income was not as buoyant as it had been, many of the commercial companies were not over-anxious to see the establishment of a second commercial television service, a factor of central importance in the developing debate about the use of the fourth channel in Wales. In April 1972, Charles Hill received a letter from Lord Aylestone, his successor as chairman of the ITA. (Aylestone was the ennobled Herbert Bowden, a Labour ex-chief whip and a native of Penarth.) In it Aylestone pointed out that 'we have a problem common to us both': that the presence of Welsh-language programmes on HTV Wales and BBC Wales led monoglot English-speaking Welsh viewers 'to deprive themselves of seeing a number of English-language programmes about the community in which they live'. The solution for the commercial sector would be to make HTV Wales an exclusively English-language service by transferring Welsh-language programmes to ITV2. Pending the allocation of the fourth channel to ITV, he suggested that 'both of us should use the unused time of BBC2 for Welsh-language material'. The letter was passed to Cardiff where Owen Edwards, Talfan Davies's successor as Wales's head of programmes, prepared suggestions for Hill's reply. Edwards pointed out that the unused hours were inconvenient and were likely to contract substantially as BBC2 came to carry the programmes of the Open University. There was no such thing as a Welsh BBC2 network, for most of the north received the service from Winter Hill in Lancashire. The Welsh governor, he wrote, 'expressed a cautious willingness to examine the possibilities of co-operation in the event of a fourth channel [but it is] a very different matter for the BBC to consider allowing ITV to encroach on an existing BBC channel . . . Co-operation on BBC2 would make co-operation on the fourth channel more remote than at present . . . If there were Welsh programmes on BBC2, that would clear the way for the fourth channel to be ITV2.' Edwards's letter is the first indication that the Welsh-language issue would feature in the Corporation's efforts to block ITV2. In replying to Aylestone, Hill, who by 1972 was very much a BBC man, used Edwards's arguments almost verbatim. He ended his letter by stating that 'we would certainly be prepared to examine the possibility of co-operation between us if the use of the fourth channel were to be allocated in Wales for Welsh programmes'.[33]

Hill's letter was a recognition that a Welsh fourth channel was hardening into a practical proposition. Developments in Wales convinced Head Office that the matter should be given serious consideration, although Wheldon continued to insist that the scheme was impractical. Curran was much disturbed by an episode at Bangor in May 1972 when two university lecturers and a minister of religion appeared before the magistrates accused of having unlicensed television sets. On informing the court that they had not bought a licence because they wished to demonstrate their support for the campaign of Cymdeithas yr Iaith Gymraeg, they were given an absolute discharge. Broadcasting in Wales was discussed by the Welsh Grand Committee in June 1972 and several Labour MPs expressed the view that a Welsh fourth channel was the only solution. Their motives perturbed Talfan Davies. 'Pan fydda i'n gweld', he stated, 'Mr George Thomas a Mr Leo Abse [Labour, Pontypool] . . . yn rhuthro i gyfleidio Dafydd Iwan, rwyf am awgrymu mai dim ond y mwyaf *naive* o blant dynion fyddai'n barod i gredu mai yr un yw eu cymhellion.'[*34]

In July 1972, the minister of posts and telecommunications, when discussing the possible use of the fourth channel, mentioned that special arrangements could be made in Wales. The way such arrangements could work was outlined in a report published by the University of Wales's broadcasting committee in June. The report envisaged the establishment of a co-ordinating authority to oversee the co-operation between the BBC and the commercial sector, a

---

*'When I see Mr George Thomas and Mr Leo Abse [Labour, Pontypool] . . . rushing to embrace Dafydd Iwan, I would suggest that it is only the most naïve of people who would believe that their motives are the same.'

suggestion which disturbed Tegai Hughes. 'Would the Authority have control over the editorial content of BBC programmes?' he asked. 'Any arrangements for the joint use of the fourth channel should be kept as simple as possible.' In the autumn of 1972 several local authorities passed resolutions supporting the University's proposals. Pembrokeshire County Council, which had frequently protested against the Welsh-language output of BBC Wales, was among them, a fact which deepened the suspicions of Talfan Davies and those who shared his views.[35]

In October, the governors asked Tegai Hughes to prepare a survey of broadcasting in Wales with a view to offering the Board a clear series of options. Wheldon was annoyed, for he wanted the 'sodding governors', as he called them, to have as little as possible to do with the running of the BBC. Tegai Hughes's paper, submitted in November 1972, is a remarkably cogent document. He stressed that the demand for broadcasts in Welsh was no mere fad, for in dealing with the language one was 'not dealing with an optional extra, but with the fabric of existence of half a million people'. He noted a 'less vocal but not insignificant demand for more English from Wales'. The situation was likely to get worse, for the extension of UHF 'will magnify rather than lessen linguistic tensions'. 'The Welsh Language Society', he noted, 'is already blackmailing us on the matter of the fourth channel.' The Society, he informed the governors, 'has a few hundred activists, a few thousand active sympathizers and perhaps a hundred thousand passive sympathizers'. Any increase in the Welsh-language output of BBC Wales beyond the seven hours aimed for was unacceptable and opt-outs from BBC2 presented problems. They would alienate opinion-makers and the service was not available in much of Welsh-speaking Wales. Tegai Hughes believed that the interim proposals of Cymdeithas yr Iaith Gymraeg were 'probably feasible', but if the fourth channel were to be granted to the Welsh language, 'a political decision of unusual firmness would be needed'. He recognized that broadcasting in Wales was already subsidized but concluded that 'the problems of Wales are so great that even more disproportionate aid is required to start solving them'. Thanking him for his paper, the BCW noted 'that it poses a series of unanswerable questions, but, as everyone knows, that is what broadcasting in Wales is all about'.[36]

Curran showed a deep interest in Tegai Hughes's paper, for he was aware of what he called 'the classical insensitivity of the English to the sensitivities of those who are not English'. 'It is a central function of the Director-General', he wrote, 'to remind his English colleagues that they are likely, by accident of birth, to be insensitive brutes.' In January 1973, he announced that he would like to see the fourth channel being used for educational programmes, but he made no comment about any different use in Wales. Tegai Hughes, encouraged by a letter in the press signed by twenty-seven prominent Welsh people calling for a Welsh fourth channel, decided that it was time for the BBC to make a statement. He contacted Sir Michael Swann, the vice-chancellor of Edinburgh University, who had replaced Hill as chairman of the governors on 20 December 1973. Swann thought that any declaration by the governors as a whole would be premature, but he had no objection if the BCW wanted to make its views known. At the Council meeting on 19 January, Tegai Hughes argued that a firm public declaration in favour of a Welsh fourth channel should be made. There were some demurrings, with two members arguing that if Welsh-speakers were to have an additional service, they should pay a differential licence fee, a notion which had been floated by George Salter, Wales's head of programme services and engineering, a year earlier. The declaration was however made. It stated that the Council favoured 'the use of the fourth channel in Wales for programmes in the Welsh language and English-language programmes of Welsh interest . . . [and urged] that the fourth network construction should start as soon as possible'.[37]

Meanwhile Cymdeithas yr Iaith Gymraeg continued its campaign. Indeed, the first three months of 1973 were the most active period in its history. There were attacks upon studios in Manchester, Bristol, Newcastle and Plymouth, a sit-in at Bush House and a demonstration in the House of Commons. Following the Manchester attack, Saunders Lewis made a public acknowledgement of his debt to the BBC, and the BCW interpreted his words as an appeal to the Society to cease attacking the Corporation. If that were the case, it was unsuccessful, for Cymdeithas yr Iaith Gymraeg held a two day sit-in at Llandaf in April. Nor was there any cessation in the complaints of those who did not want broadcasts they could not understand. References to the deprivation of the minority were countered by references to the frustration of the majority, causing Rowley's memoranda to be increasingly concerned with polarization and with the irrevocable breakdown of community relations. 'What has happened', he wrote in March 1973, 'is not any significant increase in Welsh output, but a most significant decrease in understanding and tolerance.' By then Rowley was under constant medication for chronic strain and overwork and in March his doctor insisted that he should take a Mediterranean cruise. He was away for a further seven weeks in the autumn; he took early retirement in June 1974 and was succeeded by Owen Edwards. If the linguistic condition of Wales ever created a martyr, it was John Rowley.[38]

The last months of Rowley's controllership witnessed increasing consensus on the matter of a Welsh fourth channel. On 13 March 1973, Curran met the Welsh Labour MPs and they impressed upon him that 'the situation of the language demanded urgent action'. Curran informed the BCW three days later:

> Over the last eighteen months I have been moving to a position where I can see no justification for indefinitely avoiding measures to make further provision for the Welsh language. It is part of the BBC's function to cater for minorities. Emotional reaction [in relation to] a language calls for action disporportionate to the numerical strength of its speakers . . . It would certainly minimise unrest in Wales if Welsh-language programmes could be accommodated on a fourth network.

Stressing that the BBC could not afford to pay for a new Welsh service, he stated that the Corporation would accept a government grant-in-aid, provided 'that there was no more control than was experienced with the External Service's grant-in-aid'. The BBC, he noted, had always resisted government grants for home broadcasting, but it could make an exception if 'the area was manageably small so as not to make the BBC as a whole over-dependent, and if the area is clearly identifiable so that acceptance did not spill over into other areas. The Welsh language is such an identifiable area.'[39]

In April 1973, the archbishop of Wales convened a conference which resolved to ask the Post Office to ensure 'that special consideration should be given to Wales in deciding the future of the fourth channel and that sufficient financial resources should be made available'. In July the archbishop's resolution was considered by a conference convened by the lord mayor of Cardiff and received unanimous approval. By then the Labour Party in Wales was strongly in favour of the fourth channel solution. The BBC governors had not yet fully committed themselves, but visiting Cardiff in July 1973, Michael Swann expressed 'his surprise that more emphasis had not been placed in the past on the argument that a country where there are two languages needs twice as much money for broadcasting'. 'I feel', he informed the BCW, 'that there would be advantage in pressing this argument politically.'[40]

In May 1973, the government set up a committee 'to examine the broadcasting authorities' plans for the coverage of television and sound broadcasting in Scotland, Wales, Northern Ireland and rural England'. Chaired by Sir Stewart Crawford, its members included the distinguished Welsh barrister Eifion Roberts. (In its last months, the Labour government of 1966 to 1970 had appointed Lord Annan to chair a committee to examine the entire future of broadcasting in the United Kingdom as a whole, but the incoming government of

Edward Heath dismissed Annan, deeming the exercise to be unnecessary.) In July, Swann informed the BCW that Head Office would be stressing the need for making special arrangements for Wales. In August, the BBC submitted a memorandum to the Post Office calling for a Welsh fourth channel, a document which the BCW considered to be admirable. By then, the governors were wholly committed to the proposal, Swann declaring publicly that 'we are not in any doubt . . . that some kind of fourth channel arrangement is the best way of catering for the two audiences'.[41]

The Crawford Committee visited Cardiff in November 1973 and gave the impression that it was sympathetic to the fourth channel solution. Addressing the Royal Institution in February 1974, Curran declared that 'the Welsh-language question is one which must be solved if peace of mind is to be restored to the Welsh community. The costs of doing so are a legitimate social charge.' He returned to the theme later in the year. Speaking to the BBC's education staff, he stated:

> I [see] two particular reasons as justifying the devotion of the fourth channel network to minority purposesThe first is a need for a Welsh-language solution, or rather one ought more correctly to say, an English-language solution in Wales. The problem is not the Welsh language in Wales. The problem is the English-language speakers who do not like to hear Welsh . . . If you accommodate the Welsh language on another network, you solve the English problem . . . You deal with Leo Abse, rather than with Gwynfor Evans, and politically Leo Abse is much more important . . . If you use the fourth channel in Wales for a minority purpose, it follows that you cannot use it elsewhere for a majority purpose, because if you do that you renew in Wales the sense of deprivation of a majority service which the rest of the United Kingdom is then enjoying . . . You will simply split Wales again and make the English part of Wales more English than it is. So the rest of the network, if you are going to have the Welsh language in Wales, must have a minority purpose . . . [In Wales] you have the beginnings of some kind of trust which embodies a number of different interests. I believe there are other interests in the rest of the country which can be similarly represented . . . Another ITV channel with a mass audience would be damaging to all existing services . . . The fourth channel [in the rest of the United Kingdom] should be something which represents a consortium or collegium of the various interests which would want to have running rights over it.[42]

The apparently unstoppable growth of consensus in favour of a Welsh fourth channel disturbed some Welsh-language loyalists. In particular it disturbed Jac L. Williams, the professor of education at Aberystwyth. From 1973 until his death in 1977, he bombarded the press with letters arguing that the fourth channel solution would be a disaster. To remove Welsh-language programmes from the two popular channels and exile them to an obscure frequency would create a ghetto situation. Large numbers of Welsh-speakers with only a casual loyalty to the Welsh language happened upon programmes in Welsh because they were wedged between their favourite English programmes. If a special effort had to be made to find them and if they were placed on a channel, the rest of the output of which was likely to be esoteric, they would only attract a tiny number of listeners. The ghetto argument won some support and, as will be seen, it would become central in the last months of the campaign for a Welsh fourth channel.[43] Yet, as Williams sought not only to maintain, but also to increase, Welsh-language transmissions on the popular channels, his campaign, if successful, could not have but exacerbated tensions which were already high.

A Welsh fourth channel was only feasible if the ITA was prepared to co-operate, for in the early 1970s television programme-making was confined to the BBC and the Authority's commercial companies; the notion that small-scale independent companies had a contribution to make seemed wholly futuristic. As the ITA (renamed the IBA in 1972) maintained that it wanted the fourth channel for a second ITV service, it was opposed to any suggestion that in Wales the channel should be jointly run by the BBC and the IBA. Yet it took seriously the threat of Cymdeithas yr Iaith Gymraeg, and in December 1972 Rowley informed the BCW that 'the Authority was prepared to mollify the Society if possible'. In January 1973, the IBA stated that if ITV2 were granted, it could begin in Wales ahead of the rest of the United Kingdom and could broadcast up to twelve hours of Welsh-language programmes a week. Until there was an ITV2 service for the United Kingdom as a whole, the Welsh ITV2 could devote its peak hours to Welsh-language progammes and fill the rest of its schedule by duplicating ITV1. The IBA acknowledged that the advertising income would be small, but it would be possible to compensate the Welsh contractor by reducing its rental. Several Conservatives considered the scheme attractive and suggested that the BBC could have 'placing' rights for its Welsh-language output on ITV2. In June 1973, the ACTT, the leading union in commercial television and an organization not recognized by the BBC, issued a statement opposing a Welsh fourth channel because 'it would deprive Welsh viewers of whatever alternative service was available on the channel for the rest of the United Kingdom'. It suggested, however, that the fourth channel could offer Welsh programmes until there was a general United Kingdom service, on the under-standing that they would then be moved to another channel – Channel Five.[44] The IBA, HTV and the ACTT wished the public to believe that they had practical answers to the language issue and that it was the BBC, by seeking to have joint control over a channel which should rightfully belong to the commercial sector, that was hampering the implementation of a rapid solution.

In the summer of 1973 a joint committee consisting of rep-resentatives of the BBC and the IBA's Welsh Advisory Committee began a series of meetings. The Corporation's Welsh officials also had meetings with HTV, but the BCW was informed that the main significance of both sets of meetings was the fact that they were being held at all. In October 1973, Tegai Hughes told T. Glyn Davies, the Welsh representative on the IBA, that 'our contacts with the contracting company have been so unproductive that some new approach must be sought'. By then there were signs of a 'breakaway attitude' on the part of the Welsh Committee of the IBA, and indeed it was eventually to endorse a shared channel in defiance of the views of the Authority. Yet, as the Committee only had advisory powers, the BCW could only hold discussions of substance with HTV. They were regularly reported as 'not getting anywhere', but Tegai Hughes believed that they should continue so that 'the BBC should make clear its willingness to co-operate'. 'They will not prove fruitful', he noted, 'until a decision is reached about the fourth channel.'[45]

The hope that a decision could be reached quickly seemed to be dashed in April 1974, when Roy Jenkins, the home secretary in the newly elected Labour government, announced that he was resurrecting the Annan Committee. The Corporation's charter and the IBA's licence were due to expire in July 1976. To give Annan time to consider the future of British broadcasting, both charter and licence were extended to 1979. (They were later extended to 1981 on the grounds that major technological advances were expected in the early 1980s.) It was widely assumed that the implementation of any recommendation Crawford might make would have to wait until the Annan Committee had submitted its report. Indeed, the *Western Mail* declared that the resurrection of Annan meant that 'Welsh television channel hopes are killed'. The BCW protested against any such supposition. At its meeting on 19 April, it noted that the Annan Inquiry could take up to four years and the government would want several years to make up its mind, which could mean 'that decisions regarding the fourth channel could take us to 1983'. 'In our view', declared the Council, 'it would be intolerable for the language situation to fester until then. Finance should be made available immediately to start building the fourth network in Wales without prejudice to the final decision about its allocation.' At its May meeting it was relieved to hear that the home secretary had informed Tegai Hughes that 'if Crawford produces recommendations acceptable to the government, then there would be no obligation to wait for Annan'.[46]

The Crawford Report was published in November 1974. It noted that in Wales 'both broadcasting authorities find the problem of pleasing both [language] groups insoluble within the television channels at present available and the difficulties will become increasingly acute as the switch from VHF to UHF proceeds'. The report referred to Jac L. Williams's campaign but stated that 'the greater weight of argument we heard was in favour of putting Welsh-language programmes on a separate channel'. The fourth channel should carry the Welsh-language output of the BBC and HTV and 'the co-ordinating machinery should be of the simplest and most economical'. Adapting the transmission network in Wales to carry the fourth channel would cost £4 million, 'but it would have to be done eventually in any case'. HTV's programme contributions to the channel could be partly financed 'by the adjustment of the IBA's arrangements for HTV within the ITV structure. The service, however, would need a subsidy, and this Crawford was prepared to defend.

> [A subsidy] would break new ground but in the special circumstances of the Welsh case, we do not see any objection in principle . . . The cost would represent an investment in domestic, cultural and social harmony in the United Kingdom; the money spent would, in effect, be aimed at supporting in the home the other cultural and local government expenditure which is being incurred to satisfy Welsh aspirations . . . We recommend, whatever decision may be reached about the use of the fourth channel in the rest of the United Kingdom, it should in Wales be allotted as soon as possible to a separate service on which Welsh-language programmes should be given priority.

The government accepted the recommendation and set up a working party 'to work out the arrangements required to provide a fourth television service in Wales, including timing and estimates of costs'. Chaired by John Siberry, a former under-secretary at the Welsh Office, the working party held its first meeting on 20 January 1975.[47]

II *The continuing role of sound broadcasting*

The expansion of the BBC between 1964 and 1974 – the increase in its staff, for example, from 19,722 to 23,897 – was largely caused by the demands of its television service. Yet, in terms of hours of output, the Corporation's sound-radio operation was far more prolific. In 1974, the BBC's two television services broadcast 8,142 hours of network programmes a year, compared with 26,195 hours broadcast by its four sound radio services. By 1974, the Corporation had lost its sound as well as its television monopoly, for the Conservative government which came to power in 1970 authorized the setting up of local commercial radio stations, a decision which caused the Independent Television Authority (ITA) to be renamed the Independent Broadcasting Authority (IBA). The Broadcasting Act of June 1972 legislated the BBC's sound monopoly out of existence. The monopoly effectively ended on 8 October 1973 with the launching of London's Capital Radio, but, unlike 22 September 1955 – the date of the ending of the BBC's television monopoly – the event passed almost unnoticed. Yet, even in 1964, when the fifth Charter ostensibly renewed the Corporation's sound monopoly, that monopoly was more honoured in the breach than in the observance. Radio Luxembourg had a substantial following, as did the American Forces Network in Germany. Even more threatening was the anchoring outside territorial waters of ships equipped to broadcast a continuous stream of pop music. By December 1964, there were five pirate radio ships: Caroline South near Harwich, Caroline North near the Isle of Man, Radio City near Sheerness, Radio Invicta in the Thames estuary and Radio London near Frinton. Caroline North was audible in parts of north Wales, and in 1966 the BCW was perturbed by rumours that a pirate ship was planned for the Severn Estuary; the threat, however, did not materialize.[48]

By 1965, one in five of those able to receive the pirate stations were avid listeners, and fans of Caroline and the rest were particularly common among teenagers. There was very little decline in the BBC's audience, for the devotees of the pirate stations had never been attracted to the Corporation's output. There were accusations that the pirates were giving a service that the BBC was too 'stuffy' to provide. In fact, it was one the Corporation could not provide, for the agreement with the Musicians' Union limited it to twenty-eight hours of needle-time a week. That meant one hour twenty minutes a day on each of the BBC's three services. The Performing Rights Society, which received no needle-time payments (payments for the use of records) from the pirates as it did from the BBC, pressed the Musicians' Union to make concessions. A further forty-seven hours were conceded in March 1965, but the BBC devoted thirty of them to the Music Programme (the daytime extension of the Third Programme) and only seventeen to the Light Programme, the service most capable of competing with the pirates. In 1965, a European Convention agreed to outlaw the pirates but the British government took no action. 'Labour MPs let us know privately', noted Head Office, 'that they would resist any move until the BBC is prepared to provide a substitute "pop" service.' In 1966, a government White Paper authorized the BBC to introduce such a service and promised legislation to outlaw the pirates within a year. The decision involved the splitting of the Light Programme into a 'pop' channel and one providing more traditional light entertainment. The change, put into operation on 30 September 1967, gave the Corporation an oppor-tunity to revamp and rename its entire home sound broadcasting service. From 1967, the BBC offered four sound services: Radios One and Two (the 'pop' and the 'light' service), Radio Three (an amalgam of the Third Programme, the Music Programme and the Study Session), and Radio Four (the successor to the Home Service, which henceforth would be almost entirely speech-orientated).[49]

The changes of 1967 had major implications for sound broad-casting in Wales. The concession on needle-time – vastly augmented following the launching of Radio One – meant that full-scale services heavily dependent upon records were possible in Wales; indeed, the developments in Welsh sound broadcasting in the 1970s would have been impossible had the Musicians' Union insisted on adhering to the original needle-time agreement – and it probably would have insisted had not the pirates undermined its position. Wales's radio productions, hitherto broadcast as opt-outs from the Home Service, became opt-outs from Radio Four, the middlebrow and, some claimed, the middle-aged service. Placed in such a context, there was a tendency to consider Wales's output as middlebrow and middle-aged also. That output – the Welsh-language element in particular – contained elements of all the four services, and some of its heavier programmes and many of its lighter ones sat unhappily in the context of Radio Four. 'As Radio Four is to be a speech network', noted Owen Edwards, 'it will often be difficult for us to replace like with like.' Radio One hired seventeen of the disc jockeys previously employed by the pirates and rapidly became the favourite station of the listeners of Wales. There were fears that its success would marginalize the rest of the BBC's sound output. Some Corporation officials were a little ashamed of Radio One and they would have happily concurred in the suggestion that it should be hived off and financed by advertisements. The suggestion was not pursued, largely because Radio One did not make heavy demands upon the

BBC's resources. By the mid 1970s, when it had 40 per cent of the radio audience, it received 9 per cent of the Corporation's sound budget. The figures for the other services were: Radio Two, 35 and 18; Radio Three, 2 and 20; Radio Four, 20 and 24.[50]

By the late 1960s, the sum spent on sound broadcasting was small compared with that spent on television. In 1952, the Corporation devoted three-quarters of its programme expenditure to radio and a quarter to television; by 1969 the proportions were exactly reversed. In Wales, where the devotion to sound radio was greater than it was in the United Kingdom as a whole, there was concern that the junior service should not usurp resources that should rightfully belong to the senior. The BCW was particularly anxious to support activity at Bangor and Swansea, centres which were almost exclusively involved with sound broadcasting. In 1964, it concurred in Oldfield-Davies's decision to move the Welsh-language radio drama department to Bangor, a decision which marked the beginning of the division of the BBC's operations in Wales into Welsh- and English-language components. Following the retirement of W. R. Owen in May 1970, the Bangor staff was led by John Roberts Williams, a man of great originality. By then, Bangor was producing over 450 programmes a year, a figure which would more than double by 1974. The Bangor staff also produced inserts for *Heddiw* and the television news bulletins, but as Bangor was not to have even minimal television facilities until 1971, these had to be sent to Cardiff from Manchester, causing Dyfnallt Morgan to spend much of his time toing and froing. By the late 1960s, Bryn Meirion was grossly overused and the semi-derelict Penrhyn Hall was threatened with demolition. In the 1970s, efforts to find alternative accommodation at Bangor were to absorb much of the energies of BBC officials.[51]

Corporation employees at Swansea viewed the Bangor developments with concern. In March 1965, the town's MPs wrote to Oldfield-Davies pointing out that Swansea was the centre of a far more populous area than was Bangor and requesting an assurance that its output would not be curtailed. Oldfield-Davies replied that there was no present intention of changing the status of Swansea, and, as the town was high on the BBC's local radio list, the output would almost certainly expand when decisions regarding local radio had been made. Yet, in July 1966, he informed the Corporation's Working Party on Regional Economies in confidence that when the radio studios at Llandaf were in use, the Welsh Home Service would not need a production centre at Swansea; an unattended studio would suffice. The Llandaf sound studios were in use by November 1966 and its radio complex was considered to be the BBC's finest outside London. Oldfield-Davies mishandled the Swansea situation, a rare if not unique occurrence in his distinguished career. The plan to reduce Swansea to an unattended studio had become public knowledge by the autumn of 1966 and aroused the anger of Tom Richards, the west Wales representative. Oldfield-Davies informed Richards that it was 'impossible to justify empty studios at Llandaf in order to keep Swansea ticking over'. Some of the Swansea staff could move to Cardiff, others might wish to retire and the rest would be made redundant. There were angry meetings at Swansea and Oldfield-Davies was accused of reneging on his promise of 1965. The Association of Broadcasting Staff declared that the decision was 'metropolitanization on a Welsh scale' and was equivalent to the Londonization to which Welsh broadcasters had always been opposed. 'Cardiff', stated the Association, 'is ethnically untypical', an argument which Oldfield-Davies described as 'a lot of hot air'. Glanmor Williams, a leading citizen of Swansea, was embarrassed that he was national governor at a time when the BBC's operations in his home town were being attenuated. Yet, as the decision was a management matter, he felt unable to oppose it publicly. The lease of the Alexandra Road premises was due to expire in 1971. Oldfield-Davies decided that, apart from the space occupied by the unattended studio and by an office accommodating four employees at most, the building should be left unused until the decision on the siting of local BBC stations had been announced. The case for such a station at Swansea was strong, but Head Office doubted whether the town would have one unless substantial local funding were forthcoming. 'The Post Office', it stated, 'cannot give one to Swansea gratis.' Feeling unable to offer a subsidy, the Swansea Corporation withdrew its application in July 1967. Broadcasting House at Swansea was closed on 31 December 1967, thus fulfilling the *Cambria Leader*'s prophecy of 1925 that the town would be left with 'a microphone somewhere and a telephone line to Cardiff, just enough of a concession to local feeling to allow the BBC to say that Swansea is not entirely ignored'.[52]

In Wales's sound broadcasting budget, the largest single item was the maintenance of the BBC Welsh Orchestra. (Although the orchestra was the responsibility of the BBC in Wales as a whole, its role was almost completely confined to radio; indeed, over half its broadcast programmes were contributions to the output of the Third Programme.) Its reputation was growing; in 1965, for example, it provided the music for the Third Programme's *Wrath of Achilles*, a programme which won the Italia Prize. Yet with 44 members, it lacked symphonic status and thus its repertoire was confined to lighter works. In 1967, when the Corporation was maintaining, among other orchestras, the London Symphony (91 members), the

Northern (67), and the Scottish (60), the BCW applied for money to add 10 members to the BBC Welsh Orchestra. The governors replied that the money was not available. The request coincided with Rowley's assumption of the controllership, and he proved to be far more enthusiastic than his predecessor in seeking to increase the orchestra's size and to enhance its reputation. Indeed, on his retirement he stated that it was his work on behalf of the orchestra which had given him the greatest satisfaction. In the late 1960s, the orchestra cost over £100,000 a year and broadcast about 195 programmes annually. The Welsh Arts Council organized annual series of about twenty symphony concerts by hired orchestras, but because of the small size of the BBC Welsh Orchestra it was not invited to take part in them. The concerts cost the Arts Council £39,000 a year, and it was suggested that if part of the money were spent on expanding the BBC Welsh Orchestra, the Council would enrich music-making in Wales and enable Wales's own orchestra to participate in the Arts Council's programme. The suggestion was the revival of a scheme that had previously been aired, but in the late 1960s it was pursued with greater vigour than in the past.[53]

Discussion with the Arts Council, initiated in 1967, continued over the following two years. In 1969, however, it seemed as if the whole exercise was doomed, for a report commissioned by the Corporation – *Broadcasting in the Seventies* – argued that the BBC was maintaining orchestras far in excess of its broadcasting needs and urged severe pruning. The threat that the BBC Welsh Orchestra might be disbanded caused the BCW to organize a vigorous campaign, and in June 1969 the Council won assurances that the orchestra's future was secure.

In 1970, *The Report on the Orchestra Resources of the United Kingdom* pointed out that the Welsh National Opera Company was spending £60,000 a year on hiring orchestras and recommended that the Company should divert the money to the BBC Welsh Orchestra, which could then become the Company's permanent orchestra. The idea had its attractions. The Opera Company had considered creating its own orchestra. 'Wales cannot sustain two orchestras,' argued Rowley. 'If another were to be established, ours will again be in the firing line . . . If we join with the Opera Company, that will reduce the costs to the BBC, but the orchestra's commitment to the Opera will halve the number of broadcasts we can provide, although those broadcasts will then be fully symphonic.' There were severe problems, however. The Company's workload was increasing and many of its performances were outside Wales. Rowley was not prepared to allow the BBC Welsh Orchestra to be absent from Wales for lengthy periods, and the Company refused to have one orchestra for its performances in Wales and another for its performances elsewhere. In addition, the Musicians' Union, which wanted Wales to have two orchestras, opposed the link with the Opera Company. Discussions with the Company collapsed and those with the Arts Council were resumed. The Musicians' Union again created difficulties, for it sought to insist that the Arts Council concerts provided by an augmented BBC Welsh Orchestra should be additional to the concerts the Council already organized. Between 1971 and 1973 there were protracted discussions, and the Musicians' Union was frequently obdurate. Lord Goodman, the chairman of the Arts Council of Great Britain, became involved and in January 1973 the union withdrew its objections. The Welsh Arts Council agreed to pay for sixteen extra players; furthermore, it promised that, if the funds were available, it would finance an additional three-phase expansion which would enable the orchestra to have seventy-six members by 1982. The sixty-strong orchestra, renamed the Welsh Symphony Orchestra, gave its first performance on 7 October 1973. The whole story was a striking confirmation of Maurice Gorham's dictum that 'whatever a broadcasting station starts with it inevitably ends up with a full symphony orchestra'.[54]

The report *Broadcasting in the Seventies* had implications well beyond orchestra provision. It had some bearing on television, more specifically in England, but it is its recommendations concerning sound broadcasting that attracted the widest attention, for they involved the dismantling of a system of English regional radio which had been in existence since the 1920s. The Corporation had long pondered the issue of English regionalism, an issue which became more acute as the rise of nationalism in Wales and Scotland in the 1960s was accompanied in England by a greater sense of regional identity and of regional grievance, particularly in parts of the north. Time and again regional boundaries were changed – there was an occasion when the West of England Region almost included Sussex – and conferences on the regional question were frequently held. At one such conference, a London producer stated that 'provincialism is a special kind of incompetence; professionalism is essentially a metropolitan attribute', causing Richard Hoggart to retort that 'professionalism, the current mystic word in the BBC, often [means] the prostitution of the mind'. 'Is not metropolitan v. provincial', he asked 'in reality the north v. south division in different terms?' It was left to a Welsh broadcaster to provide the classic defence of British broadcasting outside London. A few weeks before being struck by fatal illness, Hywel Davies gave one of the BBC's lunchtime lectures. Speaking on 'The Role of the Regions', he entranced his audience with his verve and cogency. Alasdair Milne felt that in explaining his role as controller Scotland, he need do no more than quote Hywel Davies, particularly Davies's comment that 'we are concerned with the delights and tribulations of being off centre'.[55]

The answer offered by *Broadcasting in the Seventies* to the problems of regionalism in England was to increase the number – and thereby decrease the influence – of English regions. It recommended that in England regional opt-outs from Radio Four should come to an end. Sound programme-making should continue at Bristol, Birmingham and Manchester, the centres of the West, Midland and Northern Regions, but those centres should devote themselves entirely to the production of material for the network. The regions themselves should be abolished and replaced by eight smaller regions, each of which should have its own local service; as resources and wavelengths became available, the BBC should increase the number of its local services until local radio was available to 90 per cent of the inhabitants of England. Opt-outs from Radio Four should continue in the 'national regions', but the report looked forward to the time when they would have their own services, either additional to or in substitution of Basic Radio Four.[56]

The implications of the report were far-reaching. If implemented – and it was – the great provincial cities would no longer have opt-out programmes of regional interest and of Radio Four standard, the content of which was the responsibility of the regional controller and the regional head of programmes. Instead, Bristol, Birmingham and Manchester would produce programmes at London's behest for a service wholly under London's control. It was proposed that the local services, when not broadcasting their own material, should opt in to either Radio One or Radio Two, a broadcasting environment which made it unlikely that the stations would produce programmes demanding sustained attention – assuming, which was also unlikely, that they would have the resources to produce such programmes. *Broadcasting in the Seventies* represented the climax of London's long radio battle against the great provincial cities – and their rout. It also represented a further differentiation in the status of the 'national regions' and that of the English regions. Furthermore, as the local stations were designed to be city-based, they were unlikely to offer much to country-dwellers, a realization which led to robust protests, particularly from south-western England. The West of England Region was permitted to continue to have a vestigial role. But it was highly vestigial. In 1973 a retired West of England producer wrote to Cardiff to ask Wales to broadcast a literary programme of interest to south-western England listeners. 'Alas', he stated, '[in England] residual regional radio has gone . . . and English authors must look enviously across the Bristol Channel to those happier and not-so-residual Welsh, among whom the new barbarism has not entirely displaced literary criticism.'[57]

When *Broadcasting in the Seventies* was published, the BBC had already involved itself with local radio. Between October 1967 and June 1968, eight stations came into existence; the first was Leicester, which was launched on 8 November 1967. The Corporation expressed its intention of adding a further twelve by 1975. All the original stations were in England, but, as has been seen, Swansea had at one time sought to be included in the second allocation. The new town of Cwmbran also put in an application and suggested that its need was great, informing the Post Office that Cwmbran 'seriously lacked cohesion as a community'. Interest was also expressed in Wrexham, Cardiff, Merthyr Tydfil and Pembrokeshire, and a group at Bangor, led by Thomas Parry, floated the idea of a Welsh-language local service for north-west Wales. All such hopes were dashed by the Broadcasting Act of June 1972, which permitted the BBC to continue with the twenty stations it had either established or planned in the late 1960s, but laid down that any additional local stations should be commercial undertakings. Thus the Corporation's intention of replacing regional broadcasting in England with local broadcasting was only partially fulfilled. By the late 1970s, when English opt-outs from Radio Four had long come to an end, large parts of England – Devon, for example, and East Anglia – had no BBC alternative to the network output. By then, BBC sound broadcasting was United Kingdom-based in England and increasingly less so in the 'national regions'. 'The one area which remains a problem for the future', wrote Curran in 1979, 'is England.'[58]

The Broadcasting Act of June 1972 specifically excluded the BBC from establishing local radio stations in the 'national regions', while encouraging the Corporation to seek ways of providing them with their own services. 'Local radio in Wales', the managing director, radio, informed the BCW in September 1972, '[will] be a station for the whole of Wales.' In 1968, when preparing its suggestions for *Broadcasting in the Seventies*, Cardiff had set up a working party on the future of radio in Wales. At that time, Wales was opting out of Radio Four for some twenty-four hours a week, with slightly over half the time devoted to programmes in Welsh. In the late 1960s, Welsh-language radio programmes created less resentment than they had in earlier decades and far less than that created by Welsh-language television programmes, although the language was more than twice as prominent on radio as it was on television. One reason for the declining resentment was the fact that radio was no longer

18. The Swansea studios on the occasion of their reopening in 1952.

19. Hywel Davies, Nan Davies and John Ormond at the Park Place studios in 1962.

20. Lord Reith (standing) and Lord Macdonald (second from left) at Cardiff Castle on the occasion of the fortieth anniversary of the BBC in Wales in 1963.

21. Mrs Rachel Jones cutting the first turf at the Llandaf site in 1963.

22. Ryan Davies and Ronnie Williams in an early series of *Ryan a Ronnie*.

23. 1959: Siân Phillips and Donald Houston in *Treason*, a translation of Saunders Lewis's *Brad*.

24. Broadcasting House, Llandaf, in the 1960s. Baynton House, visible behind the new buildings, was demolished in 1975. The School of Home Economics situated opposite Broadcasting House was bought by the BBC in 1986.

25. Alun Oldfield-Davies (right) and John Rowley, on the appointment of Rowley as controller Wales in 1967.

26. John Darren presenting *Wales Today* in the mid 1970s.

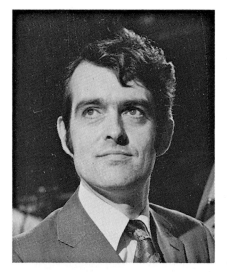

27. Controllers Wales since 1974: (from left to right) Owen Edwards (1974–1981), Geraint Stanley Jones (1981–1985), Gareth Price (1985–1990) and Geraint Talfan Davies (since 1990).

28. A scene from *Pobol y Cwm* in the late 1980s.

29. Anthony Hopkins in a networked 1993 BBC Wales production *Selected Exits*, by Alan Plater, based upon the work of Gwyn Thomas.

30. The Welsh governors since 1965: (from left to right) Glanmor Williams (1965–1971), Glyn Tegai Hughes (1971–1979), Alwyn Roberts (1979–1986), John Parry (1987–1992), Gwyn Jones (since 1992).

31. The BBC Welsh Symphony Orchestra (in 1993 renamed the BBC National Orchestra of Wales) in St David's Hall, Cardiff, in 1990 (*photograph: Eye Level Photographic*).

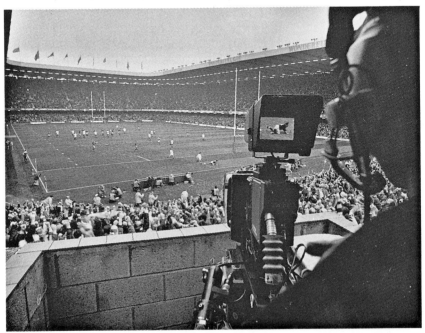

32. Ieuan Evans captured on BBC Wales camera scoring a try for Wales in 1993 (*photograph: Dave Purchase*).

central to the broadcasting experience of the public, but the main reason was the fact that other versions of Radio Four were available to the vast majority of the households of Wales. The working party pointed out that radio production in Wales was a shoestring operation. 'A twenty-minute current affairs programme in Welsh costing £325 a week', it noted, 'has made paupers of us, so narrow is the margin between solvency and bankruptcy in this region.' It regretted Head Office's decision in 1963 to cease measuring the audiences of regional opt-outs. 'There can be few services in the world', stated the working party, 'which operate "blind" as we do. The poor should know their market better than anyone else if they are to make the most of their money.' There was considerable support for opting out of all four services, with Welsh-language 'pop' programmes on Radio One, Wales's light entertainment on Radio Two, its serious programmes on Radio Three and its middlebrow output and its news and sport on Radio Four. Others argued that such a course would fragment Wales's output and create antagonism, for, unlike Radio Four, the other services did not have alternative versions available to the majority of the households of Wales.[59]

The final view favoured a demand for additional resources to enable Wales to opt out of Radio Four on a much greater scale, with the ultimate aim of taking over the channel in its entirety. 'I see Scotland does not take "The Archers",' wrote one contributor to the deliberations of the working party. 'Dare we not?' 'Ideally', wrote another contributor, 'our announcers should top and tail every programme on Radio Four.' The prospect of a progressive takeover of Radio Four was much enhanced by the decision that the service should cease to carry English regional opt-outs. When the opt-outs came to an end in 1972, the Radio Four service available to 75 per cent of the households of Wales was a single service rather than, as hitherto, the North of England service in the north, the Midland service along the border and the West of England service in the south. If the remaining 25 per cent of Welsh households had access to Basic Radio Four, it was argued, then the VHF and medium-wave frequencies carrying Radio Four on transmitters sited in Wales could instead carry a complete service exclusive to Wales.[60]

Similar arguments were put forward in Scotland, but Scotland was not faced with the problems of making extensive provision in two languages, for it paid scant attention to Gaelic. As the Welsh transmitters broadcasting Radio Four did so on two frequencies, the notion was canvassed that the VHF frequency should carry one language and the medium wave the other – an idea first mooted in the 1950s. The notion was not without its problems. During the day, the medium-wave service was clearly audible in 91 per cent of Welsh households, but during the hours of darkness only 31 per cent had satisfactory reception. Yet, with the advent of television, radio had its larger audience during the day and if the split were confined to daylight hours the medium wave's night-time problems would not be an issue. By the late 1960s, Radio Four on VHF from transmitters in Wales was available to 97 per cent of the country's inhabitants, but less than 40 per cent of Welsh households had VHF sets. The Corporation had been reluctant to stress the availability of VHF for, as a report of 1965 put it: 'We must avoid drawing public attention to our VHF coverage so forcefully as to have it turned against us at an international wavelength conference . . . While medium and long wave are still the general system, there is a technical limit to the number of radio stations that can be provided. On VHF, there is room for far more stations than the BBC is ever likely to operate, and therefore it is difficult to argue against allocating some of them to commercial radio.'[61]

Following the authorization of commercial radio, the Corporation decided that its VHF services should be heavily promoted. Radio announcements stressed that it was the quality service, the service of the future, and the public would have to get used to becoming increasingly reliant upon it. VHF car radios were available by the 1970s, and between 1970 and 1975 the price of a serviceable VHF portable radio halved in real terms. Prices fell in part because of an influx of sets from the factories of east Asia. Indeed, it could be claimed that the problem of broadcasting in two languages in Wales was solved because of the industriousness of the workers of Taiwan and South Korea.

The idea of splitting Wales's VHF and medium-wave services was strongly advocated in the document submitted by Cymdeithas yr Iaith Gymraeg to the BCW in January 1971. Although the Society's proposals regarding television were the ones which attracted the greatest attention, those regarding radio were the most feasible. The proposals included an interim plan calling for thirty-five hours a week in Welsh on VHF and thirty hours a week in English on medium wave, and an ultimate plan envisaging 112 hours a week in Welsh and in English under the control of a Welsh Broadcasting Corporation; both plans presumed the continued availability of the British sound network services. Head Office informed Rowley that the implementation of the interim plan would cost £1 million a year; the ultimate plan involved expenditure of £6 million a year, or far more if an independent Welsh Corporation came into existence, for that would be obliged 'to buy in the output of the four British services'. Rowley was at pains to emphasize that *Broadcasting in the*

Seventies had proposed a significant expansion in the radio services of the 'national regions'; the Corporation was therefore already committed to allocating additional money to sound broadcasting in Wales, and thus part at least of the £1 million operating costs of the Society's interim plan should be available. In his paper to the governors, submitted in November 1972, Tegai Hughes stated that the Society's interim plan for radio had considerable merits, although he added: 'I would not care to be a Head of Programmes having to fill two all-day services with Welsh material.' He stressed that radio programmes in Welsh could attract up to 200,000 listeners and asked: 'Is that insignificant in Radio Three terms?'[62]

By 1972, the splitting of the output of a service broadcasting on both VHF and medium wave was not a total novelty to the Corporation, for in the previous year it had arranged for Open University programmes to be broadcast on VHF while the medium wave carried material of more general interest. Furthermore, by 1973 all schools programmes were being transmitted exclusively on VHF. In September 1972, the managing director, radio, informed the BCW that money was available for a 'breakfast separation' of Welsh and English. The separation first occurred on 1 January 1973, when the early edition of the English magazine programme, *Good Morning Wales* (7.25 to 7.45) was broadcast on VHF and its Welsh equivalent, *Bore Da*, on medium wave; for the later editions (8.15 to 8.45), the arrangement was reversed. Welsh-speakers welcomed the innovation, but some who did not understand Welsh resented the necessity of changing channels in order to have a sequence of programmes they could follow. It became apparent that it would be preferable to associate one language with one frequency and the other with the other. VHF emerged as the favoured channel for Welsh-language programmes, partly because there was a perception that evening radio had a proportionately higher following among Welsh-speakers and partly because most of the areas where monolingualism in English was high could receive Radio Four on VHF from transmitters in England. A further relevant consideration was the fact that, in the early 1970s, the medium-wave service was still the majority listening channel, and there would have been strong protests if its output in Welsh were increased. Among Welsh-speakers both within and outside the Corporation, the development was viewed with foreboding. In the early 1970s, only a minority of Welsh households had VHF sets, for the Welsh, like the British generally, were 'connoisseurs of the obsolete'. There were fears that if broadcasting in Welsh were confined to a VHF frequency, the audience for Welsh-language programmes would slump, an issue on which Charles Huws, the witty broadcasting correspondent of *Y*

Faner, was particularly vocal. In 1974, some of the members of the BCW expressed concern that one of the Council's services would be confined to VHF, particularly in view of Head Office's statement that 'local radio in England had been found not to be viable when confined to VHF'. Tegai Hughes, however, stressed that the full implementation of the separation 'refers to some years ahead when the VHF take-up would have increased substantially'. While there were worries among Welsh-speakers, there was also opposition among English-speakers; in January 1975, a letter in the *Western Mail* declared that 'giving the quality VHF channel to Welsh was blatant discrimination against the English-speaking majority'. The relay companies were also annoyed, for by the 1970s they were only piping in the VHF service. According to some members of the BCW, the separation would allow Welsh-speakers to be regarded as 'a social entity and a defined community', a notion which some of the other members viewed with alarm. Yet they had no other solution to offer. As a memorandum of 1974 put it: 'At the time of Pilkington, the concept for both radio and television was still very much one of having to mix the two languages . . . However, in the light of the experience of operating such a bilingual service, with all the dissatisfaction, friction and frustration of a solution born of a compromise, there has been a shift of opinion towards a separation of the languages as far as is practicable.'[63]

In 1974, Cardiff noted with some pride that 'Radio Four (Wales) is the only service to use VHF and medium wave in a special way'. Yet the degree to which it was doing so should not be exaggerated. In January 1974, apart from a thirty-minute Sunday programme, separation had not gone beyond the early morning arrangements initiated in January 1973. There were major constraints upon the expansion of the separation. The ownership of VHF sets, although increasing rapidly in the mid 1970s, was by no means universal. With advancing technology, reception of medium wave during the hours of darkness was improving, but the problem still remained; indeed, Salter agreed that the only complete answer was the allocation to Wales of a long-wave frequency. During school terms, the VHF channel's output in the morning and the afternoon was dominated by schools programmes. VHF broadcasts from transmitters in Wales were hardly available at all outside the country. In the late 1960s, the Edinburgh police became accustomed to the sight of a middle-aged couple sitting in their car late on Sunday evenings near the summit of Arthur's Seat. They were Myrddin Lloyd, the keeper of printed books at the National Library of Scotland, and his wife, listening to *Rhwng Gŵyl a Gwaith* on medium wave on their car radio. They, and the rest of the Welsh-speakers living in England and Scotland, would have no hope of hearing such programmes on VHF, an important consideration in view of the fact that – judging by the letters received at Cardiff – interest in Welsh-language broadcasts was often greater among expatriates than it was among the residents of Wales. Above all, there was a reluctance to expand Wales's output either in English or in Welsh while a quarter of Welsh households could not receive Basic Radio Four.[64]

A further factor was the likelihood that BBC sound broadcasting in Wales would shortly be faced by a commercial competitor. By the spring of 1973 it became known that Swansea was to have a commercial station and that one in Cardiff was a strong possibility. Where Welsh-language broadcasting was concerned, the Swansea station could be a major challenger, for its hinterland included north-west Glamorgan and south-east Carmarthenshire, virtually the only areas of Wales where a high density of population and a high proportion of Welsh-speakers go hand in hand. As with commercial television, the advent of commercial radio provided an opportunity to press for additional resources, particularly in view of the fact that Radio Clyde, launched in December 1973, had made serious inroads into the audience of the BBC's Scottish output. 'We must not underrate the impact of Swansea Sound,' wrote Owen Edwards. 'It is more likely to be comparable with Radio Clyde than with LBC or Capital Radio.' Discussing the impact of commercial radio in 1972, the managing director, radio, had argued that Radio Four need not be much concerned, for the competition would only affect Radios One and Two. Yet, as the new services contemplated by Wales would, in part at least, have a local radio character, Edwards was correct in not under-rating the challenge of Swansea Sound. Following the advent of Radio Clyde, Head Office had granted Scotland an additional £40,000 to expand its radio service. In May 1973, sixteen months before the launching of Swansea Sound, Michael Brooke, Wales's chief assistant (general), argued that Wales needed an equivalent sum, 'for the development of our services has become a matter of some urgency if we are not to be seen to be belatedly responding to commercial competition'. Ideally, thought Edwards, Wales needed much more, 'for the competitive element in our production will obviously be much weaker than [in that of Scotland], for Scotland is able to concentrate almost exclusively on production in one language'. Swansea Sound, which began in September 1974, quickly established itself and did indeed represent a serious challenge to the BBC.[65]

As with television, so also with radio, there were fears that the appointment of the Annan Committee would delay the implementation of any recommendations that the Crawford Committee might make. In July 1974, the BCW was relieved to hear that 'Crawford wants progress ahead of Annan, particularly where radio is concerned'. The Council had submitted an interim statement to Crawford in June 1973, stressing its hope for two full radio services for Wales 'with no deprivation of the United Kingdom channels'. It repeated its request in November 1973, when the Committee visited Cardiff, and suggested that, pending the establishment of the new services, Wales could opt out of Radio Four for up to forty hours a week. Curran was worried by what he considered excessive opting out of Radio Four. 'It will destroy [our] capacity', he argued, 'to give a coherent news and information service to the whole of the United Kingdom.' It would be preferable, he thought, to speed up the provision of Basic Radio Four, alongside separate services for the 'national regions'. 'The tide of national sentiment in the three nations', he wrote, '[is] certain to become more significant . . . Attempts to patch up compromises between the individual national requirements and the United Kingdom need [are] doomed to friction and failure.'[66]

The BCW addressed an additional submission to Crawford in May 1974 which foresaw the establishment of Radio Cymru, broadcasting for a hundred hours a week, and Radio Wales, broadcasting for eighty hours. The services 'would be to a large part based on the style and methods of BBC local radio in England, but with a continuing heavier element to do justice to their national status'. There could be opt-outs from the two services allowing parts of Wales to have occasional specifically local programmes. The reference to the style and methods of local radio perturbed some BBC employees. 'I would be worried', wrote Owen Thomas, Wales's chief assistant, programme planning, 'if the Radio Cymru schedule were so preponderantly ephemeral as to suggest that the Welsh language is only capable of expressing day-to-day business . . . [We do not want to] reduce the BBC's radio role in Wales to continuous wallpaper talk.' In September 1974, the BCW submitted its final paper to Crawford. It suggested that managers should be appointed for the two new services and listed the additional staff that would be needed. Radio Wales on medium wave could be launched in 1977 but Radio Cymru would have to be delayed until Basic Radio Four on VHF was available to the vast majority of Welsh households. The Welsh-language service should have a somewhat heavier, and therefore more expensive, programme content than its English-language counterpart, 'to give scope for the BBC's only outlet in the Welsh language'. The separate outputs should cease at 7.00 p.m., when both wavelengths would carry a bilingual service, thus allowing Welsh-speakers outside Wales to receive at least some Welsh-language programmes on medium wave. Tegai Hughes gave a speech at Aberystwyth in October when he made public the BCW's aspirations for sound broadcasting. Most of the press comment concentrated on the Welsh-language plans. 'There seems to be little awareness', he informed the Council, 'of the benefits of an English-language service for Wales.'[67]

The Crawford Committee, reporting in November 1974, endorsed all the BCW's plans for sound broadcasting. Noting that in Scotland and Northern Ireland as well as in Wales the logical conclusion of the increased opt-outs was the establishment of a separate service for each country, it recommended that Basic Radio Four should be available everywhere. Priority should be given to providing it in west Wales, for a transmitter in Carmarthenshire would increase to 87 per cent the proportion of Welsh households able to receive it. Radio Cymru should be broadcast on VHF and Radio Wales on medium wave, and Radio Wales should be launched as soon as possible. 'Our plans have been endorsed in their entirety,' wrote Owen Edwards. 'Crawford is one of the very few reports that has been given an almost universal welcome in this odd country of ours.'[68]

III   Listeners, viewers and programmes, 1964 to 1974

The richest delights available to Welsh viewers in the later 1960s and early 1970s were the programmes of BBC2. The channel's first major series – twenty-six programmes on the First World War – were broadcast in 1964, before BBC2 was transmitted in Wales, but subsequent triumphs such as the near legendary *Forsyte Saga* (1967–8), Kenneth Clark's *Civilization* (1969), Alistair Cooke's *America* (1972), Jacob Bronowski's *Ascent of Man* (1973), and the Trollope series, *The Pallisers* (1974), were on offer to most of the viewers of Wales. BBC1's output – somewhat less serious following the advent of the new service – was the staple BBC viewing for Welsh television-owners. Its *Nine O'Clock News* was considered inferior to ITN's *News at Ten*, but its current affairs programme, *Panorama*, was widely acclaimed. The Corporation's television coverage of sport improved vastly although there were worries that it was transmitting pictures of stadium advertising hoardings. 'If the hoardings increase', noted David Bevan, Wales's head of presentation, 'we will have to withdraw our cameras.'[69] The association football programme, *Match of the Day*, was highly popular, particularly in the north, where Wales's supposed obsession with rugby was far less marked. The BBC's coverage of the Olympic Games of 1968 was considered superb and was a milestone in the Corporation's coverage of athletics. There was innovation in light entertainment, particularly with the zany *Monty Python's Flying Circus* (1969). Documentary drama became more realistic, with the police series *Softly Softly* and *Z Cars* taking the place of the bucolic cosiness of *Dixon of Dock Green. Cathy Come Home* (1968), the work of a resident of the Usk valley, was a stark dramatization of homelessness, and the BBC's attempt in 1965 to portray the aftermath of a nuclear attack in *The Wargame* was considered so harrowing that twenty years were to go by before it was broadcast. Under Hugh Carleton Greene, there was a greater readiness to deal with political controversy and in the 1960s the Corporation abandoned its policy of ensuring a political balance within each programme, opting instead to seek a balance within the output as a whole. Curran was somewhat more circumspect than his predecessor, but a programme on the Labour Party's leaders broadcast in 1971 under the title *Yesterday's Men* served to increase Harold Wilson's hostility towards the BBC. Of the Corporation's television programmes, it was those dealing with wildlife which were the most remarkable, and so great was the joy of producing them that David Attenborough gave up his prospect of becoming director-general in order to devote himself to the task. The BBC was itself responsible for 80 per cent of the material it transmitted, a proportion higher than that of any other of the world's broadcasting organizations. The other 20 per cent came largely from the United States; BBC2 broadcast some European art films, but the Corporation made very little attempt to suggest that there was a popular culture anywhere other than in Britain and the United States – and, somewhat later, in Australia. Indeed, perhaps the most serious accusation that could be levelled against the BBC is that – in its popular output at least – it savoured of an Anglo-Saxon provincialism.

In the early 1970s, the Corporation's income declined in real terms, for the government refused to sanction adequate increases in the licence fee. It believed that, although the public did not want cheap television, it wanted television on the cheap. The cost of the licence was consistently less than a year's subscription to even the cheapest daily newspaper. By 1972, recruitment had virtually come to an end, causing the controller, English regions, to comment that 'the acceptance of a no growth situation requires a new set of attitudes. The expansion of the late 1950s and 1960s has caused our younger staff to feel a sense of blockage. As the average age increases, so the organisation becomes prone to the indulgence of middle age.' BBC salaries began to lag seriously behind those paid by the commercial companies and the disparity worsened in 1975, when the Corporation was subject to a government standstill order on public-service earnings. The BBC sought to economize, particularly on its payments to broadcasters. Artists' fees represented 36 per cent of the Corporation's expenditure in 1964 and 29 per cent in 1974. Wedgwood Benn, who was appointed minister of posts and telecommunications in 1974, argued that the BBC's problems could be solved by nationalizing both it and the commercial companies and urged that the broadcasting service should be owned and controlled by its employees. Benn's scheme, stated Christopher Mayhew, was grotesque and involved handing the service over to the trade unions. In 1974 responsibility for broadcasting was transferred from the Post Office to the Home Office, thus greatly enhancing its status in the government hierarchy. At the time the home secretary was Roy Jenkins and he had no sympathy at all for Benn's ideas.[70]

Television network contributions from Wales were very few, for the advent of BBC Wales obliged Cardiff to devote its resources to home output. Network television drama production in Wales, which had been a marked feature of the late 1950s, came to an end, as did virtually all production aimed specifically at the United Kingdom as a whole. As BBC Wales's own programmes were made with far fewer resources than those of London, Head Office was prepared to accept very few of them for transmission on network. 'There [is]', wrote Rowley in April 1974, 'a marked reluctance centrally in the BBC to provide either the appropriate revenue or the facilities to produce programming which is in any way comparable with the revenue and facilities provided for network programmes . . . When we produce for the network we probably have 75 per cent of the cost of similar London programmes to spend, but for home-grown programmes the money can be as low as 10 per cent on occasion.' The reluctance to accept BBC Wales offerings for network transmission increased with the advent of colour. Until 1974, Cardiff's colour facilities were slight and the more ambitious of BBC Wales's own programmes had to be made in Birmingham. Yet some of Wales's programmes were accepted. The brilliant comedians, Ryan Davies and Ronnie Williams, made a series for BBC1 in 1971 and the whimsical travelogue, *Bus to Bosworth*, featuring Kenneth Griffith, enjoyed several network showings. Wales's most substantial input into the network was its regular contributions to *Nationwide*, a programme which began in 1969 and was broadcast between 6.15 and 6.45 p.m., a timing previously occupied by *Tonight*. 'A bold and complex venture', as Alasdair Milne called it, *Nationwide* consisted of a series of inserts provided by all the BBC's centres outside London. The BCW minuted that it disliked the title and was disturbed by the fact that Wales had no editorial control over the use made of its

317

contributions. To the extent that Wales was projected through BBC television to the rest of the United Kingdom – and to many of the Welsh people themselves, for there were among them those who could not receive BBC Wales or who chose not to view the channel – it was through *Nationwide*.[71] Between 1965 and 1974, Wales's most memorable contributions to the programme were undoubtedly its coverage of the Aberfan disaster, with pictures so poignant that the emotions of the whole world were stirred.

In addition to Wales's input into the network, London made a number of programmes of Welsh interest. They included a BBC2 investigation into Rio Tinto's mining plans in Meirionnydd, and, as the county could not receive BBC2, Head Office paid the cost of repeating it on BBC Wales. They also included a programme on the bombing-school arson of 1936; it was shown on BBC2 and BBC1, and the BCW decided, with some reluctance, to give it an additional showing on BBC Wales. In addition, Head Office took general charge of the BBC's television coverage of the investiture of Prince Charles as prince of Wales in 1969, a programme which won a prize at Cannes as the best outside broadcast.[72]

As output that was networked was slight, BBC television production in Wales between 1964 and 1974 overwhelmingly meant production for exclusive transmission on BBC Wales. During those years Channel 13 transmitted an average of eleven hours a week, six in Welsh and five in English. Almost half the time was taken up by news bulletins and the nightly topical magazine programmes, *Wales Today* and *Heddiw*. In addition, there were weekly current-affairs programmes – *Week In Week Out* and *Cywain*. Welsh-language current-affairs programmes could discuss anything for, regardless of the content, the language ensured that the programme was indubitably a fitting part of the output of BBC Wales. 'Those involved in Welsh-language programmes', noted the Annual Report of 1972, 'see the world as their oyster.' It was otherwise with English-language programmes, for as coverage of general British and world events in English was considered to be London's business, they were obliged to confine themselves to Welsh affairs. 'Gohebwyr Saesneg Cymru', wrote the journalist, Gwyn Llywelyn, 'nid y rhai Cymraeg, sy'n gorfod pori yn eu milltir sgwar.'*[73] The news in English, *Wales Today* and *Week In Week Out* were frequently acccused of dealing with trivia, and Alan Protheroe and his successor, Owen Roberts, were called before the BCW on several occasions to be informed that the output for which they were

---

*'It is the English-speaking reporters of Wales, not the Welsh-speaking ones, who are confined to their own backyards.'

responsible was over-concerned with traffic accidents, minor indus-trial disputes and other equally unscintillating matters.

Yet the fact that there was an all-Wales television news service stimulated the creation of all-Wales news. BBC Wales came into existence in the same year as the Welsh Office. Its early years coincided with the growth of political nationalism and the increasing belief that some kind of Welsh Assembly was a distinct possibility. One of the functions of the BBC, noted the BCW, will be to ensure 'a continuous critical awareness among the people of Wales' of the workings of the Assembly. The emphasis on devolution gave rise to new semi-governmental bodies – the Welsh Arts Council in 1967, for example, and the Welsh Sports Council in 1972 and the Welsh Consumer Council in 1975. TUC Wales was established in 1973; the Welsh Liberals formed their own organization and the Labour and Conservative Parties in Wales began holding annual conferences. Much of this activity was media-driven, for all-Wales institutions came into existence in part because BBC Wales was there to report their activities. Can it be that the comparative pusillanimity of the Broadcasting Council for Scotland was the result of the fact that Scotland was already a quasi nation-state and therefore broadcasting had a less vital role to play in nation-building? 'Is there a thing called Wales independent of the Wales industry?' asked Edward Nevin.[74] Wales, it has been suggested, is an artefact produced by broadcasting. Yet, ironically, the divisions created by broadcasting were in part responsible for the failure in 1979 to provide that artefact with a democratic framework and a constitutional role.

Of the television programmes produced in Wales, the most popular were those dealing with sport. 'Sport', wrote Alun Williams in 1969, 'is the only field in which we have a large and constant following.' Welsh rugby, which had years of glory in the 1960s and 1970s, was the corner-stone of BBC Wales's sports coverage. 'Our contract with the Welsh Rugby Union', noted Rowley, 'is all important to us.' Wales was fortunate in its rugby commentators. David Parry-Jones was considered to be superb, and there was annoyance in Cardiff when London preferred to employ the less talented Nigel Starmer-Smith. Sports commentaries in Welsh became firmly established, Glanmor Williams in 1971 expressing his appreciation of 'the increasing competence of Welsh-language com-mentators'. Television commentaries in English were accompanied by VHF radio commentaries in Welsh; thus, by turning off the television sound and turning on the radio, a Welsh-speaker could follow a televised match in his own language. Welsh broadcasters considered the rugby authorities to be far more co-operative than those of association football, although soccer devotees believed the

319

BBC in Wales to be excessively biased in favour of rugby. There was some truth in the accusation, for during Welsh rugby's great years BBC Wales saw it as an instrument of nation-building. The same could not be claimed for association football. Although the game had a larger following in Wales than had rugby, the teams most admired were those of England, for the Welsh teams were a minor and lacklustre part of the English League – a marked contrast with Scotland. In the 1960s, the Glamorgan Cricket Club won supporters throughout Wales, and the BBC was delighted when it secured exclusive rights to televise its matches. Ball team games wholly dominated Wales's sports output. Outdoor pursuits such as canoeing and rock-climbing, and new recreations like windsurfing and hang-gliding, were virtually ignored, although the BCW requested Onllwyn Brace to give them some attention.[75]

Sports coverage represented by far the greatest commitment by BBC Wales to outside broadcasting. Chief among the other events it broadcast was the National Eisteddfod, where it vied with HTV in displaying its wares. 'The public find difficulty', wrote Owen Edwards in 1973, 'in equating the lavish duplication of equipment, so painfully evident on the Eisteddfod field, with repeated protestations of lack of money by television authorities to expand Welsh-language services.' Outside broadcasting also became increasingly prominent in drama. In 1968, for example, a memorable production of Saunders Lewis's *Brad* made effective if somewhat chilling use of Europe's finest neo-baroque building, the Cardiff City Hall. The bulk of BBC Wales's drama was in Welsh and included the serialization of Ffowc Elis's *Lleifior* in 1970 and Marion Eames's *Ystafell Ddirgel* in 1971. Cardiff sought to broadcast a major Welsh-language drama each St David's Day, although there were doubts whether the time was well chosen, 'for the majority of Welsh-speaking viewers are [then] out at dinners' – a rather Cymmrodorion view of the five hundred thousand and more who spoke the language.[76] Back-to-back production – the use of the same cast in preparing versions in both languages – began in 1973 with *Dare to be a Daniel* and *Daniel Ddewr*. In the 1960s and 1970s, Welsh actors won world-wide acclaim, but Wales's international stars were rarely available for home-produced television plays. Welsh-language television drama relied in the main upon a pool of about twenty actors; a further hundred could be called upon on occasion, although Equity frequently created difficulties over the employment of amateurs. With the pool so small, the most talented actors appeared in almost every production; the brilliant John Ogwen, for example, seemed ubiquitous. As drama production was so expensive, Wales's television producers turned to dubbing on an extensive scale, and to hear Shane speaking Welsh was a memorable experience. In 1974, two weekly soap operas, one in English and one in Welsh, were launched under the leadership of John Hefin, the head of television drama. The English series, *Dai Macaroni*, did not find favour with viewers and was discontinued. The Welsh series, *Pobol y Cwm* ('People of the Valley'), first broadcast on Wednesday 16 October 1974, proved more durable. Indeed, it became the most long-lasting of all the Corporation's drama series; the weekly episode was expanded into five episodes a week in 1988 and *Pobol y Cwm* now appears destined to go on for ever.

BBC Wales's light entertainment had rather a bumpy start. *Studio B*, a satirical programme launched in 1965, aroused the antagonism of some of the members of the BCW, and the Council considered bringing it to an end. It desisted, however, and eventually the programme developed a satisfactory formula. The advent of the greatly talented Ryan Davies transformed the standard of Welsh-language light entertainment. The first situation comedy in Welsh, *Fo a Fe*, brilliantly written and produced by Rhydderch Jones, with much of its content revolving around north–south dialect differences, was a resounding success. 'Light entertainment', commented Glanmor Williams in 1970, 'has gone ahead in leaps and bounds.'[77] Tragically, Welsh broadcasting was to be deprived of Davies's talents for he died in 1977 at the age of forty while on tour in the United States.

Another field in which there was a marked improvement in televison output was provision for children. John Watkins became a producer of children's programmes in 1970; he was joined by Dyfed Glyn Jones in 1974, and by the mid 1970s Owen Edwards considered that children's programmes in Welsh had been transformed. The improved quality led to a demand for greater output, Mrs W. E. Jones pointing out that while English-speaking children were provided with ninety minutes of BBC programmes a day, Welsh-speaking children had to be content with sixty minutes a week. Welsh-language television provision for children became a leading issue in the late 1970s; indeed, there were ocasions when it appeared to have greater priority among language devotees than had the provision of a separate Welsh channel. Another aspect of broadcasting for children – the provision of television schools programmes – expanded markedly. The thirty Welsh-language programmes a year which Oldfield-Davies had succeeded in obtaining in the early 1960s had doubled by 1974. In addition, the BBC in Wales began broadcasting schools television programmes in English; the first series, *Five Welsh Towns*, was transmitted in 1965.[78]

Virtually from the beginning, one of the characteristics of Welsh sound broadcasting had been the emphasis on religion. It was an emphasis which was carried over to television. Professor Cochrane, a member of the BCW from 1969 to 1973, frequently commented on what he considered to be an overproduction of religious programmes and urged that the Welsh Religious Advisory Committee should include a humanist. Religion was popular. The Sunday half-hour of hymn-singing, *Dechrau Canu, Dechrau Canmol* (the prototype of *Hymns of Praise*), regularly had a larger number of viewers than had any other of BBC Wales's productions apart from sports programmes, a matter of some embarrassment to the more secular of the BBC's employees. Hymn-singing was in the traditional mould, but Tregelles Williams, Wales's head of religious broadcasting, was anxious that the rest of the output should change with the times. 'Ten years ago', he informed the BCW, 'the department was primarily engaged in relaying traditional services directed entirely at Church-attending [people]. Now we seek to appeal to the non-Church-goers and to show the relevance of the Christian faith for everyday living.'[79]

In the years 1964 to 1974, developments in sound broadcasting paralleled those in television. As with viewing, so also with listening, the people of Wales were primarily consumers of the general British services, with up to 60 per cent of them rarely straying beyond the confines of Radios One and Two. Radio Luxembourg continued to have a considerable audience, as had Radio Éireann, and following its launch in 1974, Swansea Sound attracted up to 12 per cent of the inhabitants of western Glamorgan and eastern Carmarthenshire. The BBC's radio producers in Wales, primarily involved as they were in producing opt-outs from Radio Four, had neither the time nor the resources to produce much for the network, a situation similar to that which had arisen following the establishment of BBC Wales. London did occasionally see fit to take some Welsh productions. In 1973, for example, John Ormond's series on Anglo-Welsh literature was broadcast on Basic Radio Four, which also took an English version of *Wil Six*, as did Radio Three. The BBC Welsh Orchestra frequently broadcast on Radio Three, and some of the Corporation's Welsh employees – Alun Williams, in particular – were featured on Radio Two. The disc jockeys of Radio One began to show an interest in the burgeoning Welsh pop scene, but their appreciation of groups like Anhrefn belonged to the future.[80]

By the late 1960s, Wales was producing about twenty-five hours of radio output a week, somewhat less than it had produced in the late 1930s. Of its regular programmes, the most popular by far was *Good Morning Wales*. It began as a Saturday morning programme on 5 October 1963, but from 28 September 1964 it was broadcast on five days a week – on Monday to Friday between 8.15 and 8.45. The programme was presented with great skill by Vincent Kane, the leading figure in Wales's English-language sound broadcasting for over a quarter of a century. A survey conducted in 1968 showed that up to 15 per cent of the inhabitants of Wales – 350,000 people – listened to *Good Morning Wales,* and it also had devotees beyond the border. Proportionately, it was considerably more popular than *Today,* its equivalent on Basic Radio Four. ' "Good Morning Wales" is the most vital programme of our output,' stated Onllwyn Brace. 'It is essential listening,' declared the BCW.[81]

The corresponding programme in Welsh was *Bore Da;* first broadcast on 29 September 1969, it attracted an audience of up to 150,000. *Bore Da* had several presenters, the most memorable of whom was the inimitable T. Glynne Davies. By the late 1960s, the emerging figure in Welsh-language radio was Hywel Gwynfryn, an Anglesey man with Carmarthenshire connections whose mother had been involved in broadcasting in the 1930s. His Saturday morning programme, *Helo, sut d'ach chi?* launched on 5 October 1968, quickly won popularity, except perhaps among the highbrow. More folksy than Kane, Hywel Gwynfryn's energy, wit and charm caused him to be the personification of Welsh-language broadcasting in the late twentieth century.

The impact of television on evening radio audiences, already apparent in the 1950s, intensified in the 1960s. By the 1970s, Wales's sound broadcasting was concentrated upon three periods: the early morning, lunchtime and the late afternoon. In the late 1960s, radio drama, traditionally broadcast in the evening, was still an important part of the output. Among the Welsh-language plays broadcast in that period were Max Frisch's *Biedermann und die Brandstifter* ('Y Llosgwr Tai'), Molière's *Le Misanthrope* ('Y Cybudd') and *Hedda Gabler.* The working party of 1969 doubted whether there was much point in providing plays for 'an audience which is a fraction of the already small evening audience'. The Welsh-language radio drama unit, based at Bangor since 1964, was moved back to Cardiff in 1969 and rapidly became attenuated. The working party was anxious to change the public perception of radio in Wales, and in particular to diminish the role of religion in Welsh-language production. There were suggestions that the Sunday morning service, considered by an earlier generation to be the one essential ingredient of Welsh-language broadcasting, should be curtailed. Programmes on denominational conferences,described by Owen Edwards as unutterably boring, ceased to be produced. *Caniadaeth y Cysegr,* the radio version of *Dechrau Canu, Dechrau Canmol,* was the most popular of all Welsh-language programmes, but there was a move to abolish it 'simply to change the image'. A more relaxed atmosphere was sought, partly in order to compete with Radios One and Two. In 1971, Wales had a ration of one hour's needle-time a week, which meant that less than 5 per cent of its output could be devoted to the broadcasting of recorded music. The ration was doubled in 1972, and in the late 1970s, the Musicians' Union virtually abandoned its campaign against needle-time, a fact central to the ability of Wales to expand its sound broadcasting output.[82]

There were other innovations too. On election day, 10 October 1974, Wales transmitted a radio programme on television. After closedown, BBC2 broadcast the election results in Welsh; 'it was', noted the BCW, 'by far the longest Welsh programme ever produced'. The increased availability of cassettes and recording equipment allowed Welsh people throughout the world to be correspondents of the BBC. From 1967 onwards, the programme *O Bedwar Ban* ('From the Four Corners') made extensive use of mailed recordings, and Catrin Nagashima's descriptions of Japanese female domesticity and Llew Goodstadt's accounts of the upheavals in China made admirable radio. In 1965, the BBC centrally had experimented with phone-in programmes, arranging that contributions were transmitted seven seconds after they had been made in order that indiscretions could be 'bleeped' out. In Wales, there was a general belief among broadcasters that the Welsh were too inhibited to take part in phone-ins, but in 1968 the producer Teleri Bevan adopted the practice in her programme, *Merched yn Bennaf* ('Mainly for Women'). The results delighted her. 'I felt', she wrote, 'that at last the programme was in touch with its audience.'[83]

The desire to be in touch with the audience was characteristic of the BBC by the early 1970s, for the Reithian tradition of Olympic detachment from those served by the Corporation had by then been much eroded. Rowley's concern that the existing structures of the BBC in Wales prevented it from adequately serving the people of Wales – indeed, that the pattern of its output was causing 'a most significant decrease in understanding and tolerance' – was indicative of an increasing sensitivity among officials of the Corporation to the wishes of its viewers and listeners. By 1974, Rowley and his staff, encouraged by Tegai Hughes and the BCW, and aided by the perceptiveness and magnanimity of Curran, had been successful in ensuring that the flaws in those structures would be addressed. Their success laid the foundations for the remarkable, and sometimes dramatic, developments of the following decade.

7

Annan and After:
BBC Broadcasting in Wales, 1974 –1981

I   The road to Sianel Pedwar Cymru

Ever since the appointment of Rhys Hopkin Morris in 1936, the BBC
in Wales had been fortunate in its directors and controllers. It was
particularly fortunate between 1974 and 1981; they were the years of
the controllership of Owen Edwards and were the most turbulent in
the history of broadcasting in Wales. The grandson of Sir Owen M.
Edwards, the best-loved of the leaders of the nineteenth-century
Welsh national revival, and the son of Sir Ifan ab Owain Edwards, the
founder of Urdd Gobaith Cymru, Edwards was also a descendant of
some of the leaders of early Welsh Methodism. Taking over from John
Rowley on 1 July 1974, his appointment coincided with the setting-up
of the Annan Committee and the last stages of the work of the
Crawford Committee. The Crawford Report gave rise to John
Siberry's working party, charged with the duty of examining how a
Welsh-language fourth channel would function. Siberry, a man of
charm and wit, established a harmonious relationship with Edwards,
a factor of importance in the expeditious completion of his report.

Among the issues addressed by Siberry was the question of
whether the fourth channel should be the sole outlet for Welsh-
language programmes. Impressed by Jac L. Williams's ghetto
argument, the Welsh Language Council urged that Welsh should
have a 'bridgehead presence' on the two popular channels, a view
also supported by Cymdeithas yr Iaith Gymraeg and the Welsh
Committee of the IBA. The members of the BCW disagreed, as did
the BBC's Welsh management team, for, following the establishment
of the Welsh fourth channel, they intended to relaunch BBC Wales as
an exclusively English-language service in the hope of winning back
those Welsh viewers who had tuned their aerials to transmitters in
England.[1]

In considering the sources of the additional programmes for the channel, Siberry thought solely in terms of the BBC and HTV, for small independent production companies had not yet come into existence in Wales. The two organizations doubted whether such companies would ever materialize, for they were reluctant to admit that 'good programmes could be made outside their auspices'. The additional output needed for a Welsh fourth channel, argued the Corporation, should come from the BBC and the ITV company rather than from any third body, 'since only in this way can all the benefits of a large, highly specialist organization be continued to apply to Welsh programmes'. If the two organizations were the sole sources of the fourth channel's Welsh-language output, there was an assurance that programmes in Welsh would be made in tandem with programmes in English. Hiving off Welsh-language production was anathema to the BBC. 'There can be no question', Siberry was informed, 'of the separation of location or facilities between the English- and Welsh-language output in Wales.'[2]

One of the major issues facing the Siberry working party was the way in which the BBC and HTV contributions should be scheduled. 'Interleaving [them]', it noted in its meeting of 12 March, 'would be complicated . . . and in view of this and of the Crawford Committee's call for speed and simplicity, this alternative should be rejected.' Instead, the BBC pressed for the two organizations to have three and a half days apiece, with the possibility of an annual switch of days. This had the merit of ensuring that advertisements would be confined to HTV's share of the week. The scheme involved wasteful duplication – it meant, for example, that both organizations would need full facilities for providing Welsh-language news – but it was hoped that by adopting it the co-ordinating machinery would be minimal. Both the BBC and HTV would have preferred to provide their own continuity for their half of the week, but Siberry felt that the unity of the service demanded a single continuity, which presumably would have to be provided through some form of joint operation. He also believed that the programme pattern should be broadly similar in the two halves of the week – an issue on which there was deep disagreement. The BBC wanted to emphasize the identity of its programmes by broadcasting them in a continuous block. The IBA and HTV favoured a more fragmented pattern for its Welsh-language output, with programmes for women during the day, children's programmes in the late afternoon and material of a more 'adult' nature in the late evening, all intermixed with popular programmes in English. 'Without undue cynicism', wrote Owen Edwards, '[their] plan can appear to be an attempt at a back door ITV2.' In order to fulfil Crawford's call for simplicity, the complexities of co-ordination were skated over by the Siberry working party. Alwyn Roberts, a rank-and-file member of the BCW from 1974 to 1979 and a man with a remarkable ability to get to the heart of an issue, realized that the logic of the situation demanded a more elaborate co-ordinating body, and subsequent developments amply proved the soundness of his case.[3]

The Siberry discussion hinged upon the availability of money to fund the service and its additional programmes. The Cardiff branch of the Association of Broadcasting and Allied Staff noted:

There are two arguments for a Welsh Fourth Channel: the need for Welsh programmes and the need to offload Welsh. While both arguments lead to the same conclusion, it would be naïve to assume that the proponents of the second argument share the enthusiasm of those who want more and better Welsh-language programmes. There remains therefore the task of persuading those who wish to offload Welsh . . . from existing channels that the cost of a service which will satisfy the Welsh-language lobby can be justified.

Advocates of a Welsh fourth channel were seeking twenty-five hours of Welsh-language output a week, virtually twice the existing provision of the BBC and ITV. Providing Siberry with detailed costings was a delicate matter. 'We should work with HTV to estimate costs,' wrote Owen Edwards, 'so that they should not differ so widely as to make it possible for the Home Office to divide and rule us by scaling all estimates down to the level of the lowest bidder.' In 1975, the Corporation was producing nearly seven hours in Welsh a week; it acknowledged that it had the resources to produce nine hours, but it had refrained from doing so in order to avoid increasing the antagonism of the English-speaking Welsh. To reach a BBC contribution of 12.5 hours meant the production of 3.5 hours on top of nine, a task which was impossible on Wales's current budget. Furthermore, the programme content of a separate service would need to be of a higher standard. 'Hitherto', stated Head Office, '[Welsh-language programmes] have been an opt-out operation to establish a regional presence. A fourth network would be in competition with all three existing highly professional networks. Therefore a higher quality would be needed.' It was estimated that existing Welsh-language programmes cost an average of £5,200 an hour; the budget for the additional 3.5 hours should be £11,000 an hour, bringing their total annual cost to £2 million. Such expenditure, argued Gwynfor Evans, was hardly excessive; the government, he pointed out, spent £13.2 million a year providing English-language television for forty thousand British servicemen in Germany.[4]

327

Colin Shaw, the BBC's chief secretary, advised Siberry on the financial implications for the Corporation of the establishment of a Welsh fourth channel. There would be capital costs of £6.4 million, including £1.4 million for the transmission stations, £3.75 million for additional production facilities at Cardiff and £1.5 million for additional facilities elsewhere, particularly at Bangor. The capital costs would have to be met by a grant-in-aid, for there was no possibility of financing them out of licence money. If the fourth channel generally were run by a body other than the BBC, that body could be charged the £2 million needed for the additional 3.5 hours of programmes, in the same way as the Department of Education was charged for the programmes the BBC produced for the Open University. If the BBC were wholly or partially responsible for the channel, the cost of the additional programmes would have to be taken into account when setting the new licence fee. Shaw's statement reflected the view of the Board of Governors which – despite Curran's comments in 1974 – came to the conclusion in February 1975 that it would be very reluctant 'to receive government grants to pay for programmes as opposed to capital costs'. The Association of Broadcasting Staffs urged the Board to reconsider its position, at least where non-controversial programmes – 'education, children, sport and perhaps religion' – were concerned. The BCW argued strongly that a government grant for programmes was acceptable. With its income declining in real terms, the Corporation was cutting its output and the Council feared a backlash 'if licence revenue were diverted to [additional Welsh-language programmes] when existing services are feeling the effect of restrictions'. Indeed, in March 1975, the working party considered whether, 'if the government were to pay for additional Welsh-language programmes, was there a case for it also to pay for the existing level of provision?'[5]

If Welsh-language programmes were to be moved to a fourth channel, up to seven hours a week on BBC Wales would be vacated. They could be filled with network material at no extra cost to the Corporation. Yet, as Scotland produced nine hours a week in English, and Wales five, the establishment of a Welsh fourth channel offered an opportunity to expand BBC Wales's output in English – an issue on which Welsh MPs felt strongly. For Wales to produce English-language programmes of the same quality as those of the Scots would be expensive. Compared with Wales, the BBC in Scotland had a larger programme allowance and a smaller output; in 1975, Scotland's hourly expenditure on programmes was 66 per cent higher than that of Wales. Expenditure on additional English-language programmes would have to come from the Corporation's own resources for, while the government was prepared to consider a grant for Welsh-language programmes, there was no question of such a grant for programmes in English. The need to fill the vacated hours was also an issue for HTV. In May 1974, the IBA informed the Siberry working party that it intended 'to divert from its present level of funding schedules of Welsh-language programmes such moneys as were needed to fill the six-hour gap on HTV Wales which would be left when Welsh-language programmes were moved to the fourth channel', a statement which greatly complicated the later discussions of the working party.[6]

Among Siberry's tasks was to determine when it would be practicable for a Welsh fourth channel to be operational. The IBA, which was to undertake the transmission arrangements in the United Kingdom as a whole, stated that if the work were begun in October 1975, thirty-two months would be needed to achieve parity in transmission coverage with the existing services. That meant that the Welsh fourth channel could begin in the autumn of 1978. Edwards was somewhat alarmed. 'I would be happier with a later date such as autumn 1979,' he wrote. 'However, the consensus of opinion in the working party was that the service should be in operation as soon as possible, and it would not be helpful to the BBC in Wales to be seen to be the one party which was dragging its feet. The initiative and public approval which we in the BBC have held all along by making the running in this matter would be lost to ITV who have said that they would, if it were necessary, start a service in two years from the go ahead.'[7]

The Siberry Report was delivered to the Home Office in July 1975 but was not published until November. It recommended that in Wales the fourth channel should broadcast twenty-five hours a week of Welsh-language programmes, with the BBC and HTV responsible for three and a half days apiece. There should be virtually no Welsh on the other channels. Transmission costs would amount to £2.65 million in capital outgoings and annual operation costs of £280,000. The additional programmes and 'the improvement in the mix' would involve capital expenditure of £6.2 million and £4.75 million a year in operational expenditure.[8]

The publication of the report coincided with a deepening crisis in the British economy. Although the Home Office stated in June 1975 that a Welsh fourth channel would not necessarily be held up by the economic situation, Roy Jenkins, the home secretary, announced in February 1976 that 'the government have concluded that, in the context of the recently completed review of public expenditure, the project cannot, in the present economic circumstances, command sufficient priority to justify an immediate government subvention'.

Like the government, the BBC in the mid 1970s was reluctant to commit itself to new ventures. By the spring of 1975, it had a deficit of £20 million, and the General Liaison Committee lamented the 'distraction of finding the means of surviving from day to day in an increasingly arctic financial climate'. 'We are postponing all developments for the next three years', stated Curran, 'except those in the national regions' – but, where Wales was concerned, the only developments he mentioned were in sound broadcasting.[9]

The BCW protested strongly against the home secretary's statement of February 1976, arguing that 'there is no satisfactory alternative to Channel Four'. Paul Flynn, one of the most active of the Council's members, who was later to be the Labour MP for Newport West, was particularly insistent that the fourth channel was the only answer and he deprecated any attempt to seek palliative measures lest they should cause the fourth channel to appear to be less urgent. The BCW regularly reiterated that the government had accepted the Welsh fourth channel in principle in November 1974, and in May 1976 thirty-eight prominent Welsh people, led by the archbishop of Wales, wrote to the press protesting against the government's delay in fulfilling its promise.[10]

There were other, more disheartening developments. The BCW believed that, apart from its ecclesiastical associations, the main distinction of the village of Llandaf was the fact that it was the centre of the BBC's operations in Wales. It was therefore particularly humiliating to receive a petition from the villagers in December 1975 complaining that the crane being used to build the new studio was interfering with their ability to receive broadcasts from the Mendip transmitter. More worrying were the plans for a relay for west Herefordshire. The Corporation's engineers decided that it would be more effective if it were sited on Garth Hill on the Welsh side of the border. As it was intended to serve viewers in England it would carry BBC1, not BBC Wales, thus violating the BCW's firm rule that all transmitters on Welsh soil should carry BBC Wales. The plans were far advanced when the members of the Council heard about the matter and, 'under these *wholly exceptional* circumstances', they waived their rule. The decision was given publicity in a speech by Alun Talfan Davies, the chairman of the IBA's Welsh Committee, and requests that relays should be changed to BBC1 came from Monmouth and elsewhere. They were rejected out of hand, for if acceded to there was a danger that the whole BBC Wales network would collapse.[11]

With the prospect of a Welsh fourth channel receding, Cymdeithas yr Iaith Gymraeg renewed its campaign. From December 1975 to the autumn of 1981, the Society conducted a series of raids upon BBC and ITV property and committed damage amounting to hundreds of thousands of pounds. Ffred Ffransis, the son-in-law of Gwynfor Evans, was particularly active and received a series of prison sentences amounting in all to over three years. Most of the activists were in their late teens and early twenties; they were students in the main and those responsible for their welfare became accustomed to police visits in the dead of night. The authorities felt student protest was containable but the situation changed when the law-breakers came to include figures such as the principal of a theological college, a future director of the University of Wales Press and the wife of the mid Wales representative of the Midland Bank. Members of the BCW were divided in their attitude to the activities of Cymdeithas yr Iaith Gymraeg. Tegai Hughes strongly endorsed Curran's statement that the Society's aims could not be achieved through violence and refused to meet its leaders while their threats continued. Mrs Philipps James was anxious that the Council should do nothing which might provoke the Society, and Paul Flynn came near to endorsing its activities. Violence can achieve its ends, he commented, a fact which the history of the Society had already proved. Flynn argued that the BBC should report the protests fully, otherwise the protestors would 'escalate violence to make sure they would not be ignored'. He was particuarly taken by the Society's attack on Bush House in February 1977. The episode, he thought, 'would draw attention to the absurdity of the BBC in broadcasting more radio programmes in some very obscure foreign languages . . . than it did to the indigenous Welsh-speaking population'.[12]

While these developments were taking place, the Annan Committee was pursuing its deliberations. Lord Annan, the provost of University College, London, was appointed chairman in April 1974, but the names of his fourteen fellow members were not announced until July. There was a rumour that there was a search for 'a woman who is Welsh and black'. 'Stand by, Shirley Bassey', wrote the *Observer*, 'Annan might need you.'[13] In the event, the representative from Wales – who was also asked to pay particular attention to the rural areas and to regional broadcasting generally – was Dewi Lewis, an ex-headmaster and the chairman of the Dyfed Health Authority.

While the Pilkington Committee was obliged to take for granted the continued existence of the BBC and the commercial companies, the Annan Committee was subject to no such restriction. 'It is within our terms of reference', stated Annan, 'to recommend that the BBC be abolished.' 'Be prepared to discuss the unthinkable,' Shaw, the Corporation's chief secretary, informed Edwards, 'including the division of the BBC through hiving off the regions from London.' As with Beveridge and Pilkington, the Corporation deluged Annan with paper, its total submissions representing a closely printed volume four inches thick. Head Office was confident that the BBC's existence was not under threat. Nevertheless, the Corporation considered it prudent to provide Annan with overwhelming proof of its virtues, and much of what it submitted was considered by the Committee to savour of smugness and self-satisfaction.[14]

Realizing that the main point at issue was the use of the fourth channel, the Corporation disclaimed any ambition to have the channel for itself, while at the same time seeking to undermine arguments that it should be a second outlet for the IBA. As Curran had stated in 1974, the governors' evidence to Annan stressed that an additional popular commercial channel would be harmful to all the existing networks. The fourth channel, they stated, 'should be used for specialist programmes associated with continuing education and a range of other minority services, including Welsh-language television . . . Welsh-language interests would find it more satisfactory to come to some accommodation with another specialist use for [the fourth channel] in the United Kingdom as a whole than with a new general audience service.'[15]

In October 1974, the BCW set up a committee to prepare its submissions to the Annan Committee. The statement drawn up by the committee was largely a reiteration of the submissions the Council had made to the Crawford Committee. 'The problem of bilingual broadcasting', it noted, 'will continue to dominate the plans of the BBC in Wales for the foreseeable future.' Where television was concerned, the only satisfactory solution was a Welsh fourth channel. 'Any other answer must be much later than the fourth channel for which the transmitter masts exist, the frequencies have been allotted, and, above all, for which viewers are already equipped.' The fact that viewers were already equipped differentiated the discussion of the fourth channel from those concerning the original introduction of television and the introduction of ITV and BBC2, all of which obliged viewers to acquire a television set or to pay for the modification of their existing set. Any UHF set would be able to receive the fourth channel, and thus two important pressure groups – the makers and the sellers of television sets – were less enthusiastic about it than they had been about the previous three services.[16]

The Annan Committee visited Cardiff on 2 and 3 June 1975. As the government had by then accepted the Crawford Report and had established the Siberry working party, the Committee's members assumed that, at least where Wales was concerned, the fourth channel issue had already been settled. In their meetings at Cardiff, the matter was only cursorily discussed, and while in the city Lord Annan gave a radio interview in which he endorsed Crawford's recommendations. The Committee showed more interest in the constitutional relationship between the BBC's operations in Wales and those of the Corporation as a whole. The BCW's submission to Annan had called for the strengthening of the Council's executive functions. It pointed out that where finance was concerned, it not only had no power but it was also denied vital information, a matter on which Alwyn Roberts was particularly vocal. He argued that Wales should have a block grant, a suggestion which alarmed Owen Edwards, who was more aware than were the members of the BCW of his success, and the success of his predecessors, in squeezing out of the Corporation more money than Head Office intended that Wales should have. Head Office was also concerned. 'If the powers of the Council are to be increased,' wrote Shaw, 'it may well be necessary to strengthen the hand of the Controller in order to protect the executive.'[17]

In the mid 1970s, discussion of devolution within the BBC, both in Wales and in Scotland, was complicated by the assumption that the two countries would shortly have their own assemblies. The role of the assemblies with regard to the broadcasting councils, and to broadcasting in general, was anxiously debated. The independence of the BBC rested in the last resort upon the existence in Britain of two broadly equal political parties; a party in government did not wish to seize excessive powers over broadcasting because it was aware that it would one day be the opposition. In Wales, and to a lesser extent in Scotland, there was every prospect that the assemblies would be permanently dominated by a single party; if broadcasting were to be under its control, that control would not be subject to checks which were believed to be inherent in the Westminster system. 'If we are working under a Scottish Assembly', wrote Alastair Hetherington, controller Scotland, 'we will be subject to more pressures, because we will be working in a narrower society . . . We must pre-empt the demand for Scottish Assembly control by showing that Scottish needs can be accommodated within the BBC system.'[18]

Similar arguments were put forward in Wales, where calls for a separate Broadcasting Corporation, which had been vociferous in the late 1940s, were hardly heard at all in the mid 1970s. Among its Welsh employees, noted Owen Edwards, 'there is no desire to break away from the BBC . . . Even the most committed Welsh-language supporters on the staff are strongly in favour of [the Corporation] . . . [During the Annan visit] the producers made clear their fears that an Assembly would seek to influence broadcasting in Wales.' The BCW unanimously agreed that 'it was essential to argue strongly in our evidence against an independent Welsh Broadcasting Authority, particularly in the light of the possibility of devolution.' Owen Edwards and Tegai Hughes dined with the three Plaid Cymru MPs in October 1975 and were relieved to find that 'they did not push the issue of an independent Welsh Broadcasting Authority'. In its initial submission to Annan, the BCW confined itself to calling for 'financial powers with regard to Welsh broadcasting which mirror in miniature those which the Governors have for the country as a whole'. In 1976, however, it argued that if the Welsh fourth channel materialized, and when the Council's plans for radio were implemented, 'Cardiff will be the largest BBC centre outside London, and will be as large as many of the independent broadcasting organizations of Europe . . . It will then be no longer practical for control to lie theoretically with us but for financial decisions to be made in London.' The ultimate arrangement, argued the BCW, should be for Wales to become a separate directorate with a seat on the Board of Management.[19]

The IBA's Welsh committee also told Annan that it needed greater powers. The committee had sought to assert its independence in 1973 by informing Crawford that it disagreed with the IBA generally on the issue of a Welsh fourth channel – a stance it repeated in its submission to Annan. It regarded the BCW's executive functions with envy and informed Annan that it found 'its role as an advisory body unsatisfactory and frequently frustrating'. Special arrangements should be made in Wales, it argued, for 'broadcasting plays a role in the national life of Wales which is not paralleled elsewhere in the United Kingdom'. It stressed in particular that Wales had two languages and 'a relatively small number of national institutions'.[20]

The Annan Report was published in April 1977. Elegantly written and consisting of 522 pages, it recommended that the fourth channel should be given to an Open Broadcasting Authority (OBA) which would commission programmes from any suitable source such as the Open University, existing ITV companies and 'particularly bona fide independent producers'. The channel should not be obliged to compete with other television services and its output should be paid for by block advertising and possibly by a government grant – the report was somewhat imprecise about the financial implications of its recommendations. It stated that its main aim was to encourage diversity and to break the duopoly of the BBC and ITV; to create a second ITV channel would merely confirm the duopoly. The Annan Committee thought that the BBC showed some 'loss of nerve'; it suffered from organizational weakness, its coverage of current affairs was patchy and dull and the Corporation was frequently guilty of arrogance. In marked contrast to Pilkington, Annan found virtue in the commercial sector, although some of its output was 'safe, stereotyped and dull'. The report was peppered with notes of dissent and reservation. With regard to Wales, however, it was unanimous. It assumed that the OBA would not be operational until the 1980s but it urged that a Welsh fourth channel should be launched as soon as the necessary funding was available. Initially the channel would come under the joint control of the BBC and HTV, but responsibility for it would be transferred to the OBA when that was fully functional.[21]

Reaction to the Annan Report was not enthusiastic. The Treasury disliked the references to a government grant. The suggestion of delay angered the ACTT, half of whose members were unemployed. The libertarian wing of the Conservative Party considered the rejection of another popular channel to be an élitist refusal to give the public what it wanted. The IBA argued that it could undertake the work of the OBA, and therefore an additional body was unnecessary – a view also held by William Whitelaw, the shadow home secretary. Where the Welsh fourth channel was concerned, the report did little more than restate the case put forward by Crawford twenty-nine months earlier. Some of its comments aroused concern. The reference to 'as soon as the necessary finance becomes available' seemed a loophole which would allow the project to be postponed indefinitely. The comment that 'we would regret if all Welsh programmes were banished to the fourth channel' was attacked by the BBC; 'the Committee', it stated, 'did not give enough consideration to hard practical realities.' The recommendation that the Welsh fourth channel would eventually be the responsibility of the OBA was condemned. 'It must be run in Wales by a Welsh body,' declared the *Western Mail*.[22]

Despite the endorsement of the Annan Committee, the members of the BCW were not confident that any decision on the Welsh fourth channel was likely to be speedily made. The Home Office announced in January 1977 that 'there would be no money for the channel this year'. The Council protested, arguing that 'the longer the delay, the greater the cost, financially, culturally and in terms of national harmony'. There was no need for any delay, declared Wyn Roberts, late of TWW and, since 1970, the Conservative MP for Conwy. 'A jointly-run Welsh fourth channel', he stated in April 1977, 'is as remote as ever. The channel should be given to ITV, which alone could provide it out of its own resources.'[23]

In May 1977, the Home Office established a second working party charged with the duty of updating the Siberry Report. 'This is a delaying tactic', declared Tegai Hughes, and he was undoubtedly correct, for the working party, chaired by Dennis Trevelyan, a Home Office official, took fourteen months to submit its report. The Home Office adopted the tactic because it believed that delay would undermine the consensus on the fourth channel. 'There is a belief abroad in some quarters', noted Tegai Hughes in July 1977, 'that the climate of opinion in Wales has changed.'[24] There was some foundation for the belief. Attacks on the Welsh-language broadcasts of BBC Wales and HTV Wales were far less vociferous in the late 1970s than they had been a decade earlier. That was partly because of improved television sets. In the 1960s, viewers wishing to turn away from a programme they did not understand had to tune their sets carefully in order to obtain another channel, a task which took long enough for irritation to build up. By the 1970s, it could be done by pressing a button and, with the coming of remote-control apparatus, it was not even necessary to rise from a chair in order to do so. Channel-hopping led to a decline in planned viewing, a change reflected in the drastic fall in the sale of the *Radio Times*. With fewer viewers studying the schedule, there was less awareness of the network programmes which were displaced by those in Welsh.

Furthermore, there was evidence that the loss of Welsh viewers to transmitters in England was less than had previously been believed. As Mendip aerials were a different shape from those receiving Wenvoe, a stroller in the streets of south Wales had ample evidence of the appeal of the Mendip transmitter. Installers' records indicate that in Cardiff and Swansea four out of five of the outdoor aerials were beamed on Mendip; indeed, many installers did not bother to ask what their customers wanted. Yet a fairly satisfactory Wenvoe signal could be received off the 'back end' of a Mendip aerial, and some of the houses equipped externally to receive Mendip were equipped internally to receive Wenvoe. During the Wales–Ireland rugby match in March 1979, 45.8 per cent of Welsh viewers were tuned to BBC Wales. The BCW was delighted. 'This disproves', it noted, 'the allegation that a high proportion of viewers . . . could not receive BBC Wales because their outside aerials were tuned elsewhere.'[25]

If rejection of the Welsh-based channels was not so great and if the hostility to Welsh-language programmes was in decline, would it not be better to continue to transmit them on the popular channels? Professor Jac L. Williams certainly thought so, and his relentless campaign won converts. They included Gareth Price, Wales's deputy head of programmes, who attacked the concept of a Welsh fourth channel at a private meeting; his statement was leaked to the *Guardian* and caused considerable embarrassment. Urdd Gobaith Cymru began a campaign to secure an immediate increase in the number of Welsh-language programmes for children and, by October 1977, the Trevelyan working party had come to the conclusion that 'the views of Welsh-speakers place less emphasis than hitherto on the need to transfer all Welsh-language programmes to a single channel, and are now directed more to the need to increase without delay the amount of children's programmes in Welsh'. The home secretary, Merlyn Rees, received a deputation on the matter and it was pursued with vigour by Dafydd Elis Thomas, the Plaid Cymru MP for Meirionnydd. Rees expressed willingness to consider a government grant for children's programmes; the governors were opposed to accepting such a grant and Tegai Hughes informed the BCW that he would resign if they did not withdraw their opposition. They did, and in November 1979 BBC2 began broadcasting *Yr Awr Fawr* ('The Great Hour') on Sunday mornings, a programme which won a wide following.[26]

While the children's programmes issue was attracting public attention, HTV and the IBA were becoming increasingly unwilling to countenance a Welsh fourth channel. In October 1977, Lord Harlech condemned the whole notion. 'Does this mean', asked Lucas, 'that HTV is undermining Siberry?' The IBA pointed out that HTV's involvement in Welsh-language programmes had implications for the other commercial companies. That involvement was largely responsible for the fact that HTV made sixteen hours of programmes a week, a far higher figure than that of any company except the main contractors. The IBA stated:

> The company's commitment [to the Welsh-language] is recognized by the Authority in the rental it charges HTV. If HTV were producing only as much programming as other companies of comparable advertising revenue, the rental charged would be at least £500,000 a year more than [the £800,000 charged] at present. Such an increase in the HTV rental would lead to a corresponding reduction in the rental charged to other companies . . . If the HTV rental were further reduced [in order to enable it to produce more Welsh programmes], the Authority's requirements . . . would have to be made up through an additional charge upon the other television companies.

The views of the commercial sector were carrying increasing weight in the late 1970s, largely because the BBC's deteriorating financial position was causing its rates of pay to be uncompetitive. Its staff were leaving to join commercial companies in large numbers, and part of the Corporation opposition to a second ITV channel arose from the fear that 'it would drain away BBC staff to an impossible extent'. The move to a commercial company could lead to a vastly enhanced salary. When few BBC staff were earning £15,000 a year, Emyr Daniel left to join HTV. A BBC stalwart told him: 'I won't go over to them for £30,000 a year'. 'Neither would I,' replied Daniel.[27]

All these factors were taken into consideration by the Trevelyan working party. Rumour reached the BCW that it was 'considering options less costly than the fourth channel'. 'There is no prospect whatever', Tegai Hughes informed the Council in June 1977, 'of the full Siberry proposals being implemented . . . Our public stance has been hard-nosed, but we should now consider a fall-back position.' By November, Alwyn Roberts was arguing in favour of examining new approaches, 'for channel four seems unlikely now', but Paul Flynn continued to insist that 'the channel is still very much alive'.[28] Its prospects were not improved by the fact that Charles Curran retired as director-general in December 1977. His successor, Ian Trethowan, proved far less interested in the issues involved in Welsh-language broadcasting.

Meanwhile Cymdeithas yr Iaith Gymraeg intensified its campaign. In a particularly audacious raid in January 1978, it blacked out the IBA's transmitter at Guildford and two months later it incapacitated that of the BBC on the Mendip Hills. The law-breakers, declared Merlyn Rees, should be sentenced to a month in Northern Ireland.[29] That was one of the very few statements suggesting that the conflict in Northern Ireland had any bearing upon what was happening in Wales. Yet comments on the breakdown of community relations and the need for social harmony were surely coded references to the troubles in Ulster. There was hardly any possibility that the situation in Wales could come to resemble that in Northern Ireland. Yet, as long as there was any possibility at all, Crawford's recommendation that the government should invest in social harmony made sense. After all, whatever might be the cost of a Welsh fourth channel, it was bound to be infinitesimal compared with the cost of the security operations in Northern Ireland.

Although the Trevelyan Report was not published until July 1978, its contents were known to the BCW by May. 'It is a diluted form of Siberry,' declared Tegai Hughes. There were to be twenty hours of Welsh-language programmes instead of twenty-five, and the recommended investment was less than half that suggested by Siberry. Children's programmes should be broadcast on BBC2, possibly on a permanent basis. Once Welsh went to BBC2, argued Geraint Stanley Jones, Owen Edwards's successor as head of programmes, 'the pressure on the government would be relaxed', and there was a danger that any plans for a Welsh fourth channel would be abandoned. The report made much of the potential burden to taxpayers, suggesting that they would have to pay the cost of all

Welsh-language output rather than only the programmes which were additional to those to which the BBC and ITV were already committed.[30]

Their knowledge of the contents of the Trevelyan Report did not inspire the members of the BCW with confidence. They were therefore relieved that the White Paper on Broadcasting, published on 26 July 1978 – the same day as the publication of the Trevelyan Report – endorsed virtually all Annan's proposals, at least where television was concerned. The White Paper argued that the BBC should be granted a new charter for the period 1981 to 1996 and that legislation should be introduced to allow the IBA also to continue in existence until 1996. It recommended the establishment of an Open Broadcasting Authority to run the Fourth Channel, which would have a statutory obligation to be different. In Wales, programmes in Welsh would have the first claim on the Fourth Channel and a Welsh Language Television Council should be established to supervise co-operation between the BBC, HTV and the independent companies. 'Mae'r [Papur Gwyn],' stated *Y Cymro*, 'yn fuddugoliaeth yn arbennig i Gymdeithas yr Iaith Gymraeg, a ddechreuodd ymgyrchu dros Sianel Gymraeg pan oedd pob "arbenigwr" yn wfftio'r syniad fel breuddwyd amhosibl.'*[31] The Society itself was unimpressed. 'We will continue our campaign,' declared Rhodri Williams, its chairman. 'The government has gone back on many of its promises connected with the Crawford Report.' And continue it did, particularly with major raids on transmitters at Midhurst and Sudby, when damage of thousands of pounds was committed.[32]

During the last months of the Labour government of 1974 to 1979, its continued existence was dependent on the support of the three Plaid Cymru MPs. Partly as a result, the Queen's Speech of November 1978 contained promises of legislation on a number of Welsh issues, the Welsh fourth channel among them. Yet, during the bleak, strife-torn winter of 1978–9, there was no sign of a broadcasting bill. As the precarious position of the government meant that a general election would be held sooner rather than later, and as the Conservatives announced that they wanted the fourth channel to be an ITV service, the plans for an Open Broadcasting Authority seemed likely, as the *Western Mail* put it, 'to be a major hostage to electoral fortune'. The government fell as a result of manœuvring by the SNP MPs following the Scottish and Welsh devolution referenda on 1 March 1979. The referendum result in Wales, where four out of

---

*'The White Paper is a victory especially for Cymdeithas yr Iaith Gymraeg, which started to campaign for a Welsh Channel when every "expert" was dismissing the idea as an impossible dream.'

five of those who voted rejected the proposed Welsh Assembly, was cited by several newspaper correspondents as proof that 'the Welsh fourth channel should be scrapped'.[33]

In their manifestos for the general election of May 1979, the Conservative and Labour Parties pledged that, in Wales, Welsh-language programmes should have priority on the fourth channel, although they differed in their plans for the funding and organization of the channel. Following their victory, the Conservatives repeated their pledge in the Queen's Speech of May 1979. Yet the omens were not promising. Wyn Roberts, the newly appointed minister of state at the Welsh Office, suggested that the fourth channel should transmit Welsh programmes between 4.00 and 7.00 p.m., thus ensuring that the peak hours would be exclusively in English. In July 1979, the IBA's Welsh committee changed its mind and joined HTV in expressing opposition to a Welsh fourth channel. At the BCW meeting of July 1979, Tegai Hughes mentioned the possibility that the Welsh fourth channel might be abandoned.[34] The meeting was the last he chaired. (He had been appointed for five years in 1971 and given a three-year extension in 1976.) His successor was Alwyn Roberts but the appointment was not announced until October. The head of the Extra-Mural Department at University College, Bangor, Roberts was perhaps an unexpected appointment by a Conservative government, for, whatever he was, he was certainly not a Tory. He had served with distinction on the Gwynedd County Council and was a member of the Royal Commission on Legal Services. During his years on the BCW he had earned the admiration of the BBC's Welsh officials and they greeted his appointment as Wales's national governor with much pleasure.

Between Tegai Hughes's departure and Alwyn Roberts's arrival, William Whitelaw, the home secretary, dropped his bombshell. Addressing the Royal Television Society at Cambridge on 12 September, he announced that the government was not going to proceed with a Welsh fourth channel. While it was in favour of increasing the number of hours devoted to the Welsh language, the programmes should be shared by all the channels rather than confined to one. In his autobiography, Whitelaw referred to the reasons why the government reneged on its promise:

> My colleagues in Wales [presumably Nicholas Edwards, the secretary of state, and Wyn Roberts] did not consider that the proportion of Welsh speakers could justify delivering the whole new channel to the Welsh language. I therefore proposed safeguards in the bill requiring the IBA to ensure that at least twelve hours a week of programmes broadcast in Wales should be in Welsh. Taken in common with BBC

broadcasts, that would mean up to twenty hours of airtime in Welsh. Our aim was to foster the further development of the Welsh language, while not consuming so many hours of airtime as that many good commercially produced English-language programmes might never be scheduled in Wales.[35]

Although they had read the omens, Whitelaw's speech astounded the members of the BCW. 'I am unwilling to accept', stated Paul Flynn, the Council's acting chairman, 'that [all the work put into the fourth channel] could be destroyed in a few sentences in a speech by the Home Secretary.' He announced his resignation in order to be free to oppose the decision in every possible way. The BCW minuted its extreme dismay. Whitelaw's argument, it noted, was fatally flawed. If the BBC were to expand its output in Welsh to the level suggested for the IBA, that meant depriving viewers in Wales of at least eight additional hours a week of network programmes on BBC1 and 2, which would certainly be less acceptable to those who did not understand Welsh than the fourth-channel solution. Alwyn Roberts discussed the matter with the secretary of state and was disturbed to find that 'there was little real knowledge in the Welsh Office of the costs and difficulties of expanding television output in Welsh'.[36]

The IBA was authorized to provide the necessary transmission system with the aim of launching Channel Four in the autumn of 1982. It put forward a blueprint in November 1979 which suggested that 40 per cent of the output of the new service should be provided by the main commercial contractors, 20 per cent by the regional companies, 35 per cent by the independent companies and 5 per cent by others. The independent companies, a strongly emerging force, had different ideas; they wanted to be responsible for over 50 per cent of the output and to be sure that the scheduling was completely independent of ITV. The broadcasting bill of February 1980 closely followed the IBA's blueprint. The service would be run by a board consisting of eleven members nominated by the IBA, four by the ITV companies and five by other suppliers. Channel Four would not be solely reliant upon the advertising revenue it raised, but the channel and ITV, taken together, would be dependent upon the income they jointly received. One-third of Channel Four's output should be 'popular' programmes, the exact reverse of the pattern on ITV. The new network would have no opt-outs except for programmes in Welsh.[37]

The decision to abandon the Welsh fourth channel outraged many members of Plaid Cymru (not all of them, for the party contained elements which believed that it was too closely associated with the Welsh language.) At its conference in October 1979, Plaid Cymru established a fund into which it invited those who opposed the government's plan to pay their licence fees. By April 1980, 2,000 had pledged to do so, and in the ensuing months a number received prison sentences for refusing to pay fines levied on them for having an unlicensed television set. A group of leading academics blacked out transmitters in October 1979 and Cymdeithas yr Iaith Gymraeg redoubled its efforts.[38]

But the truly dramatic development was Gwynfor Evans's announcement on 5 May 1980 that he intended to fast unto death if the decision on the Welsh fourth channel were not reversed. He nominated 6 October 1980 as the date his fast would start, and initially it was planned to take place at the Plaid Cymru office in Cathedral Road, the processional way linking Cardiff with Llandaf. Gwynfor Evans, 'the peaceful patriarch and mentor of Welsh nationalism', was sixty-nine. He had been an ardent pacificist since the days of the Peace Pledge Union, yet there was ambiguity in his attitude to violence, for he cannot but have been aware that, had he died, Wales would have become a country of chronic unrest, and, very possibly, of bloodshed. Between the announcement of his fast and its proposed beginning, Evans held a series of meetings which were attended by throngs of his admirers. He talked of his possible impending death and the occasions were remarkable for their emotional intensity. No one doubted that he was totally in earnest, and there could be few doubts too about the determination of the newly elected Thatcher government not to veer from its declared intentions – a determination it had already shown on matters such as the steel industry. Yet, unlike the government's policy on steel, its decision on the Welsh fourth channel was not central to its strategy. As Patrick Hannan put it, there was force in Gwynfor Evans's tactic, 'for he was asking for something the government could not only deliver, but which it had actually promised to deliver'.[39]

The BCW viewed Gwynfor Evans's proposed fast with the deepest concern. While some members believed that 'it would force the government to give a better deal to Welsh-language television', others argued that 'it would prevent change because the government could not be seen to be yielding to such a threat'. Owen Edwards expressed his great regret, because 'of my personal respect and concern for [Evans] and because his fast could lead to an emotional reaction which could be very disastrous . . . If the government did decide to reconsider its policy, there might be another interminable delay for a new plan to be worked out and agreed; the present plan for separate BBC and ITV services was at least workable and could be achieved without delay.' As the weeks passed, the media internationally began to show an interest, for never before had there been anyone prepared to lay down his life for a television channel. Reporters and television crews from much of Europe and from North America converged upon Gwynfor Evans's home at Llangadog in the Tywi Valley, and many of the commentators were surprised to find, not a fanatic, but a soft-spoken man unhurriedly and almost shyly stating his allegiance to an ancient culture. Visiting him to say goodbye in the summer of 1980, the distinguished academic, Owen Dudley Edwards, was reduced to tears. 'It is worse for you than it is for me,' said Evans.[40]

On 9 July, Alwyn Roberts was summoned to London to meet the home secretary, the secretary of state for Wales and leading figures in the BBC and the IBA. Whitelaw announced that he was setting up a Welsh Language Television Committee 'to reduce tension and to review . . . the two-channel arrangement . . . If its report proves that the government is wrong in its decision on channelling we shall be prepared to make changes as necessary.' The decision to establish the committee was made public on 16 July. Members of the BCW considered it to be a 'cosmetic move' and Gwynfor Evans regarded it with contempt; indeed he elaborated upon his demands, stressing the need for adequate funding for the Welsh fourth channel and for it to be launched well before Channel Four began in the United Kingdom as a whole. On 10 September, the elder statesman of Welsh politics, Cledwyn Hughes, led a deputation to see the home secretary. With him were G. O. Williams, the archbishop of Wales, and Sir Goronwy Daniel, once the head of the Welsh Office and, from 1969 to 1979, the principal of the University College of Wales, Aberystwyth. Whitelaw, who held Cledwyn Hughes in high regard, was persuaded to change his mind and to permit the setting up of a Welsh fourth channel, at least as an experiment. As Stephen Lambert put it: 'It seemed to the government that Realpolitik dictated the necessity of setting up the channel and perhaps letting the Welsh see it fail, rather than flatly denying it and allowing it to act as a lightning conductor of Welsh protest.' The government's change of mind was not immediately made apparent to Alwyn Roberts, who felt that it was time for the views of the BCW to be strongly declared. He contacted all its members and secured their approval of a forceful letter to *The Times*. The letter was delivered but a government announcement on 17 September caused Roberts to withdraw it. He gave an account of his activities to a meeting of the BCW on 19 September, when its members congratulated him on the skilful way he had handled the situation. 'The pattern of events', commented Roberts, 'are much clearer now than they were at the time.'[41]

In its announcement of 17 September, the government stated that the Fourth Channel Authority's responsibility would be limited to

England, Scotland and Northern Ireland. In Wales, a separate Fourth
Channel Board would be established; it would have its own identity
and would determine when the programmes of the general Fourth
Channel as well as those of the Welsh-language service were to be
scheduled. As Alwyn Roberts noted, the scheme was more radical
than the recommendations of either of the two Home Office working
parties. The document had been hastily put together and contained a
number of contradictions. It was not clear whether the BBC's programmes were to be broadcast in a continuous identifiable block or
whether they were to be interleaved with those of ITV and the independent production companies. The scheduling of programmes,
argued Geraint Stanley Jones, was inseparable from the process of
making them. Such considerations led the BCW to be doubtful
whether it could support the proposed scheme. Yet, as Alwyn
Roberts noted, 'the government is likely to be in no mood to compromise'. 'It would be difficult', stated Owen Edwards, 'to get public
support for the argument that the BBC's identity was not being pro-
tected.' In the end, the Council accepted the argument of John Elfed
Jones that 'having been party to forcing a shotgun marriage on the
Welsh service, [it] was in no position to dictate marriage terms or to
determine the nature of the progeny'.[42]

More crucial, perhaps, was the question of whether Gwynfor Evans
would accept the scheme. He sought further assurances, particularly
on funding, and on the evening of 17 September, at a dramatic meeting
in Crymych, he announced that he was abandoning his proposed fast.
The fast had been motivated as much by Evans's determination to
revive the confidence of the members of Plaid Cymru following the
débâcle of the referendum of 1979 as it was by his desire to see the
establishment of a Welsh fourth channel. The meetings he held in the
summer of 1980 convinced him that he was achieving his first aim if
not his second. It was a pity, he thought, that the government had
capitulated so quickly. 'Pe gwelem bum wythnos arall o'r cynnwrf a'r
deffroad yng Nghymru,' he wrote in his autobiography, 'gwelid y
Blaid . . . wedi ymsefydlu mewn safle di-syfl.'[*43]

Discussion of the government's Broadcasting Bill was well advanced when the government reversed its policy on a Welsh fourth
channel. The provisions relating to Wales were grafted on to the bill
through an amendment in the House of Lords on 6 November 1980.
A Welsh Fourth Channel Authority (W4CA) would be established.
The BBC would provide it with at least ten hours of programmes a

---

*'If we had seen another five weeks of the agitation and the reawakening in
Wales . . . we would have seen Plaid Cymru . . . established in an unassailable
position.'

week, and the government promised that when the next licence fee was fixed, provision would be made to ensure that the Corporation had sufficient resources to expand its output in Welsh. HTV would contribute up to eight hours and the smaller companies about four hours. Their programmes would be bought by the W4CA which would receive its income from the same source as the general Fourth Channel – that is, from the subscription paid by all the ITV contractors. Yet, as there would be an adjustment to the ITV levy allowing the companies to retain a larger proportion of their revenue, the contributions of HTV and the independent production companies to the W4CA would, in effect, be financed not by the ITV contractors but by the government. The bill received royal assent on 13 November 1980. Thus was the Welsh Fourth Channel won. 'For once', wrote Whitelaw in 1989, 'I had reason to be glad that I bowed to pressure, not an usual experience.'[44]

II Radio Wales and Radio Cymru

When the Crawford Report was published in November 1974, the BBC in Wales was producing twenty-six hours of radio programmes a week. When the Corporation's sixth Charter came into force in August 1981, it was broadcasting 137 hours a week. The Crawford Committee had endorsed the BCW's plan to have an English-language service for Wales on medium wave and a Welsh-language service on VHF but the implementation of the plan proceeded somewhat erratically. There were major constraints upon its full realization. Chief among them was lack of money. The language split was initiated in January 1973 and was extended in April 1974. In January 1976 the BCW noted that 'twenty-one months have passed since the last development'; it expressed its intention of pressing ahead with full services in both languages between 6.45 and 9 a.m., but in March it acknowledged that the resources to do so were not available. 'The BBC Wales radio service', it minuted, 'has expanded in the last few years far beyond the actual development money made available.' The early morning split was fully achieved in January 1977, a step made possible by savings at Head Office. 'Wales', recorded the BCW, 'has been very fairly treated by the Radio Directorate.' The governors provided a further £500,000 for radio development in Wales in December, allowing plans to be prepared to expand English-language output to thirty-five hours a week by November 1978. Thereafter, Head Office became reluctant to release further money, Aubrey Singer, the managing director, radio, informing the BCW that 'Scotland and Wales have been generously treated at the expense of London-based services'. 'The concentration of resources on regional development in recent years', declared David Webster, the Corporation's director of public affairs, 'has weakened the BBC centrally.' Scotland, with twice the population of Wales, had a larger radio budget but was seeking to build up only one radio service, while Wales was seeking to build up two. 'It has been forcefully put to me', Ian Trethowan informed the BCW, 'that each of Wales's radio services should have resources similar to Radio Scotland. There is not the remotest chance of that coming about.' Thus Wales looked with envy at Scotland, where there were thirty-seven non-specialist producers responsible for less output than were their seventeen Welsh counterparts.[45]

Finance was not the only constraint. A substantial expansion of Welsh-language transmissions on VHF was impolitic as long as a quarter of Welsh households – many of them in wholly English-speaking areas such as south Pembrokeshire – could not get Basic Radio Four on VHF. An additional consideration was the fact that on VHF the morning and afternoon were dominated in term time by schools programmes. These factors did not apply to a service on medium wave, although, as has been seen, that was subject to a different drawback – the poor quality of reception after dark. A significant increase in English-language programmes was feasible, at least during daylight hours, but there was a reluctance to expand output in English unaccompanied by an expansion in Welsh. Prospects were transformed by the Corporation's decision to broadcast Basic Radio Four on long wave, for that meant that the service would be available to every household in Wales. The change came about on 24 November 1978 and was part of a massive switch of frequencies aimed at 'giving Scotland, Wales and Northern Ireland greater programme freedom'.[46]

Eight months before the frequency switch, the BBC appointed editors for Radio Cymru and Radio Wales. The Radio Cymru post went to Meirion Edwards, who had succeeded John Roberts Williams as head of production, Bangor, in March 1976. The editorship of Radio Wales, noted the BCW, is the highest programme post in the BBC in Wales for which fluency in Welsh is not required. Ironically, the post went to a Welsh-speaker, Teleri Bevan. Although she was recognized to be the strongest candidate, there were some grumblings, almost as if the ability to speak Welsh should be looked upon as a handicap. Indeed, there were some who argued that it was, for they believed that a Welsh-speaker was unlikely to have an intuitive understanding of the needs and interests of English-speaking Wales. During the first sixty years of the BBC's operations in Wales, Teleri Bevan was the fourth woman (Nan Davies, Mai Jones and Lorraine

Davies were the other three) to hold a fairly senior position – a dismal record indeed.

The BCW decided to give priority to the launching of Radio Wales. Radio Wales and Radio Cymru were listed in the *Radio Times* as two distinct services from 1 January 1977, but at that time both were essentially opt-outs from Radio Four. Radio Wales was relaunched on 13 November 1978, when the hours of its own programmes were increased from twenty-five to forty-five hours a week. It could be argued that the establishment of Radio Wales was the single most important happening in the history of Welsh broadcasting. 'For the first time', stated Stanley Jones, 'the BBC in Wales is to set its own style of broadcasting on a service for which it is totally responsible.'[47] It was a service accessible to all the people of Wales. D. H. I. Powell had feared in 1950 that the pattern of broadcasting in Wales was resulting in 'the disintegration of our people'. With the launching of Radio Wales, there were hopes that that disintegration might be halted and reversed.

In its first months, Radio Wales was widely attacked. 'It consists of pop and prattle,' wrote the *Rhondda Leader*. Its early morning programme, *AM*, was a disaster, said Nicholas Edwards, and the bishop of Monmouth wrote to the BCW to complain of its triviality. The members of the BCW were highly critical, particularly of the early morning output. Tegai Hughes was concerned that 'we are losing opinion-formers from what had been [our] flagship programme'. Part of the Council's hostility arose from the nature of its members. They were educated high achievers and expected mental stimulation from broadcasting. Radio Four, which had a fifth of the radio audience (although it had a majority among those over sixty-five) was regularly listened to by all but one of the BCW's members. When Wales's sound broadcasts were opt-outs of Radio Four, they tended to have a Radio Four character. With the establishment of a separate service, there was a desire to win a wider audience through providing more programmes which did not demand sustained listening. When Radio Wales was not transmitting its own output, it tended to use Radio Two as the 'sustaining service'. Members of the BCW listened dutifully, but they did not care for much of what they heard. Teleri Bevan was summoned before the Council. She pointed to the enormous response to phone-in programmes and to the fact that *AM* received between 250 and 300 letters a day. If a much larger audience were to be won, she argued, the risk of losing part of the old audience was a risk worth taking.[48]

The BCW acknowledged that some of the contributors to Radio Wales were excellent. Among these were old hands, particularly

347

Alun Williams and Vincent Kane, but they also included newcomers such as Dan Damon, Noreen Bray and Chris Stuart. Yet the Council continued to have doubts, and there was much agonizing over 'the philosophy of Radio Wales'. 'The audience for programmes in Welsh', it was noted, 'is a more homogeneous group, bound together by ties of language. Radio Wales has the greater task of defining and attracting its audience.' Radio Scotland had similar problems. 'On its first birthday', noted *The Times* on 23 November 1979, '[Radio Scotland] is a bruised and demoralized bairn . . . Both the head of the service and his deputy have departed after heavy criticism of the station's output.' The Scots decided that their service could be revitalized by providing extensive opt-outs for the different communities of Scotland. The idea appealed to Welsh broadcasters for, as Dr Ross Williams, a BCW member, put it: 'The identity of Wales has different meanings in the various parts of Wales'. Gareth Bowen, the editor of Radio Wales news, was particularly enthusiastic about regional opt-outs. In parts of Wales, particularly the north-east, he argued, 'Radio Wales is seen as a south Wales service . . . There is a danger of the BBC creating in Wales precisely the same problem which [we] have complained of in respect of the network services.'[49]

Wales had already experimented with community radio. In an attempt to attract listeners to the Welsh-language output on VHF, a van carrying a mobile transmitter was borrowed from Radio Éireann. In September 1976 it broadcast for four days apiece from such places as Rhosllannerchrugog and Llwynhendy, and the response was enthusiastic. Neighbourhood radio or *radio bro* should not be confined to villages, argued Alwyn Roberts; it could play a role in urban communities, such as Canton in Cardiff. Paul Flynn agreed and listed ten communities in Newport alone where such a service would be invaluable. '*Radio Bro*', he suggested, 'would enable radio to undo some of the harm broadcasting had done to community life.' With the advent of Radio Wales, the Radio Éireann van was taken for a week apiece to Merthyr, the Rhondda, Pontypool and Wrexham, and the BCW was gratified to hear that, as a result, the new service won higher than average audiences in those four places. The *Daily Telegraph* published a glowing report on the Welsh experiments and they were the subject of a lengthy article in the *Radio Month*. The BCW sought resources to increase the number of places visited, but Head Office proved uncooperative. Neighbourhood radio, argued the managing director, radio, is not the BBC's business. 'It is just not big-time broadcasting.' Flynn was outraged. Such an attitude, he declared, was proof that broadcasters were failing the people of Wales. 'Mobile radio', he declared, 'has been by far the most successful activity of the BBC in Wales in the last few years.'[50]

Radio Wales launched a more sustained experiment in neighbourhood radio in 1980, when for sixteen weeks it provided a daily opt-out from 8.00 a.m. to 12.00 noon for the inhabitants of Deeside. Planned by Stanley Jones, who modelled it on Radio Éireann's West of Ireland Irish-language service, Radio Deeside was broadcast from a caravan at the Deeside Leisure Centre. The motive was to win an audience for Radio Wales in north-east Wales, but there was also a desire to provide a service in an area threatened by the impending closure of the Shotton steelworks. The project received the warm approval of the secretary of state, and Head Office provided half the money for the original plan, which was restricted to eight weeks. Because of local pressure and grants from the local authorities, the length of the experiment was doubled, and Radio Deeside was on the air from 3 March to 4 June. The chief executive of the Delyn District was much impressed. 'This is not', he declared, 'another travelling circus from south Wales which so unfairly dominates the radio media.' It was estimated that Radio Deeside was heard in the homes of all the Shotton workers, and during the newspaper strike of the spring of 1980 it became the notice-board for both management and unions. As the BBC had no intention of providing a permanent service for Deeside, it was somewhat alarmed by the success of its experiment. 'There is some disquiet at the BBC headquarters at Cardiff,' noted the *Liverpool Daily Post*, 'where there is a feeling that the BBC has started something in north-east Wales which has become a feature of the life of the area. There are fears that the BBC is creating a taste for local radio which it would be handing over to a commercial rival.' When it became apparent that Radio Deeside would shortly close, David Parry, a Shotton resident, organized a petition to save it. 'What Radio Deeside has done so admirably', he wrote, 'is to give this area an identity in broadcasting terms . . . It could become the forerunner of a federal Radio Wales network, which would increase the authority of Radio Wales in this area . . . The BBC will never be forgiven if, after neglecting [this part] of the Principality for so long, they leave it with no more than a token local service.' Recordings of Radio Deeside's output were played to the members of the BCW. One of them, Henry Nyman, a Cardiff solicitor, was struck by the accents of the contributors. 'I can see now', he remarked, 'why these people feel ignored by Radio Wales.'[51]

Gareth Bowen, who had taken charge of Radio Deeside, believed that the district was not large enough to sustain a permanent regional opt-out service. It would be better, he argued, to seek to serve the county of Clwyd as a whole. In its evidence to Annan, the BBC in Wales had referred to its intention of providing regional opt-outs, and mentioned specifically the Mold–Wrexham area of north-east

Wales. The Annan Report recommended that local radio services – those of the Corporation as well as those of the commercial companies – should be hived off from the BBC and the IBA and brought under a separate Local Radio Authority. As the BBC in Wales was planning local radio which would be inextricably linked with its general output, it was relieved that the government's White Paper of July 1978 ignored that part of the Annan recommendations. The White Paper was in favour of allowing both the BBC and the IBA to increase the number of their local stations, and in the late 1970s the Corporation prepared plans to add nine stations to its existing twenty. The BCW believed that full local services would only be viable in Cardiff, Swansea and Wrexham/Mold, but as it was determined to channel all its radio resources into the expansion and improvement of its networks in the two languages, it did not press for a station in any of those places. To have one at Swansea seemed superfluous, as Swansea Sound was proving successful. Cardiff's commercial station, CBC, began broadcasting on 11 April 1980; Newport and Wrexham also acquired stations, but not one of the three achieved the success of Swansea Sound, a further factor in discouraging the BCW from seeking to establish local BBC stations in Wales. It was eager, however, to pursue the notion of Clwyd opt-outs. Premises were acquired at Mold and it was proposed that Radio Clwyd should opt out from Radio Wales from 7.10 to 7.30 and from 9.00 to 10.00 a.m. The service began on 1 October 1981 and by then plans were well advanced to launch Radio Gwent from Cwmbran in 1983. The BCW drew up a list of eight other places where opt-outs would be feasible, but acknowledged that its plans would not be completed in their entirety until well into the twenty-first century.[52]

The Council was adamant that opt-outs should be confined to its English-language service. Requests that Radio Clwyd should carry some material in Welsh were firmly rejected. The BCW believed that the unity of Welsh Wales was a reality; English Wales had to be coaxed into unity through a constructive acknowledgement of its diversity. The Council's hopes seemed to be well-founded, for the initial criticism of Radio Wales ebbed away as the service took root. 'Radio Wales', stated Stanley Jones, 'found its voice through a vigorous process of editorial self-analysis.'[53] By the early 1990s, while Radio One had the largest following in Wales, Radio Wales was a close second. 'I don't like having to take a load to the East Midlands', stated a Cardiff lorry-driver in 1993, 'because once I've passed Birmingham I can't get Radio Wales.' As Welsh broadcasters had long believed that many of the people of Wales – Cardiffians in particular – rejected their output, such comments were balm indeed.

The relaunching of Radio Cymru took place just over a year after that of Radio Wales. From 19 November 1979, morning broadcasts exclusive to Radio Cymru – which hitherto had been confined to breakfast-time – came to occupy the whole of the morning. The extended service attracted a more positive initial response than had the expansion of Radio Wales. There had been fears that if an exclusively VHF Welsh-language service were provided, the numbers listening to programmes in Welsh would decline drastically. Those fears seemed to be confirmed by a survey of the village of Talybont in north Dyfed in February 1977, which showed that, since the initiation of the VHF/medium-wave split, the audience for Welsh-language programmes had decreased by 30 per cent – a figure which was extensively quoted by Jac L. Williams in his campaign against a Welsh fourth channel. Between 1977 and 1979, the BBC conducted a somewhat frenzied campaign to persuade Welsh-speakers to buy VHF sets. By the late 1970s, non-VHF receivers were reaching the end of their useful life, and those offering VHF – the products in the main of factories in east Asia – were annually becoming relatively cheaper. In 1978, 5.5 million radio sets were sold in Britain, only 600,000 of which were British-made. By the early 1980s, ownership of VHF sets was virtually universal and in March 1980 the BCW was informed that 'the initial audience figures were much better than expected'. Its most popular programme was *Helo Bobol* (7.05 to 7.45 and 8.05 to 8.45 a.m.), first broadcast on 3 January 1977 and presented by the ebullient Hywel Gwynfryn. There was also a substantial audience for *Stondin Dyddiol*, launched as a daily programme on 5 October 1981; rumours that half the Welsh-speaking housewives of Dyfed were in love with its presenter, Sulwyn Thomas, were not, however, confirmed. 'It is strange to recall', stated Alwyn Roberts in February 1982, 'that a few years ago the idea of a Welsh-language radio service on VHF seemed risky. Now it is inconceivable to many people to imagine Wales without Radio Cymru.' The London-based teacher and journalist, Hafina Clwyd, declared that it was worth returning to Wales just to receive Radio Cymru, and John Elfed Jones described the service as 'tremendous and superb'.[54]

Radio Cymru depended heavily on the output of the BBC Bangor studios, where by 1979 thirty of its fifty-five hours of weekly transmissions were produced. Indeed, it was originally suggested that the headquarters of Radio Cymru and all its continuity should be based at Bangor. (There is a widespread and wholly erroneous belief that, because the ability to speak Welsh is proportionately higher in Gwynedd than it is in the rest of Wales, the majority of Welsh-speakers live there.) The studios and offices at Bangor became grossly overcrowded. In December 1977, the BBC bought a two-acre site at Plas-y-coed on the outskirts of the city with the intention of building a new broadcasting complex. There were problems over access, and Head Office was not over-anxious to release the sums needed for building, for it considered 'developments at Bangor to be irrelevant to network needs'. There were suspicions – almost certainly well-founded – that money which could have been spent at Bangor had been diverted to building operations at Llandaf. The deteriorating financial position of the Corporation caused work on the new complex to be postponed year by year and in 1980 it was decided that the scheme should be abandoned. The Plas-y-coed site was sold and the Corporation used the money to buy Neuadd Hafren, one of the halls of residence of Y Coleg Normal. Further buildings in the vicinity of Bryn Meirion were later acquired, but the BBC's operations at Bangor remained inadequately housed. R. Alun Evans, who succeeded Meirion Edwards as head of production, Bangor, in 1978, dealt valiantly with a difficult situation, for, relative to its output, Bangor must be the most under-resourced of all the Corporation's centres of production.[55]

The needs of Radio Wales and Radio Cymru led the BBC to reconsider its policy with regard to the premises at Alexandra Road in Swansea, which since 1967 had housed little more than an unattended studio. In October 1981, the BBC began to use the entire building again, and by the mid 1980s Swansea was responsible for a significant proportion of the output of Radio Wales and Radio Cymru. The ability of the two services to draw upon contributors in all parts of Wales was greatly enhanced by the BBC's unattended radio studios. By the early 1980s, they were available at Wrexham, Newtown, Porthmadog, Aberystwyth, Carmarthen, Haverfordwest and Llandrindod, thus ensuring that – along with the facilities at Cardiff, Swansea, Bangor and Mold – hardly anyone in Wales lived more than thirty miles from a BBC microphone. The studio at Aberystwyth was especially heavily used; the lecturers of the University College proved eager to broadcast, and the college's historians were particularly voluble, if not prolix.

As in the 1960s, so also in the 1970s and early 1980s, the largest single responsibility of the radio broadcasting operations of the BBC in Wales was the orchestra. Performances for Radio Three continued to represent the greater part of its commitment to sound broadcasting, and in recognition of the fact Head Office's Radio Directorate met at least half the cost of the players' salaries. Owen Edwards enthusiastically pressed the claims of the BBC Welsh Symphony Orchestra and his successor, Geraint Stanley Jones (controller Wales, 1981–1985), was an even more ardent advocate. As has been seen, the orchestra was expanded in 1973 from forty-four members to sixty, with the Welsh Arts Council paying the salaries of the additional sixteen. Despite inflationary pressures and a shortfall in its grant, the Council struggled to fulfil its promise to finance additional expansion. It paid for a further six players in 1980, and in 1981 the BBC and the Council agreed to pay the salaries of another six players apiece, bringing the total membership to seventy-eight. The salaries were meagre and, unlike their counterparts in London, musicians at Cardiff had few opportunities to augment their income. In 1982, when the rank-and-file members of the Welsh orchestra were receiving £6,273 a year, those maintaining children were eligible for income support. Meagre though the salaries were, they represented a severe strain upon the resources of the Welsh Arts Council, and on occasion – in 1975, for example – it failed to honour its commitment. 'We look with envy', wrote Roy Bohana, the Council's director of music, 'at the maintenance and expansion of large orchestras entirely at the BBC's expense in London (101 players), Manchester (70) and Glasgow (69).'[56]

The Council's contribution helped to ensure that the BBC Welsh Symphony Orchestra was, as Head Office put it, 'somewhat apart'. 'The WSO's special relationship with the Council', noted a memorandum, 'the number and nature of its public concerts for the Council . . . and above all its implicit position as the national orchestra of Wales give it automatically a rather different musical role from the orchestras in Glasgow, Manchester and London.' The BBC's Welsh officials rightly cherished that 'rather different musical role', particularly in 1980 when the Corporation decided to disband five of its orchestras. The Welsh orchestra was not among them. 'The partnership established in 1973', wrote Bohana, 'between the BBC in Wales and the Welsh Arts Council probably ensured the exclusion of the BBC Welsh Symphony Orchestra from the proposed cuts.'[57]

Those concerned with the orchestra were anxious to broaden its role beyond sound broadcasting. 'How can music be shown on television?' asked Wales's head of music, Arnold Lewis, in 1977. The way to do so, he believed, was to televise entire symphony concerts and that was done on a sufficient scale in Wales for Head Office to note in 1980 that among the distinctive features of the Welsh orchestra was 'its regular commitment to television'. Among the most ambitious of the orchestra's television broadcasts was a performance at Dresden of Britten's *War Requiem*, organized in association with the broadcasting authorities of the German Democratic Republic, a programme which was submitted for the Italia Prize. Lewis and his colleagues looked forward eagerly to the opening of Cardiff's magnificent St David's Hall in the autumn of 1982, when they hoped that the commitment to television would be considerably expanded. Their hopes were fulfilled, and by the mid

1980s St David's Hall was described as the most televised concert hall in Britain. Stanley Jones was delighted. 'I doubt whether any other orchestra in the United Kingdom annually reaches so many people,' he wrote. By the late 1980s and the early 1990s, when more and more of the work of the BBC was put out to contract, the case for cherishing the orchestra grew ever stronger. 'The BBC in Llandaf', noted a commentator in 1990, 'will soon . . . be [only] employing a handful of journalists and a symphony orchestra.'[58]

III   Programmes, viewers and listeners, 1974 to 1981

In the mid and late 1970s, as in the mid and late 1960s, the finest broadcasting experiences available to the people of Wales were provided by BBC2. They included *I Claudius*, with a memorable performance by Siân Phillips (1976), Huw Wheldon's *Royal Heritage* (1977), *The Voyage of Charles Darwin* (1978) and *Ireland, a Television History* (1980). In 1978, BBC2 broadcast all the plays of Shakespeare and in 1979 it offered *Life on Earth*, perhaps the best natural history series ever televised. By the early 1980s, however, there were some signs of faltering and misjudgement, particularly in 1981 when the BBC's *The Borgias* contrasted painfully with Granada's superb *Brideshead Revisited*. (Ironically, Brideshead was Castle Howard, the magnificent seat of George Howard, who succeeded Michael Swann as chairman of the BBC governors in 1980.) BBC1 had its moments also, with the bizarre and highly popular *Fawlty Towers*, the fine Cornish costume drama *Poldark* and the continuously high standard of *Panorama*. Imports from the United States included the portrayal of slavery, *Roots*, a series which attracted the largest number of viewers ever recorded. Some of the BBC1 offerings, however, found less favour with Welsh viewers. A parody of 'Hen Wlad fy Nhadau' on *The Two Ronnies* in 1977 brought a flood of protest and the item was omitted from the programme's repeat.

In the mid 1970s, London's interest in Wales was slight, but as the devolution debate developed it commissioned several programmes on the implications of Scottish and Welsh assemblies. Head Office showed more interest in the arson attacks which began in 1979. In 1980, *Nationwide* featured a hooded figure purporting to be a Welsh terrorist. David Burns, the man in the hood, who had taken part in the programme out of bravado, was arrested and spent six months on remand before being found not guilty of any wrongdoing. The BCW was perturbed by the item, and wondered whether it could 'prevent staff from other parts of the BBC from coming to Wales to make programmes'. (The same problem arose in Scotland; indeed,

Alasdair Milne noted that his predecessor as controller Scotland, Andrew Stewart, came 'near to closing the border to the rest of the BBC'.) There were occasions, however, when London's intervention was welcomed. In 1982, *Nationwide* conducted an investigation into boot money for rugby players. 'It highlighted', commented Stanley Jones, 'the fact that, because of local sensitivities, some items are easier to do from London with a visiting team.' Other London productions of special interest to Wales included three programmes on Welsh localities, broadcast in 1978. One of them – that on Trawsfynydd – showed the villagers conversing almost exclusively in Welsh, and Welsh was also prominent in the programme on Ffynnongroyw – the first occasion for Head Office to commission programmes featuring the language.[59]

Welsh productions for the general British services were more numerous in the later 1970s than they had been a decade earlier. By 1975, twelve years had passed since Wales had made a network drama series. In that year *Hawkmoor*, a series starring John Ogwen and loosely based on the gentleman vagabond, Twm Siôn Catti, was broadcast at the highly popular time of 5.00 p.m. on Sunday. In 1977, the BBC in Wales produced the most ambitious series in its history – eight 50-minute programmes depicting the career of David Lloyd George. *Ennal's Point*, a seafaring saga filmed at Swansea, was broadcast in 1981 and attracted over three million viewers; the money spent on it, minuted the BCW, 'was only half that available for a London-based series'. *Ivor the Engine*, a children's series launched in 1976, was a great success and was hailed as the best programme of its kind since *Magic Roundabout*. In 1978 *Dylan*, a Welsh production for BBC2, won much praise, as did the broadcast of the Welsh National Opera's *Midsummer Night's Dream*. Max Boyce, who had originally come to prominence as a Welsh-language performer, had his own series on BBC1 in 1978; it attracted eight and a half million viewers, although Tegai Hughes thought that Boyce was 'so repetitious as to be unwatchable'. The greatest success of the 1970s was Stuart Burrows's programme on BBC1 in July 1978. It won one of the highest appreciation figures ever recorded, and the singer received over a thousand letters from his admirers.[60]

Within Wales itself, the ability to receive the programmes of BBC Wales and BBC2 was well nigh universal by the early 1980s. Phase Two – the provision of a service for communities with between 500 and 1,000 inhabitants – had been completed and George Salter, Wales's head of programme services and engineering, informed the BCW in 1981 that the BBC's hundredth UHF Welsh transmitter would be operational on 15 May. Some places were included in the second phase only with difficulty. Tegai Hughes frequently pressed the claims of Llanbryn-mair, a Montgomeryshire village with a distinguished cultural tradition. It did not qualify, argued Salter, for it had only 400 inhabitants. A council house estate built there in 1977 tipped the balance. Rhosllannerchrugog, a richly resonant mining village, also posed problems, as did the Holywell–Flint area, and some of the problems proved intractable. The standard of reception considered adequate by the BBC's engineers was high – too high in the opinion of Alwyn Roberts. When Phase Two had been completed, Salter stated that there were still some 85,000 people in Wales who lacked a UHF service, but 70 per cent of them could get a weak signal with which they seemed content. Nevertheless, he proceeded to plan Phase Three – the provision of a service for communities with between 200 and 500 inhabitants – estimating that it would take eight years to complete. He recognized, however, that there must be a 'cut-off point somewhere' and urged the BBC to follow the example of the Broadcasting Council for Scotland, which decided in 1975 not to provide transmitters once the cost of the viewers served exceeded £50 a head.[61]

With the extension of the UHF service, duplication on VHF seemed increasingly unnecessary. It had been assumed in 1967 that VHF television transmissions would come to an end in 1974, but protests from those who feared deprivation caused the Corporation to delay a decision year after year. Duplication was burdensome; as the VHF transmitters were to be phased out, there was no point in replacing them, but as they aged the cost of maintaining them rose ever higher. In July 1981 it was decided to cease VHF transmissions of BBC Wales forthwith but to continue Wenvoe's VHF BBC1 transmissions until 1986. It was acknowledged that the number who would be deprived was unknown. The only answer was to close down and await reaction. If the level of deprivation were acceptable, closure would be permanent. In the event, the only protests were those of about 2,000 viewers in the neighbourhood of Llandrindod, and special arrangements were made for them.[62]

The transmissions of BBC Wales were not only available to Welsh viewers. Television-owners along the entire east coast of the Irish Republic could receive them with ease. 'Dubliners', noted Alan Protheroe, 'watched *Wales Today* in droves', and in the 1970s Welsh visitors to the bars of the city found its inhabitants remarkably well-informed on events in Wales. They regarded the Welsh programmes as an intriguing addition to their own television fare. That was not the case in north Somerset, where some 20,000 people could not receive BBC1 from the UHF Mendip transmitter, but could receive BBC Wales from UHF Wenvoe. They reacted angrily. In November 1976, Owen Edwards was summoned to Weston-super-Mare, but he refused to go on the grounds that 'it was not a problem for which the BBC in Wales had any responsibility'. In 1977, a Somerset lorry-driver, embittered by 'Welsh gibberish on television', unsuccessfully sought to bring the BBC in Wales before the Race Relations Board. A 'Ban Welsh Telly' campaign was launched and its members vowed to go to prison rather than pay the licence fee to view Wenvoe's transmissions. Esther Rantzen, a populist broadcaster, took the matter up. 'It is monstrous', she declared, 'that viewers in the West of England are yammered at in a foreign language, complete with harps and male voice choirs.' She called for street demonstrations and for people to 'sign up with the English Nationalists'. Lucas was much perturbed. 'Both Wales and the Welsh language', he wrote, 'are now dirty words to a lot of people across the Bristol Channel.' Salter, always the voice of English common sense, thought the agitation a nonsense. 'The simple situation', he commented, 'is that those areas do not have a proper coverage of their own BBC1 service and anything they get from Wales is a bonus and not an imposition.' The Porlock transmitter came into service in 1978 and the agitation died away.[63]

Between 1974 and 1981 programmes for exclusive transmission in Wales were broadly of the same character as they had been in the previous decade. The chief difference was that, by the late 1970s, they were almost all available in colour. 'When I left the Director-Generalship in 1977,' noted Curran, 'colorization was approaching completion.' There were still some underprivileged centres. Bangor, for example, was not capable of initiating colour programmes until the 1980s. At Llandaf, the demolition of Baynton House began in May 1975 and the sod-cutting for the proposed large colour studio there was performed by Curran in March 1977. The studio, with equipment costing in excess of £3 million, was operational from December 1979. Because of lack of money, however, it was initially only used for three days a week. In 1975 it had been assumed that, with the completion of the new studio, all Cardiff's broadcasting operations would be based at the Llandaf site, but expansion between 1975 and 1979 necessitated additional premises and by 1982 200 staff members not concerned with daily studio-based programmes were housed in temporary buildings at Gabalfa. Even more exciting than the provision of the new studio was the acquisition of electronic news-gathering equipment, although its full acceptance was delayed by union opposition. Using tape not film, the equipment enabled news to be instantly transmitted. Other innovations included light, hand-held cameras, which vastly enhanced the possibilities of outside broadcasts, and greatly improved facilites for editing video tape.[64]

Of the output of BBC Wales, sport had the largest following. *Sports Line Up*, broadcast on Sunday afternoon, could attract up to half a million viewers, and the fact that 45.8 per cent of Welsh households tuned in to the 1979 Wales–Ireland rugby match has already been mentioned. 'BBC Wales', the BCW was informed in May 1976, 'will be carrying exclusive live coverage of the match between Wales and Yugoslavia . . . This sort of event is of the greatest importance in persuading viewers to make provision for watching BBC Wales.' 'Where rugby is concerned', commented Onllwyn Brace, 'we get the maximum co-operation and the standards in Wales are equal to anywhere in the world.' Association Football presented problems. While the BBC in Scotland negotiated directly with the Scottish Football League, Wales was an afterthought in discussions between Head Office and the English League. BBC Wales was permitted to show the Wales–Scotland match in 1977, but the whole issue became largely irrelevant in 1978 when ITV obtained exclusive rights to league games. BBC Wales's enthusiasm for team games was not universally shared. In 1978, when the World Cup coincided with the Urdd National Eisteddfod, the BBC decided that it would be politic to curtail its eisteddfod coverage. Its decision was attacked, particularly in view of the fact that the matches it broadcast were, as often as not, available on BBC2 and ITV.[65]

Next in popularity to sport, and representing the staple production of BBC Wales, were its news bulletins and topical magazine programmes. Industrial news continued to be thoroughly covered and in January 1980 Jack Thomas, one of the members of the BCW, paid tribute to the way BBC Wales was dealing with 'the worst trauma to hit south Wales since 1926'. The politics of Wales were admirably dealt with by Patrick Hannan in English and by Emyr Daniel in Welsh, although following the referendum of 1979 Hannan was heard to wonder whether his post as political correspondent of the BBC in Wales should be abolished. In the run-up to the referendum, the issue of a Welsh assembly was given saturation treatment. A BCW member, George Wright of the Wales TUC, had expressed concern in 1977 that, where devolution was concerned, BBC Wales was making too much use 'of MPs with eccentric views', and in January 1979 another member, Jack Thomas, stated that 'Labour rebels should not be given as much prominence as MPs supporting the official party line'.[66] Those following BBC Wales's coverage of the referendum campaign gained the impression that 'the rebels', Neil Kinnock in particular, made all the running – although, admittedly, 'the eccentric views' turned out to be those of the bulk of the Welsh electorate.

There was a widespread belief that many of the non Welsh-speaking employees of the BBC were biased against a Welsh assembly, and an even better-founded belief that the Welsh-speaking employees were biased in favour. There was also a suspicion that some of the English-speaking staff were antagonistic towards the Welsh language – hardly surprising, perhaps, in view of the fact that there were those among them who believed that their advancement was blocked by their inability to speak it. The suspicion was fed by the readiness of BBC Wales's English topical programmes to give detailed coverage to meetings of movements hostile to the Welsh language, even if they were very sparsely attended. By 1977, the practice had developed to such an extent that Trevor Fishlock, the Welsh correspondent of *The Times*, felt moved to protest against 'irresponsible, doubtful and emotive stories'. They represent, he wrote, 'a departure from accepted journalistic standards'. Among Plaid Cymru members, there was a belief that some of the staff of BBC Wales wished the party ill, a belief strengthened by a misleading BBC poll of the Carmarthen constituency conducted during the general election of 1979. Published three days before polling day, it torpedoed any chance Gwynfor Evans might have had of retaining the seat. Stanley Jones was repentant, for he doubted whether the poll met the 'agreed specifications'. Despite Plaid Cymru's suspicions, there were many outside the BBC – Welsh MPs among them – who were convinced that the Corporation in Wales was riddled with Nationalists. When Owen Edwards appeared before the Commons Committee on Welsh Affairs in 1980, Delwyn Williams (Conservative, Montgomeryshire) declared that the political convictions of the BBC's Welsh employees should be examined. He received 'an apt and entirely merited' rebuke from the committee's chairman, Leo Abse. 'There will be', said Abse, 'no McCarthy conduct in this Select Committee.'[67]

While the coverage of news and current affairs was roughly equal in the two languages, television drama production in Wales for exclusive transmission in Wales was almost wholly in Welsh. Plays included *Gwen Tomos*, an adaptation of Daniel Owen's novel, broadcast in 1981. It attracted 40 per cent of Welsh-speaking viewers, the equivalent in British terms of twenty million people. By the late 1970s, most of the energies of the drama department of BBC Wales were being devoted to the serial *Pobol y Cwm*. The serial won a devoted following. When an episode was postponed in order to pay tribute to John Lennon following his murder, the Llandaf switchboard was jammed by protesting telephone calls. 'The individual programmes', commented Alwyn Roberts rather condescingly, 'do not amount to much, but the series has acquired its own momentum.' Plans were prepared to make a back-to-back version.

They were, however, abandoned, for as an English *Pobol y Cwm* would have been BBC Wales's main if not its only English drama production specifically for viewers in Wales, and as the series would of necessity use Welsh-speaking actors, there were fears that there would be accusations that BBC Wales was unwilling to employ actors who lacked a knowledge of Welsh.[68]

The most widely enjoyed of BBC Wales's English-language drama productions was Gwenlyn Parry's *Grand Slam*, broadcast in 1975; it portrayed the adventures of a group of young rugby fans visiting Paris for an international match. The prurient were shocked but the drama was tame compared with what the largely amateur cast actually got up to during the filming. (Harri Webb's lines: 'If you thought the game was dirty / You ought to hear the songs' was only the beginning of the matter.) With *Grand Slam*, drama shaded into light entertainment, an area in which BBC Wales had traditionally been weak. Max Boyce enjoyed great popularity, especially when his repertoire was made more varied through the employment of a script-writer. Wales could not afford to produce shows featuring international Welsh stars, and there was much pleasure in 1982 at the purchase for £14,000 of twenty-four programmes featuring Tom Jones. 'Had we been able to do them,' noted Gareth Price, 'they would have cost £50,000 apiece.' Some Welsh-language light entertainment programmes were lamentably weak, with *Dr Hywel Ffiaidd* reaching the nadir of gruesome vacuity. Others were excellent. Auriol Watkin, a BCW member, considered *Fo a Fe* to be the best programme of its kind on any channel. Light entertainment in Welsh suffered a sad blow in 1974 when Derek Boote died as a result of serious burns caused when a costume he was wearing caught fire. Until Llandaf's main studio was completed, most of Wales's light entertainment programmes were made at Pebble Mill, with audiences drawn from the ageing Birmingham Welsh community. That could present difficulites, especially with situation comedies such as *Glas y Dorlan*, with its rich vein of slick *double entendre*. Cledwyn Hughes thought *Glas y Dorlan* was disgusting, but it had a large following. 'It does contain innuendo', acknowledged Jack Williams, Wales's head of light entertainment, 'but not more so than many English programmes.' In 1977, however, it was the BBC's sole light entertainment television programme in Welsh. The BCW requested Williams to tone it down, because, 'as it is the only one, it has to appeal to a wider and more sensitive audience'.[69]

The feature programmes of BBC Wales tended to be historical, a longstanding characteristic of Wales's feature production. There was much controversy in 1977 over Gwyn A. Williams's interpretation of the Merthyr Riots of 1831, particularly his linkage of the tightfistedness of the ironmasters with the Labour government's incomes policy. Critics pointed out that Williams was active in Plaid Cymru, but Stanley Jones, who was proud of the programme, insisted that 'his views are . . . basically Maoist'. *Colliers' Crusade* an account of the involvement of Welsh miners in the Spanish Civil War, broadcast in 1979, won praise, and there was appreciation too of topographical features in Welsh, such as *Dilyn Afon*. Stanley Jones was anxious to find new and unusual sources of programmes. In 1977 he acquired a series of feature films from Hungary for subtitling in Welsh. 'Increasingly', he informed the BCW, 'BBC Wales is making its own contacts, because the official BBC/EBU [European Broadcasting Union] channels do not adequately cater for [Welsh] requirements.' If Wales were to buy directly from other countries, could there not be two-way traffic? Stanley Jones went to the Cannes Festival in 1978, and noted that HTV had a stand there. Should not BBC Wales be there also, he asked? The matter was not immediately pursued, largely because the centralized nature of BBC Enterprises – the sales arm of the Corporation – meant that if BBC Wales's programmes were sold abroad, the service would gain no direct benefit.[70]

With the expansion of Radio Wales and Radio Cymru, there was a vast increase in Wales's radio output. In 1973–4, 1,625 hours of sound programmes for exclusive transmission in Wales were produced, a figure which had risen to 7,110 by 1981–2. The more than fourfold expansion in hours was accompanied by less than a fourfold increase in expenditure in absolute terms; bearing in mind the severe inflation of the period, the real increase was far smaller. Following the Annan Report, Head Office established separate Television and Radio Directorates, each of which channelled wholly distinct sums to Wales. Noting that the cost of radio programmes was on average a tenth of the cost of television programmes, Alwyn Roberts argued that 'a marginal saving in television could have a substantial effect on radio'. He wanted the BBC in Wales to have the ability to switch funds from one sector to another, part of his sustained campaign to give the BCW a degree of financial autonomy. Head Office was reluctant to agree, but 'as it admired the financial control of the BBC in Wales', it decided in 1976 to allow 5 per cent of the money Wales received to be spent on either radio or television.[71]

Until the mid 1970s, sound broadcasting in Wales conformed in general to the pattern which had been developed in the late 1930s. With the very marked expansion of output, there were considerable changes. In 1981–2, Radio Wales broadcast 3,760 hours of its own programmes and the equivalent figure for Radio Cymru was 3,344. (In that year, Wales also provided 116 hours for the network.) The transmissions of both services would have been far less numerous had the Musicians' Union not yielded on the matter of needle-time. Mike Flynn's daily programme (9.30 to 11.00 a.m.) consisted largely of record requests, and *Home Run* (4.30 to 5.58 p.m.) was a sequence of 'easy-to-listen music'. Radio Cymru also depended heavily on records, and the intrusion of song snippets on *Helo Bobol* was a cause of complaint from those who sought more nourishing fare. 'Phone-in' programmes – Radio Wales's *Helpline* and Radio Cymru's *Codi'r Ffôn*, for example – were inexpensive ways of filling airtime. Programmes such as *Alun yn Galw* – Alun Williams's telephone conversations with Welsh-speakers all over the globe – provided entertaining work for the researchers who increasingly thronged the corridors of Broadcasting House, but they were far less time-consuming than the well-crafted features of earlier years. Record and telephone programmes would have been impossible in the era of Hopkin Morris and Oldfield-Davies. Quizzes, such as Wyn Calvin's *Wyn or Lose* on Radio Wales and *Nabod y Teip* on Radio Cymru, would also have presented problems in that era, when every 'give-away' programme had to have the personal sanction of the director-general.

Yet, it is possible to exaggerate the lightweight nature of the output of the two expanded services. Both of them broadcast numerous live performances by the BBC Welsh Orchestra, and Radio Wales sought to reinvigorate the Welsh male-voice choir tradition by presenting elaborate choir competitions. Radio Cymru's *Talwrn y Beirdd* ('The Poets' Cockpit') and other poetry programmes were both stimulating and popular. Vincent Kane's discussion programme, *Meet for Lunch*, was considered superlative and the BCW formally minuted its appreciation of his work, the only occasion for it to pay such a tribute to an individual broadcaster. Among the best of Wales's productions were its Welsh-language programmes on natural history and gardening – *Seiat Holi'r Naturiaethwyr* and *Garddio*. One outstanding performer was Clay Jones, the only broadcaster speaking English with a Cardiganshire accent to win a following throughout the United Kingdom. The annual lecture, which had not stirred much interest since Saunders Lewis's celebrated contribution in 1962, experienced something of a revival in 1979 when Gwyn A. Williams asked *When was Wales?* He provided a Marxist answer, and among Welsh left-wingers his published lecture attained a status not unlike that of Mao's red book. It was intended that Radio Cymru should have a somewhat heavier programme content than Radio Wales 'to give scope to the BBC's only outlet in the Welsh language'. The degree to which the intention was carried out is not immediately apparent to a scrutinizer of the schedules. Radio Cymru certainly gave more attention to religion; on Sundays it provided four avowedly religious programmes and several others of a quasi-religious nature. Features were also more numerous on Radio Cymru, and in addition the service paid more attention to drama. In October–November 1981, for example, it broadcast a six-episode dramatization of Marion Eames's novel *I Hela Cnau*. Nevertheless, there was warm praise in 1980 for Radio Wales's *Aunty Nellie's Handbag*, a highly amusing drama series written and produced by Richard Thomas.[72]

Furthermore, much of the lighter radio output was presented with great panache. Alun Williams, who was involved with a wide variety of programmes in both languages, was considered to be 'an uniquely gifted broadcaster'. Gareth Glynne, a talented musician and a son of T. Glynne Davies, was praised as the presenter of the late-afternoon magazine programme *Post Prynhawn*. 'I am continually surprised', remarked Alwyn Roberts, 'at [his] ability to escape from convoluted sentence constructions.' Hywel Gwynfryn won increasing acclaim, at least for his work on radio. (His forays into television were considered to be less successful.) At the Cardigan National Eisteddfod in 1976, for example, his ability to conjure a programme out of impromptu comments and casual conversations was considered 'first-class'. Stanley Jones, however, feared that his 'North Wales patter was not having much impact in Llanelli', where Sulwyn Thomas, with his Carmarthenshire accent, found greater favour.[73] Complaints about the 'difficult Welsh' of Radio Cymru came frequently from eastern Carmarthenshire and western Glamorgan, where many Welsh-speakers were convinced that 'proper Welsh' was something that was spoken elsewhere, particularly in the north.

By the early 1980s, English and Welsh were not the only languages regularly included in Wales's sound broadcasting output. In December 1979, the BCW received a deputation from the Asian Society of Wales, calling for radio programmes in the languages of the Indian subcontinent. Radio Wales began transmitting a series in Hindi and Urdu in the autumn of 1980, drawing upon the advice of the Asian Programme Unit at Pebble Mill. It was a development particularly strongly supported by Mrs Betty Campbell, a member of the BCW from 1980 to 1984, and a leader of the black community in Cardiff's Butetown. Mrs Campbell was a fresh voice on the Council, raising issues relating to the portrayal of and participation by members of ethnic minorities. Such issues had not been raised before, except of course in the context of the Welsh who, while not an ethnic minority in Wales, certainly are where Britain in general is concerned. Mrs Campbell believed that the BBC could be racist and Alwyn Roberts, an advocate of positive discrimination, was not disposed to disagree with her. In 1982, a BBC2 programme on the employment of ethnic minorities came to the conclusion that the Corporation's record was poor. The record of the BBC in Wales was even poorer. 'I cannot', stated Wales's head of administration, 'recollect ever seeing an application from a member of a racial minority.'[74]

As with television, the central element in the BBC's sound broadcasting output was news and current affairs. Covering Wales continued to be difficult. The decline of the local press led to a decrease in the number of local correspondents. In 1976, Owen Roberts acknowledged that the BBC's news service had no contacts at all in Merthyr Tydfil, Aberdare and Ebbw Vale, and his successor, Arwel Ellis Owen, lamented that the coverage of mid Wales was woefully inadequate. A local staff reporter was appointed at Bangor, and in 1976 Sulwyn Thomas began his BBC career as Carmarthen's local reporter. Other local reporters were appointed in subsequent years, but the great gap was the valleys of the south Wales coalfield. They were believed to be near enough to Cardiff not to need resident correspondents, but that belief led to their neglect. 'The valleys', argued Alwyn Roberts, 'have a large indigenous Welsh population and are not adequately represented.' There were other problems too. In 1976 the secretary of state, objecting to a story about him on *Good Morning Wales*, reacted in a way which the NUJ interpreted as 'political interference with editorial processes'. BBC journalists, commented Stanley Jones, 'are particularly sensitive on this issue because of a tendency of the Information Division of the Welsh Office to regard the BBC in Wales as an arm of their operation'. In the dissemination of information, perhaps the most valued role of the BBC's Welsh broadcasting service was that which it played during emergencies. When large areas of Wales were flooded in 1979, the BBC became a clearing-house for information. Radio Wales and Radio Cymru were even more invaluable during the heavy snowstorms of 1982. With many telephones out of order, relations were contacted and emergency services alerted in a manner which won wide praise and gratitude. When the bad weather was at its worst, Radio Wales was receiving 18,000 calls a week.[75]

While the BBC was winning acclaim as the provider of a valuable community service, the Corporation was faced with a severe financial crisis. As a result, the programme hours of Radio Wales and Radio Cymru were curtailed in 1980–1 by five hours a week apiece. In the following decade, financial crises would be a recurring theme in the history of the BBC. During that decade, the Corporation would be subject to many other pressures and challenges. Not least among them was the need to react positively to the commitments it had made to Wales.

Postscript

Towards the Seventh Charter:
BBC Broadcasting in Wales since 1981

The sixth Charter, which came into force in August 1981, was granted for fifteen years. The constitutional position of the Corporation was therefore secure until 31 July 1996. Of all the periods in the history of the BBC, that since 1981 is the most difficult to assess. Furthermore, minutes, memoranda and correspondence, the essential material for the study of any institution, are far less available for the very recent past than they are for earlier years. Thus a detailed account of the history of BBC broadcasting in Wales in the 1980s and early 1990s must await a later historian. In the succeeding pages, little more will be done than to indicate what appear, from the vantage point of the mid 1990s, to be the most significant developments.

The chief agent of change was the pace of technological advance. Addressing the BCW in November 1980, Trethowan stated that 'cassettes, videotapes, teletext, cable and satellite would completely alter the structure of broadcasting in the next decade'. After visiting the United States in 1981, William Rees-Mogg, the vice-chairman of the Board of Governors, expressed his astonishment at the speed of change. A quarter of American households, he reported, had cable television, and 'if cable is developed here, the BBC's share is bound to diminish'. Prophecies of total transformation proved a little premature. Peter Jay, a former British ambassador to Washington and the founder of TV-AM, argued in the mid 1980s that in the new world that was soon to dawn 'programmes would pour out of fibre optic cables in the same way as books had poured from presses in the past'; in such a broadcasting environment, the BBC 'would be an absurdity and the proper business of the nation was to recognize its institutional redundancy'.[1] The Jay vision of the future has not materialized – at least not yet. Some forms of the new technology won rapid popularity. In the early 1980s 5 per cent of the households of the United Kingdom owned video cassette recorders (VCRs), a figure that had risen to 64 per cent by the early 1990s. VCRs were convenient for recording 'off air' programmes – an activity of doubtful legality – but they were mainly used for home viewing of films hired from the proliferating video shops; those who made a regular habit of hiring rapidly came to realize that the annual cost could far exceed the BBC's licence fee.

Cable and satellite television were slower to become established. The Hunt Report, published in September 1982, urged that Britain should be provided with multi-channel cable television as soon as possible. A Cable Authority responsible for up to thirty channels was envisaged; its service would be supplementary to the existing public service broadcasting and the Authority would be obliged to provide all the existing television networks. Legislation giving force to most of the Hunt recommendations was passed in July 1984. The Act also authorized direct broadcasting by satellite (DBS) and the satellite serving Britain was launched in 1989. The BBC was not over-enthusiastic about cable television, for it seemed unlikely that it would provide a universal service. In the United States where, by the late 1980s, cable was within the reach of 75 per cent of households, country-dwellers were almost wholly excluded. No commercial company, thought the BCW, would hasten to provide cable in rural Wales. The Corporation was far more interested in DBS, for a satellite signal could be received by any household equipped with the necessary dish. DBS also opened up the possibility that terrestrial transmitters would become unnecessary, thus relieving the BBC of the vast expense of building and maintaining them, and ensuring that even the remotest communities had full access to broadcasting. The system also allowed the BBC in Wales to receive material directly from other countries, and, through satellite news gathering, from any point in Wales. DBS cannot target a single state; the 'footprint' of Britain's satellite covers much of western Europe and the 'footprints' of the satellites of other European states cover most of Britain, thus creating the possibility that the bulk of the satellite television available in Britain would not be answerable to any British authority. Emyr Humphreys's prophecy in 1970 that 'Wales's problem today will be England's tomorrow' is likely to be fulfilled.[2]

The problems posed by DBS, in particular the technical system which should be adopted, absorbed much of the energies of the BBC's Board of Management in the mid and late 1980s. The costs were astronomical, and Alasdair Milne, who succeeded Ian Trethowan as director-general in August 1982, was obsessed by fears that a premature decision might drive the Corporation into bank-ruptcy. Rupert Murdoch launched his Sky Television in 1989, and expressed his willingness to lose billions of pounds in the early years. In 1986, the IBA had authorized a new company, British Satellite Broadcasting, to be responsible for three channels, one of which would broadcast the best of the output of the BBC and ITV, but in November 1990 financial problems forced the company to amalgamate with the Murdoch enterprise. By the mid 1990s, at least twenty satellite channels broadcasting in English were available in the United Kingdom; the BBC had some involvement with several of them, but the Corporation's hope of being the pioneer of the new technology was not realized. Take-up of cable television was slow, despite the government's anxiety to ensure that entertainment-led cable would usher in a new industrial revolution, with households plugged in to a vast array of interactive services. DBS proved more popular, particularly in Wales, and by the early 1990s several million British households had satellite dishes. As in the early years of radio, television and VCRs, the new development was scorned by the intellectual classes. In a *Sunday Times* profile of Mrs Major, the fact that her house in Huntingdon had a dish was noted in a paragraph heavy with contempt.[3]

The new technology did not immediately impinge upon the activities of the BBC in Wales. Yet, as the video vans plying their trade in the villages of Snowdonia and the dishes on the houses in the Rhondda testify, VCRs and DBS meant that, in seeking to attract Welsh viewers, the BBC had powerful new competitors – a factor of importance in assessing the viewing figures for the Corporation's output. The argument that the new technology made the BBC redundant proved to be far-fetched. As Alasdair Milne put it in 1988:

> The BBC was not conceived as a . . . demonstration laboratory for the electronically interconnected society . . . The new technology does not of itself generate the making of more programmes; it simply disseminates in different form what it can buy or find . . . Whatever fine programmes are made under other systems, the BBC is alone in having one purpose only – the making of programmes as good as we can achieve . . . You can widen viewer choice over four networks and narrow choice over forty.[4]

The challenge of the new technology was accompanied by a more insidious challenge – that of the politicians. Such hostility was no new phenomenon. 'At best', wrote Alwyn Roberts, 'the relationship between politicians and broadcasters has been one of armed neutrality with a bias towards belligerence.' In the 1970s, the attack had come from the left, with Tony Benn and his supporters, and centres devoted to media studies arguing that the BBC was an incorrigibly middle-class institution. While the Labour Party as a whole retained its belief in public service institutions and was faithful to its fundamentally liberal inheritance, the critics of the BBC included left-wingers who were contemptuous of liberal democracy. The right counter-attacked in the 1980s. 'Television man', Julian Critchley had written in 1970, 'is fundamentally on the Left, in a trendy if not in an ideological sense.' While Tory patricians such as William Whitelaw found 'it hard to understand what is supposed to be so wrong with our present arrangements', younger Conservatives of the radical right considered the Corporation to be guilty of a multitude of sins. Norman Tebbit, the chairman of the Conservative Party, conducted a sustained attack upon the BBC, showing particular venom towards Alan Protheroe, the assistant director-general. There were allegations that the Corporation was hostile to the enterprise culture, an accusation not without substance, for many of its producers considered the making of profits to be vulgar if not immoral. It was accused of being unpatriotic, perhaps even treasonable, and the accusers could point to its attempts to be evenhanded during the Falklands War in 1982 and the bombing of Libya in 1986.[5]

Above all, the BBC was perceived to be neutral with regard to anti-British terrorism in Northern Ireland. Since the early 1970s, reportage of the Ulster troubles had been central to controversy over the Corporation's coverage of current affairs. The issue erupted into a major crisis in 1985, when the BBC produced for its series *Real Lives* a programme called *At the Edge of the Union*, which gave the extremists on both sides an opportunity to explain themselves. The home secretary requested the governors not to broadcast the programme and, having seen it, they decided – with one exception – that it should not be transmitted. The exception was Alwyn Roberts, who argued that, as 'the terrorists condemned themselves out of their own mouths', the programme would inculcate revulsion towards terrorism rather than sympathy for it. Tamely to accede to a demand from the home secretary, he maintained, would seriously compromise the independence of the BBC. 'I came near to resignation on the matter,' he informed the BCW, a body which gave him full support.[6]

A further embarrassment for the BBC arose from libel actions arising from its programme *Maggie's Militant Tendency*, an examination of the extremists within the Conservative Party. The action cost the Corporation £500,000, and among those suing was Neil Hamilton, a Conservative MP and Aberystwyth graduate. Additional difficulties – this time from the other end of the political spectrum – sprang from an *Observer* article in August 1985 which alleged that MI5 routinely vetted those appointed to posts with the

BBC and that the vetting had the active connivance of the Corporation. The allegation was well-founded; where the External Services were concerned, the broadcasters themselves welcomed the vetting, 'for fear that the KGB would try to infiltrate the vernacular departments'. The practice, however, extended beyond the External Services, and Milne records that his neighbours were cross-examined about his background when he rejoined the BBC in 1967. Alwyn Roberts had queried vetting in 1980 but as it was a BBC tradition it continued, largely because of inertia. Among those mentioned in the *Observer* article was Paul Turner, a BBC Wales employee, who had had associations with the Communist Party. The BCW was informed that Turner's career 'had in no way been checked by the vetting'. He maintained and maintains otherwise, and his story is not unconvincing. The *Observer* article, noted Milne, 'had one good outcome; it reminded us to check the numbers involved and reduce them drastically. Far fewer are now vetted than were previously.'[7]

Milne was a man of many talents and great humanity, but his director-generalship proved to be increasingly accident-prone, and antagonism between him and the BBC Board of Management on the one hand, and the Board of Governors on the other, became very marked. By 1986, all the governors were appointees of the Thatcher administration and Alwyn Roberts, who had been given a two-year extension in 1984, was the only one among them whose views were left of centre. Milne had the highest respect for Roberts, regarding him as virtually his sole reliable ally among the governors. The director-general's misfortunes reached their climax in 1986, when a proposed programme on the Secret Service led to police raids on the BBC's offices in Glasgow. On 29 January 1987, Marmaduke Hussey, the chairman of the governors, informed Milne that his resignation was required immediately and that the governors were unanimous on the matter. The previous night Alwyn Roberts, whose period as Welsh governor had come to an end on 31 December 1986, had been given a farewell dinner at which he had spoken frankly about the dangers of the growing antagonism between the Board of Management and the Board of Governors. His departure determined the timing of Milne's dismissal, for Hussey deemed a unanimous decision to be essential, and unanimity would have been unlikely had Roberts still been a governor. Milne was succeeded by Michael Checkland, the first accountant to be director-general, and a man whose constructive guidance during the months leading up to the establishment of the Welsh fourth channel had caused him to be highly regarded by the BBC's Welsh management team. Alwyn Roberts was succeeded by John Parry, a Breconshire man who had been president of the British Veterinary Association and a very effective chairman of the Agricultural Advisory Committee of the BBC in Wales. Parry's term of office came to an end in 1991 and, in 1992, Gwyn Jones, previously the chairman of the Welsh Development Agency, became governor for Wales.[8]

The BBC's unpopularity with members of the government, and particularly with rank-and-file Conservative MPs, made the licence fee a matter of increasing controversy. In 1980 Ian Trethowan argued that, as nationalized utilities such as gas, electricity and the postal service were allowed to set their own charges, subject to the scrutiny of watchdog bodies, the BBC should have similar powers. It was a suggestion the government would not countenance, for apart from its right to appoint the governors, its control of the licence fee was its only way of bringing pressure to bear upon the Corporation. It did not need to exercise that control actively, for in a period of inflation the government could discipline the BBC simply by doing nothing. Mrs Thatcher was hostile to the fee, seeing it as a regressive tax – a poll tax, in fact. In 1981, it was set at £46 for colour sets and £15 for monochrome, among the lowest fees in western Europe, but reliance upon the continued growth in the acquisition of colour sets – a key factor in the finances of the BBC in the 1970s – was no longer an option, for in 1982 their acquisition peaked at 85 per cent. Between 1981 and 1985, when the income of the Corporation was virtually static, inflation was 16 per cent. At the same time, the income of ITV was increasing at around 20 per cent a year, allowing the IBA to plan a considerable expansion in hours of transmission. In calling for bids in 1980, the Authority offered a franchise for early morning television; it was won by Peter Jay's TV-AM. The BBC concluded that it could not offer a lesser service than ITV, and it launched its breakfast television on 17 January 1983, a fortnight before TV-AM began transmission. Again prompted by competition from ITV, the Corporation began an all-day service in 1986, with the budgets for the morning and afternoon programmes less than a sixth of those for programmes intended for peak-time viewing.[9]

The licence fee was due for renewal on 31 March 1985. In order to forestall any criticism of wastefulness, the BBC commissioned a firm of accountants to examine its operations. Its report, published in March 1985, identified possible savings of between 1 and 2 per cent but concluded that the licence fee was good value for money. The financial aspects of the BBC's operations in Wales were particularly well-managed. In 1980, when addressing the Commons Committee on Welsh Affairs, Trethowan paid tribute to Wales's fiscal probity, and in the early 1980s Head Office was impressed by Cardiff's ability regularly to match its expenditure with its budget. In 1983, it was pointed out that the BBC in Wales maintained two radio networks, produced its own English-language television pro-grammes, made contributions to the general British radio and television services, paid 80 to 85 per cent of the costs of the BBC Welsh Symphony Orchestra and provided half the Welsh-language output of S4C, all for the same amount of money as was expended upon the other half of the output of S4C.[10]

After a careful examination of its future needs, the Corporation concluded that in 1985 it would need an increase of £19 in the licence fee – from £46 to £65. Its meticulous presentation of its case made no impression upon the right-wing press. 'BBC blasted over bid for £65 licence,' declared the *Daily Express*. 'Attached to the bloated, overfed body of the BBC, a begging bowl is offensive. It is time Aunty's pathetic pantomime was stopped.' Answering the article, Milne wrote: 'I am tempted to ask why the *Daily Express* . . . is so expensive. Here's the BBC on air virtually round the clock, three hundred and sixty-five days a year, with all its services, at a cost of £46 a year, while the *Daily Express* (which doesn't publish on Sundays, Good Friday or Christmas Day) costs over £55 a year.' Much of the London 'quality' press was hardly more sympathetic. 'The government', wrote the Murdoch-owned *Times*, 'should concede no increase in the licence fee. It should consider quickly the establishment of a new broadcasting commission to auction franchises that are currently held by the BBC.'[11]

The government agreed to a licence fee of £58 and at the same time appointed a committee 'to assess the effects of the introduction of advertising or sponsorship on the BBC's Home Services, either as an alternative or a supplement to the income now received through the licence fee'. The committee, chaired by Professor Peacock, an ardent free marketeer, delivered its report in July 1986. It argued that the BBC should have the option of privatizing Radios One and Two and local radio, but rejected the notion that the BBC's services generally should accept advertising. It recommended that the licence fee should be linked to the Retail Price Index, a scheme which would distance the fee from political controversy but one which was likely to weaken the Corporation financially in view of the fact that broadcasting costs tended to rise more rapidly than prices in general. It also argued that, with satellite and cable channels proliferating, the consumer would eventually pay for the right to view the BBC's channels by subscription rather than by licence fee. The committee urged that ITV franchises should be put up for auction and that commercial television companies should be allowed to buy each other up. Peacock's most radical proposal was that over a ten-year period the BBC and ITV should be required to give independent producers access to 40 per cent of the total output. 'Our conclusion', stated the committee, 'is that British broadcasting should move towards a sophisticated market system based on consumer sovereignty.' To Alwyn Roberts, its report savoured of the verse by Swift, quoted in Thomas Love Peacock's *Headlong Hall*: 'All philosophers who find/ Some favourite system to their mind,/ In every point to make it fit/ Will force all nature to submit.'[12]

The government's Green and White Papers of 1987–8 and its Broadcasting Bill of December 1988 were strongly influenced by the Peacock Report. With some safeguards, the ITV franchises were to be offered to the highest bidder and provisions preventing the buying up of television companies were to be abolished. There was to be a vast expansion of commercial radio and the BBC was obliged to give up two of its sound frequencies. The Corporation, however, was to keep its existing sound and television services and to continue to be financed by the licence fee, at least until the expiration of the sixth Charter in 1996. The fee was to be linked to the Retail Price Index, but the Corporation was urged to find other sources of income. Compared with ITV, the BBC emerged relatively unscathed but the general tendency of the government's thinking caused the Corporation to feel apprehensive about the consequences of the coming discussion on what should happen to the BBC after the sixth Charter expired. The Broadcasting Bill of 1988 led to the Act of 1990 which required the BBC and ITV to ensure that within four years 25 per cent of their transmissions would be the work of independent companies. The implications were far-reaching, for fulfilling the obligation meant a marked reduction in the BBC's own output; that involved an equivalent reduction in the number of the Corporation's employees, partly because their services would no longer be needed, and partly because the outgoings represented by their salaries would have to be diverted to pay for programmes purchased from the independent companies. Other factors too were leading to a contraction in the Corporation's work-force. Faced with a fee settlement £7 lower than had been hoped for – every £1 increase in the fee represented over £18 million in additional income – Milne in May 1985 established a review body of four staff members charged with the duty of finding answers to the BBC's impending financial crisis. One of the four was Geraint Stanley Jones, controller Wales, and during the work of the review body he so impressed Head Office that in November 1985 he was transferred to London as the Corporation's director of public affairs, a post which included keeping a watching brief over the regions. The Director-General's Study Group (more commonly called 'the gang of four' or the 'black spot') urged that outside contractors should be asked to tender for the BBC's cleaning, catering, security and building maintenance operations and that their tenders should be accepted if they were lower than the cost of in-house services. Short-term contracts should be offered on a far larger scale, an option which had become realistic because, with the growth of the independent sector, there was a great increase in the number of free-lances. The competition represented by the independent sector, together with the Thatcher administration's determined attack upon trade union power, offered the opportunity, argued the review body, 'to tackle time-honoured operational practices' – a euphemism for the restrictive practices which were, in fact, far more prevalent in the commercial companies, particularly the main contractors, than they were in the BBC.[13]

Most of the suggestions of the review body were put into operation. Their implementation, and the implementation of many of the Peacock recommendations, meant that, in the mid 1980s, the total number of the BBC's direct employees peaked at 30,000 and the total number employed in Wales peaked at 1,500. In 1991, when the Gardner Merchant Company was granted the catering, security and cleaning contracts, Cardiff became the first major BBC centre drastically to slim down its in-house services. Other centres followed, a development which reduced the number on the Corporation's payroll by 5,000. Short-term contracts became the norm, causing the tradition of a lifelong career with the BBC to become a thing of the past. Experienced producers, engineers and cameramen applied for early retirement, delighted by the prospect of a late middle age cushioned by a pension and – they hoped – a constant stream of lucrative contracts. Trade-union influence rapidly declined; pressure from the ETU (later the Electrical Electronic Telecommunications Union), the NATTKE (the National Association of Theatrical, Television and Kine Employees) and the ABS (the traditionally less militant Association of Broadcasting Staff) was much reduced, and the Musicians' Union, Equity and the National Union of Journalists were shorn of much of their power.[14]

In the early 1990s, the drive for economy, and what was believed to be efficiency, was carried even further. A pattern of working associated in particular with John Birt, who became deputy director-general in 1987, director-general designate in July 1991 and director-general in December 1992 – although he was not on the Corporation's payroll in the first two capacities, nor, initially, in the third – included 'producer choice', introduced in October 1991. Under 'producer choice', the camera crew and the personnel needed by a producer could be hired either from within or from outside the Corporation, thus obliging BBC employees actively to compete with free-lances. The system also meant that the producer was an administrator as well as an artistic creator – the death blow to the rigid distinction between administrators and creators which Reith had introduced in 1933. A further aspect of 'producer choice' was the arrangement whereby internal supply departments were to be funded by selling their services to other departments and to outside bodies, an arrangement which came into operation in April 1993.

There were fears that the changes were eroding the ethos of the BBC. When Wynford Vaughan-Thomas joined the Corporation in 1936, he described the experience as being 'rather like becoming a novice in a Jesuit seminary'. By the late twentieth century, with so much toing and froing between the public and the commercial sectors, much of the feeling about the specialness of the BBC had disappeared, and Tom Burns noted that whereas the older generation talked about working for the BBC, younger colleagues talked of working at the BBC. It was a development which alarmed Alwyn Roberts: 'I am worried', he informed the BCW in 1983, 'at the apparent lack of commitment to the ideals of public service broadcasting on the part of many of the new generation of programme makers.'[15]

Roberts was far less concerned about a much more prevalent accusation against the BBC's younger generation of employees – that they were the purveyors of sex, violence and strong language. Curiously, it was strong language which aroused the greatest hostility. Kenneth Tynan's use of a four-letter word was a *cause célèbre*, and a broadcast expletive by Wales's industrial correspondent, Roy Roberts, uttered when he thought he was off the air, was widely commented upon. In 1983 Gwenlyn Parry's play, Y *Tŵr*, the first Welsh-language broadcast drama to contain some vigorous swearing, was angrily attacked. 'Somehow', remarked John Elfed Jones, 'strong language is more acceptable in English than in Welsh.' Wales's drama department doubted whether that was so. The original script of *The Mimosa Boys*, a drama concerning the Falklands War, contained 200 four-letter words; they were reduced to one. 'That is more reponsible probably', commented Gareth Price, 'but a great deal less realistic.' Mrs Whitehouse had established a south Wales branch of her organization in the 1960s, but its initial meeting was very sparsely attended and its subsequent activities amounted to little. Nevertheless there were many in Wales, particularly those with a Nonconformist background, who were unhappy about the strong language and the portrayal of sexual activities. They included some of the members of the BCW. 'Chris Stuart is in danger of becoming bawdy,' commented one; *Wastad ar y Tu Fas*, a play about homosexuality, should not have been broadcast mid evening, stated another, and several argued that *Conundrum*, a feature concerning James Morris's sex change, should never have been produced at all.[16]

The broadcast of gratuitous violence was a far more serious

matter. By the time an American was eighteen, it was estimated that he or she would have viewed 18,000 television murders, and it was difficult to deny that, for some at least, such an experience could not but result in a numbing of sensitivity. The BBC's output was tame indeed compared with what was available on video cassettes and from the satellite channels, and the nine o'clock threshold was supposed to ensure that the very young were not contaminated. Alwyn Roberts treated the matter somewhat nonchalantly. 'Japanese television,' he remarked, 'shows appalling scenes, but Japan is a very law-abiding society . . . Sex and violence were not invented by television. My own childhood in north Wales was dominated by systematic clashes with metropolitan evacuees.' The gruesome violence portrayed in the series *Bowen a'i Bartner* passed without comment. The BCW was more interested in the fact that J. W. Thomas (who played Bowen) 'is the first Welsh-speaking male actor with recognizable sex appeal'.[17]

There was some increase in the autonomy of the BBC in Wales in the early 1980s. In 1983, a new computer system allowed the devolution from London of all financial accounts, apart from matters relating to salaries. Head Office ceased to insist upon having a representative at appointments boards, thus for the first time permitting interviews to be conducted on occasion in Welsh.[18] Although much of the autonomy of the 'national regions' was undermined in the early 1990s, broadcasters in the English regions looked with envy at Cardiff, which by the mid 1980s was Britain's largest broadcasting centre outside London, a development the BCW had foreseen in its evidence to the Annan Committee.

The Welsh panel of the General Advisory Council, when selecting members of the BCW, took care to have a good geographical spread. That was not the case with the selectors of the BBC governors. 'Not a single member of the Board of Governors, apart from the National Governors,' noted Alwyn Roberts in 1984, 'lives north or west of Oxford.' On occasion, indeed, it was the national governors who spoke up for the interests of the greater part of England – that part which lies outside the 'home counties'.[19] There were grumbles, and in the late 1980s an attempt was made to advance their status to something closer to that of the 'national regions'. In 1987, the director-general established a Regional Directorate and Geraint Stanley Jones became managing director of regional broadcasting with a seat on the Board of Management. For the first time, the English regions had a clear structure and status. There was some unease in the 'national regions', for there were fears that the establishment of the directorate was an act of centralization rather than devolution.

The challenges facing the Corporation generally in the 1980s and early 1990s, and the tribulations it suffered, have been elaborated upon, for the history of the BBC in Wales is only intelligible in the context of the history of the BBC as a whole. That is particularly true where the main Welsh broadcasting innovation of the 1980s – the launching of the Welsh Fourth Channel (Sianel Pedwar Cymru – S4C) – is concerned. '[The Channel]', stated the S4C Authority in its evidence to the Peacock Committee, 'is wholly dependent upon the stability and balance of the wider British broadcasting system as a whole.' William Whitelaw's volte-face in September 1980 and the subsequent amendment to the Broadcasting Bill in November obliged the BBC's Welsh management to undertake a frenzy of activity. 'We are acutely aware', stated Owen Edwards in February 1981, 'of the shortage of time.'[20] The situation was complicated by the fact that he resigned as controller Wales on 31 April 1981 to become chief executive of S4C. Yet his change of office was also a bonus for the BBC, for it meant that the new service was headed by a man who was wholly conversant with the ways of the Corporation. Edwards was succeeded by Wales's head of programmes, Geraint Stanley Jones, whose previous post went to Gareth Price.

The first task of the BBC was to clarify its position in relation to the S4C Authority. The Broadcasting Act of 1980 gave the Authority wide powers, a far cry from the time when it was considered that a Welsh fourth channel would be jointly run by the BBC and HTV with the minimum of administrative structures. Neither the BBC nor the IBA had a statutory representative on the Authority, although its membership has consistently included the national governor for Wales. The Act of 1980 stipulated that the BBC was obliged 'to provide programmes to meet the reasonable requirements of the Authority', a statement open to several interpretations. It could mean that – at least where Welsh-language programmes were concerned – the BBC was nothing more than a facilities house, making programmes to the specification of the Authority, a situation the Corporation was determined to resist. It insisted upon having the right to decide what programmes it would supply and upon retaining full editorial control. S4C could refuse to broadcast a BBC programme but it could not instruct that alterations be made or undertake any alterations itself. The Corporation was particularly anxious that those of its staff involved with the programmes for the new service should not conceive of themselves as working for S4C rather than the BBC. It ruled that only controller Wales and the head of programmes should have contact with the staff of S4C, lest there should be 'a dividing of loyalties'.[21]

In its negotiations, the BBC was in a strong position for, unlike

HTV and the independent companies, it would not be charging S4C for its contributions. Since the establishment of BBC Wales in 1964, the Corporation had broadcast between six and seven hours of Welsh-language television programmes a week. Its initial commitment to S4C was ten hours, but it was persuaded by Goronwy Daniel, the chairman of the S4C Authority, to raise the hours to eleven. That meant an increase in its output of almost 70 per cent, and, as has been indicated already, the output would have to be more ambitious and therefore more expensive. Initially at least, all the Welsh-language programmes broadcast on S4C would be peak-time programmes. Alone among the broadcasting services of Britain, it would have no throw-away hours, although, inevitably, it would transmit many a throw-away programme. A 70 per cent increase in output, and that output of a higher quality, meant more than doubling the BBC's programme expenditure on the Welsh language. It also meant doubling the number of production and other staff involved with Welsh-language programmes. The doubling would have to happen very quickly if the deadline of autumn 1982 were to be met. In 1981, Whitelaw announced that in setting the new licence fee of £46, he had taken into account the increased cost to the BBC of its contribution to the Welsh fourth channel. Nevertheless, the Corporation was disturbed by the financial implications of the new service. The Welsh fourth channel, Milne informed the BCW in February 1981, 'potentially posed a huge financial problem for the BBC', and he asked the Council whether it would be prepared, at least temporarily, to switch money from its English productions in order to fund a stockpile of programmes for the new service. 'That', declared Owen Edwards, 'would be politically impossible.' 'It would be disastrous', argued Stanley Jones, 'if only Welsh-language programmes were produced by the BBC in Wales.' In April, the Board of Management informed the BCW that it could not support the spending of extra money in Wales 'when the BBC was surrendering fifteen hundred posts and when pay rises were below inflation'. 'Our position would be intolerable', replied the Council's members, 'if, after promoting this cause for so many years, the BBC were not able to provide on time the level of service specified by the government.'[22]

The money was found. Savings were made by sharply reducing the number of Welsh-language programmes in the run-up to the new service, a reduction which included the ending of the long-standing flagship programme, *Heddiw*. By the autumn of 1981, the main problem facing the planners of the new service was the negotiations with HTV over the content and costs of its contributions. Discussions, particularly over costs, proved protracted and on several occasions came near to breakdown. The BBC considered that it could produce its S4C contributions at an average expenditure of £20,000 an hour. HTV estimated that, for its contributions, it needed to be paid £35,000 an hour. With time desperately short, the S4C Authority was forced to accede to the commercial company's demands. There was a widespread feeling, both within and outside S4C, that in the early 1980s HTV took unfair advantage of the Authority's need to have a stockpile of programmes as soon as possible. When contracts came to be renegotiated in the late 1980s, S4C was determined not to be pressurized again, and that determination added to the problems which plagued HTV in the early 1990s. The Authority was increasingly able to look elsewhere for its programmes, because of the remarkable growth of independent Welsh-language television companies capable of producing output of high quality. William Aaron, a pioneer in the field, was asked in 1982 whether his small company was capable of making programmes as good as those of the BBC and HTV. 'We can produce much better ones,' he replied. 'I should know; I've worked for both the BBC and HTV.'[23]

Sianel Pedwar Cymru began broadcasting on All Saints' Day, 1 November 1982, one day before the launch of Channel Four – the equivalent service in England, Scotland and Northern Ireland. S4C was the first channel in the European Community with the primary duty of broadcasting in a 'lesser-used' language. Within two months it was followed by Euskal Telebista 1 (the Basque channel); Catalan and Galician channels were launched in 1983 and Canal 33 (the second Catalan service) and Canal Nou (the Valencian service) in 1989.[24]

'The preparations for S4C', Stanley Jones informed the BCW on 19 November, 'have been so heavy that there has not been time for anything else. It is a tremendous relief that it has started.' The increase in the BBC's Welsh-language output involved adding 350 employees to the Corporation's staff. 'In proportionate terms', noted the BCW, '[the development] is one of the largest ever undertaken by any part of the BBC.' The increase also placed grave pressure upon the space available at Llandaf. The Gabalfa site proved useful but the accommodation problems of the BBC in Wales were not eased until 1986 when University College, Cardiff, sold to the Corporation the buildings previously occupied by the School of Home Economics. They lay across the road from Cardiff's Broadcasting House and were given the name Tŷ Oldfield in honour of Alun Oldfield-Davies. In 1989, the Gabalfa site was given up, and all the BBC's Cardiff operations were concentrated on one side or the other of Llantrisant Road. Developments at Bangor, where a well-equipped television block was opened in 1990, also proved helpful, as did the small television installation which became available at Swansea in 1988.[25]

Initially S4C was on the air for seventy hours a week, twenty-two of which were in Welsh. The rest of the hours were devoted to a selection of the output of Channel Four. By a judicious arrangement of the scheduling, all Channel Four's more interesting programmes could be made available to the viewers of S4C. Furthermore, in the most densely populated areas of Wales, Channel Four itself was available from transmitters in England. Jeremy Isaacs, the chief executive of Channel Four, was concerned that the two channels

> could easily have been at loggerheads from the word go. [S4C], after all, prevented us from reaching into all Wales. [It] laid claims to funds which would otherwise be ours and of which we might yet stand in need . . . S4C's function was quite different from ours. We had to cater for interests the mainstream channels ignored. They were to *be* a mainstream channel, but in Welsh . . . Yet it seemed to me . . . that . . . there was much, much more to unite us than to divide us . . . Good relations between us were never ruffled.[26]

In S4C's first two months, 45 per cent of its Welsh-language transmissions were provided by the BBC, 36 per cent by HTV and 19 per cent by the independent producers. Of those receiving the highest ratings, the BBC was responsible for 60 per cent, the independent producers for 22 per cent and HTV for 18 per cent. 'This leaves HTV trailing', commented Alwyn Roberts, but he added kindly: 'Things will be better for them when their new headquarters at Culverhouse Cross is completed.' In the early months, viewing figures indicated that *Pobol y Cwm* and *Newyddion Saith* (the 7.00 p.m. news) were watched by up to 150,000 people. Compared with the mass audiences of the most popular programmes of BBC1 and ITV1, such a figure seemed derisory; ratings of the most widely watched programmes of all the television services of Britain were published weekly in *The Times* and the S4C figures provided Bernard Levin with material for several abusive articles. Yet the figure of 150,000 people represents 30 per cent of Wales's Welsh-speaking population. As Robert Silvey, the BBC's pioneer in audience research, put it: 'There is no virtue in size *per se*; all that matters is whether a broadcast attracts the audience which it is reasonable to expect of it.' In those terms, S4C was doing very well indeed. It was far more successful than was Channel Four in its early days. Initially, Channel Four attracted 6 per cent of British viewers, a figure which soon dwindled to 3 per cent. Its output was attacked as violent, iconoclastic, smutty, subversive and obscurantist. 'I was accused', wrote William Whitelaw, 'of letting the loonies on the air.' The BCW minuted in January 1983: 'S4C has established beyond doubt the appeal of a Welsh-language television service to its target audience, in stark contrast with the problems being faced by Channel Four.'[27]

Over the succeeding years, the popularity of Channel Four increased markedly and, by the 1990s, its viewers had grown to such an extent that its financial safety net was operating against it. Channel Four was secure, for unlike the ITV companies it did not have a franchise contract which could be withdrawn. S4C was not secure, for originally it had been set up for a trial period of three years. As 1985 approached, the members of the BCW became increasingly concerned about the numbers viewing the channel, for they were aware that the decision whether or not it should continue hinged upon its viewing figures. The figures presented difficulties. Television sets in two hundred of the households of Wales were equipped with meters installed by the Broadcasters' Audience Research Board (BARB), but only a minority of the households contained a Welsh-speaking family – itself an entity difficult to define. With so small a sample, the figure could be wrong to the extent of 50,000 either way. 'If 80,000', commented Glanville Price, one of the members of the BCW, 'can mean 30,000 or 130,000, what is the point of collecting the figures?' S4C conducted its own survey and discovered that 53 per cent of Welsh-speakers regularly viewed the channel. Furthermore, at least a third of those watching its Welsh-language transmissions did not consider themselves to be Welsh-speaking; indeed, where old favourites such as *Dechrau Canu, Dechrau Canmol* were concerned, up to half the viewers saw themselves as being outside the Welsh-speaking community. The S4C survey ignored viewers outside Wales. They were not negligible; by the late 1980s, some of the channel's programmes, especially *Sgorio* – a round-up of the European sports scene based on material supplied by Barcelona's Catalan service – had a large English following, particularly on Merseyside.[28]

The S4C survey, anecdotal evidence and the government's reluctance to reopen an issue which had caused it severe embarrassment, led Leon Brittan, the home secretary from 1983 to 1985, to be sympathetic towards the continuance of the Channel. S4C mounted an exhibition at Westminster in November 1984, when the BCW was told that 'the forthcoming review of S4C is unlikely to be a real threat to its existence'. The review was launched in 1985, with Alwyn Roberts successfully advocating that the views of the political parties and of individuals should be sought. 'They are likely to be overwhelmingly supportive,' he stated. Indeed they were, and in November 1985 the Home Office announced that S4C was to be a permanent part of the broadcasting services of the United Kingdom. 'The channel', wrote William Whitelaw in 1989, 'has been a great success.' 'S4C', stated Jeremy Isaacs, '. . . is one of the most remarkable living cultural phenomena of our time. It is a mark of generosity in the political practice of the United Kingdom that there should be a general will to preserve and maintain it for the future.'[29]

The BBC's senior Welsh officials were not uncritical of the way S4C developed. Their hope that the Corporation's output would be broadcast in continuous blocks was frustrated, and the interleaving of its programmes with those of HTV and the independent production companies made it difficult for them to stand out as BBC productions. S4C did not want them to stand out and it applied annually to the Corporation to reduce its identification captions. The BBC particularly disliked a clause in the Broadcasting Act of 1990 which removed restrictions upon the transmission of commercial breaks before, during and after Corporation productions broadcast on S4C. It was felt that BBC programmes suffered because of what were considered to be S4C's poor presentation methods, but the Corporation was powerless to change them. The new service constantly sought to expand its Welsh-language transmissions; by the mid 1990s, they had increased to thirty-five hours a week and the consequent strain upon the resources of the BBC was considerable. S4C, with over eighty employees, felt itself to be a powerful, independent concern, and on occasion its officials commented publicly on the relative quality of the programmes it received from its three sources of supply. 'The BBC', Stanley Jones informed the BCW, 'has been meticulous in avoiding any public criticism of S4C . . . but this restraint cannot be maintained for ever.'[30]

Yet the overall feeling was one of pride. During a Board of Governors meeting in the Highlands of Scotland, Alwyn Roberts discovered that 'there is a great deal of informed interest there in the recent developments in Welsh-language broadcasting'. Controller Scotland is reputed to have said: 'Would that we had academics who climbed masts.' Wales became the model for those seeking an improved Gaelic television service, and BBC Scotland's successful Gaelic serial, *Machair*, was closely modelled on Wales's *Pobol y Cwm*. There was particular pride in the BBC's Welsh-language news service, especially its coverage of international events. Cardiff had to set up its own system of news-gathering, a novel development, for never before had a British broadcasting centre outside London been involved in collating international news. There were fears that a news service run by Welsh-speakers – many of whom had Nationalist sympathies – would be accused of bias towards Plaid Cymru and, indeed, one member of the BCW believed that he could detect a sneer on the face of the talented broadcaster, Beti George, when she mentioned Mrs Thatcher's name.[31] The issue of Nationalist bias had been extensively aired at the hearings of the Commons Select Committee on Welsh Affairs in December 1980. In the 1980s and early 1990s, attacks were far less virulent although one or two MPs continued to show a dogged interest in the matter. It was decided that the BBC should supply S4C's news bulletins and HTV its current affairs programmes, an arrangement which resulted in part from ITN's refusal to provide international material unless it was allowed to retain editorial and production control. HTV's reportage for the new channel was considered to be bolder than that of the BBC. To some extent, that might be explained by the fact that the company's collective memory did not include the trauma of the David Llewellyn inquiry. A more likely explanation, however, is that current affairs programmes offer broadcasters more stimulating challenges than do the preparation of news bulletins.

The employment opportunities provided by the BBC as a result of the establishment of S4C meant that able Welsh-speaking graduates were disproportionately drawn to broadcasting, causing worries that other, more traditional, callings – teaching in particular – would suffer. The expansion of the BBC, and the concomitant expansion of HTV and of the independent companies, created a new social phenomenon. Never before had there been a fairly numerous group of people, mainly young, employed in a well-paid, glamorous profession and working through the medium of Welsh. The 'Cuppies' (the Welsh-speaking Yuppies) came into existence almost exclusively because of media expansion and their life-style was the subject of envy and much head-shaking. (Oldfield-Davies's suggested name for Llandaf's Broadcasting House may well have been prescient.)

The development was mainly centred upon Cardiff, but Gwynedd too had its 'Cuppies', particularly among those employed in the independent production companies. By 1988, 25 per cent of such employees lived in and around Caernarfon, a town which benefited by £6 million a year from their expenditure. The investment by the companies of millions of pounds in the Barcud studios and facilities centre at Caernarfon was a very striking sign of confidence in the future of broadcasting in Wales. 'S4C's most remarkable achievement', wrote Jeremy Isaacs, 'was to bring into being in Wales an independent production sector of programme-makers working on film and video, and in Welsh. In doing so it overcame the scepticism of all those who doubted that there could ever be an alternative to the conventional broadcasting institutions as purveyors of programming.' 'The independents', noted Clare Hudson, 'argued that [the new arrangements] gave . . . much better value for money.' 'There is something strange', she continued, 'in the spectacle of a largely radical, critical body of Welsh independent producers making common cause with the Thatcherite vision of a cost-effective future.'[32]

The architect of S4C, Owen Edwards, retired in 1989. Among the Channel's boldest ventures during his term of office was the decision to turn *Pobol y Cwm* – the Corporation's most long-lived soap opera – into a daily serial, with much of the action being produced on the day it was broadcast. The initiator of the venture was Teleri Bevan who became deputy head of programmes in 1981; it was widely considered to be an incredibly foolhardy step, but when the daily serial was launched on 5 September 1988, it proved to be highly successful. Owen Edwards was succeeded at S4C by Geraint Stanley Jones, a man who was particularly eager that Wales should reach out beyond England when searching for and when providing broadcasting material. He was instrumental in expanding Mentrau, the sales arm of S4C, which by the 1990s was selling programmes to over fifty countries. *Pobol y Cwm*, for example, was screened with Dutch subtitles on Netherlands television in 1991, although the experiment proved short-lived. The Channel's success in selling animated programmes was particularly striking, a development which caused Cardiff to become one of Europe's chief centres for the production of such programmes. Stanley Jones's term of office came to an end in 1994, when the post went to Huw Jones, the first head of any British broadcasting service to have come to the top through the independent production company sector.

By the mid 1990s, S4C was so much an established fact that – as had been the case earlier with Radio Cymru – it was difficult to imagine Wales without it. The expansion of subtitles on Ceefax allowed the Channel to gain viewers well beyond the Welsh-language community. In week 5 of 1994, an episode of *Pobol y Cwm* attracted 350,000 viewers.[33] Referring to the soap opera's rapist, a girl on the Newport–Chepstow train cried: 'I couldn't believe it was Barry John.' 'Join me for a pint tonight,' said a young man in Flint. 'Before or after *Sgorio*,' replied his friend. After the years of antagonism and bitterness, such eavesdroppings are a delight indeed.

The establishment of S4C could not but have a marked impact upon Wales's English-language television output. During the BCW's discussion in October 1980 of the proposed amendment to the Broadcasting Bill, the Council stressed that the government's change of mind meant that 'for the first time, Wales could have a proper television service for non-Welsh-speakers'. There was evidence that most viewers would be content if the hours on BBC Wales previously filled with Welsh-language programmes were given over to the network output, but the BCW was determined that as many as possible of them should be devoted to Welsh programmes in English. The Welsh MPs agreed. At the Commons Select Committee on Welsh Affairs in December 1980, they demanded a substantial increase in Wales's English-language output, accompanied by enhanced employment opportunities for their non-Welsh-speaking constituents. Stanley Jones felt strongly on the matter. 'S4C', he informed the BCW, 'should be beneficial to both linguistic groups.' He warned the Council, however, 'that this view is not fully accepted centrally in the BBC'. Providing money for Welsh-language programmes, argued Head Office, was one thing, for such programmes were unique. Advancing additional money to Wales for English-language programmes was quite another matter. That would arouse the antagonism of the English regions which had suffered disproportionately as a result of the cuts imposed during the Corporation's financial crisis of 1979.[34]

Initially the BCW sought an extra hour in English a week, at an annual cost of almost a million pounds. Head Office was unenthusiastic, but it did provide money for the relaunch of BBC Wales as an exclusively English-language service. The relaunch, which occurred at the same time as the opening of S4C, was marked by the broadcast of the first of the Tom Jones programmes which had been acquired in 1982. BBC Cymru/Wales was renamed BBC Wales, for it was felt that the service needed a wholly English title to stress its wholly English content. It was again renamed in 1984, when it became BBC1 Wales, a change which allowed BBC2 to become BBC2 Wales. Welsh opt-outs on BBC2 were intended to be somewhat 'heavier'. They included, for example, *Wales! Wales?*, Dai Smith's personal and stimulating interpretation of modern Welsh history. Cardiff also began contributing a twelve-minute slot to the BBC's breakfast television service.[35]

The results of these developments were heartening. In 1983, a survey showed that only 16 per cent of the inhabitants of Wales made no use at all of the services broadcast by the transmitters sited on Welsh soil. Sales of the Wales edition of the *Radio Times* leapt up; by 1985, 120,000 copies a week were sold, which meant that its circulation in Wales was far higher than the circulations of the North and West editions. The Broadcasting Act of 1990, however, created an open market in programme listings, and brasher, cheaper magazines became available which listed all the broadcasting services in Britain. Sales of the *Radio Times* as a whole slumped and on 31 August 1991 the Wales edition was merged with that of the West, a change which followed the sad demise of *The Listener* six months earlier.[36]

The need for additional resources to increase the English-language productions of the BBC in Wales is the theme which recurs most frequently in the annual reports of the BCW in the late 1980s and the early 1990s. By 1994, Wales's weekly television broadcasts in English had risen to 10.25 hours, 7.75 of which were transmitted on BBC1 Wales and 2.5 on BBC2 Wales. In addition, HTV was responsible for between nine and eleven hours a week of English programmes for transmission exclusively in Wales. Thus, by 1994, television specifically intended for viewers in Wales amounted to about twenty hours a week in English and thirty-five in Welsh. At both the BBC and HTV, much of the time given over to Welsh productions in English was devoted to news bulletins. Where non-news programmes were concerned, the difference between the output in English and that in Welsh was very marked indeed. The difference was a matter of deep concern to spokesmen of English-speaking Wales such as Dai Smith, Gwyn A. Williams and the distinguished film producer, Karl Francis, and there were the beginnings of an agitation in favour of an English-language television channel for Wales.[37]

Expensive programmes in English for exclusive transmission in Wales were beyond the means of the Corporation. That meant that plays in particular could only be produced if they were transmitted on the entire British network. Those acceptable to Head Office included *District Nurse*, a sentimental serial set in the 1930s, and two plays concerning the Falklands War – *The Mimosa Boys* and *Bluff Cove*. Unlike BBC broadcasters in Scotland, whose demands that their productions should be transmitted on the network became almost frenetic in the 1970s and 1980s, BBC broadcasters in Wales were more concerned to supply their own home audience. 'Within the United Kingdom', argued Owen Edwards in a BBC lunch-time lecture in 1976, 'the effectiveness with which nation shall speak unto nation depends upon the extent to which nation can adequately discharge its prime function and its privilege of properly speaking to itself.' 'We are of interest to others', wrote Dai Smith in 1993, 'the more we interest ourselves.' There was general regret in Welsh broadcasting circles, however, that the most splendid television drama of the 1980s set in Wales – *Morgan's Boy*, a poignant portrayal of life in the Black Mountains – was the work of BBC2. *Penyberth*, a Welsh-language dramatization of the Bombing School episode of 1936, was transmitted on the BBC2 network with subtitles in 1985. It won warm praise, but when it was shown on BBC1 Wales there were vigorous protests against what was seen as the re-invasion by Welsh of an English-only channel. 'Some of the old venom is still there,' noted Stanley Jones sadly.[38]

The BBC's great worry was that HTV would invest heavily in English-language drama for exclusive transmission in Wales. 'They have the resources to do so', noted the BCW, 'and if they do, BBC Wales would not be able to compete.'[39] By the early 1990s, however, it was HTV which was unable to compete. The Peacock Report's recommendation that television franchises should be put out to tender was included in the Broadcasting Act of 1990. HTV was obliged to pay £20.53 million a year for its right to broadcast, a painful contrast with the £2,000 paid by STV. The burden of the bid payments, the recession, some injudicious investments by the company and the contraction in the number of programmes it supplied to S4C caused severe financial embarrassment for HTV, and for a period in the 1990s it was largely ineffective as a competitor with the BBC. (Admittedly, its shares rose in 1993–4 from 13p to 161p and, as a result, the pubs of Pontcanna – Cardiff's media suburb – were loud with the lamentations of those whose suspicion of the Stock Exchange had robbed them of the opportunity of clearing their mortgages.)

While television took by far the largest share of the resources available to the BBC in Wales, its radio output was much greater. A week before the launching of S4C, Radio Wales transmissions were increased by between two and three hours a day. In January 1985, the service filled its final daytime gap by occupying the period 1.15 to 2.00 p.m. It was therefore on the air continuously from 6.00 a.m. to 6.00 p.m. In the main, the style of Radio Wales continued to be based upon that of Radio Two, although there were attempts to introduce some heavier material; in the spring of 1985, for example, it broadcast six plays by new Welsh playwrights, 'the first major English-language radio drama series to be produced for many years'. Its audience continued to grow and in 1994 525,000 of the inhabitants of Wales were regular listeners to Radio Wales. Regional opt-outs, on which great hopes had been pinned, proved to be a disappointment. The Clwyd opt-outs won some additional listeners to Radio Wales, but those in Gwent, which began in 1985, failed to find an audience, despite the fact that Red Dragon Radio – an amalgam of CBC and the Gwent commercial station – had a considerable following in the former county of Monmouthshire. The Gwent opt-outs came to an end on 12 April 1991, and thereafter the BBC's Welsh management team was disinclined to plan other opt-out ventures.[40] On ceasing to be editor of Radio Wales in 1981, Teleri Bevan was succeeded by Robin Atkins; the post went to Megan Stuart in 1987, to Gaynor Vaughan Jones in 1991 and to Dai Smith in 1993. Smith's appointment was particularly imaginative; a distinguished historian and intellectual, he had emerged as the most articulate spokesman of English-speaking Wales, although there were Welsh-speakers who felt threatened by some of his opinions.

By the late 1980s, radio programmes produced in Wales were not only much more numerous than ever before, they were also of a better sound quality. Stereophonic sound had been provided at Wenvoe since 1974. It was extended to Blaenplwyf and Haverfordwest in 1983 and to the transmitters serving north Wales in 1985. In 1990, the BBC launched a fifth network radio station. Radio Five, a news, sports and education service, brought the number of the BBC radio services available throughout the United Kingdom to six, for there was good reception of the World Service as well as of the five domestic services. Scotland and Northern Ireland had seven services, but Wales topped everywhere else by having eight.

The additional service was, of course, Radio Cymru. Whereas Radio Wales became a continuous twelve-hour service in 1985, that was not possible on Radio Cymru because its frequency carried schools programmes. In 1987, it ceased to carry them in the morning, thus permitting a continuous Welsh-language service from 7 a.m. to 2 p.m. Some contributions to the 90-minute afternoon sequence of schools programmes were in Welsh, but there were a number in English and they were deemed to impede the flow of the Welsh-language service. In 1993 the sequence was reduced to thirty minutes and to contributions in Welsh only, thus allowing Radio Cymru to offer a full daytime service throughout the year. The original plans had not envisaged that there should be much in the way of an evening service on Radio Cymru. The matter was reconsidered following the launching of S4C. As the Channel's Welsh-language output almost always came to an end by 9.30 p.m., Radio Cymru could be dovetailed into the new service by broadcasting in the late evening. The additional programmes, mainly updates of the news and pop music for young people, meant that there was a broadcasting service in Welsh, on either radio or television, from 6.00 a.m. to 11.00 p.m. With the distribution of the Welsh-speaking population so very different from that of the population as a whole, surveying the audience of Radio Cymru proved as difficult as did measuring the viewing figures of S4C. The BCW was surprised to discover in 1984 that, when interviews were conducted in homes rather than on the street, the viewing figures for Radio Cymru increased by 50 per cent. In 1994, audience research indicated that the daily reach of Radio Cymru (the number of people over fifteen years of age listening to the service for more than five consecutive minutes in any given day) was 122,000, although there are some doubts about the reliability of the figure.[41] Initially, the service was the responsibility of Meirion Edwards. He became head of radio in 1987, with responsibility for both services, but left for the private sector in 1991. He was replaced as editor of Radio Cymru by Lyn Jones.

The movement of staff became increasingly characteristic of the Corporation in the later decades of the twentieth century. By the 1990s, Oldfield-Davies's twenty-two years as controller Wales seemed to be part of a vanished, more stable past. George Salter, a key figure in the BBC's Welsh operations in the 1970s, left to work for the IBA in 1981 and his post as head of programme services and engineering went to John Corbett. When Stanley Jones became the BBC's director of public affairs in 1985, he was succeeded by Gareth Price, with Teleri Bevan as head of programmes. Price left to become the Thomson Foundation's controller of broadcasting in April 1990; after an interregnum under Teleri Bevan, the controllership passed in September to Geraint Talfan Davies, the director of programmes at Tyne-Tees Television and a former assistant director of programmes at HTV.

Talfan Davies was the first head of the BBC in Wales since Hopkin Morris not to have been previously employed by the Corporation. Yet, as the son of Aneirin Talfan Davies, the BBC was hardly unfamiliar to him. 'I grew up with the BBC,' he wrote in 1990, '[but] I have never worked for the Corporation . . . I [went] off into newspapers to avoid the tediously predictable charge of nepotism.' On his appointment, Talfan Davies was immediately faced with the problems arising from the inadequacy of the licence fee. He brought in a firm of management consultants and their recommendations led to savings of £2.8 million a year and the loss of 147 posts.[42] There was considerable ill-feeling at Llandaf and elsewhere, but among Talfan Davies's changes there were some which were warmly welcomed. Among them was his decision to carry out a version of the scheme which had been suggested by John Rowley in 1972. He secured the appointment of two heads of programmes. In 1991, Michael Chaplin took charge of BBC Wales's output in English and Gwynn Pritchard took charge of its output in Welsh.

The consolidation of the changes introduced by Talfan Davies coincided with the seventieth anniversary of BBC broadcasting in Wales, the occasion of several celebratory programmes. There was much to celebrate, in particular the remarkable development of radio and television in the Welsh language. 'The success of programming in the Welsh language', wrote Stanley Jones, 'has been one of the broadcasting miracles of the late twentieth century. For just over half a million people to be able to sustain a complex radio and television service in their historically buffeted language is a creative, political and economic achievement of some magnitude.'

There are those who would argue that the achievement was made possible by the diversion of resources which could otherwise have been used to provide broadcasts intelligible to the population of Wales as a whole. Yet there have been significant developments in the Welsh output in English also, and it is probable that, had Wales not had the energizing factor represented by the Welsh language, its status within the BBC would resemble that of an English region. As Jeremy Isaacs put it: 'The language had a life force within it that could not be denied.'[43]

Huw Wheldon – 'without question the greatest broadcasting figure to have come from Wales', as the BCW described him – looked upon the British Broadcasting Corporation as 'one of the jewels of western civilization'. Alastair Hetherington defined it more prosaically as 'this benign machine'.[44] After a very shaky start, the BBC has treated Wales with benignity – with particular benignity in more recent years. With the whole concept of public service broadcasting now coming under attack, it surely behoves the Welsh to regard the BBC with benignity. The story of BBC broadcasting in Wales is the most remarkable example in Welsh history of the playing of the patriot game. The game was lost; and the game was won. And it will have to be won again.

Appendix 1

A. *Chairmen of the Board of Governors of the BBC*

Earl of Clarendon	1927–1930
J. H. Whitley	1930–1935
Viscount Bridgeman	1935
R.C. Norman	1935–1939
Allan Powell	1939–1946
Lord Inman	1947
Lord Simon of Wythenshawe	1947–1952
Alexander Cadogan	1952–1957
Arthur fforde	1958–1964
James Duff	1964
Lord Normanbrook	1964–1967
Lord Hill of Luton	1967–1972
Michael Swann	1973–1980
George Howard	1980–1983
Stuart Young	1983–1986
Marmaduke Hussey	1987–

B. *Directors-General of the BBC*

John Reith	1927–1938
F. W. Ogilvie	1938–1941
R. W. Foot C. Graves } joint Directors-General	1942–1943
R. W. Foot	1943–1944
William Haley	1944–1952
Ian Jacob	1952–1959
H. Carleton Greene	1960–1969
Charles Curran	1969–1977
Ian Trethowan	1977–1982

Appendix

Alasdair Milne	1982–1987
Michael Checkland	1987–1992
John Birt	1992–

C. *National Governors for Wales*

Lord Macdonald of Gwaenysgor	1952–1960
Rachel Jones	1960–1965
Glanmor Williams	1965–1971
Glyn Tegai Hughes	1971–1979
Alwyn Roberts	1979–1986
John Parry	1987–1991
Gwyn Jones	1992 –

D. *The Heads of BBC Broadcasting in Wales*

Rex Palmer 1923
Frederick Roberts 1923
Rex Palmer 1923 } Cardiff Station Directors
Cecil Lewis 1923
Arthur Corbett-Smith 1923–1924

Ernest Robert Appleton 1923–1936 — Cardiff Station Director until 1929
West Regional Director 1929–1935
The Welsh and the West of England Regional Director 1935–1936

Rhys Hopkin Morris 1936–1945 — Welsh Regional Director 1936–1939
Welsh Director 1939–1945

Alun Oldfield-Davies 1945–1967 — Welsh Director 1945–1948
Controller Wales 1948–1967

John Rowley 1967–1974
Owen Edwards 1974–1981
Geraint Stanley Jones 1981–1985 } Controllers Wales
Gareth Price 1985–1990
Teleri Bevan 1990 – Acting Controller
Geraint Talfan Davies 1990–

Appendix 2

Some significant dates in the history of broadcasting in Wales:

18 October 1922	Inauguration of the British Broadcasting Company
14 December 1922	John Reith is appointed manager of the Company
13 February 1923	Cardiff station (5WA) is brought into service
1 March 1923	First broadcast talk in the Welsh language
28 September 1923	Publication of the first issue of *Radio Times*
17 March 1924	Cardiff station moves to Park Place
12 December 1924	Swansea relay station (5SX) is brought into service
22 February 1925	First broadcast of a Welsh-language religious service
27 July 1925	Opening at Daventry of the BBC's first long-wave transmitter
1 January 1927	Inauguration of the British Broadcasting Corporation under the first Charter
12 May 1928	First broadcast by the National Orchestra of Wales
30 May 1928	First meeting between Reith and representatives of the University of Wales
16 January 1929	Publication of the first issue of *The Listener*
4 February 1929	The Cardiff station director becomes the director of the West Region
2 May 1932	Broadcasting House in Portland Place, London, becomes the headquarters of the BBC
28 May 1933	The West transmitter at Washford comes into service
1 January 1934	Broadcast of the first Welsh-language news bulletin

7 October 1934	Daventry (5XX) is superseded by Droitwich
31 July 1935	A half of the households of Wales are licensed to receive radio broadcasts
4 September 1935	First use of the term 'Welsh Region'
1 November 1935	Opening of the BBC studios at Bangor
8 November 1935	First broadcast from Bangor
14 March 1936	First broadcast of *Noson Lawen*
1 September 1936	Appointment of a separate director for the Welsh Region
2 November 1936	Inauguration of London's television service
1 January 1937	The BBC receives its second Charter
1 February 1937	Opening of the Penmon transmitter
4 July 1937	The Welsh Region begins broadcasting on its own wavelength
1 October 1937	Opening of the Swansea studios in Alexandra Road
19 July 1938	First broadcast of *Welsh Rarebit*
2 September 1939	The National and Regional Services are replaced by the unified Home Service
7 January 1940	Launching of the Forces Programme
21 February 1941	The BBC studios at Swansea are destroyed in a bombing raid
27 July 1945	First issue of the Welsh edition of the *Radio Times*
29 July 1945	Inauguration of the Light Programme and of the Regional Home Services (including the Welsh Home Service)
7 June 1946	Resumption of the television service in London
29 September 1946	Inauguration of the Third Programme
1 January 1947	The BBC receives its third Charter
13 February 1947	First meeting of the BBC's Welsh Advisory Council
17 December 1949	Sutton Coldfield television station is brought into service
18 January 1951	Publication of the Beveridge Report
12 October 1951	Holme Moss television station is brought into service
1 May 1952	Reopening of the BBC's Swansea Studios in Alexandra Road
1 July 1952	The BBC receives its fourth Charter
15 August 1952	Wenvoe television station is brought into service
6 January 1953	First meeting of the Broadcasting Council for Wales

1	March 1953	First broadcast of a Welsh-language television programme
2	May 1955	First VHF broadcasting station brought into service at Wrotham
27	July 1955	Postmaster-general bans regional party political broadcasts
22	September 1955	Inauguration of London's ITV service
2	October 1955	Temporary VHF station at Penmon brought into service
20	December 1955	Welsh Home Service becomes available on VHF from Wenvoe
30	January 1956	Debate in the House of Commons on bias in the Welsh Home Service
12	February 1956	Inauguration of Birmingham's ITV service
3	May 1956	Inauguration of Manchester's ITV service
6	December 1956	Publication of the Ince Report
19	December 1957	Launching of Granada's Welsh-language programmes
30	December 1957	BBC launches a daily Welsh-language television programme
14	February 1958	Inauguration of service by Television Wales and the West (TWW) from the St Hilary transmitter
31	March 1959	Half the households of Wales are licensed to receive television broadcasts
17	April 1961	First broadcast of *Heddiw*
13	February 1962	Saunders Lewis's *Tynged yr Iaith* is broadcast
27	June 1962	Publication of the Pilkington Report
14	September 1962	Inauguration of Television Wales West and North (TWWN)
1	January 1964	Merger of the output of TWWN with that of TWW
9	February 1964	BBC Wales is brought into service at Wenvoe on Band III
20	April 1964	Inauguration at Crystal Palace of BBC2 on 625 UHF
30	July 1964	The BBC receives its fifth Charter
28	September 1964	*Good Morning Wales* first becomes a five-day-a-week programme
6	December 1964	BBC2 becomes available in the English Midlands
12	September 1965	BBC2 becomes available from Wenvoe
31	October 1965	BBC2 becomes available from Winter Hill in Lancashire

1	March 1967	Broadcasting House, Llandaf, is opened
21	August 1967	BBC2 begins regular colour television transmission
30	September 1967	Radios 1, 2, 3 and 4 replace the Light, Home and Third radio services
8	November 1967	Inauguration at Leicester of the BBC's first local radio station
31	December 1967	Swansea becomes an unmanned radio studio
15	March 1968	HTV replaces TWW
11	May 1968	The first protest relating to broadcasting by Cymdeithas yr Iaith Gymraeg
29	September 1969	The first broadcast of Bore Da
15	November 1969	Colour television is extended to BBC1 and ITV on 625 UHF
9	July 1970	BBC Wales first broadcasts in colour
1	February 1971	The radio-only licence is abolished
1	January 1973	The VHF and medium-wave services of Radio Four in Wales are first used to provide Welsh and English programmes on different wavelengths
7	October 1973	First performance of the BBC Welsh Symphony Orchestra
8	October 1973	Inauguration in London of Capital Radio, Britain's first commercial radio station
30	September 1974	Inauguration of Swansea Sound
16	October 1974	First broadcast of *Pobol y Cwm*
21	November 1974	Publication of the Crawford Report
12	May 1975	Demolition of Baynton House, Llandaf, begins
28	November 1975	Publication of the Siberry Report
1	January 1977	*Radio Times* first lists Radio Cymru and Radio Wales as separate services
3	January 1977	First broadcast of *Helo Bobol*
24	March 1977	Publication of the Annan Report
26	July 1978	Publication of the Trevelyan Report
13	November 1978	Relaunch of Radio Wales
24	November 1978	Basic Radio Four first broadcast on long wave
12	September 1979	William Whitelaw states that the government will not proceed with a Welsh fourth channel
19	November 1979	Relaunch of Radio Cymru
3	March 1980	Inauguration of Radio Deeside (until 4 June 1980)
11	April 1980	Inauguration of the Cardiff Broadcasting Company (CBC)
5	May 1980	Gwynfor Evans announces that he will begin his fast on 6 October 1980

17 September 1980	The government announces that the Welsh Fourth Channel will be established
6 November 1980	The bill establishing the Welsh Fourth Channel and Channel 4 becomes law
31 July 1981	The BBC receives its sixth Charter
1 October 1981	Launching of the Clwyd radio opt-outs
19 October 1981	Swansea studios again used on an extensive scale
1 November 1982	Inauguration of Sianel Pedwar Cymru
2 November 1982	Inauguration of Channel 4
1 January 1985	Radio Wales first broadcasts continuously for twelve hours a day
1 January 1988	*Pobol y Cwm* is first broadcast five times a week
20 September 1993	Radio Cymru becomes permanently committed to broadcasting at least twelve hours a day throughout the year

Notes

Abbreviations

MBCW: Minutes of the Broadcasting Council for Wales
NLW: The National Library of Wales
WAC: The BBC Written Archives Centre, Caversham
WRC: The BBC Wales Record Centre, Llandaf

Chapter 1: The Beginnings, 1923–1927

1 *Western Mail*, 14 February 1923.
2 Ibid.; Programmes as Broadcast (WRC).
3 A. Briggs, *The History of Broadcasting in the United Kingdom*, vol.I, *The Birth of Broadcasting* (1961) (henceforth referred to as A. Briggs, I), pp.68–89.
4 P. Eckersley, *Power behind the Microphone* (1941), p.59.
5 P. Scannell and D. Cardiff, *A Social History of British Broadcasting*, vol.I, *1922–1939* (1991), pp.5–6.
6 A. Briggs, I, pp.91–134.
7 *Radio Times*, October 1925. Cardiff also broadcast a concert sponsored by Fry's Chocolate.
8 General Report of the British Broadcasting Company, 4 January 1923 (WAC CO 7); minutes of the British Broadcasting Company, 13 June 1923 (ibid.).
9 M. Daunton, *Coal Metropolis, Cardiff, 1870–1914* (1977), *passim*.
10 *News Chronicle*, 17 October 1936.
11 Lloyd George resigned on 6 October 1922. Reith's secretary, Miss F. I. Shields, was appointed on the recommendation of Frances Stevenson, later Countess Lloyd-George.
12 The Free Church of Scotland, created as a result of the 'Disruption' of 1843, had a profound influence upon Welsh Nonconformity. The United Free Church came into existence in 1900 through the union of the Free Church and the United Presbyterian Church. In 1929, the United Free Church reunited with the Church of Scotland. The reunited church, the established Church of Scotland, has a relationship with the state similar to that which Reith sought for the BBC.
13 I. McIntyre, *The Expense of Glory: A Life of John Reith* (1993), *passim*.
14 See, for example, the entry of 1 January 1936: 'Honours irritated me as usual.

Notes

It is monstrous that the king hasn't given me a GCVO, and I should also like a KCMG' (WAC S 60).

15 Quoted in E. E. Ellis, *T.J.: A Life of Dr Thomas Jones, CH* (1992), p.391.
16 Reith Diary, 8 March 1932 (WAC S 60).
17 Programmes as Broadcast (WRC); P. Scannell and D. Cardiff, op.cit., p.292.
18 R.Lucas, *The Voice of a Nation?* (1981), p.15. Burrows stated that the Company had to make do with inadequate premises because Cardiff's shipping boom meant that 'every inch of office space [was] occupied'. (A. R. Burrows, *The Story of Broadcasting* (1924), p.156.) Lucas states that the studio was above a cinema but in his reminiscences Arthur Trimmell is clear that it was above a shop. Trimmell to Rowley, 15 February 1973 (WRC 3600).
19 Ibid.
20 Reminiscences of Mrs Wynford Vaughan-Thomas (*Western Mail*, 10 February 1983).
21 WAC R 13/380. Corbett-Smith was offered the post on 5 February 1923 (Reith Diary, 5 February 1923: WAC S 60).
22 *Western Mail*, 10 February 1983; *Daily Mirror*, 18 January 1945; *Daily Mail*, 20 January 1945.
23 Note by Grace Williams, 15 February 1973 (WRC 3600).
24 Ibid.; letters, 15 June and 7 July 1927 (WAC R 13/380).
25 *Radio Times, passim*; Programmes as Broadcast (WRC). Corbett-Smith's successor considered the Urdd to be 'a very stupid movement' (memorandum 1931: WAC R 34/427/1).
26 Programmes as Broadcast (WRC); I. G. Jones (ed.), *Gwilym Davies, 1879–1955* (1972), p.48.
27 So great was the strain of the work that Corbett-Smith urged that all stations should close for one day a week. There were precedents elsewhere. Stations in Chicago did not broadcast on Mondays. (Minutes of the meetings of the station directors, 8 April 1923: WAC CO 9).
28 J. Reith, *Broadcast over Britain* (1924), pp.34–5.
29 Report on the West Region (WAC R 13/381).
30 P. Eckersley, op.cit., p.129.
31 Minutes of the Control Board, 18 May 1926 (WAC R 3/3). Corbett-Smith's position may also have been jeopardized by an attack in the House of Commons on a controversial talk on Danzig broadcast from Cardiff in 1924 (*Parliamentary Debates*, fifth series, vol.172, col.1169).
32 E. Pawley, *BBC Engineering, 1922–1972* (1972), p.59.
33 R. Silvey, *Who's Listening?* (1974), chap.1.
34 *Henry IV, Part One*, Act IV, scene 1:
    And those musicians that shall play to you
    Hang in the air a thousand leagues from hence
    And straight they shall be here.
35 *Western Mail*, 13 February 1923; minutes of the meeting of the station directors, 18 April 1923 (WAC CO 9).
36 R. Lucas, op.cit., p.38; A. Briggs, I, p.79.
37 *South Wales Daily News*, 13 December 1924; *Merthyr Express*, 3 March 1923.
38 Ibid., 24 February and 17 March 1923; *Western Mail*, 1923, passim; *Welsh in Education and Life* (1927), p.174.
39 R. H. Morgan, 'The development of the electricity supply industry in Wales', *Welsh History Review*, vol.11, no.3 (June 1983); A. Briggs, I, pp.85–6, 231; advertisements in *Western Mail*, 1923; Hopkin Morris to the director of regional relations, 28 September 1937 (WRC 2153).
40 *Y Llenor* XIII, 1 (Spring 1934), p.4; Davies to Jones, 18 February 1930 (NLW,

Thomas Jones Collection, Class H, vol.18, no.25). *Diwifr* (wireless) continued to be used in Welsh until the 1950s but, as in English, it was increasingly replaced by *radio*.

41 A. Briggs, I, p.219.

42 The wavelength was changed to 435 in December 1923 but, as the change proved unsatisfactory, Cardiff reverted within a few weeks to 353 (*Radio Times*, 18 January 1924). In January 1929, the station began transmitting on 323.3 metres.

43 *Western Mail*, 29 February 1923; E. Pawley, op.cit., pp.21–2.

44 Report on the West Region (WAC R 13/381).

45 P. Eckersley, op.cit., pp.79–80; Programmes as Broadcast (WRC).

46 *Western Mail*, 29 February 1923 and 18 March 1925.

47 Memorandum, 12 March 1925 (WAC CO 7/3); Appleton to Reith, 6 September 1928 (WAC R 13/380).

48 The high ground behind Margam prevented Swansea from receiving Cardiff, but Swansea frequently received a good signal from Bournemouth.

49 P. Eckersley, op.cit., p.67. Eckersley was in no sense a socialist; in the 1930s he was closely involved with Mosley's Union of Fascists (*History Today*, vol.40, March 1992).

50 The United States never adopted the long wave. As the advertisers who controlled broadcasting were only interested in mass audiences, they had no use for a waveband which could reach thinly populated rural areas. Thus, American-made radio sets did not cater for long-wave reception and the introduction of a long-wave service in Britain meant they were unsaleable there. This restriction upon Free Trade was far more effective than any tariff and was the cause of much delight to British radio manufacturers.

51 Reith to Joynson-Hicks, 5 April 1923, quoted in A. Briggs, I, pp.154–5.

52 Ibid., pp.164–77, 192.

53 The statement in Report on the West Region (WAC R 13/381) that Cardiff in November 1923 was the first provincial station to provide an SB for all British stations finds no confirmation in the *Radio Times*. In fact, Cardiff was one of the last stations to provide a general SB.

54 Minutes of the meeting of the station directors, 11 December 1923 (WAC CO 9). Although there were nine main stations, the scheme only involved seven. London was excluded, as was Belfast; not surprisingly, there were no land lines linking Belfast with the other stations of the United Kingdom.

55 Minutes of the Control Board, 14 January 1924 (WAC CO 7/2).

56 P. Scannell and D. Cardiff, op.cit., pp.315–16.

57 A. Briggs, I, pp.256, 292–4; minutes of the meeting of the station directors, 15 December 1927 (WAC CO 9).

58 Ibid., 17 December 1926 (ibid.); memorandum by Reith, 14 July 1925 (WAC R 34/731/1).

59 P. Scannell and D. Cardiff, op.cit., p.304.

60 A. Briggs, *The Golden Age of Wireless* (1965) (henceforth referred to as A. Briggs, II), p.308. See also D. Read, *The English Provinces, 1760–1960* (1964), *passim*, especially pp.252–6.

61 Report on the West Region (WAC R 13/381); *Radio Times*, 23 February 1934; Reith Diary, 27 April 1927 (WAC S 60).

62 *South Wales Echo*, 8 October 1930.

63 A. Llywelyn-Williams, *Gwanwyn yn y Ddinas* (1975), pp. 118–19.

64 Report on the Cardiff Station, 24 November 1925 (WAC R 13/380); memorandum by Appleton, 9 April 1936 (WRC 2152).

65 *BBC Handbook* 1928, p.177.

66 Report on West Region (WAC R 13/381); report on 5WA, July 1924 (WAC R 13/380).

67 Davies to Jones, 18 February 1930 (NLW, Thomas Jones Collection, class H, vol.18, no.25).
68 *Bristol Evening Echo*, 29 September 1926; *Bristol Evening Express*, 7 March 1927.
69 Report on the West Region (WAC R 13/381).
70 Ibid.; A. Briggs, I, p.284; file on the orchestra (WRC 1007). A short-lived Welsh Symphony Orchestra had been created on the occasion of the Pontypool National Eisteddfod of 1924 (*Radio Times*, 6 April 1928).
71 Report on the West Region (WAC R 13/381).
72 *Radio Times, passim*; memorandum by Appleton, 24 November 1924 (WAC R 13/380).
73 Report on a visit to the Cardiff station, 24 November 1925 (ibid.); report on the West Region (WAC R 13/381).
74 The other stations were Aberdeen and Nottingham (memorandum of Reith, 1 December 1925: WAC CO 9); *Western Mail*, 5 December 1925. The monthly *Beacon* came to an end during the General Strike.
75 Memorandum, 30 November 1925 (WAC R 34/731/1).
76 P. Eckersley, op.cit., p.6.
77 *Herald of Wales*, 23 February 1924; minutes of the Broadcasting Board, 30 April 1924 (WAC CO 60/65).
78 The only main station not to transmit it was Manchester which carried a programme celebrating the opening of its new studio.
79 *Cambria Leader*, 13 December 1924. Evans was still alive twenty-five years later when he took part in Swansea's anniversary celebrations (*Western Mail*, 12 December 1949).
80 Reith Diary, 12 December 1950 (WAC S 60). (A pencilled note adds: 'but didn't until February 1936'); memorandum, 8 June 1927 (WAC R 34/738/1);. memorandum, 12 March 1935 (WAC R 13/386/2).
81 Report on the West Region (WAC R 13/381).
82 J. Reith, op.cit., p.62.
83 Memorandum by Reith, 12 March 1925 (WAC CO 7/3).
84 *South Wales Daily News*, 13 December 1924.
85 J. Reith, op.cit., p.63.
86 *Cambria Leader*, 9 December 1924. According to the Census of 1921, 51 per cent of the 472,000 people living within fifteen miles of Swansea – 240,000 people in all – were Welsh-speaking; the equivalent figures for Cardiff were 14 per cent, 656,000 and 93,000.
87 *Cambria Leader*, 17 April 1925; *Bristol Wireless World*, 1925, *passim*.
88 Minutes of the Broadcasting Board, 28 May 1924 (WAC CO 64); E. Pawley, op.cit., p.21–36.
89 A. Briggs, I, p.192.
90 *South Wales Daily News*, 13 December 1924. For reception at Aberystwyth, see the *Cambrian News*, 2 July 1926.
91 A. Briggs, I, pp.222–4. 5XX was first listed in the *Radio Times* on 15 December 1924.
92 Minutes of the meeting of the station directors, 27 May 1924 (WAC CO 9).
93 Burrows to the Control Board, 3 March 1925 (WAC R 34/731/1).
94 A. Briggs, I, p.397.
95 P. Eckersley, op.cit., pp.81–103. Listeners to the Swansea Station suffered from interference from Frankfurt (*Cambria Leader*, 8 September 1926).
96 Minutes of the Control Board, 17 November 1926 (WAC R 3/3).
97 P. Scannell and D. Cardiff, op.cit, pp.321–2.
98 Memorandum by the Manchester station director, 27 September 1927 (WAC R 34/738/1).

99 Memorandum by Reith, 9 October 1925 (WAC R 34/731/1).

100 *Radio Times, passim.* In 1926, the eisteddfod authorities refused to allow the National Eisteddfod at Swansea to be broadcast, partly because they feared a fall in attendances and partly because the sum offered by the Company was considered to be insufficient. The sum of £100 was offered; the festival cost £17,000 (*South Wales Evening Post*, 26 October 1925; *Western Mail*, 11 June 1926).

101 P. Scannell and D. Cardiff, op.cit., p.13.

102 Memorandum by Appleton, 1 September 1925 (WAC R 13/380).

103 Appleton to Reith, 2 and 12 March 1935 (WAC R 6/208/1).

104 D. H. Davies, *The Welsh Nationalist Party, 1925–45: A Call to Nationhood* (1983), pp.142–4; J. E. Jones, *Tros Gymru: J.E. a'r Blaid* (1970), pp.130–6.

105 Appleton to Reith, 12 March 1935 (WAC R 208/1).

106 Lewis to Jones, February 1925 (NLW, Cylch Dewi Collection).

107 Jones to Appleton, 1 May 1925 (ibid.); Appleton to Jones, 2 May 1925 (ibid.); *Radio Times*, in listing the programmes, makes no mention of Cylch Dewi.

108 *BBC Handbook*, 1928, p.177.

109 *Cambria Leader*, 9 November 1925.

110 Ibid., 5 December 1925.

111 Minutes of the Control Board, 17 November 1926 (WAC R 3/3); minutes of a meeting between the Control Board and the regional directors, 19 November 1929 (WAC R 3/3/6).

112 Hughes to Jones, 15 February 1930 (NLW, Thomas Jones Collection, class H, vol.18, no.24).

113 Minutes of the Control Board, 3 November 1926 (WAC R 3/3).

114 *Parliamentary Debates*, fifth series, vol.199, col.1595 (15 November 1926).

115 *Manchester Guardian*, 5 October 1926; *Liverpool Evening Express*, 1 March 1927.

116 Memorandum, 5 February 1926 (WAC R 34/731/1).

117 Memorandum by Ashbridge, November 1928 (WAC R 34/427/1); *BBC Handbook*, 1928, p.177. In the inter-war years, Welsh-speakers were by far the largest of England's linguistic minorities. In 1931, 350,000 people born in Wales were living in England. Their birthplaces and age structure suggest that a knowledge of Welsh was more prevalent among them than it was among the generality of the people of Wales; in addition, many had English-born Welsh-speaking children. Thus, in the 1930s, England had between 150,000 and 200,000 Welsh-speakers. The second largest linguistic minority were the Yiddish-speakers among the 80,000 migrants from Poland and Russia.

118 *Western Mail*, 13 February 1926.

119 *Report of the Broadcasting Committee* (1925: Cd.2599). The committee consisted of five Scots and two Englishmen.

120 A. Briggs, I, pp.348–60. In 1926, the Conservative government also established the General Electricity Authority and British Airways.

121 Hartshorn effectively placed political broadcasting in the hands of the party whips. Thus politicians unpopular with the party leadership – Churchill in the 1930s for example – were rarely allowed to broadcast. Furthermore, there was no provision for parties outside the British mainstream, a cause of much complaint by Plaid Cymru in the 1940s and 1950s.

122 J. Dimbleby, *Richard Dimbleby, a Biography* (1975), p.66.

123 A. Briggs, I, pp.360–84; P. Scannell and D. Cardiff, op.cit., pp.103–13.

124 *Radio Times*; Programmes as Broadcast (WRC). There is no equivalent volume for Swansea.

125 J. Reith, *Into the Wind* (1949), p.99.

Chapter 2: The Struggle for the Welsh Region, 1927–1937

1 Letters, September and December 1926 (WAC R 34/31/1).
2 Memorandum, 8 June 1927 (WAC R 34/738/1).
3 Ibid. Appleton's copy was accompanied by a letter from Reith which stated: 'You will, I know, be tactful to Mr Parsons.'
4 *Radio Times, passim; Herald of Wales*, 3 November 1934.
5 Reith to Livening, 6 September 1927, cited in A. Briggs, *The Golden Age of Broadcasting* (1965) (henceforth referred to as A. Briggs, II), p.317.
6 Letters by Appleton, 1927–9 (WAC R 13/380).
7 P. Scannell and D. Cardiff, *A Social History of British Broadcasting* (1991), p.328; minutes of the meeting of the Board of the British Broadcasting Company, 7 August and 13 November 1924 (WAC CO 72).
8 Allowances, 1927 (WAC R 34/731/1).
9 D. C. Thomson, *Radio is Changing Us* (1937), p.140.
10 Assistant controller to controller, 10 June 1930 (WAC R 34/731/2); Reith to regional directors (ibid.).
11 P. Eckersley, *Power Behind the Microphone* (1941), pp.22, 128.
12 Stobart to assistant controller (programmes), 21 May 1928; memorandum on regional policy, 30 May 1928 (WAC R 34/38/2).
13 D. C. Thomson, op.cit., p.140.
14 Report on the West Region (WAC R 13/381).
15 Reith Diary, 6 July 1927 (WAC S 60).
16 R. Eckersley to Reith, 13 November 1928 (WAC R 34/731/1); P. Scannell and D. Cardiff, op.cit., p.322.
17 *Cambria Leader*, 3 October 1928.
18 Jones to Lewis, 16 May 1930 (NLW, Thomas Jones Papers, Class H, vol.18, no.28).
19 Report on the West Region (WAC R 13/381); *Western Mail*, 23 December 1931.
20 R. Eckersley to Reith, 13 November 1928 (WAC R 34/731/1).
21 Minutes of the meeting of the station directors, 17 December 1926 (WAC CO 9).
22 Lord Gainford also had an estate in County Durham.
23 A. Briggs, II, pp.483–4.
24 R. Eckersley to the station directors, 28 November 1928 (WAC R 34/738/2).
25 *Western Mail*, 12 June 1930.
26 Siepmann to Reith, 12 May 1932 (WAC R 34/731/2).
27 A. Calder-Marshall, *The Changing Scene* (1937), p.91, quoted in P. Scannell and D.Cardiff, op.cit., p.18.
28 P. Eckersley, op.cit., pp.181, 245.
29 Cardiff weekly staff file, 1930–7 (WAC R 13/36).
30 Minutes of the Control Board, 16 June 1926 (WAC R 3/3); memorandum, 16 March 1939 (WRC 2151).
31 A greater number of Welsh-language programmes would, if provided, not only imply greater autonomy for Cardiff; it would also undermine the basic principle of the Regional Scheme – that London dealt with the universal and the regions with the local. A service in Welsh would have to deal with the universal and the local.
32 *Western Mail*, 11 February 1927.
33 Ibid., 8 March 1927.
34 *Cambria Leader*, 18 November 1929.
35 *Western Mail*, 31 August 1927.
36 Ibid., 26 February 1927.

[37] Ibid., 12 September 1928. The play complained of was Saunders Lewis's *Eve of St John*. There were similar complaints in the *South Wales Echo*, 2 September 1927.

[38] *Y Cerddor Newydd*, March 1927, March 1928; M. Gorham, *Forty Years of Irish Broadcasting* (1967), p.44. Further programmes were broadcast from Dublin in 1936. They were the work of the distinguished Cardiff schoolmaster, W. C. Elvet-Thomas. (*Y Brython*, 24 December 1936).

[39] Hughes to Jones, 15 February 1930 (NLW, Thomas Jones Papers, class H, vol.18, no.24).

[40] *Welsh in Education and Life* (1927), p.175.

[41] The series from Ireland was not broadcast weekly and was only partially in Welsh. The comment ignored the fact that the BBC had broadcast a number of Welsh-language programmes, although, admittedly, not on a regular basis. In the 1920s, British broadcasters considered regular programming to be an undesirable trait of American radio.

[42] *Welsh in Education and Life*, pp.174–5.

[43] *Western Mail*, 30 August 1927.

[44] *Y Llenor*, VI, 3 (October 1927), p.133.

[45] The first broadcast in Breton was transmitted from Cardiff in 1939. During the Second World War, the German occupying forces permitted broadcasts in Breton, causing advocates of Breton broadcasting to be viewed as collaborationists.

[46] A Welsh monoglot appearing before a court in Wales had to pay for the services of an interpreter; speakers of other languages lacking a knowledge of English did not. The distinction was abolished by the Welsh Courts Act of 1942.

[47] *Welsh Outlook*, May 1925; memorandum by Rendall, February 1935 (WAC R 13/386/2).

[48] In June 1930, there were 118,018 licences in force in Wales and 190,000 in the area defined in 1927 as south-western England (*BBC Handbook*, 1931, pp.33–4).

[49] Evans to Jones, 20 December 1927 (NLW Thomas Jones Papers, class H, vol.5, no.62).

[50] E. E. Ellis, *T.J.: A Life of Thomas Jones, CH* (1992), pp.322–3.

[51] List of the members of the Welsh Advisory Committee (NLW, Thomas Jones Papers, class H, vol.18, no.23); Gruffydd to Appleton, February 1928 (NLW, W. J. Gruffydd Collection, no.138).

[52] Reith Diary, 30 November 1928 (WAC S 60); correspondence and memoranda, 1928 (WAC R 34/427/1).

[53] *Western Mail*, 6 July 1929; *Welsh Outlook*, August 1929. The BBC had already abolished adult education talks from all regions except Scotland.

[54] File on the Welsh Children's Message (WAC R 11/79); I. G. Jones (ed.), *Gwilym Davies, 1879–1955* (1972), pp.40–7.

[55] *Manchester Guardian*, 1 August 1929. In the party's earliest days, it made no approach to the broadcasting authorities in London, for its original policy was to ignore the existence of British institutions (D. H. Davies, *The Welsh Nationalist Party, 1925–45* (1983), pp.132–3).

[56] *Western Mail*, 3 August 1929.

[57] Ibid., 12 March 1930; *News Chronicle*, 13 August 1931; *Welsh Nationalist*, April and August 1932. The chief reason for installing the 'little nationals' was the electrical interference suffered by Daventry transmissions in some densely populated areas (A. Briggs, II, p.314).

[58] Memoranda concerning the meeting with the University of Wales, 1929 (WAC R 34/427/1). Those present were William George, W. J. Gruffydd, J. R.

Rees (principal of University College, Cardiff), W. Jenkins, (Labour MP for Neath), and Jenkin James (secretary of the University Council).

59 Reith Diary, 23 May 1930 (WAC S 60).
60 E. E. Ellis, op.cit., p.323.
61 E.g., *News Chronicle*, 12 September 1930. The BBC sought to restrict the word 'station' to the actual transmitter.
62 Reith was aware of accusations that the BBC was pro-Scottish. See Reith to Jones, 1 September 1931 (NLW, Thomas Jones Papers, class H, vol.18, no.41). The number of Scottish and the lack of Welsh employees at Head Office was a matter of comment (*Wireless World*, 25 February 1931).
63 Conversation with the late J. E. Jones.
64 *The Broadcasting Service in Wales* and *Y Gwasanaeth Darlledu yng Nghymru* (1931). Five thousand English and seven thousand Welsh copies were distributed. Another pamplet was published in 1932.
65 Minutes of meetings, 9 October 1929 and 27 May 1930 (WAC R 3/3/6).
66 Letters concerning Edgar Jones in NLW, Thomas Jones Papers, class H, vol.18; minutes of the Control Board, 1 April 1931 (WAC R 3/3); report on the West Region (WAC R 13/381).
67 Ibid.; Reith Diary, 19 March 1931 and 8 March 1932 (WAC S 60); Reith to Jones, 1 September 1931 (NLW, Thomas Jones Papers, class H, vol.18, no.41).
68 Ibid. All three were to have governors under the charter of 1952, much to the annoyance of the Corporation.
69 Report on the West Region (WAC R 13/381); Reith to Jones, 1 September 1931 (NLW, Thomas Jones Papers, class H, vol.18, no.41).
70 Appleton to Reith, 22 June 1931 (WAC R 34/945/5); memorandum, 26 May 1932 (WAC R 34/427/2).
71 Assistant director of programmes to Appleton, 21 October 1931 (WAC R 34/427/1); Appleton to assistant director of programmes, 28 October 1931 (WAC R 11/79); Reith Diary, 15 July 1936 (WAC S 60).
72 J. E. Jones, *Tros Gymru: J.E. a'r Blaid* (1970), p.132; *Daily Herald*, 1 July 1931.
73 *Western Mail*, 25 July 1931.
74 I. G. Jones (ed.), op.cit., p.52; I. C. Peate, *Rhwng Dau Fyd* (1976), pp.93–6; file on I. C. Peate (WRC 2156); *Liverpool Daily Post*, 8 March 1930; *Western Mail*, 26 May 1931; *News Chronicle*, 23 February 1933.
75 Appleton to Reith, 22 June 1931 (WAC R 34/427/1).
76 *BBC Handbook*, 1932, p.31; ibid., 1933, p.65; note, June 1931 (WAC R 34/427/1).
77 Appleton to the director of information and publications, 16 June 1932 (WAC R 34/427/2).
78 NLW, Thomas Jones Papers, class H, vol.18, letters nos. 42 to 51, especially no.45. At the interview, Carpendale asked Sam Jones: 'Why do you speak Welsh?' Jones answered: 'Why do you speak English?' (Conversation with Elwyn Evans).
79 Appleton to the director of programmes, 7 July 1932 (WAC R 34/427/2); Appleton to Reith, 10 November 1932 (ibid.).
80 Reith to the director of information and publications, 2 January 1933 (ibid.); Reith Diary, 19 July 1933 (WAC S 60); report on the West Region (WAC R 13/381). 'The BBC', declared the *Welsh Nationalist* of January 1934, 'chooses the tamest body it can find among its critics.'
81 Reith to Appleton, 6 March 1935 (WAC R 208/1); report on the West Region (WAC R 13/381).
82 Appleton to the assistant controller (information), 28 April 1933 (WAC R 34/427/2); E. Pawley, *BBC Engineering, 1922–1972* (1972), pp.90–1.
83 *Western Mail*, 17 November and 1 December 1933.

84 Sutthery to Nicolls, 10 January 1934 (WAC R 13/386/2).
85 *BBC Handbook*, 1935, pp.187–90; *Bristol Evening News*, 14 July 1934.
86 P. Gould and R. White, *Mental Maps* (1986), p.32; memorandum of Rendall, February 1935 (WAC R 13/386/2).
87 *Evening World*, 27 January 1931 and 27 February 1934; *Bodmin Post*, 9 February 1934; *South Wales Evening Post*, 12 February 1934.
88 BBC memorandum, November 1933 (WAC R 6/208/1); memorandum of the University of Wales, 12 December 1933 (WAC R 6/209); minutes of the meeting of 9 February 1934 (ibid.).
89 The director of information and publications to Reith, 31 January 1934 (WAC R 13/384/1).
90 *Welsh Nationalist*, February 1933; *Western Mail*, 14 February 1933; Bowen to the Marconi Company, 25 January 1934 (WAC R 6/208/1).
91 WAC R 34/472/2; *Western Mail*, 14 October 1930; Reith Diary, 9 February 1934 (WAC S 60).
92 Ibid.; minutes of the meeting of 9 February 1934 (WAC R 6/209); memorandum by the director of programme administration (WAC R 6/208/2); Lewis to Jones, 31 August 1968 (NLW, David Jones Papers (1985), group C, box 5).
93 Minutes of the meeting of 9 February 1934 (WAC R 6/209); report on the West Region (WAC R 13/381); minutes of the Control Board, 14 June 1932 (WAC R 3/3).
94 Minutes of the Director-General's Meeting, 18 September 1934 (WAC R 3/11/1).
95 William George, *Atgof a Myfyr* (1948), p.197; minutes of the meeting of 26 October 1934 (WAC R 6/209). See also J. E. Jones, op.cit., pp. 130–6. Saunders Lewis, in commenting upon his visit to London's Broadcasting House, stated: 'It stinks of wealth, but I have seen more genuine thought in the kitchens of the Welsh unemployed.' (*News Chronicle*, 2 March 1934).
96 The vice-chancellor's statement on broadcasting in Wales, 13 December 1934 (WAC R 6/208/1).
97 Minutes of the meeting of 9 February 1934 (WAC R 6/209); note on the Welsh Advisory Committee (WAC R 34/427/1).
98 Gwyn Jones, 'The first forty years: some notes on Anglo-Welsh literature', in *Triskel One* (1971), p.82.
99 Staff file, 1935–9 (WRC 2159).
100 Statement, November 1956 (WRC 2142).
101 Memorandum, 25 August 1936 (WRC 2146).
102 *Western Mail*, 10 March 1933 and 12 April 1935; memorandum by Appleton, 15 May 1935 (WAC R 6/208/1).
103 Memorandum by Rendall, 16 May 1935 (WAC R 6/208/1).
104 Memorandum by Rendall, February 1935 (WAC 13/386/2).
105 E. Evans, 'Deuparth Gwaith', in D. Morgan (ed.), *Babi Sam* (1985), p.33; Appleton to Nicolls, 25 February 1935 (WAC R 3/386/2).
106 John to Reith, 22 February 1935 (WAC R 6/208/1); Reith to Appleton, 28 February 1935 (ibid.); Appleton to Reith, 2 March 1935 (ibid); *Western Mail*, 21 February 1935.
107 Reith to Appleton, 6 March 1935 (WAC R 6/208/1); Appleton to Reith, 12 March 1935 (ibid.).
108 Reith to Carpendale, 4 March 1935 (ibid.); Reith to Nicolls, 12 April 1935 (WAC R 13/386/2).
109 E. Pawley, op.cit., p.91; minutes of the Director-General's Meeting, 2 April 1935 (WAC 3/20).
110 Ibid., 13 March 1935 (ibid.); memoranda by Reith, 2 and 4 April 1935 (WAC R

6/208/1); record of the discussion of 11 April 1935 (ibid.).

111 Ibid.; Reith Diary, 11 April 1935 (WAC S 60).

112 *North Wales Chronicle*, 12 April 1935; *Western Mail*, 12 and 20 April 1935; *Bristol Evening News*, 24 April 1935.

113 Memorandum, 22 May 1935 (WAC R 6/208/1). The final decision on synchronization was not taken until 4 June 1936 (Reith Diary: WAC S 60).

114 *News Chronicle*, 27 April 1935; *Western Mail*, 28 May 1935; *Y Ddraig Goch*, May and September 1935; *Welsh Nationalist*, June 1935. Lewis claimed that 'there had never been any technical difficulties. The only difficulty was the obduracy of the BBC.' (*News Chronicle*, 24 April 1935).

115 Reith Diary, 15 March 1935 (WAC S 60); J. Reith, *Into the Wind* (1949), p.219.

116 Those questioned were Edgar (Midland), Livening (North) and Dinwoodie (Scotland) (A. Briggs, II, pp.487–8).

117 Appleton to Nicolls, 28 January 1936 (WAC R 13/378/2); *South Wales Evening Post*, 23 May 1935. Salaries varied from £600 for the programme director to £260 for studio assistants.

118 Memoranda (WAC R 6/208/1 and R 13/378/1 and 2); note on staff in Wales, 1935–9 (WRC 2159).

119 Ibid.; auditions of Welsh announcers, 1935 (WAC R 13/378/1); notes on candidates (WAC R 13/378/2); A. L. James, *The Broadcast Word* (1935), especially pp.64–73.

120 C. Stuart (ed.), *The Reith Diaries* (1975), p.510.

121 A. Llywelyn-Williams, *Gwanwyn yn y Ddinas* (1975), p.112; Appleton to Nicolls, 11 January 1935 (WAC R 13/378/2). In fact, Llywelyn-Williams had left Plaid Genedlaethol Cymru in 1932.

122 Nicolls to Reith, 21 March 1935 (WRC 2159); E. Evans, 'Deuparth Gwaith', in D. Morgan (ed.), op.cit., p.34; Rendall to Nicolls, 23 March 1935 (WAC R 13/386/2); Appleton to Nicolls, 23 March 1935 (ibid.); Reith to Appleton, 12 March 1935 (ibid.); memorandum, 12 March 1935 (ibid.); Appleton to Reith, 12 April 1935 (ibid.).

123 *Western Mail*, 8 and 13 August 1935; notes for the conference with the University of Wales (WAC R 6/208/2); *News Chronicle*, 14 February 1936; A. Llywelyn-Williams, op.cit., p.129; D. Ifans (ed.), *Annwyl Kate, Annwyl Saunders* (1992), p.114; file on I. C. Peate (WRC 2156); *Baner ac Amserau Cymru*, 25 February 1936; I. C. Peate, 'Y Radio yng Nghymru', *Y Llenor*, XVI, 2 (Summer 1937), pp.94–5.

124 Appleton to Nicolls, 16 April 1935 (WAC R 13/386/2); letters, September 1935 (WAC R 6/208/2); minutes of the meeting of 24 October 1935 (WAC R 6/209).

125 Minutes of the Control Board, 17 December 1935 (WAC R 3/20); R. Lucas, *The Voice of a Nation?* (1981), pp.76–9; V. Williams, 'Yr "SM" cyntaf', in D. Morgan (ed.), op.cit., pp.48–9; report on the West Region (WAC R 13/381).

126 *Parliamentary Debates*, fifth series, vol.302, col.1535; A. Briggs, II, p.331.

127 Report on the Regions, January 1936 (WRC 2156).

128 Minutes of the Control Board, 7 July 1936 (WAC R 3/20).

129 Note on staff in Wales, 1935–9 (WRC 2159).

130 *The Report of the Ullswater Committee* (1936: Cmd.5091); *Parliamentary Debates*, fifth series, vol.314, cols.896–8, 924–8, 935–6. Clement Davies, a member of the Ullswater Committee, spoke in the debate but did not mention broadcasting in Wales.

131 Wellington to Rendall, 11 March 1936 (WAC R 34/945/1).

132 Reith Diary, 29 August and 1 and 28 October 1936, 12 and 13 March and 9 July 1937 (WAC S 60); minutes of the Control Board, 27 October 1936 (WAC

R 3/20); minutes of the meetings of the Board of Governors, 22 July, 23 September, 14 October and 28 October 1936, 10 and 24 March 1937 (WAC R 3/20).

133 Minutes of the Control Board, 26 May and 16 June 1936 (ibid.); note on staff in Wales, 1935 (WAC R 13/378/2); *Western Mail*, 17 June and 9 July 1936; list of applications for the post of Welsh regional director (WAC R 13/374/2).

134 P. J. Madgwick, *The Politics of Rural Wales* (1973), p.49; H. M. Jones, *Doctor in the Whips' Room* (1955), p.82.

135 *Western Mail*, 30 December 1931, 22 January and 13 February 1932.

136 J. Reith, op.cit., pp.287, 288.

137 See, for example, a letter from Nantlais Williams suggesting that, in choosing Hopkin Morris, Reith had been directly inspired by the Almighty. As he believed that that was true of all his decisions, Reith would no doubt have agreed (Williams to Hopkin Morris, 12 November 1936: WRC 3719).

138 Parry-Williams to Jones, 17 June 1936 (NLW, Thomas Jones Papers, class V, vol.2).

139 A. Llywelyn-Williams, op.cit., p.133.

140 D. C. Thomson, op.cit., p.64.

141 *Western Mail*, 20 October 1936; *Cardiff Times*, 24 October 1936; *Herald of Wales*, 24 October 1936.

142 Minutes of the meetings of 1 May and 27 November 1936 (WAC R 6/209); *Liverpool Daily Post*, 29 December 1936.

143 Memoranda and letters, 1936 (WAC R 34/940); *Bristol Evening World*, 2 February 1934.

144 Minutes of the Control Board, 8 December 1936 (WAC R 3/20); memorandum, 16 December 1936 (WAC R 34/940); E. Pawley, op.cit., p.97.

145 Reith Diary, 3 July 1937 (WAC S 60); J. Reith, op.cit., p.288.

146 Board Report, July to September 1937 (WRC 2140).

147 Reith Diary, 3 July 1937 (WAC S 60).

148 *Y Cymro*, 7 December 1936.

149 J. Reith, op.cit., p.288; I. G. Jones (ed.), op.cit., pp.54–5; Reith Diary, 4 December 1937 (WAC S 60).

150 Ibid., 18 May 1938 (ibid.).

151 M. Gorham, op.cit., p.29.

152 *BBC Handbooks*, 1931–5, 1938–40; *BBC Annuals*, 1935–7. Until 1936, the Corporation considered Monmouthshire to be in England; the Monmouthshire figures have been added to the BBC's figures for Wales.

153 *BBC Handbook*, 1931, p.33.

154 Memorandum of the University of Wales, 12 December 1933 (WAC R 6/209); *BBC Handbook*, 1932, p.31. The BBC argued that as licence-holders in Wales represented one-thirtieth of those of the United Kingdom, there was no case for giving Wales one of its nine medium wavelengths (ibid., 1933, p.66).

155 M. Gorham, op.cit., p.99. The numbers prosecuted for not buying a licence rose rapidly in the last months of the Company. Six hundred were fined in the twelve months up to 28 February 1927 (*Parliamentary Debates*, fifth series, vol.203, col.1386).

156 A. Briggs, II, pp.253–4, 314.

157 Ibid., p.357–61, 494–8; *News Chronicle*, 10 February 1934; *Rhondda Gazette*, 17 February 1934; *Western Mail*, 8 December 1934.

158 Memoranda by Parry (WRC 2152); review of 1937 (WRC 2153); notes on the regions (WRC 3600); *Daily Express*, 29 July 1935; E. H. F. Mills, 'Wireless in the south Wales coalfield', *Cambria*, 2 (Summer 1930), pp.53–4; A. Briggs, II, p.74.

159 Ibid., p.271; P. Scannell and D. Cardiff, op.cit., p.373.

160 Memorandum by Rendall, 4 December 1935 (WRC 2146).
161 *Radio Times, passim;* A. Briggs, II, p.364.
162 P. Scannell and D. Cardiff, op.cit., p.277–303.The members of the committee were two professors of phonetics (Lloyd James and Daniel Jones), C. T. Onions, the Cardiff-born editor of the *Oxford Dictionary*, Bernard Shaw, Robert Bridges and Logan Pearsall Smith (A. Briggs, II, p.469).
163 File on the Cardiff City Hall (WRC 3719); *Western Mail,* 2 March 1935; memorandum by Sutthery, 15 February 1934 (WAC R 34/237); Rendall to R. Eckersley, 2 March 1935 (ibid.).
164 A. Briggs, II, pp.306–9, 327; memorandum by Wellington, 19 December 1933 (WAC R 34/945/1); memorandum, 22 October 1935 (WAC R 34/731/2).
165 *Radio Times, passim.*
166 List of allowances (WAC R 34/371/1); note on allowances, 1935–6 (WAC R 20/196/3).
167 Memorandum by Sutthery, April 1934 (WAC R 34/945/1); note on organization (WRC 2156).
168 Memorandum by Appleton, 16 August 1934 (WAC R 20/196/2).
169 A. Briggs, IV, p.90; *Times,* 4 November 1963.
170 *BBC Handbook,* 1929, p.71; Marshall to Dawnay, 19 December 1935, quoted in A. Briggs, II, pp.51–2.
171 Sutthery to Wellington, 5 January 1934 (WAC R 34/237/1).
172 Reminiscences of Grace Williams (WRC 3600).
173 Memorandum, 3 March 1938 (WAC R 34/944).
174 Report on the West Region (WAC R 13/381); file on the orchestra (WRC 2156); *Cambria Leader,* 18 January 1926.
175 Memorandum, 3 March 1938 (WAC R 34/944).
176 P. Scannell and D. Cardiff, op.cit., pp.181–2.
177 File labelled 'Aberystwyth' (WRC 3719); A. Briggs, II, p.126.
178 Ibid., pp.124–7; P. Scannell and D. Cardiff, op.cit., pp.57–71; *Listener,* 1 February 1933.
179 *Daily Herald,* 19 April 1934, 2 May 1935 and 10 October 1936; *South Wales Argus,* 14 May 1934.
180 Memoranda, April 1933, April 1934 and March 1935 (WRC 2142).
181 *Western Mail,* 6, 8 and 14 October 1936.
182 Memoranda, 5 January and 8 June 1934 (WAC R 34/237).
183 *Western Mail,* 3 February 1937; note on Caradoc Evans (WRC 2142).
184 S. Lewis, *The Banned Wireless Talk on Welsh Nationalism* (1930); *Western Mail,* 8 December 1930.
185 G. Erfyl (ed.), *Radio Cymru* (1989), p.ix.
186 Minutes of the meeting of 26 October 1934 (WAC R 6/209); notes on a Welsh *Listener,* 1934–6 (WRC 3600).
187 A. Briggs, II, pp.147–8, 153–60; J. Dimbleby, *Richard Dimbleby: A Biography* (1975), pp.68–9.
188 Minutes of the meeting of the station directors, 15 December 1927 (WAC CO 9).
189 Memoranda on the Welsh regional news (WAC R 13/376). The discontinuance of the late evening news gave London the opportunity to press Cardiff to cease employing 'your night stenographer'.
190 A. Llywelyn-Williams, op.cit., p.148; *Radio Times, passim; Western Mail,* 20 and 27 November 1933; memorandum on the news, 16 April 1936 (WRC 2146); *News Chronicle,* 30 October 1936.
191 R. Lucas, op.cit., p.34; *Cambria Leader,* 24 February 1925.
192 Memorandum, 16 November 1928 (WAC R 13/380).
193 Memorandum, 14 February 1932 (WAC R 20/196/1); memorandum, 21

November 1935 (WRC 3600); R. Lucas, op.cit., pp.114–15. The prayer was concerned with the conversion of Wales to 'the true faith'.
[194] Memorandum, 16 November 1928 (WAC R 13/380); report on the West Region (WAC R 13/381).
[195] Minutes of the Control Board, 21 May 1929 (WAC R 3/3).
[196] *Radio Times, passim*; R. Lucas, op.cit., pp.108–13.
[197] Ibid., p.111; *South Wales News*, 25 January 1928; *South Wales Evening Post*, 9 January 1934; memorandum, 2 December 1936 (WRC 2153); *News Chronicle*, 16 October 1936.
[198] Ibid; R. Lucas, op.cit., pp.112–22; *Yr Efrydydd*, October 1937.
[199] Memoranda, 1929 (WAC R 19/280/1).
[200] Memoranda, 1936 (WRC 2146); *Radio Times, passim*.
[201] *Radio Times*, 22 February 1957.
[202] Memorandum, 10 February 1937 (WAC R 34/237).
[203] J. S. Lewis, *Buchedd Garmon* (1937).

Chapter 3: The Welsh Region, 1937–1945

[1] E. M. Humphreys, 'Y darl
lediad cyntaf', in G. Erfyl (ed.), *Radio Cymru* (1989), p.69; A. Llywelyn-Williams, *Gwanwyn yn y Ddinas* (1975), p.131; *News Chronicle*, 10 December 1938.
[2] M. Gorham, *Forty Years of Irish Broadcasting* (1967), pp.200–1.
[3] Minutes of the Control Board, 6 January 1939 (WAC R 3/20).
[4] *Western Mail*, 5 July 1937.
[5] Board Report, May–June 1937 (WRC 2140).
[6] A. Briggs, *The Golden Age of Wireless* (1965) (henceforth referred to as A. Briggs, II), p.268.
[7] Memorandum by Hopkin Morris, 28 September 1937 (WRC 2153).
[8] R. Silvey, *Who's Listening?* (1974), pp.69, 78.
[9] J. Jones, *Me and Mine* (1946), pp.81–2.
[10] Notes on programme finance (WAC R 20/196/4).
[11] Minutes of the meetings of the regional directors, 1937–9 (WRC 2153).
[12] Memoranda, 1937 (WAC R 34/944); notes on programme finance (WAC R 20/196/4).
[13] *South Wales Evening Post*, 1 October 1937; minutes of the meeting of the regional directors, 9 September 1937 (WRC 2153).
[14] Memorandum, 22 March 1938 (WAC R 34/940); memoranda, 1937–9 (WAC R 20/196/4); memoranda, 1938–9 (WAC R 34/945/2); memorandum by Rowland Hughes, 10 March 1938 (WRC 2142).
[15] Board Report, April–May, 1938 (WRC 2140); *Western Mail*, 26 March and 5 May 1938.
[16] *South Wales Evening Post*, 30 September 1937; file on Swansea (WRC 2159); memorandum, 3 June 1936 (WRC 2146).
[17] Conversation with Elwyn Evans; note, 1938 (WRC 3619); D. Morgan (ed.), *Babi Sam* (1985), p.35.
[18] Ibid., pp.17–18.
[19] Memorandum by Jones, 28 November 1937 (WRC 2142); *Radio Times, passim*.
[20] Report of the public relations officer, December 1937 (WRC 2140); *Western Mail*, 20 October 1936.
[21] Memorandum, 15 April 1936 (WRC 2138).
[22] *News Chronicle*, 9 April 1938; *Y Cymro*, 9 April 1938; *Daily Herald*, 21 January 1939.

23 *Ariel*, June 1937; conversation with Elwyn Evans; minutes of the Programme Board (WRC 2153); minutes of the University Committee, 26 October 1934 (WAC R 6/209).

24 *Western Mail*, 8 July 1935; A. Llywelyn-Williams, op.cit., pp.144–9; memoranda by Llywelyn-Williams (WRC 2152); memoranda, 1938–9 (WRC 2142); T. J. Morgan, 'Darlledu yng Nghymru', *Y Llenor*, XVII, 3 (Autumn 1938), pp.150–62; I. C. Peate, 'Y Radio yng Nghymru', ibid., XVI, 2 (Summer 1937), pp.88–97.

25 Memoranda, 1938 (WRC 2153); *News Chronicle*, 26 July 1938; *Y Cymro*, 15 September 1938; minutes of the Programme Board (WRC 2153).

26 Ibid.; Reith Diary, 13 July 1937 (WAC S 60); A. Briggs, II, pp.146–7; *Daily Herald*, 21 August 1937.

27 Programme Analysis, 1939 (WRC 2153).

28 Statement of the music director, 17 December 1937 (WRC 2142); Board Report, April 1939 (WRC 2140).

29 Ibid., May–June 1938 (WRC 2140).

30 Memorandum, 28 November 1937 (WRC 2142).

31 Ibid.

32 File on Peate (WRC 2156); memorandum by Llywelyn-Williams, 22 December 1937 (WRC 2142).

33 Board Report, March 1939 (WRC 2140); A. Llywelyn-Williams, op.cit., pp.136–44.

34 Ibid., pp.138–9.

35 *Yr Efrydydd*, March 1938; report, 1937 (WRC 3600).

36 Memorandum by Vaughan-Thomas, 25 January 1938 (WRC 2142); Board Report, May 1939 (WRC 2140); W. Vaughan-Thomas, *Trust to Talk* (1980), pp.25–42.

37 *Western Mail*, 5 and 6 August 1938; *News Chronicle*, 6 and 9 August 1938.

38 *South Wales Argus*, 16 April 1934.

39 A. Llywelyn-Williams, op.cit., p.130; minutes of the meeting of the regional directors, 4 April 1939 (WRC 2153); *Daily Herald*, 17 and 24 August 1937.

40 Letter by Gwent ap Glasnant, 25 November 1936 (WRC 2152). Ap Glasnant gave a talk in Welsh on rugby in November 1936 (note, 12 November 1936: WRC 2152); E. Davies, 'Arloesi', in G. Erfyl (ed.), op.cit., pp.52–3.

41 *Observer*, 6 March, 11 September and 25 December 1938; P. Scannell and D. Cardiff, *A Social History of British Broadcasting* (1991), pp.134–51.

42 Review of 1937 (WRC 2153).

43 *News Chronicle*, 26 March 1938; *North Wales Chronicle*, 1 April 1938; *Western Mail*, 4 April 1938; *Liverpool Echo*, 27 April 1938; Board Report, December 1938–January 1939 (WRC 2140).

44 *Radio Times*, passim; *South Wales Echo*, 26 July 1937; *Y Cloriannydd*, 27 April 1938.

45 R. Lucas, *The Voice of a Nation?* (1981), pp.118–22; Monthly Report, October 1938 (WRC 2149); Board Report, December 1938–January 1939 (WRC 2140).

46 Memorandum, 27 May 1937 (WAC R 13/378/2); memorandum by Hopkin Morris (ibid.). The Ullswater Report asserted that the fact that 116 of the BBC's non-engineering salaried graduates were educated at Oxford or Cambridge and 75 at other universities disproved the allegation that 'undue preference was given to candidates with Oxford and Cambridge degrees' (*Ullswater Report*, p.13).

47 *Y Llan*, 6 and 23 December 1938.

48 *Radio Times*, passim; Board Report, November 1938 (WRC 2140).

49 Ibid., June–July 1937 (ibid.); *Liverpool Daily Post*, 25 October 1936.

⁵⁰ Board Report, October–November 1937 (WRC 2140).
⁵¹ Ibid.; *Manchester Guardian*, 11 May 1938.
⁵² *Y Cymro*, 12 April 1938; memorandum by Dafydd Gruffydd, 2 December 1937 (WRC 2142); Hopkin Morris to Cynan, 22 December 1936 (WRC 2152).
⁵³ Note on Welsh staff, May 1935 (WRC 2159); *BBC Annual*, 1936, p.44; *News Chronicle*, 2 April 1938; conversation with Elwyn Evans; A. Llywelyn-Williams, op.cit., p.134.
⁵⁴ Memoranda, April 1936 (WRC 2152); Board Report, July–December 1938 (WRC 2140).
⁵⁵ R. Lucas, op.cit., pp.103–5; *Western Mail*, 29 December 1934; A. Briggs, II, p.118; P. Scannell and D. Cardiff, op.cit., p.227.
⁵⁶ *Y Cymro*, 12 December 1936; *South Wales Evening Post*, 21 October 1933.
⁵⁷ D. Morgan (ed.), op.cit., pp.14–15.
⁵⁸ Ibid., pp.81–2; conversation with Elwyn Evans; *BBC Yearbook*, 1949, pp.40–3; *North Wales Chronicle*, 1 October 1937; W. D. Williams, 'Cofio Sam Jones', *Y Genhinen*, 28 (1978), pp.73–5, 148–53.
⁵⁹ A. Briggs, *The War of Words* (1970) (henceforth referred to as A. Briggs, III), p.83.
⁶⁰ Lee to Nicolls, 10 October 1939 (file labelled 'Welsh Broadcasting, War Emergency': WAC R 34/943).
⁶¹ *Radio Times*, September 1938; A. Briggs, III, pp.92–4. The programmes cancelled in September 1938 were concerts by the BBC Welsh Orchestra and by the Merthyr and District Philharmonic Society and a talk by Richard Hughes. Programmes as Broadcast (WRC) has no entries for September 1939.
⁶² Memoranda, 1939 (WAC R 34/943).
⁶³ Ibid.; correspondence, 1939 (WRC 3716); minutes of the Programme Board, 4 September 1939 (WRC 2153).
⁶⁴ Memoranda, 1939 (WAC R 34/943).
⁶⁵ Hopkin Morris to Nicolls, 18 September 1939 (ibid.). According to J. E. Jones, Hopkin Morris threatened to resign and to seek to rouse Wales in protest if the Corporation refused to broadcast any Welsh at all (J. E. Jones, *Tros Gymru: J. E. a'r Blaid* (1970), p.284).
⁶⁶ A. Llywelyn-Williams, op.cit., pp.160–1. The bulletin was first broadcast on 17 September and was originally called *Crynodeb o'r Cyhoeddiadau Swyddogol yn Gymraeg* ('A Summary of the Official Announcements in Welsh'). The title was changed to *Newyddion a Chyhoeddiadau* ('News and Announcements') on 8 October.
⁶⁷ Memorandum, 21 September 1939 (WRC 2153); memorandum, 24 September (WAC R 34/943).
⁶⁸ Minutes of the Control Board, 29 September 1939 (WRC 2141).
⁶⁹ Memoranda, 1939 (WAC R 34/943); *BBC Handbook*, 1940, p.46.
⁷⁰ Hopkin Morris to Nicolls, 4 October 1939 (WAC R 34/943).
⁷¹ Memorandum, 11 October 1939 (ibid.).
⁷² Memorandum by Lee, 12 October 1939 (ibid.).
⁷³ Memorandum by Nicolls, 12 October 1939 (ibid.); Nicolls to Hopkin Morris, 16 October 1939 (ibid.); Lee to Wellington, 20 October 1939 (ibid.); Scottish director to Welsh director, 25 November 1940 (WRC 2153).
⁷⁴ Hopkin Morris to Nicolls, 13 November 1939 (WAC R 34/943); memorandum by Nicolls, 27 October 1939 (ibid.).
⁷⁵ Memoranda, 6 October and 6 and 9 November 1939 (ibid.). Predictably, Wynn, a member of the Welsh landed class, was more hostile to Welsh-language broadcasts than was any other senior official at Head Office.
⁷⁶ A. Briggs, III, pp.126–40.
⁷⁷ Memorandum, 19 December 1939 (WAC R 34/943).

[78] Daily digest of foreign broadcasts, December 1939 (WAC).

[79] Note on broadcasts from Wales (WAC R 34/945/2); *Radio Times, passim.*

[80] Ibid.; A. Llywelyn-Williams, op.cit., pp.160–73; R. Lucas, op.cit., pp.135–7.

[81] Ibid., p.136. The texts for the period 2 January 1940 to 30 June 1945 are in WRC 3716, 3717 and 3718.

[82] *Radio Times, passim,* especially 2 August 1940; memorandum, 16 July 1940 (WAC R 34/945/2); memorandum, 5 August 1940 (WAC R 20/196/4); *Manchester Guardian,* 17 July and 6 August 1940.

[83] A. Briggs, III, p.116; memorandum, 26 February 1942 (WRC 2152); *Sheffield Star,* 9 July 1940; W. McDouall, *A History of BBC Broadcasting in Scotland* (1993), pp.42–52.

[84] *Radio Times, passim; Western Mail,* 20 February 1940; *Manchester Guardian,* 20 February 1940; *News Chronicle,* 22 February 1940; R. Lucas, op.cit., pp.124–5.

[85] Note of the Home Board, 14 February 1940 (WAC R 34/943); the director of religious broadcasting to controller (programmes), 5 February 1940 (ibid.).

[86] Memorandum, 10 February 1940 (ibid.).

[87] Memorandum by Nicolls, 13 November 1940 (ibid.); J. E. Jones, *Llais y Cymry yn Lluoedd Lloegr* (1944).

[88] Nicolls to Hopkin Morris, 7 March 1940 (WAC R 34/943).

[89] N. Bradney, 'Welsh broadcasting in wartime' (WRC 3718); Ellis to Ogilvie, 8 February 1940 (WAC R 34/943).

[90] Letters, February 1940 (ibid.).

[91] *News Chronicle,* 5 March 1940; *Heddiw,* V, 10 (March 1940), pp.471–2; Jones to Hopkin Morris, n.d. (WRC 2153).

[92] *Radio Times, passim; Listener,* 28 December 1939.

[93] A. Oldfield-Davies, 'Y BBC a Chymru', *Y Genhinen,* XII, 1 (1961), p.50.

[94] 'Maintenance of broadcasting services under emergency conditions' (WRC 2152); file labelled 'Secret Documents' (WRC 2158).

[95] Memorandum, 20 December 1941 (ibid.); minutes of the Regional Board, 4 December 1941 (WRC 2141); note on D. R. Jenkins (WRC 2158); A.Briggs, III, p.205.

[96] Memoranda, 13 January and 11 February 1942 (WAC R 34/945/3); memoranda, 17 May 1940 and 23 April 1942 (WAC R 11/80).

[97] E. Forster, 'Welsh working holiday', in D. Morgan (ed.), op.cit., pp.61–2; *Liverpool Daily Post,* 11 November 1985; file on Bangor (WRC 2142); *North Wales Chronicle,* 9 July 1943; R. Lucas, op.cit., pp.130–1; M. Gorham, *Sound and Fury* (1948), p.98; A. Briggs, III, p.571.

[98] Ibid., pp.29–30; memorandum, 5 March 1942 (WRC 2145); memorandum, 29 October 1942 (WRC 2159); memoranda, 1942 (WAC R 13/375); file on Bangor (WRC 2142).

[99] Ibid.; W. Pickles, *Between You and Me* (1949), p.149.

[100] *Luftwaffe over Swansea* (1965), *passim; Welshman,* 5 January 1943; documents on Aberdare (WRC 2158). No BBC employee was killed in the attack on Swansea's Broadcasting House, but Myfyr Arfon Williams, a BBC engineer at Swansea, was killed in a raid in July 1943 (*Liverpool Daily Post,* 19 July 1943).

[101] A. Briggs, III, pp.6, 551; staff lists (WRC 2156); notes on regional establishments (WRC 2153); minutes of the meeting of the regional directors, 7 July 1944 (WRC 2145).

[102] W. Vaughan-Thomas, op.cit., pp.143–87; staff file, especially report, 29 October 1942 (WRC 2159); memorandum by Hopkin Morris, 4 January 1943 (WRC 2145); *Welsh Review,* IV, 3 (September 1945), p.155.

[103] Conversation with the late Gwilym R. Jones; N. Bradney, op.cit.(WRC 3718); staff file (2159); G. T. Davies, 'Behind the chair', in P. Hannan (ed.), *Wales in*

Vision (1990), p.27; I. Rees (ed.), *Bro a Bywyd Aneirin Talfan Davies* (1992).
[104] A. Briggs, III, pp.361, 363, 552–5.
[105] Ibid., p.550; file on regional directors (2153); memorandum, 29 June 1942 (ibid.); memorandum, 2 September 1943 (WRC 2156); minutes of the meeting of the regional directors, 7 July 1944 (WRC 2145).
[106] Memorandum, April 1942 (WRC 2142); *Observer*, 10 May 1942; N. Bradney, op.cit. (WRC 3718); *Manchester Guardian*, 7 July 1942 and 22 June 1943.
[107] Text of the news, August 1942 to January 1943 (WRC 3719); W. Vaughan-Thomas, op.cit., pp.151–7; A. Briggs, III, p.48.
[108] Ibid., pp.68–9; *Observer*, 18 July 1943.
[109] Memorandum, 27 May 1940 (WRC 2153).
[110] Announcement, 26 February 1943 (WRC 3717); text of news, 26 March 1944 and 1 October 1944 (WRC 3718); R. E. Griffith, *Urdd Gobaith Cymru, 1922–45* (1971), pp.334–5; N. Bradney, op.cit. (WRC 3718). There is a full set of *Seren y Dwyrain* (October 1943 to October 1945) in NLW.
[111] File on Tabernacl (WRC 3719); *Western Mail*, 21 September 1942; N. Bradney, op.cit. (WRC 3718).
[112] Ibid.; text of news, 2 March 1943 (WRC 3717); memorandum, 27 April 1942 (WAC R 34/945/3).
[113] *Parliamentary Debates*, fifth series, vol.361, cols.780–1 and vol. 370, col.424; *Western Mail*, 31 March and 19 December 1941; *Flintshire County Herald*, 19 September 1941.
[114] Memorandum, 28 February 1941 (WAC R 34/945/3); memorandum, 30 December 1942 (WRC 2140); Nicolls to Foot, 28 August 1942 (WAC R 34/943).
[115] A. Briggs, III, p.265; *Caernarvon and Denbigh Herald*, 12 September 1941 and 11 September and 9 October 1942; memorandum, 21 July 1942 (WAC R 34/945/3).
[116] *Carmarthen Journal*, 6 March 1942.
[117] *Y Cymro*, 17 October and 21 November 1942; *Caernarvon and Denbigh Herald*, 14 February 1941; memorandum, 20 March 1942 (WAC R 34/945/3); Nicolls to Graves, 1 April 1942 (ibid.).
[118] *Y Cymro*, 21 November 1942.
[119] *Western Mail*, 24 October 1942; memorandum, 27 August 1942 (WRC 2153); memorandum, 21 February 1944 (WAC R 34/731/3); note, 16 July 1943 (WAC R 34/945/3); minutes of the meeting of the regional directors, 9 February 1944 (WRC 2157); press cuttings, February 1943 (WAC P 562).
[120] *Western Mail*, 10 March 1943.
[121] *Reynolds News*, 21 June 1942; *South Wales Evening Post*, 25 March 1943; *Welsh Review*, IV, 3 (September 1945) p.158; *Western Mail*, 24 April 1943; memorandum, 2 January 1946 (WRC 2145).
[122] Text of news, 23 August 1944 (WRC 3718).
[123] *South Wales Evening Post*, 25 September 1945; memoranda, 1942 and 1945 (WRC 2158); memorandum, 9 June 1945 (WRC 3718); W. Vaughan-Thomas, op.cit., pp.186–7.
[124] Ellis to Ogilvie, 8 February 1940 (WAC R 34/943); R. Silvey, op.cit., pp.110–11; A. Briggs, III, pp.714–26; A. Briggs, *Sound and Vision* (henceforth referred to as A. Briggs, IV), pp.93–4.
[125] Ibid., pp.88, 91.
[126] *Y Cymro*, 4 July 1942; *Observer*, 10 September 1944.
[127] *Parliamentary Debates*, fifth series, vol.388, col.867; A. Briggs, III, p.574.
[128] Ibid., pp.714–18.
[129] A. Briggs, IV, p.87; *South Wales Evening Post*, 21 July 1945; minutes of the meeting of the regional directors, 7 March 1945 (WAC R 34/731/2).

[130] Ibid., 7 February 1945 (WRC 2157); file on post-war reorganization (WRC 2156).

[131] A. Briggs, III, p.722.

[132] Some of the BBC's employees who had spent the war in the armed forces were taken aback by Oldfield-Davies's promotion. 'Pan ddes i a'm cyfeillion yn ôl o'r fyddin', wrote Elwyn Evans, 'fe gawsom fod yr hen Alun wedi dringo o'r swydd ddi-nod [o gynhyrchydd rhaglenni i ysgolion] i fod yn Rheolwr y Rhanbarth yn lle Hopkin Morris. Cyfnewidiad rhyfeddol.' ('When my friends and I returned from the army, we found that old Alun had climbed from the obscure post [of producer of schools' programmes] to be the Director of the Region instead of Hopkin Morris. A wondrous transformation.') (Text of a lecture by Elwyn Evans.) Three producers who had distinguished themselves before the war – Elwyn Evans, Geraint Dyfnallt Owen and Alun Llywelyn-Williams – returned to work for the BBC in Wales after the war, but eventually opted for careers elsewhere.

[133] *South Wales Evening Post*, 1 August 1945.

Chapter 4: From the End of the War to the Beveridge Committee, 1945–1952

[1] *Daily Herald*, 4 July 1945; *Liverpool Daily Post*, 7 August 1945.

[2] Ibid., 7 July 1945; statement of 2 January 1946 (WRC 2145).

[3] Memoranda of the regional director in residence, 12 and 25 July 1945 (WRC 2157).

[4] *South Wales Argus*, 28 July 1945.

[5] *Caernarvon and Denbigh Herald*, 24 August 1945; *Parliamentary Debates*, fifth series, vol.416, col.232.

[6] *Liverpool Daily Post*, 9 October and 27 November 1945; *Reynolds News*, 2 July 1945.

[7] *Welsh Review*, IV, 3 (September 1945), pp.158, 159; Rhys to Ward, 6 September 1946 (WRC 2145).

[8] Memorandum, 8 January 1946 (ibid.).

[9] See the forthcoming history of *Woman's Hour* by Sally Thompson.

[10] Memoranda on regional finance (WRC 2135); *BBC Annual Report and Accounts*, 1950–1 (1951), pp.98–9.

[11] BBC memorandum for Beveridge, no.13 (WRC 2139). Scotland's allowance was raised to £1,750 in 1947 and to £2,000 in 1949; that of North was raised from £1,750 in 1947 to £2,250 in 1949 (ibid., no.28: WRC 2138).

[12] *Welsh Review*, IV, 3 (September 1945), p.158.

[13] *Llanelly Mercury*, 15 August 1946; *Liverpool Daily Post*, 14 November 1949; memorandum, 6 June 1946 (WRC 2145); memorandum, 11 July 1949 (WRC 2157); Oldfield-Davies to Lloyd George, 3 February 1950 (WRC 2138).

[14] *Western Mail*, 16 October 1943.

[15] A. Briggs, *The War of Words* (1970) (henceforth referred to as A. Briggs, III), p.584; minutes of the meeting of the regional controllers, 3 March 1948 (WRC 2157).

[16] *Liverpool Daily Post*, 28 January 1946; *South Wales Evening Post*, 5 June 1946; file on the orchestra (WRC 2156).

[17] Ibid.; P. Ferris, *Sir Huge: The Life of Huw Wheldon* (1990), p.74.

[18] Memorandum, 15 March 1946 (WRC 2145); *Liverpool Daily Post*, 19 March 1946.

[19] A. Briggs, *Sound and Vision* (1979) (henceforth referred to as A. Briggs, IV), pp.43–5.

[20] *Manchester Guardian*, 11 February 1946; *Observer*, 14 April 1946; *Y Cymro*, 29 March 1946; *Liverpool Daily Post*, 19 February, 26 March, 9 April and 11 June 1946.

[21] Oldfield-Davies to Cecil-Williams, 5 March 1946 (WRC 2145).

[22] *Liverpool Daily Post*, 5 and 11 June 1946; A. Briggs, IV, p.101.

[23] Haley to Oldfield-Davies, 13 March 1946 (WRC 2145).

[24] Memoranda on regional programmes (WAC R 34/731/3).

[25] Memoranda, 20 August 1946 and 21 June 1949 (WRC 2153); memorandum, 5 July 1950 (WRC 2145).

[26] Memorandum, 2 July 1948 (WRC 2157); E. Evans, 'Deuparth gwaith', in D. Morgan (ed.), *Babi Sam* (1985), p.36. Of the forty engineers at Cardiff in 1950, three were Welsh-speakers (minutes of the Welsh Advisory Committee, 30 June 1950: WAC R 6/207).

[27] Memoranda (WRC 2153).

[28] Staff file, 1939–52 (ibid.).

[29] Oldfield-Davies to Cecil-Williams, 5 March 1946 (WRC 2145).

[30] *Times*, 26 June 1946.

[31] *Y Cymro*, 29 March 1946.

[32] *Times*, 11 and 16 April and 16 July 1946; *Welsh Review*, IV, 3 (September 1945), p.155.

[33] But see J. Hale, *Radio Power: Propaganda and International Broadcasting* (1975), p.48.

[34] H. Grisewood, *One Thing at a Time* (1968), p.177.

[35] In 1974, broadcasting became the responsibility of the home secretary; it was transferred to the heritage secretary in 1992.

[36] *Parliamentary Debates*, fifth series, 1945–6, vol.425, cols.116–1123.

[37] A. Briggs, IV, p.187. *Y Cymro* (29 March 1946) noted that the proposed centres were London, Birmingham, Huddersfield, Falkirk and Bristol, but the report mentions no specific centres.

[38] Memorandum, 15 November 1946 (WRC 2157). All regions were charged for television to the extent of 11.08 per cent of net sound licence revenue, regardless of when they might expect to receive the service (BBC memorandum for Beveridge, no.245: WRC 2138).

[39] A. Briggs, IV, pp.189–90; P. Ferris, op.cit., p.83; A. Milne, *D.G.: The Memoirs of a British Broadcaster* (1988), p.9.

[40] *Aberdare Leader*, 3 July 1948.

[41] *BBC Handbook*, 1947, p.22.

[42] A. Briggs, IV, pp.65–7.

[43] Ibid., p.77; note on the Third Programme (WAC R 9/9/12).

[44] R. Silvey, *Who's Listening?* (1977), p.71.

[45] Oldfield-Davies to Haley, 6 September 1946; Nicolls to Haley, September 1946 (WAC R 6/206).

[46] Note by Haley, 8 January 1948; Beadle to Nicolls, 12 January 1948 (ibid.); minutes of the Welsh Advisory Council, 13 February 1947 (ibid.).

[47] *Liverpool Daily Post*, 12 July 1949.

[48] Minutes of the Welsh Advisory Council, 24 September 1948 (WAC R 6/207).

[49] Haley to Nicolls, 24 March 1948; Oldfield-Davies to Nicolls, 31 March 1948 (WAC R 34/945/4).

[50] Memorandum by Haley, 25 October 1948 (WAC R 6/206).

[51] *South Wales Echo*, 28 January 1949.

[52] Letter by Weekes, 9 December 1949 (WAC R 6/206); *South Wales Evening Post*,

3 January 1950. The Welsh Republican Movement put forward a similar argument (*Western Mail*, 16 January 1950).

53 *Manchester Guardian*, 12 October 1949.
54 Correspondence, May and June, 1950 (WRC 3718); audience research reports (WAC R 9/5/80–5); D. Balsom and others, 'The political consequences of Welsh identity', *Ethnic and Racial Studies*, VII (1984), p.160.
55 *South Wales Echo*, 11 March 1949; *Merthyr Express*, 17 December 1949; minutes of the Welsh Advisory Council, 26 September 1947, 9 December 1949, 24 March 1950, 8 June 1951 and 28 September 1951 (WAC R 6/207); M. Aspel, *Polly Wants a Zebra* (1974), p.103.
56 Minutes of the Welsh Advisory Council, 26 September 1947 (WAC R 6/207); *North Wales Chronicle*, 24 December 1947.
57 Haley to Parry-Williams, 26 July 1949 (WAC R 6/206); *Daily Herald*, 23 July 1949; minutes of the Welsh Advisory Council, 13 February 1947 and 18 March 1948 (WAC R 6/207).
58 *North Wales Chronicle*, 8 February 1949; *Cambrian News*, 8 July 1949; reports, 13 February 1948 and 31 March 1949 (WRC 2146).
59 Memorandum, 22 September 1948 (WAC R 6/206).
60 Minutes of the Welsh Advisory Council, 8 December 1950 (WAC R 6/207).
61 Ibid., 24 September 1948 (WAC R 6/206); Ashbridge to Jacob, 22 September 1948 (ibid.).
62 Memorandum, 26 April 1950 (WRC 2159); notes on appointments (WRC 2138).
63 Oldfield-Davies to Aaron, 4 July 1963 (WRC 1007); D. Jones, *Music in Wales* (1961) p.38; minutes of the Welsh Advisory Council, 25 April 1947 (WAC R 6/207).
64 Ibid., 30 September 1949 (ibid.); Monthly Report, March 1949 (WRC 2154); R. Lucas, *The Voice of a Nation?* (1981), pp.168, 202.
65 Note, January 1952 (WRC 2146).
66 *Carmarthen Journal*, 10 May 1946 and 6 July 1946; *South Wales Evening Post*, 4 June 1946.
67 Ibid., 1 May 1952.
68 *Liverpool Daily Post*, 18 March 1946 and 30 September 1947; memorandum, 11 June 1946 (WRC 2138); minutes of the Welsh Advisory Council, 26 September 1947 (WAC R 6/207).
69 *Wrexham Leader*, 18 November 1949.
70 Papers concerning Scottish MPs (WAC R 34/566); *Merthyr Express*, 6 April 1949.
71 File labelled 'Welsh Regional Council of Labour' (WRC 2163).
72 Ibid.
73 Report, 13 December 1950 (WRC 2159); *Liverpool Daily Post*, 29 March 1949 and 29 September 1950.
74 Haley to Parry-Williams, 5 February 1948 (WAC R 6/206); report of a meeting, 17 February 1955 (WRC 2163).
75 *Liverpool Daily Post*, 9 April 1952; minutes of the General Advisory Council, 12 May 1952 (WRC 2145).
76 Memoranda (WAC R 34/529 and R 32/570).
77 *Montgomeryshire Times*, 12 November 1949; *South Wales Echo*, 18 May 1949; licence figures, 31 May 1950–2 (WRC 2151).
78 Ibid.
79 *South Wales Echo*, 22 July 1949; *Herald of Wales*, 16 November 1951.
80 *Western Mail*, 12 November 1949; *South Wales Evening Post*, 14 June 1949.
81 Ibid., 22 October 1949; *Liverpool Daily Post*, 9 August 1949 and 2 May 1952.
82 *Y Faner*, 14 February 1951.

[83] J. Eilian, 'Y BBC a chenedl y Cymry', *Y Llenor* XXX, 1 (Spring, 1950), pp.44, 45.

[84] *Western Mail*, 17 December 1949; minutes of the meeting of the director of home broadcasting, 14 June 1949 (WRC 2146).

[85] Ibid., 30 November 1949 (WRC 2146); *Parliamentary Debates*, fifth series, vol.469, col.1998.

[86] Report by Ashbridge, 28 April 1950 (WAC T 16/235/1); report, 19 July 1950 (ibid.); minutes of the Welsh Advisory Council, 30 June 1950 (WAC R 6/207).

[87] Ibid., 8 December 1950 (ibid.); R. Lucas, op.cit., pp.167–8; *Liverpool Daily Post*, 27 May 1952.

[88] *Y Faner*, 20 August 1952.

[89] File labelled 'Wenvoe Opening Ceremony' (WRC 2162); *Western Mail*, 26 May and 18 August 1952.

[90] A. Briggs, IV, pp.291–420, especially p.338; notes on the Beveridge visit to Cardiff, 3 May 1950 (WRC 2138).

[91] M. Stocks, *My Commonplace Book* (1970), p.174. See also Lord Simon of Wythenshawe, *The BBC from Within* (1953), p.151.

[92] *Western Mail*, 23 January 1950; memorandum, July 1950 (WRC 2139).

[93] Notes on the subcommittee of the Advisory Council (WRC 2138); Wheldon to Oldfield-Davies, 2 February 1950 (ibid.). Mrs Snowden was a governor from 1927 to 1933, and, according to Reith, considered that it was incumbent upon her to harry the director-general (J. Reith, *Into the Wind* (1949), pp.117–24).

[94] Minutes of the special meeting of the Welsh Advisory Council, 27 January 1950 (WAC R 6/207).

[95] J. Cain, *Seventy Years of Broadcasting* (1992), p.69; BBC memorandum for Beveridge, no.245 (WRC 2138); the BBC's answers to written questions, no.28 (ibid.).

[96] *Y Faner*, 5 April 1950; *Y Cymro*, 14 and 21 April 1950; *Liverpool Daily Post*, 2 March and 12 July 1949; *South Wales Evening Post*, 19 January and 25 April 1950; *South Wales Echo*, 27 January 1950.

[97] Oldfield-Davies to Walters, 30 November 1949 (WRC 2152); Oldfield-Davies to Lloyd George, 3 February 1950 (WAC 2138).

[98] J. Cain, op.cit., p.70; A. Briggs, IV, pp.372–91.

[99] Ibid., pp.381, 383; R. Lucas, op.cit., p.162; *Y Cymro*, 26 January 1951; *South Wales Evening Post*, 19 January 1951; minutes of the Welsh Advisory Council, 9 March 1951 (WAC R 6/207).

[100] Ibid., 9 March and 2 April 1951 (ibid.); Nicolls to the regional controllers, 26 January 1951 (WRC 2138); memorandum, February 1951 (ibid.).

[101] A. Briggs, IV, p.399; *New Statesman*, 21 July 1951; *Western Mail*, 4 August 1951; observations of the governors, July 1951 (WRC 2138); *Parliamentary Debates*, fifth series, vol.490, cols.1423–1541; report, 11 October 1951 (WRC 2146).

[102] C. Stuart, *The Reith Diary* (1975), p.475; C. Curran, *A Seamless Robe* (1979), p.55.

[103] Minutes of the Welsh Advisory Council, 23 May and 24 October 1952 (WAC R 6/207).

[104] *BBC Annual Report and Accounts*, 1952–3, p.111.

[105] R. Silvey, op.cit., pp.43–57; note on listener research (WRC 2151); *South Wales Evening Post*, 6 April 1948; *South Wales Echo*, 11 February 1949.

[106] Memorandum on audiences (WRC 2139); report, 1948 (WAC R 9/9/12).

[107] Ibid.; audience research reports (WAC R 9/5/80–5); report on audience research (WRC 2151); *Wrexham Leader*, 18 November 1949.

[108] Report, 1948 (WAC R 9/9/12).

[109] Memorandum on audiences (WRC 2139); note on Radio Luxembourg, November 1949 (WRC 2157); memorandum on Sunday policy, 30 January 1952 (WRC 2156).

[110] Reports, 14 January 1948, 19 September 1949 and 21 June 1951 (WRC 2146); *Liverpool Echo*, 27 April 1948.

[111] Monthly Report, December 1948 (WRC 2154); *Daily Mail*, 15 September 1949 and 26 January 1950; *Manchester Guardian*, 10 February 1950; *Daily Herald*, 20 March 1950.

[112] Memorandum, 11 March 1948 (WRC 2157); *South Wales Evening Post*, 25 November 1947; *Carmarthen Journal*, 7 December 1949; *Radio Times, passim*.

[113] Ibid.; *BBC Handbook*, 1951, pp.62–4; letter from Gaiman (WRC 2138); report, December 1948 (WRC 2154); *Herald of Wales*, 1 October 1949.

[114] *Radio Times, passim*; minutes of the Welsh Advisory Committee, 9 December 1949 (WAC R 6/207).

[115] There is more than one definition of Reithianism. Nicholas Fraser defined it as 'a high minded racket whereby the good and the great were able to keep their paws on British broadcasting, while professing the best of intentions' (*Sunday Times*, 29 August 1993).

[116] Note on audience research (WRC 2151); text of a speech by Oldfield-Davies, 13 February 1948 (WRC 2138); Monthly Report, June 1949 (WRC 2154); *South Wales Evening Post*, 21 September 1948; *Reynolds News*, 1 May 1949; *Herald of Wales*, 1 October 1949; *Liverpool Daily Post*, 16 December 1947.

[117] Ibid., 14 November 1949; *News Chronicle*, 3 March 1949; *Y Faner*, 7 September 1949; memorandum by Talfan Davies, 11 December 1947 (WRC 2143).

[118] *Radio Times, passim*.

[119] Note on the use of the gramophone (WRC 2139); report, March 1950 (WRC 2154).

[120] Note by Davies (WAC R 11/80); report, 17 September 1948 (WRC 2146); report, November 1949 (WRC 2154); audience research reports (WAC R 9/5/81–2).

[121] Report on home orchestras, 1951 (WRC 2156); memorandum, 13 November 1951 (ibid.); note, 28 April 1950 (WRC 2138).

[122] Quarterly Reports, 12 April and 11 October 1951 (WRC 2146); report, June 1948 (WRC 2154); *Radio Times, passim*; *BBC Handbook*, 1950, p.103.

[123] *South Wales Echo*, 18 March 1949; I. B. Griffith, 'A Personal Note', in D. Morgan (ed.), op.cit., p.125; audience research reports, 1945–51 (WAC R 9/5/80–5).

[124] Ibid.; report, June 1954 (WRC 2148); *BBC Handbook*, 1947, p.64; note, 27 March 1951 (WAC R 9/5/85).

[125] *Liverpool Daily Post*, 12 March 1946; *Western Mail*, 17 October 1949; M. Richards (ed.), *Meddai Syr Ifor* (1968).

[126] A. Briggs, IV, pp.605–12; audience research reports (WAC R 9/5/80–5); memorandum, 7 April 1948 (WRC 2142). In the late 1940s, the Labour and Conservative Parties were granted an equal number of broadcasts, with occasional broadcasts for the Liberals (memorandum, 30 April 1948: WRC 2148).

[127] BBC document for Beveridge, no.26 (WRC 2139); memorandum, 20 April 1948 (WRC 2156); note, 1950 (WRC 2148); note on Nicholas (ibid.).

[128] Report, August 1945 (WRC 2157); memorandum, 26 September 1956 (WRC 2142); J. Dimbleby, *Richard Dimbleby: A Biography* (1975), pp.204, 270–1.

[129] Note on local correspondents (WRC 2157); memorandum, 2 November 1950 (WRC 2145).

[130] Report, 13 December 1950 (WRC 2159); file on the complaints of the Welsh Regional Council of Labour (WRC 2163); memorandum on Pugh (WRC 2142); file on Pugh (WRC 2159); audience research reports (WAC R 9/5/80–5).

[131] Report, September 1948 (WRC 2143); report, February 1949 (WRC 2154); *Liverpool Daily Post*, 26 October 1948.

[132] M. Aspel, op.cit., p.77.

[133] Report on schools' broadcasts (WRC 2148); R. Lucas, op.cit., pp.154–5.

[134] Ibid., p.156; note on religious programmes, 26 April 1950 (WRC 2159); note for Beveridge (WRC 2138).

[135] Report, 29 April 1950 (WRC 2159); note, 2 December 1951 (WAC R 9/5/85); *Weekly Mail*, 25 September 1948; *Radio Times, passim*; memorandum on religious programmes, 26 April 1950 (WRC 2159).

[136] Audience research reports (WAC R 9/5/80–5); note by Jones, 29 November 1948 (WRC 2143); *BBC Handbook*, 1949, pp.40–3.

[137] A. Briggs, *The BBC, The First Fifty Years* (1985), p.248; Listeners' Research Bulletin, October 1947 (WRC 2151); report, 17 September 1948 (WRC 2146); Quarterly Report, 12 April 1951 (ibid.); *Merthyr Express*, 5 March 1949; *South Wales Echo*, 18 March 1949; *Radio Times, passim*.

[138] Memorandum by Evans, 19 March 1946 (WRC 2159); memorandum by Talfan Davies, 20 March 1946 (ibid.).

[139] Quarterly Report, 12 April 1951 (WRC 2146); audience research reports (WAC R 9/5/83); Monthly Report, January 1950 (WRC 2154).

[140] Memorandum by Gruffydd, 31 December 1946 (WRC 2143).

[141] *South Wales Evening Post*, 26 April 1949; audience research reports (WAC R 9/5/80–5).

[142] Ibid.; Monthly Report, April 1949 (WRC 2154); Quarterly Report, 31 March 1949 (WRC 2146); memorandum for the Beveridge Committee (WRC 2139); *Radio Times, passim*.

[143] Memorandum, 31 December 1946 (WRC 2143); Monthly Report, June 1951 (WRC 2146); audience research reports (WAC R 9/5/85).

[144] Ibid.; *Radio Times, passim; Cambrian News*, 1 April 1949.

Chapter 5: *The Era of the Fourth Charter, 1952–1964*

[1] List of licences (WRC 2151); note on licence-holders, September 1953 (WAC T 16/235/1); BCW Annual Report, 1954–5 (WRC 3626); *Daily Mail*, 14 August 1952; A. D. Bain, *The Growth of Television Ownership in the United Kingdom* (1964); *Western Mail*, 18 August 1952.

[2] Ibid., 1 September 1952; *Manchester Evening Chronicle*, 23 June 1949; *South Wales Argus*, 23 August 1952; report, 1949 (WRC 2145); A. Briggs, *Sound and Vision* (1979) (henceforth referred to as A. Briggs, IV), p.245.

[3] Ibid., p.243; *Cardiff Times*, 2 August 1952.

[4] Memorandum on reception (WRC 3626); C. Curran, *A Seamless Robe* (1979), p.292.

[5] R. Silvey, *Who's Listening?* (1974), p.156; *Liverpool Daily Post*, 25 July 1952.

[6] Note by Fraser, March 1955, quoted in B. Sendall, *Independent Television in Britain*, vol.I (1982) (henceforth referred to as B. Sendall, I), p.96.

[7] *Liverpool Daily Post*, 13 May 1952; *Daily Mail*, 14 August 1982; *Radio Times*, 8 August 1952; text of talk, 15 August 1952 (WRC 2161); note on expenditure, 14 May 1952 (ibid.); *Western Mail*, 26 May 1952.

[8] Ibid., 1 September 1952; *Liverpool Daily Post*, 9 September 1952.

[9] Ibid., 22 January and 3 March 1953; *Western Mail*, 16 February and 2 and 4 March 1953; *News Chronicle*, 4 March 1953; *Radio Times, passim*.

[10] Parry-Williams to Oldfield-Davies, 22 March 1953 (WRC 2155); file on competition (WRC 2138); MBCW, 18 May 1953 (WAC R 6/10/1).

11 Ibid., 15 July 1953 (ibid.); *South Wales Echo*, 10 April 1953; *Western Mail*, 20 July 1953.

12 Minutes of the meeting of the regional controllers, 5 July 1957 (WRC 3620); *Daily Telegraph*, 26 May 1952; memorandum by controller West, 11 March 1952 (WRC 2161).

13 Report on regional broadcasting, 22 December 1958 (WAC 3626).

14 A. Oldfield-Davies, 'Dwy flynedd ar hugain fel rheolwr y BBC yng Nghymru', in G. Erfyl (ed.), *Radio Cymru* (1989), p.71. See also A. Oldfield-Davies, 'Y BBC a Chymru', *Y Genhinen*, XII, 1 (Winter 1961–2).

15 Statement on hours, 3 June 1955 (WRC 2160); MBCW, 21 September, 19 October and 16 November 1955 (WRC 3626); memorandum by Oldfield-Davies, 20 June 1955 (WRC 2160); minutes of the meetings of the regional controllers, 11 November 1953 and 8 November 1955 (WRC 3620).

16 Ibid., 5 September 1955 (ibid.); report on regional broadcasting, 22 December 1958 (WRC 3626).

17 Report, 30 June 1955 (WRC 2148); *South Wales Evening Post*, 9 July and 10 September 1954; A.Briggs, IV, p.7.

18 *Western Mail*, 30 August 1954; report, 31 March 1955 (WRC 2148); R. Lucas, *Voice of a Nation?* (1981), p.168; *Y Cymro*, 30 May 1952; list of BBC property (WRC 1009); note, 24 October 1957 (WRC 2147); minutes of the meeting of the regional controllers, 8 November 1955 (WRC 3620).

19 Report, 31 December 1955 (WRC 2148); *Radio Times, passim*.

20 Ibid.; note by Watkin Jones, 4 March 1957 (WAC T 16/685); J. Ormond, 'Beginnings', in P. Hannan (ed.), *Wales in Vision* (1990), pp.1–4.

21 Davies to Jones, February 1956 (WAC T 16/235/1); Oldfield-Davies to Barnes, February 1956 (ibid.); Oldfield-Davies to Roberts, 26 February 1957 (WAC T 16/685); Oldfield-Davies to Beadle, 1 April 1957 (ibid.); Beadle to Oldfield-Davies, 26 March 1957 (ibid.); minutes of the meeting of the regional controllers, 3 April 1957 (WRC 3620); MBCW, 10 February 1959 (WRC 3626); ibid., 20 July 1960 (WRC 3691); A. Briggs, IV, p.795.

22 Ibid., pp.882–976, especially 898, 912, 913; B. Sendall, I, Part 1; H. H. Wilson, *Pressure Group: The Campaign for Commercial Television* (1961); *South Wales Echo*, 23 April 1954; C. Mayhew, *Time to Explain* (1987), p.130.

23 *Liverpool Daily Post*, 7 July 1953; *South Wales Echo*, 30 July 1954; B. Sendall, I, p.14.

24 Ibid., p.51; *Parliamentary Debates*, fifth series, vol.527, cols.375–540; *South Wales Echo*, 23 April 1954; report on regional broadcasting, 22 December 1958 (WRC 3626).

25 B. Sendall, I, pp.118–19, 303–14; S. Lambert, *Channel Four* (1982), pp.11–12.

26 Memorandum by controller North, 20 December 1954 (WRC 2160).

27 MBCW, 19 September 1956 (WRC 2626); report, 30 September 1957 (WRC 2148); memorandum, 7 October 1957 (WAC T 16/235/2); minutes of the meeting of the regional controllers, 1 October 1957 (WAC T 16/685).

28 Oldfield-Davies to Beadle, 4 October 1957 (ibid.).

29 Ibid., 15 October 1957 (ibid.); Beadle to Oldfield-Davies, 8 October 1957 and 28 October 1958 (WAC T 16/235/2).

30 B. Sendall, I, pp.204, 212, 217–18.

31 Ibid., p.136; A. Briggs, *The BBC: The First Fifty Years* (1985), p.300; R. Silvey, op.cit., p.174–95; G. W. Goldie, *Facing the Nation* (1977), p.111; M. Tracey, *A Variety of Lives: A Biography of Sir Hugh Greene* (1983), p.157.

32 Ibid., pp.160–5; C. Mayhew, op.cit., p.132.

33 G. W. Goldie, op.cit., p.112–13; T. Burns, *The BBC: Public Institution and Private World* (1977), pp.65–6.

34 BCW Annual Report, 1957–8 (WAC T 16/235/2).

35 MBCW, 1957–60, especially 21 November 1956 and 17 December 1958 (WRC 3626 and 3691); *The Place of Welsh and English in the Schools of Wales* (1953); Hill to Cecil-Williams, 18 April 1955 (WRC 2160).

36 Oldfield-Davies to the director of sound broadcasting, 6 May 1958 (WRC 3619).

37 Memorandum, 22 September 1955 (WAC T 16/235/2); minutes of the meeting of the regional controllers, 1 October 1957 (WAC T 16/685); report, 31 December 1957 (WRC 2148); minutes of the meetings of the television service controllers, 8 October and 10 December 1957 (WRC 2161).

38 Report, 30 June 1956 (WRC 2148).

39 *Radio Times, passim*; minutes of the meetings of the regional controllers, 8 February and 3 April 1957 (WRC 3620); memorandum, 21 March 1957 (WRC 2161); reports, 30 June and 31 December 1957 (WRC 2148).

40 Jacob to Fraser, 9 April 1958 (WAC T 16/685); B. Sendall, I, pp.218–19.

41 Ibid., pp.49–50, 63; Oldfield-Davies to Jacob, 7 June 1958 (WAC T 16/235/2); memorandum, 22 July 1958 (WAC T 16/685).

42 Director of engineering to Oldfield-Davies, 8 July 1958 (WAC T 16/235/2); MBCW, 18 June and 15 October 1958 and 20 April 1960 (WRC 3626).

43 Ibid., 18 November 1958 (ibid.); BCW statement, December 1958 (WAC T 16/685); press announcement, 19 November 1958 (ibid.).

44 Note by Oldfield-Davies, 15 August 1960 (ibid.); Bevins to fforde, 1 August 1961 (WRC 3420); fforde to Bevins, 4 August 1961 (ibid.); minutes of the meeting of the regional controllers, 7 December 1960 (WRC 3620).

45 Ibid., 9 July, 7 September and 9 November 1960 (ibid.).

46 R. Cathcart, *The Most Contrary Region: The BBC in Northern Ireland, 1924–84* (1984), p.85; memorandum of Oldfield-Davies, 7 June 1958 (WAC T 16/235/2); note by Davies, 27 February 1962 (WAC T 16/685); note by the pre-sentation director, 5 April 1962 (ibid.); MBCW, 19 November 1958 (WRC 3626).

47 Beadle to Jacob, 5 November 1959 (WAC T 16/656); Oldfield-Davies to Beadle, 5 November 1959 (ibid.); controller of television administration to Oldfield-Davies, 9 March 1961 (WRC 2353).

48 Minutes of the meeting of the regional controllers, 1 March 1961 (WRC 3620).

49 C. Jenkins, *Power behind the Screen* (1961), p.218; A. Briggs, *Governing the BBC* (1979), p.105; Shaw to Oldfield-Davies, 12 June 1959 (WRC 3420).

50 Oldfield-Davies to Beadle, 10 August 1960 (WAC T 16/685); memorandum of Oldfield-Davies, 30 September 1960 (ibid.); B. Sendall, *Independent Television in Britain*, vol.II (1983) (henceforth referred to as B. Sendall, II), pp.70–82.

51 Ibid. It was unprecedented for the postmaster-general to lay down rules about programme content.

52 Minutes of the meetings of the regional controllers, 3 May and 5 July 1961 (WRC 3620); MBCW, 23 June 1961 (WRC 3691).

53 B. Sendall, II, pp.76–7.

54 A. Oldfield-Davies, op.cit., in G. Erfyl (ed.), op.cit., p.72; B. Sendall, II, pp.75, 79.

55 Sodlau Prysur (A. T. Davies), *Teledu Mamon* (n.d).

56 B. Sendall, II, pp.80–2.

57 A. Briggs, *The First Fifty Years*, p.326; M. Tracey, op.cit., p.190; MBCW, 18 May 1960 (WRC 3691).

58 A. D. Rees, *Dear Sir Harry Pilkington* (n.d.).

59 B. Sendall, I, p.335, II, pp.85–9; *The Report of the Committee on Broadcasting 1960* (1962: Cmnd.1753); A. Briggs., *The First Fifty Years*, pp.326–7.

60 Ibid., pp.328–9; teleprint from controller North, 30 December 1963 (WRC 3430). The government had decided on its policy before the publication of the Pilkington Report (R. Bevins, *The Greasy Pole* (1965), p.80).

Notes

Parliamentary Debates, fifth series, vol.679, cols.996–9; *Parliamentary Debates* (House of Lords), fifth series, vol.252, cols.525–46; B. Sendall, II, p.185.

Ibid., pp.210–12; *Western Mail*, 20 November 1963.

R. Sampson, *Anatomy of Britain* (1965), p.664.

Correspondence in file labelled 'ITA' (WRC 3430); MBCW, 23 June 1961 (WRC 3691).

ITA proposals (WAC T 16/685); response of the BBC, 10 October 1962 (WRC 3430); correspondence on overlapping (ibid.); MBCW, 10 October 1962 (WRC 3691).

J. Cain, *The BBC: Seventy Years of Broadcasting* (1992), p.76.

Western Mail, 9 June 1952.

Ibid., 30 December 1952; *South Wales Echo*, 17 October 1952; file labelled 'National Broadcasting Council, 1952' (WRC 2155); Oldfield-Davies to Grisewood, 22 January 1953 (WAC R 34/237); *Times*, 30 December 1952.

MBCW, 1953 (WAC R 6/10/1); director-general to controller Wales and controller Scotland, 27 September 1953 (WRC 2145); T. M. Jones, *Going Public* (1987), pp.145–51.

C. Curran, op.cit., p.157; note, 16 October 1954 (WAC R 34/237/2); text of talk by Wynn (ibid.); *Y Faner*, 30 April 1952; *Y Cymro*, 12 December 1952; *Cardigan and Tivyside Advertiser*, 20 February and 13 March 1953.

Reports, 19 March, 30 September and 31 December 1953 and 31 March and 30 September 1954 (WRC 2157); *Y Faner*, 3 and 24 March 1954; *Liverpool Daily Post*, 3 November 1954; *Western Mail*, 11 October 1954; *Y Cymro*, 8 October 1954; *Wrexham Leader*, 15 October 1954; MBCW, 1953–5 (WAC R 6/10/2 and WRC 3626).

Ibid.; *Western Mail*, 18 and 20 October 1954.

Ibid., 12 October and 8 November 1954; *Daily Mail*, 9 July 1955; *Caernarvon and Denbigh Herald*, 22 October and 19 November 1954; minutes of the Board of Governors, 31 March 1955 (WRC 2147); Annual Report of the BCW, 1953–4 (WAC R 34/237); MBCW 17 November 1954 (WRC 3626).

Y Cymro, 16 December 1954; *Y Faner*, 7 April 1954 and 23 February 1955; *Yr Herald Gymraeg*, 13 December 1954; *Western Mail*, 19 January and 5 July 1955; *Daily Mail*, 21 June 1955.

Minutes of the meetings of the regional controllers, 11 November and 2 December 1953 and 11 October 1954 (WRC 3620); *South Wales Echo*, 21 July 1954; *South Wales Argus*, 25 March 1955; C. Curran, op.cit., p.170.

Report on regional broadcasting, 22 December 1958 (WRC 3626); memorandum by Oldfield-Davies, 29 August 1958 (WRC 2335).

U. Wiliam, 'Broadcasting in Wales today', *Dock Leaves* 5, 14 (Summer 1954), pp.29–33; memoranda by Jacobs, 27 January and 28 May 1953 (WRC 2155 and 2145).

Memorandum by Oldfield-Davies, 20 June 1953 (WRC 3626); letters, 1956 (WRC 2141); letters, 1949–56 (WRC 2155).

South Wales Echo, 18 September 1953; *Western Mail*, 16 July 1953.

A. Briggs, IV, p.627; MBCW, 6 January 1953 (WAC R 6/10/1).

Ibid., 5 April, 24 July and 16 September 1953 (ibid.); note, April 1953 (ibid.); note by Jacob, February 1953 (ibid.); note by Grisewood, 1 April 1953 (WRC 2155); note, April 1953 (WAC R 34/237).

Macdonald to Oldfield-Davies, 18 September 1953 (WRC 2155); minutes of meeting of the Board of Governors, 3 September 1953 (WAC R 34/43). Macdonald always wrote to controller Wales in Welsh, and began almost every sentence with the splendid but somewhat archaic word *parthed* (with reference to).

83 Note, September 1953 (ibid.); the solicitor to Jacob, 20 November 1953 (ibid.).

84 Minutes of meeting of the Board of Governors, 10 February 1954 (ibid.); Macdonald to Oldfield-Davies, 12 January 1954 (WRC 2155); report of a meeting, 17 February 1955 (WRC 2162); MBCW, 15 June and 14 September 1954 (WAC R 6/10/2); *Liverpool Daily Post*, 14 September 1954 .

85 Ibid., 21 September 1954; *Western Mail*, 10 and 22 September and 1 October 1954; G. Jones, 'The use of government power by notice under the licence and agreement' (1988) (WAC C 146); A. Briggs, IV, pp.641–4, 655, 671.

86 MBCW, 19 October 1954 (WAC R 6/10/2); statement of Oldfield-Davies, 23 November 1954 (WRC 2150); Jacob to Cadogan, 9 November 1954 (WAC R 34/237/3)

87 Note by Grisewood, 24 November 1954 (ibid.); memorandum by Oldfield-Davies, 25 November 1954 (ibid.); memorandum by the parliamentary correspondent, 1 December 1954 (ibid.).

88 Memorandum by Grisewood, 30 December 1954 (WAC R 34/237/3); memorandum, 20 December 1954 (ibid.); opinion of the law officers, 20 December 1954 (ibid.); minutes of the meeting of the Board of Governors, 13 January 1955 (ibid.).

89 G. Jones, op.cit. (WAC C 146); note on party political broadcasts (WAC R 34/524/3).

90 Minutes of the meeting of the regional controllers, 1 March 1955 (WRC 3620); note on a meeting with Hill, 1955 (WRC 3626); MBCW, 20 April 1955 (WRC 3626).

91 Statement of the postmaster-general (WRC 3626); Hill to Cadogan, 27 July 1955 (ibid.). Hill also used the occasion to reconfirm the Fourteen-Day Rule (G. Jones, op.cit.: WAC C 146).

92 *Times*, 28 July and 15 August 1955; G. W. Goldie, op.cit., pp.136–43; *Parliamentary Debates*, fifth series, vol.548, cols.615–717.

93 Minutes of the meeting of the Board of Governors, 29 September 1955 (WRC 2147); minutes of the meeting of the regional controllers, 5 February and 1 October 1958 and 6 April 1959 (WRC 3620); MBCW, 18 December 1957 (WRC 3626); report, 18 December 1959 (WRC 2150).

94 *Parliamentary Debates*, fifth series, vol.548, cols.615–19.

95 Ibid., 615–717; minutes of the meeting of the regional controllers, 6 February 1956 (WRC 3620).

96 Minutes of the meeting of the Board of Governors, 2 February 1956 (WRC 2147); minutes of the meeting of the General Advisory Council, December 1955 and March 1956 (WRC 2149); minutes of the meeting of the General Liaison Committee, 10 April 1956 (WRC 2145); *Times*, 2 March 1956.

97 Letters of Llewellyn, January 1956 (WRC 2141); memorandum by Richards, 10 January 1956 (WRC 2142); Edwards to Oldfield-Davies, 4 February 1956 (ibid.); Oldfield-Davies to Edwards, 7 February 1956 (ibid.).

98 Oldfield-Davies to Watkins, 29 April 1955 (ibid.); MBCW, 18 November 1953 and 20 January 1954 (WAC R 6/10); *Parliamentary Debates*, fifth series, vol.548, cols.615–717.

99 Llewellyn to Oldfield-Davies, 13 April 1956 (WRC 2141).

100 Files on the allegations (WRC 2141, 2142, 2156).

101 MBCW, 15 February 1956 (WRC 3626); Jacob to Oldfield-Davies, 10 February 1956 (WRC 2141); Cadbury to Ince, 27 April 1957 (ibid.); Association of Broadcasting Staffs to Ince, 17 April 1956 (ibid.); file on the allegations (WRC 2142); *Times*, 2 March 1956; minutes of the meeting of the General Advisory Council, 10 April 1956 (WRC 2145).

102 Ince to Llewellyn, 7 May 1956 (WRC 2142); Ince to Oldfield-Davies, 4 September 1956 (WRC 2141); Jones to Oldfield-Davies, 20 May 1956 (ibid.).

[103] *Ince Report* (1956) (copy in WRC 2141).
[104] *Western Mail*, 19 December 1956; *Times*, 19 December 1956; statement of Plaid Cymru (WRC 2141); report of Hole (WRC 2156); the BCW's observations on *Ince Report*, 21 January 1957 (WRC 2145); MBCW, 14 April 1961 (WRC 3691).
[105] Ibid., 23 June 1960 (ibid.); statement of the BCW, June 1960 (WRC 3626); *Charter of Incorporation* (1952: Cmd.8605), p.7.
[106] Press statement of Lord Macdonald, June 1960 (WRC 3691); MBCW, 20 July 1960 (ibid.); *Parliamentary Debates*, fifth series, vol.62, cols.339–72. James Griffiths's motion condemning the appointment was defeated by 240 votes to 171.
[107] fforde to Brooke, 29 July 1960 (WRC 3430); fforde to Oldfield-Davies, 29 July 1960 (ibid.); Brooke to fforde, 11 August 1960 (ibid.); Oldfield-Davies to fforde, 17 August 1960 (ibid.).
[108] MBCW, 22 May 1964 and 25 June 1965 (WRC 3691).
[109] Ibid., 17 February, 21 July and 31 October 1961 and 14 June 1963 (ibid.).
[110] *Report of the Committee on Broadcasting 1960*, p.94; *White Paper*, July 1962.
[111] *Listener*, 15 February 1962; memorandum on local broadcasting, 30 May 1962 (WRC 3694); note on experiments at Swansea and Wrexham (ibid.); note on the meeting of the General Advisory Council (WRC 3620); MBCW, 17 November and 8 December 1961 (WRC 3691).
[112] *Aberdare Leader*, 19 July 1952.
[113] *South Wales Echo*, 25 September 1952; A. Briggs, IV, pp.258, 688; A. Sampson, op.cit., p.666; conversation with Emyr Daniel; J. Iverson, 'The man who used to be . . .', in P. Hannan (ed.), op.cit., p.105; P. Ferris, *Sir Huge: The Life of Huw Wheldon* (1990), p.84.
[114] A. Milne, *D.G.: The Memoirs of a British Broadcaster* (1988), p.8; J. Dimbleby, *Richard Dimbleby: A Biography* (1975), p.361; T. Burns, op.cit., p.151.
[115] A. Milne, op.cit., pp.40–58; B. Sendall, II, p.182; M. Tracey, op.cit., p.288.
[116] C. Curran, op.cit., p.276; R. Bevins, op.cit., p.119.
[117] T. Burns, op.cit., pp.270–1; M. Gorham, *Forty Years of Irish Broadcasting* (1967), p.271.
[118] *Radio Times, passim*; J. Dowling and L. Doolan, *Sit Down and be Counted* (1969), pp.23, 25, 30.
[119] Memorandum on regional broadcasting, 22 December 1958 (WRC 3620).
[120] Ibid.; H. Williams, 'Confessions of a TV Critic', in P. Hannan (ed.), op.cit., p.89; J. Ormond, 'Beginnings', in ibid., pp.6–10; R. Lucas, *Voice of a Nation?* (1981), pp.186–8; MBCW, 23 March 1960 (WRC 3691).
[121] A. Briggs, *The Collected Essays of Asa Briggs*, vol.III (1991), p.106.
[122] R. Silvey, op.cit., p.208; statement by controller North, 10 January 1956 (WRC 2147).
[123] Minutes of the meeting of the regional controllers, 6 June 1956 (WRC 2147); memorandum on regional broadcasting, 22 December 1958 (WRC 3620).
[124] Statement by controller North, 10 January 1956 (WRC 2147); statement by controller Wales, 17 February 1956 (ibid.); statement by Jacob, 8 April 1957 (WRC 2145).
[125] *Montgomeryshire Express*, 14 March 1953.
[126] *South Wales Evening Post*, 14 October 1952.
[127] Report, 19 March 1954 (WRC 2157); A. Milne, op. cit., pp.13–14; minutes of the meeting of the regional controllers, 13 October 1955 (WRC 3620).
[128] *Western Mail*, 17 November 1952; note, 1951 (WRC 2155); Oldfield-Davies to Lewis, 1 March 1955 (ibid.); note, 10 May 1957 (WRC 2147); R. Cathcart, op.cit., *passim*.
[129] Memorandum by Jones, 15 February 1955 (WAC R 34/945/5); memorandum by controller Home Service, 18 February 1955 (ibid.).

[130] *Sunday Times*, 11 January 1953; Monthly Reports, 1952–4 (WRC 2157); *Western Mail*, 20 July 1953 and 26 February 1954.

[131] Memorandum by Oldfield-Davies, 13 January 1955 (WRC 2147).

[132] MBCW, 15 June 1954 (WAC R 6/10/2); report, 30 June 1954 (WRC 2157); minutes of the meeting of the Board of Governors, 2 June 1954 (WRC 2147).

[133] MBCW, 28 January (WAC R 6/10/1); ibid., 11 October 1963 (WRC 3691); report, March 1955 (WRC 2147).

[134] Report, September 1956 (WRC 2147); *South Wales Evening Post*, 24 March 1953; *Liverpool Daily Post*, 18 January 1955.

[135] *Yr Herald Gymraeg*, 4 April 1955; *Western Mail*, 23 February 1953.

[136] *Y Faner*, 8 April 1953.

[137] *Western Mail*, 3 November 1952; *Herald of Wales*, 9 May 1953; report, 30 June 1954 (WRC 2157); report, October 1954 (WRC 2143); *Yr Herald Gymraeg*, 16 April 1952.

[138] Ibid., 13 December 1954. Cardiff's drama department noted that 'we can take credit that [Siwan] was written at all, having chased him for months' (report, January 2954: WRC 2143); *Manchester Guardian*, 20 March 1962. *Excelsior* was eventually published in 1980. See its introduction.

[139] S. Lewis, *Tynged yr Iaith* (1962) (There is a translation in *Planet* 4, February/March 1971.); J. Davies, 'Hanes cynnar Cymdeithas yr Iaith Gymraeg', in A. Eirug (ed.), *Tân a Daniwyd* (1976).

Chapter 6: From BBC Wales to the Crawford Report, 1964–1974

[1] Note, 20 February 1963 (WAC T 16/235/4); note, 20 March 1963 (WAC T 16/236); MBCW, 17 May and 14 June 1963 and 14 February 1964 (WRC 3691).

[2] Ibid., 13 March 1964 (ibid.)

[3] Ibid., 14 February 1964 (ibid.); letters, March and April 1964 (WRC 3630); memorandum by Baverstock, 16 April 1964 (WAC T 16/685).

[4] MBCW, 13 March, 10 April and 11 June 1964 (WRC 3691); memoranda, January 1966 (WRC 3430).

[5] *Cambrian News*, 31 January 1964. Welsh-speakers living in Cardiff tended to assume that the entire native population west of the linguistic line could speak Welsh. They therefore found difficulty in accepting the fact that places like Aberystwyth had indigenous inhabitants who were monoglot English-speakers.

[6] MBCW, 11 June and 13 November 1964 (WRC 3691).

[7] Ibid., 11 September 1964 (ibid.); ibid., 19 June 1970 (WRC 3695); *Report of the Committee on Broadcast Coverage* (1974), chapter 5.

[8] R. Silvey, *Who's Listening?* (1974), p.203.

[9] Memorandum, 28 June 1965 (WRC 3430); T. Burns, *The BBC: Public Institution and Private World* (1977), pp.223–9; A. Briggs, *The BBC: The First Fifty Years* (1985), p.348; report, March 1965 (WRC 3619); file labelled 'Premises General' (WRC 1009).

[10] File on the death of Hywel Davies (WRC 3430).

[11] Adams to Oldfield-Davies, 28 January 1965 (WAC T 16/685).

[12] M. Tracey, *A Variety of Lives: A Biography of Sir Hugh Greene* (1983), pp.202, 254–5; G. Williams, 'Fighting under the bedclothes', in P. Hannan (ed.), *Wales in Vision* (1990), p.147; M. Leapman, *The Last Days of the Beeb* (1986), pp.50–1.

[13] Conversation with Selwyn Roderick and Wyndham Richards.

[14] C. Stuart (ed.), *The Reith Diaries* (1975), pp. 510, 514; M. Tracey, op.cit., p.230; A. Briggs, *The First Fifty Years*, pp.332, 352.

15 Ibid., p.353; A. Sampson, *Anatomy of Britain* (1965), p.664; C. Curran, *A Seamless Robe* (1979), p.257; M. Tracey, op.cit., p.292. The BBC governor, Robert Lusty, claimed that he was the author of the comment on Rommel (R. Lusty, *Bound to be Read* (1975), p.253).

16 J. Morgan, 'Winning the franchise', in P. Hannan (ed.), *Wales on the Wireless* (1988), pp.173–4; C. Hill, *Behind the Screen* (1974), pp.48–51, 55–8; B. Sendall, *Independent Television in Britain*, vol.II (1983) (henceforth referred to as B. Sendall, II), pp.354–61.

17 Ibid., p.365; G. Williams, op.cit., in P. Hannan (ed.), *Wales in Vision*, p.152; MBCW, 16 June 1967 (WRC 3691).

18 Ibid., 17 February 1967 and 19 September 1969 (ibid.); ibid., 15 September 1972 (WRC 3695); *Report of the Committee on Broadcasting Coverage* (1974).

19 MBCW, 19 May 1972 and 20 July 1973 (WRC 3695); file labelled 'Premises General' (WRC 1009).

20 *Report of the Committee on Broadcast Coverage*; report, 1974 (WRC 3420); BBC Wales Paper for Annan, 1974 (WRC 1008); MBCW, 17 January 1969 (WRC 3691); ibid., 19 November 1971 and 20 October 1972 (WRC 3695). There was a widespread assumption that 'when *Heddiw* comes on the air, BBC Wales goes over to Welsh only' (note by Vaughan, 11 January 1965: WRC 3619).

21 Controller North to Rowley, 13 February 1968 (WRC 3430); memorandum by Talfan Davies, February 1968 (ibid.); Rowley to controller North (ibid.).

22 MBCW, 19 November 1971 and 12 March 1972 (WRC 3695); letter of protest, 4 July 1974 (WRC 3430).

23 MBCW, 16 January and 19 June 1970, 20 October 1972 and 15 March 1974 (WRC 3695).

24 Minutes of the meeting of the regional controllers, 5 April 1966 (WRC 3619); D. Rosser, *Dragon in the House* (1987), pp.88–93; letter by Davies, 21 January 1970 (WRC 3430); Callaghan to Curran, 5 February 1970 (ibid.); memorandum by Talfan Davies, February 1970 (ibid.); correspondence concerning Plwm (WRC 3430); MBCW, 20 February 1970 and 14 May 1971 (WRC 3695).

25 Rowley to Probert, 22 February 1972 (WRC 3430); letters of protest, June 1971 (WRC 2334); minutes of the meeting of the regional controllers, 1 December 1965 (WRC 3619); memorandum by Talfan Davies, 1970 (WRC 3430); MBCW, 14 January 1966 and 21 April 1967 (WRC 3691); ibid., 25 June 1971 and 16 June 1972 (WRC 3695).

26 Ibid., 21 June 1968 (WRC 3691); ibid., 20 February 1970 (WRC 3695); file on Welsh broadcasts from English transmitters (WRC 3430).

27 MBCW, 17 May, 18 October and 20 December 1968 (WRC 3691); ; ibid., 15 January 1971 (WRC 3695); G. Tudur, *Wyt Ti'n Cofio?* (1989), pp.55, 57; *S4C: Pwy Dalodd Amdani?* (1985), pp.13–15; memorandum by Rowley, 7 February 1969 (WRC 1009); A. Briggs, *Governing the BBC* (1979), p.145.

28 Note on the conference of 31 January 1970 (WRC 2334); 'The future of broadcasting: a symposium', *Planet*, 2 (October/November 1970); Wheldon to Rowley, 2 December 1970 (WRC 3430); MBCW, 16 October 1970 (WRC 3695).

29 Ibid., 18 December 1970 (ibid.); *S4C: Pwy Dalodd Amdani?*, pp.18–19; file on the proposals of the Welsh Language Society (WRC 3420); Rowley to Adams, February 1971 (ibid.). The proposals were drawn up by Ffred Ffransis, Gwyneth Wiliam, Arfon Gwilym and Gronw ap Islwyn.

30 Notes by Rowley, 14 December 1971 (WRC 3430); memorandum by Rowley, April 1971 (ibid.); *S4C: Pwy Dalodd Amdani?*, p.24; *Barn*, September 1971; MBCW, 25 June and 17 September 1971 and 18 February 1972 (WRC 3695).

31 A. T. Davies, 'Y Sianel' in G. Erfyl (ed.), *Radio Cymru* (1989), p.94; file on the proposals of the Welsh Language Society (WRC 3430); MBCW, 23 April and

17 September 1971 (WRC 3695).

32 Ibid., 19 November 1971 and 18 February 1972 (ibid.); survey of television in Europe, 21 January 1972 (WRC 3430); *Parliamentary Debates*, fifth series, vol.828, col.87.

33 Aylestone to Hill, 10 April 1972 (WRC 3430); memorandum by Edwards, 14 April 1972 (ibid.); Hill to Aylestone, 17 May 1972 (ibid.). It was widely believed that, of the independent companies, only Associated Television was eager to have a second TV channel (A. Sampson, op.cit., p.665). On retiring from the chairmanship, Hill informed the BCW that 'he could not fail to admire that very remarkable, delicate, and sometimes dangerous institution, the BBC . . . We have in this country a system that we would tamper with at our peril' (MBCW 17 November 1972: WRC 3695).

34 A. T. Davies, 'Y Sianel', in G. Erfyl (ed.), op.cit., p.73; Rowley to Adams, May 1972 (WRC 3430); *Western Mail*, 10 May 1972; MBCW, 16 June 1972 (WRC 3695).

35 Ibid., 15 September and 15 December 1972 (ibid.).

36 Memorandum by Tegai Hughes, 24 October 1972 (WRC 2430); Wheldon to Rowley, 22 September 1972 (WRC 3430); MBCW, 17 November 1972 (WRC 3695).

37 Ibid., 15 December 1972 and 19 January 1973 (ibid.); minutes of the meeting of the BCW and the IBA Welsh Committee, 15 December 1972 (WRC 1009); statement of the BCW, 19 January 1973 (WRC 3430); Curran to Rowley, 31 October 1972 (ibid.); C. Curran, op.cit., p.219.

38 *S4C: Pwy Dalodd Amdani?*, pp.40, 44; G. Tudur, op.cit., p.10; memorandum by Rowley, 13 March 1973 (WRC 3430); note, December 1972 (WRC 2334); note, February 1973 (WRC 1009); MBCW, 16 March 1973 (WRC 3695).

39 Ibid., 16 March 1973 (ibid.).

40 Ibid., 18 May and 20 July 1973 (ibid.); note on the Lord Mayor's Conference, 3 July 1973 (WRC 3430).

41 MBCW, 20 July 1973 (WRC 3695); *Report of the Committee on Broadcast Coverage* (1974); transcript of an interview with Swann, 20 September 1973 (WRC 3430); *Western Mail*, 13 August 1973.

42 Text of a lecture by Curran, 1 February 1974 (WRC 3600); ibid., 19 November 1974 (WRC 3430).

43 *S4C: Pwy Dalodd Amdani?*, pp.95–100.

44 Statement by the IBA, 2 January 1973 (WRC 1009); statement by the ACCT, 27 June 1973 (ibid.); memorandum by Tegai Hughes, 24 October 1972 (WRC 3430); MBCW, 15 December 1972 (WRC 3695).

45 Ibid., 17 March and 16 June 1972 and 19 September and 16 November 1973 (ibid.); Tegai Hughes to Davies, 9 October 1973 (WRC 1009); memorandum by the Welsh Committee of the IBA, March 1975 (WRC 1008).

46 J. Cain, *The BBC: Seventy Years of Broadcasting* (1992), pp.113–19; *Western Mail*, 11 April 1974; MBCW, 19 April and 17 May 1974 (WRC 3695); statement by the BCW, 19 April 1974 (WRC 1008).

47 *Report of the Committee on Broadcasting Coverage* (1974), especially chapter 3.

48 *BBC Handbook*, 1965, p.147, 1975, pp.79, 124–5; MBCW, 20 May 1966 (WRC 3691); report of the director of sound broadcasting, December 1964 (WRC 3619).

49 Ibid., March 1965 (ibid.); statement by Curran, 15 May 1964 (WRC 3430); *Annual Register*, 1966, p.460; R. Silvey, op.cit., pp.211–13.

50 Ibid., p.213; C. Curran, op.cit., p.268; MBCW, 19 February 1971 (WRC 3695). Of the rest of the BBC's radio outgoings, 13 per cent was spent on regional radio, 11 per cent on local radio and 5 per cent on transmission.

[51] MBCW, 16 February and 15 June 1973 (ibid.); D. Morgan (ed.), *Babi Sam* (1985), p.17.

[52] File on Swansea (WRC 2335); *Cambria Leader*, 5 December 1926; MBCW, 12 March 1965, 15 July 1966 and 16 June and 21 July 1967 (WRC 3691).

[53] Ibid., 16 June 1967 (ibid.); Rowley to Trimmell, 12 March 1973 (WRC 3600); report, September 1965 (WRC 3619); files on the orchestra (WRC 1007).

[54] Ibid.; MBCW, 28 April 1972 (WRC 3695); report, 1974 (WRC 3430); A. Briggs, *The First Fifty Years*, p.354; M. Gorham, *Forty Years of Irish Broadcasting* (1967), p.43.

[55] Report on a conference, 20 December 1964 (WRC 3430); H. Davies, *The Role of the Regions* (1965); A. Milne, *DG: The Memoirs of a British Broadcaster* (1988), pp.67–8.

[56] A. Briggs, *The First Fifty Years*, pp.355–6; *Broadcasting in the Seventies* (1969), *passim*.

[57] Hawkins to the BBC in Wales, 27 April 1973 (WRC 3430).

[58] File on local broadcasting (ibid.); C. Curran, op.cit, p.219.

[59] MBCW, 15 September 1972 (WRC 3695); report of working party, 20 January 1969 (WRC 2335). Scotland did opt out of Radio Two, particularly with sports programmes on Saturday afternoons.

[60] Report of working party, 20 January 1969 (WRC 2335).

[61] Ibid.; report by the director of sound broadcasting, March 1965 (WRC 3619).

[62] Comments on the proposals of the Welsh Language Society (WRC 3430); memorandum by Tegai Hughes, 24 October 1972 (ibid.).

[63] *Radio Times*, January 1973; BBC Wales Paper for Annan (WRC 1008); MBCW, 15 September 1972, 19 February 1973 and 19 April 1974 (WRC 3695); file labelled 'Radio Development' (WRC 1009); *Western Mail*, 12 January 1975; BBC Wales Paper for Annan (WRC 1008).

[64] Ibid.; MBCW, 20 November 1970 and 15 September 1972 (WRC 3695); file labelled 'Radio Development' (WRC 1009).

[65] Memorandum by Edwards, 19 March 1974 (WRC 1009); memorandum by Brooke, 23 May 1974 (ibid.); MBCW, 15 September 1972 (WRC 3695).

[66] MBCW, 19 July 1974 (WRC 3695); BBC Wales Paper for Annan (WRC 1008); C. Curran, op.cit., p.167; file labelled 'Radio Development' (WRC 1009).

[67] Ibid.; text of speech, 15 October 1974 (ibid.); papers for Crawford and Annan (WRC 1008); MBCW, 18 October and 15 November 1974 (WRC 3695); *Western Mail*, 17 October 1974.

[68] *Report of the Committee on Broadcasting Coverage* (1974), *passim*; memorandum by Edwards, 2 December 1974 (WRC 1009).

[69] Memorandum by Bevan, 20 June 1964 (WRC 1008).

[70] Statement by controller, English regions (ibid.); T. Burns, op.cit., p.226; C. Mayhew, *Time to Explain* (1987), p.201.

[71] Rowley to Thomas, 11 April 1974 (WRC 3430); A. Milne, op.cit., p.74; MBCW, 19 September 1969 (WRC 3691).

[72] Ibid., 15 May 1970 (WRC 3695); note, June 1972 (WRC 2334).

[73] G. Llewelyn, *Hel Straeon* (1973), p.58; Annual Report of the BBC in Wales, 1972–3 (WRC 3430).

[74] Note, 6 February 1976 (WRC 1008); E. Nevin, 'Is the King naked', in P. Hannan (ed.), *Wales in Vision*, p.130.

[75] Report, 20 January 1969 (WRC 2335); note, February 1974 (WRC 3430); MBCW, 12 February 1967 (WRC 3691); ibid., 23 April 1971 and 18 January 1974 (WRC 3695).

[76] Ibid., 1 March 1972 (ibid.); memorandum by Edwards, 1973 (WRC 1009).

[77] Memorandum by Williams, 5 April 1965 (WRC 3619); G. Williams, op.cit., in

P. Hannan (ed.), *Wales in Vision*, p.148; MBCW, 18 December 1970 (WRC 3695).

78 Ibid., 16 June 1972 (ibid.); Edwards to Davies, 2 October 1975 (WRC 3430).

79 MBCW, 14 December 1973 and 20 July 1973 (WRC 3695).

80 Ibid., 16 March 1973 (ibid.); note on Swansea Sound, 18 May 1977 (WRC 3695).

81 MBCW, 16 July 1976 (WRC 3695); BBC Wales Paper for Annan (WRC 1008); report, 20 January 1969 (WRC 2335).

82 Ibid.; MBCW, 15 January 1971 (WRC 3695).

83 Ibid., 15 February 1974 (ibid.); memorandum, 27 April 1965 (WRC 3620); memorandum by Bevan, 4 July 1968 (ibid.).

Chapter 7: Annan and After, 1974–1981

1 File labelled 'Home Office Working Party' (WRC 1008).

2 Ibid.; BBC Paper for Annan (ibid.); S. Lambert, *Channel Four* (1982), p.38; MBCW, 21 March 1975 (WRC 3695).

3 Ibid., 13 December 1974 (ibid.); Edwards to Wheldon, 16 December 1974 (WRC 1009); file labelled 'Home Office Working Party' (WRC 1008).

4 Ibid.; *Liverpool Daily Post*, 13 December 1977.

5 File labelled 'Home Office Working Party' (WRC 1008).

6 Ibid.; MBCW, 20 June 1975 (WRC 3695).

7 File labelled 'Home Office Working Party' (WRC 1008).

8 *Report of the Working Party on a Fourth Channel Television Service for Wales* (Cmnd. 6290, 1975).

9 *Parliamentary Debates*, fifth series, vol.905, col.788 (written answers); *S4C: Pwy Dalodd Amdani?* (1985), p.51; statement by Curran, 10 March 1975 (WRC 3430); minutes of the meeting of the General Liaison Committee, 14 April 1975 (ibid.); MBCW, 18 July 1975 and 20 February 1976 (WRC 3695).

10 Ibid., 20 February and 19 March 1976 (ibid.); *Western Mail*, 17 May 1976.

11 MBCW, 18 July, 12 September and 12 December 1975 (WRC 3695).

12 Ibid., 18 February, 18 March and 15 April 1977 (ibid.); *S4C: Pwy Dalodd Amdani?*, pp.57–65; G. Tudur, *Wyt Ti'n Cofio?* (1989), pp.137, 145.

13 Cutting from the *Observer* (WRC 1008).

14 Text of an interview with Annan, 4 June 1975 (ibid.); Shaw to Edwards, June 1975 (ibid.); *Report of the Committee on the Future of Broadcasting* (1977: Cmnd. 6753), especially pp.81–2.

15 Memorandum, 4 September 1975 (WRC 1008).

16 BBC Wales Paper for Annan (ibid.); MBCW, 18 October 1974 (WRC 3695).

17 Ibid., 17 September 1976 (ibid.); note on the visit of the Annan Committee, June 1975 (WRC 1008); text of an interview with Annan, 4 June 1975 (ibid.); comments on the Charter, March 1975 (WRC 3430).

18 Memorandum by Shaw, 1975 (WRC 1008); memorandum by controller Scotland, 20 March 1976 (ibid.).

19 Memorandum by controller Wales, January 1975 (ibid.); Edwards to Shaw, 5 June 1975 (ibid.); MBCW, 21 February 1975 and 14 November 1975 and 11 June 1976 (WRC 3695); BBC Wales Paper for Annan (WRC 1008).

20 Statement of the Welsh Committee of the IBA (ibid.).

21 *Report of the Committee on the Future of Broadcasting, passim.*

22 S. Lambert, op.cit., pp.73–80; *Western Mail*, 25 March and 6 July 1977.

23 *North Wales Weekly News*, 7 April 1977; MBCW, 21 January and 18 February 1977 (WRC 3695).

[24] Ibid., 20 May and 22 July 1977 (ibid.).

[25] Ibid., 16 March 1979 (ibid.); minutes of the meeting of the Home Office Working Party, 19 May 1975 (WRC 1008).

[26] *Guardian*, 12 January 1979; *Y Cymro*, 16 January 1979; minutes of the meeting of the Trevelyan Committee, 11 October 1977 (WRC 1008); MBCW, 21 October 1977 and 19 January 1979 (WRC 3695).

[27] Ibid., 22 July 1977 (ibid.); memorandum by the IBA, 7 February 1977 (WRC 3695); conversation with Emyr Daniel.

[28] MBCW, 17 June, 16 September and 18 November 1977 (WRC 3695).

[29] *Western Mail*, 28 February 1977.

[30] MBCW, 26 May 1978 (WRC 3695); *Times*, 25 April 1978; Report of the Home Office Working Party (WRC 1008).

[31] *Y Cymro*, 1 August 1978; White Paper, July 1978.

[32] *Liverpool Daily Post*, 17 August 1977; G. Tudur, op.cit., p.153.

[33] *Western Mail*, 8 November 1978 and 26 March 1979.

[34] MBCW, 18 May and 20 July 1979 (WRC 3695).

[35] W. Whitelaw, *The Whitelaw Memoirs* (1989), p.217; *Western Mail*, 13 September 1979.

[36] MBCW, 21 September and 14 December 1979 (WRC 3694).

[37] *Annual Register*, 1979, p.430; S. Lambert, op.cit., pp.80–1.

[38] *S4C: Pwy Dalodd Amdani?* pp.79–85; G. Tudur, op.cit., pp.153, 155, 158.

[39] Ibid., p.159; S. Lambert, op.cit., pp.110–11; P. Hannan (ed.), *Wales in Vision* (1990), p.140.

[40] Conversation with Dudley Edwards; MBCW, 20 June 1980 (WRC 3694).

[41] Ibid., 18 July and 19 September 1980 (ibid.); W. Whitelaw, op.cit., p.218; S. Lambert, op.cit., p.112; *S4C: Pwy Dalodd Amdani?*, p.92. Cymdeithas yr Iaith Gymraeg had planned massive disruption in London on 11 October (ibid., p.90).

[42] MBCW, 19 September 1980 (WRC 3694).

[43] G. Evans, *Bywyd Cymro* (1982), p.319.

[44] W. Whitelaw, op.cit., p.219; S. Lambert, op.cit., pp.110–12; *Listener*, 2 October 1980.

[45] MBCW, 16 January, 19 March and 19 April 1974 and 21 May 1976 (WRC 3695); ibid., 16 March and 16 November 1979 (WRC 3694); minutes of the joint meeting of the BCW and the Board of Governors, 9 October 1980 (ibid.).

[46] C. Curran, *A Seamless Robe* (1979), p.169; MBCW, 20 June 1975 and 21 July 1978 (WRC 3695).

[47] Ibid., 14 October and 15 December 1978 (ibid.).

[48] Ibid., 17 November and 15 December 1978 and 19 January 1979 (WRC 3695); ibid., 22 October 1982 (WRC 3694); *Rhondda Leader*, 2 March 1979; *Western Mail*, 21 January 1979.

[49] MBCW, 20 April 1979 (WRC 3695); ibid., 20 June and 10 October 1980 and 28 November 1981 (WRC 3694); *Times*, 23 November 1979; W. McDouall, *A History of BBC Broadcasting in Scotland* (1992), p. 261.

[50] *Daily Telegraph*, 20 October 1979; *Radio Month*, February 1979; *Western Mail*, 7 September 1979; MBCW, 19 November and 9 December 1976 and 15 September and 17 November 1979 (WRC 3695); ibid., 21 September 1979 (WRC 3694).

[51] Ibid., 10 October 1980 (ibid.); file on Radio Deeside (WRC 3691); *Liverpool Daily Post*, 31 March 1980.

[52] *Report of the Committee on the Future of Broadcasting*, pp.73, 105–7; file on local broadcasting (WRC 3694); MBCW, 19 December 1980 and 20 November 1981 (WRC 3694).

53 Ibid., 23 October 1981 (ibid.); G. S. Jones, 'A sense of place', in P. Hannan (ed.), op.cit., p.158.

54 MBCW, 14 October 1978 (WRC 3695); ibid., 28 March 1980 and 12 February and 17 December 1982 (WRC 3694); *Y Cymro*, 25 January 1977; *Daily Telegraph*, 25 July 1978.

55 MBCW, 18 November 1977 and 15 June 1979 (WRC 3695); ibid., 18 April and 23 May 1980 (WRC 3694); file labelled 'Bangor Premises' (WRC 1010).

56 MBCW, 21 March and 16 May 1975 (WRC 3695); file labelled 'Welsh Symphony Orchestra' (WRC 1007).

57 Ibid.

58 Ibid.; D. W. Jones, 'Variations on a Welsh theme', in P. Hannan (ed.), op.cit., p.75; MBCW, 18 February 1977 (WRC 3695). In 1987, the orchestra was expanded by a further ten string players, bringing it to full symphonic strength. Part of the expansion was financed by the Welsh Fourth Channel, which joined the Arts Council and the BBC as partners in funding the orchestra (*BBC Annual Report and Accounts*, 1986–7, p.18).

59 J. Davies and others, *Political Policing in Wales* (1984), *passim*; A. Milne, *D.G: The Memoirs of a British Broadcaster* (1988), p.69; MBCW, 28 March 1980 and 17 December 1982 (WRC 3694).

60 Ibid., 20 February 1976 and 24 February, 21 July and 15 September 1978 (WRC 3695); ibid., 12 February 1982 (WRC 3694); *Private Eye*, 6 December 1976.

61 MBCW, 23 April and 19 November 1976 and 20 January 1978 (WRC 3695); ibid., 28 March and 23 May 1980 and 24 April 1981 (WRC 3694).

62 Ibid., 17 July and 18 December 1981 (WRC 3694).

63 A. Protheroe, 'News on wheels', in P. Hannan (ed.), op.cit., p.15; *Western Mail*, 20 April, 27 August and 14 September 1977; *Daily Telegraph*, 18 May 1977; memorandum by Lucas, 11 February 1977 (WRC 3694); memorandum by Salter, 5 May 1977 (ibid.); MBCW, 9 December 1976 (WRC 3695).

64 Ibid., 14 December 1979 (WRC 3695); ibid., 12 February and 12 March 1982 (WRC 3694); C. Curran, op.cit., p.281.

65 MBCW, 17 October 1975, 21 May 1976 and 24 February and 17 March 1978 (WRC 3695).

66 Ibid., 21 January 1977 and 19 January 1979 (WRC 3695); ibid., 25 January 1980 (WRC 3694).

67 Ibid., 18 May 1979 (WRC 3695); ibid., 19 December 1980 (WRC 3694); *Times*, 24 May 1977; *Western Mail*, 10 December 1980.

68 MBCW, 21 March 1975 (WRC 3695); ibid., 26 October 1979, 19 December 1980 and 18 December 1981 (WRC 3694).

69 Ibid., 15 October 1976, 16 December 1977 and 19 January 1979 (WRC 3695); ibid., 14 May 1982 (WRC 5694).

70 Ibid., 18 March and 22 July 1977 and 26 May 1978 (WRC 3695).

71 Ibid., 14 November 1975 and 11 June and 17 September 1976 (ibid.).

72 Ibid., 21 May 1976 (ibid.); ibid., 20 June 1980 (WRC 3694); file labelled 'Radio Development' (WRC 1009); *Radio Times, passim*.

73 MBCW, 14 December 1979 (WRC 3694); ibid., 17 September and 9 December 1976 and 17 February 1984 (WRC 3695).

74 Ibid., 14 December (WRC 3694); ibid., 23 January and 16 July 1982 (WRC 3695). The situation had improved somewhat by the 1990s.

75 Ibid., 15 October and 17 September 1976 and 22 October 1962 and 21 January 1983 (ibid.); ibid., 22 January 1982 (WRC 3694); *BBC Annual Report and Handbook*, 1983, p.89.

Postscript: Towards the Seventh Charter: BBC Broadcasting in Wales since 1981

[1] MBCW, 21 November 1980 and 20 November 1981 (WRC 3694); A. Milne, *D.G.: The Memoirs of a British Broadcaster* (1988), pp.224, 226.

[2] Ibid., pp.144–56; MBCW, 23 September 1983 (WRC 3695); *Annual Register*, 1989, pp.481–2.

[3] Ibid., 1990, pp.500–1; J. Cain, *The BBC: Seventy Years of Broadcasting* (1992), pp.119, 121–4; A. Milne, op.cit., pp.155–6.

[4] Ibid., pp.152, 224, 279.

[5] Ibid., pp.252–3; W. Whitelaw, *The Whitelaw Memoirs* (1989), p.163; A. Roberts, 'From a beleagured city', *Planet*, 63 (June/July 1987), p.10; *Annual Register*, 1970, p.452.

[6] Ibid., 1985, p.433; MBCW, 27 September 1985 (WRC 3695).

[7] Ibid., 27 February 1985 (ibid.); *Observer*, 18 August 1985; A. Milne, op.cit., pp.196, 250–2.

[8] Ibid., pp.107, 192, 245, 246, 266; M. Leapman, *The Last Days of the Beeb* (1986), *passim*; MBCW, 15 February and 14 June 1985 (WRC 3695).

[9] Ibid., 18 July 1980 (WRC 3694); *Annual Register*, 1980, pp.427–8.

[10] MBCW, 19 December 1980 (WRC 3694); ibid., 18 March 1983 (WRC 3695); J. Cain, op.cit., p.132; A. Milne, op.cit., pp.167–8.

[11] Ibid., pp.166, 169.

[12] Ibid., pp.217–35; J. Cain, op.cit., pp.132–3; *Annual Register*, 1986, pp.444–5; A. Roberts, op.cit., p.12.

[13] A. Milne, op.cit., pp.183–5; MBCW, 19 July 1985 (WRC 3695).

[14] *Annual Register*, 1985, pp.433–4; *BBC Annual Report and Handbook*, 1985–7; *BBC Annual Report and Accounts*, 1986–92.

[15] MBCW, 21 January 1983 (WRC 3695); W. Vaughan-Thomas, *Trust to Talk* (1980), p.124; T. Burns, *The BBC: Public Institution and Private World* (1977), p.67.

[16] MBCW, 19 December 1980 (WRC 3694); ibid., 18 February 1983 and 14 June 1985 (WRC 3695).

[17] Ibid., 14 April 1984, 15 March 1985 and 18 April 1986 (ibid.).

[18] Ibid., 18 March 1983 (ibid.).

[19] Ibid., 20 July 1984 and 18 October 1985 (ibid.).

[20] MBCW, 20 February 1981 (WRC 3694); ibid., 10 December 1985 (WRC 3695).

[21] Ibid., 19 June and 1 July 1981 (WRC 3694); minutes of the joint meeting of the BCW and the Board of Governors, 9 October 1980 (ibid.).

[22] MBCW, 20 February and 24 April 1981 (ibid.).

[23] Ibid., 23 October 1981 (ibid.); C. Hudson, 'TV world turned upside down', *Planet*, 63 (June/July 1987), pp.111–16; conversation with William Aaron.

[24] J. Davies (ed.), *The Mercator Media Guide* (1993), *passim*.

[25] MBCW, 19 November 1982 (WRC 3695); *BBC Annual Report and Handbook*, 1983, p.86; *BBC Annual Report and Accounts*, 1986–7, p.18, 1988–9, pp.23–5, 1990–1, pp.10–11.

[26] J. Isaacs, *Storm over 4: A Personal Account* (1989), pp.95, 96.

[27] Ibid., pp.61–2; MBCW, 19 November and 21 January 1983 (WRC 3695); R. Silvey, *Who's Listening?* (1974), pp.101, 185; W. Whitelaw, op.cit., p.240.

[28] *Times*, 25 May 1994; MBCW, 1982–5, especially 15 July 1983 and 14 September 1984 (WRC 3695). By 1994, BARB was monitoring 850 Welsh households, 472 of which were Welsh-speaking (*Audience Research, BBC Cymru/Wales*, January/February 1994, p.20).

[29] MBCW, 16 November 1984 and 19 April 1985 (ibid.); W. Whitelaw, op.cit., p.240; J. Isaacs, op.cit., p.96.

[30] MBCW, 19 November 1982, 27 April 1984 and 15 April 1986 (WRC 3695).

[31] Ibid., 19 November 1982 and 15 July 1983 (ibid.).

[32] J. Isaacs, op.cit., p.96; C. Hudson, op.cit., p.116; P. Cooke and C. Gahan, *The Television Industry in Wales* (1988), p.ii.

[33] *Audience Research, BBC Cymru/Wales*, January/February 1994.

[34] Minutes of the joint meeting of the BCW and the Board of Governors, 9 October 1980 (WRC 3694); MBCW, 18 December 1981 (ibid.).

[35] Ibid., 22 January and 22 October 1982 and 16 March and 20 July 1984 (WRC 3695).

[36] Ibid., 17 June 1983 and 15 March 1985 (WRC 3695). The *Radio Times* began to carry the ITV schedules on 23 February 1991.

[37] Calculated from the *Radio Times*, 30 October to 5 November 1993. See also 'Now – an English channel', *Planet*, 54 (December/January 1985–6), pp.120–1.

[38] A. Milne, op.cit., p.68; W. McDouall, *A History of BBC Broadcasting in Scotland* (1993), *passim*; O. Edwards, *Nation or Region?* (Lunchtime Lectures, eleventh series, 1976), p.60; application of Smith, 1993 (copy given to the author); MBCW, 27 September 1985 (WRC 3695).

[39] Ibid., 14 December 1984 (ibid.).

[40] *Radio Times, passim; Gwifren*, 6 (May 1994), p.3; *BBC Annual Report and Handbook*, 1987, pp.79–84; *BBC Annual Report and Accounts*, 1990–1, pp.10–11.

[41] MBCW, 14 September 1984 (WRC 3695); *Audience Research, BBC Cymru/Wales*, January/February 1994, p.6.

[42] *BBC Annual Report and Accounts*, 1990–1, p.10; G. T. Davies, op.cit., in P. Hannan (ed.), *Wales in Vision* (1990), p.24.

[43] G. S. Jones, 'A sense of place', in ibid., p.157; J. Isaacs, op.cit., p.92.

[44] MBCW, 25 March 1986 (WRC 3695); memorandum of Hetherington, 20 March 1976 (WRC 1008). Whether Hetherington continued to hold that view after the governors removed him from the post of controller Scotland is open to doubt. See W. McDouall, op.cit., p.253.

Index

Index

Parry-Jones, Glyn, 150, 166, 194
Parry-Williams, T. H., 78, 160, 204, 236
Parsons, C. K., 25, 39, 217
party political broadcasts, 74, 161, 170–1, 242–8, 256–7, 287–8
Peacock Committee and Report, 371–2, 373, 376, 386
Peate, Iorwerth, 55, 73, 92, 112, 133
Peate, Nansi, 55
Peers, Donald, 188
Philipps-James, Mrs, 331
Phillips, D. H. I., 162, 284
Phillips, Morgan, 168
Phillips, Siân, 271, 354
Pickering, Tom, 75, 105–6, 135, 167
Pickles, Wilfred, 135, 184
Pilkington Committee and Report, 222–4, 230–3, 248, 256–7, 312, 331–2, 335
Pitt, Percy, 7–8, 41
Planet, 289
Plwm, Mici, 287
Pontypool, 348
Porthmadog, 352
postmaster-general, 2–3, 17, 24, 35, 37, 38, 77–8, 157–8, 218
Powell, D. H. I., 162, 172–3, 178, 347
Preece, William, 12
Price, Gareth, 336, 360, 374, 376, 388
Price, Glanville, 380
Price-White, D. A., 174
Pritchard, Gwynn, 388
Probert, Arthur, 287
programmes
Alun yn Galw, 362
AM, 347
Amenity Maketh Man, 112
Antigone, 197
Army Sings, The, 140
Arts Magazine, 196
Aunty Nellie's Handbag, 363
Awr Fawr, Yr, 337
Battle for Coal, The, 185
Birds of a Feather, 158–9, 172
Black Parade, 91–2
Blodeuwedd, 197
Bluff Cove, 385
Bore Da, 311, 323
Borrowed Pastures, 263
Bowen a'i Bartner, 375
Brad, 320
Brenin Llŷr, Y, 197
Bristol Pageant, The, 16
Buchedd Garmon, 99–100
Bus to Bosworth, 317
Calling Gibraltar, 140
Camgymeriadau, 195
Caniadaeth y Cysegr, 270, 323
Cap Wil Tomos, 209
Cefndir, 209

Cenwch im' yr hen ganiadau, 188
Children's Corner, 18
Children's Hour, 9, 14, 25, 40, 96, 115–16, 127, 133, 136, 138, 186, 192–3, 269, 271
Choir Practice, 172
Codi'r Ffôn, 362
Colliers' Crusade, 361
Conflict in the Coalfield, 91
Conundrum, 374
Cornel y Llenor, 149
Country Magazine, 190
Crefft Geiriau, 190
Cross Section, 112
Crugybar, 118
Cwrs y Byd, 96–7, 116
Cymru Fodern, 195
Cywain, 318
Dai Macaroni, 321
Dare to be a Daniel/Daniel Ddewr, 320
Dechrau Canu, Dechrau Canmol, 322, 380
Dewraf o'n Hawduron, Y, 196
Dilyn Afon, 361
District Nurse, 385
Dr Hywel Ffiaidd, 360
Disc a Dawn, 287
Drwmwr Bach, Y, 284
Dydd, Y, 262
Dylan, 355
Ein Pentref Ni, 115
Ennal's Point, 355
Eosiaid, Y, 99
Excelsior, 272
Ffasiwn, Y, 122
Five Welsh Towns, 321
Fo a Fe, 321, 360
Full Moon, 99
Garddio, 362
Gari Tryfan, 193, 271
Gazooka, 267
Glas y Dorlan, 360
Glo Caled, 271
Good Morning Wales, 311, 322–3, 364
Grand Slam, 360
Gwen Tomos, 359
Gwlad y Gân, 220
Hawkmoor, 355
Hedda Gabler, 197
Heddiw, 131, 262, 274, 282, 288, 303, 318, 377
Helo Bobol, 351, 362
Helo, sut d'ach chi?, 323
Helpline, 362
Hen Atgofion, 190
Home Life of the Carrion Crow, The, 38
Home Fires Burning, 132
Home Run, 362
Hour of the Kiddiewinks, 9
Hywel ab Owain Gwynedd, 268
Iarlles Cathleen, Yr, 271

440

Index